Case Studies in Contemporary Criticism

THOMAS HARDY

Tess of the d'Urbervilles

Case Studies in Contemporary Criticism
SERIES EDITOR: Ross C Murfin

Charlotte Brontë, *Jane Eyre*
EDITED BY Beth Newman, Southern Methodist University

Emily Brontë, *Wuthering Heights*
EDITED BY Linda H. Peterson, Yale University

Geoffrey Chaucer, *The Wife of Bath*
EDITED BY Peter G. Beidler, Lehigh University

Kate Chopin, *The Awakening*
EDITED BY Nancy A. Walker, Vanderbilt University

Joseph Conrad, *Heart of Darkness,* Second Edition
EDITED BY Ross C Murfin, University of Miami

Charles Dickens, *Great Expectations*
EDITED BY Janice Carlisle, Tulane University

Nathaniel Hawthorne, *The Scarlet Letter*
EDITED BY Ross C Murfin, University of Miami

Henry James, *The Turn of the Screw*
EDITED BY Peter G. Beidler, Lehigh University

James Joyce, *The Dead*
EDITED BY Daniel R. Schwarz, Cornell University

James Joyce, *A Portrait of the Artist as a Young Man*
EDITED BY R. B. Kershner, University of Florida

James Joyce, *A Companion to James Joyce's* Ulysses
EDITED BY Margot Norris, University of California, Irvine

Thomas Mann, *Death in Venice*
EDITED BY Naomi Ritter, University of Missouri

William Shakespeare, *Hamlet*
EDITED BY Susanne L. Wofford, University of Wisconsin–Madison

Mary Shelley, *Frankenstein*
EDITED BY Johanna M. Smith, University of Texas at Arlington

Jonathan Swift, *Gulliver's Travels*
EDITED BY Christopher Fox, University of Notre Dame

Edith Wharton, *The House of Mirth*
EDITED BY Shari Benstock, University of Miami

Case Studies in Contemporary Criticism

SERIES EDITOR: Ross C Murfin, *Southern Methodist University*

THOMAS HARDY
Tess of the d'Urbervilles

Complete, Authoritative Text with Biographical and Historical Contexts, Critical History, and Essays from Five Contemporary Critical Perspectives

EDITED BY

John Paul Riquelme
Boston University

Bedford Books
BOSTON NEW YORK

For Bedford Books
President and Publisher: Charles H. Christensen
General Manager and Associate Publisher: Joan E. Feinberg
Managing Editor: Elizabeth M. Schaaf
Development Editor: Stephen A. Scipione
Editorial Assistant: Maura E. Shea
Assistant Managing Editor: John Amburg
Production Editor: Julie Sullivan
Copyeditor: Marie Salter
Text Designer: Sandra Rigney, The Book Department
Cover Design: Richard Emery Design, Inc.
Cover Art: Stonehenge. Photograph by Jeffrey Sylvester/FPG International LLC.

Library of Congress Catalog Card Number: 97–74961

Manufactured in the United States of America.

3 2 1 0 9 8
f e d c b a

For information, write: Bedford Books, 75 Arlington Street, Boston, MA 02116 (617–426–7440)

ISBN: 0–312–10688–2 (paperback)
ISBN: 0–312–16375–4 (hardcover)

Published and distributed outside North America by:

MACMILLAN PRESS LTD.
Houndmills, Basingstoke, Hampshire RG21 2XS and London
Companies and representatives throughout the world.

ISBN: 0–333–69094–X

About the Series

Volumes in the Case Studies in Contemporary Criticism series provide college students with an entrée into the current critical and theoretical ferment in literary studies. Each volume reprints the complete text of a classic literary work and presents critical essays that approach the work from different theoretical perspectives, together with the editors' introductions to both the literary work and the critics' theoretical perspectives.

The volume editor of each Case Study has selected and prepared an authoritative text of the classic work, written an introduction to the work's biographical and historical contexts, and surveyed the critical responses to the work since its initial publication. Thus situated biographically, historically, and critically, the work is examined in five critical essays, each representing a theoretical perspective of importance to contemporary literary studies. These essays, prepared especially for undergraduates, show theory in praxis; whether written by established scholars or exceptional young critics, they demonstrate how current theoretical approaches can generate compelling readings of great literature.

As series editor, I have prepared introductions, with bibliographies, to the theoretical perspectives represented in the five critical essays. Each introduction presents the principal concepts of a particular theory in their historical context and discusses the major figures and key works that have influenced their formulation. It is my hope that these introductions will reveal to students that effective criticism is informed by a set of coherent assumptions, and will encourage them to recognize and examine their own assumptions about literature. After each introduction, a selective bibliography presents a partially annotated list of important works from the literature of the particular theoretical perspective, including the most recent and readily available editions and translations of the works cited in the introduction. Finally, I have compiled a glossary of key terms that recur in these volumes and in the discourse of contemporary theory and criticism. We hope that the Case Studies in Contemporary Criticism series will reaffirm the richness of its literary works, even as it introduces invigorating new ways to mine their apparently inexhaustible wealth.

Ross C Murfin
Series Editor
Southern Methodist University

About This Volume

The text of *Tess of the d'Urbervilles* reprinted here is the 1920 reimpression of the novel from the collected Wessex Edition of 1912, for which *Tess* was Volume One. *Tess* appeared in various forms during Hardy's lifetime, beginning with its serial publication in the *Graphic* and in *Harper's Bazaar* in 1891. Hardy made numerous changes when the narrative appeared first in a three-volume edition (1891), then in a one-volume edition (1892), later as Volume One of a collected edition (1895), and in a paperback edition (1900). The 1912 Wessex Edition has special standing among the versions of *Tess* because it was the last edition for which Hardy clearly read the proofs. Although it does not appear that Hardy read the proofs of the 1920 reimpression, he did send a list of changes to the publisher that were incorporated in that reprinting. The text provided here, then, has the authority of being the final one in which the author played a significant role in the production process.

Part One reprints *Tess* preceded by my biographical and historical introduction. Part Two opens with my history of critical commentary on the novel and includes five essays formulated with distinctive theoretical perspectives in mind: new historical (Catherine Gallagher), feminist and gender-oriented (Ellen Rooney), deconstructive (myself), reader-response (Garrett Stewart), and cultural criticism (Jennifer

Wicke). All these essays, which have been written or revised specifically for this volume, approach *Tess* through interpretive concepts and strategies that are of contemporary concern to teachers, scholars, and students of literature. I have chosen these particular scholar-teachers to contribute their commentaries for two primary reasons: first, we are all deeply committed to teaching and interpreting this memorable text by Thomas Hardy; and, second, we have each been working on projects of research and writing to which our readings of *Tess* are directly relevant. It is with pleasure that we invite you to participate with us in our attempt to bring out the complexity and the value of a seminal novel in the history of modern fiction.

Acknowledgments

I am grateful to Simon Gatrell for providing a copy of the 1920 reprinting of *Tess* for my use in the making of this edition. Anyone interested in exploring the variations among the significant editions of *Tess* published while Hardy was alive can consult the textual notes in the Clarendon Press edition of *Tess* (Oxford, corrected reprinting 1986), edited by Gatrell and Juliet Grindle. Ellen Rooney's essay is an abridged, revised version of the essay that appeared in *Rape and Representation,* edited by Lynn A. Higgins and Brenda R. Silver (New York: Columbia University Press, 1991). Columbia University Press kindly allowed the use of the revised essay. Beth Newman brought Rooney's essay to my attention.

Any editor who attempts to annotate *Tess,* a novel that has been annotated many times, owes debts to earlier editors. In making my own notes I consulted editions by Scott Elledge, P. N. Furbank, James Gibson, Simon Gatrell, David Skilton, and Carl J. Weber. I acknowledge their work with thanks. My research assistant during this project, Colin Harris, contributed substantially to my attempts to meet deadlines in a coherent way. Shawna McAlearney, the secretary of my department, and Harriet Lane, my administrative assistant, helped make the work on this edition possible for me with their perennial good will and efficiency. Valuable advice and generous amounts of patience came from Ross Murfin and Steve Scipione. At Bedford Books, Maura Shea, among others, helped ensure that the late stages of the work moved smoothly. Julie Sullivan, the project manager, was more careful and resourceful than any editor could expect. The forbearance of Victor, Louis, and Irene in allowing me time to work at the start and in the middle of my editing was greater than I can acknowledge adequately in this or any other place. Marie-Anne Verougstraete's patience, understanding, and encouragement during the concluding phase of the project made completion a joyful task.

John Paul Riquelme
Boston University

Contents

Case Studies in Contemporary Criticism

THOMAS HARDY

Tess of the d'Urbervilles

PART ONE

Tess of the d'Urbervilles: The Complete Text

Introduction: Biographical and Historical Contexts

Thomas Hardy, born (June 2, 1840) in Higher Bockhampton, a village in the country parish of Stinsford near Dorchester, an important market town in Dorset, was the younger contemporary of the major Victorian writers. Because of his long life, which extended into his eighty-eighth year, Hardy eventually became the older contemporary of the first generation of modernists. A number of the most prominent early modernist writers, including T. S. Eliot (b. 1888), James Joyce (b. 1882), D. H. Lawrence (b. 1885), Ezra Pound (b. 1885), and Virginia Woolf (b. 1882) were born while Hardy was in his forties. Like William Butler Yeats (1865–1939), arguably the elder statesman among the poets of modernism, who also reached maturity in the nineteenth century, Hardy lived long enough to experience and respond to the Boer War (1899–1902) and World War I (1914–18). But Hardy was twenty-five years older than Yeats; when he was born (in the year of the Great Irish famine), a large proportion of the villagers in Bockhampton would have had memories or impressions of the Napoleonic Wars (1805–14). Only the career of Henry James (1843–1916), among the other novelists of the late nineteenth century who lived into the twentieth century and influenced modernism, approaches the span and the effect of Hardy's almost six decades of active publishing. But James died during World War I, and his literary connections, his education in Europe and at Harvard, and his convoluted late style distinguish him from Hardy. Hardy not only continued to write for a decade after the armistice that ended World War I until his death in 1928, but to do so for a broad audience composed of people from various classes and walks of life.

Many of the great Victorian writers of the preceding generation, including Charles Dickens (1812–1870), George Eliot (1819–1880), and Matthew Arnold (1822–1888), were dead by the time Hardy wrote *Tess of the d'Urbervilles* (1889–91). Dickens, who brought out *Pickwick Papers* (1837) three years prior to Hardy's birth, died before Hardy published his first novel. During the first ten years of Hardy's life, Charlotte Brontë's *Jane Eyre* (1847) appeared, as did her sister Emily's *Wuthering Heights* (1848), Dickens's *David Copperfield* (1849–50), and William Makepeace Thackeray's *Vanity Fair* (1847–48). Alfred Lord Tennyson (1809–1892), who had succeeded William Wordsworth as poet laureate on Wordsworth's death in 1850, died the year after *Tess* appeared as a book. Hardy's contemporary, Walter Pater (1839–1894), the influential Oxford don whose essays on art inaugurated the Aesthetic Movement at the time Hardy was becoming established as a novelist, was already dead by 1900. And Oscar Wilde (1854–1900), the most flamboyant and promising of Hardy's younger contemporaries, had his career truncated even before his early death when he was arrested and convicted in 1895 for "'indecent acts'" (qtd. in Ellmann 456). In short, Hardy is exceptional among writers who were well established in the last two decades of the nineteenth century for maintaining an active, influential writing career into the 1920s.

Among the twentieth-century writers indebted to his work are Ezra Pound, D. H. Lawrence, W. H. Auden, Philip Larkin, Marianne Moore, and Dylan Thomas. Larkin claimed that he would not want Hardy's *Collected Poems* (1930), which contains more than nine hundred items, to be shorter by even a single page. Lawrence wrote an important critical study of Hardy's novels and clearly felt that Hardy provided the precedent for the novelist who is also a poet. It is fair to say that Hardy gave younger poets a model for emulation that was distinctly different from the neo-Romantic modernism of W. B. Yeats and the more radical, fragmented modernism of T. S. Eliot and Ezra Pound. Because of the character of his late fiction writing, especially *Tess* and *Jude the Obscure*, and the influence of his poetry, most of which was published in the twentieth century, it is reasonable to treat Hardy, like Wilde, as more an originator of modernism than a late Victorian writer. His works point forward in their attitudes and their styles, even though they are necessarily closely allied to the traditions and conventions of late nineteenth-century writing.

Hardy's life and career can be mapped in three phases: his early life and young adulthood (1840–72) until the time that he gave up writing poetry and established himself as a novelist; his middle adulthood (1873–97), when he was engaged in writing the most ambitious and successful of his fourteen published novels; and his late life (1897–1928), during which he gave up novel writing and devoted his energies primarily to writing poetry. In his extremely long and active writing career, Hardy, who was not university educated, became a novelist of the first rank and then a poet of the first rank, though his poetry continues to be less widely read and appreciated than his novels, five of which are frequently taught in college and university literature courses: *Far From the Madding Crowd* (1874), *The Return of the Native* (1878), *The Mayor of Casterbridge* (1886), *Tess of the d'Urbervilles* (1891), and *Jude the Obscure* (1895). A sixth novel, *The Woodlanders* (1887), though not taught as frequently, is considered by some critics to be the equal of the other five. Hardy grouped these six novels along with *Under the Greenwood Tree* (1872) as his "Novels of Character and Environment" in the collected "Wessex Edition" of 1912. Two of Hardy's novels have been made into films of note, *Far From the Madding Crowd* (1967) by John Schlesinger and *Tess* (1980) by Roman Polanski. The quality and quantity of his fiction put Hardy in the company of the most highly regarded nineteenth- and twentieth-century novelists, including Jane Austen, Charles Dickens, George Eliot, Joseph Conrad, Henry James, and William Faulkner. Hardy's abundant, technically accomplished poetry makes him unusual among these or any other group of English and American novelists.

EARLY LIFE AND YOUNG ADULTHOOD (1840–72): TOWARD A WRITING CAREER

Hardy achieved a level of success and prominence that could not have been predicted from his obscure origins. He was the first child of Jemima (Hand) and Thomas Hardy. Because the elder Hardy was a stonemason, that is, a skilled workman, the family was socially slightly superior to some others of the working class but was no better off financially. Hardy's father passed on an enthusiasm for music to his son, who grew up hearing the music of the parish church and local celebrations. Hardy's schooling, which ended when he was sixteen, was not meant to be a prelude for university studies. It would be a mistake, however, to believe that Hardy's limited formal education deprived him of learning or subtlety. The harsh quality of some of his later writing in both prose and verse arose from choice, not from lack of literary ability, experience, or knowledge. Hardy studied first in the village school and then, from age nine, at a day school in Dorchester, where the curriculum included some Latin and French. At sixteen he became apprenticed to John Hicks, a church architect in Dorchester. Coincidentally, Hicks's offices were next door to the school run by the philologist and dialect poet, William Barnes (1800–1886), the teacher of some of Hardy's closest friends. Eventually, the apprentice-architect, who admired Barnes's poetry but did not emulate his writing in dialect, established collegial relations with the poet, reviewed (1879) Barnes's *Poems of Rural Life in the Dorset Dialect*, wrote a memorable obituary notice about the poet, and edited a selection of Barnes's poetry (1908).

After his apprenticeship (1856–59), Hardy became John Hicks's assistant (1860–61). But he was intellectually ambitious and energetic in ways that his architectural work did not exhaust. During the six years of his apprenticeship and early career with Hicks, according to Hardy's own account, he studied Greek and Latin in the early mornings before work and went out in the evenings to indulge his love of music by playing the fiddle at country dances. His earliest surviving poems, such as "Domicilium" (1857–60), were written during this period, probably before he was twenty. Desiring wider horizons, Hardy decided on a life in the city, and in 1862, he moved to London, where he lived for five years. During that time, he found employment assisting the well-known architect, Arthur Blomfield, was elected to the Architectural Association, won recognition for his architectural work, pursued his interests in music, art, and the theater, and continued writing poetry, for which he was unable to find a publisher.

In the 1860s, Charles Darwin's *The Origin of Species* (1859) was causing consternation because of its implications concerning the biblical account of creation. Darwin followed it a dozen years later with *The Descent of Man* (1871). Hardy attended to the controversies surrounding these works and became familiar with the writings of Herbert Spencer (1820–1903; another important evolutionary thinker), John Stuart Mill (1806–1873), and Thomas Henry Huxley (1825–1895). During the 1860s, he lost his religious faith. In a number of poems from this time, Hardy wrote about Victorian religious doubts and what eventually came to be known as the death of God. "The Respectable Burgher on 'The Higher Criticism'" is particularly revealing of Hardy's attention to contemporary intellectual currents. By its humorous excesses, the poem shows as well his mixed response to the loss of belief in the myths associated with Christianity and to the skeptical posturings of some intellectuals:

> Since Reverend Doctors now declare
> That clerks and people must prepare
> To doubt if Adam ever were;
>
> . . . .
>
> To argue, though the stolid stare,
>
> . . . .
>
> That David was no giant-slayer,
>
> . . . .
>
> But rather was a debonair
> Shrewd bandit, skilled as banjo-player:
>
> . . . .
>
> — Since thus they hint, nor turn a hair,
> All churchgoing will I forswear,
> And sit on Sundays in my chair,
> And read that moderate man Voltaire.
>
> (Gibson 159–60; Hynes 1: 198–99)

The Higher Criticism, which involved a demystifying reappraisal of biblical stories, was influenced by German writers of the late eighteenth and early nineteenth centuries, such as David Strauss (1808–1874) and Ludwig Feuerbach (1804–1872), some of whose works George Eliot had translated in the 1840s and 1850s.

In 1867 Hardy returned to Dorset, where he worked again for his former employer and began writing novels instead of poetry. Around this time, he seems to have had an unfulfilling affair with a relative, Tryphena Sparks. But we know little about the intimate details of Hardy's life at that time or later, for he was a reticent man who destroyed many of his personal papers before he died. In the next five years, Hardy wrote four novels, three of which were published. He discarded the manuscript of the first one after George Meredith, the sympathetic evaluator of the submission for a publisher, befriended Hardy and told him that publication of the novel would hurt his career. Meredith's advice that Hardy write a novel with a stronger narrative line led to the anonymous publication in 1871 of *Desperate Remedies,* which was not commercially successful. In 1872, Hardy made a decision that moved his career toward the success that he would eventually achieve when he gave up architecture to devote all his energies to his writing. Hardy's prudence had kept him from taking this risk sooner. In that year, Leslie Stephen, the well-known editor and intellectual, asked him to write a novel in serial form for *The Cornhill Magazine,* a widely read periodical. The novel that he produced in response to Stephen's invitation, *Far From the Madding Crowd,* established him as an accomplished and popular writer of fiction.

MIDDLE ADULTHOOD (1873–97): HARDY THE SUCCESSFUL NOVELIST

Beginning with his third novel, *A Pair of Blue Eyes* (1873), Hardy published his longer fiction serially. When the installments were subsequently collected and published as volumes, they generally appeared in the traditional mid-Victorian two- or three-volume format. This was the case with *Far From the Madding Crowd,* Hardy's fourth novel, which was published in two volumes after having been serialized in *Cornhill* (1874). In the year of its publication, Hardy married Emma Lavinia Gifford, whom he had met four years earlier, in March 1870, when he visited North Cornwall to restore the church of St. Juliot. (Church restoration was his main architectural work.) Emma was the rector's sister-in-law. Their courtship (1870–74) and early marriage (1874–78) appear to have been a time of great happiness in Hardy's life. Hardy's memories of these years and his wife's written recollections of them became important in his later writing, particularly in the poetry he wrote subsequent to Emma's death in 1912 after a long period of difficulty in their childless marriage. After their wedding they lived in London briefly before moving in 1875 to Dorset, where for most of the next decade (except for 1878–81 in London) they lived in various lodgings until he designed (and his brother built) Max Gate, the home on the edge of Dorchester in which Hardy resided for the remainder of his life.

In the dozen years from 1875–86, Hardy was tremendously productive, publishing six novels, three in 1880–82 alone, including most notably *The Return of the Native* and *The Mayor of Casterbridge.* These were the years in which Henry James began publishing his mature novels (*Roderick Hudson,* 1876), work toward *The Oxford English Dictionary* was started, and Thomas Edison invented the incandescent light bulb. Hardy also now published short stories regularly, beginning with "The Distracted Young Preacher" in 1879; eventually he would publish over fifty tales. Hardy's marital difficulties seem to have begun around the time *The Return of the Native* appeared. His literary and social success, reflected in many ways, as in his becoming a member of London's Savile Club, may well have contributed to his deteriorating relations with Emma. In 1880, he had a serious illness, which lasted several months, but for most of the 1880s he was active not only writing but also pursuing his interest in art, including impressionism, and traveling to Europe (to Paris early in the decade and to Italy and France late in the decade).

From 1887–97, Hardy produced fewer novels, but at least two of the four that he published during that time, *Tess* and *Jude,* are generally considered to be more accomplished and memorable than even *The Mayor of Casterbridge,* itself a vividly rendered tragic narrative. All of Hardy's longer narratives rely on a strong realistic element. They concern characters and events that might have existed in a social and natural world that are recognizable. It would be a mistake, however, to consign Hardy narrowly to the tradition of realism in English fiction, particularly considering the developments in his late novels. As Hardy says in his third-person autobiography in the entry for August 5, 1890, "'realism' is not art" (Millgate 239). Naturalism was important to the final decades of the nineteenth century, with Emile Zola, whose *Nana* was published in 1880, as its primary exponent. Hardy expressed his admiration for Zola when Zola died in 1902, but he was no naturalist either.

Stylistically, Hardy's novels became more discontinuous, allusive, and antirealistic as his career proceeds. This is especially evident in *Tess,* where there are characters bearing allegorical names, such as Angel, and frequent changes in register among the report of dialogue, the report of thought, and the narrator's comments, which are filled with anger, bitterness, and evident learning. By drawing attention to itself, the narration regularly pulls us away from the illusion of realistic narrative. Hardy's narration develops into a stylized mask that asks us both to see the style and to see through it as we encounter character and event. The swerve from realism does not, however, involve an escape into fantasy, for Hardy's narratives concern relations of power in society, particularly the relations between men and women and between individuals and the larger controlling, often cruelly limiting, tendencies of their society. There is, in fact, an affinity between Hardy's antirealism and his presentation of individuals facing the overwhelming odds of a social and natural world that does not satisfy their needs. The conventions of society that insist on rigid, constricting roles for most women and men are as arbitrary and deforming as the conventions of realism that please those who willingly conform to society's pressures. Like the societally scripted position of rurally born, working-class men and women in the cultural hierarchy, the realistic style in fiction can, through Hardy's writing, be recognized for what it is, a convention best not taken at face value that can be variously interpreted, judged, modified, and even discarded. Along with Henry James, Oscar Wilde, and the first generation of modernists, Hardy combines in his work issues of aesthetic form with questions of value that are political and ethical. The conjunction of the aesthetic and the political places him at the beginning of significant developments in literature that are often associated with later, more obviously experimental writers.

The second phase of Hardy's career begins to reach its culmination and to develop into the third phase when he turns his attention in 1887 to the material that ultimately became *Tess*, which was published in 1891, first serially in the *Graphic*, then in three volumes by Osgood, McIlvaine & Co., a new publisher for Hardy. The decade from 1887 to 1897 is the period of Hardy's transition from fiction to poetry, even though he publishes no poetry during these years. He was, however, writing poetry again toward the end of that time, and his shift of interest toward poetic language can be discerned in his fiction at an earlier point. Although Hardy is not writing verse while working on *Tess*, the entries in his third-person autobiography for 1889 to 1892 indicate that he intended to turn his energy away from fiction and toward poetry. I have already described briefly some aspects of Hardy's style of narration as it develops toward the allusive, sometimes antirealistic style of *Tess*. In certain regards the most poetic of Hardy's novels, *Tess* is premonitory of Hardy's shift in artistic interests. It contains, for example, much repetition of word and phrase and many other instances of echoic language, that is, language that echoes other writers' words or that contains a repetition of sounds. The mythological figure of Echo has traditionally been associated with poetry because rhyme is a form of echo. Aspects of Tess's character link her to Echo. The verb of speaking that Hardy uses most frequently to describe Tess's voice, for example, is *murmur*, which with its internal repetition of the sound *-ur* is an example of echoic language that duplicates the repetition in d'*Ur*b*er*ville.

Like Wilde's Salomé, Tess is a woman character under intense social pressure whose echoic language makes her a figure representing the artist. For this reason, in the history of Hardy's shift from fiction to poetry, *Tess* is the prose, novelistic counterpart for "Wessex

Heights" (composed in 1896 but published in *Satires of Circumstance* in 1914), the poem in which the speaker shifts his allegiance within Wessex, the world of his imaginative production, from its lowlands to its heights. Like Tess, the poet speaker of "Wessex Heights" finds no comfort on the plain or in the town:

> I cannot go to the great grey Plain; there's a figure against the moon,
> Nobody sees it but I, and it makes my breast beat out of tune;
> I cannot go to the tall-spired town, being barred by the forms now passed
> For everybody but me, in whose long vision they stand there fast.
>
> (Gibson 319; Hynes II: 26)

The continuity between *Tess* and the poetry that Hardy begins writing in the 1890s involves as well Hardy's stance toward the public. His difficulties with editors and reviewers because of *Tess* caused him to take stands of principle on issues that were public matters rather than private ones. Before the 1890s, Hardy produced no public verse. When he returned to poetry-writing, however, he did so with a sense of public engagement that can be explained only partly by the freedom to speak out that Hardy felt because of his increased stature as a writer. Hardy the poet during the last three decades of his life often writes about private matters, but he is now as willing to dissent publicly in his poetry from popular causes, such as the Boer War, as he was earlier to object to the imposing of conventional morality on novelists. He writes poetry about his personal relations with his wife after her death, but he also produces the more impersonal writing of *The Dynasts* (1903–08), an epical drama about the Napoleonic Wars that mixes verse and prose.

During the decade before he stopped writing novels, Hardy collected for the first time and published as books his shorter narratives, *Wessex Tales* (1888), *A Group of Noble Dames* (1891), and *Life's Little Ironies* (1894). In addition, he published three important essays about fiction, "The Profitable Reading of Fiction" (1888), "Candour in English Fiction" (1890), and "The Science of Fiction" (1891). It is clear from Hardy's diversifying of his literary forms to include shorter tales and essays and from the substance of the essays that he was reconsidering intently his relation to his medium and his relation to his audience while he was writing *Tess*. In particular, "Candour in English Fiction" reveals Hardy's anger at the conventional expectations of the editors and the audience for the periodicals in which his fiction appeared. The decisions that editors made about *Tess* resulted in its initial rejection and eventual publication in an altered form after Hardy exercised self-censorship on the manuscript. Hardy's anger apparently led him to decide that at some point he would make an issue about the limitations that authors of fiction faced in publishing narratives about sensitive topics, such as premarital sexuality, births out of wedlock, and adultery.

After the manuscript of *Tess* was rejected in 1889 by the periodical that had commissioned it, Hardy arranged for publication in another periodical. At the same time, however, he sent the manuscript for evaluation to two other periodicals, which he knew would impose the same attitudes and restrictions as had the first one. In their rejections, the editors responded amply and frankly to his invitation for comment (Gatrell xxvi–xxvii). The responses, which Hardy preserved, substantiate his complaints about the situation of the writer in "Candour in English Fiction." When *Tess* appeared in book form, Hardy replaced many of the deletions and modifications with the original passages, which he had set aside with the evident intention of restoring them. At that time, he also emphasized his positive judgment of Tess and his empathy for her by adding the subtitle, with its ascription of purity, and the epigraph from Shakespeare. The objections to the novel then became public through some of the reviews that appeared. These Hardy responded to in the Preface to the Fifth Edition, which is now normally printed with the text (as it is here) and has become, in effect, a permanent part of it.

The controversy that resulted from the publication of *Tess* after its serialization should not distract us from the fact that the novel was well received by the public and, in many cases, by reviewers. It sold extremely well. Although the sales of Hardy's novels were never as great as those of popular novelists, such as Mrs. Humphry Ward, his success as a novelist resulted in the plan by his new publisher, Osgood, McIlvaine, to collect and reprint Hardy's fiction under the rubric "Wessex Novels." This they did from 1895–97. Hardy made *Tess* volume one of the edition. His new novel, *Jude the Obscure* (1895), first appeared in book form in this collected edition, as did his last published novel, *The Well-Beloved* (1897), a version of which had been published serially five years earlier. The collected edition gave Hardy the opportunity to revise his novels and to bring the references to his imaginary Wessex into closer conformity. In 1878 Hardy published as part of *The Return of the Native* a map of the novel's setting, but he did not carefully orchestrate the place names of the Wessex novels until the collected edition of 1895–97, for which he drew a map. Ultimately, when his works were collected again in 1912 for Macmillan's "Wessex Edition," a more elaborate map of Wessex, which included both the fictitious and the real names of places, was appended to the novels.

When they were first published in book form, both *Jude* and *The Well-Beloved* appeared as single volumes, not as two-volume or three-volume books, as was the Victorian publishing convention. *Tess* was the last of Hardy's volumes of fiction to be published originally in three volumes after serialization. When it was reprinted in the collected edition, it appeared, as did Hardy's other novels, as a single volume. This may seem a small matter, but in fact it is a mark of Hardy's modernity. Like Yeats, Hardy began his writing career under circumstances of publishing and audience that were determined by the mores and economics of nineteenth-century British culture, but by 1895, which turns out to be not the end of his writing career, only its midpoint, the earlier circumstances had been replaced by ones that were much closer to those his younger contemporaries faced in the opening decades of the twentieth century.

LATE LIFE (1897–1928): HARDY THE POET

The conflict surrounding Hardy's fiction that began with *Tess* continued with *Jude,* which was reviewed sharply. The reviews confirmed Hardy's already largely made decision to give up the writing of novels, although he did revise *The Well-Beloved* for book publication. The option to write fiction again was, however, always open to him, and he did produce a few tales (two short stories in 1899) and respond politely as late as 1905 to editors who wanted stories. Instead of writing any new novels, however, Hardy dramatized *Tess* in 1895 and in the next year produced his first significant poems since the 1860s, including "Wessex Heights" and the three poems of "In Tenebris." In 1898, he published his first collection of verse, *Wessex Poems,* containing about fifty poems written primarily in the 1860s and the 1890s.

The shift of attention to poetry came at the same time that the difficulties of Hardy's marriage intensified. With the publication of *Tess,* Hardy's relations with his wife worsened, and he developed an attachment, apparently unrequited, to Florence Henniker, a married woman, whom he advised about her writing. His emotional and intellectual estrangement from Emma, which became marked after *Jude* appeared, became even greater at the end of the decade. It is not possible to determine in exactly what measure the various factors, including Hardy's anger at editors and reviewers, his marital unhappiness, and his literary ambitions, contributed to his decision to concentrate in future on his poetry. Whatever the precise causes, the decision was momentous for Hardy's career. In the 1890s, he was at the acme of a fiction-writing career that had lasted more than a quarter of a century. Hardy was a highly successful man of letters, an active presence in English artistic life, a part of fashionable London society, and sufficiently rich to have built Max Gate. Although he did not completely turn his back on all that, he did largely withdraw to Dorset to take the risk of publicly becoming a poet. The results were worth the gamble, for Hardy produced a substantial body of poetry that is distinctly modern in character, though its roots are in the nineteenth century. The 1890s turned out to be the end of Hardy's long career as a novelist and the middle of an even more ambitious literary career that lasted six decades.

The frequent concern with loss in Hardy's poetry invites comparisons with the work of his Romantic and Victorian precursors, but its tough-minded quality and its sensitivity to ambivalence set it apart. In Hardy's poetry, which is often lyrical without being quite personal, loss is expressed but, because of life's tragic character, a lack of consolation is recognized and accepted, not lamented in a sentimental way. Easy consolation is no more available in Hardy's poetry than it is in his fiction. We can see one aspect of Hardy's modernity in the impersonal lyrical mixture of elements in poems such as "During Wind and Rain" (1917). The poem is lyric utterance, but without, strictly speaking, a personal "I." The emphasis is on third-person pronouns, as is clear in the poem's first stanza:

> They sing their dearest songs —
> He, she, all of them — yea,
> Treble and tenor and bass,
>   And one to play;
> With the candles mooning each face. . . .
>   Ah, no; the years O!
> How the sick leaves reel down in throngs!
> (Gibson 495; Hynes II: 239)

"I" is expressed indirectly later in the poem by the homonym "aye," which, because it means yes, repeats its anagram, "yea." The "O" of apostrophe, typical of lyric poetry, is balanced by its counterpart, "no." In this poem about death and change, Hardy combines an acceptance of loss with an emphasis on human work, including the act of writing represented in the carving of names on headstones, that transforms the potentially gloomy rain into a humanized but not sentimentalized plough:

> Ah, no; the years, the years;
> Down their carved names the rain-drop ploughs.
> (Gibson 496; Hynes II: 240)

The combination typifies Hardy's originality and his achievement as a poet. The connection Hardy makes between writing and working in stone, which he would have known from his father's stonemasonry and his experience with architecture, puts him in the line of poets that stand behind Seamus Heaney's metaphor (in his poem "Digging") of digging with a pen.

Besides being a lyric poet, Hardy was a strong-minded public poet from near the start of his renewed poetic career. He responded to the Boer War (1899–1902) in verse in ways that were politically courageous. "Drummer Hodge" (1899) is probably the best known of his poems expressing skepticism about the War. Hardy's second volume of verse, *Poems of the Past and the Present* (1901), which included his War Poems, was received more positively than the first and established for his audience Hardy's new writing persona as a poet. In the year of its appearance, Queen Victoria, who ascended the throne three years before Hardy's birth, died.

During the remainder of the first decade of the century, Hardy published, in three parts (I, 1903; II, 1906; III, 1908), a substantial, unusual epic drama, mostly in verse, of the Napoleonic era, *The Dynasts,* an important but still underrated work. While he was composing *The Dynasts,* Hardy's mother died (1904), and he met Florence Dugdale, who eventually became his wife. Hardy was awarded the Order of Merit in the year that Edward VII died (1910), the year following the publication of his third volume of poetry, *Time's Laughingstocks* (1909). That collection contains a poem in terza rima on the death of Hardy's friend and former mentor, the novelist George Meredith, whom he had known for almost forty years. Hardy succeeded Meredith as President of the Society of Authors.

Macmillan, who had become Hardy's publisher early in the new century, began publication of his second collected edition, the Wessex Edition, in 1912. Hardy again chose to make *Tess* volume one. For the Wessex Edition, Hardy wrote a "General Preface to the Novels and

Poems," in which he explains that he has arranged his narratives under three broad headings: "Novels of Character and Environment" (by far the largest group), "Romances and Fantasies," and "Novels of Ingenuity." The penultimate sentence of the general preface captures succinctly Hardy's sensibility in 1911 at age seventy-one: "The more written the more seems to remain to be written; and the night cometh."

In 1912 Hardy also published his fourth volume of short narratives, *A Changed Man and Other Tales,* and began to write elegiac poems about Emma after her death in November. Hardy found among her effects an exercise book containing recollections about her childhood and their romance. The recollections apparently intensified his sense of their marriage's loss and tragedy. Hardy responded to his grief by revisiting the locales of his courtship of Emma in Cornwall. The initial poetic results were the twenty-one elegiac "Poems of 1912–13," whose subtitle, *Veteris vestigia flammae,* means "traces of an old fire." Hardy published these poems, which are among the greatest of his career, in *Satires of Circumstance* (1914). The volume also contains a group of poems bearing the book's title and one of his best-known poems, "The Convergence of the Twain," concerning the horrific loss of the luxury liner, the *Titanic,* on its initial Atlantic crossing in 1912. "A Singer Asleep," Hardy's metrically virtuosic elegy for a poet he admired greatly, A. C. Swinburne (1837–1909), appears in the volume as well. In a later poem, "A Refusal," published in *Human Shows* (1925), Hardy derided the decision not to bury Swinburne in Westminster Abbey because of puritanical objections to his moral character. In 1914 Hardy married Florence Dugdale, but he continued to write elegiac poetry concerning his relations with his first wife for the remainder of his career.

During World War I, Hardy wrote his "Poems of War and Patriotism," which were published in his sixth volume of poems, *Moments of Vision* (1917). Unlike the poems written during the Boer War, some of these later poems, such as "A Call to National Service," explicitly supported the war effort. Others, however, including "In Time of 'The Breaking of Nations,'" put war in the context of work, love, and the passage of time with no hint of nationalistic feeling:

Yonder a maid and her wight
  Come whispering by:
War's annals will cloud into night
  Ere their story die.

(Gibson 543; Hynes II: 296)

And the closing poem of the group, "I Looked Up from My Writing," suggests that the poet bears some culpability for the deaths of young soldiers because of his writing during wartime. The poem's self-indicting aspect is evident in the pun on "indicting," which means *writing,* in the first stanza:

> I looked up from my writing,
>   And gave a start to see,
> As if rapt in my inditing,
>   The moon's full gaze on me.
>   (Gibson 551; Hynes II: 305)

Hardy's *Selected Poems* (1916), which he edited himself, appeared during the war, followed by his *Collected Poems* (1919) and the deluxe "Mellstock Edition" of his work. In the next decade, Hardy published two volumes of poetry and a verse drama before his death: *Late Lyrics and Earlier* (1922; the year of both Eliot's *The Waste Land* and Joyce's *Ulysses*); *Human Shows* (1925); and *The Famous Tragedy of the Queen of Cornwall* (1923). *Late Lyrics* contains a long prefatory "Apology" in which Hardy reflects on criticism of his work as pessimistic and on the need for poetry to effect the unlikely conjunction of science and religion. Hardy's final volume of poems, *Winter Words* (1928), was published posthumously. The fourth edition of *Collected Poems,* published two years after Hardy's death, contains 918 poems, most of them written after 1890. Hardy's second wife published her modified version of the third-person autobiography that he had dictated to her, *The Early Life of Thomas Hardy* (1928) and *The Later Years of Thomas Hardy* (1930). Both volumes carried her name as author.

Thomas Hardy was buried in a way that drew criticism from some, including T. S. Eliot in an editorial in *The Monthly Criterion* (March 1928). He had wanted to be buried in the churchyard at Stinsford with his first wife, but instead his heart was buried there and his ashes were interred in Westminster Abbey, along with the remains of many other writers important to England's national heritage. The dismemberment and split burial close in an oddly apt way the life of a reticent, private, uncompromising individual whose ambition, talent, principles, and achievements thrust him into the eye of the public and into the company of his country's greatest writers.

John Paul Riquelme

WORKS CITED

Ellmann, Richard. *Oscar Wilde.* New York: Knopf, 1988.

Gatrell, Simon. "Note on the Text." In *Tess of the d'Urbervilles.* Oxford and New York: Oxford UP, 1988. xxv–xxx.

Gibson, James, ed. *The Complete Poems of Thomas Hardy.* New York: Macmillan, 1976.

Heaney, Seamus. *Selected Poems, 1966–1987.* New York: Farrar, 1990.

Hynes, Samuel, ed. *The Complete Poetical Works of Thomas Hardy. Vol. 1* (Oxford: Clarendon, 1982) and *Vol. II* (rpt. with corrections, 1987; Oxford: Clarendon, 1984).

Millgate, Michael. *The Life and Work of Thomas Hardy by Thomas Hardy.* Athens, GA: U of Georgia P, 1985.

SELECTED BIOGRAPHIES OF THOMAS HARDY

Gittings, Robert. *Young Thomas Hardy.* Boston: Little, 1975.

———. *Thomas Hardy's Later Years.* Boston: Little, 1978.

Millgate, Michael. *Thomas Hardy: A Biography.* New York: Random, 1982.

Seymour-Smith, Martin. *Hardy.* New York: St. Martin's, 1995.

TESS OF THE D'URBERVILLES

A PURE WOMAN

FAITHFULLY PRESENTED BY

THOMAS HARDY

'. . . Poor wounded name! My bosom as a bed
Shall lodge thee.'

— W. Shakespeare.°

MACMILLAN AND CO., LIMITED
ST. MARTIN'S STREET, LONDON
1920

'. . . Poor wounded name! . . . : *Two Gentlemen of Verona* 1.2.115–16. In Shakespeare's play, the lines are spoken by a character who has, in order to create an effect on the person watching her, just torn up a letter containing the name of her beloved, the fragments of which she places in her cleavage. The implied meaning for *Tess* concerns Tess's reputation, or name, but also the mutilated character of the book. As Hardy suggests in the "Explanatory Note to the First Edition" (see p. 24), the narrative's "trunk and limbs" were separated by the cuts and other changes he made in order to meet the expectations of editors and some readers when he published *Tess* in installments.

GENERAL PREFACE TO THE NOVELS AND POEMS

In accepting a proposal for a definitive edition of these productions in prose and verse I have found an opportunity of classifying the novels under heads that show approximately the author's aim, if not his achievement, in each book of the series at the date of its composition. Sometimes the aim was lower than at other times; sometimes, where the intention was primarily high, force of circumstances (among which the chief were the necessities of magazine publication) compelled a modification, great or slight, of the original plan. Of a few, however, of the longer novels, and of many of the shorter tales, it may be assumed that they stand to-day much as they would have stood if no accidents had obstructed the channel between the writer and the public. That many of them, if any, stand as they would stand if written *now* is not to be supposed.

In the classification of these fictitious chronicles — for which the name of 'The Wessex Novels' was adopted, and is still retained — the first group is called 'Novels of Character and Environment,' and contains those which approach most nearly to uninfluenced works; also one or two which, whatever their quality in some few of their episodes, may claim a verisimilitude in general treatment and detail.

The second group is distinguished as 'Romances and Fantasies,' a sufficiently descriptive definition. The third class — 'Novels of Ingenuity' — show a not infrequent disregard of the probable in the chain of events, and depend for their interest mainly on the incidents themselves. They might also be characterized as 'Experiments,' and were written for the nonce simply; though despite the artificiality of their fable some of their scenes are not without fidelity to life.

It will not be supposed that these differences are distinctly perceptible in every page of every volume. It was inevitable that blendings and alternations should occur in all. Moreover, as it was not thought desirable in every instance to change the arrangement of the shorter stories to which readers have grown accustomed, certain of these may be found under headings to which an acute judgment might deny appropriateness.

It has sometimes been conceived of novels that evolve their action on a circumscribed scene — as do many (though not all) of these — that they cannot be so inclusive in their exhibition of human nature as novels wherein the scenes cover large extents of country, in which events figure amid towns and cities, even wander over the four quarters of the globe. I am not concerned to argue this point further than to suggest that the conception is an untrue one in respect of the elementary passions. But I would state that the geographical limits of the stage here trodden were not absolutely forced upon the writer by circumstances; he forced them upon himself from judgment. I considered that our magnificent heritage from the Greeks in dramatic literature found sufficient room for a large proportion of its action in an extent of their country not much larger than the half-dozen counties here reunited under the old name of Wessex, that the domestic emotions have throbbed in Wessex nooks with as much intensity as in the palaces of Europe, and that, anyhow, there was quite enough human nature in Wessex for one man's literary purpose. So far was I possessed by this idea that I kept within the frontiers when it would have been easier to overleap them and give more cosmopolitan features to the narrative.

Thus, though the people in most of the novels (and in much of the shorter verse) are dwellers in a province bounded on the north by the Thames, on the south by the English Channel, on the east by a line running from Hayling Island to Windsor Forest, and on the west by the Cornish coast, they were meant to be typically and essentially those of any and every place where

Thought's the slave of life, and life time's fool,

— beings in whose hearts and minds that which is apparently local should be really universal.

But whatever the success of this intention, and the value of these novels as delineations of humanity, they have at least a humble supplementary quality of which I may be justified in reminding the reader, though it is one that was quite unintentional and unforeseen. At the dates represented in the various narrations things were like that in Wessex: the inhabitants lived in certain ways, engaged in certain occupations, kept alive certain customs, just as they are shown doing in these pages. And in particularizing such I have often been reminded of Boswell's remarks on the trouble to which he was put and the pilgrimages he was obliged to make to authenticate some detail, though the labour was one which would bring him no praise. Unlike his achievement, however, on which an error would as he says have brought discredit, if these country customs and vocations, obsolete and obsolescent, had been detailed wrongly, nobody would have discovered such errors to the end of Time. Yet I have instituted inquiries to correct tricks of memory, and striven against temptations to exaggerate, in order to preserve for my own satisfaction a fairly true record of a vanishing life.

It is advisable also to state here, in response to inquiries from readers interested in landscape, prehistoric antiquities, and especially old English architecture, that the description of these backgrounds has been done from the real — that is to say, has something real for its basis, however illusively treated. Many features of the first two kinds have been given under their existing names; for instance, the Vale of Blackmoor or Blakemore, Hambledon Hill, Bulbarrow, Nettlecombe Tout, Dogbury Hill, High-Stoy, Bubb-Down Hill, The Devil's Kitchen, Cross-in-Hand, Long-Ash Lane, Benvill Lane, Giant's Hill, Crimmercrock Lane, and Stonehenge. The rivers Froom, or Frome, and Stour, are, of course, well known as such. And the further idea was that large towns and points tending to mark the outline of Wessex — such as Bath, Plymouth, The Start, Portland Bill, Southampton, etc., — should be named clearly. The scheme was not greatly elaborated, but, whatever its value, the names remain still.

In respect of places described under fictitious or ancient names in the novels — for reasons that seemed good at the time of writing them — and kept up in the poems — discerning people have affirmed in print that they clearly recognize the originals: such as Shaftesbury in 'Shaston,' Sturminster Newton in 'Stourcastle,' Dorchester in 'Casterbridge,' Salisbury Plain in 'The Great Plain,' Cranborne Chase in 'The Chase,' Beaminster in 'Emminster,' Bere Regis in 'Kingsbere,' Woodbury Hill in 'Greenhill,' Wool Bridge in 'Wellbridge,' Hartfoot or Harput Lane in 'Stagfoot Lane,' Hazlebury in 'Nuttlebury,' Bridport in 'Port Bredy,' Maiden Newton in 'Chalk Newton,' a farm near Nettlecombe Tout in 'Flintcomb Ash,' Sherborne in 'Sherton Abbas,' Milton Abbey in 'Middleton Abbey,' Cerne Abbas in 'Abbot's Cernel,' Evershot in 'Evershed,' Taunton in 'Toneborough,' Bournemouth in 'Sandbourne,' Winchester in 'Wintoncester,' Oxford in 'Christminster,' Reading in 'Aldbrickham,' Newbury in 'Kennetbridge,' Wantage in 'Alfredston,' Basingstoke in 'Stoke Barehills,' and so on. Subject to the qualifications above given, that no detail is guaranteed, — that the portraiture of fictitiously named towns and villages was only suggested by certain real places, and wantonly wanders from inventorial descriptions of them — I do not contradict these keen hunters for the real; I am satisfied with their statements as at least an indication of their interest in the scenes.

Thus much for the novels. Turning now to the verse — to myself the more individual part of my literary fruitage — I would say that, unlike some of the fiction, nothing interfered with the writer's freedom in respect of its form or context. Several of the poems — indeed many — were produced before novel-writing had been thought of as a pursuit; but few saw the light till all the novels had been published. The limited stage to which the majority of the latter confine their exhibitions has not been adhered to here in the same proportion, the dramatic part especially having a very broad theatre of action. It may thus relieve the circumscribed areas treated in the prose, if such relief be needed. To be sure, one might argue that by surveying Europe from a celestial point of vision — as in *The Dynasts* — that continent becomes virtually a province — a Wessex, an Attica, even a mere garden — and hence is made to conform to the principle of the novels, however far it outmeasures their region. But that may be as it will.

The few volumes filled by the verse cover a producing period of some eighteen years first and last, while the seventeen or more volumes of novels represent correspondingly about four-and-twenty years. One is reminded by this disproportion in time and result how much more concise and quintessential expression becomes when given in rhythmic form than when shaped in the language of prose.

One word on what has been called the present writer's philosophy of life, as exhibited more particularly in this metrical section of his compositions. Positive views on the Whence and the Wherefore of things have never been advanced by this pen as a consistent philosophy. Nor is it likely, indeed, that imaginative writings extending over more than forty years would exhibit a coherent scientific theory of the universe even if it had been attempted — of that universe concerning which Spencer owns to the 'paralyzing thought' that possibly there exists no comprehension of it anywhere. But such objectless consistency never has been attempted, and the sentiments in the following pages have been stated truly to be mere impressions of the moment, and not convictions or arguments.

That these impressions have been condemned as 'pessimistic' — as if that were a very wicked adjective — shows a curious muddle-mindedness. It must be obvious that there is a higher characteristic of philosophy than pessimism, or than meliorism, or even than the optimism of these critics — which is truth. Existence is either ordered in a certain way, or it is not so ordered, and conjectures which harmonize best with experience are removed above all comparison with other conjectures which do not so harmonize. So that to say one view is worse than other views without proving it erroneous implies the possibility of a false view being better or more expedient than a true view; and no pragmatic proppings can make that *idolum specus* stand on its feet, for it postulates a prescience denied to humanity.

And there is another consideration. Differing natures find their tongue in the presence of differing spectacles. Some natures become vocal at tragedy, some are made vocal by comedy, and it seems to me that to whichever of these aspects of life a writer's instinct for expression the more readily responds, to that he should allow it to respond. That before a contrasting side of things he remains undemonstrative need not be assumed to mean that he remains unperceiving.

It was my hope to add to these volumes of verse as many more as would make a fairly comprehensive cycle of the whole. I had wished that those in dramatic, ballad, and narrative form should include most of the cardinal situations which occur in social and public life, and those in lyric form a round of emotional experiences of some completeness. But

The petty done, the undone vast!

The more written the more seems to remain to be written; and the night cometh. I realize that these hopes and plans, except possibly to the extent of a volume or two, must remain unfulfilled.

T. H.
October 1911.

EXPLANATORY NOTE TO THE FIRST EDITION

The main portion of the following story appeared — with slight modifications — in the *Graphic* newspaper; other chapters, more especially addressed to adult readers, in the *Fortnightly Review* and the *National Observer*, as episodic sketches. My thanks are tendered to the editors and proprietors of those periodicals for enabling me now to piece the trunk and limbs of the novel together, and print it complete, as originally written two years ago.

I will just add that the story is sent out in all sincerity of purpose, as an attempt to give artistic form to a true sequence of things; and in respect of the book's opinions and sentiments, I would ask any too genteel reader, who cannot endure to have said what everybody nowadays thinks and feels, to remember a well-worn sentence of St. Jerome's: If an offence come out of the truth, better is it that the offence come than that the truth be concealed.

T. H.
November 1891.

PREFACE TO THE FIFTH AND LATER EDITIONS

This novel being one wherein the great campaign of the heroine begins after an event in her experience which has usually been treated as fatal to her part of protagonist, or at least as the virtual ending of her enterprises and hopes, it was quite contrary to avowed conventions that the public should welcome the book, and agree with me in holding that there was something more to be said in fiction than had been said about the shaded side of a well-known catastrophe. But the responsive spirit in which *Tess of the d'Urbervilles* has been received by the readers of England and America, would seem to prove that the plan of laying down a story on the lines of tacit opinion, instead of making it to square with the merely vocal formulæ of society, is not altogether a wrong one, even when exemplified in so unequal and partial an achievement as the present. For this responsiveness I cannot refrain from expressing my thanks; and my regret is that, in a world where one so often hungers in vain for friendship, where even not to be wilfully misunderstood is felt as a kindness, I shall never meet in person these appreciative readers, male and female, and shake them by the hand.

I include amongst them the reviewers — by far the majority — who have so generously welcomed the tale. Their words show that they, like the others, have only too largely repaired my defects of narration by their own imaginative intuition.

Nevertheless, though the novel was intended to be neither didactic nor aggressive, but in the scenic parts to be representative simply, and in the contemplative to be oftener charged with impressions than with convictions, there have been objectors both to the matter and to the rendering.

The more austere of these maintain a conscientious difference of opinion concerning, among other things, subjects fit for art, and reveal an inability to associate the idea of the sub-title adjective with any but the artificial and derivative meaning which has resulted to it from the ordinances of civilization. They ignore the meaning of the word in Nature, together with all æsthetic claims upon it, not to mention the spiritual interpretation afforded by the finest side of their own Christianity. Others dissent on grounds which are intrinsically no more than an assertion that the novel embodies the views of life prevalent at the end of the nineteenth century, and not those of an earlier and simpler generation — an assertion which I can only hope may be well founded. Let me repeat that a novel is an impression, not an argument; and there the matter must rest; as one is reminded by a passage which occurs in the letters of Schiller to Goethe on judges of this class: 'They are those who seek only their own ideas in a representation, and prize that which should be as higher than what is. The cause of the dispute, therefore, lies in the very first principles, and it would be utterly impossible to come to an understanding with them.' And again: 'As soon as I observe that any one, when judging of poetical representations, considers anything more important than the inner Necessity and Truth, I have done with him.'

In the introductory words to the first edition I suggested the possible advent of the genteel person who would not be able to endure something or other in these pages. That person duly appeared among the aforesaid objectors. In one case he felt upset that it was not possible for him to read the book through three times, owing to my not having made that critical effort which 'alone can prove the salvation of such an one.' In another, he objected to such vulgar articles as the Devil's pitchfork, a lodging-house carving-knife, and a shame-bought parasol, appearing in a respectable story. In another place he was a gentleman who turned Christian for half-an-hour the better to express his grief that a disrespectful phrase about the Immortals should have been used; though the same innate gentility compelled him to excuse the author in words of pity that one cannot be too thankful for: 'He does but give us of his best.' I can assure this great critic that to exclaim illogically against the gods, singular or plural, is not such an original sin of mine as he seems to imagine. True, it may have some local originality; though if Shakespeare were an authority on history, which perhaps he is not, I could show that the sin was introduced into Wessex as early as the Heptarchy° itself. Says Glo'ster in *Lear,* otherwise Ina, king of that country:

Heptarchy: The loose confederation of the seven Anglo-Saxon kingdoms (East Anglia, Essex, Kent, Mercia, Northumbria, Sussex, and Wessex) from the fifth to the ninth century.

As flies to wanton boys are to the gods;
They kill us for their sport.°

The remaining two or three manipulators of *Tess* were of the predetermined sort whom most writers and readers would gladly forget; professed literary boxers, who put on their convictions for the occasion; modern 'Hammers of Heretics'; sworn Discouragers, ever on the watch to prevent the tentative half-success from becoming the whole success later on; who pervert plain meanings, and grow personal under the name of practising the great historical method. However, they may have causes to advance, privileges to guard, traditions to keep going; some of which a mere tale-teller, who writes down how the things of the world strike him, without any ulterior intentions whatever, has overlooked, and may by pure inadvertence have run foul of when in the least aggressive mood. Perhaps some passing perception, the outcome of a dream hour, would, if generally acted on, cause such an assailant considerable inconvenience with respect to position, interests, family, servant, ox, ass, neighbour, or neighbour's wife. He therefore valiantly hides his personality behind a publisher's shutters, and cries 'Shame!' So densely is the world thronged that any shifting of positions, even the best warranted advance, galls somebody's kibe.° Such shiftings often begin in sentiment, and such sentiment sometimes begins in a novel.

July 1892.

The foregoing remarks were written during the early career of this story, when a spirited public and private criticism of its points was still fresh to the feelings. The pages are allowed to stand for what they are worth, as something once said; but probably they would not have been written now. Even in the short time which has elapsed since the book was first published, some of the critics who provoked the reply have 'gone down into silence,' as if to remind one of the infinite unimportance of both their say and mine.

January 1895.

The present edition of this novel contains a few pages that have never appeared in any previous edition. When the detached episodes

As flies to wanton boys . . . : *King Lear* 4:1.36–37. **galls somebody's kibe:** The statement echoes *Hamlet* 5.1.141, where it refers to the peasant's toe coming so close to the courtier's heel as to chafe the courtier's chilblain, an itching swollen place on the foot. Hardy is comparing himself to the peasant.

were collected as stated in the preface of 1891, these pages were overlooked, though they were in the original manuscript. They occur in Chapter X.

Respecting the sub-title, to which allusion was made above, I may add that it was appended at the last moment, after reading the final proofs, as being the estimate left in a candid mind of the heroine's character — an estimate that nobody would be likely to dispute. It was disputed more than anything else in the book. *Melius fuerat non scribere.*° But there it stands.

The novel was first published complete, in three volumes, in November 1891.

T. H.
March 1912.

Melius fuerat non scribere: "It would have been better not to write it." (Latin)

CONTENTS

PHASE THE FIRST

PHASE THE SECOND

PHASE THE THIRD

PHASE THE FOURTH

PHASE THE FIFTH

PHASE THE SIXTH

PHASE THE SEVENTH

Map reprinted from Vol. I of the Wessex Edition of *The Works of Thomas Hardy in Prose and Verse.*

PHASE THE FIRST. THE MAIDEN

I

On an evening in the latter part of May a middle-aged man was walking homeward from Shaston to the village of Marlott, in the adjoining Vale of Blakemore or Blackmoor. The pair of legs that carried him were rickety, and there was a bias in his gait which inclined him somewhat to the left of a straight line. He occasionally gave a smart nod, as if in confirmation of some opinion, though he was not thinking of anything in particular. An empty egg-basket was slung upon his arm, the nap of his hat was ruffled, a patch being quite worn away at its brim where his thumb came in taking it off. Presently he was met by an elderly parson astride on a gray mare, who, as he rode, hummed a wandering tune.

'Good night t'ee,' said the man with the basket.

'Good night, Sir John,' said the parson.

The pedestrian, after another pace or two, halted, and turned round.

'Now, sir, begging your pardon; we met last market-day on this road about this time, and I zaid "Good night," and you made reply "*Good night, Sir John,*" as now.'

'I did,' said the parson.

'And once before that — near a month ago.'

'I may have.'

'Then what might your meaning be in calling me "Sir John" these different times, when I be plain Jack Durbeyfield, the haggler?'°

The parson rode a step or two nearer.

'It was only my whim,' he said; and, after a moment's hesitation: 'It was on account of a discovery I made some little time ago, whilst I was hunting up pedigrees for the new county history. I am Parson Tringham, the antiquary, of Stagfoot Lane. Don't you really know, Durbeyfield, that you are the lineal representative of the ancient and knightly family of the d'Urbervilles, who derive their descent from Sir Pagan d'Urberville, that renowned knight who came from Normandy with William the Conqueror, as appears by Battle Abbey Roll?'°

haggler: An itinerant dealer (*OED*). **Battle Abbey Roll:** "This is popularly supposed to have been a list of William the Conqueror's companions preserved at Battle Abbey, on the site of his great victory over Harold. . . . It is not a list of individuals, but only of family surnames, and it seems to have been intended to show which families had 'come over with the Conqueror,' and to have been compiled about the 14th century." (*Enc. Brit.* 3:534)

'Never heard it before, sir!'

'Well it's true. Throw up your chin a moment, so that I may catch the profile of your face better. Yes, that's the d'Urberville nose and chin — a little debased. Your ancestor was one of the twelve knights who assisted the Lord of Estremavilla in Normandy in his conquest of Glamorganshire. Branches of your family held manors over all this part of England; their names appear in the Pipe Rolls in the time of King Stephen.° In the reign of King John one of them was rich enough to give a manor to the Knights Hospitallers; and in Edward the Second's time your forefather Brian was summoned to Westminster to attend the great Council there. You declined a little in Oliver Cromwell's time, but to no serious extent, and in Charles the Second's reign you were made Knights of the Royal Oak for your loyalty. Aye, there have been generations of Sir Johns among you, and if knighthood were hereditary, like a baronetcy, as it practically was in old times, when men were knighted from father to son, you would be Sir John now.'

'Ye don't say so!'

'In short,' concluded the parson, decisively smacking his leg with his switch, 'there's hardly such another family in England.'

'Daze my eyes, and isn't there?' said Durbeyfield. 'And here have I been knocking about, year after year, from pillar to post, as if I was no more than the commonest feller in the parish. . . . And how long hev this news about me been knowed, Pa'son Tringham?'

The clergyman explained that, as far as he was aware, it had quite died out of knowledge, and could hardly be said to be known at all. His own investigations had begun on a day in the preceding spring when, having been engaged in tracing the vicissitudes of the d'Urberville family, he had observed Durbeyfield's name on his waggon, and had thereupon been led to make inquiries about his father and grandfather till he had no doubt on the subject.

'At first I resolved not to disturb you with such a useless piece of information,' said he. 'However, our impulses are too strong for our judgment sometimes. I thought you might perhaps know something of it all the while.'

Pipe Rolls in the time of King Stephen . . . : Financial records of the Exchequer, or royal treasury. The reigns of the kings mentioned are as follows: King Stephen (1135–54); King John (1199–1216); Edward III (1307–27); Charles II (1660–85). Oliver Cromwell (1599–1658) was Lord Protector of England (1653–58) until his death shortly before the restoration of the monarchy under Charles II. Knights Hospitallers, or Knights of St. John of Jerusalem, were members of a religious order that protected Crusaders and pilgrims on their way to the Holy Land.

'Well, I have heard once or twice, 'tis true, that my family had seen better days afore they came to Blackmoor. But I took no notice o't, thinking it to mean that we had once kept two horses where we now keep only one. I've got a wold° silver spoon, and a wold graven seal at home, too; but, Lord, what's a spoon and seal? . . . And to think that I and these noble d'Urbervilles were one flesh all the time. 'Twas said that my gr't-grandfer had secrets, and didn't care to talk of where he came from. . . . And where do we raise our smoke, now, parson, if I may make so bold; I mean, where do we d'Urbervilles live?'

'You don't live anywhere. You are extinct — as a county family.'

'That's bad.'

'Yes — what the mendacious family chronicles call extinct in the male line — that is, gone down — gone under.'

'Then where do we lie?'

'At Kingsbere-sub-Greenhill: rows and rows of you in your vaults, with your effigies under Purbeck-marble canopies.'

'And where be our family mansions and estates?'

'You haven't any.'

'Oh? No lands neither?'

'None; though you once had 'em in abundance, as I said, for your family consisted of numerous branches. In this county there was a seat of yours at Kingsbere, and another at Sherton, and another at Millpond, and another at Lullstead, and another at Wellbridge.'

'And shall we ever come into our own again?'

'Ah — that I can't tell!'

'And what had I better do about it, sir?' asked Durbeyfield, after a pause.

'Oh — nothing, nothing; except chasten yourself with the thought of "how are the mighty fallen."° It is a fact of some interest to the local historian and genealogist, nothing more. There are several families among the cottagers of this county of almost equal lustre. Good night.'

'But you'll turn back and have a quart of beer wi' me on the strength o't, Pa'son Tringham? There's a very pretty brew in tap at The Pure Drop — though, to be sure, not so good as at Rolliver's.'

'No, thank you — not this evening, Durbeyfield. You've had enough already.' Concluding thus the parson rode on his way, with doubts as to his discretion in retailing this curious bit of lore.

wold: Old (dialect). **"how are the mighty fallen":** Quoted from 2 Samuel 1:19, 25, and 27, where it appears as part of David's lament for Saul and Jonathan.

When he was gone Durbeyfield walked a few steps in a profound reverie, and then sat down upon the grassy bank by the roadside, depositing his basket before him. In a few minutes a youth appeared in the distance, walking in the same direction as that which had been pursued by Durbeyfield. The latter, on seeing him, held up his hand, and the lad quickened his pace and came near.

'Boy, take up that basket! I want 'ee to go on an errand for me.'

The lath-like stripling frowned. 'Who be you, then, John Durbeyfield, to order me about and call me "boy"? You know my name as well as I know yours!'

'Do you, do you? That's the secret — that's the secret! Now obey my orders, and take the message I'm going to charge 'ee wi'. . . . Well, Fred, I don't mind telling you that the secret is that I'm one of a noble race — it has been just found out by me this present afternoon, P.M.' And as he made the announcement, Durbeyfield, declining from his sitting position, luxuriously stretched himself out upon the bank among the daisies.

The lad stood before Durbeyfield, and contemplated his length from crown to toe.

'Sir John d'Urberville — that's who I am,' continued the prostrate man. 'That is if knights were baronets — which they be. 'Tis recorded in history all about me. Dost know of such a place, lad, as Kingsbere-sub-Greenhill?'

'Ees. I've been there to Greenhill Fair.'

'Well, under the church of that city there lie ——'

''Tisn't a city, the place I mean; leastwise 'twaddn' when I was there — 'twas a little one-eyed, blinking sort o' place.'

'Never you mind the place, boy, that's not the question before us. Under the church of that there parish lie my ancestors — hundreds of 'em — in coats of mail and jewels, in gr't lead coffins weighing tons and tons. There's not a man in the county o' South-Wessex that's got grander and nobler skillentons in his family than I.'

'Oh?'

'Now take up that basket, and goo on to Marlott, and when you've come to The Pure Drop Inn, tell 'em to send a horse and carriage to me immed'ately, to carry me hwome. And in the bottom o' the carriage they be to put a noggin o' rum in a small bottle, and chalk it up to my account. And when you've done that goo on to my house with the basket, and tell my wife to put away that washing, because she needn't finish it, and wait till I come hwome, as I've news to tell her.'

As the lad stood in a dubious attitude, Durbeyfield put his hand in his pocket, and produced a shilling, one of the chronically few that he possessed.

'Here's for your labour, lad.'

This made a difference in the young man's estimate of the position.

'Yes, Sir John. Thank 'ee. Anything else I can do for 'ee, Sir John?'

'Tell 'em at hwome that I should like for supper, — well, lamb's fry if they can get it; and if they can't, black-pot; and if they can't get that, well, chitterlings will do.'

'Yes, Sir John.'

The boy took up the basket, and as he set out the notes of a brass band were heard from the direction of the village.

'What's that?' said Durbeyfield. 'Not on account o' I?'

''Tis the women's club-walking,° Sir John. Why, your da'ter is one o' the members.'

'To be sure — I'd quite forgot it in my thoughts of greater things! Well, vamp° on to Marlott, will ye, and order that carriage, and maybe I'll drive round and inspect the club.'

The lad departed, and Durbeyfield lay waiting on the grass and daisies in the evening sun. Not a soul passed that way for a long while, and the faint notes of the band were the only human sounds audible within the rim of blue hills.

II

The village of Marlott lay amid the north-eastern undulations of the beautiful Vale of Blakemore or Blackmoor aforesaid, an engirdled and secluded region, for the most part untrodden as yet by tourist or landscape-painter, though within a four hours' journey from London.

It is a vale whose acquaintance is best made by viewing it from the summits of the hills that surround it — except perhaps during the droughts of summer. An unguided ramble into its recesses in bad weather is apt to engender dissatisfaction with its narrow, tortuous, and miry ways.

This fertile and sheltered tract of country, in which the fields are never brown and the springs never dry, is bounded on the south by the bold chalk ridge that embraces the prominences of Hambledon

women's club-walking: "A procession by the members of a local club or clubs; esp. the annual festival of a benefit club or friendly society" (*OED*); here the club is a parish group. **vamp:** Trudge, tramp, walk (dialect).

Hill, Bulbarrow, Nettlecombe-Tout, Dogbury, High Stoy, and Bubb Down. The traveller from the coast, who, after plodding northward for a score of miles over calcareous downs and corn-lands, suddenly reaches the verge of one of these escarpments, is surprised and delighted to behold, extended like a map beneath him, a country differing absolutely from that which he has passed through. Behind him the hills are open, the sun blazes down upon fields so large as to give an unenclosed character to the landscape, the lanes are white, the hedges low and plashed, the atmosphere colourless. Here, in the valley, the world seems to be constructed upon a smaller and more delicate scale; the fields are mere paddocks, so reduced that from this height their hedgerows appear a network of dark green threads overspreading the paler green of the grass. The atmosphere beneath is languorous, and is so tinged with azure that what artists call the middle distance partakes also of that hue, while the horizon beyond is of the deepest ultramarine. Arable lands are few and limited; with but slight exceptions the prospect is a broad rich mass of grass and trees, mantling minor hills and dales within the major. Such is the Vale of Blackmoor.

The district is of historic, no less than of topographical interest. The Vale was known in former times as the Forest of White Hart, from a curious legend of King Henry III's reign, in which the killing by a certain Thomas de la Lynd of a beautiful white hart which the king had run down and spared, was made the occasion of a heavy fine. In those days, and till comparatively recent times, the country was densely wooded. Even now, traces of its earlier condition are to be found in the old oak copses and irregular belts of timber that yet survive upon its slopes, and the hollow-trunked trees that shade so many of its pastures.

The forests have departed, but some old customs of their shades remain. Many, however, linger only in a metamorphosed or disguised form. The May-Day dance, for instance, was to be discerned on the afternoon under notice, in the guise of the club revel, or 'club-walking,' as it was there called.

It was an interesting event to the younger inhabitants of Marlott, though its real interest was not observed by the participators in the ceremony. Its singularity lay less in the retention of a custom of walking in procession and dancing on each anniversary than in the members being solely women. In men's clubs such celebrations were, though expiring, less uncommon; but either the natural shyness of the softer sex, or a sarcastic attitude on the part of male relatives, had denuded such women's clubs as remained (if any other did) of this their glory and consummation. The club of Marlott alone lived to uphold the local Cerealia.° It had walked for hundreds of years, if not as benefit-club, as votive sisterhood of some sort; and it walked still.

The banded ones were all dressed in white gowns — a gay survival from Old Style days,° when cheerfulness and May-time were synonyms — days before the habit of taking long views had reduced emotions to a monotonous average. Their first exhibition of themselves was in a processional march of two and two round the parish. Ideal and real clashed slightly as the sun lit up their figures against the green hedges and creeper-laced house-fronts; for, though the whole troop wore white garments, no two whites were alike among them. Some approached pure blanching; some had a bluish pallor; some worn by the older characters (which had possibly lain by folded for many a year) inclined to a cadaverous tint, and to a Georgian style.

In addition to the distinction of a white frock, every woman and girl carried in her right hand a peeled willow wand, and in her left a bunch of white flowers. The peeling of the former, and the selection of the latter, had been an operation of personal care.

There were a few middle-aged and even elderly women in the train, their silver-wiry hair and wrinkled faces, scourged by time and trouble, having almost a grotesque, certainly a pathetic, appearance in such a jaunty situation. In a true view, perhaps, there was more to be gathered and told of each anxious and experienced one, to whom the years were drawing nigh when she should say, 'I have no pleasure in them,'° than of her juvenile comrades. But let the elder be passed over here for those under whose bodices the life throbbed quick and warm.

The young girls formed, indeed, the majority of the band, and their heads of luxuriant hair reflected in the sunshine every tone of gold, and black, and brown. Some had beautiful eyes, others a beautiful nose, others a beautiful mouth and figure: few, if any, had all. A difficulty of arranging their lips in this crude exposure to public scrutiny, an inability to balance their heads, and to dissociate self-consciousness from their features, was apparent in them, and showed that they were genuine country girls, unaccustomed to many eyes.

And as each and all of them were warmed without by the sun, so each had a private little sun for her soul to bask in; some dream, some affection, some hobby, at least some remote and distant hope which,

Cerealia: Celebration in honour of Ceres, Roman goddess of harvest. **Old Style days:** The time before 1752 when Great Britain replaced the Julian Calendar, or old-style dating, with Gregorian, or new-styling dating. **'I have no pleasure in them':** Ecclesiastes 12.1.

though perhaps starving to nothing, still lived on, as hopes will. Thus they were all cheerful, and many of them merry.

They came round by The Pure Drop Inn, and were turning out of the high road to pass through a wicket-gate into the meadows, when one of the women said —

'The Lord-a-Lord! Why, Tess Durbeyfield, if there isn't thy father riding hwome in a carriage!'

A young member of the band turned her head at the exclamation. She was a fine and handsome girl — not handsomer than some others, possibly — but her mobile peony mouth and large innocent eyes added eloquence to colour and shape. She wore a red ribbon in her hair, and was the only one of the white company who could boast of such a pronounced adornment. As she looked round Durbeyfield was seen moving along the road in a chaise belonging to The Pure Drop, driven by a frizzle-headed brawny damsel with her gown-sleeves rolled above her eyebrows. This was the cheerful servant of that establishment, who, in her part of factotum, turned groom and ostler at times. Durbeyfield, leaning back, and with his eyes closed luxuriously, was waving his hand above his head, and singing in a slow recitative —

'I've-got-a-gr't-family-vault-at-Kingsbere — and knighted-fore-fathers-in-lead-coffins-there!'

The clubbists tittered, except the girl called Tess — in whom a slow heat seemed to rise at the sense that her father was making himself foolish in their eyes.

'He's tired, that's all,' she said hastily, 'and he has got a lift home, because our own horse has to rest to-day.'

'Bless thy simplicity, Tess,' said her companions. 'He's got his market-nitch.° Haw-haw!'

'Look here; I won't walk another inch with you, if you say any jokes about him!' Tess cried, and the colour upon her cheeks spread over her face and neck. In a moment her eyes grew moist, and her glance drooped to the ground. Perceiving that they had really pained her they said no more, and order again prevailed. Tess's pride would not allow her to turn her head again, to learn what her father's meaning was, if he had any; and thus she moved on with the whole body to the enclosure where there was to be dancing on the green. By the time the spot was reached she had recovered her equanimity, and tapped her neighbour with her wand and talked as usual.

market-nitch: The amount of alcohol that he would normally drink on a market day.

Tess Durbeyfield at this time of her life was a mere vessel of emotion untinctured by experience. The dialect was on her tongue to some extent, despite the village school: the characteristic intonation of that dialect for this district being the voicing approximately rendered by the syllable UR, probably as rich an utterance as any to be found in human speech. The pouted-up deep red mouth to which this syllable was native had hardly as yet settled into its definite shape, and her lower lip had a way of thrusting the middle of her top one upward, when they closed together after a word.

Phases of her childhood lurked in her aspect still. As she walked along to-day, for all her bouncing handsome womanliness, you could sometimes see her twelfth year in her cheeks, or her ninth sparkling from her eyes; and even her fifth would fit over the curves of her mouth now and then.

Yet few knew, and still fewer considered this. A small minority, mainly strangers, would look long at her in casually passing by, and grow momentarily fascinated by her freshness, and wonder if they would ever see her again: but to almost everybody she was a fine and picturesque country girl, and no more.

Nothing was seen or heard further of Durbeyfield in his triumphal chariot under the conduct of the ostleress, and the club having entered the allotted space, dancing began. As there were no men in the company the girls danced at first with each other, but when the hour for the close of labour drew on, the masculine inhabitants of the village, together with other idlers and pedestrians, gathered round the spot, and appeared inclined to negotiate for a partner.

Among these on-lookers were three young men of a superior class, carrying small knapsacks strapped to their shoulders, and stout sticks in their hands. Their general likeness to each other, and their consecutive ages, would almost have suggested that they might be, what in fact they were, brothers. The eldest wore the white tie, high waistcoat, and thin-brimmed hat of the regulation curate; the second was the normal undergraduate; the appearance of the third and youngest would hardly have been sufficient to characterize him; there was an uncribbed, uncabined° aspect in his eyes and attire, implying that he had hardly as yet found the entrance to his professional groove. That he was a desultory tentative student of something and everything might only have been predicted of him.

uncribbed, uncabined: After murdering Banquo, in *Macbeth* (3.4.24–25), Macbeth refers to himself as "cabined, cribbed, confined."

These three brethren told casual acquaintance that they were spending their Whitsun holidays° in a walking tour through the Vale of Blackmoor, their course being south-westerly from the town of Shaston on the north-east.

They leant over the gate by the highway, and inquired as to the meaning of the dance and the white-frocked maids. The two elder of the brothers were plainly not intending to linger more than a moment, but the spectacle of a bevy of girls dancing without male partners seemed to amuse the third, and make him in no hurry to move on. He unstrapped his knapsack, put it, with his stick, on the hedge-bank, and opened the gate.

'What are you going to do, Angel?' asked the eldest.

'I am inclined to go and have a fling with them. Why not all of us — just for a minute or two — it will not detain us long?'

'No — no; nonsense!' said the first. 'Dancing in public with a troop of country hoydens — suppose we should be seen! Come along, or it will be dark before we get to Stourcastle, and there's no place we can sleep at nearer than that; besides, we must get through another chapter of *A Counterblast to Agnosticism*° before we turn in, now I have taken the trouble to bring the book.'

'All right — I'll overtake you and Cuthbert in five minutes; don't stop; I give my word that I will, Felix.'

The two elder reluctantly left him and walked on, taking their brother's knapsack to relieve him in following, and the youngest entered the field.

'This is a thousand pities,' he said gallantly, to two or three of the girls nearest him, as soon as there was a pause in the dance. 'Where are your partners, my dears?'

'They've not left off work yet', answered one of the boldest. 'They'll be here by and by. Till then, will you be one, sir?'

'Certainly. But what's one among so many!'

'Better than none. 'Tis melancholy work facing and footing it to one of your own sort, and no clipsing and colling° at all. Now, pick and choose.'

' 'Ssh — don't be so for'ard!' said a shyer girl.

Whitsun holidays: The time around the seventh Sunday after Easter, Whitsuntide or Whit Sunday. Club-walking and other festivities were held in parishes at Whitsuntide. ***A Counterblast to Agnosticism:*** A fictitious or unidentified work whose character is reflected in its title. **clipsing and colling:** Hugging (dialect).

The young man, thus invited, glanced them over, and attempted some discrimination; but, as the group were all so new to him, he could not very well exercise it. He took almost the first that came to hand, which was not the speaker, as she had expected; nor did it happen to be Tess Durbeyfield. Pedigree, ancestral skeletons, monumental record, the d'Urberville lineaments, did not help Tess in her life's battle as yet, even to the extent of attracting to her a dancing-partner over the heads of the commonest peasantry. So much for Norman blood unaided by Victorian lucre.

The name of the eclipsing girl, whatever it was, has not been handed down; but she was envied by all as the first who enjoyed the luxury of a masculine partner that evening. Yet such was the force of example that the village young men, who had not hastened to enter the gate while no intruder was in the way, now dropped in quickly, and soon the couples became leavened with rustic youth to a marked extent, till at length the plainest woman in the club was no longer compelled to foot it on the masculine side of the figure.

The church clock struck, when suddenly the student said that he must leave — he had been forgetting himself — he had to join his companions. As he fell out of the dance his eyes lighted on Tess Durbeyfield, whose own large orbs wore, to tell the truth, the faintest aspect of reproach that he had not chosen her. He, too, was sorry then that, owing to her backwardness, he had not observed her; and with that in his mind he left the pasture.

On account of his long delay he started in a flying-run down the lane westward, and had soon passed the hollow and mounted the next rise. He had not yet overtaken his brothers, but he paused to get breath, and looked back. He could see the white figures of the girls in the green enclosure whirling about as they had whirled when he was among them. They seemed to have quite forgotten him already.

All of them, except, perhaps, one. This white shape stood apart by the hedge alone. From her position he knew it to be the pretty maiden with whom he had not danced. Trifling as the matter was, he yet instinctively felt that she was hurt by his oversight. He wished that he had asked her; he wished that he had inquired her name. She was so modest, so expressive, she had looked so soft in her thin white gown that he felt he had acted stupidly.

However, it could not be helped, and turning, and bending himself to a rapid walk, he dismissed the subject from his mind.

III

As for Tess Durbeyfield, she did not so easily dislodge the incident from her consideration. She had no spirit to dance again for a long time, though she might have had plenty of partners; but, ah! they did not speak so nicely as the strange young man had done. It was not till the rays of the sun had absorbed the young stranger's retreating figure on the hill that she shook off her temporary sadness and answered her would-be partner in the affirmative.

She remained with her comrades till dusk, and participated with a certain zest in the dancing; though, being heart-whole as yet, she enjoyed treading a measure purely for its own sake; little divining when she saw 'the soft torments, the bitter sweets, the pleasing pains, and the agreeable distresses' of those girls who had been wooed and won, what she herself was capable of in that kind. The struggles and wrangles of the lads for her hand in a jig were an amusement to her — no more; and when they became fierce she rebuked them.

She might have stayed even later, but the incident of her father's odd appearance and manner returned upon the girl's mind to make her anxious, and wondering what had become of him she dropped away from the dancers and bent her steps towards the end of the village at which the parental cottage lay.

While yet many score yards off, other rhythmic sounds than those she had quitted became audible to her; sounds that she knew well — so well. They were a regular series of thumpings from the interior of the house, occasioned by the violent rocking of a cradle upon a stone floor, to which movement a feminine voice kept time by singing, in a vigorous gallopade, the favourite ditty of 'The Spotted Cow' —

I saw her lie do′ — own in yon′ — der green gro′ — ove;
Come, love!′ and I'll tell you where!′

The cradle-rocking and the song would cease simultaneously for a moment, and an exclamation at highest vocal pitch would take the place of the melody.

'God bless thy diment° eyes! And thy waxen cheeks! And thy cherry mouth! And thy Cubit's° thighs! And every bit o' thy blessed body!'

After this invocation the rocking and the singing would recommence, and the 'Spotted Cow' proceed as before. So matters stood

diment: Diamond (dialect). **Cubit's:** Cupid's.

when Tess opened the door, and paused upon the mat within it surveying the scene.

The interior, in spite of the melody, struck upon the girl's senses with an unspeakable dreariness. From the holiday gaieties of the field — the white gowns, the nosegays, the willow-wands, the whirling movements on the green, the flash of gentle sentiment towards the stranger — to the yellow melancholy of this one-candled spectacle, what a step! Besides the jar of contrast there came to her a chill self-reproach that she had not returned sooner, to help her mother in these domesticities, instead of indulging herself out-of-doors.

There stood her mother amid the group of children, as Tess had left her, hanging over the Monday washing-tub, which had now, as always, lingered on to the end of the week. Out of that tub had come the day before — Tess felt it with a dreadful sting of remorse — the very white frock upon her back which she had so carelessly greened about the skirt on the damping grass — which had been wrung up and ironed by her mother's own hands.

As usual, Mrs. Durbeyfield was balanced on one foot beside the tub, the other being engaged in the aforesaid business of rocking her youngest child. The cradle-rockers had done hard duty for so many years, under the weight of so many children, on that flagstone floor, that they were worn nearly flat, in consequence of which a huge jerk accompanied each swing of the cot, flinging the baby from side to side like a weaver's shuttle, as Mrs. Durbeyfield, excited by her song, trod the rocker with all the spring that was left in her after a long day's seething in the suds.

Nick-knock, nick-knock, went the cradle; the candle-flame stretched itself tall, and began jigging up and down; the water dribbled from the matron's elbows, and the song galloped on to the end of the verse, Mrs. Durbeyfield regarding her daughter the while. Even now, when burdened with a young family, Joan Durbeyfield was a passionate lover of tune. No ditty floated into Blackmoor Vale from the outer world but Tess's mother caught up its notation in a week.

There still faintly beamed from the woman's features something of the freshness, and even the prettiness, of her youth; rendering it probable that the personal charms which Tess could boast of were in main part her mother's gift, and therefore unknightly, unhistorical.

'I'll rock the cradle for 'ee, mother,' said the daughter gently. 'Or I'll take off my best frock and help you wring up? I thought you had finished long ago.'

Her mother bore Tess no ill-will for leaving the house-work to her single-handed efforts for so long; indeed, Joan seldom upbraided her thereon at any time, feeling but slightly the lack of Tess's assistance whilst her instinctive plan for relieving herself of her labours lay in postponing them. To-night, however, she was even in a blither mood than usual. There was a dreaminess, a preoccupation, an exaltation, in the maternal look which the girl could not understand.

'Well, I'm glad you've come,' her mother said, as soon as the last note had passed out of her. 'I want to go and fetch your father; but what's more'n that, I want to tell 'ee what have happened. Y'll be fess° enough, my poppet,° when th'st know!' (Mrs. Durbeyfield habitually spoke the dialect; her daughter, who had passed the Sixth Standard in the National School° under a London-trained mistress, spoke two languages; the dialect at home, more or less; ordinary English abroad and to persons of quality.)

'Since I've been away?' Tess asked.

'Ay!'

'Had it anything to do with father's making such a mommet° of himself in thik carriage this afternoon? Why did 'er? I felt inclined to sink into the ground with shame!'

'That wer all a part of the larry!° We've been found to be the greatest gentlefolk in the whole county — reaching all back along before Oliver Grumble's° time — to the days of the Pagan Turks — with monuments, and vaults, and crests, and 'scutcheons, and the Lord knows what all. In Saint Charles's days we was made Knights o' the Royal Oak, our real name being d'Urberville! . . . Don't that make your bosom plim°? 'Twas on this account that your father rode home in the vlee;° not because he'd been drinking, as people supposed.'

'I'm glad of that. Will it do us any good, mother?'

'O yes! 'Tis thoughted that great things may come o't. No doubt a mampus° of volk of our own rank will be down here in their carriages as soon as 'tis known. Your father learnt it on his way hwome from Shaston, and he has been telling me the whole pedigree of the matter.'

'Where is father now?' asked Tess suddenly.

Her mother gave irrelevant information by way of answer: 'He

fess: Pleased (dialect). **poppet:** Puppet (obsolete usage) (*OED*). **Sixth Standard in the National School:** The highest level available in a school supported by government funds and run by the National Society for Promoting the Education of the Poor in the Principles of the Established Church. The first schools were established in 1811. **mommet:** Variant of *maumet;* a term of abuse or contempt (dialect) (*OED*). **larry:** Commotion, disturbance (dialect). **Oliver Grumble's:** Oliver Cromwell. **plim:** Swell (dialect). **vlee:** Fly; a one-horse hackney-carriage (dialect). **mampus:** Crowd (dialect).

called to see the doctor to-day in Shaston. It is not consumption at all, it seems. It is fat round his heart, 'a says. There, it is like this.' Joan Durbeyfield, as she spoke, curved a sodden thumb and forefinger to the shape of the letter C, and used the other forefinger as a pointer. '"At the present moment," he says to your father, "your heart is enclosed all round there, and all round there; this space is still open," 'a says. "As soon as it do meet, so,"' — Mrs. Durbeyfield closed her fingers into a circle complete — "off you will go like a shadder, Mr. Durbeyfield," 'a says. "You mid last ten years; you mid go off in ten months, or ten days."'

Tess looked alarmed. Her father possibly to go behind the eternal cloud so soon, notwithstanding this sudden greatness!

'But where *is* father?' she asked again.

Her mother put on a deprecating look. 'Now don't you be bursting out angry! The poor man — he felt so rafted° after his uplifting by the pa'son's news — that he went up to Rolliver's half an hour ago. He do want to get up his strength for his journey to-morrow with that load of beehives, which must be delivered, family or no. He'll have to start shortly after twelve to-night, as the distance is so long.'

'Get up his strength!' said Tess impetuously, the tears welling to her eyes. 'O my God! Go to a public-house to get up his strength! And you as well agreed as he, mother!'

Her rebuke and her mood seemed to fill the whole room, and to impart a cowed look to the furniture, and candle, and children playing about, and to her mother's face.

'No,' said the latter touchily, 'I be not agreed. I have been waiting for 'ee to bide and keep house while I go to fetch him.'

'I'll go.'

'O no, Tess. You see, it would be no use.'

Tess did not expostulate. She knew what her mother's objection meant. Mrs. Durbeyfield's jacket and bonnet were already hanging slily upon a chair by her side, in readiness for this contemplated jaunt, the reason for which the matron deplored more than its necessity.

'And take the *Compleat Fortune-Teller* to the outhouse,'° Joan continued, rapidly wiping her hands, and donning the garments.

The *Compleat Fortune-Teller* was an old thick volume, which lay on a table at her elbow, so worn by pocketing that the margins had reached the edge of the type. Tess took it up, and her mother started.

rafted: Disturbed, unsettled (dialect). **outhouse:** A subsidiary building adjoining the house; probably not a privy in nineteenth-century British usage (*OED*).

This going to hunt up her shiftless husband at the inn was one of Mrs. Durbeyfield's still extant enjoyments in the muck and muddle of rearing children. To discover him at Rolliver's, to sit there for an hour or two by his side and dismiss all thought and care of the children during the interval, made her happy. A sort of halo, an occidental glow, came over life then. Troubles and other realities took on themselves a metaphysical impalpability, sinking to mere mental phenomena for serene contemplation, and no longer stood as pressing concretions which chafed body and soul. The youngsters, not immediately within sight, seemed rather bright and desirable appurtenances than otherwise; the incidents of daily life were not without humorousness and jollity in their aspect there. She felt a little as she had used to feel when she sat by her now wedded husband in the same spot during his wooing, shutting her eyes to his defects of character, and regarding him only in his ideal presentation as lover.

Tess, being left alone with the younger children, went first to the outhouse with the fortune-telling book, and stuffed it into the thatch. A curious fetichistic fear of this grimy volume on the part of her mother prevented her ever allowing it to stay in the house all night, and hither it was brought back whenever it had been consulted. Between the mother, with her fast-perishing lumber of superstitions, folk-lore, dialect, and orally transmitted ballads, and the daughter, with her trained National teachings and Standard knowledge under an infinitely Revised Code,° there was a gap of two hundred years as ordinarily understood. When they were together the Jacobean and the Victorian ages were juxtaposed.

Returning along the garden path Tess mused on what the mother could have wished to ascertain from the book on this particular day. She guessed the recent ancestral discovery to bear upon it, but did not divine that it solely concerned herself. Dismissing this, however, she busied herself with sprinkling the linen dried during the daytime, in company with her nine-year-old brother Abraham, and her sister Eliza-Louisa of twelve and a half, called ''Liza-Lu,' the youngest ones being put to bed. There was an interval of four years and more between Tess and the next of the family, the two who had filled the gap having died in their infancy, and this lent her a deputy-maternal atti-

Revised Code: The Education Department's Revised Codes of 1862 and 1867 linked the funding for schools to their size and to student performance on standardized assessment examinations.

tude when she was alone with her juniors. Next in juvenility to Abraham came two more girls, Hope and Modesty; then a boy of three, and then the baby, who had just completed his first year.

All these young souls were passengers in the Durbeyfield ship — entirely dependent on the judgment of the two Durbeyfield adults for their pleasures, their necessities, their health, even their existence. If the heads of the Durbeyfield household chose to sail into difficulty, disaster, starvation, disease, degradation, death, thither were these half-dozen little captives under hatches compelled to sail with them — six helpless creatures, who had never been asked if they wished for life on any terms, much less if they wished for it on such hard conditions as were involved in being of the shiftless house of Durbeyfield. Some people would like to know whence the poet whose philosophy is in these days deemed as profound and trustworthy as his song is breezy and pure, gets his authority for speaking of 'Nature's holy plan.'°

It grew later, and neither father nor mother reappeared. Tess looked out of the door, and took a mental journey through Marlott. The village was shutting its eyes. Candles and lamps were being put out everywhere: she could inwardly behold the extinguisher and the extended hand.

Her mother's fetching simply meant one more to fetch. Tess began to perceive that a man in indifferent health, who proposed to start on a journey before one in the morning, ought not to be at an inn at this late hour celebrating his ancient blood.

'Abraham,' she said to her little brother, 'do you put on your hat — you bain't afraid? — and go up to Rolliver's, and see what has gone wi' father and mother.'

The boy jumped promptly from his seat, and opened the door, and the night swallowed him up. Half an hour passed yet again; neither man, woman, nor child returned. Abraham, like his parents, seemed to have been limed° and caught by the ensnaring inn.

'I must go myself,' she said.

'Liza-Lu then went to bed, and Tess, locking them all in, started on her way up the dark and crooked lane or street not made for hasty progress; a street laid out before inches of land had value, and when one-handed clocks sufficiently subdivided the day.

'Nature's holy plan': Wordsworth, "Lines Written in Early Spring" (line 22).
limed: Abraham is compared to a bird ensnared in bird-lime.

IV

Rolliver's inn, the single alehouse at this end of the long and broken village, could only boast of an off-license;° hence, as nobody could legally drink on the premises, the amount of overt accommodation for consumers was strictly limited to a little board about six inches wide and two yards long, fixed to the garden palings by pieces of wire, so as to form a ledge. On this board thirsty strangers deposited their cups as they stood in the road and drank, and threw the dregs on the dusty ground to the pattern of Polynesia,° and wished they could have a restful seat inside.

Thus the strangers. But there were also local customers who felt the same wish; and where there's a will there's a way.

In a large bedroom upstairs, the window of which was thickly curtained with a great woollen shawl lately discarded by the landlady Mrs. Rolliver, were gathered on this evening nearly a dozen persons, all seeking beatitude; all old inhabitants of the nearer end of Marlott, and frequenters of this retreat. Not only did the distance to The Pure Drop, the fully-licensed tavern at the further part of the dispersed village, render its accommodation practically unavailable for dwellers at this end; but the far more serious question, the quality of the liquor, confirmed the prevalent opinion that it was better to drink with Rolliver in a corner of the housetop than with the other landlord in a wide house.°

A gaunt four-post bedstead which stood in the room afforded sitting-space for several persons gathered round three of its sides; a couple more men had elevated themselves on a chest of drawers; another rested on the oak-carved 'cwoffer'; two on the wash-stand; another on the stool; and thus all were, somehow, seated at their ease. The stage of mental comfort to which they had arrived at this hour was one wherein their souls expanded beyond their skins, and spread their personalities warmly through the room. In this process the chamber and its furniture grew more and more dignified and luxurious; the shawl hanging at the window took upon itself the richness of tapestry; the brass handles of the chest of drawers were as golden knockers; and the carved bed-posts seemed to have some kinship with the magnificent pillars of Solomon's temple.°

off-license: Rolliver's is not licensed to sell alcohol for consumption on the premises. **pattern of Polynesia:** A pattern like that of a group of islands. **wide house:** Proverbs 21.9: "It is better to dwell in a corner of the housetop, than with a brawling woman in a wide house." **Solomon's temple:** The building of Solomon's temple is contained in 1 Kings 7.

Mrs. Durbeyfield, having quickly walked hitherward after parting from Tess, opened the front door, crossed the downstairs room, which was in deep gloom, and then unfastened the stair-door like one whose fingers knew the tricks of the latches well. Her ascent of the crooked staircase was a slower process, and her face, as it rose into the light above the last stair, encountered the gaze of all the party assembled in the bedroom.

'—— Being a few private friends I've asked in to keep up club-walking at my own expense,' the landlady exclaimed at the sound of footsteps, as glibly as a child repeating the Catechism, while she peered over the stairs. 'Oh, 'tis you, Mrs. Durbeyfield — Lard — how you frightened me! — I thought it might be some gaffer° sent by Gover'-ment.'

Mrs. Durbeyfield was welcomed with glances and nods by the remainder of the conclave, and turned to where her husband sat. He was humming absently to himself, in a low tone: 'I be as good as some folks here and there! I've got a great family vault at Kingsbere-sub-Greenhill, and finer skillentons than any man in Wessex!'

'I've something to tell 'ee that's come into my head about that — a grand projick!' whispered his cheerful wife. 'Here, John, don't 'ee see me?' She nudged him, while he, looking through her as through a windowpane, went on with his recitative.

'Hush! Don't 'ee sing so loud, my good man,' said the landlady; 'in case any member of the Gover'ment should be passing, and take away my licends.'

'He's told 'ee what's happened to us, I suppose?' asked Mrs. Durbeyfield.

'Yes — in a way. D'ye think there's any money hanging by it?'

'Ah, that's the secret,' said Joan Durbeyfield sagely. 'However, 'tis well to be kin to a coach, even if you don't ride in 'en.' She dropped her public voice, and continued in a low tone to her husband: 'I've been thinking since you brought the news that there's a great rich lady out by Trantridge, on the edge o' The Chase, of the name of d'Urberville.'

'Hey — what's that?' said Sir John.

She repeated the information. 'That lady must be our relation,' she said. 'And my projick is to send Tess to claim kin.'

'There *is* a lady of the name, now you mention it,' said Durbeyfield. 'Pa'son Tringham didn't think of that. But she's nothing beside

gaffer: A person entitled to respect (*OED*); apparently, an official.

we — a junior branch of us, no doubt, hailing long since King Norman's day.'

While this question was being discussed neither of the pair noticed, in their preoccupation, that little Abraham had crept into the room, and was awaiting an opportunity of asking them to return.

'She is rich, and she'd be sure to take notice o' the maid,' continued Mrs. Durbeyfield; 'and 'twill be a very good thing. I don't see why two branches o' one family should not be on visiting terms.'

'Yes; and we'll all claim kin!' said Abraham brightly from under the bedstead. 'And we'll all go and see her when Tess had gone to live with her; and we'll ride in her coach and wear black clothes!'

'How do you come here, child? What nonsense be ye talking! Go away, and play on the stairs till father and mother be ready! . . . Well, Tess ought to go to this other member of our family. She'd be sure to win the lady — Tess would; and likely enough 'twould lead to some noble gentleman marrying her. In short, I know it.'

'How?'

'I tried her fate in the *Fortune-Teller*, and it brought out that very thing! . . . You should ha' seen how pretty she looked to-day; her skin is as sumple° as a duchess's.'

'What says the maid herself to going?'

'I've not asked her. She don't know there is any such lady-relation yet. But it would certainly put her in the way of a grand marriage, and she won't say nay to going.'

'Tess is queer.'

'But she's tractable at bottom. Leave her to me.'

Though this conversation had been private, sufficient of its import reached the understandings of those around to suggest to them that the Durbeyfields had weightier concerns to talk of now than common folks had, and that Tess, their pretty eldest daughter, had fine prospects in store.

'Tess is a fine figure o' fun, as I said to myself to-day when I zeed her vamping round parish with the rest,' observed one of the elderly boozers in an undertone. 'But Joan Durbeyfield must mind that she don't get green malt in floor.'° It was a local phrase which had a peculiar meaning, and there was no reply.

The conversation became inclusive, and presently other footsteps were heard crossing the room below.

sumple: Supple (dialect). **green malt in floor:** The expression refers to pregnancy before marriage.

'—— Being a few private friends asked in to-night to keep up club-walking at my own expense.' The landlady had rapidly re-used the formula she kept on hand for intruders before she recognized that the newcomer was Tess.

Even to her mother's gaze the girl's young features looked sadly out of place amid the alcoholic vapours which floated here as no unsuitable medium for wrinkled middle-age; and hardly was a reproachful flash from Tess's dark eyes needed to make her father and mother rise from their seats, hastily finish their ale, and descend the stairs behind her, Mrs. Rolliver's caution following their footsteps.

'No noise, please, if ye'll be so good, my dears; or I mid lose my licends, and be summons'd, and I don't know what all! 'Night t'ye!'

They went home together, Tess holding one arm of her father, and Mrs. Durbeyfield the other. He had, in truth, drunk very little — not a fourth of the quantity which a systematic tippler could carry to church on a Sunday afternoon without a hitch in his eastings or genuflections; but the weakness of Sir John's constitution made mountains of his petty sins in this kind. On reaching the fresh air he was sufficiently unsteady to incline the row of three at one moment as if they were marching to London, and at another as if they were marching to Bath — which produced a comical effect, frequent enough in families on nocturnal homegoings; and, like most comical effects, not quite so comic after all. The two women valiantly disguised these forced excursions and countermarches as well as they could from Durbeyfield their cause, and from Abraham, and from themselves; and so they approached by degrees their own door, the head of the family bursting suddenly into his former refrain as he drew near, as if to fortify his soul at sight of the smallness of his present residence —

'I've got a fam — ily vault at Kingsbere!'

'Hush — don't be silly, Jacky,' said his wife. 'Yours is not the only family that was of 'count in wold days. Look at the Anktells, and Horseys, and the Tringhams themselves — gone to seed a'most as much as you — though you was bigger folks than they, that's true. Thank God, I was never of no family, and have nothing to be ashamed of in that way!'

'Don't you be so sure o' that. From your nater° 'tis my belief you've disgraced yourselves more than any o' us, and was kings and queens outright at one time.'

nater: Nature (dialect).

Tess turned the subject by saying what was far more prominent in her own mind at the moment than thoughts of her ancestry —

'I am afraid father won't be able to take the journey with the beehives to-morrow so early.'

'I? I shall be all right in an hour or two,' said Durbeyfield.

It was eleven o'clock before the family were all in bed, and two o'clock next morning was the latest hour for starting with the beehives if they were to be delivered to the retailers in Casterbridge before the Saturday market began, the way thither lying by bad roads over a distance of between twenty and thirty miles, and the horse and waggon being of the slowest. At half-past one Mrs. Durbeyfield came into the large bedroom where Tess and all her little brothers and sisters slept.

'The poor man can't go,' she said to her eldest daughter, whose great eyes had opened the moment her mother's hand touched the door.

Tess sat up in bed, lost in a vague interspace between a dream and this information.

'But somebody must go,' she replied. 'It is late for the hives already. Swarming will soon be over for the year; and if we put off taking 'em till next week's market the call for 'em will be past, and they'll be thrown on our hands.'

Mrs. Durbeyfield looked unequal to the emergency. 'Some young feller, perhaps, would go? One of them who were so much after dancing with 'ee yesterday,' she presently suggested.

'O no — I wouldn't have it for the world!' declared Tess proudly. 'And letting everybody know the reason — such a thing to be ashamed of! I think *I* could go if Abraham could go with me to kip me company.'

Her mother at length agreed to this arrangement. Little Abraham was aroused from his deep sleep in a corner of the same apartment, and made to put on his clothes while still mentally in the other world. Meanwhile Tess had hastily dressed herself; and the twain, lighting a lantern, went out to the stable. The rickety little waggon was already laden, and the girl led out the horse Prince, only a degree less rickety than the vehicle.

The poor creature looked wonderingly round at the night, at the lantern, at their two figures, as if he could not believe that at that hour, when every living thing was intended to be in shelter and at rest, he was called upon to go out and labour. They put a stock of candle-ends into the lantern, hung the latter to the off-side of the load, and directed the horse onward, walking at his shoulder at first during the uphill parts of the way, in order not to overload an animal of so little vigour. To cheer themselves as well as they could, they made an artificial morning with the lantern, some bread and butter, and their own conversation, the real morning being far from come. Abraham, as he more fully awoke (for he had moved in a sort of trance so far), began to talk of the strange shapes assumed by the various dark objects against the sky; of this tree that looked like a raging tiger springing from a lair; of that which resembled a giant's head.

When they had passed the little town of Stourcastle, dumbly somnolent under its thick brown thatch, they reached higher ground. Still higher, on their left, the elevation called Bulbarrow or Bealbarrow, well-nigh the highest in South Wessex, swelled into the sky, engirdled by its earthen trenches. From hereabout the long road was fairly level for some distance onward. They mounted in front of the waggon, and Abraham grew reflective.

'Tess!' he said in a preparatory tone, after a silence.

'Yes, Abraham.'

'Bain't you glad that we've become gentlefolk?'

'Not particular glad.'

'But you be glad that you 'm going to marry a gentleman?'

'What?' said Tess, lifting her face.

'That our great relation will help 'ee to marry a gentleman.'

'I? Our great relation? We have no such relation. What has put that into your head?'

'I heard 'em talking about it up at Rolliver's when I went to find father. There's a rich lady of our family out at Trantridge, and mother said that if you claimed kin with the lady, she'd put 'ee in the way of marrying a gentleman.'

His sister became abruptly still, and lapsed into a pondering silence. Abraham talked on, rather for the pleasure of utterance than for audition, so that his sister's abstraction was of no account. He leant back against the hives, and with upturned face made observations on the stars, whose cold pulses were beating amid the black hollows above, in serene dissociation from these two wisps of human life. He asked how far away those twinklers were, and whether God was on the other side of them. But ever and anon his childish prattle recurred to what impressed his imagination even more deeply than the wonders of creation. If Tess were made rich by marrying a gentleman, would she have money enough to buy a spy-glass so large that it would draw the stars as near to her as Nettlecombe-Tout?

The renewed subject, which seemed to have impregnated the whole family, filled Tess with impatience.

'Never mind that now!' she exclaimed.

'Did you say the stars were worlds, Tess?'

'Yes.'

'All like ours?'

'I don't know; but I think so. They sometimes seem to be like the apples on our stubbard-tree.° Most of them splendid and sound — a few blighted.'

'Which do we live on — a splendid one or a blighted one?'

'A blighted one.'

''Tis very unlucky that we didn't pitch on a sound one, when there were so many more of 'em!'

'Yes.'

'Is it like that *really*, Tess?' said Abraham, turning to her much impressed, on reconsideration of this rare information. 'How would it have been if we had pitched on a sound one?'

'Well, father wouldn't have coughed and creeped about as he does, and wouldn't have got too tipsy to go this journey; and mother wouldn't have been always washing, and never getting finished.'

'And you would have been a rich lady ready-made, and not have had to be made rich by marrying a gentleman?'

'O Aby, don't — don't talk of that any more!'

Left to his reflections Abraham soon grew drowsy. Tess was not skilful in the management of a horse, but she thought that she could take upon herself the entire conduct of the load for the present, and allow Abraham to go to sleep if he wished to do so. She made him a sort of nest in front of the hives, in such a manner that he could not fall, and, taking the reins into her own hands, jogged on as before.

Prince required but slight attention, lacking energy for superfluous movements of any sort. With no longer a companion to distract her, Tess fell more deeply into reverie than ever, her back leaning against the hives. The mute procession past her shoulders of trees and hedges became attached to fantastic scenes outside reality, and the occasional heave of the wind became the sigh of some immense sad soul, conterminous with the universe in space, and with history in time.

Then, examining the mesh of events in her own life, she seemed to see the vanity of her father's pride; the gentlemanly suitor awaiting herself in her mother's fancy; to see him as a grimacing personage,

stubbard-tree: A kind of apple tree.

laughing at her poverty, and her shrouded knightly ancestry. Everything grew more and more extravagant, and she no longer knew how time passed. A sudden jerk shook her in her seat, and Tess awoke from the sleep into which she, too, had fallen.

They were a long way further on than when she had lost consciousness, and the waggon had stopped. A hollow groan, unlike anything she had ever heard in her life, came from the front, followed by a shout of 'Hoi there!'

The lantern hanging at her waggon had gone out, but another was shining in her face — much brighter than her own had been. Something terrible had happened. The harness was entangled with an object which blocked the way.

In consternation Tess jumped down, and discovered the dreadful truth. The groan had proceeded from her father's poor horse Prince. The morning mail-cart, with its two noiseless wheels, speeding along these lanes like an arrow, as it always did, had driven into her slow and unlighted equipage. The pointed shaft of the cart had entered the breast of the unhappy Prince like a sword, and from the wound his life's blood was spouting in a stream, and falling with a hiss into the road.

In her despair Tess sprang forward and put her hand upon the hole, with the only result that she became splashed from face to skirt with the crimson drops. Then she stood helplessly looking on. Prince also stood firm and motionless as long as he could; till he suddenly sank down in a heap.

By this time the mail-cart man had joined her, and began dragging and unharnessing the hot form of Prince. But he was already dead, and, seeing that nothing more could be done immediately, the mail-cart man returned to his own animal, which was uninjured.

'You was on the wrong side,' he said. 'I am bound to go on with the mail-bags, so that the best thing for you to do is to bide here with your load. I'll send somebody to help you as soon as I can. It is getting daylight, and you have nothing to fear.'

He mounted and sped on his way; while Tess stood and waited. The atmosphere turned pale, the birds shook themselves in the hedges, arose, and twittered; the lane showed all its white features, and Tess showed hers, still whiter. The huge pool of blood in front of her was already assuming the iridescence of coagulation; and when the sun rose a hundred prismatic hues were reflected from it. Prince lay alongside still and stark; his eyes half open, the hole in his chest looking scarcely large enough to have let out all that had animated him.

' 'Tis all my doing — all mine!' the girl cried, gazing at the spectacle. 'No excuse for me — none. What will mother and father live on now? Aby, Aby!' She shook the child, who had slept soundly through the whole disaster. 'We can't go on with our load — Prince is killed!'

When Abraham realized all, the furrows of fifty years were extemporized on his young face.

'Why, I danced and laughed only yesterday!' she went on to herself. 'To think that I was such a fool!'

' 'Tis because we be on a blighted star, and not a sound one, isn't it, Tess?' murmured Abraham through his tears.

In silence they waited through an interval which seemed endless. At length a sound, and an approaching object, proved to them that the driver of the mail-cart had been as good as his word. A farmer's man from near Stourcastle came up, leading a strong cob. He was harnessed to the waggon of beehives in the place of Prince, and the load taken on towards Casterbridge.

The evening of the same day saw the empty waggon reach again the spot of the accident. Prince had lain there in the ditch since the morning; but the place of the blood-pool was still visible in the middle of the road, though scratched and scraped over by passing vehicles. All that was left of Prince was now hoisted into the waggon he had formerly hauled, and with his hoofs in the air, and his shoes shining in the setting sunlight, he retraced the eight or nine miles to Marlott.

Tess had gone back earlier. How to break the news was more than she could think. It was a relief to her tongue to find from the faces of her parents that they already knew of their loss, though this did not lessen the self-reproach which she continued to heap upon herself for her negligence.

But the very shiftlessness of the household rendered the misfortune a less terrifying one to them than it would have been to a striving family, though in the present case it meant ruin, and in the other it would only have meant inconvenience. In the Durbeyfield countenances there was nothing of the red wrath that would have burnt upon the girl from parents more ambitious for her welfare. Nobody blamed Tess as she blamed herself.

When it was discovered that the knacker and tanner would give only a few shillings for Prince's carcase because of his decrepitude, Durbeyfield rose to the occasion.

'No,' said he stoically, 'I won't sell his old body. When we d'Urbervilles was knights in the land, we didn't sell our chargers for cat's meat. Let 'em keep their shillings! He 've served me well in his lifetime, and I won't part from his now.'

He worked harder the next day in digging a grave for Prince in the garden than he had worked for months to grow a crop for his family. When the hole was ready, Durbeyfield and his wife tied a rope round the horse and dragged him up the path towards it, the children following in funeral train. Abraham and 'Liza-Lu sobbed, Hope and Modesty discharged their griefs in loud blares which echoed from the walls; and when Prince was tumbled in they gathered round the grave. The bread-winner had been taken away from them; what would they do?

'Is he gone to heaven?' asked Abraham, between the sobs.

Then Durbeyfield began to shovel in the earth, and the children cried anew. All except Tess. Her face was dry and pale, as though she regarded herself in the light of a murderess.

V

The haggling business, which had mainly depended on the horse, became disorganized forthwith. Distress, if not penury, loomed in the distance. Durbeyfield was what was locally called a slack-twisted fellow; he had good strength to work at times; but the times could not be relied on to coincide with the hours of requirement; and, having been unaccustomed to the regular toil of the day-labourer, he was not particularly persistent when they did so coincide.

Tess, meanwhile, as the one who had dragged her parents into this quagmire, was silently wondering what she could do to help them out of it; and then her mother broached her scheme.

'We must take the ups wi' the downs, Tess,' said she; 'and never could your high blood have been found out at a more called-for moment. You must try your friends. Do ye know that there is a very rich Mrs. d'Urberville living on the outskirts o' The Chase, who must be our relation? You must go to her and claim kin, and ask for some help in our trouble.'

'I shouldn't care to do that,' says Tess. 'If there is such a lady, 'twould be enough for us if she were friendly — not to expect her to give us help.'

'You could win her round to do anything, my dear. Besides, perhaps there's more in it than you know of. I've heard what I've heard, good-now.'

The oppressive sense of the harm she had done led Tess to be more deferential than she might otherwise have been to the maternal wish; but she could not understand why her mother should find such satisfaction in contemplating an enterprise of, to her, such doubtful profit. Her mother might have made inquiries, and have discovered that this Mrs. d'Urberville was a lady of unequalled virtues and charity. But Tess's pride made the part of poor relation one of particular distaste to her.

'I'd rather try to get work,' she murmured.

'Durbeyfield, you can settle it,' said his wife, turning to where he sat in the background. 'If you say she ought to go, she will go.'

'I don't like my children going and making themselves beholden to strange kin,' murmured he. 'I'm the head of the noblest branch o' the family, and I ought to live up to it.'

His reasons for staying away were worse to Tess than her own objection to going. 'Well, as I killed the horse, mother,' she said mournfully, 'I suppose I ought to do something. I don't mind going and seeing her, but you must leave it to me about asking for help. And don't go thinking about her making a match for me — it is silly.'

'Very well said, Tess!' observed her father sententiously.

'Who said I had such a thought?' asked Joan.

'I fancy it is in your mind, mother. But I'll go.'

Rising early next day she walked to the hill-town called Shaston, and there took advantage of a van which twice in the week ran from Shaston eastward to Chaseborough, passing near Trantridge, the parish in which the vague and mysterious Mrs. d'Urberville had her residence.

Tess Durbeyfield's route on this memorable morning lay amid the north-eastern undulations of the Vale in which she had been born, and in which her life had unfolded. The Vale of Blackmoor was to her the world, and its inhabitants the races thereof. From the gates and stiles of Marlott she had looked down its length in the wondering days of infancy, and what had been mystery to her then was not much less than mystery to her now. She had seen daily from her chamber-window towers, villages, faint white mansions; above all the town of Shaston standing majestically on its height; its windows shining like lamps in the evening sun. She had hardly ever visited the place, only a small tract even of the Vale and its environs being known to her by close inspection. Much less had she been far outside the valley. Every contour of the surrounding hills was as personal to her as that of her relatives' faces; but for what lay beyond her judgment was dependent on the teaching of the village school, where she had held a leading place at the time of her leaving, a year or two before this date.

In those early days she had been much loved by others of her own sex and age, and had used to be seen about the village as one of three — all nearly of the same year — walking home from school side by side; Tess the middle one — in a pink print pinafore, of a finely reticulated pattern, worn over a stuff frock that had lost its original colour for a nondescript tertiary — marching on upon long stalky legs, in tight stockings, which had little ladder-like holes at the knees, torn by kneeling in the roads and banks in search of vegetable and mineral treasures; her then earth-coloured hair hanging like pot-hooks; the arms of the two outside girls resting round the waist of Tess; her arms on the shoulders of the two supporters.

As Tess grew older, and began to see how matters stood, she felt quite a Malthusian° towards her mother for thoughtlessly giving her so many little sisters and brothers, when it was such a trouble to nurse and provide for them. Her mother's intelligence was that of a happy child: Joan Durbeyfield was simply an additional one, and that not the eldest, to her own long family of waiters on Providence.

However, Tess became humanely beneficent towards the small ones, and to help them as much as possible she used, as soon as she left school, to lend a hand at haymaking or harvesting on neighbouring farms; or, by preference, at milking or butter-making processes, which she had learnt when her father had owned cows; and being deft-fingered it was a kind of work in which she excelled.

Every day seemed to throw upon her young shoulders more of the family burdens, and that Tess should be the representative of the Durbeyfields at the d'Urberville mansion came as a thing of course. In this instance it must be admitted that the Durbeyfields were putting their fairest side outward.

She alighted from the van at Trantridge Cross, and ascended on foot a hill in the direction of the district known as The Chase, on the borders of which, as she had been informed, Mrs. d'Urberville's seat, The Slopes, would be found. It was not a manorial home in the ordinary sense, with fields, and pastures, and a grumbling farmer, out of whom the owner had to squeeze an income for himself and his family by hook or by crook. It was more, far more; a country-house built for enjoyment pure and simple, with not an acre of troublesome land at-

Malthusian: A follower of Robert Malthus (1766–1834), known for his writings against overpopulation.

tached to it beyond what was required for residential purposes, and for a little fancy farm kept in hand by the owner, and tended by a bailiff.

The crimson brick lodge came first in sight, up to its eaves in dense evergreens. Tess thought this was the mansion itself till, passing through the side wicket with some trepidation, and onward to a point at which the drive took a turn, the house proper stood in full view. It was of recent erection — indeed almost new — and of the same rich red colour that formed such a contrast with the evergreens of the lodge. Far behind the corner of the house — which rose like a geranium bloom against the subdued colours around — stretched the soft azure landscape of The Chase — a truly venerable tract of forest land, one of the few remaining woodlands in England of undoubted primæval date, wherein Druidical mistletoe° was still found on aged oaks, and where enormous yew-trees, not planted by the hand of man, grew as they had grown when they were pollarded for bows.° All this sylvan antiquity, however, though visible from The Slopes, was outside the immediate boundaries of the estate.

Everything on this snug property was bright, thriving, and well kept; acres of glass-houses stretched down the inclines to the copses at their feet. Everything looked like money — like the last coin issued from the Mint. The stables, partly screened by Austrian pines and evergreen oaks, and fitted with every late appliance, were as dignified as Chapels-of-Ease.° On the extensive lawn stood an ornamental tent, its door being towards her.

Simple Tess Durbeyfield stood at gaze, in a half-alarmed attitude, on the edge of the gravel sweep. Her feet had brought her onward to this point before she had quite realized where she was; and now all was contrary to her expectation.

'I thought we were an old family; but this is all new!' she said, in her artlessness. She wished that she had not fallen in so readily with her mother's plans for 'claiming kin,' and had endeavoured to gain assistance nearer home.

The d'Urbervilles — or Stoke-d'Urbervilles, as they at first called themselves — who owned all this, were a somewhat unusual family to

Druidical mistletoe: To the Druids, mistletoe was sacred. **pollarded for bows:** Had their boughs severed to make bows. **Chapels-of-Ease:** Chapels built for the use of parishioners living far from the church *(OED)*.

find in such an old-fashioned part of the country. Parson Tringham had spoken truly when he said that our shambling John Durbeyfield was the only really lineal representative of the old d'Urberville family existing in the county, or near it; he might have added, what he knew very well, that the Stoke-d'Urbervilles were no more d'Urbervilles of the true tree than he was himself. Yet it must be admitted that this family formed a very good stock whereon to regraft a name which sadly wanted such renovation.

When old Mr. Simon Stoke, latterly deceased, had made his fortune as an honest merchant (some said money-lender) in the North, he decided to settle as a county man in the South of England, out of hail of his business district; and in doing this he felt the necessity of recommencing with a name that would not too readily identify him with the smart tradesman of the past, and that would be less commonplace than the original bald stark words. Conning for an hour in the British Museum the pages of works devoted to extinct, half-extinct, obscured, and ruined families appertaining to the quarter of England in which he proposed to settle, he considered that *d'Urberville* looked and sounded as well as any of them: and d'Urberville accordingly was annexed to his own name for himself and his heirs eternally. Yet he was not an extravagant-minded man in this, and in constructing his family tree on the new basis was duly reasonable in framing his intermarriages and aristocratic links, never inserting a single title above a rank of strict moderation.

Of this work of imagination poor Tess and her parents were naturally in ignorance — much to their discomfiture; indeed, the very possibility of such annexations was unknown to them; who supposed that, though to be well-favoured might be the gift of fortune, a family name came by nature.

Tess still stood hesitating like a bather about to make his plunge, hardly knowing whether to retreat or to persevere, when a figure came forth from the dark triangular door of the tent. It was that of a tall young man, smoking.

He had an almost swarthy complexion, with full lips, badly moulded, though red and smooth, above which was a well-groomed black moustache with curled points, though his age could not be more than three- or four-and-twenty. Despite the touches of barbarism in his contours, there was a singular force in the gentleman's face, and in his bold rolling eye.

'Well, my Beauty, what can I do for you?' said he, coming forward. And perceiving that she stood quite confounded: 'Never mind me. I am Mr. d'Urberville. Have you come to see me or my mother?'

This embodiment of a d'Urberville and a namesake differed even more from what Tess had expected than the house and grounds had differed. She had dreamed of an aged and dignified face, the sublimation of all the d'Urberville lineaments, furrowed with incarnate memories representing in hieroglyphic the centuries of her family's and England's history. But she screwed herself up to the work in hand, since she could not get out of it, and answered —

'I came to see your mother, sir.'

'I am afraid you cannot see her — she is an invalid,' replied the present representative of the spurious house; for this was Mr. Alec, the only son of the lately deceased gentleman. 'Cannot I answer your purpose? What is the business you wish to see her about?'

'It isn't business — it is — I can hardly say what!'

'Pleasure?'

'Oh no. Why, sir, if I tell you, it will seem —— '

Tess's sense of a certain ludicrousness in her errand was now so strong that, notwithstanding her awe of him, and her general discomfort at being here, her rosy lips curved towards a smile, much to the attraction of the swarthy Alexander.

'It is so very foolish,' she stammered; 'I fear I can't tell you!'

'Never mind; I like foolish things. Try again, my dear,' said he kindly.

'Mother asked me to come,' Tess continued; 'and, indeed, I was in the mind to do so myself likewise. But I did not think it would be like this. I came, sir to tell you that we are of the same family as you.'

'Ho! Poor relations?'

'Yes.'

'Stokes?'

'No; d'Urbervilles.'

'Ay, ay; I mean d'Urbervilles.'

'Our names are worn away to Durbeyfield; but we have several proofs that we are d'Urbervilles. Antiquarians hold we are, — and — and we have an old seal, marked with a ramping lion on a shield, and a castle over him. And we have a very old silver spoon, round in the bowl like a little ladle, and marked with the same castle. But it is so worn that mother uses it to stir the pea-soup.'

'A castle argent is certainly my crest,' said he blandly. 'And my arms a lion rampant.'

'And so mother said we ought to make ourselves beknown to you — as we've lost our horse by a bad accident, and are the oldest branch o' the family.'

'Very kind of your mother, I'm sure. And I, for one, don't regret her step.' Alec looked at Tess as he spoke, in a way that made her blush a little. 'And so, my pretty girl, you've come on a friendly visit to us, as relations?'

'I suppose I have,' faltered Tess, looking uncomfortable again.

'Well — there's no harm in it. Where do you live? What are you?'

She gave him brief particulars; and responding to further inquiries told him that she was intending to go back by the same carrier who had brought her.

'It is a long while before he returns past Trantridge Cross. Supposing we walk round the grounds to pass the time, my pretty Coz?'

Tess wished to abridge her visit as much as possible; but the young man was pressing, and she consented to accompany him. He conducted her about the lawns, and flower-beds, and conservatories; and thence to the fruit-garden and green-houses, where he asked her if she liked strawberries.

'Yes,' said Tess, 'when they come.'

'They are already here.' D'Urberville began gathering specimens of the fruit for her, handing them back to her as he stooped; and, presently, selecting a specially fine product of the 'British Queen' variety, he stood up and held it by the stem to her mouth.

'No — no!' she said quickly, putting her fingers between his hand and her lips. 'I would rather take it in my own hand.'

'Nonsense!' he insisted; and in a slight distress she parted her lips and took it in.

They had spent some time wandering desultorily thus, Tess eating in a half-pleased, half-reluctant state whatever d'Urberville offered her. When she could consume no more of the strawberries he filled her little basket with them; and then the two passed round to the rose trees, whence he gathered blossoms and gave her to put in her bosom. She obeyed like one in a dream, and when she could affix no more he himself tucked a bud or two into her hat, and heaped her basket with others in the prodigality of his bounty. At last, looking at his watch, he said, 'Now, by the time you have had something to eat, it will be time for you to leave, if you want to catch the carrier to Shaston. Come here, and I'll see what grub I can find.'

Stoke-d'Urberville took her back to the lawn and into the tent, where he left her, soon reappearing with a basket of light luncheon, which he put before her himself. It was evidently the gentleman's wish not to be disturbed in this pleasant *tête-à-tête* by the servantry.

'Do you mind my smoking?' he asked.

'Oh, not at all, sir.'

He watched her pretty and unconscious munching through the skeins of smoke that pervaded the tent, and Tess Durbeyfield did not divine, as she innocently looked down at the roses in her bosom, that there behind the blue narcotic haze was potentially the 'tragic mischief' of her drama — one who stood fair to be the blood-red ray in the spectrum of her young life. She had an attribute which amounted to a disadvantage just now; and it was this that caused Alec d'Urberville's eyes to rivet themselves upon her. It was a luxuriance of aspect, a fullness of growth, which made her appear more of a woman than she really was. She had inherited the feature from her mother without the quality it denoted. It had troubled her mind occasionally, till her companions had said that it was a fault which time would cure.

She soon had finished her lunch. 'Now I am going home, sir,' she said, rising.

'And what do they call you?' he asked, as he accompanied her along the drive till they were out of sight of the house.

'Tess Durbeyfield, down at Marlott.'

'And you say your people have lost their horse?'

'I — killed him!' she answered, her eyes filling with tears as she gave particulars of Prince's death. 'And I don't know what to do for father on account of it!'

'I must think if I cannot do something. My mother must find a berth for you. But, Tess, no nonsense about "d'Urberville"; — "Durbeyfield" only, you know — quite another name.'

'I wish for no better, sir,' said she with something of dignity.

For a moment — only for a moment — when they were in the turning of the drive, between the tall rhododendrons and conifers, before the lodge became visible, he inclined his face towards her as if — but, no: he thought better of it, and let her go.

Thus the thing began. Had she perceived this meeting's import she might have asked why she was doomed to be seen and coveted that day by the wrong man, and not by some other man, the right and desired one in all respects — as nearly as humanity can supply the right and desired; yet to him who amongst her acquaintance might have approximated to this kind, she was but a transient impression, half forgotten.

In the ill-judged execution of the well-judged plan of things the call seldom produces the comer, the man to love rarely coincides with the hour for loving. Nature does not often say 'See!' to her poor creature at a time when seeing can lead to happy doing; or reply 'Here!' to a body's cry of 'Where?' till the hide-and-seek has become an irksome, outworn game. We may wonder whether at the acme and summit of the human progress these anachronisms will be corrected by a finer intuition, a closer interaction of the social machinery than that which now jolts us round and along; but such completeness is not to be prophesied, or even conceived as possible. Enough that in the present case, as in millions, it was not the two halves of a perfect whole that confronted each other at the perfect moment; a missing counterpart wandered independently about the earth waiting in crass obtuseness till the late time came. Out of which maladroit delay sprang anxieties, disappointments, shocks, catastrophes, and passing-strange destinies.

When d'Urberville got back to the tent he sat down astride on a chair reflecting, with a pleased gleam in his face. Then he broke into a loud laugh.

'Well, I'm damned! What a funny thing! Ha-ha-ha! And what a crumby° girl!'

VI

Tess went down the hill to Trantridge Cross, and inattentively waited to take her seat in the van returning from Chaseborough to Shaston. She did not know what the other occupants said to her as she entered, though she answered them; and when they had started anew she rode along with an inward and not an outward eye.

One among her fellow-travellers addressed her more pointedly than any had spoken before: 'Why, you be quite a posy! And such roses in early June!'

Then she became aware of the spectacle she presented to their surprised vision: roses at her breast; roses in her hat; roses and strawberries in her basket to the brim. She blushed, and said confusedly that the flowers had been given to her. When the passengers were not looking she stealthily removed the more prominent blooms from her hat and placed them in the basket, where she covered them with her handkerchief. Then she fell to reflecting again, and in looking downwards a thorn of the rose remaining in her breast accidentally pricked her chin. Like all the cottagers in Blackmoor Vale, Tess was steeped in fancies and prefigurative superstitions; she thought this an ill omen — the first she had noticed that day.

The van travelled only so far as Shaston, and there were several

crumby: Attractive.

miles of pedestrian descent from that mountain-town into the vale to Marlott. Her mother had advised her to stay here for the night, at the house of a cottage-woman they knew, if she should feel too tired to come on; and this Tess did, not descending to her home till the following afternoon.

When she entered the house she perceived in a moment from her mother's triumphant manner that something had occurred in the interim.

'Oh yes; I know all about it! I told 'ee it would be all right, and now 'tis proved!'

'Since I've been away? What has?' said Tess rather wearily.

Her mother surveyed the girl up and down with arch approval, and went on banteringly: 'So you've brought 'em round!'

'How do you know, mother?'

'I've had a letter.'

Tess then remembered that there would have been time for this.

'They say — Mrs. d'Urberville says — that she wants you to look after a little fowl-farm which is her hobby. But this is only her artful way of getting 'ee there without raising your hopes. She's going to own 'ee as kin — that's the meaning o't.'

'But I didn't see her.'

'You zid somebody, I suppose?'

'I saw her son.'

'And did he own 'ee?'

'Well — he called me Coz.'

'An' I knew it! Jacky — he called her Coz!' cried Joan to her husband. 'Well, he spoke to his mother, of course, and she do want 'ee there.'

'But I don't know that I am apt at tending fowls,' said the dubious Tess.

'Then I don't know who is apt. You've be'n born in the business, and brought up in it. They that be born in a business always know more about it than any 'prentice. Besides, that's only just a show of something for you to do, that you midn't feel beholden.'

'I don't altogether think I ought to go,' said Tess thoughtfully. 'Who wrote the letter? Will you let me look at it?'

'Mrs. d'Urberville wrote it. Here it is.'

The letter was in the third person, and briefly informed Mrs. Durbeyfield that her daughter's services would be useful to that lady in the management of her poultry-farm, that a comfortable room would be provided for her if she could come, and that the wages would be on a liberal scale if they liked her.

'Oh — that's all!' said Tess.

'You couldn't expect her to throw her arms round 'ee, an' to kiss and to coll 'ee all at once.'

Tess looked out of the window.

'I would rather stay here with father and you,' she said.

'But why?'

'I'd rather not tell you why, mother; indeed, I don't quite know why.'

A week afterwards she came in one evening from an unavailing search for some light occupation in the immediate neighbourhood. Her idea had been to get together sufficient money during the summer to purchase another horse. Hardly had she crossed the threshold before one of the children danced across the room, saying, 'The gentleman's been here!'

Her mother hastened to explain, smiles breaking from every inch of her person. Mrs. d'Urberville's son had called on horseback, having been riding by chance in the direction of Marlott. He had wished to know, finally, in the name of his mother, if Tess could really come to manage the old lady's fowl-farm or not; the lad who had hitherto superintended the birds having proved untrustworthy. 'Mr. d'Urberville says you must be a good girl if you are at all as you appear; he knows you must be worth your weight in gold. He is very much interested in 'ee — truth to tell.'

Tess seemed for the moment really pleased to hear that she had won such high opinion from a stranger when, in her own esteem, she had sunk so low.

'It is very good of him to think that,' she murmured; 'and if I was quite sure how it would be living there, I would go any-when.'

'He is a mighty handsome man!'

'I don't think so,' said Tess coldly.

'Well, there's your chance, whether or no; and I'm sure he wears a beautiful diamond ring!'

'Yes,' said little Abraham, brightly, from the window-bench; 'and I seed it! and it did twinkle when he put his hand up to his mistarshers. Mother, why did our grand relation keep on putting his hand up to his mistarshers?'

'Hark at that child!' cried Mrs. Durbeyfield, with parenthetic admiration.

'Perhaps to show his diamond ring,' murmured Sir John, dreamily, from his chair.

'I'll think it over,' said Tess, leaving the room.

'Well, she's made a conquest o' the younger branch of us, straight off,' continued the matron to her husband, 'and she's a fool if she don't follow it up.'

'I don't quite like my children going away from home,' said the haggler. 'As the head of the family, the rest ought to come to me.'

'But do let her go, Jacky,' coaxed his poor witless wife. 'He's struck wi' her — you can see that. He called her Coz! He'll marry her, most likely, and make a lady of her; and then she'll be what her forefathers was.'

John Durbeyfield had more conceit than energy or health, and this supposition was pleasant to him.

'Well, perhaps, that's what young Mr. d'Urberville means,' he admitted; 'and sure enough he mid have serious thoughts about improving his blood by linking on to the old line. Tess, the little rogue! And have she really paid 'em a visit to such an end as this?'

Meanwhile Tess was walking thoughtfully among the gooseberry-bushes in the garden, and over Prince's grave. When she came in her mother pursued her advantage.

'Well, what be you going to do?' she asked.

'I wish I had seen Mrs. d'Urberville,' said Tess.

'I think you mid as well settle it. Then you'll see her soon enough.'

Her father coughed in his chair.

'I don't know what to say!' answered the girl restlessly. 'It is for you to decide. I killed the old horse, and I suppose I ought to do something to get ye a new one. But — but — I don't quite like Mr. d'Urberville being there!'

The children, who had made use of this idea of Tess being taken up by their wealthy kinsfolk (which they imagined the other family to be) as a species of dolorifuge after the death of the horse, began to cry at Tess's reluctance, and teased and reproached her for hesitating.

'Tess won't go — o — o and be made a la — a — dy of ! — no, she says she wo — o — on't!' they wailed, with square mouths. 'And we shan't have a nice new horse, and lots o' golden money to buy fairlings! And Tess won't look pretty in her best cloze no mo — o — ore!'

Her mother chimed in to the same tune: a certain way she had of making her labours in the house seem heavier than they were by prolonging them indefinitely, also weighed in the argument. Her father alone preserved an attitude of neutrality.

'I will go,' said Tess at last.

Her mother could not repress her consciousness of the nuptial Vision conjured up by the girl's consent.

'That's right! For such a pretty maid as 'tis, this is a fine chance!'

Tess smiled crossly.

'I hope it is a chance for earning money. It is no other kind of chance. You had better say nothing of that silly sort about parish.'

Mrs. Durbeyfield did not promise. She was not quite sure that she did not feel proud enough, after the visitor's remarks, to say a good deal.

Thus it was arranged; and the young girl wrote, agreeing to be ready to set out on any day on which she might be required. She was duly informed that Mrs. d'Urberville was glad of her decision, and that a spring-cart should be sent to meet her and her luggage at the top of the Vale on the day after the morrow, when she must hold herself prepared to start. Mrs. d'Urberville's handwriting seemed rather masculine.

'A cart?' murmured Joan Durbeyfield doubtingly. 'It might have been a carriage for her own kin!'

Having at last taken her course Tess was less restless and abstracted, going about her business with some self-assurance in the thought of acquiring another horse for her father by an occupation which would not be onerous. She had hoped to be a teacher at the school, but the fates seemed to decide otherwise. Being mentally older than her mother she did not regard Mrs. Durbeyfield's matrimonial hopes for her in a serious aspect for a moment. The light-minded woman had been discovering good matches for her daughter almost from the year of her birth.

VII

On the morning appointed for her departure Tess was awake before dawn — at the marginal minute of the dark when the grove is still mute, save for one prophetic bird who sings with a clear-voiced conviction that he at least knows the correct time of day, the rest preserving silence as if equally convinced that he is mistaken. She remained upstairs packing till breakfast-time, and then came down in her ordinary weekday clothes, her Sunday apparel being carefully folded in her box.

Her mother expostulated. 'You will never set out to see your folks without dressing up more the dand than that?'

'But I am going to work!' said Tess.

'Well, yes,' said Mrs. Durbeyfield; and in a private tone, 'at first there mid be a little pretence o't. . . . But I think it will be wiser of 'ee to put your best side outward,' she added.

'Very well; I suppose you know best,' replied Tess with calm abandonment.

And to please her parent the girl put herself quite in Joan's hands, saying serenely — 'Do what you like with me, mother.'

Mrs. Durbeyfield was only too delighted at this tractability. First she fetched a great basin, and washed Tess's hair with such thoroughness that when dried and brushed it looked twice as much as at other times. She tied it with a broader pink ribbon than usual. Then she put upon her the white frock that Tess had worn at the club-walking, the airy fullness of which, supplementing her enlarged *coiffure,* imparted to her developing figure an amplitude which belied her age, and might cause her to be estimated as a woman when she was not much more than a child.

'I declare there's a hole in my stocking-heel!' said Tess.

'Never mind holes in your stockings — they don't speak! When I was a maid, so long as I had a pretty bonnet the devil might ha' found me in heels.'

Her mother's pride in the girl's appearance led her to step back, like a painter from his easel, and survey her work as a whole.

'You must zee yourself!' she cried. 'It is much better than you was t'other day.'

As the looking-glass was only large enough to reflect a very small portion of Tess's person at one time, Mrs. Durbeyfield hung a black cloak outside the casement, and so made a large reflector of the panes, as it is the wont of bedecking cottagers to do. After this she went downstairs to her husband, who was sitting in the lower room.

'I'll tell 'ee what 'tis, Durbeyfield,' said she exultingly; 'he'll never have the heart not to love her. But whatever you do, don't zay too much to Tess of his fancy for her, and this chance she has got. She is such an odd maid that it mid zet her against him, or against going there, even now. If all goes well, I shall certainly be for making some return to that pa'son at Stagfoot Lane for telling us — dear, good man!'

However, as the moment for the girl's setting out drew nigh, when the first excitement of the dressing had passed off, a slight misgiving found place in Joan Durbeyfield's mind. It prompted the matron to say that she would walk a little way — as far as to the point where the acclivity from the valley began its first steep ascent to the outer world. At the top Tess was going to be met with the spring-cart sent by the Stoke-d'Urbervilles, and her box had already been wheeled ahead towards this summit by a lad with trucks,° to be in readiness.

Seeing their mother put on her bonnet the younger children clamoured to go with her.

'I do want to walk a little-ways wi' Sissy, now she's going to marry our gentleman-cousin, and wear fine cloze!'

'Now,' said Tess, flushing and turning quickly, 'I'll hear no more o' that! Mother, how could you ever put such stuff into their heads?'

'Going to work, my dears, for our rich relation, and help get enough money for a new horse,' said Mrs. Durbeyfield pacifically.

'Good-bye, father,' said Tess, with a lumpy throat.

'Good-bye, my maid,' said Sir John, raising his head from his breast as he suspended his nap, induced by a slight excess this morning in honour of the occasion. 'Well, I hope my young friend will like such a comely sample of his own blood. And tell'n, Tess, that being sunk, quite, from our former grandeur, I'll sell him the title — yes, sell it — and at no onreasonable figure.'

'Not for less than a thousand pound!' cried Lady Durbeyfield.

'Tell'n — I'll take a thousand pound. Well, I'll take less, when I come to think o't. He'll adorn it better than a poor lammicken feller like myself can. Tell'n he shall hae it for a hundred. But I won't stand upon trifles — tell'n he shall hae it for fifty — for twenty pound! Yes, twenty pound — that's the lowest. Dammy, family honour is family honour, and I won't take a penny less!'

Tess's eyes were too full and her voice too choked to utter the sentiments that were in her. She turned quickly, and went out.

So the girls and their mother all walked together, a child on each side of Tess, holding her hand, and looking at her meditatively from time to time, as at one who was about to do great things; her mother just behind with the smallest; the group forming a picture of honest beauty flanked by innocence, and backed by simple-souled vanity. They followed the way till they reached the beginning of the ascent, on the crest of which the vehicle from Trantridge was to receive her, this limit having been fixed to save the horse the labour of the last slope. Far away behind the first hills the cliff-like dwellings of Shaston

trucks: Wheeled handcarts for luggage and other items.

broke the line of the ridge. Nobody was visible in the elevated road which skirted the ascent save the lad whom they had sent on before them, sitting on the handle of the barrow that contained all Tess's worldly possessions.

'Bide here a bit, and the cart will soon come, no doubt,' said Mrs. Durbeyfield. 'Yes, I see it yonder!'

It had come — appearing suddenly from behind the forehead of the nearest upland, and stopping beside the boy with the barrow. Her mother and the children thereupon decided to go no farther, and bidding them a hasty good-bye Tess bent her steps up the hill.

They saw her white shape draw near to the spring-cart, on which her box was already placed. But before she had quite reached it another vehicle shot out from a clump of trees on the summit, came round the bend of the road there, passed the luggage-cart, and halted beside Tess, who looked up as if in great surprise.

Her mother perceived, for the first time, that the second vehicle was not a humble conveyance like the first, but a spick-and-span gig or dog-cart, highly varnished and equipped. The driver was a young man of three- or four-and-twenty, with a cigar between his teeth; wearing a dandy cap, drab jacket, breeches of the same hue, white neckcloth, stick-up collar, and brown driving-gloves — in short, he was the handsome, horsey young buck who had visited Joan a week or two before to get her answer about Tess.

Mrs. Durbeyfield clapped her hands like a child. Then she looked down, then stared again. Could she be deceived as to the meaning of this?

'Is dat the gentleman-kinsman who'll make Sissy a lady?' asked the youngest child.

Meanwhile the muslined form of Tess could be seen standing still, undecided, beside this turn-out, whose owner was talking to her. Her seeming indecision was, in fact, more than indecision: it was misgiving. She would have preferred the humble cart. The young man dismounted, and appeared to urge her to ascend. She turned her face down the hill to her relatives, and regarded the little group. Something seemed to quicken her to a determination; possibly the thought that she had killed Prince. She suddenly stepped up; he mounted beside her, and immediately whipped on the horse. In a moment they had passed the slow cart with the box, and disappeared behind the shoulder of the hill.

Directly Tess was out of sight, and the interest of the matter as a drama was at an end, the little ones' eyes filled with tears. The youngest child said, 'I wish poor, poor Tess wasn't gone away to be a lady!' and, lowering the corners of his lips, burst out crying. The new point of view was infectious, and the next child did likewise, and then the next, till the whole three of them wailed loud.

There were tears also in Joan Durbeyfield's eyes as she turned to go home. But by the time she had got back to the village she was passively trusting to the favour of accident. However, in bed that night she sighed, and her husband asked her what was the matter.

'Oh, I don't know exactly,' she said. 'I was thinking that perhaps it would ha' been better if Tess had not gone.'

'Oughtn't ye to have thought of that before?'

'Well, 'tis a chance for the maid —— Still, if 'twere the doing again, I wouldn't let her go till I had found out whether the gentleman is really a goodhearted young man and choice over her as his kinswoman.'

'Yes, you ought, perhaps, to ha' done that,' snored Sir John.

Joan Durbeyfield always managed to find consolation somewhere: 'Well, as one of the genuine stock, she ought to make her way with 'en, if she plays her trump card aright. And if he don't marry her afore he will after. For that he's all afire wi' love for her any eye can see.'

'What's her trump card? Her d'Urberville blood, you mean?'

'No, stupid; her face — as 'twas mine.'

VIII

Having mounted beside her, Alec d'Urberville drove rapidly along the crest of the first hill, chatting compliments to Tess as they went, the cart with her box being left far behind. Rising still, an immense landscape stretched around them on every side; behind, the green valley of her birth, before, a gray country of which she knew nothing except from her first brief visit to Trantridge. Thus they reached the verge of an incline down which the road stretched in a long straight descent of nearly a mile.

Ever since the accident with her father's horse Tess Durbeyfield, courageous as she naturally was, had been exceedingly timid on wheels; the least irregularity of motion startled her. She began to get uneasy at a certain recklessness in her conductor's driving.

'You will go down slow, sir, I suppose?' she said with attempted unconcern.

D'Urberville looked round upon her, nipped his cigar with the tips of his large white centre-teeth, and allowed his lips to smile slowly of themselves.

'Why, Tess,' he answered, after another whiff or two, 'it isn't a brave bouncing girl like you who asks that? Why, I always go down at full gallop. There's nothing like it for raising your spirits.'

'But perhaps you need not now?'

'Ah,' he said, shaking his head, 'there are two to be reckoned with. It is not me alone. Tib has to be considered, and she has a very queer temper.'

'Who?'

'Why, this mare. I fancy she looked round at me in a very grim way just then. Didn't you notice it?'

'Don't try to frighten me, sir,' said Tess stiffly.

'Well, I don't. If any living man can manage this horse I can: — I won't say any living man can do it — but if such has the power, I am he.'

'Why do you have such a horse?'

'Ah, well may you ask it! It was my fate, I suppose. Tib has killed one chap; and just after I bought her she nearly killed me. And then, take my word for it, I nearly killed her. But she's touchy still, very touchy; and one's life is hardly safe behind her sometimes.'

They were just beginning to descend; and it was evident that the horse, whether of her own will or of his (the latter being the more likely), knew so well the reckless performance expected of her that she hardly required a hint from behind.

Down, down, they sped, the wheels humming like a top, the dog-cart rocking right and left, its axis acquiring a slightly oblique set in relation to the line of progress; the figure of the horse rising and falling in undulations before them. Sometimes a wheel was off the ground, it seemed, for many yards; sometimes a stone was sent spinning over the hedge, and flinty sparks from the horse's hoofs outshone the daylight. The aspect of the straight road enlarged with their advance, the two banks dividing like a splitting stick; one rushing past at each shoulder.

The wind blew through Tess's white muslin to her very skin, and her washed hair flew out behind. She was determined to show no open fear, but she clutched d'Urberville's rein-arm.

'Don't touch my arm! We shall be thrown out if you do! Hold on round my waist!'

She grasped his waist, and so they reached the bottom.

'Safe, thank God, in spite of your fooling!' said she, her face on fire.

'Tess — fie! that's temper!' said d'Urberville.

''Tis truth.'

'Well, you need not let go your hold of me so thanklessly the moment you feel yourself out of danger.'

She had not considered what she had been doing; whether he were man or woman, stick or stone, in her involuntary hold on him. Recovering her reserve she sat without replying, and thus they reached the summit of another declivity.

'Now then, again!' said d'Urberville.

'No, no!' said Tess. 'Show more sense, do, please.'

'But when people find themselves on one of the highest points in the county, they must get down again,' he retorted.

He loosened rein, and away they went a second time. D'Urberville turned his face to her as they rocked, and said, in playful raillery: 'Now then, put your arms round my waist again, as you did before, my Beauty.'

'Never!' said Tess independently, holding on as well as she could without touching him.

'Let me put one little kiss on those holmberry lips, Tess, or even on that warmed cheek, and I'll stop — on my honour, I will!'

Tess, surprised beyond measure, slid farther back still on her seat, at which he urged the horse anew, and rocked her the more.

'Will nothing else do?' she cried at length, in desperation, her large eyes staring at him like those of a wild animal. This dressing her up so prettily by her mother had apparently been to lamentable purpose.

'Nothing, dear Tess,' he replied.

'Oh, I don't know — very well; I don't mind!' she panted miserably.

He drew rein, and as they slowed he was on the point of imprinting the desired salute, when, as if hardly yet aware of her own modesty, she dodged aside. His arms being occupied with the reins there was left him no power to prevent her manœuvre.

'Now, damn it — I'll break both our necks!' swore her capriciously passionate companion. 'So you can go from your word like that, you young witch, can you?'

'Very well,' said Tess, 'I'll not move since you be so determined! But I — thought you would be kind to me, and protect me, as my kinsman!'

'Kinsman be hanged! Now!'

'But I don't want anybody to kiss me, sir!' she implored, a big tear beginning to roll down her face, and the corners of her mouth trembling in her attempts not to cry. 'And I wouldn't ha' come if I had known!'

He was inexorable, and she sat still, and d'Urberville gave her the kiss of mastery. No sooner had he done so than she flushed with shame, took out her handkerchief, and wiped the spot on her cheek that had been touched by his lips. His ardour was nettled at the sight, for the act on her part had been unconsciously done.

'You are mighty sensitive for a cottage girl!' said the young man.

Tess made no reply to this remark, of which, indeed, she did not quite comprehend the drift, unheeding the snub she had administered by her instinctive rub upon her cheek. She had, in fact, undone the kiss, as far as such a thing was physically possible. With a dim sense that he was vexed she looked steadily ahead as they trotted on near Melbury Down and Wingreen, till she saw, to her consternation, that there was yet another descent to be undergone.

'You shall be made sorry for that!' he resumed, his injured tone still remaining, as he flourished the whip anew. 'Unless, that is, you agree willingly to let me do it again, and no handkerchief.'

She sighed. 'Very well, sir!' she said. 'Oh — let me get my hat!'

At the moment of speaking her hat had blown off into the road, their present speed on the upland being by no means slow. D'Urberville pulled up, and said he would get it for her, but Tess was down on the other side.

She turned back and picked up the article.

'You look prettier with it off, upon my soul, if that's possible,' he said, contemplating her over the back of the vehicle. 'Now then, up again! What's the matter?'

The hat was in place and tied, but Tess had not stepped forward.

'No, sir,' she said, revealing the red and ivory of her mouth as her eye lit in defiant triumph; 'not again, if I know it!'

'What — you won't get up beside me?'

'No; I shall walk.'

''Tis five or six miles yet to Trantridge.'

'I don't care if 'tis dozens. Besides, the cart is behind.'

'You artful hussy! Now, tell me — didn't you make that hat blow off on purpose? I'll swear you did!'

Her strategic silence confirmed his suspicion.

Then d'Urberville cursed and swore at her, and called her everything he could think of for the trick. Turning the horse suddenly he tried to drive back upon her, and so hem her in between the gig and the hedge. But he could not do this short of injuring her.

'You ought to be ashamed of yourself for using such wicked words!' cried Tess with spirit, from the top of the hedge into which she had scrambled. 'I don't like 'ee at all! I hate and detest you! I'll go back to mother, I will!'

D'Urberville's bad temper cleared up at sight of hers; and he laughed heartily.

'Well, I like you all the better,' he said. 'Come, let there be peace. I'll never do it any more against your will. My life upon it now!'

Still Tess could not be induced to remount. She did not, however, object to his keeping his gig alongside her; and in this manner, at a slow pace, they advanced towards the village of Trantridge. From time to time d'Urberville exhibited a sort of fierce distress at the sight of the tramping he had driven her to undertake by his misdemeanour. She might in truth have safely trusted him now; but he had forfeited her confidence for the time, and she kept on the ground, progressing thoughtfully, as if wondering whether it would be wiser to return home. Her resolve, however, had been taken, and it seemed vacillating even to childishness to abandon it now, unless for graver reasons. How could she face her parents, get back her box, and disconcert the whole scheme for the rehabilitation of her family on such sentimental grounds?

A few minutes later the chimneys of The Slopes appeared in view, and in a snug nook to the right the poultry-farm and cottage of Tess's destination.

IX

The community of fowls to which Tess had been appointed as supervisor, purveyor, nurse, surgeon, and friend, made its headquarters in an old thatched cottage standing in an enclosure that had once been a garden, but was now a trampled and sanded square. The house was overrun with ivy, its chimney being enlarged by the boughs of the parasite to the aspect of a ruined tower. The lower rooms were entirely given over to the birds, who walked about them with a proprietary air, as though the place had been built by themselves, and not by certain dusty copyholders° who now lay east and west in the churchyard. The descendants of these bygone owners felt it almost as a slight to their family when the house which had so much of their affection, had cost so much of their forefathers' money, and had been in their possession for several generations before the d'Urbervilles came and built here,

copyholders: Possessors of the land at the will of the lord of the manor, who, by custom, normally allowed tenants to stay for longer than the life of the original tenant.

was indifferently turned into a fowlhouse by Mrs. Stoke-d'Urberville as soon as the property fell into hand according to law. ''Twas good enough for Christians in grandfather's time,' they said.

The rooms wherein dozens of infants had wailed at their nursing now resounded with the tapping of nascent chicks. Distracted hens in coops occupied spots where formerly stood chairs supporting sedate agriculturists. The chimney-corner and once blazing hearth was now filled with inverted beehives, in which the hens laid their eggs; while out of doors the plots that each succeeding householder had carefully shaped with his spade were torn by the cocks in wildest fashion.

The garden in which the cottage stood was surrounded by a wall, and could only be entered through a door.

When Tess had occupied herself about an hour the next morning in altering and improving the arrangements, according to her skilled ideas as the daughter of a professed poulterer, the door in the wall opened and a servant in white cap and apron entered. She had come from the manor-house.

'Mrs. d'Urberville wants the fowls as usual,' she said; but perceiving that Tess did not quite understand, she explained, 'Mis'ess is a old lady, and blind.'

'Blind!' said Tess.

Almost before her misgiving at the news could find time to shape itself she took, under her companion's direction, two of the most beautiful of the Hamburghs in her arms, and followed the maid-servant, who had likewise taken two, to the adjacent mansion, which, though ornate and imposing, showed traces everywhere on this side that some occupant of its chambers could bend to the love of dumb creatures — feathers floating within view of the front, and hen-coops standing on the grass.

In a sitting-room on the ground-floor, ensconced in an armchair with her back to the light, was the owner and mistress of the estate, a white-haired woman of not more than sixty, or even less, wearing a large cap. She had the mobile face frequent in those whose sight has decayed by stages, has been laboriously striven after, and reluctantly let go, rather than the stagnant mien apparent in persons long sightless or born blind. Tess walked up to this lady with her feathered charges — one sitting on each arm.

'Ah, you are the young woman come to look after my birds?' said Mrs. d'Urberville, recognizing a new footstep. 'I hope you will be kind to them. My bailiff tells me you are quite the proper person. Well, where are they? Ah, this is Strut! But he is hardly so lively to-day, is he? He is alarmed at being handled by a stranger, I suppose. And Phena too — yes, they are a little frightened — aren't you, dears? But they will soon get used to you.'

While the old lady had been speaking Tess and the other maid, in obedience to her gestures, had placed the fowls severally in her lap, and she had felt them over from head to tail, examining their beaks, their combs, the manes of the cocks, their wings, and their claws. Her touch enabled her to recognize them in a moment, and to discover if a single feather were crippled or draggled. She handled their crops, and knew what they had eaten, and if too little or too much; her face enacting a vivid pantomime of the criticisms passing in her mind.

The birds that the two girls had brought in were duly returned to the yard, and the process was repeated till all the pet cocks and hens had been submitted to the old woman — Hamburghs, Bantams, Cochins, Brahmas, Dorkings, and such other sorts as were in fashion just then — her perception of each visitor being seldom at fault as she received the bird upon her knees.

It reminded Tess of a Confirmation, in which Mrs. D'Urberville was the bishop, the fowls the young people presented, and herself and the maid-servant the parson and curate of the parish bringing them up. At the end of the ceremony Mrs. d'Urberville abruptly asked Tess, wrinkling and twitching her face into undulations, 'Can you whistle?'

'Whistle, Ma'am?'

'Yes, whistle tunes.'

Tess could whistle like most other country girls, though the accomplishment was one which she did not care to profess in genteel company. However, she blandly admitted that such was the fact.

'Then you will have to practise it every day. I had a lad who did it very well, but he has left. I want you to whistle to my bullfinches; as I cannot see them I like to hear them, and we teach 'em airs that way. Tell her where the cages are, Elizabeth. You must begin to-morrow, or they will go back in their piping. They have been neglected these several days.'

'Mr. d'Urberville whistled to 'em this morning, ma'am,' said Elizabeth.

'He! Pooh!'

The old lady's face creased into furrows of repugnance, and she made no further reply.

Thus the reception of Tess by her fancied kinswoman terminated, and the birds were taken back to their quarters. The girl's surprise at Mrs. d'Urberville's manner was not great; for since seeing the size of the house she had expected no more. But she was far from being aware that the old lady had never heard a word of the so-called kinship. She gathered that no great affection flowed between the blind woman and her son. But in that, too, she was mistaken. Mrs. d'Urberville was not the first mother compelled to love her offspring resentfully, and to be bitterly fond.

In spite of the unpleasant initiation of the day before, Tess inclined to the freedom and novelty of her new position in the morning when the sun shone, now that she was once installed there; and she was curious to test her powers in the unexpected direction asked of her, so as to ascertain her chance of retaining her post. As soon as she was alone within the walled garden she sat herself down on a coop, and seriously screwed up her mouth for the long-neglected practice. She found her former ability to have degenerated to the production of a hollow rush of wind through the lips, and no clear note at all.

She remained fruitlessly blowing and blowing, wondering how she could have so grown out of the art which had come by nature, till she became aware of a movement among the ivy-boughs which cloaked the garden-wall no less than the cottage. Looking that way she beheld a form springing from the coping to the plot. It was Alec d'Urberville, whom she had not set eyes on since he had conducted her the day before to the door of the gardener's cottage where she had lodgings.

'Upon my honour!' cried he, 'there was never before such a beautiful thing in Nature or Art as you look, "Cousin" Tess ["Cousin" had a faint ring of mockery]. I have been watching you from over the wall — sitting like *Im*-patience on a monument,° and pouting up that pretty red mouth to whistling shape, and whooing and whooing, and privately swearing, and never being able to produce a note. Why, you are quite cross because you can't do it.'

'I may be cross, but I didn't swear.'

'Ah! I understand why you are trying — those bullies! My mother wants you to carry on their musical education. How selfish of her! As if attending to these curst cocks and hens here were not enough work for any girl. I would flatly refuse, if I were you.'

'But she wants me particularly to do it, and to be ready by tomorrow morning.'

'Does she? Well then — I'll give you a lesson or two.'

like *Im*-patience on a monument: A reversal of the statement by Viola in *Twelfth Night* that "She sat like Patience on a monument, / Smiling at grief" (2.4.114–5).

'Oh no, you won't!' said Tess, withdrawing towards the door.

'Nonsense; I don't want to touch you. See — I'll stand on this side of the wire-netting, and you can keep on the other; so you may feel quite safe. Now, look here; you screw up your lips too harshly. There 'tis — so.'

He suited the action to the word, and whistled a line of 'Take, O take those lips away.'° But the allusion was lost upon Tess.

'Now try,' said d'Urberville.

She attempted to look reserved; her face put on a sculptural severity. But he persisted in his demand, and at last, to get rid of him, she did put up her lips as directed for producing a clear note; laughing distressfully, however, and then blushing with vexation that she had laughed.

He encouraged her with 'Try again!'

Tess was quite serious, painfully serious by this time; and she tried — ultimately and unexpectedly emitting a real round sound. The momentary pleasure of success got the better of her; her eyes enlarged, and she involuntarily smiled in his face.

'That's it! Now I have started you — you'll go on beautifully. There — I said I would not come near you; and, in spite of such temptation as never before fell to mortal man, I'll keep my word. . . . Tess, do you think my mother a queer old soul?'

'I don't know much of her yet, sir.'

'You'll find her so; she must be, to make you learn to whistle to her bullfinches. I am rather out of her books just now, but you will be quite in favour if you treat her live-stock well. Good morning. If you meet with any difficulties and want help here, don't go to the bailiff, come to me.'

It was in the economy of this *régime* that Tess Durbeyfield had undertaken to fill a place. Her first day's experiences were fairly typical of those which followed through many succeeding days. A familiarity with Alec d'Urberville's presence — which that young man carefully cultivated in her by playful dialogue, and by jestingly calling her his cousin when they were alone — removed much of her original shyness of him, without, however, implanting any feeling which could engender shyness of a new and tenderer kind. But she was more pliable under his hands than a mere companionship would have made her, owing to her unavoidable dependence upon his mother, and, through that lady's comparative helplessness, upon him.

'Take, O take those lips away': *Measure for Measure* 4.1.1.

She soon found that whistling to the bullfinches in Mrs. d'Urberville's room was no such onerous business when she had regained the art, for she had caught from her musical mother numerous airs that suited those songsters admirably. A far more satisfactory time than when she practised in the garden was this whistling by the cages each morning. Unrestrained by the young man's presence she threw up her mouth, put her lips near the bars, and piped away in easeful grace to the attentive listeners.

Mrs. d'Urberville slept in a large four-post bedstead hung with heavy damask curtains, and the bullfinches occupied the same apartment, where they flitted about freely at certain hours, and made little white spots on the furniture and upholstery. Once while Tess was at the window where the cages were ranged, giving her lesson as usual, she thought she heard a rustling behind the bed. The old lady was not present, and turning round the girl had an impression that the toes of a pair of boots were visible below the fringe of the curtains. Thereupon her whistling became so disjointed that the listener, if such there were, must have discovered her suspicion of his presence. She searched the curtains every morning after that, but never found anybody within them. Alec d'Urberville had evidently thought better of his freak to terrify her by an ambush of that kind.

X

Every village has its idiosyncrasy, its constitution, often its own code of morality. The levity of some of the younger women in and about Trantridge was marked, and was perhaps symptomatic of the choice spirit who ruled The Slopes in that vicinity. The place had also a more abiding defect; it drank hard. The staple conversation on the farms around was on the uselessness of saving money; and smock-frocked arithmeticians, leaning on their ploughs or hoes, would enter into calculations of great nicety to prove that parish relief was a fuller provision for a man in his old age than any which could result from savings out of their wages during a whole lifetime.

The chief pleasure of these philosophers lay in going every Saturday night, when work was done, to Chaseborough, a decayed market-town two or three miles distant; and, returning in the small hours of the next morning, to spend Sunday in sleeping off the dyspeptic effects of the curious compounds sold to them as beer by the monopolizers of the once independent inns.

For a long time Tess did not join in the weekly pilgrimages. But under pressure from matrons not much older than herself — for a field-man's wages being as high at twenty-one as at forty, marriage was early here — Tess at length consented to go. Her first experience of the journey afforded her more enjoyment than she had expected, the hilariousness of the others being quite contagious after her monotonous attention to the poultry-farm all the week. She went again and again. Being graceful and interesting, standing moreover on the momentary threshold of womanhood, her appearance drew down upon her some sly regards from loungers in the streets of Chaseborough; hence, though sometimes her journey to the town was made independently, she always searched for her fellows at nightfall, to have the protection of their companionship homeward.

This had gone on for a month or two when there came a Saturday in September, on which a fair and a market coincided; and the pilgrims from Trantridge sought double delights at the inns on that account. Tess's occupations made her late in setting out, so that her comrades reached the town long before her. It was a fine September evening, just before sunset, when yellow lights struggle with blue shades in hairlike lines, and the atmosphere itself forms a prospect without aid from more solid objects, except the innumerable winged insects that dance in it. Through this low-lit mistiness Tess walked leisurely along.

She did not discover the coincidence of the market with the fair till she had reached the place, by which time it was close upon dusk. Her limited marketing was soon completed; and then as usual she began to look about for some of the Trantridge cottagers.

At first she could not find them, and she was informed that most of them had gone to what they called a private little jig at the house of a hay-trusser and peat-dealer who had transactions with their farm. He lived in an out-of-the-way nook of the townlet, and in trying to find her course thither her eyes fell upon Mr. d'Urberville standing at a street corner.

'What — my Beauty? You here so late?' he said.

She told him that she was simply waiting for company homeward.

'I'll see you again,' said he over her shoulder as she went on down the back lane.

Approaching the hay-trussers she could hear the fiddled notes of a reel proceeding from some building in the rear; but no sound of dancing was audible — an exceptional state of things for these parts, where as a rule the stamping drowned the music. The front door being open she could see straight through the house into the garden at the back as far as the shades of night would allow; and nobody appearing to her knock she traversed the dwelling and went up the path to the outhouse whence the sound had attracted her.

It was a windowless erection used for storage, and from the open door there floated into the obscurity a mist of yellow radiance, which at first Tess thought to be illuminated smoke. But on drawing nearer she perceived that it was a cloud of dust, lit by candles within the outhouse, whose beams upon the haze carried forward the outline of the doorway into the wide night of the garden.

When she came close and looked in she beheld indistinct forms racing up and down to the figure of the dance, the silence of their footfalls arising from their being overshoe in 'scroff' — that is to say, the powdery residuum from the storage of peat and other products, the stirring of which by their turbulent feet created the nebulosity that involved the scene. Through this floating, fusty *débris* of peat and hay, mixed with the perspirations and warmth of the dancers, and forming together a sort of vegeto-human pollen, the muted fiddles feebly pushed their notes, in marked contrast to the spirit with which the measure was trodden out. They coughed as they danced, and laughed as they coughed. Of the rushing couples there could barely be discerned more than the high lights — the indistinctness shaping them to satyrs° clasping nymphs° — a multiplicity of Pans° whirling a multiplicity of Syrinxes;° Lotis attempting to elude Priapus,° and always failing.

At intervals a couple would approach the doorway for air, and the haze no longer veiling their features, the demigods resolved themselves into the homely personalities of her own next-door neighbours. Could Trantridge in two or three short hours have metamorphosed itself thus madly!

Some Sileni° of the throng sat on benches and hay-trusses by the wall; and one of them recognized her.

'The maids don't think it respectable to dance at "The Flower-de-Luce,"' he explained. 'They don't like to let everybody see which be their fancy-men. Besides, the house sometimes shuts up just when their jints begin to get greased. So we come here and send out for liquor.'

satyrs: In classical mythology, these were part-human creatures with goats' legs and tails. **nymphs:** Minor divinities in the form of beautiful young women. **Pans:** Greek god with the legs, ears, and horns of a goat, noted for his lust. **Syrinxes:** Syrinx was pursued by Pan, but the gods turned her into a reed, from which Pan then made his pipe. **Lotis . . . Priapus:** Priapus, another lustful god, pursued Lotis, who was turned into a lotus flower. **Sileni:** Plural form of Silenus; a satyr or follower of Bacchus.

'But when be any of you going home?' asked Tess with some anxiety.

'Now — a'most directly. This is all but the last jig.'

She waited. The reel drew to a close, and some of the party were in the mind for starting. But others would not, and another dance was formed. This surely would end it, thought Tess. But it merged in yet another. She became restless and uneasy; yet, having waited so long, it was necessary to wait longer; on account of the fair the roads were dotted with roving characters of possibly ill intent; and, though not fearful of measurable dangers, she feared the unknown. Had she been near Marlott she would have had less dread.

'Don't ye be nervous, my dear good soul,' expostulated, between his coughs, a young man with a wet face, and his straw hat so far back upon his head that the brim encircled it like the nimbus of a saint. 'What's yer hurry? To-morrow is Sunday, thank God, and we can sleep it off in church-time. Now, have a turn with me?'

She did not abhor dancing, but she was not going to dance here. The movement grew more passionate: the fiddlers behind the luminous pillar of cloud now and then varied the air by playing on the wrong side of the bridge or with the back of the bow. But it did not matter; the panting shapes spun onwards.

They did not vary their partners if their inclination were to stick to previous ones. Changing partners simply meant that a satisfactory choice had not as yet been arrived at by one or other of the pair, and by this time every couple had been suitably matched. It was then that the ecstasy and the dream began, in which emotion was the matter of the universe, and matter but an adventitious intrusion likely to hinder you from spinning where you wanted to spin.

Suddenly there was a dull thump on the ground: a couple had fallen, and lay in a mixed heap. The next couple, unable to check its progress, came toppling over the obstacle. An inner cloud of dust rose around the prostrate figures amid the general one of the room, in which a twitching entanglement of arms and legs was discernible.

'You shall catch it for this, my gentleman, when you get home!' burst in female accents from the human heap — those of the unhappy partner of the man whose clumsiness had caused the mishap; she happened also to be his recently married wife, in which assortment there was nothing unusual at Trantridge as long as any affection remained between wedded couples; and, indeed, it was not uncustomary in their later lives, to avoid making odd lots of the single people between whom there might be a warm understanding.

A loud laugh from behind Tess's back, in the shade of the garden, united with the titter within the room. She looked round, and saw the red coal of a cigar: Alec d'Urberville was standing there alone. He beckoned to her, and she reluctantly retreated towards him.

'Well, my Beauty, what are you doing here?'

She was so tired after her long day and her walk that she confided her trouble to him — that she had been waiting ever since he saw her to have their company home, because the road at night was strange to her. 'But it seems they will never leave off, and I really think I will wait no longer.'

'Certainly do not. I have only a saddle-horse here to-day; but come to "The Flower-de-Luce," and I'll hire a trap, and drive you home with me.'

Tess, though flattered, had never quite got over her original mistrust of him, and, despite their tardiness, she preferred to walk home with the work-folk. So she answered that she was much obliged to him, but would not trouble him. 'I have said that I will wait for 'em, and they will expect me to now.'

'Very well, Miss Independence. Please yourself. . . . Then I shall not hurry. . . . My good Lord, what a kick-up they are having there!'

He had not put himself forward into the light, but some of them had perceived him, and his presence led to a slight pause and a consideration of how the time was flying. As soon as he had re-lit a cigar and walked away the Trantridge people began to collect themselves from amid those who had come in from other farms, and prepared to leave in a body. Their bundles and baskets were gathered up, and half an hour later, when the clock-chime sounded a quarter past eleven, they were straggling along the lane which led up the hill towards their homes.

It was a three-mile walk, along a dry white road, made whiter to-night by the light of the moon.

Tess soon perceived as she walked in the flock, sometimes with this one, sometimes with that, that the fresh night air was producing staggerings and serpentine courses among the men who had partaken too freely; some of the more careless women also were wandering in their gait — to wit, a dark virago, Car Darch, dubbed Queen of Spades, till lately a favourite of d'Urberville's; Nancy, her sister, nicknamed the Queen of Diamonds; and the young married woman who had already tumbled down. Yet however terrestrial and lumpy their appearance just now to the mean unglamoured eye, to themselves the case was different. They followed the road with a sensation that they were soaring along in a supporting medium, possessed of original and profound thoughts, themselves and surrounding nature forming an organism of which all the parts harmoniously and joyously interpenetrated each other. They were as sublime as the moon and stars above them, and the moon and stars were as ardent as they.

Tess, however, had undergone such painful experiences of this kind in her father's house, that the discovery of their condition spoilt the pleasure she was beginning to feel in the moonlight journey. Yet she stuck to the party, for reasons above given.

In the open highway they had progressed in scattered order; but now their route was through a field-gate, and the foremost finding a difficulty in opening it they closed up together.

This leading pedestrian was Car the Queen of Spades, who carried a wicker-basket containing her mother's groceries, her own draperies, and other purchases for the week. The basket being large and heavy, Car had placed it for convenience of porterage on the top of her head, where it rode on in jeopardized balance as she walked with arms akimbo.

'Well — whatever is that a-creeping down thy back, Car Darch?' said one of the group suddenly.

All looked at Car. Her gown was a light cotton print, and from the back of her head a kind of rope could be seen descending to some distance below her waist, like a Chinaman's queue.

''Tis her hair falling down,' said another.

No; it was not her hair: it was a black stream of something oozing from her basket, and it glistened like a slimy snake in the cold still rays of the moon.

''Tis treacle,' said an observant matron.

Treacle it was. Car's poor old grandmother had a weakness for the sweet stuff. Honey she had in plenty out of her own hives, but treacle was what her soul desired, and Car had been about to give her a treat of surprise. Hastily lowering the basket the dark girl found that the vessel containing the syrup had been smashed within.

By this time there had arisen a shout of laughter at the extraordinary appearance of Car's back, which irritated the dark queen into getting rid of the disfigurement by the first sudden means available, and independently of the help of the scoffers. She rushed excitedly into the field they were about to cross, and flinging herself flat on her back upon the grass, began to wipe her gown as well as she could by spinning horizontally on the herbage and dragging herself over it upon her elbows.

The laughter rang louder; they clung to the gate, to the posts, rested on their staves, in the weakness engendered by their convulsions at the spectacle of Car. Our heroine, who had hitherto held her peace, at this wild moment could not help joining in with the rest.

It was a misfortune — in more ways than one. No sooner did the dark queen hear the soberer richer note of Tess among those of the other work-people than a long smouldering sense of rivalry inflamed her to madness. She sprang to her feet and closely faced the object of her dislike.

'How darest th' laugh at me, hussy!' she cried.

'I couldn't really help it when t'others did,' apologized Tess, still tittering.

'Ah, th'st think th' beest everybody, dostn't, because th' beest first favourite with He just now! But stop a bit, my lady, stop a bit! I'm as good as two of such! Look here — here's at 'ee!'

To Tess's horror the dark queen began stripping off the bodice of her gown — which for the added reason of its ridiculed condition she was only too glad to be free of — till she had bared her plump neck, shoulders, and arms to the moonshine, under which they looked as luminous and beautiful as some Praxitelean creation,° in their possession of the faultless rotundities of a lusty country girl. She closed her fists and squared up at Tess.

'Indeed, then, I shall not fight!' said the latter majestically; 'and if I had known you was of that sort, I wouldn't have so let myself down as to come with such a whorage as this is!'

The rather too inclusive speech brought down a torrent of vituperation from other quarters upon fair Tess's unlucky head, particularly from the Queen of Diamonds, who having stood in the relations to d'Urberville that Car had also been suspected of, united with the latter against the common enemy. Several other women also chimed in, with an animus which none of them would have been so fatuous as to show but for the rollicking evening they had passed. Thereupon, finding Tess unfairly browbeaten, the husbands and lovers tried to make peace by defending her; but the result of that attempt was directly to increase the war.

Tess was indignant and ashamed. She no longer minded the loneliness of the way and the lateness of the hour; her one object was to get away from the whole crew as soon as possible. She knew well enough

Praxitelean creation: Like the work of Praxiteles, Greek sculptor of the fourth century B.C. known for his sensual statues.

that the better among them would repent of their passion next day. They were all now inside the field, and she was edging back to rush off alone when a horseman emerged almost silently from the corner of the hedge that screened the road, and Alec d'Urberville looked round upon them.

'What the devil is all this row about, work-folk?' he asked.

The explanation was not readily forthcoming; and, in truth, he did not require any. Having heard their voices while yet some way off he had ridden creepingly forward, and learnt enough to satisfy himself.

Tess was standing apart from the rest, near the gate. He bent over towards her. 'Jump up behind me,' he whispered, 'and we'll get shot of the screaming cats in a jiffy!'

She felt almost ready to faint, so vivid was her sense of the crisis. At almost any other moment of her life she would have refused such proffered aid and company, as she had refused them several times before; and now the loneliness would not of itself have forced her to do otherwise. But coming as the invitation did at the particular juncture when fear and indignation at these adversaries could be transformed by a spring of the foot into a triumph over them, she abandoned herself to her impulse, climbed the gate, put her toe upon his instep, and scrambled into the saddle behind him. The pair were speeding away into the distant gray by the time that the contentious revellers became aware of what had happened.

The Queen of Spades forgot the stain on her bodice, and stood beside the Queen of Diamonds and the new-married, staggering young woman — all with a gaze of fixity in the direction in which the horse's tramp was diminishing into silence on the road.

'What be ye looking at?' asked a man who had not observed the incident.

'Ho-ho-ho!' laughed dark Car.

'Hee-hee-hee!' laughed the tippling bride, as she steadied herself on the arm of her fond husband.

'Heu-heu-heu!' laughed dark Car's mother, stroking her moustache as she explained laconically: 'Out of the frying-pan into the fire!'

Then these children of the open air, whom even excess of alcohol could scarce injure permanently, betook themselves to the field-path; and as they went there moved onward with them, around the shadow of each one's head, a circle of opalized light, formed by the moon's rays upon the glistening sheet of dew. Each pedestrian could see no halo but his or her own, which never deserted the head-shadow, whatever its vulgar unsteadiness might be; but adhered to it, and persistently beautified it; till the erratic motions seemed an inherent part of the irradiation, and the fumes of their breathing a component of the night's mist; and the spirit of the scene, and of the moonlight, and of Nature, seemed harmoniously to mingle with the spirit of wine.

XI

The twain cantered along for some time without speech, Tess as she clung to him still panting in her triumph, yet in other respects dubious. She had perceived that the horse was not the spirited one he sometimes rode, and felt no alarm on that score, though her seat was precarious enough despite her tight hold of him. She begged him to slow the animal to a walk, which Alec accordingly did.

'Neatly done, was it not, dear Tess?' he said by and by.

'Yes!' said she. 'I am sure I ought to be much obliged to you.'

'And are you?'

She did not reply.

'Tess, why do you always dislike my kissing you?'

'I suppose —— because I don't love you.'

'You are quite sure?'

'I am angry with you sometimes!'

'Ah, I half feared as much.' Nevertheless, Alec did not object to that confession. He knew that anything was better than frigidity. 'Why haven't you told me when I have made you angry?'

'You know very well why. Because I cannot help myself here.'

'I haven't offended you often by love-making?'

'You have sometimes.'

'How many times?'

'You know as well as I — too many times.'

'Every time I have tried?'

She was silent, and the horse ambled along for a considerable distance, till a faint luminous fog, which had hung in the hollows all the evening, became general and enveloped them. It seemed to hold the moonlight in suspension, rendering it more pervasive than in clear air. Whether on this account, or from absent-mindedness, or from sleepiness, she did not perceive that they had long ago passed the point at which the lane to Trantridge branched from the highway, and that her conductor had not taken the Trantridge track.

She was inexpressibly weary. She had risen at five o'clock every morning of that week, had been on foot the whole of each day, and on this evening had in addition walked the three miles to Chaseborough, waited three hours for her neighbours without eating or drinking, her impatience to start them preventing either; she had then walked a mile of the way home, and had undergone the excitement of the quarrel, till, with the slow progress of their steed, it was now nearly one o'clock. Only once, however, was she overcome by actual drowsiness. In that moment of oblivion her head sank gently against him.

D'Urberville stopped the horse, withdrew his feet from the stirrups, turned sideways on the saddle, and enclosed her waist with his arm to support her.

This immediately put her on the defensive, and with one of those sudden impulses of reprisal to which she was liable she gave him a little push from her. In his ticklish position he nearly lost his balance and only just avoided rolling over into the road, the horse, though a powerful one, being fortunately the quietest he rode.

'That is devilish unkind!' he said. 'I mean no harm — only to keep you from falling.'

She pondered suspiciously; till, thinking that this might after all be true, she relented, and said quite humbly, 'I beg your pardon, sir.'

'I won't pardon you unless you show some confidence in me. Good God!' he burst out, 'what am I, to be repulsed so by a mere chit like you? For near three mortal months have you trifled with my feelings, eluded me, and snubbed me; and I won't stand it!'

'I'll leave you to-morrow, sir.'

'No, you will not leave me to-morrow! Will you, I ask once more, show your belief in me by letting me clasp you with my arm? Come, between us two and nobody else, now. We know each other well; and you know that I love you, and think you the prettiest girl in the world, which you are. Mayn't I treat you as a lover?'

She drew a quick pettish breath of objection, writhing uneasily on her eat, looked far ahead, and murmured, 'I don't know — I wish — how can I say yes or no when —— '

He settled the matter by clasping his arm round her as he desired, and Tess expressed no further negative. Thus they sidled slowly onward till it struck her they had been advancing for an unconscionable time — far longer than was usually occupied by the short journey from Chaseborough, even at this walking pace, and that they were no longer on hard road, but in a mere trackway.

'Why, where be we?' she exclaimed.

'Passing by a wood.'

'A wood — what wood? Surely we are quite out of the road?'

'A bit of The Chase — the oldest wood in England. It is a lovely night, and why should we not prolong our ride a little?'

'How could you be so treacherous!' said Tess, between archness and real dismay, and getting rid of his arm by pulling open his fingers one by one, though at the risk of slipping off herself. 'Just when I've been putting such trust in you, and obliging you to please you, because I thought I had wronged you by that push! Please set me down, and let me walk home.'

'You cannot walk home, darling, even if the air were clear. We are miles away from Trantridge, if I must tell you, and in this growing fog you might wander for hours among these trees.'

'Never mind that,' she coaxed. 'Put me down, I beg you. I don't mind where it is; only let me get down, sir, please!'

'Very well, then, I will — on one condition. Having brought you here to this out-of-the-way place, I feel myself responsible for your safe-conduct home, whatever you may yourself feel about it. As to your getting to Trantridge without assistance, it is quite impossible; for, to tell the truth, dear, owing to this fog, which so disguises everything, I don't quite know where we are myself. Now, if you will promise to wait beside the horse while I walk through the bushes till I come to some road or house, and ascertain exactly our whereabouts, I'll deposit you here willingly. When I come back I'll give you full directions, and if you insist upon walking you may; or you may ride — at your pleasure.'

She accepted these terms, and slid off on the near side, though not till he had stolen a cursory kiss. He sprang down on the other side.

'I suppose I must hold the horse?' said she.

'Oh no; it's not necessary,' replied Alec, patting the panting creature. 'He's had enough of it for to-night.'

He turned the horse's head into the bushes, hitched him on to a bough, and made a sort of couch or nest for her in the deep mass of dead leaves.

'Now, you sit there,' he said. 'The leaves have not got damp as yet. Just give an eye to the horse — it will be quite sufficient.'

He took a few steps away from her, but, returning, said, 'By the bye, Tess, your father has a new cob to-day. Somebody gave it to him.'

'Somebody? You!'

D'Urberville nodded.

'O how very good of you that is!' she exclaimed, with a painful sense of the awkwardness of having to thank him just then.

'And the children have some toys.'

'I didn't know — you ever sent them anything!' she murmured, much moved. 'I almost wish you had not — yes, I almost wish it!'

'Why, dear?'

'It — hampers me so.'

'Tessy — don't you love me ever so little now?'

'I'm grateful,' she reluctantly admitted. 'But I fear I do not —— ' The sudden vision of his passion for herself as a factor in this result so distressed her that, beginning with one slow tear, and then following with another, she wept outright.

'Don't cry, dear, dear one! Now sit down here, and wait till I come.' She passively sat down amid the leaves he had heaped, and shivered slightly. 'Are you cold?' he asked.

'Not very — a little.'

He touched her with his fingers, which sank into her as into down. 'You have only that puffy muslin dress on — how's that?'

'It's my best summer one. 'Twas very warm when I started, and I didn't know I was going to ride, and that it would be night.'

'Nights grow chilly in September. Let me see.' He pulled off a light overcoat that he had worn, and put it round her tenderly. 'That's it — now you'll feel warmer,' he continued. 'Now, my pretty, rest there; I shall soon be back again.'

Having buttoned the overcoat round her shoulders he plunged into the webs of vapour which by this time formed veils between the trees. She could hear the rustling of the branches as he ascended the adjoining slope, till his movements were no louder than the hopping of a bird, and finally died away. With the setting of the moon the pale light lessened, and Tess became invisible as she fell into reverie upon the leaves where he had left her.

In the meantime Alec d'Urberville had pushed on up the slope to clear his genuine doubt as to the quarter of The Chase they were in. He had, in fact, ridden quite at random for over an hour, taking any turning that came to hand in order to prolong companionship with her, and giving far more attention to Tess's moonlit person than to any wayside object. A little rest for the jaded animal being desirable, he did not hasten his search for landmarks. A clamber over the hill into the adjoining vale brought him to the fence of a highway whose contours he recognized, which settled the question of their whereabouts.

D'Urberville thereupon turned back; but by this time the moon had quite gone down, and partly on account of the fog The Chase was wrapped in thick darkness, although morning was not far off. He was obliged to advance with outstretched hands to avoid contact with the boughs, and discovered that to hit the exact spot from which he had started was at first entirely beyond him. Roaming up and down, round and round, he at length heard a slight movement of the horse close at hand; and the sleeve of his overcoat unexpectedly caught his foot.

'Tess!' said d'Urberville.

There was no answer. The obscurity was now so great that he could see absolutely nothing but a pale nebulousness at his feet, which represented the white muslin figure he had left upon the dead leaves. Everything else was blackness alike. D'Urberville stooped; and heard a gentle regular breathing. He knelt and bent lower, till her breath warmed his face, and in a moment his cheek was in contact with hers. She was sleeping soundly, and upon her eyelashes there lingered tears.

Darkness and silence ruled everywhere around. Above them rose the primeval yews and oaks of The Chase, in which were poised gentle roosting birds in their last nap; and about them stole the hopping rabbits and hares. But, might some say, where was Tess's guardian angel? where was the providence of her simple faith? Perhaps, like that other god of whom the ironical Tishbite° spoke, he was talking, or he was pursuing, or he was in a journey, or he was sleeping and not to be awaked.

Why it was that upon this beautiful feminine tissue, sensitive as gossamer, and practically blank as snow as yet, there should have been traced such a coarse pattern as it was doomed to receive; why so often the coarse appropriates the finer thus, the wrong man the woman, the wrong woman the man, many thousand years of analytical philosophy have failed to explain to our sense of order. One may, indeed, admit the possibility of a retribution lurking in the present catastrophe. Doubtless some of Tess d'Urberville's mailed ancestors rollicking home from a fray had dealt the same measure even more ruthlessly towards peasant girls of their time. But though to visit the sins of the fathers° upon the children may be a morality good enough for divinities, it is scorned by average human nature; and it therefore does not mend the matter.

Tishbite: Elijah, who in 1 Kings 18 mocks the god worshipped by the priests of Baal.
sins of the fathers: Exodus 20.5: "I the Lord thy God am a jealous God, visiting the iniquity of the fathers upon the children unto the third and fourth generation of them that hate me."

As Tess's own people down in those retreats are never tired of saying among each other in their fatalistic way: 'It was to be.' There lay the pity of it. An immeasurable social chasm was to divide our heroine's personality thereafter from that previous self of hers who stepped from her mother's door to try her fortune at Trantridge poultry-farm.

End of Phase the First

PHASE THE SECOND. MAIDEN NO MORE

XII

The basket was heavy and the bundle was large, but she lugged them along like a person who did not find her especial burden in material things. Occasionally she stopped to rest in a mechanical way by some gate or post; and then, giving the baggage another hitch upon her full round arm, went steadily on again.

It was a Sunday morning in late October, about four months after Tess Durbeyfield's arrival at Trantridge, and some few weeks subsequent to the night ride in The Chase. The time was not long past daybreak, and the yellow luminosity upon the horizon behind her back lighted the ridge towards which her face was set — the barrier of the vale wherein she had of late been a stranger — which she would have to climb over to reach her birthplace. The ascent was gradual on this side, and the soil and scenery differed much from those within Blakemore Vale. Even the character and accent of the two peoples had shades of difference, despite the amalgamating effects of a roundabout railway; so that, though less than twenty miles from the place of her sojourn at Trantridge, her native village had seemed a far-away spot. The field-folk shut in there traded northward and westward, travelled, courted, and married northward and westward, thought northward and westward; those on this side mainly directed their energies and attention to the east and south.

The incline was the same down which d'Urberville had driven with her so wildly on that day in June. Tess went up the remainder of its length without stopping, and on reaching the edge of the escarpment gazed over the familiar green world beyond, now half-veiled in mist. It was always beautiful from here; it was terribly beautiful to Tess to-day, for since her eyes last fell upon it she had learnt that the serpent hisses where the sweet birds sing,° and her views of life had been totally changed for her by the lesson. Verily another girl than the simple one she had been at home was she who, bowed by thought, stood still here, and turned to look behind her. She could not bear to look forward into the Vale.

Ascending by the long white road that Tess herself had just laboured up, she saw a two-wheeled vehicle, beside which walked a man, who held up his hand to attract her attention.

She obeyed the signal to wait for him with unspeculative repose, and in a few minutes man and horse stopped beside her.

'Why did you slip away by stealth like this?' said d'Urberville, with upbraiding breathlessness; 'on a Sunday morning, too, when people were all in bed! I only discovered it by accident, and I have been driving like the deuce to overtake you. Just look at the mare. Why go off like this? You know that nobody wished to hinder your going. And how unnecessary it has been for you to toil along on foot, and encumber yourself with this heavy load! I have followed like a madman, simply to drive you the rest of the distance, if you won't come back.'

'I shan't come back,' said she.

'I thought you wouldn't — I said so! Well, then, put up your baskets, and let me help you on.'

She listlessly placed her basket and bundle within the dog-cart, and stepped up, and they sat side by side. She had no fear of him now, and in the cause of her confidence her sorrow lay.

D'Urberville mechanically lit a cigar, and the journey was continued with broken unemotional conversation on the commonplace objects by the wayside. He had quite forgotten his struggle to kiss her when, in the early summer, they had driven in the opposite direction along the same road. But she had not, and she sat now, like a puppet, replying to his remarks in monosyllables. After some miles they came in view of the clump of trees beyond which the village of Marlott stood. It was only then that her still face showed the least emotion, a tear or two beginning to trickle down.

'What are you crying for?' he coldly asked.

'I was only thinking that I was born over there,' murmured Tess.

'Well — we must all be born somewhere.'

'I wish I had never been born — there or anywhere else!'

the serpent hisses . . . : Tess is being implicitly compared to Lucretia (see note to Chapter LIII). In Shakespeare's *The Rape of Lucrece,* Lucrece says, "The adder hisses where the sweet birds sing" (line 871).

'Pooh! Well, if you didn't wish to come to Trantridge why did you come?'

She did not reply.

'You didn't come for love of me, that I'll swear.'

''Tis quite true. If I had gone for love o' you, if I had ever sincerely loved you, if I loved you still, I should not so loathe and hate myself for my weakness as I do now! . . . My eyes were dazed by you for a little, and that was all.'

He shrugged his shoulders. She resumed —

'I didn't understand your meaning till it was too late.'

'That's what every woman says.'

'How can you dare to use such words!' she cried, turning impetuously upon him, her eyes flashing as the latent spirit (of which he was to see more some day) awoke in her. 'My God! I could knock you out of the gig! Did it never strike your mind that what every woman says some women may feel?'

'Very well,' he said, laughing; 'I am sorry to wound you. I did wrong — I admit it.' He dropped into some little bitterness as he continued: 'Only you needn't be so everlastingly flinging it in my face. I am ready to pay to the uttermost farthing. You know you need not work in the fields or the dairies again. You know you may clothe yourself with the best, instead of in the bald plain way you have lately affected, as if you couldn't get a ribbon more than you earn.'

Her lip lifted slightly, though there was little scorn, as a rule, in her large and impulsive nature.

'I have said I will not take anything more from you, and I will not — I cannot! I *should* be your creature to go on doing that, and I won't!'

'One would think you were a princess from your manner, in addition to a true and original d'Urberville — ha! ha! Well, Tess, dear, I can say no more. I suppose I am a bad fellow — a damn bad fellow. I was born bad, and I have lived bad, and I shall die bad in all probability. But, upon my lost soul, I won't be bad towards you again, Tess. And if certain circumstances should arise — you understand — in which you are in the least need, the least difficulty, send me one line, and you shall have by return whatever you require. I may not be at Trantridge — I am going to London for a time — I can't stand the old woman. But all letters will be forwarded.'

She said that she did not wish him to driver her further, and they stopped just under the clump of trees. D'Urberville alighted, and lifted her down bodily in his arms, afterwards placing her articles on the ground beside her. She bowed to him slightly, her eye just lingering in his; and then she turned to take the parcels for departure.

Alec d'Urberville removed his cigar, bent towards her, and said —

'You are not going to turn away like that, dear? Come!'

'If you wish,' she answered indifferently. 'See how you've mastered me!'

She thereupon turned round and lifted her face to his, and remained like a marble term° while he imprinted a kiss upon her cheek — half perfunctorily, half as if zest had not yet quite died out. Her eyes vaguely rested upon the remotest trees in the lane while the kiss was given, as though she were nearly unconscious of what he did.

'Now the other side, for old acquaintance' sake.'

She turned her head in the same passive way, as one might turn at the request of a sketcher or hairdresser, and he kissed the other side, his lips touching cheeks that were damp and smoothly chill as the skin of the mushrooms in the fields around.

'You don't give me your mouth and kiss me back. You never willingly do that — you'll never love me, I fear.'

'I have said so, often. It is true. I have never really and truly loved you, and I think I never can.' She added mournfully, 'Perhaps, of all things, a lie on this thing would do the most good to me now; but I have honour enough left, little as 'tis, not to tell that lie. If I did love you I may have the best o' causes for letting you know it. But I don't.'

He emitted a laboured breath, as if the scene were getting rather oppressive to his heart, or to his conscience, or to his gentility.

'Well, you are absurdly melancholy, Tess. I have no reason for flattering you now, and I can say plainly that you need not be so sad. You can hold your own for beauty against any woman of these parts, gentle or simple; I say it to you as a practical man and well-wisher. If you are wise you will show it to the world more than you do before it fades. . . . And yet, Tess, will you come back to me? Upon my soul I don't like to let you go like this!'

'Never, never! I made up my mind as soon as I saw — what I ought to have seen sooner; and I won't come.'

'Then good morning, my four months' cousin — good-bye!'

He leapt up lightly, arranged the reins, and was gone between the tall red-berried hedges.

Tess did not look after him, but slowly wound along the crooked

marble term: A post that marks a boundary, often in the shape of a pillar topped with a head and torso.

lane. It was still early, and though the sun's lower limb was just free of the hill, his rays, ungenial and peering, addressed the eye rather than the touch as yet. There was not a human soul near. Sad October and her sadder self seemed the only two existences haunting that lane.

As she walked, however, some footsteps approached behind her, the footsteps of a man; and owing to the briskness of his advance he was close at her heels and had said 'Good morning' before she had been long aware of his propinquity. He appeared to be an artisan of some sort, and carried a tin pot of red paint in his hand. He asked in a business-like manner if he should take her basket, which she permitted him to do, walking beside him.

'It is early to be astir this Sabbath morn!' he said cheerfully.

'Yes,' said Tess.

'When most people are at rest from their week's work.'

She also assented to this.

'Though I do more real work to-day than all the week besides.'

'Do you?'

'All the week I work for the glory of man, and on Sunday for the glory of God. That's more real than the other — hey? I have a little to do here at this stile.' The man turned as he spoke to an opening at the roadside leading into a pasture. 'If you'll wait a moment,' he added, 'I shall not be long.'

As he had her basket she could not well do otherwise; and she waited, observing him. He set down her basket and the tin pot, and stirring the paint with the brush that was in it began painting large square letters on the middle board of the three composing the stile, placing a comma after each word, as if to give pause while that word was driven well home to the reader's heart —

THY, DAMNATION, SLUMBERETH, NOT.
2 PET. ii. 3.

Against the peaceful landscape, the pale, decaying tints of the copses, the blue air of the horizon, and the lichened stile-boards, these staring vermilion words shone forth. They seemed to shout themselves out and make the atmosphere ring. Some people might have cried 'Alas, poor Theology!' at the hideous defacement — the last grotesque phase of a creed which had served mankind well in its time. But the words entered Tess with accusatory horror. It was as if this man had known her recent history; yet he was a total stranger.

Having finished his text he picked up her basket, and she mechanically resumed her walk beside him.

'Do you believe what you paint?' she asked in low tones.

'Believe that tex? Do I believe in my own existence!'

'But,' said she tremulously, 'suppose your sin was not of your own seeking?'

He shook his head.

'I cannot split hairs on that burning query,' he said. 'I have walked hundreds of miles this past summer, painting these texes on every wall, gate, and stile in the length and breadth of this district. I leave their application to the hearts of the people who read 'em.'

'I think they are horrible,' said Tess. 'Crushing! killing!'

'That's what they are meant to be!' he replied in a trade voice. 'But you should read my hottest ones — them I kips for slums and seaports. They'd make ye wriggle! Not but what this is a very good tex for rural districts. . . . Ah — there's a nice bit of blank wall up by that barn standing to waste. I must put one there — one that it will be good for dangerous young females like yerself to heed. Will ye wait, missy?'

'No,' said she; and taking her basket Tess trudged on. A little way forward she turned her head. The old gray wall began to advertise a similar fiery lettering to the first, with a strange and unwonted mien, as if distressed at duties it had never before been called upon to perform. It was with a sudden flush that she read and realized what was to be the inscription he was not half-way through —

THOU, SHALT, NOT, COMMIT — °

Her cheerful friend saw her looking, stopped his brush, and shouted —

'If you want to ask for edification on these things of moment, there's a very earnest good man going to preach a charity-sermon to-day in the parish you are going to — Mr. Clare of Emminster. I'm not of his persuasion now, but he's a good man, and he'll expound as well as any parson I know. 'Twas he began the work in me.'

But Tess did not answer; she throbbingly resumed her walk, her eyes fixed on the ground. 'Pooh — I don't believe God said such things!' she murmured contemptuously when her flush had died away.

A plume of smoke soared up suddenly from her father's chimney, the sight of which made her heart ache. The aspect of the interior, when she reached it, made her heart ache more. Her mother, who had

Thou, Shalt, Not, Commit — : The seventh commandment, against adultery (Exodus 20.14).

just come down stairs, turned to greet her from the fireplace, where she was kindling barked-oak twigs under the breakfast kettle. The young children were still above, as was also her father, it being Sunday morning, when he felt justified in lying an additional half-hour.

'Well! — my dear Tess!' exclaimed her surprised mother, jumping up and kissing the girl. 'How be ye? I didn't see you till you was in upon me! Have you come home to be married?'

'No, I have not come for that, mother.'

'Then for a holiday?'

'Yes — for a holiday; for a long holiday,' said Tess.

'What, isn't your cousin going to do the handsome thing?'

'He's not my cousin, and he's not going to marry me.'

Her mother eyed her narrowly.

'Come, you have not told me all,' she said.

Then Tess went up to her mother, put her face upon Joan's neck, and told.

'And yet th'st not got him to marry 'ee!' reiterated her mother. 'Any woman would have done it but you, after that!'

'Perhaps any woman would except me.'

'It would have been something like a story to come back with, if you had!' continued Mrs. Durbeyfield, ready to burst into tears of vexation. 'After all the talk about you and him which has reached us here, who would have expected it to end like this! Why didn't ye think of doing some good for your family instead o' thinking only of yourself? See how I've got to teave° and slave, and your poor weak father with his heart clogged like a dripping-pan.° I did hope for something to come out o' this! To see what a pretty pair you and he made that day when you drove away together four months ago! See what he has given us — all, as we thought, because we were his kin. But if he's not, it must have been done because of his love for 'ee. And yet you've not got him to marry!'

Get Alec d'Urberville in the mind to marry her! He marry *her!* On matrimony he had never once said a word. And what if he had? How a convulsive snatching at social salvation might have impelled her to answer him she could not say. But her poor foolish mother little knew her present feeling towards this man. Perhaps it was unusual in the circumstances, unlucky, unaccountable; but there it was; and this, as she had said, was what made her detest herself. She had never wholly cared

teave: Work or struggle (dialect). **clogged like a dripping-pan:** A pan used for roasting in which the drippings of fat have been allowed to congeal.

for him, she did not at all care for him now. She had dreaded him, winced before him, succumbed to adroit advantages he took of her helplessness; then, temporarily blinded by his ardent manners, had been stirred to confused surrender awhile: had suddenly despised and disliked him, and had run away. That was all. Hate him she did not quite; but he was dust and ashes° to her, and even for her name's sake she scarcely wished to marry him.

'You ought to have been more careful if you didn't mean to get him to make you his wife!'

'O mother, my mother!' cried the agonized girl, turning passionately upon her parent as if her poor heart would break. 'How could I be expected to know? I was a child when I left this house four months ago. Why didn't you tell me there was danger in men-folk? Why didn't you warn me? Ladies know what to fend hands against, because they read novels that tell them of these tricks; but I never had the chance o' learning in that way, and you did not help me!'

Her mother was subdued.

'I thought if I spoke of his fond feelings and what they might lead to, you would be hontish° wi' him and lose your chance,' she murmured, wiping her eyes with her apron. 'Well, we must make the best of it, I suppose. 'Tis nater, after all, and what do please God!'

XIII

The event of Tess Durbeyfield's return from the manor of her bogus kinsfolk was rumoured abroad, if rumour be not too large a word for a space of a square mile. In the afternoon several young girls of Marlott, former schoolfellows and acquaintances of Tess, called to see her, arriving dressed in their best starched and ironed, as became visitors to a person who had made a transcendent conquest (as they supposed), and sat round the room looking at her with great curiosity. For the fact that it was this said thirty-first cousin, Mr. d'Urberville, who had fallen in love with her, a gentleman not altogether local, whose reputation as a reckless gallant and heart-breaker was beginning to spread beyond the immediate boundaries of Trantridge, lent Tess's supposed position, by its fearsomeness, a far higher fascination than it would have exercised if unhazardous.

Their interest was so deep that the younger ones whispered when her back was turned —

dust and ashes: Job 42.6. **hontish:** Haughty (dialect).

'How pretty she is; and how that best frock do set her off! I believe it cost an immense deal, and that it was a gift from him.'

Tess, who was reaching up to get the tea-things from the corner-cupboard, did not hear these commentaries. If she had heard them, she might soon have set her friends right on the matter. But her mother heard, and Joan's simple vanity, having been denied the hope of a dashing marriage, fed itself as well as it could upon the sensation of a dashing flirtation. Upon the whole she felt gratified, even though such a limited and evanescent triumph should involve her daughter's reputation; it might end in marriage yet, and in the warmth of her responsiveness to their admiration she invited her visitors to stay to tea.

Their chatter, their laughter, their good-humoured innuendoes, above all, their flashes and flickerings of envy, revived Tess's spirits also; and, as the evening wore on, she caught the infection of their excitement, and grew almost gay. The marble hardness left her face, she moved with something of her old bounding step, and flushed in all her young beauty.

At moments, in spite of thought, she would reply to their inquiries with a manner of superiority, as if recognizing that her experiences in the field of courtship had, indeed, been slightly enviable. But so far was she from being, in the words of Robert South,° 'in love with her own ruin,' that the illusion was transient as lightning; cold reason came back to mock her spasmodic weakness; the ghastliness of her momentary pride would convict her, and recall her to reserved listlessness again.

And the despondency of the next morning's dawn, when it was no longer Sunday, but Monday; and no best clothes; and the laughing visitors were gone, and she awoke alone in her old bed, the innocent younger children breathing softly around her. In place of the excitement of her return, and the interest it had inspired, she saw before her a long and stony highway which she had to tread, without aid, and with little sympathy. Her depression was then terrible, and she could have hidden herself in a tomb.

In the course of a few weeks Tess revived sufficiently to show herself so far as was necessary to get to church one Sunday morning. She liked to hear the chanting — such as it was — and the old Psalms, and to join the Morning Hymn. That innate love of melody, which she had inherited from her ballad-singing mother, gave the simplest music a power over her which could well-nigh drag her heart out of her bosom at times.

words of Robert South: English divine (1634–1716).

To be as much out of observation as possible for reasons of her own, and to escape the gallantries of the young men, she set out before the chiming began, and took a back seat under the gallery, close to the lumber, where only old men and women came, and where the bier stood on end among the churchyard tools.

Parishioners dropped in by twos and threes, deposited themselves in rows before her, rested three-quarters of a minute on their foreheads as if they were praying, though they were not; then sat up, and looked around. When the chants came on one of her favourites happened to be chosen among the rest — the old double chant 'Langdon'° — but she did not know what it was called, though she would have much liked to know. She thought, without exactly wording the thought, how strange and godlike was a composer's power, who from the grave could lead through sequences of emotion, which he alone had felt at first, a girl like her who had never heard of his name, and never would have a clue to his personality.

The people who had turned their heads turned them again as the service proceeded; and at last observing her they whispered to each other. She knew what their whispers were about, grew sick at heart, and felt that she could come to church no more.

The bedroom which she shared with some of the children formed her retreat more continually than ever. Here, under her few square yards of thatch, she watched winds, and snows, and rains, gorgeous sunsets, and successive moons at their full. So close kept she that at length almost everybody thought she had gone away.

The only exercise that Tess took at this time was after dark; and it was then, when out in the woods, that she seemed least solitary. She knew how to hit to a hair's-breadth that moment of evening when the light and the darkness are so evenly balanced that the constraint of day and the suspense of night neutralize each other, leaving absolute mental liberty. It is then that the plight of being alive becomes attenuated to its least possible dimensions. She had no fear of the shadows; her sole idea seemed to be to shun mankind — or rather that cold accretion called the world, which, so terrible in the mass, is so unformidable, even pitiable, in its units.

On these lonely hills and dales her quiescent glide was of a piece with the element she moved in. Her flexuous and stealthy figure became an integral part of the scene. At times her whimsical fancy would

old double chant 'Langdon': A chant in the Anglican Church double the normal length, in this case named after the English composer, Robert Langdon (1730–1803).

intensify natural processes around her till they seemed a part of her own story. Rather they became a part of it; for the world is only a psychological phenomenon, and what they seemed they were. The midnight airs and gusts, moaning amongst the tightly-wrapped buds and bark of the winter twigs, were formulæ of bitter reproach. A wet day was the expression of irremediable grief at her weakness in the mind of some vague ethical being whom she could not class definitely as the God of her childhood, and could not comprehend as any other.

But this encompassment of her own characterization, based on shreds of convention, peopled by phantoms and voices antipathetic to her, was a sorry and mistaken creation of Tess's fancy — a cloud of moral hobgoblins by which she was terrified without reason. It was they that were out of harmony with the actual world, not she. Walking among the sleeping birds in the hedges, watching the skipping rabbits on a moonlit warren, or standing under a pheasant-laden bough, she looked upon herself as a figure of Guilt intruding into the haunts of Innocence. But all the while she was making a distinction where there was no difference. Feeling herself in antagonism she was quite in accord. She had been made to break an accepted social law, but no law known to the environment in which she fancied herself such an anomaly.

XIV

It was a hazy sunrise in August. The denser nocturnal vapours, attacked by the warm beams, were dividing and shrinking into isolated fleeces within hollows and coverts, where they waited till they should be dried away to nothing.

The sun, on account of the mist, had a curious sentient, personal look, demanding the masculine pronoun for its adequate expression. His present aspect, coupled with the lack of all human forms in the scene, explained the old-time heliolatries° in a moment. One could feel that a saner religion had never prevailed under the sky. The luminary was a golden-haired, beaming, mild-eyed, God-like creature, gazing down in the vigour and intentness of youth upon an earth that was brimming with interest for him.

His light, a little later, broke through chinks of cottage shutters, throwing stripes like red-hot pokers upon cupboards, chests of drawers, and other furniture within; and awakening harvesters who were not already astir.

heliolatries: Religions in which the sun is worshipped.

But of all ruddy things that morning the brightest were two broad arms of painted wood, which rose from the margin of a yellow cornfield hard by Marlott village. They, with two others below, formed the revolving Maltese cross° of the reaping-machine, which had been brought to the field on the previous evening to be ready for operations this day. The paint with which they were smeared, intensified in hue by the sunlight, imparted to them a look of having been dipped in liquid fire.

The field had already been 'opened'; that is to say, a lane a few feet wide had been hand-cut through the wheat along the whole circumference of the field, for the first passage of the horses and machine.

Two groups, one of men and lads, the other of women, had come down the lane just at the hour when the shadows of the eastern hedgetop struck the west hedge midway, so that the heads of the groups were enjoying sunrise while their feet were still in the dawn. They disappeared from the lane between the two stone posts which flanked the nearest field-gate.

Presently there arose from within a ticking like the love-making of the grasshopper. The machine had begun, and a moving concatenation of three horses and the aforesaid long rickety machine was visible over the gate, a driver sitting upon one of the hauling horses, and an attendant on the seat of the implement. Along one side of the field the whole wain° went, the arms of the mechanical reaper revolving slowly, till it passed down the hill quite out of sight. In a minute it came up on the other side of the field at the same equable pace; the glistening brass star in the forehead of the fore horse first catching the eye as it rose into view over the stubble, then the bright arms, and then the whole machine.

The narrow lane of stubble encompassing the field grew wider with each circuit, and the standing corn was reduced to smaller area as the morning wore on. Rabbits, hares, snakes, rats, mice, retreated inwards as into a fastness, unaware of the ephemeral nature of their refuge, and of the doom that awaited them later in the day when, their covert shrinking to a more and more horrible narrowness, they were huddled together, friends and foes, till the last few yards of upright wheat fell also under the teeth of the unerring reaper, and they were every one put to death by the sticks and stones of the harvesters.

Maltese cross: A cross with arms of equal length that broaden outward, often with indented ends. **wain:** Large open farm wagon.

The reaping-machine left the fallen corn behind it in little heaps, each heap being of the quantity for a sheaf; and upon these the active binders in the rear laid their hands — mainly women, but some of them men in print shirts, and trousers supported round their waists by leather straps, rendering useless the two buttons behind, which twinkled and bristled with sunbeams at every movement of each wearer, as if they were a pair of eyes in the small of his back.

But those of the other sex were the most interesting of this company of binders, by reason of the charm which is acquired by woman when she becomes part and parcel of outdoor nature, and is not merely an object set down therein as at ordinary times. A field man is a personality afield; a field-woman is a portion of the field; she has somehow lost her own margin, imbibed the essence of her surrounding, and assimilated herself with it.

The women — or rather girls, for they were mostly young — wore drawn cotton bonnets with great flapping curtains to keep off the sun, and gloves to prevent their hands being wounded by the stubble. There was one wearing a pale pink jacket, another in a cream-coloured tight-sleeved gown, another in a petticoat as red as the arms of the reaping-machine; and others, older, in the brown-rough 'wropper' or over-all — the old-established and most appropriate dress of the field-woman, which the young ones were abandoning. This morning the eye returns involuntarily to the girl in the pink cotton jacket, she being the most flexuous and finely-drawn figure of them all. But her bonnet is pulled so far over her brow that none of her face is disclosed while she binds, though her complexion may be guessed from a stray twine or two of dark brown hair which extends below the curtain of her bonnet. Perhaps one reason why she seduces casual attention is that she never courts it, though the other women often gaze around them.

Her binding proceeds with clock-like monotony. From the sheaf last finished she draws a handful of ears, patting their tips with her left palm to bring them even. Then stooping low she moves forward, gathering the corn with both hands against her knees, and pushing her left gloved hand under the bundle to meet the right on the other side, holding the corn in an embrace like that of a lover. She brings the ends of the bond together, and kneels on the sheaf while she ties it, beating back her skirts now and then when lifted by the breeze. A bit of her naked arm is visible between the buff leather of the gauntlet and the sleeve of her gown; and as the day wears on its feminine smoothness becomes scarified by the stubble, and bleeds.

At intervals she stands up to rest, and to retie her disarranged apron, or to pull her bonnet straight. Then one can see the oval face of a handsome young woman with deep dark eyes and long heavy clinging tresses, which seem to clasp in a beseeching way anything they fall against. The cheeks are paler, the teeth more regular, the red lips thinner than is usual in a country-bred girl.

It is Tess Durbeyfield, otherwise d'Urberville, somewhat changed — the same, but not the same; at the present stage of her existence living as a stranger and an alien here, though it was no strange land° that she was in. After a long seclusion she had come to a resolve to undertake outdoor work in her native village, the busiest season of the year in the agricultural world having arrived, and nothing that she could do within the house being so remunerative for the time as harvesting in the fields.

The movements of the other women were more or less similar to Tess's, the whole bevy of them drawing together like dancers in a quadrille° at the completion of a sheaf by each, every one placing her sheaf on end against those of the rest, till a shock, or 'stitch' as it was here called, of ten or a dozen was formed.

They went to breakfast, and came again, and the work proceeded as before. As the hour of eleven drew near a person watching her might have noticed that every now and then Tess's glance flitted wistfully to the brow of the hill, though she did not pause in her sheafing. On the verge of the hour the heads of a group of children, of ages ranging from six to fourteen, rose above the stubbly convexity of the hill.

The face of Tess flushed slightly, but still she did not pause.

The eldest of the comers, a girl who wore a triangular shawl, its corner draggling on the stubble, carried in her arms what at first sight seemed to be a doll, but proved to be an infant in long clothes. Another brought some lunch. The harvesters ceased working, took their provisions, and sat down against one of the shocks. Here they fell to, the men plying a stone jar freely, and passing round a cup.

Tess Durbeyfield had been one of the last to suspend her labours. She sat down at the end of the shock, her face turned somewhat away from her companions. When she had deposited herself a man in a rabbit-skin cap and with a red handkerchief tucked into his belt, held the cup of ale over the top of the shock for her to drink. But she did

a stranger . . . no strange land: In Exodus 2.22, Moses in Egypt refers to himself as a stranger in a strange land. **quadrille:** A square dance made up of five figures performed by four pairs of dancers; French in origin.

not accept his offer. As soon as her lunch was spread she called up the big girl her sister, and took the baby of her, who, glad to be relieved of the burden, went away to the next shock and joined the other children playing there. Tess, with a curiously stealthy yet courageous movement, and with a still rising colour, unfastened her frock and began suckling the child.

The men who sat nearest considerately turned their faces towards the other end of the field, some of them beginning to smoke; one, with absent-minded fondness, regretfully stroking the jar that would no longer yield a stream. All the women but Tess fell into animated talk, and adjusted the disarranged knots of their hair.

When the infant had taken its fill the young mother sat it upright in her lap, and looking into the far distance dandled it with a gloomy indifference that was almost dislike; then all of a sudden she fell to violently kissing it some dozens of times, as if she could never leave off, the child crying at the vehemence of an onset which strangely combined passionateness with contempt.

'She's fond of that there child, though she mid pretend to hate en, and say she wishes the baby and her too were in the churchyard,' observed the woman in the red petticoat.

'She'll soon leave off saying that,' replied the one in buff. 'Lord, 'tis wonderful what a body can get used to o' that sort in time!'

'A little more than persuading had to do wi' the coming o't, I reckon. There were they that heard a sobbing one night last year in The Chase; and it mid ha' gone hard wi' a certain party if folks had come along.'

'Well, a little more, or a little less, 'twas a thousand pities that it should have happened to she, of all others. But 'tis always the comeliest! The plain ones be as safe as churches — hey, Jenny?' The speaker turned to one of the group who certainly was not ill-defined as plain.

It was a thousand pities, indeed; it was impossible for even an enemy to feel otherwise on looking at Tess as she sat there, with her flower-like mouth and large tender eyes, neither black nor blue nor gray nor violet; rather all those shades together, and a hundred others, which could be seen if one looked into their irises — shade behind shade — tint beyond tint — around pupils that had no bottom; an almost standard woman, but for the slight incautiousness of character inherited from her race.

A resolution which had surprised herself had brought her into the fields this week for the first time during many months. After wearing and wasting her palpitating heart with every engine of regret that lonely inexperience could devise, common-sense had illumined her. She felt that she would do well to be useful again — to taste anew sweet independence at any price. The past was past; whatever it had been it was no more at hand. Whatever its consequences, time would close over them; they would all in a few years be as if they had never been, and she herself grassed down and forgotten. Meanwhile the trees were just as green as before; the birds sang and the sun shone as clearly now as ever. The familiar surroundings had not darkened because of her grief, nor sickened because of her pain.

She might have seen that what had bowed her head so profoundly — the thought of the world's concern at her situation — was founded on an illusion. She was not an existence, an experience, a passion, a structure of sensations, to anybody but herself. To all humankind besides Tess was only a passing thought. Even to friends she was no more than a frequently passing thought. If she made herself miserable the livelong night and day it was only this much to them — 'Ah, she makes herself unhappy.' If she tried to be cheerful, to dismiss all care, to take pleasure in the daylight, the flowers, the baby, she could only be this idea to them — 'Ah, she bears it very well.' Moreover, alone in a desert island would she have been wretched at what had happened to her? Not greatly. If she could have been but just created, to discover herself as a spouseless mother, with no experience of life except as the parent of a nameless child, would the position have caused her to despair? No, she would have taken it calmly, and found pleasures therein. Most of the misery had been generated by her conventional aspect, and not by her innate sensations.

Whatever Tess's reasoning, some spirit had induced her to dress herself up neatly as she had formerly done, and come out into the fields, harvest-hands being greatly in demand just then. This was why she had borne herself with dignity, and had looked people calmly in the face at times, even when holding the baby in her arms.

The harvest-men rose from the shock of corn, and stretched their limbs, and extinguished their pipes. The horses, which had been unharnessed and fed, were again attached to the scarlet machine. Tess, having quickly eaten her own meal, beckoned to her eldest sister to come and take away the baby, fastened her dress, put on the buff gloves again, and stooped anew to draw a bond from the last completed sheaf for the tying of the next.

In the afternoon and evening the proceedings of the morning were continued, Tess staying on till dusk with the body of harvesters. Then they all rode home in one of the largest wagons, in the company of a broad tarnished moon that had risen from the ground to the eastwards, its face resembling the outworn gold-leaf halo of some worm-eaten Tuscan saint.° Tess's female companions sang songs, and showed themselves very sympathetic and glad at her reappearance out of doors, though they could not refrain from mischievously throwing in a few verses of the ballad about the maid who went to the merry green wood and came back a changed state. There are counterpoises and compensations in life; and the event which had made of her a social warning had also for the moment made her the most interesting personage in the village to many. Their friendliness won her still farther away from herself, their lively spirits were contagious, and she became almost gay.

But now that her moral sorrows were passing away a fresh one arose on the natural side of her which knew no social law. When she reached home it was to learn to her grief that the baby had been suddenly taken ill since the afternoon. Some such collapse had been probable, so tender and puny was its frame; but the event came as a shock nevertheless.

The baby's offence against society in coming into the world was forgotten by the girl-mother; her soul's desire was to continue that offence by preserving the life of the child. However, it soon grew clear that the hour of emancipation for that little prisoner of the flesh was to arrive earlier than her worst misgivings had conjectured. And when she had discovered this she was plunged into a misery which transcended that of the child's simple loss. Her baby had not been baptized.

Tess had drifted into a frame of mind which accepted passively the consideration that if she should have to burn for what she had done, burn she must, and there was an end to it. Like all village girls she was well grounded in the Holy Scriptures, and had dutifully studied the histories of Aholah and Aholibah,° and knew the inferences to be drawn therefrom. But when the same question arose with regard to the baby, it had a very different colour. Her darling was about to die, and no salvation.

It was nearly bedtime, but she rushed downstairs and asked if she might send for the parson. The moment happened to be one at which her father's sense of the antique nobility of his family was highest, and his sensitiveness to the smudge which Tess had set upon that nobility

Tuscan saint: Refers to the images typical of Florentine art during the Renaissance.
Aholah and Aholibah: Two sisters who were prostitutes; Ezekiel predicts that not only they but their children will be punished (Ezek. 23).

most pronounced, for he had just returned from his weekly booze at Rolliver's Inn. No parson should come inside his door, he declared, prying into his affairs, just then, when, by her shame, it had become more necessary than ever to hide them. He locked the door and put the key in his pocket.

The household went to bed, and, distressed beyond measure, Tess retired also. She was continually waking as she lay, and in the middle of the night found that the baby was still worse. It was obviously dying — quietly and painlessly, but none the less surely.

In her misery she rocked herself upon the bed. The clock struck the solemn hour of one, that hour when fancy stalks outside reason, and malignant possibilities stand rock-firm as facts. She thought of the child consigned to the nethermost corner of hell, as its double doom for lack of baptism and lack of legitimacy; saw the arch-fiend tossing it with his three-pronged fork, like the one they used for heating the oven on baking days; to which picture she added many other quaint and curious details of torment sometimes taught the young in this Christian country. The lurid presentment so powerfully affected her imagination in the silence of the sleeping house that her nightgown became damp with perspiration, and the bedstead shook with each throb of her heart.

The infant's breathing grew more difficult, and the mother's mental tension increased. It was useless to devour the little thing with kisses; she could stay in bed no longer, and walked feverishly about the room.

'O merciful God, have pity; have pity upon my poor baby!' she cried. 'Heap as much anger as you want to upon me, and welcome; but pity the child!'

She leant against the chest of drawers, and murmured incoherent supplications for a long while, till she suddenly started up.

'Ah, perhaps baby can be saved! Perhaps it will be just the same!'

She spoke so brightly that it seemed as though her face might have shone in the gloom surrounding her.

She lit a candle, and went to a second and a third bed under the wall, where she awoke her young sisters and brothers, all of whom occupied the same room. Pulling out the washing-stand so that she could get behind it, she poured some water from a jug, and made them kneel around, putting their hands together with fingers exactly vertical. While the children, scarcely awake, awe-stricken at her manner, their eyes growing larger and larger, remained in this position, she took the baby from her bed — a child's child — so immature as scarce to seem a sufficient personality to endow its producer with the maternal title. Tess then stood erect with the infant on her arm beside the basin, the next sister held the Prayer-Book open before her, as the clerk at church held it before the parson; and thus the girl set about baptizing her child.

Her figure looked singularly tall and imposing as she stood in her long white nightgown, a thick cable of twisted dark hair hanging straight down her back to her waist. The kindly dimness of the weak candle abstracted from her form and features the little blemishes which sunlight might have revealed — the stubble scratches upon her wrists, and the weariness of her eyes — her high enthusiasm having a transfiguring effect upon the face which had been her undoing, showing it as a thing of immaculate beauty, with a touch of dignity which was almost regal. The little ones kneeling round, their sleepy eyes blinking and red, awaited her preparations full of a suspended wonder which their physical heaviness at that hour would not allow to become active.

The most impressed of them said:

'Be you really going to christen him, Tess?'

The girl-mother replied in a grave affirmative.

'What's his name going to be?'

She had not thought of that, but a name suggested by a phrase in the book of Genesis° came into her head as she proceeded with the baptismal service, and now she pronounced it:

'SORROW, I baptize thee in the name of the Father, and of the Son, and of the Holy Ghost.'

She sprinkled the water, and there was silence.

'Say "Amen," children.'

The tiny voices piped in obedient response 'Amen!'

Tess went on:

'We receive this child' — and so forth — 'and do sign him with the sign of the Cross.'

Here she dipped her hand into the basin, and fervently drew an immense cross upon the baby with her forefinger, continuing with the customary sentences as to his manfully fighting against sin, the world, and the devil, and being a faithful soldier and servant unto his life's end. She duly went on with the Lord's Prayer, the children lisping it after her in a thin gnat-like wail, till, at the conclusion, raising their voices to clerk's pitch, they again piped into the silence, 'Amen!'

a phrase in the book of Genesis: In Genesis, God's curse on woman after the fall is to bring forth children in "sorrow" (Gen. 3.16).

Then their sister, with much augmented confidence in the efficacy of this sacrament, poured forth from the bottom of her heart the thanksgiving that follows, uttering it boldly and triumphantly in the stopt-diapason note° which her voice acquired when her heart was in her speech, and which will never be forgotten by those who knew her. The ecstasy of faith almost apotheosized her; it set upon her face a glowing irradiation, and brought a red spot into the middle of each cheek; while the miniature candle-flame inverted in her eye-pupils shone like a diamond. The children gazed up at her with more and more reverence, and no longer had a will for questioning. She did not look like Sissy to them now, but as a being large, towering, and awful — a divine personage with whom they had nothing in common.

Poor Sorrow's campaign against sin, the world, and the devil° was doomed to be of limited brilliancy — luckily perhaps for himself, considering his beginnings. In the blue of the morning that fragile soldier and servant breathed his last, and when the other children awoke they cried bitterly, and begged Sissy to have another pretty baby.

The calmness which had possessed Tess since the christening remained with her in the infant's loss. In the daylight, indeed, she felt her terrors about his soul to have been somewhat exaggerated; whether well founded or not she had no uneasiness now, reasoning that if Providence would not ratify such an act of approximation she, for one, did not value the kind of heaven lost by the irregularity — either for herself or for her child.

So passed away Sorrow the Undesired — that intrusive creature, that bastard gift of shameless Nature who respects not the social law; a waif to whom eternal Time had been a matter of days merely, who knew not that such things as years and centuries ever were; to whom the cottage interior was the universe, the week's weather climate, newborn babyhood human existence, and the instinct to suck human knowledge.

Tess, who mused on the christening a good deal, wondered if it were doctrinally sufficient to secure a Christian burial for the child. Nobody could tell this but the parson of the parish, and he was a newcomer, and did not know her. She went to his house after dusk, and stood by the gate, but could not summon courage to go in. The enterprise would have been abandoned if she had not by accident met him

stopt-diapason note: Suggests that her voice, like an organ with stops, or tuned sets of pipes, is characterized by a full range of harmonious sound. **sin, the world, and the devil:** A reference to "the world, the flesh, and the devil," traditional temptations to sin mentioned in *The Book of Common Prayer*.

coming homeward as she turned away. In the gloom she did not mind speaking freely.

'I should like to ask you something, sir.'

He expressed his willingness to listen, and she told the story of the baby's illness and the extemporized ordinance.

'And now, sir,' she added earnestly, 'can you tell me this — will it be just the same for him as if you had baptized him?'

Having the natural feelings of a tradesman at finding that a job he should have been called in for had been unskilfully botched by his customers among themselves, he was disposed to say no. Yet the dignity of the girl, the strange tenderness in her voice, combined to affect his nobler impulses — or rather those that he had left in him after ten years of endeavour to graft technical belief on actual scepticism. The man and the ecclesiastic fought within him, and the victory fell to the man.

'My dear girl,' he said, 'it will be just the same.'

'Then will you give him a Christian burial?' she asked quickly.

The Vicar felt himself cornered. Hearing of the baby's illness, he had conscientiously gone to the house after nightfall to perform the rite, and, unaware that the refusal to admit him had come from Tess's father and not from Tess, he could not allow the plea of necessity for its irregular administration.

'Ah — that's another matter,' he said.

'Another matter — why?' asked Tess, rather warmly.

'Well — I would willingly do so if only we two were concerned. But I must not — for certain reasons.'

'Just for once, sir!'

'Really I must not.'

'O sir!' She seized his hand as she spoke.

He withdrew it, shaking his head.

'Then I don't like you!' she burst out, 'and I'll never come to your church no more!'

'Don't talk so rashly.'

'Perhaps it will be just the same to him if you don't? . . . Will it be just the same? Don't for God's sake speak as saint to sinner, but as you yourself to me myself — poor me!'

How the Vicar reconciled his answer with the strict notions he supposed himself to hold on these subjects it is beyond a layman's power to tell, though not to excuse. Somewhat moved, he said in this case also —

'It will be just the same.'

So the baby was carried in a small deal box, under an ancient woman's shawl, to the churchyard that night, and buried by lantern-light, at the cost of a shilling and a pint of beer to the sexton, in that shabby corner of God's allotment where He lets the nettles grow, and where all unbaptized infants, notorious drunkards, suicides, and others of the conjecturally damned are laid. In spite of the untoward surroundings, however, Tess bravely made a little cross of two laths and a piece of string, and having bound it with flowers, she stuck it up at the head of the grave one evening when she could enter the churchyard without being seen, putting at the foot also a bunch of the same flowers in a little jar of water to keep them alive. What matter was it that on the outside of the jar the eye of mere observation noted the words 'Keelwell's Marmalade'? The eye of maternal affection did not see them in its vision of higher things.

XV

'By experience,' says Roger Ascham,° 'we find out a short way by a long wandering.' Not seldom that long wandering unfits us for further travel, and of what use is our experience to us then? Tess Durbeyfield's experience was of this incapacitating kind. At last she had learned what to do; but who would now accept her doing?

If before going to the d'Urbervilles' she had vigorously moved under the guidance of sundry gnomic texts° and phrases known to her and to the world in general, no doubt she would never have been imposed on. But it had not been in Tess's power — nor is it in anybody's power — to feel the whole truth of golden opinions while it is possible to profit by them. She — and how many more — might have ironically said to God with Saint Augustine:° 'Thou hast counselled a better course than Thou hast permitted.'

She remained in her father's house during the winter months, plucking fowls, or cramming turkeys and geese, or making clothes for her sisters and brothers out of some finery which d'Urberville had given her, and she had put by with contempt. Apply to him she would not. But she would often clasp her hands behind her head and muse when she was supposed to be working hard.

She philosophically noted dates as they came past in the revolution

Roger Ascham: A sentence (slightly misquoted) from Ascham's *The Schoolmaster* (1570). **gnomic texts:** Texts that express general truths in an aphoristic manner, such as that of Roger Ascham. **Saint Augustine:** The quotation comes from the *Confessions* 10.29 of Augustine (354–430), a famous Father of the early church.

of the year; the disastrous night of her undoing at Trantridge with its dark background of The Chase; also the dates of the baby's birth and death; also her own birthday; and every other day individualized by incidents in which she had taken some share. She suddenly thought one afternoon, when looking in the glass at her fairness, that there was yet another date, of greater importance to her than those; that of her own death, when all these charms would have disappeared; a day which lay sly and unseen among all the other days of the year, giving no sign or sound when she annually passed over it; but not the less surely there. When was it? Why did she not feel the chill of each yearly encounter with such a cold relation? She had Jeremy Taylor's thought° that some time in the future those who had known her would say: 'It is the —th, the day that poor Tess Durbeyfield died;' and there would be nothing singular to their minds in the statement. Of that day, doomed to be her terminus in time through all the ages, she did not know the place in month, week, season, or year.

Almost at a leap Tess thus changed from simple girl to complex woman. Symbols of reflectiveness passed into her face, and a note of tragedy at times into her voice. Her eyes grew larger and more eloquent. She became what would have been called a fine creature; her aspect was fair and arresting; her soul that of a woman whom the turbulent experiences of the last year or two had quite failed to demoralize. But for the world's opinion those experiences would have been simply a liberal education.

She had held so aloof of late that her trouble, never generally known, was nearly forgotten in Marlott. But it became evident to her that she could never be really comfortable again in a place which had seen the collapse of her family's attempt to 'claim kin' — and, through her, even closer union — with the rich d'Urbervilles. At least she could not be comfortable there till long years should have obliterated her keen consciousness of it. Yet even now Tess felt the pulse of hopeful life still warm within her; she might be happy in some nook which had no memories. To escape the past and all that appertained thereto was to annihilate it, and to do that she would have to get away.

Was once lost always lost really true of chastity? she would ask herself. She might prove it false if she could veil bygones. The recuperative power which pervaded organic nature was surely not denied to maidenhood alone.

Jeremy Taylor's thought: In *The Rule and Exercises of Holy Dying* (1651) by this seventeenth-century Anglican divine.

She waited a long time without finding opportunity for a new departure. A particularly fine spring came round, and the stir of germination was almost audible in the buds; it moved her, as it moved the wild animals, and made her passionate to go. At last, one day in early May, a letter reached her from a former friend of her mother's, to whom she had addressed inquiries long before — a person whom she had never seen — that a skilful milkmaid was required at a dairy-house many miles to the southward, and that the dairyman would be glad to have her for the summer months.

It was not quite so far off as could have been wished; but it was probably far enough, her radius of movement and repute having been so small. To persons of limited spheres, miles are as geographical degrees, parishes as counties, counties as provinces and kingdoms.

On one point she was resolved: there should be no more d'Urberville air-castles in the dreams and deeds of her new life. She would be the dairymaid Tess, and nothing more. Her mother knew Tess's feeling on this point so well, though no words had passed between them on the subject, that she never alluded to the knightly ancestry now.

Yet such is human inconsistency that one of the interests of the new place to her was the accidental virtue of its lying near her forefathers' country (for they were not Blakemore men, though her mother was Blakemore to the bone). The dairy called Talbothays, for which she was bound, stood not remotely from some of the former estates of the d'Urbervilles, near the great family vaults of her granddames and their powerful husbands. She would be able to look at them, and think not only that d'Urberville, like Babylon,° had fallen, but that the individual innocence of a humble descendant could lapse as silently. All the while she wondered if any strange good thing might come of her being in her ancestral land; and some spirit within her rose automatically as the sap in the twigs. It was unexpended youth, surging up anew after its temporary check, and bringing with it hope, and the invincible instinct towards self-delight.

End of Phase the Second

Babylon: A capital city noted for its vice and corruption, whose destruction is mentioned in several places in the Bible, including Revelation 14.8.

PHASE THE THIRD. THE RALLY

XVI

On a thyme-scented, bird-hatching morning in May, between two and three years after the return from Trantridge — silent reconstructive years for Tess Durbeyfield — she left her home for the second time.

Having packed up her luggage so that it could be sent to her later, she started in a hired trap for the little town of Stourcastle, through which it was necessary to pass on her journey, now in a direction almost opposite to that of her first adventuring. On the curve of the nearest hill she looked back regretfully at Marlott and her father's house, although she had been so anxious to get away.

Her kindred dwelling there would probably continue their daily lives as heretofore, with no great diminution of pleasure in their consciousness, although she would be far off, and they deprived of her smile. In a few days the children would engage in their games as merrily as ever without the sense of any gap left by her departure. This leaving of the younger children she had decided to be for the best; were she to remain they would probably gain less good by her precepts than harm by her example.

She went through Stourcastle without pausing, and onward to a junction of highways, where she could await a carrier's van that ran to the south-west; for the railways which engirdled this interior tract of country had never yet struck across it. While waiting, however, there came along a farmer in his spring cart, driving approximately in the direction that she wished to pursue. Though he was a stranger to her she accepted his offer of a seat beside him, ignoring that its motive was a mere tribute to her countenance. He was going to Weatherbury, and by accompanying him thither she could walk the remainder of the distance instead of travelling in the van by way of Casterbridge.

Tess did not stop at Weatherbury, after this long drive, further than to make a slight nondescript meal at noon at a cottage to which the farmer recommended her. Thence she started on foot, basket in hand, to reach the wide upland of heath dividing this district from the low-lying meads of a further valley in which the dairy stood that was the aim and end of her day's pilgrimage.

Tess had never before visited this part of the country, and yet she felt akin to the landscape. Not so very far to the left of her she could discern a dark patch in the scenery, which inquiry confirmed her in supposing to be trees marking the environs of Kingsbere — in the church of which parish the bones of her ancestors — her useless ancestors — lay entombed.

She had no admiration for them now; she almost hated them for the dance they had led her; not a thing of all that had been theirs did she retain but the old seal and spoon. 'Pooh — I have as much of mother as father in me!' she said. 'All my prettiness comes from her, and she was only a dairymaid.'

The journey over the intervening uplands and lowlands of Egdon, when she reached them, was a more troublesome walk than she had anticipated, the distance being actually but a few miles. It was two hours, owing to sundry wrong turnings, ere she found herself on a summit commanding the long-sought-for vale, the Valley of the Great Dairies, the valley in which milk and butter grew to rankness, and were produced more profusely, if less delicately, than at her home — the verdant plain so well watered by the river Var or Froom.

It was intrinsically different from the Vale of Little Dairies, Blackmoor Vale, which, save during her disastrous sojourn at Trantridge, she had exclusively known till now. The world was drawn to a larger pattern here. The enclosures numbered fifty acres instead of ten, the farmsteads were more extended, the groups of cattle formed tribes hereabout; there only families. These myriads of cows stretching under her eyes from the far east to the far west outnumbered any she had ever seen at one glance before. The green lea was speckled as thickly with them as a canvas by Van Alsloot or Sallaert° with burghers. The ripe hues of the red and dun kine absorbed the evening sunlight, which the white-coated animals returned to the eye in rays almost dazzling, even at the distant elevation on which she stood.

The bird's-eye perspective before her was not so luxuriantly beautiful, perhaps, as that other one which she knew so well; yet it was more cheering. It lacked the intensely blue atmosphere of the rival vale, and its heavy soils and scents; the new air was clear, bracing, ethereal. The river itself, which nourished the grass and cows of these renowned dairies, flowed not like the streams in Blackmoor. Those were slow, silent, often turbid; flowing over beds of mud into which the incautious wader might sink and vanish unawares. The Froom waters were clear as the pure River of Life shown to the Evangelist,° rapid as the

Van Alsloot or Sallaert: Seventeenth-century Flemish painters of village life. **River of Life shown to the Evangelist:** The pure river from John the Evangelist's vision of heaven in Revelation 22.1.

shadow of a cloud, with pebbly shallows that prattled to the sky all day long. There the water-flower was the lily; the crow-foot here.

Either the change in the quality of the air from heavy to light, or the sense of being amid new scenes where there were no invidious eyes upon her, sent up her spirits wonderfully. Her hopes mingled with the sunshine in an ideal photosphere which surrounded her as she bounded along against the soft south wind. She heard a pleasant voice in every breeze, and in every bird's note seemed to lurk a joy.

Her face had latterly changed with changing states of mind, continually fluctuating between beauty and ordinariness, according as the thoughts were gay or grave. One day she was pink and flawless; another pale and tragical. When she was pink she was feeling less than when pale; her more perfect beauty accorded with her less elevated mood; her more intense mood with her less perfect beauty. It was her best face physically that was now set against the south wind.

The irresistible, universal, automatic tendency to find sweet pleasure somewhere, which pervades all life, from the meanest to the highest, had at length mastered Tess. Being even now only a young woman of twenty, one who mentally and sentimentally had not finished growing, it was impossible that any event should have left upon her an impression that was not in time capable of transmutation.

And thus her spirits, and her thankfulness, and her hopes, rose higher and higher. She tried several ballads, but found them inadequate; till, recollecting the psalter° that her eyes had so often wandered over of a Sunday morning before she had eaten of the tree of knowledge, she chanted: 'O ye Sun and Moon . . . O ye Stars . . . ye Green Things upon the Earth . . . ye Fowls of the Air . . . Beasts and Cattle . . . Children of Men . . . bless ye the Lord, praise Him and magnify Him for ever!'°

She suddenly stopped and murmured: 'But perhaps I don't quite know the Lord as yet.'

And probably the half-unconscious rhapsody was a Fetichistic utterance in a Monotheistic setting; women whose chief companions are the forms and forces of outdoor Nature retain in their souls far more of the Pagan fantasy of their remote forefathers than of the

psalter: Often a book containing part or all of the Book of Psalms, usually with a musical setting, but in this case, Tess is thinking of the psalm that is part of the "Invitatory and Psalter" of the Daily Morning Prayer in *The Book of Common Prayer*. The psalm is sung or said before the Benedicite. **'O ye Sun and Moon . . .':** From the Benedicite, or "Song of Creation," of the Daily Morning Prayer in *The Book of Common Prayer*, which is sung after the psalter.

systematized religion taught their race at later date. However, Tess found at least approximate expression for her feelings in the old *Benedicite* that she had lisped from infancy; and it was enough. Such high contentment with a slight initial performance as that of having started towards a means of independent living was a part of the Durbeyfield temperament. Tess really wished to walk uprightly, while her father did nothing of the kind; but she resembled him in being content with immediate and small achievements, and in having no mind for laborious effort towards such petty social advancement as could alone be effected by a family so heavily handicapped as the once powerful d'Urbervilles were now.

There was, it might be said, the energy of her mother's unexpended family, as well as the natural energy of Tess's years, rekindled after the experience which had so overwhelmed her for the time. Let the truth be told — women do as a rule live through such humiliations, and regain their spirits, and again look about them with an interested eye. While there's life there's hope is a conviction not so entirely unknown to the 'betrayed' as some amiable theorists would have us believe.

Tess Durbeyfield, then, in good heart, and full of zest for life, descended the Egdon slopes lower and lower towards the dairy of her pilgrimage.

The marked difference, in the final particular, between the rival vales now showed itself. The secret of Blackmoor was best discovered from the heights around; to read aright the valley before her it was necessary to descend into its midst. When Tess had accomplished this feat she found herself to be standing on a carpeted level, which stretched to the east and west as far as the eye could reach.

The river had stolen from the higher tracts and brought in particles to the vale all this horizontal land; and now, exhausted, aged, and attenuated, lay serpentining along through the midst of its former spoils.

Not quite sure of her direction Tess stood still upon the hemmed expanse of verdant flatness, like a fly on a billiard-table of indefinite length, and of no more consequence to the surroundings than that fly. The sole effect of her presence upon the placid valley so far had been to excite the mind of a solitary heron, which, after descending to the ground not far from her path, stood with neck erect, looking at her.

Suddenly there arose from all parts of the lowland a prolonged and repeated call —

'Waow! waow! waow!'

From the furthest east to the furthest west the cries spread as if by contagion, accompanied in some cases by the barking of a dog. It was not the expression of the valley's consciousness that beautiful Tess had arrived, but the ordinary announcement of milking-time — half-past four o'clock, when the dairymen set about getting in the cows.

The red and white herd nearest at hand, which had been phlegmatically waiting for the call, now trooped towards the steading in the background, their great bags of milk swinging under them as they walked. Tess followed slowly in their rear, and entered the barton by the open gate through which they had entered before her. Long thatched sheds stretched round the enclosure, their slopes encrusted with vivid green moss, and their eaves supported by wooden posts rubbed to a glossy smoothness by the flanks of infinite cows and calves of bygone years, now passed to an oblivion almost inconceivable in its profundity. Between the posts were ranged the milchers, each exhibiting herself at the present moment to a whimsical eye in the rear as a circle on two stalks, down the centre of which a switch moved pendulum-wise; while the sun, lowering itself behind this patient row, threw their shadows accurately inwards upon the wall. Thus it threw shadows of these obscure and homely figures every evening with as much care over each contour as if it had been the profile of a Court beauty on a palace wall; copied them as diligently as it had copied Olympian shapes° on marble *façades* long ago, or the outline of Alexander, Cæsar, and the Pharaohs.

They were the less restful cows that were stalled. Those that would stand still of their own will were milked in the middle of the yard, where many of such better behaved ones stood waiting now — all prime milchers, such as were seldom seen out of this valley, and not always within it; nourished by the succulent feed which the water-meads supplied at this prime season of the year. Those of them that were spotted with white reflected the sunshine in dazzling brilliancy, and the polished brass knobs on their horns glittered with something of military display. Their large-veined udders hung ponderous as sandbags, the teats sticking out like the legs of a gipsy's crock; and as each animal lingered for her turn to arrive the milk oozed forth and fell in drops to the ground.

Olympian shapes: The shapes of the Greek gods, who lived on Mount Olympus.

XVII

The dairymaids and men had flocked down from their cottages and out of the dairy-house with the arrival of the cows from the meads; the maids walking in pattens, not on account of the weather, but to keep their shoes above the mulch of the barton. Each girl sat down on her three-legged stool, her face sideways, her right cheek resting against the cow; and looked musingly along the animal's flank at Tess as she approached. The male milkers, with hat-brims turned down, resting flat on their foreheads and gazing on the ground, did not observe her.

One of these was a sturdy middle-aged man — whose long white 'pinner'° was somewhat finer and cleaner than the wraps of the others, and whose jacket underneath had a presentable marketing aspect — the master-dairyman, of whom she was in quest, his double character as a working milker and butter-maker here during six days, and on the seventh as a man in shining broad-cloth in his family pew at church, being so marked as to have inspired a rhyme —

Dairyman Dick
All the week: —
On Sundays Mister Richard Crick.

Seeing Tess standing at gaze he went across to her.

The majority of dairymen have a cross manner at milking-time, but it happened that Mr. Crick was glad to get a new hand — for the days were busy ones now — and he received her warmly; inquiring for her mother and the rest of the family — (though this as a matter for form merely, for in reality he had not been aware of Mrs. Durbeyfield's existence till apprised of the fact, by a brief business-letter about Tess).

'Oh — ay, as a lad I knowed your part o' the country very well,' he said terminatively. 'Though I've never been there since. And a aged woman of ninety that used to live nigh here, but is dead and gone long ago, told me that a family of some such name as yours in Blackmoor Vale came originally from these parts, and that 'twere a old ancient race that had all but perished off the earth — though the new generations didn't know it. But, Lord, I took no notice of the old woman's ramblings, not I.'

'Oh no — it is nothing,' said Tess.

Then the talk was of business only.

'pinner': A pinafore or apron with a bib (dialect) (*OED*).

'You can milk 'em clean, my maidy? I don't want my cows going azew at this time o' year.'

She reassured him on that point, and he surveyed her up and down. She had been staying indoors a good deal, and her complexion had grown delicate.

'Quite sure you can stand it? 'Tis comfortable enough here for rough folk; but we don't live in a cowcumber frame.'

She declared that she could stand it, and her zest and willingness seemed to win him over.

'Well, I suppose you'll want a dish o' tay, or victuals of some sort, hey? Not yet? Well, do as ye like about it. But faith, if 'twas I, I should be as dry as a kex° wi' travelling so far.'

'I'll begin milking now, to get my hand in,' said Tess.

She drank a little milk as temporary refreshment — to the surprise — indeed, slight contempt — of Dairyman Crick, to whose mind it had apparently never occurred that milk was good as a beverage.

'Oh, if ye can swaller that, be it so,' he said indifferently, while one held up the pail that she sipped from. ''Tis what I hain't touched for years — not I. Rot the stuff; it would lie in my innerds like lead. You can try your hand upon she,' he pursued, nodding to the nearest cow. 'Not but what she do milk rather hard. We've hard ones and we've easy ones, like other folks. However, you'll find out that soon enough.'

When Tess had changed her bonnet for a hood, and was really on her stool under the cow, and the milk was squirting from her fists into the pail, she appeared to feel that she really had laid a new foundation for her future. The conviction bred serenity, her pulse slowed, and she was able to look about her.

The milkers formed quite a little battalion of men and maids, the men operating on the hard-teated animals, the maids on the kindlier natures. It was a large dairy. There were nearly a hundred milchers under Crick's management, all told; and of the herd the master-dairyman milked six or eight with his own hands, unless away from home. These were the cows that milked hardest of all; for his journey milkmen being more or less casually hired, he would not entrust this half-dozen to their treatment, lest, from indifference, they should not milk them fully; nor to the maids, lest they should fail in the same way for lack of finger-grip; with the result that in course of time the cows would 'go azew' — that is, dry up. It was not the loss for the moment

kex: The dry, usually hollow, stem of various herbaceous plants (dialect) (*OED*).

that made slack milking so serious, but that with the decline of demand there came decline, and ultimately cessation, of supply.

After Tess had settled down to her cow there was for a time no talk in the barton, and not a sound interfered with the purr of the milk-jets into the numerous pails, except a momentary exclamation to one or other of the beasts requesting her to turn round or stand still. The only movements were those of the milkers' hands up and down, and the swing of the cows' tails. Thus they all worked on, encompassed by the vast flat mead which extended to either slope of the valley — a level landscape compounded of old landscapes long forgotten, and, no doubt, differing in character very greatly from the landscape they composed now.

'To my thinking,' said the dairyman, rising suddenly from a cow he had just finished off, snatching up his three-legged stool in one hand and the pail in the other, and moving on to the next hard-yielder in his vicinity; 'to my thinking, the cows don't gie down their milk to-day as usual. Upon my life, if Winker do begin keeping back like this, she'll not be worth going under by midsummer.'

''Tis because there's a new hand come among us,' said Jonathan Kail. 'I've noticed such things afore.'

'To be sure. It may be so. I didn't think o't.'

'I've been told that it goes up into their horns at such times,' said a dairymaid.

'Well, as to going up into their horns,' replied Dairyman Crick dubiously, as though even witchcraft might be limited by anatomical possibilities, 'I couldn't say; I certainly could not. But as nott cows° will keep it back as well as the horned ones, I don't quite agree to it. Do ye know that riddle about the nott cows, Jonathan? Why do nott cows give less milk in a year than horned?'

'I don't!' interposed the milkmaid. 'Why do they?'

'Because there bain't so many of 'em,' said the dairyman. 'Howsomever, these gam'sters do certainly keep back their milk to-day. Folks, we must lift up a stave° or two — that's the only cure for't.'

Songs were often resorted to in dairies hereabout as an enticement to the cows when they showed signs of withholding their usual yield; and the band of milkers at this request burst into melody — in purely business-like tones, it is true, and with no great spontaneity; the result, according to their own belief, being a decided improvement during

nott cows: Cows without horns (dialect). **stave:** A "verse" or stanza of a poem, song, etc. (*OED*).

the song's continuance. When they had gone through fourteen or fifteen verses of a cheerful ballad about a murderer who was afraid to go to bed in the dark because he saw certain brimstone flames around him, one of the male milkers said —

'I wish singing on the stoop didn't use up so much of a man's wind! You should get your harp, sir; not but what a fiddle is best.'

Tess, who had given ear to this, thought the words were addressed to the dairyman, but she was wrong. A reply, in the shape of 'Why?' came as it were out of the belly of a dun cow in the stalls; it had been spoken by a milker behind the animal, whom she had not hitherto perceived.

'Oh yes; there's nothing like a fiddle,' said the dairyman. 'Though I do think that bulls are more moved by a tune than cows — at least that's my experience. Once there was a old aged man over at Mellstock — William Dewy by name — one of the family that used to do a good deal of business as tranters° over there, Jonathan, do ye mind? — I knowed the man by sight as well as I know my own brother, in a manner of speaking. Well, this man was a coming homealong from a wedding where he had been playing his fiddle, one fine moonlight night, and for shortness' sake he took a cut across Forty-acres, a field lying that way, where a bull was out to grass. The bull seed William, and took after him, horns aground, begad; and though William runned his best, and hadn't *much* drink in him (considering 'twas a wedding, and the folks well off), he found he'd never reach the fence and get over in time to save himself. Well, as a last thought, he pulled out his fiddle as he runned, and struck up a jig, turning to the bull, and backing towards the corner. The bull softened down, and stood still, looking hard at William Dewy, who fiddled on and on; till a sort of a smile stole over the bull's face. But no sooner did William stop his playing and turn to get over hedge than the bull would stop his smiling and lower his horns towards the seat of William's breeches. Well, William had to turn about and play on, willy-nilly; and 'twas only three o'clock in the world, and 'a knowed that nobody would come that way for hours, and he so leery and tired that 'a didn't know what to do. When he had scraped till about four o'clock he felt that he verily would have to give over soon, and he said to himself, "There's only this last tune between me and eternal welfare! Heaven save me, or I'm a done man." Well, then he called to mind how he'd seen the cattle kneel o' Christmas Eves in the dead o' night. It was not

tranters: Carriers; hawkers (dialect).

Christmas Eve then, but it came into his head to play a trick upon the bull. So he broke into the 'Tivity Hymn, just as at Christmas carol-singing; when, lo and behold, down went the bull on his bended knees, in his ignorance, just as if 'twere the true 'Tivity night and hour. As soon as his horned friend were down, William turned, clinked off like a long-dog, and jumped safe over hedge, before the praying bull had got on his feet again to take after him. William used to say that he'd seen a man look a fool a good many times, but never such a fool as that bull looked when he found his pious feelings had been played upon, and 'twas not Christmas Eve. . . . Yes, William Dewy, that was the man's name; and I can tell you to a foot where's he a-lying in Mellstock Churchyard at this very moment — just between the second yew-tree and the north aisle.'

'It's a curious story; it carries us back to mediæval times, when faith was a living thing!'

The remark, singular for a dairy-yard, was murmured by the voice behind the dun cow; but as nobody understood the reference no notice was taken, except that the narrator seemed to think it might imply scepticism as to his tale.

'Well, 'tis quite true, sir, whether or no. I knowed the man well.'

'Oh yes; I have no doubt of it,' said the person behind the dun cow.

Tess's attention was thus attracted to the dairyman's interlocutor, of whom she could see but the merest patch, owing to his burying his head so persistently in the flank of the milcher. She could not understand why he should be addressed as 'sir' even by the dairyman himself. But no explanation was discernible; he remained under the cow long enough to have milked three, uttering a private ejaculation now and then, as if he could not get on.

'Take it gentle, sir; take it gentle,' said the dairyman. ''Tis knack, not strength that does it.'

'So I find,' said the other, standing up at last and stretching his arms. 'I think I have finished her, however, though she made my fingers ache.'

Tess could then see him at full length. He wore the ordinary white pinner and leather leggings of a dairy-farmer when milking, and his boots were clogged with the mulch of the yard; but this was all his local livery. Beneath it was something educated, reserved, subtle, sad, differing.

But the details of his aspect were temporarily thrust aside by the discovery that he was one whom she had seen before. Such vicissitudes had Tess passed through since that time that for a moment she could not remember where she had met him; and then it flashed upon her that he was the pedestrian who had joined in the club-dance at Marlott — the passing stranger who had come she knew not whence, had danced with others but not with her, had slightingly left her, and gone on his way with his friends.

The flood of memories brought back by this revival of an incident anterior to her troubles produced a momentary dismay lest, recognizing her also, he should by some means discover her story. But it passed away when she found no sign of remembrance in him. She saw by degrees that since their first and only encounter his mobile face had grown more thoughtful, and had acquired a young man's shapely moustache and beard — the latter of the palest straw colour where it began upon his cheeks, and deepening to a warm brown farther from its root. Under his linen milking-pinner he wore a dark velveteen jacket, cord breeches and gaiters, and a starched white shirt. Without the milking-gear nobody could have guessed what he was. He might with equal probability have been an eccentric landowner or a gentlemanly plough-man. That he was but a novice at dairy-work she had realized in a moment, from the time he had spent upon the milking of one cow.

Meanwhile many of the milkmaids had said to one another of the new-comer, 'how pretty she is!' with something of real generosity and admiration, though with a half hope that the auditors would qualify the assertion — which, strictly speaking, they might have done, prettiness being an inexact definition of what struck the eye in Tess. When the milking was finished for the evening they straggled indoors, where Mrs. Crick, the dairyman's wife — who was too respectable to go out milking herself, and wore a hot stuff gown in warm weather because the dairymaids wore prints — was giving an eye to the leads° and things.

Only two or three of the maids, Tess learnt, slept in the dairy-house besides herself; most of the helpers going to their homes. She saw nothing at suppertime of the superior milker who had commented on the story, and asked no questions about him, the remainder of the evening being occupied in arranging her place in the bed-chamber. It was a large room over the milk-house, some thirty feet long; the sleeping-cots of the other three indoor milkmaids being in the same apartment. They were blooming young women, and, except one,

leads: Milk pans made of lead.

rather older than herself. By bedtime Tess was thoroughly tired, and fell asleep immediately.

But one of the girls who occupied an adjoining bed was more wakeful than Tess, and would insist upon relating to the latter various particulars of the homestead into which she had just entered. The girl's whispered words mingled with the shades, and, to Tess's drowsy mind, they seemed to be generated by the darkness in which they floated.

'Mr. Angel Clare — he that is learning milking, and that plays the harp — never says much to us. He is a pa'son's son, and is too much taken up wi' his own thoughts to notice girls. He is the dairyman's pupil — learning farming in all its branches. He has learnt sheep-farming at another place, and he's now mastering dairy-work.... Yes, he is quite the gentleman-born. His father is the Reverent Mr. Clare at Emminster — a good many miles from here.'

'Oh — I have heard of him,' said her companion, now awake. 'A very earnest clergyman, is he not?'

'Yes — that he is — the earnestest man in all Wessex, they say — the last of the old Low Church sort, they tell me — for all about here be what they call High. All his sons, except our Mr. Clare, be made pa'sons too.'

Tess had not at this hour the curiosity to ask why the present Mr. Clare was not made a parson like his brethren, and gradually fell asleep again, the words of her informant coming to her along with the smell of the cheeses in the adjoining cheese-loft, and the measured dripping of the whey from the wrings° downstairs.

XVIII

Angel Clare rises out of the past not altogether as a distinct figure, but as an appreciative voice, a long regard of fixed, abstracted eyes, and a mobility of mouth somewhat too small and delicately lined for a man's, though with an unexpectedly firm close of the lower lip now and then; enough to do away with any inference of indecision. Nevertheless, something nebulous, preoccupied, vague, in his bearing and regard, marked him as one who probably had no very definite aim or concern about his material future. Yet as a lad people had said of him that he was one who might do anything if he tried.

He was the youngest son of his father, a poor parson at the other end of the county, and had arrived at Talbothays Dairy as a six

wrings: Cheese presses (*OED*).

months' pupil, after going the round of some other farms, his object being to acquire a practical skill in the various processes of farming, with a view either to the Colonies, or the tenure of a home-farm, as circumstances might decide.

His entry into the ranks of the agriculturists and breeders was a step in the young man's career which had been anticipated neither by himself nor by others.

Mr. Clare the elder, whose first wife had died and left him a daughter, married a second late in life. This lady had somewhat unexpectedly brought him three sons, so that between Angel, the youngest, and his father the vicar there seemed to be almost a missing generation. Of these boys the aforesaid Angel, the child of his old age, was the only son who had not taken a University degree, though he was the single one of them whose early promise might have done full justice to an academical training.

Some two or three years before Angel's appearance at the Marlott dance, on a day when he had left school and was pursuing his studies at home, a parcel came to the vicarage from the local bookseller's, directed to the Reverend James Clare. The vicar having opened it and found it to contain a book, read a few pages; whereupon he jumped up from his seat and went straight to the shop with the book under his arm.

'Why has this been sent to my house?' he asked peremptorily, holding up the volume.

'It was ordered, sir.'

'Not by me, or any one belonging to me, I am happy to say.'

The shopkeeper looked into his order-book.

'Oh, it has been misdirected, sir,' he said. 'It was ordered by Mr. Angel Clare, and should have been sent to him.'

Mr. Clare winced as if he had been struck. He went home pale and dejected, and called Angel into his study.

'Look into this book, my boy,' he said. 'What do you know about it?'

'I ordered it,' said Angel simply.

'What for?'

'To read.'

'How can you think of reading it?'

'How can I? Why — it is a system of philosophy. There is no more moral, or even religious, work published.'

'Yes — moral enough; I don't deny that. But religious! — and for *you*, who intend to be a minister of the Gospel!'

'Since you have alluded to the matter, father,' said the son, with anxious thought upon his face, 'I should like to say, once for all, that I should prefer not to take Orders.° I fear I could not conscientiously do so. I love the Church as one loves a parent. I shall always have the warmest affection for her. There is no institution for whose history I have a deeper admiration; but I cannot honestly be ordained her minister, as my brothers are, while she refuses to liberate her mind from an untenable redemptive theolatry.'°

It had never occurred to the straightforward and simple-minded Vicar that one of his own flesh and blood could come to this! He was stultified, shocked, paralyzed. And if Angel were not going to enter the Church, what was the use of sending him to Cambridge? The University as a step to anything but ordination seemed, to this man of fixed ideas, a preface without a volume. He was a man not merely religious, but devout; a firm believer — not as the phrase is now elusively construed by theological thimble-riggers° in the Church and out of it, but in the old and ardent sense of the Evangelical school: one who could

> Indeed opine
> That the Eternal and Divine
> Did, eighteen centuries ago
> In very truth . . .°

Angel's father tried argument, persuasion, entreaty.

'No, father; I cannot underwrite Article Four° (leave alone the rest), taking it "in the literal and grammatical sense" as required by the Declaration; and, therefore, I can't be a parson in the present state of affairs,' said Angel. 'My whole instinct in matters of religion is towards reconstruction; to quote your favourite Epistle to the Hebrews, "*the removing of those things that are shaken, as of things that are made, that those things which cannot be shaken may remain.*"' °

His father grieved so deeply that it made Angel quite ill to see him.

'What is the good of your mother and me economizing and stinting ourselves to give you a University education, if it is not to be used for the honour and glory of God?' his father repeated.

to take Orders: To become an ordained minister. **redemptive theolatry:** The worship of a god that promises redemption, as in Christianity. **thimble-riggers:** Cheaters or swindlers, such as those who organize games of thimblerig, in which bets are taken concerning which of three thimbles covers an object. **Indeed opine...:** From "Easter Day" by Robert Browning. **Article Four:** The fourth of the Thirty-Nine Articles of the Church of England asserts the literal resurrection of Christ from the dead. ***the removing of those things that are shaken, . . .":*** Hebrews 12.27.

'Why, that it may be used for the honour and glory of man, father.'

Perhaps if Angel had persevered he might have gone to Cambridge like his brothers. But the Vicar's view of that seat of learning as a stepping-stone to Orders alone was quite a family tradition; and so rooted was the idea in his mind that perseverance began to appear to the sensitive son akin to an intent to misappropriate a trust, and wrong the pious heads of the household, who had been and were, as his father had hinted, compelled to exercise much thrift to carry out this uniform plan of education for the three young men.

'I will do without Cambridge,' said Angel at last. 'I feel that I have no right to go there in the circumstances.'

The effects of this decisive debate were not long in showing themselves. He spent years and years in desultory studies, undertakings, and meditations; he began to evince considerable indifference to social forms and observances. The material distinctions of rank and wealth he increasingly despised. Even the 'good old family' (to use a favourite phrase of a late local worthy) had no aroma for him unless there were good new resolutions in its representatives. As a balance to these austerities, when he went to live in London to see what the world was like, and with a view to practising a profession or business there, he was carried off his head, and nearly entrapped by a woman much older than himself, though luckily he escaped not greatly the worse for the experience.

Early association with country solitudes had bred in him an unconquerable, and almost unreasonable, aversion to modern town life, and shut him out from such success as he might have aspired to by following a mundane calling in the impracticability of the spiritual one. But something had to be done; he had wasted many valuable years; and having an acquaintance who was starting on a thriving life as a Colonial farmer, it occurred to Angel that this might be a lead in the right direction. Farming, either in the Colonies, America, or at home — farming, at any rate, after becoming well qualified for the business by a careful apprenticeship — that was a vocation which would probably afford an independence without the sacrifice of what he valued even more than a competency — intellectual liberty.

So we find Angel Clare at six-and-twenty here at Talbothays as a student of kine, and, as there were no houses near at hand in which he could get a comfortable lodging, a boarder at the dairyman's.

His room was an immense attic which ran the whole length of the dairy-house. It could only be reached by a ladder from the cheese-loft, and had been closed up for a long time till he arrived and selected it as his retreat. Here Clare had plenty of space, and could often be heard by the dairy-folk pacing up and down when the household had gone to rest. A portion was divided off at one end by a curtain, behind which was his bed, the outer part being furnished as a homely sitting-room.

At first he lived up above entirely, reading a good deal, and strumming upon an old harp which he had bought at a sale, saying when in a bitter humour that he might have to get his living by it in the streets some day. But he soon preferred to read human nature by taking his meals downstairs in the general dining-kitchen, with the dairyman and his wife, and the maids and men, who all together formed a lively assembly; for though but few milking hands slept in the house, several joined the family at meals. The longer Clare resided here the less objection had he to his company, and the more did he like to share quarters with them in common.

Much to his surprise he took, indeed, a real delight in their companionship. The conventional farm-folk of his imagination — personified in the newspaper-press by the pitiable dummy known as Hodge° — were obliterated after a few days' residence. At close quarters no Hodge was to be seen. At first, it is true, when Clare's intelligence was fresh from a contrasting society, these friends with whom he now hobnobbed seemed a little strange. Sitting down as a level member of the dairyman's household seemed at the outset an undignified proceeding. The ideas, the modes, the surroundings, appeared retrogressive and unmeaning. But with living on there, day after day, the acute sojourner became conscious of a new aspect in the spectacle. Without any objective change whatever, variety had taken the place of monotonousness. His host and his host's household, his men and his maids, as they became intimately known to Clare, began to differentiate themselves as in a chemical process. The thought of Pascal's° was brought home to him: 'A mesure qu'on a plus d'esprit, on trouve qu'il y a plus d'hommes originaux. Les gens du commun ne trouvent pas de différence entre les hommes.' The typical and unvarying Hodge ceased to exist. He had been disintegrated into a number of varied fellow-creatures — beings of many minds, beings infinite in difference; some

Hodge: A familiar term for an agricultural laborer in England; shortened form of Roger.
thought of Pascal's: "To the same degree as one has intelligence, one notices that many individuals possess distinctive qualities. People of an ordinary kind do not notice the differences between individuals." From the *Pensées* of Blaise Pascal (1602–1674), French philosopher and mathematician.

happy, many serene, a few depressed, one here and there bright even to genius, some stupid, others wanton, others austere; some mutely Miltonic, some potentially Cromwellian;° into men who had private views of each other, as he had of his friends; who could applaud or condemn each other, amuse or sadden themselves by the contemplation of each other's foibles or vices; men every one of whom walked in his own individual way the road to dusty death.°

Unexpectedly he began to like the outdoor life for its own sake, and for what it brought, apart from its bearing on his own proposed career. Considering his position he became wonderfully free from the chronic melancholy which is taking hold of the civilized races with the decline of belief in a beneficent Power. For the first time of late years he could read as his musings inclined him, without any eye to cramming for a profession, since the few farming handbooks which he deemed it desirable to master occupied him but little time.

He grew away from old associations, and saw something new in life and humanity. Secondarily, he made close acquaintance with phenomena which he had before known but darkly — the seasons in their moods, morning and evening, night and noon, winds in their different tempers, trees, waters and mists, shades and silences, and the voices of inanimate things.

The early mornings were still sufficiently cool to render a fire acceptable in the large room wherein they breakfasted; and, by Mrs. Crick's orders, who held that he was too genteel to mess at their table, it was Angel Clare's custom to sit in the yawning chimney-corner during the meal, his cup-and-saucer and plate being placed on a hinged flap at his elbow. The light from the long, wide, mullioned window opposite shone in upon his nook, and, assisted by a secondary light of cold blue quality which shone down the chimney, enabled him to read there easily whenever disposed to do so. Between Clare and the window was the table at which his companions sat, their munching profiles rising sharp against the panes; while to the side was the milk-house door, through which were visible the rectangular leads in rows, full to the brim with the morning's milk. At the further end the great churn could be seen revolving, and its slip-slopping heard — the moving power being discernible through the window in the form of a spiritless horse walking in a circle and driven by a boy.

some mutely Miltonic, some potentially Cromwellian: An allusion to Thomas Gray's "Elegy Written in a Country Churchyard" (lines 59–60). **dusty death:** A phrase from *Macbeth* 5.5.23.

For several days after Tess's arrival Clare, sitting abstractedly reading from some book, periodical, or piece of music just come by post, hardly noticed that she was present at table. She talked so little, and the other maids talked so much, that the babble did not strike him as possessing a new note, and he was ever in the habit of neglecting the particulars of an outward scene for the general impression. One day, however, when he had been conning one of his music-scores, and by force of imagination was hearing the tune in his head, he lapsed into listlessness, and the music-sheet rolled to the hearth. He looked at the fire of logs, with its one flame pirouetting on the top in a dying dance after the breakfast-cooking and boiling, and it seemed to jig to his inward tune; also at the two chimney crooks dangling down from the cotterel or cross-bar, plumed with soot which quivered to the same melody; also at the half-empty kettle whining an accompaniment. The conversation at the table mixed in with his phantasmal orchestra till he thought: 'What a fluty voice one of those milkmaids has! I suppose it is the new one.'

Clare looked round upon her, seated with the others.

She was not looking towards him. Indeed, owing to his long silence, his presence in the room was almost forgotten.

'I don't know about ghosts,' she was saying; 'but I do know that our souls can be made to go outside our bodies when we are alive.'

The dairyman turned to her with his mouth full, his eyes charged with serious inquiry, and his great knife and fork (breakfasts were breakfasts here) planted erect on the table, like the beginning of a gallows.

'What — really now? And is it so, maidy?' he said.

'A very easy way to feel 'em go,' continued Tess, 'is to lie on the grass at night and look straight up at some big bright star; and, by fixing your mind upon it, you will soon find that you are hundreds and hundreds o' miles away from your body, which you don't seem to want at all.'

The dairyman removed his hard gaze from Tess, and fixed it on his wife.

'Now that's a rum thing, Christianner — hey? To think o' the miles I've vamped o' starlight nights these last thirty year, courting, or trading, or for doctor, or for nurse, and yet never had the least notion o' that till now, or feeled my soul rise so much as an inch above my shirt-collar.'

The general attention being drawn to her, including that of the dairyman's pupil, Tess flushed, and remarking evasively that it was only a fancy, resumed her breakfast.

Clare continued to observe her. She soon finished her eating, and having a consciousness that Clare was regarding her, began to trace imaginary patterns on the tablecloth with her forefinger with the constraint of a domestic animal that perceives itself to be watched.

'What a fresh and virginal daughter of Nature that milkmaid is!' he said to himself.

And then he seemed to discern in her something that was familiar, something which carried him back into a joyous and unforeseeing past, before the necessity of taking thought had made the heavens gray. He concluded that he had beheld her before; where he could not tell. A casual encounter during some country ramble it certainly had been, and he was not greatly curious about it. But the circumstance was sufficient to lead him to select Tess in preference to the other pretty milkmaids when he wished to contemplate contiguous womankind.

XIX

In general the cows were milked as they presented themselves, without fancy or choice. But certain cows will show a fondness for a particular pair of hands, sometimes carrying this predilection so far as to refuse to stand at all except to their favourite, the pail of a stranger being unceremoniously kicked over.

It was Dairyman Crick's rule to insist on breaking down these partialities and aversions by constant interchange, since otherwise, in the event of a milkman or maid going away from the dairy, he was placed in a difficulty. The maids' private aims, however, were the reverse of the dairyman's rule, the daily selection by each damsel of the eight or ten cows to which she had grown accustomed rendering the operation on their willing udders surprisingly easy and effortless.

Tess, like her compeers, soon discovered which of the cows had a preference for her style of manipulation, and her fingers having become delicate from the long domiciliary imprisonments to which she had subjected herself at intervals during the last two or three years, she would have been glad to meet the milchers' views in this respect. Out of the whole ninety-five there were eight in particular — Dumpling, Fancy, Lofty, Mist, Old Pretty, Young Pretty, Tidy, and Loud — who, though the teats of one or two were as hard as carrots, gave down to her with a readiness that made her work on them a mere touch of the fingers. Knowing, however, the dairyman's wish, she endeavoured conscientiously to take the animals just as they came, excepting the very hard yielders which she could not yet manage.

But she soon found a curious correspondence between the ostensibly chance position of the cows and her wishes in this matter, till she felt that their order could not be the result of accident. The dairyman's pupil had lent a hand in getting the cows together of late, and at the fifth or sixth time she turned her eyes, as she rested against the cow, full of sly inquiry upon him.

'Mr. Clare, you have ranged the cows!' she said, blushing; and in making the accusation symptoms of a smile gently lifted her upper lip in spite of her, so as to show the tips of her teeth, the lower lip remaining severely still.

'Well, it makes no difference,' said he. 'You will always be here to milk them.'

'Do you think so? I *hope* I shall! But I don't *know*.'

She was angry with herself afterwards, thinking that he, unaware of her grave reasons for liking this seclusion, might have mistaken her meaning. She had spoken so earnestly to him, as if his presence were somehow a factor in her wish. Her misgiving was such that at dusk, when the milking was over, she walked in the garden alone, to continue her regrets that she had disclosed to him her discovery of his considerateness.

It was a typical summer evening in June, the atmosphere being in such delicate equilibrium and so transmissive that inanimate objects seemed endowed with two or three senses, if not five. There was no distinction between the near and the far, and an auditor felt close to everything within the horizon. The soundlessness impressed her as a positive entity rather than as the mere negation of noise. It was broken by the strumming of strings.

Tess had heard those notes in the attic above her head. Dim, flattened, constrained by their confinement, they had never appealed to her as now, when they wandered in the still air with a stark quality like that of nudity. To speak absolutely, both instrument and execution were poor; but the relative is all, and as she listened Tess, like a fascinated bird, could not leave the spot. Far from leaving she drew up towards the performer, keeping behind the hedge that he might not guess her presence.

The outskirt of the garden in which Tess found herself had been left uncultivated for some years, and was now damp and rank with juicy grass which sent up mists of pollen at a touch; and with tall blooming weeds emitting offensive smells — weeds whose red and yellow and purple hues formed a polychrome as dazzling as that of cultivated flowers. She went stealthily as a cat through this profusion of growth, gathering cuckoo-spittle on her skirts, cracking snails that were underfoot, staining her hands with thistle-milk and slug-slime, and rubbing off upon her naked arms sticky blights which, though snow-white on the apple-tree trunks, made madder stains on her skin; thus she drew quite near to Clare, still unobserved of him.

Tess was conscious of neither time nor space. The exaltation which she had described as being producible at will by gazing at a star, came now without any determination of hers; she undulated upon the thin notes of the second-hand harp, and their harmonies passed like breezes through her, bringing tears into her eyes. The floating pollen seemed to be his notes made visible, and the dampness of the garden the weeping of the garden's sensibility. Though near nightfall, the rank-smelling weed-flowers flowed as if they would not close for intentness, and the waves of colour mixed with the waves of sound.

The light which still shone was derived mainly from a large hole in the western bank of cloud; it was like a piece of day left behind by accident, dusk having closed in elsewhere. He concluded his plaintive melody, a very simple performance, demanding no great skill; and she waited, thinking another might be begun. But, tired of playing, he had desultorily come round the fence, and was rambling up behind her. Tess, her cheeks on fire, moved away furtively, as if hardly moving at all.

Angel, however, saw her light summer gown, and he spoke; his low tones reaching her, though he was some distance off.

'What makes you draw off in that way, Tess?' said he. 'Are you afraid?'

'Oh no, sir . . . not of outdoor things; especially just now when the apple-blooth° is falling, and everything so green.'

'But you have your indoor fears — eh?'

'Well — yes, sir.'

'What of?'

'I couldn't quite say.'

'The milk turning sour?'

'No.'

'Life in general?'

'Yes, sir.'

'Ah — so have I, very often. This hobble of being alive is rather serious, don't you think so?'

'It is — now you put it that way.'

apple-blooth: Apple blossom.

'All the same, I shouldn't have expected a young girl like you to see it so just yet. How is it you do?'

She maintained a hesitating silence.

'Come, Tess, tell me in confidence.'

She thought that he meant what were the aspects of things to her, and replied shyly —

'The trees have inquisitive eyes, haven't they? — that is, seem as if they had. And the river says, — "Why do ye trouble me with your looks?" And you seem to see numbers of to-morrows just all in a line, the first of them the biggest and clearest, the others getting smaller and smaller as they stand farther away; but they all seem very fierce and cruel and as if they said, "I'm coming! Beware of me! Beware of me!" . . . But *you,* sir, can raise up dreams with your music, and drive all such horrid fancies away!'

He was surprised to find this young woman — who though but a milkmaid had just that touch of rarity about her which might make her the envied of her housemates — shaping such sad imaginings. She was expressing in her own native phrases — assisted a little by her Sixth Standard training — feelings which might almost have been called those of the age — the ache of modernism. The perception arrested him less when he reflected that what are called advanced ideas are really in great part but the latest fashion in definition — a more accurate expression, by words in *logy* and *ism,* of sensations which men and women have vaguely grasped for centuries.

Still, it was strange that they should have come to her while yet so young; more than strange; it was impressive, interesting, pathetic. Not guessing the cause, there was nothing to remind him that experience is as to intensity, and not as to duration. Tess's passing corporeal blight had been her mental harvest.

Tess, on her part, could not understand why a man of clerical family and good education, and above physical want, should look upon it as a mishap to be alive. For the unhappy pilgrim herself there was very good reason. But how could this admirable and poetic man ever have descended into the Valley of Humiliation,° have felt with the man of Uz° — as she herself had felt two or three years ago — 'My soul chooseth strangling and death rather than my life. I loathe it; I would not live alway.'°

Valley of Humiliation: From Part I (1678) and Part II (1684) of John Bunyan's *Pilgrim's Progress.* **man of Uz:** Job. **My soul chooseth strangling . . . :** Job 7.15–16.

It was true that he was at present out of his class. But she knew that was only because, like Peter the Great° in a shipwright's yard, he was studying what he wanted to know. He did not milk cows because he was obliged to milk cows, but because he was learning how to be a rich and prosperous dairyman, landowner, agriculturist, and breeder of cattle. He would become an American or Australian Abraham, commanding like a monarch his flocks and his herds, his spotted and his ring-straked, his men-servants and his maids. At times, nevertheless, it did seem unaccountable to her that a decidedly bookish, musical, thinking young man should have chosen deliberately to be a farmer, and not a clergyman, like his father and brothers.

Thus, neither having the clue to the other's secret, they were respectively puzzled at what each revealed, and awaited new knowledge of each other's character and moods without attempting to pry into each other's history.

Every day, every hour, brought to him one more little stroke of her nature, and to her one more of his. Tess was trying to lead a repressed life, but she little divined the strength of her own vitality.

At first Tess seemed to regard Angel Clare as an intelligence rather than as a man. As such she compared him with herself; and at every discovery of the abundance of his illuminations, of the distance between her own modest mental standpoint and the unmeasurable, Andean altitude of his, she became quite dejected, disheartened from all further effort on her own part whatever.

He observed her dejection one day, when he had casually mentioned something to her about pastoral life in ancient Greece. She was gathering the buds called 'lords and ladies' from the bank while he spoke.

'Why do you look so woebegone all of a sudden?' he asked.

'Oh, 'tis only — about my own self,' she said, with a frail laugh of sadness, fitfully beginning to peel 'a lady' meanwhile. 'Just a sense of what might have been with me! My life looks as if it had been wasted for want of chances! When I see what you know, what you have read, and seen, and thought, I feel what a nothing I am! I'm like the poor Queen of Sheba° who lived in the Bible. There is no more spirit in me.'

Peter the Great: Before becoming Emperor of Russia, Peter (1682–1725) studied shipbuilding. **Queen of Sheba:** Refers to the Queen's dispirited feeling after she experiences the wisdom and wealth of Solomon (1 Kings 10.3–5).

'Bless my soul, don't go troubling about that! Why,' he said with some enthusiasm, 'I should be only too glad, my dear Tess, to help you to anything in the way of history, or any line of reading you would like to take up —— '

'It is a lady again,' interrupted she, holding out the bud she had peeled.

'What?'

'I meant that there are always more ladies than lords when you come to peel them.'

'Never mind about the lords and ladies. Would you like to take up any course of study — history, for example?'

'Sometimes I feel I don't want to know anything more about it than I know already.'

'Why not?'

'Because what's the use of learning that I am one of a long row only — finding out that there is set down in some old book somebody just like me, and to know that I shall only act her part; making me sad, that's all. The best is not to remember that your nature and your past doings have been just like thousands' and thousands', and that your coming life and doings 'll be like thousands' and thousands'.'

'What, really, then, you don't want to learn anything?'

'I shouldn't mind learning why — why the sun do shine on the just and the unjust alike,'° she answered, with a slight quaver in her voice. 'But that's what books will not tell me.'

'Tess, fie for such bitterness!' Of course he spoke with a conventional sense of duty only, for that sort of wondering had not been unknown to himself in bygone days. And as he looked at the unpractised mouth and lips, he thought that such a daughter of the soil could only have caught up the sentiment by rote. She went on peeling the lords and ladies till Clare, regarding for a moment the wave-like curl of her lashes as they drooped with her bent gaze on her soft cheek, lingeringly went away. When he was gone she stood awhile, thoughtfully peeling the last bud; and then, awakening from her reverie, flung it and all the crowd of floral nobility impatiently on the ground, in an ebullition of displeasure with herself for her *niaiseries,*° and with a quickening warmth in her heart of hearts.

How stupid he must think her! In an access of hunger for his good opinion she bethought herself of what she had latterly endeavoured to

shine on the just and the unjust alike: An echo of the Sermon on the Mount (Matt. 5.45). ***niaiseries:*** Nonsense, foolish thought (Fr.).

forget, so unpleasant had been its issues — the identity of her family with that of the knightly d'Urbervilles. Barren attribute as it was, disastrous as its discovery had been in many ways to her, perhaps Mr. Clare, as a gentleman and a student of history, would respect her sufficiently to forget her childish conduct with the lords and ladies if he knew that those Purbeck-marble and alabaster people in Kingsbere Church really represented her own lineal forefathers; that she was no spurious d'Urberville, compounded of money and ambition like those at Trantridge, but true d'Urberville to the bone.

But, before venturing to make the revelation, dubious Tess indirectly sounded the dairyman as to its possible effect upon Mr. Clare, by asking the former if Mr. Clare had any great respect for old county families when they had lost all their money and land.

'Mr. Clare,' said the dairyman emphatically, 'is one of the most rebellest rozums you ever knowed — not a bit like the rest of his family; and if there's one thing that he do hate more than another 'tis the notion of what's called a' old family. He says that it stands to reason that old families have done their spurt of work in past days, and can't have anything left in 'em now. There's the Billetts and the Drenkhards and the Greys and the St. Quintins and the Hardys and the Goulds, who used to own the lands for miles down this valley; you could buy 'em all up now for an old song a'most. Why, our little Retty Priddle here, you know, is one of the Paridelles — the old family that used to own lots o' the lands out by King's-Hintock now owned by the Earl o' Wessex, afore even he or his was heard of. Well, Mr. Clare found this out, and spoke quite scornful to the poor girl for days. "Ah!" he says to her, "you'll never make a good dairymaid! All your skill was used up ages ago in Palestine, and you must lie fallow for a thousand years to git strength for more deeds!" A boy came here t'other day asking for a job, and said his name was Matt, and when we asked him his surname he said he'd never heard that 'a had any surname, and when we asked why, he said he supposed his folks hadn't been 'stablished long enough. "Ah! you're the very boy I want!" says Mr. Clare, jumping up and shaking hands wi'en; "I've great hopes of you;" and gave him half-a-crown. O no! he can't stomach old families!'

After hearing this caricature of Clare's opinions poor Tess was glad that she had not said a word in a weak moment about her family — even though it was so unusually old as almost to have gone round the circle and become a new one. Besides, another dairy-girl was as good as she, it seemed, in that respect. She held her tongue about the d'Urberville vault, and the Knight of the Conqueror whose name she bore. The insight afforded into Clare's character suggested to her that it was largely owing to her supposed untraditional newness that she had won interest in his eyes.

XX

The season developed and matured. Another year's instalment of flowers, leaves, nightingales, thrushes, finches, and such ephemeral creatures, took up their positions where only a year ago others had stood in their place when these were nothing more than germs and inorganic particles. Rays from the sunrise drew forth the buds and stretched them into long stalks, lifted up sap in noiseless streams, opened petals, and sucked out scents in invisible jets and breathings.

Dairyman Crick's household of maids and men lived on comfortably, placidly, even merrily. Their position was perhaps the happiest of all positions in the social scale, being above the line at which neediness ends, and below the line at which the *convenances*° begin to cramp natural feeling, and the stress of threadbare modishness makes too little of enough.

Thus passed the leafy time when arborescence seems to be the one thing aimed at out of doors. Tess and Clare unconsciously studied each other, ever balanced on the edge of a passion, yet apparently keeping out of it. All the while they were converging, under an irresistible law, as surely as two streams in one vale.

Tess had never in her recent life been so happy as she was now, possibly never would be so happy again. She was, for one thing, physically and mentally suited among these new surroundings. The sapling which had rooted down to a poisonous stratum on the spot of its sowing had been transplanted to a deeper soil. Moreover she, and Clare also, stood as yet on the debatable land between predilection and love; where no profundities have been reached; no reflections have set in, awkwardly inquiring, 'Whither does this new current tend to carry me? What does it mean to my future? How does it stand towards my past?'

Tess was the merest stray phenomenon to Angel Clare as yet — a rosy warming apparition which had only just acquired the attribute of persistence in his consciousness. So he allowed his mind to be occupied with her, deeming his preoccupation to be no more than a philosopher's regard of an exceedingly novel, fresh, and interesting specimen of womankind.

convenances: Social conventions (Fr.).

They met continually; they could not help it. They met daily in that strange and solemn interval, the twilight of the morning, in the violet or pink dawn; for it was necessary to rise early, so very early, here. Milking was done betimes; and before the milking came the skimming, which began at a little past three. It usually fell to the lot of some one or other of them to wake the rest, the first being aroused by an alarm-clock; and, as Tess was the latest arrival, and they soon discovered that she could be depended upon not to sleep through the alarm as the others did, this task was thrust most frequently upon her. No sooner had the hour of three struck and whizzed, than she left her room and ran to the dairyman's door; then up the ladder to Angel's, calling him in a loud whisper; then woke her fellow-milkmaids. By the time that Tess was dressed Clare was downstairs and out in the humid air. The remaining maids and the dairyman usually gave themselves another turn on the pillow, and did not appear till a quarter of an hour later.

The gray half-tones of daybreak are not the gray half-tones of the day's close, though the degree of their shade may be the same. In the twilight of the morning light seems active, darkness passive; in the twilight of evening it is the darkness which is active and crescent, and the light which is the drowsy reverse.

Being so often — possibly not always by chance — the first two persons to get up at the dairy-house, they seemed to themselves the first persons up of all the world. In these early days of her residence here Tess did not skim, but went out of doors at once after rising, where he was generally awaiting her. The spectral, half-compounded, aqueous light which pervaded the open mead, impressed them with a feeling of isolation, as if they were Adam and Eve. At this dim inceptive stage of the day Tess seemed to Clare to exhibit a dignified largeness both of disposition and physique, and almost regnant power, possibly because he knew that at that preternatural time hardly any woman so well endowed in person as she was likely to be walking in the open air within the boundaries of his horizon; very few in all England. Fair women are usually asleep at midsummer dawns. She was close at hand, and the rest were nowhere.

The mixed, singular, luminous gloom in which they walked along together to the spot where the cows lay, often made him think of the Resurrection hour. He little thought that the Magdalen° might be at

Magdalen: Mary Magdalen was a fallen woman. Christ's appearance to her after his Resurrection occurs in Mark 16.

his side. Whilst all the landscape was in neutral shade his companion's face, which was the focus of his eyes, rising above the mist stratum, seemed to have a sort of phosphorescence upon it. She looked ghostly, as if she were merely a soul at large. In reality her face, without appearing to do so, had caught the cold gleam of day from the north-east; his own face, though he did not think of it, wore the same aspect to her.

It was then, as has been said, that she impressed him most deeply. She was no longer the milkmaid, but a visionary essence of woman — a whole sex condensed into one typical form. He called her Artemis, Demeter,° and other fanciful names half teasingly, which she did not like because she did not understand them.

'Call me Tess,' she would say askance; and he did.

Then it would grow lighter, and her features would become simply feminine; they had changed from those of a divinity who could confer bliss to those of a being who craved it.

At these non-human hours they could get quite close to the waterfowl. Herons came, with a great bold noise as of opening doors and shutters, out of the boughs of a plantation which they frequented at the side of the mead; or, if already on the spot, hardily maintained their standing in the water as the pair walked by, watching them by moving their heads round in a slow, horizontal, passionless wheel, like the turn of puppets by clockwork.

They could then see the faint summer fogs in layers, woolly, level, and apparently no thicker than counterpanes, spread about the meadows in detached remnants of small extent. On the gray moisture of the grass were marks where the cows had lain through the night — dark-green islands of dry herbage the size of their carcases, in the general sea of dew. From each island proceeded a serpentine trail, by which the cow had rambled away to feed after getting up, at the end of which trail they found her; the snoring puff from her nostrils, when she recognized them, making an intenser little fog of her own amid the prevailing one. Then they drove the animals back to the barton, or sat down to milk them on the spot, as the case might require.

Or perhaps the summer fog was more general, and the meadows lay like a white sea, out of which the scattered trees rose like dangerous rocks. Birds would soar through it into the upper radiance, and hang on the wing sunning themselves, or alight on the wet rails subdividing

Artemis, Demeter: Goddesses associated with chastity, but the former also connected with hunting and both understood in the early anthropology of Hardy's time as fertility goddesses.

the mead, which now shone like glass rods. Minute diamonds of moisture from the mist hung, too, upon Tess's eyelashes, and drops upon her hair, like seed pearls. When the day grew quite strong and commonplace these dried off her; moreover, Tess then lost her strange and ethereal beauty; her teeth, lips, and eyes scintillated in the sunbeams, and she was again the dazzlingly fair dairymaid only, who had to hold her own against the other women of the world.

About this time they would hear Dairyman Crick's voice, lecturing the non-resident milkers for arriving late, and speaking sharply to old Deborah Fyander for not washing her hands.

'For Heaven's sake, pop thy hands under the pump, Deb! Upon my soul, if the London folk only knowed of thee and thy slovenly ways, they'd swaller their milk and butter more mincing than they do a'ready; and that's saying a good deal.'

The milking progressed, till towards the end Tess and Clare, in common with the rest, could hear the heavy breakfast table dragged out from the wall in the kitchen by Mrs. Crick, this being the invariable preliminary to each meal; the same horrible scrape accompanying its return journey when the table had been cleared.

XXI

There was a great stir in the milk-house just after breakfast. The churn revolved as usual, but the butter would not come. Whenever this happened the dairy was paralyzed. Squish, squash, echoed the milk in the great cylinder, but never arose the sound they waited for.

Dairyman Crick and his wife, the milkmaids Tess, Marian, Retty Priddle, Izz Huett, and the married ones from the cottages; also Mr. Clare, Jonathan Kail, old Deborah, and the rest, stood gazing hopelessly at the churn; and the boy who kept the horse going outside put on moon-like eyes to show his sense of the situation. Even the melancholy horse himself seemed to look in at the window in inquiring despair at each walk round.

''Tis years since I went to Conjuror Trendle's son in Egdon — years!' said the dairyman bitterly. 'And he was nothing to what his father had been. I have said fifty times, if I have said once, that I don't believe in en; though he do cast folks' waters very true. But I shall have to go to 'n if he's alive. O yes, I shall have to go to 'n, if this sort of thing continnys!'

Even Mr. Clare began to feel tragical at the dairyman's desperation.

'Conjuror Fall, t'other side of Casterbridge, that they used to call "Wide-O," was a very good man when I was a boy,' said Jonathan Kail. 'But he's rotten as touchwood by now.'

'My grandfather used to go to Conjuror Mynterne, out at Owlscombe, and a clever man a' were, so I've heard grandf'er say,' continued Mr. Crick. 'But there's no such genuine folk about nowadays!'

Mrs. Crick's mind kept nearer to the matter in hand.

'Perhaps somebody in the house is in love,' she said tentatively. 'I've heard tell in my younger days that that will cause it. Why, Crick — that maid we had years ago, do ye mind, and how the butter didn't come then —— '

'Ah yes, yes! — but that isn't the rights o't. It had nothing to do with the love-making. I can mind all about it — 'twas the damage to the churn.'

He turned to Clare.

'Jack Dollop, a 'hore's-bird of a fellow we had here as milker at one time, sir, courted a young woman over at Mellstock, and deceived her as he had deceived many afore. But he had another sort o' woman to reckon wi' this time, and it was not the girl herself. One Holy Thursday, of all days in the almanack, we was here as we mid be now, only there was no churning in hand, when we zid the girl's mother coming up to the door, wi' a great brass-mounted umbrella in her hand that would ha' felled an ox, and saying "Do Jack Dollop work here? — because I want him! I have a big bone to pick with he, I can assure 'n!" And some way behind her mother walked Jack's young woman, crying bitterly into her handkercher. "O Lard, here's a time!" said Jack, looking out o' winder at 'em. "She'll murder me! Where shall I get — where shall I —— ? Don't tell her where I be!" And with that he scrambled into the churn through the trap-door, and shut himself inside, just as the young woman's mother busted into the milk-house. "The villain — where is he?" says she, "I'll claw his face for'n, let me only catch him!" Well, she hunted about everywhere, ballyragging Jack by side and by seam, Jack lying a'most stifled inside the churn, and the poor maid — or young woman rather — standing at the door crying her eyes out. I shall never forget it, never! 'Twould have melted a marble stone! But she couldn't find him nowhere at all.'

The dairyman paused, and one or two words of comment came from the listeners.

Dairyman Crick's stories often seemed to be ended when they were not really so, and strangers were betrayed into premature interjections of finality; though old friends knew better. The narrator went on —

'Well, how the old woman should have had the wit to guess it I could never tell, but she found out that he was inside that there churn. Without saying a word she took hold of the winch (it was turned by handpower then), and round she swung him, and Jack began to flop about inside. "O Lard! stop the churn! let me out!" says he, popping out his head, "I shall be churned into a pummy!"° (he was a cowardly chap in his heart, as such men mostly be). "Not till ye make amends for ravaging her virgin innocence!" says the old woman. "Stop the churn, you old witch!" screams he. "You call me old witch, do ye, you deceiver!" says she, "when ye ought to ha' been calling me mother-law these last five months!" And on went the churn, and Jack's bones rattled round again. Well, none of us ventured to interfere; and at last 'a promised to make it right wi' her. "Yes — I'll be as good as my word!" he said. And so it ended that day.'

While the listeners were smiling their comments there was a quick movement behind their backs, and they looked round. Tess, pale-faced, had gone to the door.

'How warm 'tis to-day!' she said, almost inaudibly.

It was warm, and none of them connected her withdrawal with the reminiscences of the dairyman. He went forward, and opened the door for her, saying with tender raillery —

'Why, maidy' (he frequently, with unconscious irony, gave her this pet name), 'the prettiest milker I've got in my dairy; you mustn't get so fagged as this at the first breath of summer weather, or we shall be finely put to for want of 'ee by dog-days, shan't we, Mr. Clare?'

'I was faint — and — I think I am better out o' doors,' she said mechanically; and disappeared outside.

Fortunately for her the milk in the revolving churn at that moment changed its squashing for a decided flick-flack.

''Tis coming!' cried Mrs. Crick, and the attention of all was called off from Tess.

That fair sufferer soon recovered herself externally; but she remained much depressed all the afternoon. When the evening milking was done she did not care to be with the rest of them, and went out of doors wandering along she knew not whither. She was wretched — O so wretched — at the perception that to her companions the dairyman's story had been rather a humorous narration than otherwise;

pummy: Or pommey; ground apples in the process of cider making (*OED*).

none of them but herself seemed to see the sorrow of it; to a certainty, not one knew how cruelly it touched the tender place in her experience. The evening sun was now ugly to her, like a great inflamed wound in the sky. Only a solitary cracked-voiced reed-sparrow greeted her from the bushes by the river, in a sad, machine-made tone, resembling that of a past friend whose friendship she had outworn.

In these long June days the milkmaids, and, indeed, most of the household, went to bed at sunset or sooner, the morning work before milking being so early and heavy at a time of full pails. Tess usually accompanied her fellows upstairs. To-night, however, she was the first to go to their common chamber; and she had dozed when the other girls came in. She saw them undressing in the orange light of the vanished sun, which flushed their forms with its colour; she dozed again, but she was reawakened by their voices, and quietly turned her eyes towards them.

Neither of her three chamber-companions had got into bed. They were standing in a group, in their nightgowns, barefooted, at the window, the last red rays of the west still warming their faces and necks, and the walls around them. All were watching somebody in the garden with deep interest, their three faces close together: a jovial and round one, a pale one with dark hair, and a fair one whose tresses were auburn.

'Don't push! You can see as well as I,' said Retty, the auburn-haired and youngest girl, without removing her eyes from the window.

''Tis no use for you to be in love with him any more than me, Retty Priddle,' said jolly-faced Marian, the eldest, slily. 'His thoughts be of other cheeks than thine!'

Retty Priddle still looked, and the others looked again.

'There he is again!' cried Izz Huett, the pale girl with dark damp hair and keenly cut lips.

'You needn't say anything, Izz,' answered Retty. 'For I zid you kissing his shade.'

'*What* did you see her doing?' asked Marian.

'Why — he was standing over the whey-tub to let off the whey, and the shade of his face came upon the wall behind, close to Izz, who was standing there filling a vat. She put her mouth against the wall and kissed the shade of his mouth; I zid her, though he didn't.'

'O Izz Huett!' said Marian.

A rosy spot came into the middle of Izz Huett's cheek.

'Well, there was no harm in it,' she declared, with attempted coolness. 'And if I be in love wi'en, so is Retty, too; and so be you, Marian, come to that.'

Marian's full face could not blush past its chronic pinkness.

'I!' she said. 'What a tale! Ah, there he is again! Dear eyes — dear face — dear Mr. Clare!'

'There — you've owned it!'

So have you — so have we all,' said Marian, with the dry frankness of complete indifference to opinion. 'It is silly to pretend otherwise amongst ourselves, though we need not own it to other folks. I would just marry 'n to-morrow!'

'So would I — and more,' murmured Izz Huett.

'And I too,' whispered the more timid Retty.

The listener grew warm.

'We can't all marry him,' said Izz.

'We shan't, either of us; which is worse still,' said the eldest. 'There he is again!'

They all three blew him a silent kiss.

'Why?' asked Retty quickly.

'Because he likes Tess Durbeyfield best,' said Marian, lowering her voice. 'I have watched him every day, and have found it out.'

There was a reflective silence.

'But she don't care anything for 'n?' at length breathed Retty.

'Well — I sometimes think that too.'

'But how silly all this is!' said Izz Huett impatiently. 'Of course he won't marry any one of us, or Tess either — a gentleman's son, who's going to be a great landowner and farmer abroad! More likely to ask us to come wi'en as farm-hands at so much a year!'

One sighed, and another sighed, and Marian's plump figure sighed biggest of all. Somebody in bed hard by sighed too. Tears came into the eyes of Retty Priddle, the pretty red-haired youngest — the last bud of the Paridelles, so important in the county annals. They watched silently a little longer, their three faces still close together as before, and the triple hues of their hair mingling. But the unconscious Mr. Clare had gone indoors, and they saw him no more; and, the shades beginning to deepen, they crept into their beds. In a few minutes they heard him ascend the ladder to his own room. Marian was soon snoring, but Izz did not drop into forgetfulness for a long time. Retty Priddle cried herself to sleep.

The deeper-passioned Tess was very far from sleeping even then. This conversation was another of the bitter pills she had been obliged to swallow that day. Scarce the least feeling of jealousy arose in her breast. For that matter she knew herself to have the preference. Being more finely formed, better educated, and, though the youngest except Retty, more woman than either, she perceived that only the slightest ordinary care was necessary for holding her own in Angel Clare's heart against these her candid friends. But the grave question was, ought she to do this? There was, to be sure, hardly a ghost of a chance for either of them, in a serious sense; but there was, or had been, a chance of one or the other inspiring him with a passing fancy for her, and enjoying the pleasure of his attentions while he stayed here. Such unequal attachments had led to marriage; and she had heard from Mrs. Crick that Mr. Clare had one day asked, in a laughing way, what would be the use of his marrying a fine lady, and all the while ten thousand acres of Colonial pasture to feed, and cattle to rear, and corn to reap. A farm-woman would be the only sensible kind of wife for him. But whether Mr. Clare had spoken seriously or not, why should she, who could never conscientiously allow any man to marry her now, and who had religiously determined that she never would be tempted to do so, draw off Mr. Clare's attention from other women, for the brief happiness of sunning herself in his eyes while he remained at Talbothays?

XXII

They came downstairs yawning next morning; but skimming and milking were proceeded with as usual, and they went indoors to breakfast. Dairyman Crick was discovered stamping about the house. He had received a letter, in which a customer had complained that the butter had a twang.

'And begad, so 't have!' said the dairyman, who held in his left hand a wooden slice on which a lump of butter was stuck. 'Yes — taste for yourself!'

Several of them gathered round him; and Mr. Clare tasted, Tess tasted, also the other indoor milkmaids, one or two of the milking-men, and last of all Mrs. Crick, who came out from the waiting breakfast-table. There certainly was a twang.

The dairyman, who had thrown himself into abstraction to better realize the taste, and so divine the particular species of noxious weed to which it appertained, suddenly exclaimed —

' 'Tis garlic! and I thought there wasn't a blade left in that mead!'

Then all the old hands remembered that a certain dry mead, into which a few of the cows had been admitted of late, had, in years gone by, spoilt the butter in the same way. The dairyman had not recognized the taste at that time, and thought the butter bewitched.

'We must overhaul that mead,' he resumed; 'this mustn't continny!'

All having armed themselves with old pointed knives they went out together. As the inimical plant could only be present in very microscopic dimensions to have escaped ordinary observation, to find it seemed rather a hopeless attempt in the stretch of rich grass before them. However, they formed themselves into line, all assisting, owing to the importance of the search; the dairyman at the upper end with Mr. Clare, who had volunteered to help; then Tess, Marian, Izz Huett, and Retty; then Bill Lewell, Jonathan, and the married dairywomen — Beck Knibbs, with her woolly black hair and rolling eyes; and flaxen Frances, consumptive from the winter damps of the watermeads — who lived in their respective cottages.

With eyes fixed upon the ground they crept slowly across a strip of the field, returning a little further down in such a manner that, when they should have finished, not a single inch of the pasture but would have fallen under the eye of some one of them. It was a most tedious business, not more than half a dozen shoots of garlic being discoverable in the whole field; yet such was the herb's pungency that probably one bite of it by one cow had been sufficient to season the whole dairy's produce for the day.

Differing one from another in natures and moods so greatly as they did, they yet formed, bending, a curiously uniform row — automatic, noiseless; and an alien observer passing down the neighbouring lane might well have been excused for massing them as 'Hodge.' As they crept along, stooping low to discern the plant, a soft yellow gleam was reflected from the buttercups into their shaded faces, giving them an elfish, moonlit aspect, though the sun was pouring upon their backs in all the strength of noon.

Angel Clare, who communistically stuck to his rule of taking part with the rest in everything, glanced up now and then. It was not, of course, by accident that he walked next to Tess.

'Well, how are you?' he murmured.

'Very well, thank you, sir,' she replied demurely.

As they had been discussing a score of personal matters only half-an-hour before, the introductory style seemed a little superfluous. But they got no further in speech just then. They crept and crept, the hem of her petticoat just touching his gaiter, and his elbow sometimes brushing hers. At last the dairyman, who came next, could stand it no longer.

'Upon my soul and body, this here stooping do fairly make my back open and shut!' he exclaimed, straightening himself slowly with an excruciated look till quite upright. 'And you, maidy Tess, you wasn't well a day or two ago — this will make your head ache finely! Don't do any more, if you feel fainty; leave the rest to finish it.'

Dairyman Crick withdrew, and Tess dropped behind. Mr. Clare also stepped out of line, and began privateering about for the weed. When she found him near her, her very tension at what she had heard the night before made her the first to speak.

'Don't they look pretty?' she said.

'Who?'

'Izzy Huett and Retty.'

Tess had moodily decided that either of these maidens would make a good farmer's wife, and that she ought to recommend them, and obscure her own wretched charms.

'Pretty? Well, yes — they are pretty girls — fresh looking. I have often thought so.'

'Though, poor dears, prettiness won't last long!'

'O no, unfortunately.'

'They are excellent dairywomen.'

'Yes: though not better than you.'

'They skim better than I.'

'Do they?'

Clare remained observing them — not without their observing him.

'She is colouring up,' continued Tess heroically.

'Who?'

'Retty Priddle.'

'Oh! Why is that?'

'Because you are looking at her.'

Self-sacrificing as her mood might be Tess could not well go further and cry, 'Marry one of them, if you really do want a dairywoman and not a lady; and don't think of marrying me!' She followed Dairyman Crick, and had the mournful satisfaction of seeing that Clare remained behind.

From this day she forced herself to take pains to avoid him — never allowing herself, as formerly, to remain long in his company, even if their juxtaposition were purely accidental. She gave the other three every chance.

Tess was woman enough to realize from their avowals to herself that Angel Clare had the honour of all the dairymaids in his keeping, and her perception of his care to avoid compromising the happiness of either in the least degree bred a tender respect in Tess for what she deemed, rightly or wrongly, the self-controlling sense of duty shown by him, a quality which she had never expected to find in one of the opposite sex, and in the absence of which more than one of the simple hearts who were his housemates might have gone weeping on her pilgrimage.

XXIII

The hot weather of July had crept upon them unawares, and the atmosphere of the flat vale hung heavy as an opiate over the dairy-folk, the cows, and the trees. Hot steaming rains fell frequently, making the grass where the cows fed yet more rank, and hindering the late hay-making in the other meads.

It was Sunday morning; the milking was done; the outdoor milkers had gone home. Tess and the other three were dressing themselves rapidly, the whole bevy having agreed to go together to Mellstock Church, which lay some three or four miles distant from the dairy-house. She had now been two months at Talbothays, and this was her first excursion.

All the preceding afternoon and night heavy thunderstorms had hissed down upon the meads, and washed some of the hay into the river; but this morning the sun shone out all the more brilliantly for the deluge, and the air was balmy and clear.

The crooked lane leading from their own parish to Mellstock ran along the lowest levels in a portion of its length, and when the girls reached the most depressed spot they found that the result of the rain had been to flood the lane over-shoe to a distance of some fifty yards. This would have been no serious hindrance on a week-day; they would have clicked through it in their high pattens and boots quite unconcerned; but on this day of vanity, this Sun's-day, when flesh went forth to coquet with flesh while hypocritically affecting business with spiritual things; on this occasion for wearing their white stockings and thin shoes, and their pink, white, and lilac gowns, on which every mud spot would be visible, the pool was an awkward impediment. They could hear the churchbell calling — as yet nearly a mile off.

'Who would have expected such a rise in the river in summer-time!' said Marian, from the top of the roadside-bank on which they had climbed, and were maintaining a precarious footing in the hope of creeping along its slope till they were past the pool.

'We can't get there anyhow, without walking right through it, or else going round the Turnpike way; and that would make us so very late!' said Retty, pausing hopelessly.

'And I do colour up so hot, walking into church late, and all the people staring round,' said Marian, 'that I hardly cool down again till we get into the That-it-may-please-Thees.'

While they stood clinging to the bank they heard a splashing round the bend of the road, and presently appeared Angel Clare, advancing along the lane towards them through the water.

Four hearts gave a big throb simultaneously.

His aspect was probably as un-Sabbatarian° a one as a dogmatic parson's son often presented; his attire being his dairy clothes, long wading boots, a cabbage-leaf inside his hat to keep his head cool, with a thistle-spud to finish him off.

'He's not going to church,' said Marian.

'No — I wish he was!' murmured Tess.

Angel, in fact, rightly or wrongly (to adopt the safe phrase of evasive controversialists), preferred sermons in stones° to sermons in churches and chapels on fine summer days. This morning, moreover, he had gone out to see if the damage to the hay by the flood was considerable or not. On his walk he observed the girls from a long distance, though they had been so occupied with their difficulties of passage as not to notice him. He knew that the water had risen at that spot, and that it would quite check their progress. So he had hastened on, with a dim idea of how he could help them — one of them in particular.

The rosy-cheeked, bright-eyed quartet looked so charming in their light summer attire, clinging to the roadside bank like pigeons on a roof-slope, that he stopped a moment to regard them before coming close. Their gauzy skirts had brushed up from the grass innumerable flies and butterflies which, unable to escape, remained caged in the transparent tissue as in an aviary. Angel's eye at last fell upon Tess, the hindmost of the four; she, being full of suppressed laughter at their dilemma, could not help meeting his glance radiantly.

He came beneath them in the water, which did not rise over his long boots; and stood looking at the entrapped flies and butterflies.

'Are you trying to get to church?' he said to Marian, who was in front, including the next two in his remark, but avoiding Tess.

un-Sabbatarian: Unlike a Sabbatarian, who observes the Sabbath strictly. **sermons in stones:** *As You Like It* 2.1.17.

'Yes, sir; and 'tis getting late; and my colour do come up so —— '

'I'll carry you through the pool — every Jill of you.'

The whole four flushed as if one heart beat through them.

'I think you can't, sir,' said Marian.

'It is the only way for you to get past. Stand still. Nonsense — you are not too heavy! I'd carry you all four together. Now, Marian, attend,' he continued, 'and put your arms round my shoulders, so. Now! Hold on. That's well done.'

Marian had lowered herself upon his arm and shoulder as directed, and Angel strode off with her, his slim figure, as viewed from behind, looking like the mere stem to the great nosegay suggested by hers. They disappeared round the curve of the road, and only his sousing footsteps and the top ribbon of Marian's bonnet told where they were. In a few minutes he reappeared. Izz Huett was the next in order upon the bank.

'Here he comes,' she murmured, and they could hear that her lips were dry with emotion. 'And I have to put my arms round his neck and look into his face as Marian did.'

'There's nothing in that,' said Tess quickly.

'There's a time for everything,' continued Izz, unheeding. 'A time to embrace, and a time to refrain from embracing;° the first is now going to be mine.'

'Fie — it is Scripture, Izz!'

'Yes,' said Izz, 'I've always a' ear at church for pretty verses.'

Angel Clare, to whom three-quarters of this performance was a commonplace act of kindness, now approached Izz. She quietly and dreamily lowered herself into his arms, and Angel methodically marched off with her. When he was heard returning for the third time Retty's throbbing heart could be almost seen to shake her. He went up to the red-haired girl, and while he was seizing her he glanced at Tess. His lips could not have pronounced more plainly, 'It will soon be you and I.' Her comprehension appeared in her face; she could not help it. There was an understanding between them.

Poor little Retty, though by far the lightest weight, was the most troublesome of Clare's burdens. Marian had been like a sack of meal, a dead weight of plumpness under which he had literally staggered. Izz had ridden sensibly and calmly. Retty was a bunch of hysterics.

However, he got through with the disquieted creature, deposited her, and returned. Tess could see over the hedge the distant three in a

A time to embrace, . . . : Ecclesiastes 3.5.

group, standing as he had placed them on the next rising ground. It was now her turn. She was embarrassed to discover that excitement at the proximity of Mr. Clare's breath and eyes, which she had contemned in her companions, was intensified in herself; and as if fearful of betraying her secret she paltered with him at the last moment.

'I may be able to clim' along the bank perhaps — I can clim' better than they. You must be so tired, Mr. Clare!'

'No, no, Tess,' said he quickly. And almost before she was aware she was seated in his arms and resting against his shoulder.

'Three Leahs to get one Rachel,'° he whispered.

'They are better women than I,' she replied, magnanimously sticking to her resolve.

'Not to me,' said Angel.

He saw her grow warm at this; and they went some steps in silence.

'I hope I am not too heavy?' she said timidly.

'O no. You should lift Marian! Such a lump. You are like an undulating billow warmed by the sun. And all this fluff of muslin about you is the froth.'

'It is very pretty — if I seem like that to you.'

'Do you know that I have undergone three-quarters of this labour entirely for the sake of the fourth quarter?'

'No.'

'I did not expect such an event to-day.'

'Nor I. . . . The water came up so sudden.'

That the rise in the water was what she understood him to refer to, the state of her breathing belied. Clare stood still and inclined his face towards hers.

'O Tessy!' he exclaimed.

The girl's cheeks burned to the breeze, and she could not look into his eyes for her emotion. It reminded Angel that he was somewhat unfairly taking advantage of an accidental position; and he went no further with it. No definite words of love had crossed their lips as yet, and suspension at this point was desirable now. However, he walked slowly, to make the remainder of the distance as long as possible; but at last they came to the bend, and the rest of their progress was in full view of the other three. The dry land was reached, and he set her down.

Three Leahs to get one Rachel: In Genesis 29, Jacob works for seven years in order to marry Rachel but is given her sister, Leah, instead and must work an additional seven years before he is allowed to marry Rachel.

Her friends were looking with round thoughtful eyes at her and him, and she could see that they had been talking of her. He hastily bade them farewell, and splashed back along the stretch of submerged road.

The four moved on together as before, till Marian broke the silence by saying —

'No — in all truth; we have no chance against her!' She looked joylessly at Tess.

'What do you mean?' asked the latter.

'He likes 'ee best — the very best! We could see it as he brought 'ee. He would have kissed 'ee, if you had encouraged him to do it, ever so little.'

'No, no,' said she.

The gaiety with which they had set out had somehow vanished; and yet there was no enmity or malice between them. They were generous young souls; they had been reared in the lonely country nooks where fatalism is a strong sentiment, and they did not blame her. Such supplanting was to be.

Tess's heart ached. There was no concealing from herself the fact that she loved Angel Clare, perhaps all the more passionately from knowing that the others had also lost their hearts to him. There is contagion in this sentiment, especially among women. And yet that same hungry heart of hers compassionated her friends. Tess's honest nature had fought against this, but too feebly, and the natural result had followed.

'I will never stand in your way, nor in the way of either of you!' she declared to Retty that night in the bedroom (her tears running down). 'I can't help this, my dear! I don't think marrying is in his mind at all; but if he were even to ask me I should refuse him, as I should refuse any man.'

'Oh! would you? Why?' said wondering Retty.

'It cannot be! But I will be plain. Putting myself quite on one side, I don't think he will choose either of you.'

'I have never expected it — thought of it!' moaned Retty. 'But O! I wish I was dead!'

The poor child, torn by a feeling which she hardly understood, turned to the other two girls who came upstairs just then.

'We be friends with her again,' she said to them. 'She thinks no more of his choosing her than we do.'

So the reserve went off, and they were confiding and warm.

'I don't seem to care what I do now,' said Marian, whose mood was tuned to its lowest bass. 'I was going to marry a dairyman at Stickleford, who's asked me twice; but — my soul — I would put an end to myself rather'n be his wife now! Why don't ye speak, Izz?'

'To confess, then,' murmured Izz, 'I made sure to-day that he was going to kiss me as he held me; and I lay still against his breast, hoping and hoping, and never moved at all. But he did not. I don't like biding here at Talbothays any longer! I shall go hwome.'

The air of the sleeping-chamber seemed to palpitate with the hopeless passion of the girls. They writhed feverishly under the oppressiveness of an emotion thrust on them by cruel Nature's law — an emotion which they had neither expected nor desired. The incident of the day had fanned the flame that was burning the inside of their hearts out, and the torture was almost more than they could endure. The differences which distinguished them as individuals were abstracted by this passion, and each was but portion of one organism called sex. There was so much frankness and so little jealousy because there was no hope. Each one was a girl of fair common sense, and she did not delude herself with any vain conceits, or deny her love, or give herself airs, in the idea of outshining the others. The full recognition of the futility of their infatuation, from a social point of view; its purposeless beginning; its self-bounded outlook; its lack of everything to justify its existence in the eye of civilization (while lacking nothing in the eye of Nature); the one fact that it did exist, ecstasizing them to a killing joy; all this imparted to them a resignation, a dignity, which a practical and sordid expectation of winning him as a husband would have destroyed.

They tossed and turned on their little beds, and the cheese-wring dripped monotonously downstairs.

'B' you awake, Tess?' whispered one, half-an-hour later.

It was Izz Huett's voice.

Tess replied in the affirmative, whereupon also Retty and Marian suddenly flung the bedclothes off them, and sighed —

'So be we!'

'I wonder what she is like — the lady they say his family have looked out for him!'

'I wonder,' said Izz.

'Some lady looked out for him?' gasped Tess, starting. 'I have never heard o' that!'

'O yes — 'tis whispered; a young lady of his own rank, chosen by his family; a Doctor of Divinity's daughter near his father's parish of

Emminster; he don't much care for her, they say. But he is sure to marry her.'

They had heard so little of this; yet it was enough to build up wretched dolorous dreams upon, there in the shade of the night. They pictured all the details of his being won round to consent, of the wedding preparations, of the bride's happiness, of her dress and veil, of her blissful home with him, when oblivion would have fallen upon themselves as far as he and their love were concerned. Thus they talked, and ached, and wept till sleep charmed their sorrow away.

After this disclosure Tess nourished no further foolish thought that there lurked any grave and deliberate import in Clare's attentions to her. It was a passing summer love of her face, for love's own temporary sake — nothing more. And the thorny crown of this sad conception was that she whom he really did prefer in a cursory way to the rest, she who knew herself to be more impassioned in nature, cleverer, more beautiful than they, was in the eyes of propriety far less worthy of him than the homelier ones whom he ignored.

XXIV

Amid the oozing fatness and warm ferments of the Var Vale, at a season when the rush of juices could almost be heard below the hiss of fertilization, it was impossible that the most fanciful love should not grow passionate. The ready bosoms existing there were impregnated by their surroundings.

July passed over their heads, and the Thermidorean weather° which came in its wake seemed an effort on the part of Nature to match the state of hearts at Talbothays Dairy. The air of the place, so fresh in the spring and early summer, was stagnant and enervating now. Its heavy scents weighed upon them, and at mid-day the landscape seemed lying in a swoon. Ethiopic scorchings browned the upper slopes of the pastures, but there was still bright green herbage here where the watercourses purled. And as Clare was oppressed by the outward heats, so was he burdened inwardly by waxing fervour of passion for the soft and silent Tess.

The rains having passed the uplands were dry. The wheels of the dairyman's spring cart, as he sped home from market, licked up the

Thermidorean weather: Thermidor was the month from July 19 to August 17 in the French calendar instituted in 1793 after the Revolution.

pulverized surface of the highway, and were followed by white ribands of dust, as if they had set a thin powder-train on fire. The cows jumped wildly over the five-barred barton-gate, maddened by the gad-fly; Dairyman Crick kept his shirt-sleeves permanently rolled up from Monday to Saturday: open windows had no effect in ventilation without open doors, and in the dairy-garden the blackbirds and thrushes crept about under the currant-bushes, rather in the manner of quadrupeds than of winged creatures. The flies in the kitchen were lazy, teasing, and familiar, crawling about in unwonted places, on the floor, into drawers, and over the backs of the milkmaids' hands. Conversations were concerning sunstroke; while butter-making, and still more butter-keeping, was a despair.

They milked entirely in the meads for coolness and convenience, without driving in the cows. During the day the animals obsequiously followed the shadow of the smallest tree as it moved round the stem with the diurnal roll; and when the milkers came they could hardly stand still for the flies.

On one of these afternoons four or five unmilked cows chanced to stand apart from the general herd, behind the corner of a hedge, among them being Dumpling and Old Pretty, who loved Tess's hands above those of any other maid. When she rose from her stool under a finished cow Angel Clare, who had been observing her for some time, asked her if she would take the aforesaid creatures next. She silently assented, and with her stool at arm's length, and the pail against her knee, went round to where they stood. Soon the sound of Old Pretty's milk fizzing into the pail came through the hedge, and then Angel felt inclined to go round the corner also, to finish off a hard-yielding milcher who had strayed there, he being now as capable of this as the dairyman himself.

All the men, and some of the women, when milking, dug their foreheads into the cows and gazed into the pail. But a few — mainly the younger ones — rested their heads sideways. This was Tess Durbeyfield's habit, her temple pressing the milcher's flank, her eyes fixed on the far end of the meadow with the quiet of one lost in meditation. She was milking Old Pretty thus, and the sun chancing to be on the milking-side it shone flat upon her pink-gowned form and her white curtain-bonnet, and upon her profile, rendering it keen as a cameo cut from the dun background of the cow.

She did not know that Clare had followed her round, and that he sat under his cow watching her. The stillness of her head and features was remarkable: she might have been in a trance, her eyes open, yet unseeing. Nothing in the picture moved but Old Pretty's tail and Tess's pink hands, the latter so gently as to be a rhythmic pulsation only, as if they were obeying a reflex stimulus, like a beating heart.

How very lovable her face was to him. Yet there was nothing ethereal about it; all was real vitality, real warmth, real incarnation. And it was in her mouth that this culminated. Eyes almost as deep and speaking he had seen before, and cheeks perhaps as fair; brows as arched, a chin and throat almost as shapely; her mouth he had seen nothing to equal on the face of the earth. To a young man with the least fire in him that little upward lift in the middle of her red top lip was distracting, infatuating, maddening. He had never before seen a woman's lips and teeth which forced upon his mind with such persistent iteration the old Elizabethan simile of roses filled with snow.° Perfect, he, as a lover, might have called them off-hand. But no — they were not perfect. And it was the touch of the imperfect upon the would-be perfect that gave the sweetness, because it was that which gave the humanity.

Clare had studied the curves of those lips so many times that he could reproduce them mentally with ease: and now, as they again confronted him, clothed with colour and life, they sent an *aura* over his flesh, a breeze through his nerves, which wellnigh produced a qualm; and actually produced, by some mysterious physiological process, a prosaic sneeze.

She then became conscious that he was observing her; but she would not show it by any change of position, though the curious dream-like fixity disappeared, and a close eye might easily have discerned that the rosiness of her face deepened, and then faded till only a tinge of it was left.

The influence that had passed into Clare like an excitation from the sky did not die down. Resolutions, reticences, prudences, fears, fell back like a defeated battalion. He jumped up from his seat, and, leaving his pail to be kicked over if the milcher had such a mind, went quickly towards the desire of his eyes, and, kneeling down beside her, clasped her in his arms.

Tess was taken completely by surprise, and she yielded to his embrace with unreflecting inevitableness. Having seen that it was really her lover who had advanced, and no one else, her lips parted, and she sank upon him in her momentary joy, with something very like an ecstatic cry.

roses filled with snow: The comparison occurs in a poem by Thomas Campion (1567–1620), "There is a Garden in Her Face."

He had been on the point of kissing that too tempting mouth, but he checked himself, for tender conscience' sake.

'Forgive me, Tess dear!' he whispered. 'I ought to have asked. I — did not know what I was doing. I do not mean it as a liberty. I am devoted to you, Tessy, dearest, in all sincerity!'

Old Pretty by this time had looked round, puzzled; and seeing two people crouching under her where, by immemorial custom, there should have been only one, lifted her hind leg crossly.

'She is angry — she doesn't know what we mean — she'll kick over the milk!' exclaimed Tess, gently striving to free herself, her eyes concerned with the quadruped's actions, her heart more deeply concerned with herself and Clare.

She slipped up from her seat, and they stood together, his arm still encircling her. Tess's eyes, fixed on distance, began to fill.

'Why do you cry, my darling?' he said.

'O — I don't know!' she murmured.

As she saw and felt more clearly the position she was in she became agitated and tried to withdraw.

'Well, I have betrayed my feeling, Tess, at last,' said he, with a curious sigh of desperation, signifying unconsciously that his heart had outrun his judgment. 'That I — love you dearly and truly I need not say. But I — it shall go no further now — it distresses you — I am as surprised as you are. You will not think I have presumed upon your defencelessness — been too quick and unreflecting, will you?'

'N' — I can't tell.'

He had allowed her to free herself; and in a minute or two the milking of each was resumed. Nobody had beheld the gravitation of the two into one; and when the dairyman came round by that screened nook a few minutes later there was not a sign to reveal that the markedly sundered pair were more to each other than mere acquaintance. Yet in the interval since Crick's last view of them something had occurred which changed the pivot of the universe for their two natures; something which, had he known its quality, the dairyman would have despised, as a practical man; yet which was based upon a more stubborn and resistless tendency than a whole heap of so-called practicalities. A veil had been whisked aside; the tract of each one's outlook was to have a new horizon thenceforward — for a short time or for a long.

End of Phase the Third

PHASE THE FOURTH. THE CONSEQUENCE

XXV

Clare, restless, went out into the dusk when evening drew on, she who had won him having retired to her chamber.

The night was as sultry as the day. There was no coolness after dark unless on the grass. Roads, garden-paths, the house-fronts, the barton-walls were warm as hearths, and reflected the noontide temperature into the noctambulist's face.

He sat on the east gate of the dairy-yard, and knew not what to think of himself. Feeling had indeed smothered judgment that day.

Since the sudden embrace, three hours before, the twain had kept apart. She seemed stilled, almost alarmed, at what had occurred, while the novelty, unpremeditation, mastery of circumstance disquieted him — palpitating, contemplative being that he was. He could hardly realize their true relations to each other as yet, and what their mutual bearing should be before third parties thenceforward.

Angel had come as pupil to this dairy in the idea that his temporary existence here was to be the merest episode in his life, soon passed through and early forgotten; he had come as to a place from which as from a screened alcove he could calmly view the absorbing world without, and, apostrophizing it with Walt Whitman — °

Crowds of men and women attired in the usual costumes,
How curious you are to me! —

resolve upon a plan for plunging into that world anew. But, behold, the absorbing scene had been imported hither. What had been the engrossing world had dissolved into an uninteresting outer dumb-show; while here, in this apparently dim and unimpassioned place, novelty had volcanically started up, as it had never, for him, started up elsewhere.

Every window of the house being open Clare could hear across the yard each trivial sound of the retiring household. That dairy-house, so humble, so insignificant, so purely to him a place of constrained sojourn that he had never hitherto deemed it of sufficient importance to

Walt Whitman: The quotation from Whitman (1819–1892) is from the opening of "Crossing Brooklyn Ferry."

be reconnoitred as an object of any quality whatever in the landscape; what was it now? The aged and lichened brick gables breathed forth 'Stay!' The windows smiled, the door coaxed and beckoned, the creeper blushed confederacy. A personality within it was so far-reaching in her influence as to spread into and make the bricks, mortar, and whole overhanging sky throb with a burning sensibility. Whose was this mighty personality? A milkmaid's.

It was amazing, indeed, to find how great a matter the life of the obscure dairy had become to him. And though new love was to be held partly responsible for this it was not solely. Many besides Angel have learnt that the magnitude of lives is not as to their external displacements, but as to their subjective experiences. The impressionable peasant leads a larger, fuller, more dramatic life than the pachydermatous king. Looking at it thus he found that life was to be seen of the same magnitude here as elsewhere.

Despite his heterodoxy, faults, and weaknesses, Clare was a man with a conscience. Tess was no insignificant creature to toy with and dismiss; but a woman living her precious life — a life which, to herself who endured or enjoyed it, possessed as great a dimension as the life of the mightiest to himself. Upon her sensations the whole world depended to Tess; through her existence all her fellow-creatures existed, to her. The universe itself only came into being for Tess on the particular day in the particular year in which she was born.

This consciousness upon which he had intruded was the single opportunity of existence ever vouch-safed to Tess by an unsympathetic First Cause — her all; her every and only chance. How then should he look upon her as of less consequence than himself; as a pretty trifle to caress and grow weary of; and not deal in the greatest seriousness with the affection which he knew that he had awakened in her — so fervid and so impressionable as she was under her reserve; in order that it might not agonize and wreck her?

To encounter her daily in the accustomed manner would be to develop what had begun. Living in such close relations, to meet meant to fall into endearment; flesh and blood could not resist it; and, having arrived at no conclusion as to the issue of such a tendency, he decided to hold aloof for the present from occupations in which they would be mutually engaged. As yet the harm done was small.

But it was not easy to carry out the resolution never to approach her. He was driven towards her by every heave of his pulse.

He thought he would go and see his friends. It might be possible to sound them upon this. In less than five months his term here would have ended, and after a few additional months spent upon other farms he would be fully equipped in agricultural knowledge, and in a position to start on his own account. Would not a farmer want a wife, and should a farmer's wife be a drawing-room wax-figure, or a woman who understood farming? Notwithstanding the pleasing answer returned to him by the silence he resolved to go his journey.

One morning when they sat down to breakfast at Talbothays Dairy some maid observed that she had not seen anything of Mr. Clare that day.

'O no,' said Dairyman Crick. 'Mr. Clare has gone hwome to Emminster to spend a few days wi' his kinsfolk.'

For four impassioned ones around that table the sunshine of the morning went out at a stroke, and the birds muffled their song. But neither girl by word or gesture revealed her blankness.

'He's getting on towards the end of his time wi' me,' added the dairyman, with a phlegm which unconsciously was brutal; 'and so I suppose he is beginning to see about his plans elsewhere.'

'How much longer is he to bide here?' asked Izz Huett, the only one of the gloom-stricken bevy who could trust her voice with the question.

The others waited for the dairyman's answer as if their lives hung upon it; Retty, with parted lips, gazing on the table-cloth, Marian with heat added to her redness, Tess throbbing and looking out at the meads.

'Well, I can't mind the exact day without looking at my memorandum-book,' replied Crick, with the same intolerable unconcern. 'And even that may be altered a bit. He'll bide to get a little practice in the calving out at the straw-yard, for certain. He'll hang on till the end of the year I should say.'

Four months or so of torturing ecstasy in his society — of 'pleasure girdled about with pain.'° After that the blackness of unutterable night.

At this moment of the morning Angel Clare was riding along a narrow lane ten miles distant from the breakfasters, in the direction of his father's vicarage at Emminster, carrying, as well as he could, a little basket which contained some black-puddings and a bottle of mead, sent by Mrs. Crick, with her kind respects, to his parents. The white

'pleasure girdled about with pain': From a chorus in *Atalanta in Calydon* by A. C. Swinburne (1837–1909).

lane stretched before him, and his eyes were upon it; but they were staring into next year, and not at the lane. He loved her; ought he to marry her? Dared he to marry her? What would his mother and his brothers say? What would he himself say a couple of years after the event? That would depend upon whether the germs of staunch comradeship underlay the temporary emotion, or whether it were a sensuous joy in her form only, with no substratum of everlastingness.

His father's hill-surrounded little town, the Tudor church-tower of red stone, the clump of trees near the vicarage, came at last into view beneath him, and he rode down towards the well-known gate. Casting a glance in the direction of the church before entering his home, he beheld standing by the vestry-door a group of girls, of ages between twelve and sixteen, apparently awaiting the arrival of some other one, who in a moment became visible; a figure somewhat older than the school-girls, wearing a broad-brimmed hat and highly-starched cambric morning-gown, with a couple of books in her hand.

Clare knew her well. He could not be sure that she observed him; he hoped she did not, so as to render it unnecessary that he should go and speak to her, blameless creature that she was. An overpowering reluctance to greet her made him decide that she had not seen him. The young lady was Miss Mercy Chant, the only daughter of his father's neighbour and friend, whom it was his parents' quiet hope that he might wed some day. She was great at Antinomianism° and Bible-classes, and was plainly going to hold a class now. Clare's mind flew to the impassioned, summer-steeped heathens in the Var Vale, their rosy faces court-patched with cow-droppings; and to one the most impassioned of them all.

It was on the impulse of the moment that he had resolved to trot over to Emminster, and hence had not written to apprise his mother and father, aiming, however, to arrive about the breakfast hour, before they should have gone out to their parish duties. He was a little late, and they had already sat down to the morning meal. The group at table jumped up to welcome him as soon as he entered. They were his father and mother, his brother the Reverend Felix — curate at a town in the adjoining county, home for the inside of a fortnight — and his other brother, the Reverend Cuthbert, the classical scholar, and Fellow and Dean of his College, down from Cambridge for the long va-

great at Antinomianism: She has come to understand various Christian doctrines, such as this one, which holds that salvation depends solely on faith and grace.

cation. His mother appeared in a cap and silver spectacles, and his father looked what in fact he was — an earnest, God-fearing man, somewhat gaunt, in years about sixty-five, his pale face lined with thought and purpose. Over their heads hung the picture of Angel's sister, the eldest of the family, sixteen years his senior, who had married a missionary and gone out to Africa.

Old Mr. Clare was a clergyman of a type which, within the last twenty years, has wellnigh dropped out of contemporary life. A spiritual descendant in the direct line from Wycliff, Huss, Luther, Calvin; an Evangelical of the Evangelicals, a Conversionist,° a man of Apostolic simplicity in life and thought, he had in his raw youth made up his mind once for all on the deeper questions of existence, and admitted no further reasoning on them thenceforward. He was regarded even by those of his own date and school of thinking as extreme; while, on the other hand, those totally opposed to him were unwillingly won to admiration for his thoroughness, and for the remarkable power he showed in dismissing all question as to principles in his energy for applying them. He loved Paul of Tarsus, liked St. John, hated St. James as much as he dared, and regarded with mixed feelings Timothy, Titus, and Philemon. The New Testament was less a Christiad than a Pauliad° to his intelligence — less an argument than an intoxication. His creed of determinism was such that it almost amounted to a vice, and quite amounted, on its negative side, to a renunciative philosophy which had cousinship with that of Schopenhauer and Leopardi. He despised the Canons and Rubric, swore by the Articles, and deemed himself consistent through the whole category — which in a way he might have been. One thing he certainly was — sincere.

To the æsthetic, sensuous, pagan pleasure in natural life and lush womanhood which his son Angel had lately been experiencing in Var Vale, his temper would have been antipathetic in a high degree, had he either by inquiry or imagination been able to apprehend it. Once upon a time Angel had been so unlucky as to say to his father, in a moment of irritation, that it might have resulted far better for mankind if Greece had been the source of the religion of modern civilization, and not Palestine; and his father's grief was of that blank description which

Conversionist: A form of Evangelical belief that claims that even members of the Church must experience a personal conversion in order to be saved. **Paul of Tarsus . . . a Pauliad:** Mr. Clare's religious attitudes are dominated by those aspects of Paul's teachings that emphasize salvation through grace and belief, which come through emotional responses rather than logical ones.

could not realize that there might lurk a thousandth part of a truth, much less a half truth or a whole truth, in such a proposition. He had simply preached austerely at Angel for some time after. But the kindness of his heart was such that he never resented anything for long, and welcomed his son to-day with a smile which was as candidly sweet as a child's.

Angel sat down, and the place felt like home; yet he did not so much as formerly feel himself one of the family gathered there. Every time that he returned hither he was conscious of this divergence, and since he had last shared in the Vicarage life it had grown even more distinctly foreign to his own than usual. Its transcendental aspirations — still unconsciously based on the geocentric view of things, a zenithal paradise, a nadiral hell — were as foreign to his own as if they had been the dreams of people on another planet. Latterly he had seen only Life, felt only the great passionate pulse of existence, unwarped, uncontorted, untrammelled by those creeds which futilely attempt to check what wisdom would be content to regulate.

On their part they saw a great difference in him, a growing divergence from the Angel Clare of former times. It was chiefly a difference in his manner that they noticed just now, particularly his brothers. He was getting to behave like a farmer; he flung his legs about; the muscles of his face had grown more expressive; his eyes looked as much information as his tongue spoke, and more. The manner of the scholar had nearly disappeared; still more the manner of the drawing-room young man. A prig would have said that he had lost culture, and a prude that he had become coarse. Such was the contagion of domiciliary fellowship with the Talbothays nymphs and swains.

After breakfast he walked with his two brothers, non-evangelical, well-educated, hall-marked young men, correct to their remotest fibre; such unimpeachable models as are turned out yearly by the lathe of a systematic tuition. They were both somewhat shortsighted, and when it was the custom to wear a single eyeglass and string they wore a single eyeglass and string; when it was the custom to wear a double glass they wore a double glass; when it was the custom to wear spectacles they wore spectacles straightway, all without reference to the particular variety of defect in their own vision. When Wordsworth was enthroned they carried pocket copies; and when Shelley° was belittled they allowed him to grow dusty on their shelves. When Correggio's

Wordsworth . . . Shelley: British Romantic poets whose writings are markedly different.

Holy Families were admired, they admired Correggio's Holy Families; when he was decried in favour of Velasquez,° they sedulously followed suit without any personal objection.

If these two noticed Angel's growing social ineptness, he noticed their growing mental limitations. Felix seemed to him all Church; Cuthbert all College. His Diocesan Synod and Visitations° were the mainsprings of the world to the one; Cambridge to the other. Each brother candidly recognized that there were a few unimportant scores of millions of outsiders in civilized society, persons who were neither University men nor churchmen; but they were to be tolerated rather than reckoned with and respected.

They were both dutiful and attentive sons, and were regular in their visits to their parents. Felix, though an offshoot from a far more recent point in the devolution of theology than his father, was less self-sacrificing and disinterested. More tolerant than his father of a contradictory opinion, in its aspect as a danger to its holder, he was less ready than his father to pardon it as a slight to his own teaching. Cuthbert was, upon the whole, the more liberal-minded, though, with greater subtlety, he had not so much heart.

As they walked along the hillside Angel's former feeling revived in him — that whatever their advantages by comparison with himself, neither saw or set forth life as it really was lived. Perhaps, as with many men, their opportunities of observation were not so good as their opportunities of expression. Neither had an adequate conception of the complicated forces at work outside the smooth and gentle current in which they and their associates floated. Neither saw the difference between local truth and universal truth; that what the inner world said in their clerical and academic hearing was quite a different thing from what the outer world was thinking.

'I suppose it is farming or nothing for you now, my dear fellow,' Felix was saying, among other things, to his youngest brother, as he looked through his spectacles at the distant fields with sad austerity. 'And, therefore, we must make the best of it. But I do entreat you to endeavour to keep as much as possible in touch with moral ideals. Farming, of course, means roughing it externally; but high thinking may go with plain living, nevertheless.'

Correggio's Holy Families . . . Velasquez: The style of the Italian painter Correggio (1495–1534) is quite different from that of the Spanish painter Velasquez (1599–1660). **Diocesan Synod and Visitations:** A synod is the gathering of all the clergy in a diocese to discuss church business and policy. Visitations are official visits by the bishop in charge of the diocese.

'Of course it may,' said Angel. 'Was it not proved nineteen hundred years ago — if I may trespass upon your domain a little? Why should you think, Felix, that I am likely to drop my high thinking and my moral ideals?'

'Well, I fancied, from the tone of your letters and our conversation — it may be fancy only — that you were somehow losing intellectual grasp. Hasn't it struck you, Cuthbert?'

'Now, Felix,' said Angel drily, 'we are very good friends, you know; each of us treading our allotted circles; but if it comes to intellectual grasp, I think you, as a contented dogmatist, had better leave mine alone, and inquire what has become of yours.'

They returned down the hill to dinner, which was fixed at any time at which their father's and mother's morning work in the parish usually concluded. Convenience as regarded afternoon callers was the last thing to enter into the consideration of unselfish Mr. and Mrs. Clare; though the three sons were sufficiently in unison on this matter to wish that their parents would conform a little to modern notions.

The walk had made them hungry, Angel in particular, who was now an outdoor man, accustomed to the profuse *dapes inemptæ*° of the dairyman's somewhat coarsely-laden table. But neither of the old people had arrived, and it was not till the sons were almost tired of waiting that their parents entered. The self-denying pair had been occupied in coaxing the appetites of some of their sick parishioners, whom they, somewhat inconsistently, tried to keep imprisoned in the flesh, their own appetites being quite forgotten.

The family sat down to table, and a frugal meal of cold viands was deposited before them. Angel looked round for Mrs. Crick's black-puddings,° which he had directed to be nicely grilled, as they did them at the dairy, and of which he wished his father and mother to appreciate the marvellous herbal savours as highly as he did himself.

'Ah! you are looking for the black-puddings, my dear boy,' observed Clare's mother. 'But I am sure you will not mind doing without them, as I am sure your father and I shall not, when you know the reason. I suggested to him that we should take Mrs. Crick's kind present to the children of the man who can earn nothing just now because of his attacks of delirium tremens; and he agreed that it would be a great pleasure to them; so we did.'

dapes inemptæ: "Unpurchased banquet" (Latin); refers to the dairyman's self-sufficiency in producing food. **black-puddings:** Dark sausages made with meat and seasoned blood.

'Of course,' said Angel cheerfully, looking round for the mead.

'I found the mead so extremely alcoholic,' continued his mother, 'that it was quite unfit for use as a beverage, but as valuable as rum or brandy in an emergency; so I have put it in my medicine-closet.'

'We never drink spirits at this table; on principle,' added his father.

'But what shall I tell the dairyman's wife?' said Angel.

'The truth, of course,' said his father.

'I rather wanted to say we enjoyed the mead and the black-puddings very much. She is a kind, jolly sort of body, and is sure to ask me directly I return.'

'You cannot, if we did not,' Mr. Clare answered lucidly.

'Ah — no; though that mead was a drop of pretty tipple.'

'A what?' said Cuthbert and Felix both.

'Oh — 'tis an expression they use down at Talbothays,' replied Angel, blushing. He felt that his parents were right in their practice if wrong in their want of sentiment, and said no more.

XXVI

It was not till the evening, after family prayers, that Angel found opportunity of broaching to his father one or two subjects near his heart. He had strung himself up to the purpose while kneeling behind his brothers on the carpet, studying the little nails in the heels of their walking boots. When the service was over they went out of the room with their mother, and Mr. Clare and himself were left alone.

The young man first discussed with the elder his plans for the attainment of his position as a farmer on an extensive scale — either in England or in the Colonies. His father then told him that, as he had not been put to the expense of sending Angel up to Cambridge, he had felt it his duty to set by a sum of money every year towards the purchase or lease of land for him some day, that he might not feel himself unduly slighted.

'As far as worldly wealth goes,' continued his father, 'you will no doubt stand far superior to your brothers in a few years.'

This considerateness on old Mr. Clare's part led Angel onward to the other and dearer subject. He observed to his father that he was then six-and-twenty, and that when he should start back in the farming business he would require eyes in the back of his head to see to all matters — some one would be necessary to superintend the domestic labours of his establishment whilst he was afield. Would it not be well, therefore, for him to marry?

His father seemed to think this idea not unreasonable; and then Angel put the question —

'What kind of wife do you think would be best for me as a thrifty hard-working farmer?'

'A truly Christian woman, who will be a help and a comfort to you in your goings-out and your comings-in. Beyond that, it really matters little. Such an one can be found; indeed, my earnest-minded friend and neighbour, Dr. Chant —— '

'But ought she not primarily to be able to milk cows, churn good butter, make immense cheeses; know how to sit hens and turkeys, and rear chickens, to direct a field of labourers in an emergency, and estimate the value of sheep and calves?'

'Yes; a farmer's wife; yes, certainly. It would be desirable.' Mr. Clare, the elder, had plainly never thought of these points before. 'I was going to add,' he said, 'that for a pure and saintly woman you will not find one more to your true advantage, and certainly not more to your mother's mind and my own, than your friend Mercy, whom you used to show a certain interest in. It is true that my neighbour Chant's daughter has lately caught up the fashion of the younger clergy round about us for decorating the Communion-table — altar, as I was shocked to hear her call it one day — with flowers and other stuff on festival occasions. But her father, who is quite as opposed to such flummery as I, says that can be cured. It is a mere girlish outbreak which, I am sure, will not be permanent.'

'Yes, yes; Mercy is good and devout, I know. But, father, don't you think that a young woman equally pure and virtuous as Miss Chant, but one who, in place of that lady's ecclesiastical accomplishments, understands the duties of farm life as well as a farmer himself, would suit me infinitely better?'

His father persisted in his conviction that a knowledge of a farmer's wife's duties came second to a Pauline view of humanity; and the impulsive Angel, wishing to honour his father's feelings and to advance the cause of his heart at the same time, grew specious. He said that fate or Providence had thrown in his way a woman who possessed every qualification to be the helpmate of an agriculturist, and was decidedly of a serious turn of mind. He would not say whether or not she had attached herself to the sound Low Church School of his father; but she would probably be open to conviction on that point; she was a regular church-goer of simple faith; honest-hearted, receptive, intelligent, graceful to a degree, chaste as a vestal, and, in personal appearance, exceptionally beautiful.

'Is she of a family such as you would care to marry into — a lady, in short?' asked his startled mother, who had come softly into the study during the conversation.

'She is not what in common parlance is called a lady,' said Angel, unflinchingly, 'for she is a cottager's daughter, as I am proud to say. But she *is* a lady, nevertheless — in feeling and nature.'

'Mercy Chant is of a very good family.'

'Pooh! — what's the advantage of that, mother?' said Angel quickly. 'How is family to avail the wife of a man who has to rough it as I have, and shall have to do?'

'Mercy is accomplished. And accomplishments have their charm,' returned his mother, looking at him through her silver spectacles.

'As to external accomplishments, what will be the use of them in the life I am going to lead? — while as to her reading, I can take that in hand. She'll be apt pupil enough, as you would say if you knew her. She's brim full of poetry — actualized poetry, if I may use the expression. She *lives* what paper-poets only write. . . . And she is an unimpeachable Christian, I am sure; perhaps of the very tribe, genus, and species you desire to propagate."

'O Angel, you are mocking!'

'Mother, I beg pardon. But as she really does attend Church almost every Sunday morning, and is a good Christian girl, I am sure you will tolerate any social shortcomings for the sake of that quality, and feel that I may do worse than choose her.' Angel waxed quite earnest on that rather automatic orthodoxy in his beloved Tess which (never dreaming that it might stand him in such good stead) he had been prone to slight when observing it practised by her and the other milkmaids, because of its obvious unreality amid beliefs essentially naturalistic.

In their sad doubts as to whether their son had himself any right whatever to the title he claimed for the unknown young woman, Mr. and Mrs. Clare began to feel it as an advantage not to be overlooked that she at least was sound in her views; especially as the conjunction of the pair must have arisen by an act of Providence; for Angel never would have made orthodoxy a condition of his choice. They said finally that it was better not to act in a hurry, but that they would not object to see her.

Angel therefore refrained from declaring more particulars now. He felt that, single-minded and self-sacrificing as his parents were, there yet existed certain latent prejudices of theirs, as middle-class people, which it would require some tact to overcome. For though legally at liberty to do as he chose, and though their daughter-in-law's qualifications could make no practical difference to their lives, in the probability of her living far away from them, he wished for affection's sake not to wound their sentiment in the most important decision of his life.

He observed his own inconsistencies in dwelling upon accidents in Tess's life as if they were vital features. It was for herself that he loved Tess; her soul, her heart, her substance — not for her skill in the dairy, her aptness as his scholar, and certainly not for her simple formal faith-professions. Her unsophisticated open-air existence required no varnish of conventionality to make it palatable to him. He held that education had as yet but little affected the beats of emotion and impulse on which domestic happiness depends. It was probable that, in the lapse of ages, improved systems of moral and intellectual training would appreciably, perhaps considerably, elevate the involuntary and even the unconscious instincts of human nature; but up to the present day culture, as far as he could see, might be said to have affected only the mental epiderm of those lives which had been brought under its influence. This belief was confirmed by his experience of women, which, having latterly been extended from the cultivated middle-class into the rural community, had taught him how much less was the intrinsic difference between the good and wise woman of one social stratum and the good and wise woman of another social stratum, than between the good and bad, the wise and the foolish, of the same stratum or class.

It was the morning of his departure. His brothers had already left the vicarage to proceed on a walking tour in the north, whence one was to return to his college, and the other to his curacy. Angel might have accompanied them, but preferred to rejoin his sweetheart at Talbothays. He would have been an awkward member of the party; for, though the most appreciative humanist, the most ideal religionist, even the best-versed Christologist of the three, there was alienation in the standing consciousness that his squareness would not fit the round hole that had been prepared for him. To neither Felix nor Cuthbert had he ventured to mention Tess.

His mother made him sandwiches, and his father accompanied him, on his own mare, a little way along the road. Having fairly well advanced his own affairs Angel listened in a willing silence, as they jogged on together through the shady lanes, to his father's account of his parish difficulties, and the coldness of brother clergymen whom he loved, because of his strict interpretations of the New Testament by the light of what they deemed a pernicious Calvinistic doctrine.°

'Pernicious!' said Mr. Clare, with genial scorn; and he proceeded to recount experiences which would show the absurdity of that idea. He told of wondrous conversions of evil livers of which he had been the instrument, not only amongst the poor, but amongst the rich and well-to-do; and he also candidly admitted many failures.

As an instance of the latter, he mentioned the case of a young upstart squire named d'Urberville, living some forty miles off, in the neighbourhood of Trantridge.

'Not one of the ancient d'Urbervilles of Kingsbere and other places?' asked his son. 'That curiously historic worn-out family with its ghostly legend of the coach-and-four?'

'O no. The original d'Urbervilles decayed and disappeared sixty or eighty years ago — at least, I believe so. This seems to be a new family which has taken the name; for the credit of the former knightly line I hope they are spurious, I'm sure. But it is odd to hear you express interest in old families. I thought you set less store by them even than I.'

'You misapprehend me, father; you often do,' said Angel with a little impatience. 'Politically I am skeptical as to the virtue of their being old. Some of the wise even among themselves "exclaim against their own succession," as Hamlet puts it;° but lyrically, dramatically, and even historically, I am tenderly attached to them.'

This distinction, though by no means a subtle one, was yet too subtle for Mr. Clare the elder, and he went on with the story he had been about to relate; which was that after the death of the senior so-called d'Urberville the young man developed the most culpable passions, though he had a blind mother, whose condition should have made him know better. A knowledge of his career having come to the ears of Mr. Clare, when he was in that part of the country preaching missionary sermons, he boldly took occasion to speak to the delinquent on his spiritual state. Though he was a stranger, occupying another's pulpit, he had felt this to be his duty, and took for his text the words from St. Luke:° 'Thou fool, this night thy soul shall be required of thee!' The young man much resented this directness of attack, and

Calvinistic doctrine: The teachings of John Calvin (1509–1564), Swiss Protestant theologian, emphasize salvation through God's grace. **as Hamlet puts it:** *Hamlet* 2.2.351. **from St. Luke:** Luke 12.20.

in the war of words which followed when they met he did not scruple publicly to insult Mr. Clare, without respect for his gray hairs.

Angel flushed with distress.

'Dear father,' he said sadly, 'I wish you would not expose yourself to such gratuitous pain from scoundrels!'

'Pain?' said his father, his rugged face shining in the ardour of self-abnegation. 'The only pain to me was pain on his account, poor, foolish young man. Do you suppose his incensed words could give me any pain, or even his blows? "Being reviled we bless; being persecuted we suffer it; being defamed we entreat; we are made as the filth of the world, and as the offscouring of all things unto this day."° Those ancient and noble words to the Corinthians are strictly true at this present hour.'

'Not blows, father? He did not proceed to blows?'

'No, he did not. Though I have borne blows from men in a mad state of intoxication.'

'No!'

'A dozen times, my boy. What then? I have saved them from the guilt of murdering their own flesh and blood thereby; and they have lived to thank me, and praise God.'

'May this young man do the same!' said Angel fervently. 'But I fear otherwise, from what you say.'

'We'll hope, nevertheless,' said Mr. Clare. 'And I continue to pray for him, though on this side of the grave we shall probably never meet again. But, after all, one of those poor words of mine may spring up in his heart as a good seed some day.'

Now, as always, Clare's father was sanguine as a child; and though the younger could not accept his parent's narrow dogma he revered his practice, and recognized the hero under the pietist. Perhaps he revered his father's practice even more now than ever, seeing that, in the question of making Tessy his wife, his father had not once thought of inquiring whether she were well provided or penniless. The same unworldliness was what had necessitated Angel's getting a living as a farmer, and would probably keep his brothers in the position of poor parsons for the term of their activities; yet Angel admired it none the less. Indeed, despite his own heterodoxy, Angel often felt that he was nearer to his father on the human side than was either of his brethren.

"Being reviled we bless . . .": 1 Corinthians 4.12–13.

XXVII

An up-hill and down-dale ride of twenty-odd miles through a garish mid-day atmosphere brought him in the afternoon to a detached knoll a mile or two west of Talbothays, whence he again looked into that green trough of sappiness and humidity, the valley of the Var or Froom. Immediately he began to descend from the upland to the fat alluvial soil below, the atmosphere grew heavier; the languid perfume of the summer fruits, the mists, the hay, the flowers, formed therein a vast pool of odour which at this hour seemed to make the animals, the very bees and butterflies, drowsy. Clare was now so familiar with the spot that he knew the individual cows by their names when, a long distance off, he saw them dotted about the meads. It was with a sense of luxury that he recognized his power of viewing life here from its inner side, in a way that had been quite foreign to him in his student-days; and, much as he loved his parents, he could not help being aware that to come here, as now, after an experience of home-life, affected him like throwing off splints and bandages; even the one customary curb on the humours of English rural societies being absent in this place, Talbothays having no resident landlord.

Not a human being was out of doors at the dairy. The denizens were all enjoying the usual afternoon nap of an hour or so which the exceedingly early hours kept in summer-time rendered a necessity. At the door the wood-hooped pails, sodden and bleached by infinite scrubbings, hung like hats on a stand upon the forked and peeled limb of an oak fixed there for that purpose; all of them ready and dry for the evening milking. Angel entered, and went through the silent passages of the house to the back quarters, where he listened for a moment. Sustained snores came from the cart-house, where some of the men were lying down; the grunt and squeal of sweltering pigs arose from the still further distance. The large-leaved rhubarb and cabbage plants slept too, their broad limp surfaces hanging in the sun like half-closed umbrellas.

He unbridled and fed his horse, and as he re-entered the house the clock struck three. Three was the afternoon skimming-hour; and, with the stroke, Clare heard the creaking of the floor-boards above, and then the touch of a descending foot on the stairs. It was Tess's, who in another moment came down before his eyes.

She had not heard him enter, and hardly realized his presence there. She was yawning, and he saw the red interior of her mouth as if it had been a snake's. She had stretched one arm so high above her coiled-up cable of hair that he could see its satin delicacy above the sunburn; her face was flushed with sleep, and her eyelids hung heavy over their pupils. The brim-fulness of her nature breathed from her. It was a moment when a woman's soul is more incarnate than at any other time; when the most spiritual beauty bespeaks itself flesh; and sex takes the outside place in the presentation.

Then those eyes flashed brightly through their filmy heaviness, before the remainder of her face was well awake. With an oddly compounded look of gladness, shyness, and surprise, she exclaimed —

'O Mr. Clare! How you frightened me — I —— '

There had not at first been time for her to think of the changed relations which his declaration had introduced; but the full sense of the matter rose up in her face when she encountered Clare's tender look as he stepped forward to the bottom stair.

'Dear, darling Tessy!' he whispered, putting his arm round her, and his face to her flushed cheek. 'Don't, for Heaven's sake, Mister me any more. I have hastened back so soon because of you!'

Tess's excitable heart beat against his by way of reply; and there they stood upon the red-brick floor of the entry, the sun slanting in by the window upon his back, as he held her tightly to his breast; upon her inclining face, upon the blue veins of her temple, upon her naked arm, and her neck, and into the depths of her hair. Having been lying down in her clothes she was warm as a sunned cat. At first she would not look straight up at him, but her eyes soon lifted, and his plumbed the deepness of the ever-varying pupils, with their radiating fibrils of blue, and black, and gray, and violet, while she regarded him as Eve at her second waking might have regarded Adam.

'I've got to go a-skimming,' she pleaded, 'and I have on'y old Deb to help me to-day. Mrs. Crick is gone to market with Mr. Crick, and Retty is not well, and the others are gone out somewhere, and won't be home till milking.'

As they retreated to the milk-house Deborah Fyander appeared on the stairs.

'I have come back, Deborah,' said Mr. Clare, upwards. 'So I can help Tess with the skimming; and, as you are very tired, I am sure, you needn't come down till milking-time.'

Possibly the Talbothays milk was not very thoroughly skimmed that afternoon. Tess was in a dream wherein familiar objects appeared as having light and shade and position, but no particular outline. Every time she held the skimmer under the pump to cool it for the work her hand trembled, the ardour of his affection being so palpable that she seemed to flinch under it like a plant in too burning a sun.

Then he pressed her again to his side, and when she had done running her forefinger round the leads to cut off the cream-edge, he cleaned it in nature's way; for the unconstrained manners of Talbothays dairy came convenient now.

'I may as well say it now as later, dearest,' he resumed gently. 'I wish to ask you something of a very practical nature, which I have been thinking of ever since that day last week in the meads. I shall soon want to marry, and, being a farmer, you see I shall require for my wife a woman who knows all about the management of farms. Will you be that woman, Tessy?'

He put it in that way that she might not think he had yielded to an impulse of which his head would disapprove.

She turned quite careworn. She had bowed to the inevitable result of proximity, the necessity of loving him; but she had not calculated upon this sudden corollary, which, indeed, Clare had put before her without quite meaning himself to do it so soon. With pain that was like the bitterness of dissolution she murmured the words of her indispensable and sworn answer as an honourable woman.

'O Mr. Clare — I cannot be your wife — I cannot be!'

The sound of her own decision seemed to break Tess's very heart, and she bowed her face in her grief.

'But Tess!' he said, amazed at her reply, and holding her still more greedily close. 'Do you say no? Surely you love me?'

'O yes, yes! And I would rather be yours than anybody's in the world,' returned the sweet and honest voice of the distressed girl. 'But I *cannot* marry you!'

'Tess,' he said, holding her at arm's length, 'you are engaged to marry some one else!'

'No, no!'

'Then why do you refuse me?'

'I don't want to marry! I have not thought o' doing it. I cannot! I only want to love you.'

'But why?'

Driven to subterfuge, she stammered —

'Your father is a parson, and your mother wouldn' like you to marry such as me. She will want you to marry a lady.'

'Nonsense — I have spoken to them both. That was partly why I went home.'

'I feel I cannot — never, never!' she echoed.

'Is it too sudden to be asked thus, my Pretty?'

'Yes — I did not expect it.'

'If you will let it pass, please, Tessy, I will give you time,' he said. 'It was very abrupt to come home and speak to you all at once. I'll not allude to it again for a while.'

She again took up the shining skimmer, held it beneath the pump, and began anew. But she could not, as at other times, hit the exact under-surface of the cream with the delicate dexterity required, try as she might: sometimes she was cutting down into the milk, sometimes in the air. She could hardly see, her eyes having filled with two blurring tears drawn forth by a grief which, to this her best friend and dear advocate, she could never explain.

'I can't skim — I can't!' she said, turning away from him.

Not to agitate and hinder her longer the considerate Clare began talking in a more general way:

'You quite misapprehend my parents. They are the most simple-mannered people alive, and quite unambitious. They are two of the few remaining Evangelical school. Tessy, are you an Evangelical?'

'I don't know.'

'You go to church very regularly, and our parson here is not very High, they tell me.'

Tess's ideas on the views of the parish clergyman, whom she heard every week, seemed to be rather more vague than Clare's, who had never heard him at all.

'I wish I could fix my mind on what I hear there more firmly than I do,' she remarked as a safe generality. 'It is often a great sorrow to me.'

She spoke so unaffectedly that Angel was sure in his heart that his father could not object to her on religious grounds, even though she did not know whether her principles were High, Low, or Broad.° He himself knew that, in reality, the confused beliefs which she held, apparently imbibed in childhood, were, if any thing, Tractarian° as to phraseology, and Pantheistic° as to essence. Confused or otherwise, to disturb them was his last desire:

High, Low, or Broad: Three groups within the Anglican Church. Stressing historical continuity in Catholic Christianity, the High-Church orientation advocates traditional rituals of worship. By contrast, the Low opposes these rituals and favors Evangelical doctrines, especially salvation through belief. In the late nineteenth century, the Broad-Church group advocated liberalized ritual and doctrine. **Tractarian:** Derived from the Oxford Movement, which, among High-Church Anglicans, emphasized the connection to the Catholic Church most strongly. **Pantheistic:** Identifying God with the entire world.

Leave thou thy sister, when she prays,
Her early Heaven, her happy views;
Nor thou with shadow'd hint confuse
A life that leads melodious days.°

He had occasionally thought the counsel less honest than musical; but he gladly conformed to it now.

He spoke further of the incidents of his visit, of his father's mode of life, of his zeal for his principles; she grew serener, and the undulations disappeared from her skimming; as she finished one lead after another he followed her, and drew the plugs for letting down the milk.

'I fancied you looked a little downcast when you came in,' she ventured to observe, anxious to keep away from the subject of herself.

'Yes — well, my father has been talking a good deal to me of his troubles and difficulties, and the subject always tends to depress me. He is so zealous that he gets many snubs and buffetings from people of a different way of thinking from himself, and I don't like to hear of such humiliations to a man of his age, the more particularly as I don't think earnestness does any good when carried so far. He has been telling me of a very unpleasant scene in which he took part quite recently. He went as the deputy of some missionary society to preach in the neighbourhood of Trantridge, a place forty miles from here, and made it his business to expostulate with a lax young cynic he met with somewhere about there — son of some landowner up that way — and who has a mother afflicted with blindness. My father addressed himself to the gentleman point-blank, and there was quite a disturbance. It was very foolish of my father, I must say, to intrude his conversation upon a stranger when the probabilities were so obvious that it would be useless. But whatever he thinks to be his duty, that he'll do, in season or out of season; and, of course, he makes many enemies, not only among the absolutely vicious, but among the easy-going, who hate being bothered. He says he glories in what happened, and that good may be done indirectly; but I wish he would not so wear himself out now he is getting old, and would leave such pigs to their wallowing.'

Tess's look had grown hard and worn, and her ripe mouth tragical; but she no longer showed any tremulousness. Clare's revived thoughts of his father prevented his noticing her particularly; and so they went on down the white row of liquid rectangles till they had finished and drained them off, when the other maids returned, and took their pails,

Leave thou thy sister . . . : From *In Memoriam* (XXXIII.5–8) by Alfred Lord Tennyson (1809–1892).

and Deb came to scald out the leads for the new milk. As Tess withdrew to go afield to the cows he said to her softly —

'And my question, Tessy?'

'O no — no!' replied she with grave hopelessness, as one who had heard anew the turmoil of her own past in the allusion to Alec d'Urberville. 'It *can't* be!'

She went out towards the mead, joining the other milkmaids with a bound, as if trying to make the open air drive away her sad constraint. All the girls drew onward to the spot where the cows were grazing in the farther mead, the bevy advancing with the bold grace of wild animals — the reckless unchastened motion of women accustomed to unlimited space — in which they abandoned themselves to the air as a swimmer to the wave. It seemed natural enough to him now that Tess was again in sight to choose a mate from unconstrained Nature, and not from the abodes of Art.

XXVIII

Her refusal, though unexpected, did not permanently daunt Clare. His experience of women was great enough for him to be aware that the negative often meant nothing more than the preface to the affirmative; and it was little enough for him not to know that in the manner of the present negative there lay a great exception to the dallyings of coyness. That she had already permitted him to make love to her he read as an additional assurance, not fully trowing that in the fields and pastures to 'sigh gratis'° is by no means deemed waste; love-making being here more often accepted inconsiderately and for its own sweet sake than in the carking anxious homes of the ambitious, where a girl's craving for an establishment paralyzes her healthy thought of a passion as an end.

'Tess, why did you say "no" in such a positive way?' he asked her in the course of a few days.

She started.

'Don't ask me. I told you why — partly. I am not good enough — not worthy enough.'

'How? Not fine lady enough?'

'Yes — something like that,' murmured she. 'Your friends would scorn me.'

'Indeed, you mistake them — my father and mother. As for my

'sigh gratis': Act or feel without expecting reward; *Hamlet* 2.2.323.

brothers, I don't care —— ' He clasped his fingers behind her back to keep her from slipping away. 'Now — you did not mean it, sweet? — I am sure you did not! You have made me so restless that I cannot read, or play, or do anything. I am in no hurry, Tess, but I want to know — to hear from your own warm lips — that you will some day be mine — any time you may choose; but some day?'

She could only shake her head and look away from him.

Clare regarded her attentively, conned the characters of her face as if they had been hieroglyphics. The denial seemed real.

'Then I ought not to hold you in this way — ought I? I have no right to you — no right to seek out where you are, or to walk with you! Honestly, Tess, do you love any other man?'

'How can you ask?' she said, with continued self-suppression.

'I almost know that you do not. But then, why do you repulse me?'

'I don't repulse you. I like you to — tell me you love me; and you may always tell me so as you go about with me — and never offend me.'

'But you will not accept me as a husband?'

'Ah — that's different — it is for your good, indeed my dearest! O, believe me, it is only for your sake! I don't like to give myself the great happiness o' promising to be yours in that way — because — because I am *sure* I ought not to do it.'

'But you will make me happy!'

'Ah — you think so, but you don't know!'

At such times as this, apprehending the grounds of her refusal to be her modest sense of incompetence in matters social and polite, he would say that she was wonderfully well-informed and versatile — which was certainly true, her natural quickness, and her admiration for him, having led her to pick up his vocabulary, his accent, and fragments of his knowledge, to a surprising extent. After these tender contests and her victory she would go away by herself under the remotest cow, if at milking-time, or into the sedge, or into her room, if at a leisure interval, and mourn silently, not a minute after an apparently phlegmatic negative.

The struggle was so fearful; her own heart was so strongly on the side of his — two ardent hearts against one poor little conscience — that she tried to fortify her resolution by every means in her power. She had come to Talbothays with a made-up mind. On no account could she agree to a step which might afterwards cause bitter rueing to her husband for his blindness in wedding her. And she held that what her conscience had decided for her when her mind was unbiassed ought not to be overruled now.

'Why don't somebody tell him all about me?' she said. 'It was only forty miles off — why hasn't it reached here? Somebody must know!'

Yet nobody seemed to know; nobody told him.

For two or three days no more was said. She guessed from the sad countenances of her chamber companions that they regarded her not only as the favourite, but as the chosen; but they could see for themselves that she did not put herself in his way.

Tess had never before known a time in which the thread of her life was so distinctly twisted of two strands, positive pleasure and positive pain. At the next cheese-making the pair were again left alone together. The dairyman himself had been lending a hand; but Mr. Crick, as well as his wife, seemed latterly to have acquired a suspicion of mutual interest between these two; though they walked so circumspectly that suspicion was but of the faintest. Anyhow, the dairyman left them to themselves.

They were breaking up the masses of curd before putting them into the vats. The operation resembled the act of crumbling bread on a large scale; and amid the immaculate whiteness of the curds Tess Durbeyfield's hands showed themselves of the pinkness of the rose. Angel, who was filling the vats with his handfuls, suddenly ceased, and laid his hands flat upon hers. Her sleeves were rolled far above the elbow, and bending lower he kissed the inside vein of her soft arm.

Although the early September weather was sultry, her arm, from her dabbling in the curds, was as cold and damp to his mouth as a new-gathered mushroom, and tasted of the whey. But she was such a sheaf of susceptibilities that her pulse was accelerated by the touch, her blood driven to her finger-ends, and the cool arms flushed hot. Then, as though her heart had said, 'Is coyness longer necessary? Truth is truth between man and woman, as between man and man,' she lifted her eyes, and they beamed devotedly into his, as her lip rose in a tender half-smile.

'Do you know why I did that, Tess?' he said.

'Because you love me very much!'

'Yes, and as a preliminary to a new entreaty.'

'Not *again!*'

She looked a sudden fear that her resistance might break down under her own desire.

'O, Tessy!' he went on, 'I *cannot* think why you are so tantalizing. Why do you disappoint me so? You seem almost like a coquette, upon my life you do — a coquette of the first urban water! They blow hot and blow cold, just as you do; and it is the very last sort of thing to expect to find in a retreat like Talbothays. . . . And yet, dearest,' he quickly added, observing how the remark had cut her, 'I know you to be the most honest, spotless creature that ever lived. So how can I suppose you a flirt? Tess, why don't you like the idea of being my wife, if you love me as you seem to do?'

'I have never said I don't like the idea, and I never could say it; because — it isn't true!'

The stress now getting beyond endurance her lip quivered, and she was obliged to go away. Clare was so pained and perplexed that he ran after and caught her in the passage.

'Tell me, tell me!' he said, passionately clasping her, in forgetfulness of his curdy hands: 'do tell me that you won't belong to anybody but me!'

'I will, I will tell you!' she exclaimed. 'And I will give you a complete answer, if you will let me go now. I will tell you my experiences — all about myself — all!'

'Your experiences, dear; yes, certainly; any number.' He expressed assent in loving satire, looking into her face. 'My Tess has, no doubt, almost as many experiences as that wild convolvulus out there on the garden hedge, that opened itself this morning for the first time. Tell me anything, but don't use that wretched expression any more about not being worthy of me.'

'I will try — not! And I'll give you my reasons to-morrow — next week.'

'Say on Sunday?'

'Yes, on Sunday.'

At last she got away, and did not stop in her retreat till she was in the thicket of pollard willows at the lower side of the barton, where she could be quite unseen. Here Tess flung herself down upon the rustling undergrowth of spear-grass, as upon a bed, and remained crouching in palpitating misery broken by momentary shoots of joy, which her fears about the ending could not altogether suppress.

In reality, she was drifting into acquiescence. Every see-saw of her breath, every wave of her blood, every pulse singing in her ears, was a voice that joined with nature in revolt against her scrupulousness. Reckless, inconsiderate acceptance of him; to close with him at the altar, revealing nothing, and chancing discovery; to snatch ripe pleasure before the iron teeth of pain could have time to shut upon her: that was what love counselled; and in almost a terror of ecstasy Tess divined that, despite her many months of lonely self-chastisement, wrestlings, communings, schemes to lead a future of austere isolation, love's counsel would prevail.

The afternoon advanced, and still she remained among the willows. She heard the rattle of taking down the pails from the forked stands; the 'waow-waow!' which accompanied the getting together of the cows. But she did not go to the milking. They would see her agitation; and the dairyman, thinking the cause to be love alone, would good-naturedly tease her; and that harassment could not be borne.

Her lover must have guessed her overwrought state, and invented some excuse for her non-appearance, for no inquiries were made or calls given. At half-past six the sun settled down upon the levels, with the aspect of a great forge in the heavens, and presently a monstrous pumpkin-like moon arose on the other hand. The pollard willows, tortured out of their natural shape by incessant choppings, became spiny-haired monsters as they stood up against it. She went in, and upstairs without a light.

It was now Wednesday. Thursday came, and Angel looked thoughtfully at her from a distance, but intruded in no way upon her. The indoor milkmaids, Marian and the rest, seemed to guess that something definite was afoot, for they did not force any remarks upon her in the bedchamber. Friday passed; Saturday. To-morrow was the day.

'I shall give way — I shall say yes — I shall let myself marry him — I cannot help it!' she jealously panted, with her hot face to the pillow that night, on hearing one of the other girls sigh his name in her sleep. 'I can't bear to let anybody have him but me! Yet it is a wrong to him, and may kill him when he knows! O my heart — O — O — O!'

XXIX

'Now, who mid ye think I've heard news o' this morning?' said Dairyman Crick, as he sat down to breakfast next day, with a riddling gaze round upon the munching men and maids. 'Now, just who mid ye think?'

One guessed, and another guessed. Mrs. Crick did not guess, because she knew already.

'Well,' said the dairyman, ''tis that slack-twisted 'hore's-bird of a feller, Jack Dollop. He's lately got married to a widow-woman.'

'Not Jack Dollop? A villain — to think o' that!' said a milker.

The name entered quickly into Tess Durbeyfield's consciousness, for it was the name of the lover who had wronged his sweetheart, and had afterwards been so roughly used by the young woman's mother in the butter-churn.

'And has he married the valiant matron's daughter, as he promised?' asked Angel Clare absently, as he turned over the newspaper he was reading at the little table to which he was always banished by Mrs. Crick, in her sense of his gentility.

'Not he, sir. Never meant to,' replied the dairyman. 'As I say, 'tis a widow-woman, and she had money, it seems — fifty poun' a year or so; and that was all he was after. They were married in a great hurry; and then she told him that by marrying she had lost her fifty poun' a year. Just fancy the state o' my gentleman's mind at that news! Never such a cat-and-dog life as they've been leading ever since! Serves him well beright. But onluckily the poor woman gets the worst o't.'

'Well, the silly body should have told en sooner that the ghost of her first man would trouble him' said Mrs. Crick.

'Ay; ay,' responded the dairyman indecisively. 'Still, you can see exactly how 'twas. She wanted a home, and didn't like to run the risk of losing him. Don't ye think that was something like it, maidens?'

He glanced towards the row of girls.

'She ought to ha' told him just before they went to church, when he could hardly have backed out,' exclaimed Marian.

'Yes, she ought,' agreed Izz.

'She must have seen what he was after, and should ha' refused him,' cried Retty spasmodically.

'And what do you say, my dear?' asked the dairyman of Tess.

'I think she ought — to have told him the true state of things — or else refused him — I don't know,' replied Tess, the bread-and-butter choking her.

'Be cust if I'd have done either o't,' said Beck Knibbs, a married helper from one of the cottages. 'All's fair in love and war. I'd ha' married en just as she did, and if he'd said two words to me about not telling him beforehand anything whatsomdever about my first chap that I hadn't chose to tell, I'd ha' knocked him down wi' the rolling-pin — a scram little feller like he! Any woman could do it.'

The laughter which followed this sally was supplemented only by a sorry smile, for form's sake, from Tess. What was comedy to them was tragedy to her; and she could hardly bear their mirth. She soon rose from table, and, with an impression that Clare would follow her, went along a little wriggling path, now stepping to one side of the irrigating channels, and now to the other, till she stood by the main stream of the Var. Men had been cutting the water-weeds higher up the river, and masses of them were floating past her — moving islands of green crow-foot, whereon she might almost have ridden; long locks of which weed had lodged against the piles driven to keep the cows from crossing.

Yes, there was the pain of it. This question of a woman telling her story — the heaviest of crosses to herself — seemed but amusement to others. It was as if people should laugh at martyrdom.

'Tessy!' came from behind her, and Clare sprang across the gully, alighting beside her feet. 'My wife — soon!'

'No, no; I cannot. For your sake, O Mr. Clare; for your sake, I say no!'

'Tess!'

'Still I say no!' she repeated.

Not expecting this he had put his arm lightly round her waist the moment after speaking, beneath her hanging tail of hair. (The younger dairymaids, including Tess, breakfasted with their hair loose on Sunday mornings before building it up extra high for attending church, a style they could not adopt when milking with their heads against the cows.) If she had said 'Yes' instead of 'No' he would have kissed her; it had evidently been his intention; but her determined negative deterred his scrupulous heart. Their condition of domiciliary comradeship put her, as the woman, to such disadvantage by its enforced intercourse, that he felt it unfair to her to exercise any pressure of blandishment which he might have honestly employed had she been better able to avoid him. He released her momentarily-imprisoned waist, and withheld the kiss.

It all turned on that release. What had given her strength to refuse him this time was solely the tale of the widow told by the dairyman; and that would have been overcome in another moment. But Angel said no more; his face was perplexed; he went away.

Day after day they met — somewhat less constantly than before; and thus two or three weeks went by. The end of September drew near, and she could see in his eye that he might ask her again.

His plan of procedure was different now — as though he had made up his mind that her negatives were, after all, only coyness and youth startled by the novelty of the proposal. The fitful evasiveness of her manner when the subject was under discussion countenanced the idea. So he played a more coaxing game; and while never going beyond words, or attempting the renewal of caresses, he did his utmost orally.

In this way Clare persistently wooed her in undertones like that of the purling milk — at the cow's side, at skimmings, at butter-makings, at cheese-makings, among broody poultry,° and among farrowing pigs — as no milkmaid was ever wooed before by such a man.

Tess knew that she must break down. Neither a religious sense of a certain moral validity in the previous union nor a conscientious wish for candour could hold out against it much longer. She loved him so passionately, and he was so godlike in her eyes; and being, though untrained, instinctively refined, her nature cried for his tutelary guidance. And thus, though Tess kept repeating to herself, 'I can never be his wife,' the words were vain. A proof of her weakness lay in the very utterance of what calm strength would not have taken the trouble to formulate. Every sound of his voice beginning on the old subject stirred her with a terrifying bliss, and she coveted the recantation she feared.

His manner was — what man's is not? — so much that of one who would love and cherish and defend her under any conditions, changes, charges, or revelations, that her gloom lessened as she basked in it. The season meanwhile was drawing onward to the equinox, and though it was still fine, the days were much shorter. The dairy had again worked by morning candle-light for a long time; and a fresh renewal of Clare's pleading occurred one morning between three and four.

She had run up in her bedgown to his door to call him as usual; then had gone back to dress and call the others; and in ten minutes was walking to the head of the stairs with the candle in her hand. At the same moment he came down his steps from above in his shirt-sleeves and put his arm across the stairway.

'Now, Miss Flirt, before you go down,' he said peremptorily. 'It is a fortnight since I spoke, and this won't do any longer. You *must* tell what you mean, or I shall have to leave this house. My door was ajar just now, and I saw you. For your own safety I must go. You don't know. Well? Is it to be yes at last?'

'I am only just up, Mr. Clare, and it is too early to take me to task!' she pouted. 'You need not call me Flirt. 'Tis cruel and untrue. Wait till by and by. Please wait till by and by! I will really think seriously about it between now and then. Let me go downstairs!'

She looked a little like what he said she was as, holding the candle sideways, she tried to smile away the seriousness of her words.

'Call me Angel, then, and not Mr. Clare.'

broody poultry: Hens sitting on their eggs.

'Angel.'

'Angel dearest — why not?'

''Twould mean that I agree, wouldn't it?'

'It would only mean that you love me, even if you cannot marry me; and you were so good as to own that long ago.'

'Very well, then, "Angel dearest," if I *must*,' she murmured, looking at her candle, a roguish curl coming upon her mouth, notwithstanding her suspense.

Clare had resolved never to kiss her until he had obtained her promise; but somehow, as Tess stood there in her prettily tucked-up milking gown, her hair carelessly heaped upon her head till there should be leisure to arrange it when skimming and milking were done, he broke his resolve, and brought his lips to her cheek for one moment. She passed downstairs very quickly, never looking back at him or saying another word. The other maids were already down, and the subject was not pursued. Except Marian they all looked wistfully and suspiciously at the pair, in the sad yellow rays which the morning candles emitted in contrast with the first cold signals of the dawn without.

When skimming was done — which, as the milk diminished with the approach of autumn, was a lessening process day by day — Retty and the rest went out. The lovers followed them.

'Our tremulous lives are so different from theirs, are they not?' he musingly observed to her, as he regarded the three figures tripping before him through the frigid pallor of opening day.

'Not so very different, I think,' she said.

'Why do you think that?'

'There are very few women's lives that are not — tremulous,' Tess replied, pausing over the new word as if it impressed her. 'There's more in those three than you think.'

'What is in them?'

'Almost either of 'em,' she began, 'would make — perhaps would make — a properer wife than I. And perhaps they love you as well as I — almost.'

'O, Tessy!'

There were signs that it was an exquisite relief to her to hear the impatient exclamation, though she had resolved so intrepidly to let generosity make one bid against herself. That was now done, and she had not the power to attempt self-immolation a second time then. They were joined by a milker from one of the cottages, and no more was said on that which concerned them so deeply. But Tess knew that this day would decide it.

In the afternoon several of the dairyman's household and assistants went down to the meads as usual, a long way from the dairy, where many of the cows were milked without being driven home. The supply was getting less as the animals advanced in calf, and the supernumerary milkers of the lush green season had been dismissed.

The work progressed leisurely. Each pailful was poured into tall cans that stood in a large spring-waggon which had been brought upon the scene; and when they were milked the cows trailed away.

Dairyman Crick, who was there with the rest, his wrapper gleaming miraculously white against a leaden evening sky, suddenly looked at his heavy watch.

'Why, 'tis later than I thought,' he said. 'Begad! We shan't be soon enough with this milk at the station, if we don't mind. There's no time to-day to take it home and mix it with the bulk afore sending off. It must go to station straight from here. Who'll drive it across?'

Mr. Clare volunteered to do so, though it was none of his business, asking Tess to accompany him. The evening, though sunless, had been warm and muggy for the season, and Tess had come out with her milking-hood only, naked-armed and jacketless; certainly not dressed for a drive. She therefore replied by glancing over her scant habiliments; but Clare gently urged her. She assented by relinquishing her pail and stool to the dairyman to take home; and mounted the spring-waggon beside Clare.

XXX

In the diminishing daylight they went along the level roadway through the meads, which stretched away into gray miles, and were backed in the extreme edge of distance by the swarthy and abrupt slopes of Egdon Heath. On its summit stood clumps and stretches of fir-trees, whose notched tips appeared like battlemented towers crowning black-fronted castles of enchantment.

They were so absorbed in the sense of being close to each other that they did not begin talking for a long while, the silence being broken only by the clucking of the milk in the tall cans behind them. The lane they followed was so solitary that the hazel nuts had remained on the boughs till they slipped from their shells, and the blackberries hung in heavy clusters. Every now and then Angel would fling the lash of his whip round one of these, pluck it off, and give it to his companion.

The dull sky soon began to tell its meaning by sending down herald-drops of rain, and the stagnant air of the day changed into a fitful breeze which played about their faces. The quicksilvery glaze on the rivers and pools vanished; from broad mirrors of light they changed to lustreless sheets of lead, with a surface like a rasp. But that spectacle did not affect her preoccupation. Her countenance, a natural carnation slightly embrowned by the season, had deepened its tinge with the beating of the rain-drops; and her hair, which the pressure of the cows' flanks had, as usual, caused to tumble down from its fastenings and stray beyond the curtain of her calico bonnet, was made clammy by the moisture, till it hardly was better than seaweed.

'I ought not to have come, I suppose,' she murmured, looking at the sky.

'I am sorry for the rain,' said he. 'But how glad I am to have you here!'

Remote Egdon disappeared by degrees behind the liquid gauze. The evening grew darker, and the roads being crossed by gates it was not safe to drive faster than at a walking pace. The air was rather chill.

'I am so afraid you will get cold, with nothing upon your arms and shoulders,' he said. 'Creep close to me, and perhaps the drizzle won't hurt you much. I should be sorrier still if I did not think that the rain might be helping me.'

She imperceptibly crept closer, and he wrapped round them both a large piece of sail-cloth, which was sometimes used to keep the sun off the milk-cans. Tess held it from slipping off him as well as herself, Clare's hands being occupied.

'Now we are all right again. Ah — no we are not! It runs down into my neck a little, and it must still more into yours. That's better. Your arms are like wet marble, Tess. Wipe them in the cloth. Now, if you stay quiet, you will not get another drop. Well, dear — about that question of mine — that long-standing question?'

The only reply that he could hear for a little while was the smack of the horse's hoofs on the moistening road, and the cluck of the milk in the cans behind them.

'Do you remember what you said?'

'I do,' she replied.

'Before we get home, mind.'

'I'll try.'

He said no more then. As they drove on the fragment of an old manor house of Caroline date° rose against the sky, and was in due course passed and left behind.

'That,' he observed, to entertain her, 'is an interesting old place — one of the several seats which belonged to an ancient Norman family formerly of great influence in this county, the d'Urbervilles. I never pass one of their residences without thinking of them. There is something very sad in the extinction of a family of renown, even if it was fierce, domineering, feudal renown.'

'Yes,' said Tess.

They crept along towards a point in the expanse of shade just at hand at which a feeble light was beginning to assert its presence, a spot where, by day, a fitful white streak of steam at intervals upon the dark green background denoted intermittent moments of contact between their secluded world and modern life. Modern life stretched out its steam feeler to this point three or four times a day, touched the native existences, and quickly withdrew its feeler again, as if what it touched had been uncongenial.

They reached the feeble light, which came from the smoky lamp of a little railway station; a poor enough terrestrial star, yet in one sense of more importance to Talbothays Dairy and mankind than the celestial ones to which it stood in such humiliating contrast. The cans of new milk were unladen in the rain, Tess getting a little shelter from a neighbouring holly tree.

Then there was the hissing of a train, which drew up almost silently upon the wet rails, and the milk was rapidly swung can by can into the truck. The light of the engine flashed for a second upon Tess Durbeyfield's figure, motionless under the great holly tree. No object could have looked more foreign to the gleaming cranks and wheels than this unsophisticated girl, with the round bare arms, the rainy face and hair, the suspended attitude of a friendly leopard at pause, the print gown of no date or fashion, and the cotton bonnet drooping on her brow.

She mounted again beside her lover, with a mute obedience characteristic of impassioned natures at times, and when they had wrapped themselves up over head and ears in the sail-cloth again, they plunged back into the now thick night. Tess was so receptive that the few minutes of contact with the whirl of material progress lingered in her thought.

Caroline date: The seventeenth century, during the reign of Charles I (1625–49) or Charles II (1660–85).

'Londoners will drink it at their breakfasts tomorrow, won't they?' she asked. 'Strange people that we have never seen.'

'Yes — I suppose they will. Though not as we send it. When its strength has been lowered, so that it may not get up into their heads.'

'Noble men and noble women, ambassadors and centurions, ladies and tradeswomen, and babies who have never seen a cow.'

'Well, yes; perhaps; particularly centurions.'

'Who don't know anything of us, and where it comes from; or think how we two drove miles across the moor to-night in the rain that it might reach 'em in time?'

'We did not drive entirely on account of these precious Londoners; we drove a little on our own — on account of that anxious matter which you will, I am sure, set at rest, dear Tess. Now, permit me to put it in this way. You belong to me already, you know; your heart, I mean. Does it not?'

'You know as well as I. O yes — yes!'

'Then, if your heart does, why not your hand?'

'My only reason was on account of you — on account of a question. I have something to tell you —— '

'But suppose it to be entirely for my happiness, and my worldly convenience also?'

'O yes; if it is for your happiness and worldly convenience. But my life before I came here — I want —— '

'Well, it is for my convenience as well as my happiness. If I have a very large farm, either English or colonial, you will be invaluable as a wife to me; better than a woman out of the largest mansion in the country. So please — please, dear Tessy, disabuse your mind of the feeling that you will stand in my way.'

'But my history. I want you to know it — you must let me tell you — you will not like me so well!'

'Tell it if you wish to, dearest. This precious history then. Yes, I was born at so and so, Anno Domini —— '

'I was born at Marlott,' she said, catching at his words as a help, lightly as they were spoken. 'And I grew up there. And I was in the Sixth Standard when I left school, and they said I had great aptness, and should make a good teacher, so it was settled that I should be one. But there was trouble in my family; father was not very industrious, and he drank a little.'

'Yes, yes. Poor child! Nothing new.' He pressed her more closely to his side.

'And then — there is something very unusual about it — about me. I — I was —— '

Tess's breath quickened.

'Yes, dearest. Never mind.'

'I — I — am not a Durbeyfield, but a d'Urberville — a descendant of the same family as those that owned the old house we passed. And — we are all gone to nothing!'

'A d'Urberville! — Indeed! And is that all the trouble, dear Tess?'

'Yes,' she answered faintly.

'Well — why should I love you less after knowing this?'

'I was told by the dairyman that you hated old families.'

He laughed.

'Well, it is true, in one sense. I do hate the aristocratic principle of blood before everything, and do think that as reasoners the only pedigrees we ought to respect are those spiritual ones of the wise and virtuous, without regard to corporeal paternity. But I am extremely interested in this news — you can have no idea how interested I am! Are not you interested yourself in being one of that well-known line?'

'No. I have thought it sad — especially since coming here, and knowing that many of the hills and fields I see once belonged to my father's people. But other hills and fields belonged to Retty's people, and perhaps others to Marian's, so that I don't value it particularly.'

'Yes — it is surprising how many of the present tillers of the soil were once owners of it, and I sometimes wonder that a certain school of politicians don't make capital of the circumstance; but they don't seem to know it. . . . I wonder that I did not see the resemblance of your name to d'Urberville, and trace the manifest corruption. And this was the carking secret!'

She had not told. At the last moment her courage had failed her, she feared his blame for not telling him sooner; and her instinct of self-preservation was stronger than her candour.

'Of course,' continued the unwitting Clare, 'I should have been glad to know you to be descended exclusively from the long-suffering, dumb, unrecorded rank and file of the English nation, and not from the self-seeking few who made themselves powerful at the expense of the rest. But I am corrupted away from that by my affection for you, Tess [he laughed as he spoke], and made selfish likewise. For your own sake I rejoice in your descent. Society is hopelessly snobbish, and this fact of your extraction may make an appreciable difference to its acceptance of you as my wife, after I have made you the well-read woman that I mean to make you. My mother too, poor soul, will think so much better of you on account of it. Tess, you must spell your name correctly — d'Urberville — from this very day.'

'I like the other way rather best.'

'But you *must*, dearest! Good heavens, why dozens of mushroom millionaires would jump at such a possession! By the bye, there's one of that kidney who has taken the name — where have I heard of him? — Up in the neighbourhood of The Chase, I think. Why, he is the very man who had that rumpus with my father I told you of. What an odd coincidence!'

'Angel, I think I would rather not take the name! It is unlucky, perhaps!'

She was agitated.

'Now then, Mistress Teresa d'Urberville, I have you. Take my name, and so you will escape yours! The secret is out, so why should you any longer refuse me?'

'If it is *sure* to make you happy to have me as your wife, and you feel that you do wish to marry me, *very, very* much —— '

'I do, dearest, of course!'

'I mean, that it is only your wanting me very much, and being hardly able to keep alive without me, whatever my offences, that would make me feel I ought to say I will.'

'You will — you do say it, I know! You will be mine for ever and ever.'

He clasped her close and kissed her.

'Yes!'

She had no sooner said it than she burst into a dry hard sobbing, so violent that it seemed to rend her. Tess was not a hysterical girl by any means, and he was surprised.

'Why do you cry, dearest?'

'I can't tell — quite! — I am so glad to think — of being yours, and making you happy!'

'But this does not seem very much like gladness, my Tessy!'

'I mean — I cry because I have broken down in my vow! I said I would die unmarried!'

'But, if you love me you would like me to be your husband?'

'Yes, yes, yes! But O, I sometimes wish I had never been born!'

'Now, my dear Tess, if I did not know that you are very much excited, and very inexperienced, I should say that remark was not very complimentary. How came you to wish that if you care for me? Do you care for me? I wish you would prove it in some way.'

'How can I prove it more than I have done?' she cried, in a distraction of tenderness. 'Will this prove it more?'

She clasped his neck, and for the first time Clare learnt what an impassioned woman's kisses were like upon the lips of one whom she loved with all her heart and soul, as Tess loved him.

'There — now do you believe?' she asked, flushed, and wiping her eyes.

'Yes. I never really doubted — never, never!'

So they drove on through the gloom, forming one bundle inside the sail-cloth, the horse going as he would, and the rain driving against them. She had consented. She might as well have agreed at first. The 'appetite for joy' which pervades all creation, that tremendous force which sways humanity to its purpose, as the tide sways the helpless weed, was not to be controlled by vague lucubrations over the social rubric.

'I must write to my mother,' she said. 'You don't mind my doing that?'

'Of course not, dear child. You are a child to me, Tess, not to know how very proper it is to write to your mother at such a time, and how wrong it would be in me to object. Where does she live?'

'At the same place — Marlott. On the further side of Blackmoor Vale.'

'Ah, then I *have* seen you before this summer ——'

'Yes; at that dance on the green; but you would not dance with me. O, I hope that is of no ill-omen for us now!'

XXXI

Tess wrote a most touching and urgent letter to her mother the very next day, and by the end of the week a response to her communication arrived in Joan Durbeyfield's wandering last-century hand.

> DEAR TESS, — J write these few lines Hoping they will find you well, as they leave me at Present, thank God for it. Dear Tess, we are all glad to Hear that you are going really to be married soon. But with respect to your question, Tess, J say between ourselves, quite private but very strong, that on no account do you say a word of your Bygone Trouble to him. J did not tell everything to your Father, he being so Proud on account of his Respectability, which, perhaps, your Intended is the same. Many a woman — some of the Highest in the Land — have had a Trouble in their time; and why should you Trumpet yours when others don't

Trumpet theirs? No girl would be such a Fool, specially as it is so long ago, and not your Fault at all. J shall answer the same if you ask me fifty times. Besides, you must bear in mind that, knowing it to be your Childish Nature to tell all that's in your heart — so simple! — J made you promise me never to let it out by Word or Deed, having your Welfare in my Mind; and you most solemnly did promise it going from this Door. J have not named either that Question or your coming marriage to your Father, as he would blab it everywhere, poor Simple Man.

Dear Tess, keep up your Spirits, and we mean to send you a Hogshead of Cyder for your Wedding, knowing there is not much in your parts, and thin Sour Stuff what there is. So no more at present, and with kind love to your Young Man. — From your affectte. Mother,

J. DURBEYFIELD.

'O mother, mother!' murmured Tess.

She was recognizing how light was the touch of events the most oppressive upon Mrs. Durbeyfield's elastic spirit. Her mother did not see life as Tess saw it. That haunting episode of bygone days was to her mother but a passing accident. But perhaps her mother was right as to the course to be followed, whatever she might be in her reasons. Silence seemed, on the face of it, best for her adored one's happiness: silence it should be.

Thus steadied by a command from the only person in the world who had any shadow of right to control her action, Tess grew calmer. The responsibility was shifted, and her heart was lighter than it had been for weeks. The days of declining autumn which followed her assent, beginning with the month of October, formed a season through which she lived in spiritual altitudes more nearly approaching ecstasy than any other period of her life.

There was hardly a touch of earth in her love for Clare. To her sublime trustfulness he was all that goodness could be — knew all that a guide, philosopher, and friend should know. She thought every line in the contour of his person the perfection of masculine beauty, his soul the soul of a saint, his intellect that of a seer. The wisdom of her love for him, as love, sustained her dignity; she seemed to be wearing a crown. The compassion of his love for her, as she saw it, made her lift up her heart to him in devotion. He would sometimes catch her large, worshipful eyes, that had no bottom to them, looking at him from their depths, as if she saw something immortal before her.

She dismissed the past — trod upon it and put it out, as one treads on a coal that is smouldering and dangerous.

She had not known that men could be so disinterested, chivalrous, protective, in their love for women as he. Angel Clare was far from all that she thought him in this respect; absurdly far, indeed; but he was, in truth, more spiritual than animal; he had himself well in hand, and was singularly free from grossness. Though not cold-natured, he was rather bright than hot — less Byronic than Shelleyan;° could love desperately, but with a love more especially inclined to the imaginative and ethereal; it was a fastidious emotion which could jealously guard the loved one against his very self. This amazed and enraptured Tess, whose slight experiences had been so infelicitous till now; and in her reaction from indignation against the male sex she swerved to excess of honour for Clare.

They unaffectedly sought each other's company; in her honest faith she did not disguise her desire to be with him. The sum of her instincts on this matter, if clearly stated, would have been that the elusive quality in her sex which attracts men in general might be distasteful to so perfect a man after an avowal of love, since it must in its very nature carry with it a suspicion of art.

The country custom of unreserved comradeship out of doors during betrothal was the only custom she knew, and to her it had no strangeness; though it seemed oddly anticipative to Clare till he saw how normal a thing she, in common with all the other dairy-folk, regarded it. Thus, during this October month of wonderful afternoons they roved along the meads by creeping paths which followed the brinks of trickling tributary brooks, hopping across by little wooden bridges to the other side, and back again. They were never out of the sound of some purling weir, whose buzz accompanied their own murmuring, while the beams of the sun, almost as horizontal as the mead itself, formed a pollen of radiance over the landscape. They saw tiny blue fogs in the shadows of trees and hedges, all the time that there was bright sunshine elsewhere. The sun was so near the ground, and the sward so flat, that the shadows of Clare and Tess would stretch a quarter of a mile ahead of them, like two long fingers pointing afar to where the green alluvial reaches abutted against the sloping sides of the vale.

less Byronic than Shelleyan: Less passionate than spiritual in inclination.

Men were at work here and there — for it was the season for 'taking up' the meadows, or digging the little waterways clear for the winter irrigation, and mending their banks where trodden down by the cows. The shovelfuls of loam, black as jet, brought there by the river when it was as wide as the whole valley, were an essence of soils, pounded champaigns° of the past, steeped, refined, and subtilized to extra-ordinary richness, out of which came all the fertility of the mead, and of the cattle grazing there.

Clare hardily kept his arm round her waist in sight of these watermen, with the air of a man who was accustomed to public dalliance, though actually as shy as she who, with lips parted and eyes askance on the labourers, wore the look of a wary animal the while.

'You are not ashamed of owning me as yours before them!' she said gladly.

'O no!'

'But if it should reach the ears of your friends at Emminster that you are walking about like this with me, a milkmaid —— '

'The most bewitching milkmaid ever seen.'

'They might feel it a hurt to their dignity.'

'My dear girl — a d'Urberville hurt the dignity of a Clare! It is a grand card to play — that of your belonging to such a family, and I am reserving it for a grand effect when we are married, and have the proofs of your descent from Parson Tringham. Apart from that, my future is to be totally foreign to my family — it will not affect even the surface of their lives. We shall leave this part of England — perhaps England itself — and what does it matter how people regard us here? You will like going, will you not?'

She could answer no more than a bare affirmative, so great was the emotion aroused in her at the thought of going through the world with him as his own familiar friend. Her feelings almost filled her ears like a babble of waves, and surged up to her eyes. She put her hand in his, and thus they went on, to a place where the reflected sun glared up from the river, under a bridge, with a molten-metallic glow that dazzled their eyes, though the sun itself was hidden by the bridge. They stood still, whereupon little furred and feathered heads popped up from the smooth surface of the water; but, finding that the disturbing presences had paused, and not passed by, they disappeared again. Upon this river-brink they lingered till the fog began to close round them — which was very early in the evening at this time of the year —

champaigns: Plains; level, open country.

settling on the lashes of her eyes, where it rested like crystals, and on his brows and hair.

They walked later on Sundays, when it was quite dark. Some of the dairy-people, who were also out of doors on the first Sunday evening after their engagement, heard her impulsive speeches, ecstasized to fragments, though they were too far off to hear the words discoursed; noted the spasmodic catch in her remarks, broken into syllables by the leapings of her heart, as she walked leaning on his arm; her contented pauses, the occasional little laugh upon which her soul seemed to ride — the laugh of a woman in company with the man she loves and has won from all other women — unlike anything else in nature. They marked the buoyancy of her tread, like the skim of a bird which has not quite alighted.

Her affection for him was now the breath and life of Tess's being; it enveloped her as a photosphere, irradiated her into forgetfulness of her past sorrows, keeping back the gloomy spectres that would persist in their attempts to touch her — doubt, fear, moodiness, care, shame. She knew that they were waiting like wolves just outside the circumscribing light, but she had long spells of power to keep them in hungry subjection there.

A spiritual forgetfulness co-existed with an intellectual remembrance. She walked in brightness, but she knew that in the background those shapes of darkness were always spread. They might be receding, or they might be approaching, one or the other, a little every day.

One evening Tess and Clare were obliged to sit indoors keeping house, all the other occupants of the domicile being away. As they talked she looked thoughtfully up at him, and met his two appreciative eyes.

'I am not worthy of you — no, I am not!' she burst out, jumping up from her low stool as though appalled at his homage, and the fulness of her own joy thereat.

Clare, deeming the whole basis of her excitement to be that which was only the smaller part of it, said —

'I won't have you speak like it, dear Tess! Distinction does not consist in the facile use of a contemptible set of conventions, but in being numbered among those who are true, and honest, and just, and pure, and lovely, and of good report° — as you are, my Tess.'

those who are true . . . : The list of virtues comes from Paul; Philippians 4.8.

She struggled with the sob in her throat. How often had that string of excellences made her young heart ache in church of late years, and how strange that he should have cited them now.

'Why didn't you stay and love me when I — was sixteen; living with my little sisters and brothers, and you danced on the green? O, why didn't you, why didn't you!' she said, impetuously clasping her hands.

Angel began to comfort and reassure her, thinking to himself, truly enough, what a creature of moods she was, and how careful he would have to be of her when she depended for her happiness entirely on him.

'Ah, — why didn't I stay!' he said. 'That is just what I feel. If I had only known! But you must not be so bitter in your regret — why should you be?'

With the woman's instinct to hide she diverged hastily —

'I should have had four years more of your heart than I can ever have now. Then I should not have wasted my time as I have done — I should have had so much longer happiness!'

It was no mature woman with a long dark vista of intrigue behind her who was tormented thus; but a girl of simple life, not yet one-and-twenty, who had been caught during her days of immaturity like a bird in a springe. To calm herself the more completely she rose from her little stool and left the room, overturning the stool with her skirts as she went.

He sat on by the cheerful firelight thrown from a bundle of green ash-sticks laid across the dogs; the sticks snapped pleasantly, and hissed out bubbles of sap from their ends. When she came back she was herself again.

'Do you not think you are just a wee bit capricious, fitful, Tess?' he said, good humouredly, as he spread a cushion for her on the stool, and seated himself in the settle beside her. 'I wanted to ask you something, and just then you ran away.'

'Yes, perhaps I am capricious,' she murmured. She suddenly approached him, and put a hand upon each of his arms. 'No, Angel, I am not really so — by Nature, I mean!' The more particularly to assure him that she was not, she placed herself close to him in the settle, and allowed her head to find a resting-place against Clare's shoulder. 'What did you want to ask me — I am sure I will answer it,' she continued humbly.

'Well, you love me, and have agreed to marry me, and hence there follows a thirdly, "When shall the day be?"'

'I like living like this.'

'But I must think of starting in business on my own hook with the new year, or a little later. And before I get involved in the multifarious details of my new position, I should like to have secured my partner.'

'But,' she timidly answered, 'to talk quite practically, wouldn't it be best not to marry till after all that? — Though I can't bear the thought o' your going away and leaving me here!'

'Of course you cannot — and it is not best in this case. I want you to help me in many ways in making my start. When shall it be? Why not a fortnight from now?'

'No,' she said, becoming grave; 'I have so many things to think of first.'

'But —— '

He drew her gently nearer to him.

The reality of marriage was startling when it loomed so near. Before discussion of the question had proceeded further there walked round the corner of the settle into the full firelight of the apartment Mr. Dairyman Crick, Mrs. Crick, and two of the milkmaids.

Tess sprang like an elastic ball from his side to her feet, while her face flushed and her eyes shone in the firelight.

'I knew how it would be if I sat so close to him!' she cried, with vexation. 'I said to myself, they are sure to come and catch us! But I wasn't really sitting on his knee, though it might ha' seemed as if I was almost!'

'Well — if so be you hadn't told us, I am sure we shouldn't ha' noticed that ye had been sitting anywhere at all in this light,' replied the dairyman. He continued to his wife, with the stolid mien of a man who understood nothing of the emotions relating to matrimony — 'Now, Christianer, that shows that folks should never fancy other folks be supposing things when they bain't. O no, I should never ha' thought a word of where she was a sitting to, if she hadn't told me — not I.'

'We are going to be married soon,' said Clare, with improvised phlegm.

'Ah — and be ye! Well, I am truly glad to hear it, sir. I've thought you mid do such a thing for some time. She's too good for a dairy-maid — I said so the very first day I zid her — and a prize for any man; and what's more, a wonderful woman for a gentleman-farmer's wife; he won't be at the mercy of his baily° wi' her at his side.'

baily: Bailiff; in England, a steward or manager of a farm or estate.

Somehow Tess disappeared. She had been even more struck with the look of the girls who followed Crick than abashed by Crick's blunt praise.

After supper, when she reached her bedroom, they were all present. A light was burning, and each damsel was sitting up whitely in her bed, awaiting Tess, the whole like a row of avenging ghosts.

But she saw in a few moments that there was no malice in their mood. They could scarcely feel as a loss what they had never expected to have. Their condition was objective, contemplative.

'He's going to marry her!' murmured Retty, never taking eyes off Tess. 'How her face do show it!'

'You *be* going to marry him?' asked Marian.

'Yes,' said Tess.

'When?'

'Some day.'

They thought that this was evasiveness only.

'*Yes* — going to *marry* him — a gentleman!' repeated Izz Huett.

And by a sort of fascination the three girls, one after another, crept out of their beds, and came and stood barefooted round Tess. Retty put her hands upon Tess's shoulders, as if to realize her friend's corporeality after such a miracle, and the other two laid their arms round her waist, all looking into her face.

'How it do seem! Almost more than I can think of!' said Izz Huett.

Marian kissed Tess. 'Yes,' she murmured as she withdrew her lips.

'Was that because of love for her, or because other lips have touched there by now?' continued Izz drily to Marian.

'I wasn't thinking o' that,' said Marian simply. 'I was on'y feeling the strangeness o't — that she is to be his wife, and nobody else. I don't say nay to it, nor either of us, because we did not think of it — only loved him. Still, nobody else is to marry'n in the world — no fine lady, nobody in silks and satins; but she who do live like we.'

'Are you sure you don't dislike me for it?' said Tess in a low voice.

They hung about her in their white nightgowns before replying, as if they considered their answer might lie in her look.

'I don't know — I don't know,' murmured Retty Priddle. 'I want to hate 'ee; but I cannot!'

'That's how I feel,' echoed Izz and Marian. 'I can't hate her. Somehow she hinders me!'

'He ought to marry one of you,' murmured Tess.

'Why?'

'You are all better than I.'

'We better than you?' said the girls in a low, slow whisper. 'No, no, dear Tess!'

'You are!' she contradicted impetuously. And suddenly tearing away from their clinging arms she burst into a hysterical fit of tears, bowing herself on the chest of drawers and repeating incessantly, 'O yes, yes, yes!'

Having once given way she could not stop her weeping.

'He ought to have had one of you!' she cried. 'I think I ought to make him even now! You would be better for him than — I don't know what I'm saying! O! O!'

They went up to her and clasped her round, but still her sobs tore her.

'Get some water,' said Marian. 'She's upset by us, poor thing, poor thing!'

They gently led her back to the side of her bed, where they kissed her warmly.

'You are best for'n,' said Marian. 'More ladylike, and a better scholar than we, especially since he has taught 'ee so much. But even you ought to be proud. You *be* proud, I'm sure!'

'Yes, I am,' she said; 'and I am ashamed at so breaking down!'

When they were all in bed, and the light was out, Marian whispered across to her —

'You will think of us when you be his wife, Tess, and of how we told 'ee that we loved him, and how we tried not to hate you, and did not hate you, and could not hate you, because you were his choice, and we never hoped to be chose by him.'

They were not aware that, at these words, salt, stinging tears trickled down upon Tess's pillow anew, and how she resolved, with a bursting heart, to tell all her history to Angel Clare, despite her mother's command — to let him for whom she lived and breathed despise her if he would, and her mother regard her as a fool, rather than preserve a silence which might be deemed a treachery to him, and which somehow seemed a wrong to these.

XXXII

This penitential mood kept her from naming the wedding-day. The beginning of November found its date still in abeyance, though he asked her at the most tempting times. But Tess's desire seemed to be for a perpetual betrothal in which everything should remain as it was then.

The meads were changing now; but it was still warm enough in early afternoons before milking to idle there awhile, and the state of dairy-work at this time of year allowed a spare hour for idling. Looking over the damp sod in the direction of the sun, a glistening ripple of gossamer webs was visible to their eyes under the luminary, like the track of moonlight on the sea. Gnats, knowing nothing of their brief glorification, wandered across the shimmer of this pathway, irradiated as if they bore fire within them, then passed out of its line, and were quite extinct. In the presence of these things he would remind her that the date was still the question.

Or he would ask her at night, when he accompanied her on some mission invented by Mrs. Crick to give him the opportunity. This was mostly a journey to the farmhouse on the slopes above the vale, to inquire how the advanced cows were getting on in the straw-barton to which they were relegated. For it was a time of the year that brought great changes to the world of kine. Batches of the animals were sent away daily to this lying-in hospital, where they lived on straw till their calves were born, after which event, and as soon as the calf could walk, mother and offspring were driven back to the dairy. In the interval which elapsed before the calves were sold there was, of course, little milking to be done, but as soon as the calf had been taken away the milkmaids would have to set to work as usual.

Returning from one of these dark walks they reached a great gravel-cliff immediately over the levels, where they stood still and listened. The water was now high in the streams, squirting through the weirs, and tinkling under culverts; the smallest gullies were all full; there was no taking short cuts anywhere, and foot-passengers were compelled to follow the permanent ways. From the whole extent of the invisible vale came a multitudinous intonation; it forced upon their fancy that a great city lay below them, and that the murmur was the vociferation of its populace.

'It seems like tens of thousands of them,' said Tess; 'holding public-meetings in their market-places, arguing, preaching, quarrelling, sobbing, groaning, praying, and cursing.'

Clare was not particularly heeding.

'Did Crick speak to you to-day, dear, about his not wanting much assistance during the winter months?'

'No.'

'The cows are going dry rapidly.'

'Yes. Six or seven went to the straw-barton yesterday, and three the day before, making nearly twenty in the straw already. Ah — is it that the farmer don't want my help for the calving? O, I am not wanted here any more! And I have tried so hard to ——'

'Crick didn't exactly say that he would no longer require you. But, knowing what our relations were, he said in the most good-natured and respectful manner possible that he supposed on my leaving at Christmas I should take you with me, and on my asking what he would do without you he merely observed that, as a matter of fact, it was a time of year when he could do with a very little female help. I am afraid I was sinner enough to feel rather glad that he was in this way forcing your hand.'

'I don't think you ought to have felt glad, Angel. Because 'tis always mournful not to be wanted, even if at the same time 'tis convenient.'

'Well, it is convenient — you have admitted that.' He put his finger upon her cheek. 'Ah!' he said.

'What?'

'I feel the red rising up at her having been caught! But why should I trifle so! We will not trifle — life is too serious.'

'It is. Perhaps I saw that before you did.'

She was seeing it then. To decline to marry him after all — in obedience to her emotion of last night — and leave the dairy, meant to go to some strange place, not a dairy; for milkmaids were not in request now calving-time was coming on; to go to some arable farm where no divine being like Angel Clare was. She hated the thought, and she hated more the thought of going home.

'So that, seriously, dearest Tess,' he continued, 'since you will probably have to leave at Christmas, it is in every way desirable and convenient that I should carry you off then as my property. Besides, if you were not the most uncalculating girl in the world you would know that we could not go on like this for ever.'

'I wish we could. That it would always be summer and autumn, and you always courting me, and always thinking as much of me as you have done through the past summer-time!'

'I always shall.'

'O, I know you will!' she cried, with a sudden fervour of faith in him. 'Angel, I will fix the day when I will become yours for always!'

Thus at last it was arranged between them, during that dark walk home, amid the myriads of liquid voices on the right and left.

When they reached the dairy Mr. and Mrs. Crick were promptly told — with injunctions to secrecy; for each of the lovers was desirous that the marriage should be kept as private as possible. The dairyman, though he had thought of dismissing her soon, now made a great concern about losing her. What should he do about his skimming? Who would make the ornamental butter-pats for the Anglebury and Sandbourne ladies? Mrs. Crick congratulated Tess on the shilly-shallying having at last come to an end, and said that directly she set eyes on Tess she divined that she was to be the chosen one of somebody who was no common outdoor man; Tess had looked so superior as she walked across the barton on that afternoon of her arrival; that she was of a good family she could have sworn. In point of fact Mrs. Crick did remember thinking that Tess was graceful and good-looking as she approached; but the superiority might have been a growth of the imagination aided by subsequent knowledge.

Tess was now carried along upon the wings of the hours, without the sense of a will. The word had been given; the number of the day written down. Her naturally bright intelligence had begun to admit the fatalistic convictions common to field-folk and those who associate more extensively with natural phenomena than with their fellow-creatures; and she accordingly drifted into that passive responsiveness to all things her lover suggested, characteristic of the frame of mind.

But she wrote anew to her mother, ostensibly to notify the wedding-day; really to again implore her advice. It was a gentleman who had chosen her, which perhaps her mother had not sufficiently considered. A post-nuptial explanation, which might be accepted with a light heart by a rougher man, might not be received with the same feeling by him. But this communication brought no reply from Mrs. Durbeyfield.

Despite Angel Clare's plausible representations to himself and to Tess of the practical need for their immediate marriage, there was in truth an element of precipitancy in the step, as became apparent at a later date. He loved her dearly, though perhaps rather ideally and fancifully than with the impassioned thoroughness of her feeling for him. He had entertained no notion, when doomed as he had thought to an unintellectual bucolic life, that such charms as he beheld in this idyllic creature would be found behind the scenes. Unsophistication was a thing to talk of; but he had not known how it really struck one until he came here. Yet he was very far from seeing his future track clearly, and it might be a year or two before he would be able to consider himself fairly started in life. The secret lay in the tinge of recklessness imparted to his career and character by the sense that he had been made to miss his true destiny through the prejudices of his family.

'Don't you think 'twould have been better for us to wait till you were quite settled in your midland farm?' she once asked timidly. (A midland farm was the idea just then.)

'To tell the truth, my Tess, I don't like you to be left anywhere away from my protection and sympathy.'

The reason was a good one, so far as it went. His influence over her had been so marked that she had caught his manner and habits, his speech and phrases, his likings and his aversions. And to leave her in farmland would be to let her slip back again out of accord with him. He wished to have her under his charge for another reason. His parents had naturally desired to see her once at least before he carried her off to a distant settlement, English or colonial; and as no opinion of theirs was to be allowed to change his intention, he judged that a couple of months' life with him in lodgings whilst seeking for an advantageous opening would be of some social assistance to her at what she might feel to be a trying ordeal — her presentation to his mother at the Vicarage.

Next, he wished to see a little of the working of a flour-mill, having an idea that he might combine the use of one with corn-growing. The proprietor of a large old water-mill at Wellbridge — once the mill of an Abbey — had offered him the inspection of his time-honoured mode of procedure, and a hand in the operations for a few days, whenever he should choose to come. Clare paid a visit to the place, some few miles distant, one day at this time, to inquire particulars, and returned to Talbothays in the evening. She found him determined to spend a short time at the Wellbridge flour-mills. And what had determined him? Less the opportunity of an insight into grinding and bolting° than the casual fact that lodgings were to be obtained in that very farmhouse which, before its mutilation, had been the mansion of a branch of the d'Urberville family. This was always how Clare settled practical questions; by a sentiment which had nothing to do with them. They decided to go immediately after the wedding, and remain for a fortnight, instead of journeying to towns and inns.

'Then we will start off to examine some farms on the other side of London that I have heard of,' he said, 'and by March or April we will pay a visit to my father and mother.'

Questions of procedure such as these arose and passed, and the day, the incredible day, on which she was to become his, loomed large in the near future. The thirty-first of December, New Year's Eve, was the date. His wife, she said to herself. Could it ever be? Their two

bolting: Passing of ground material, such as flour, through a sieve.

selves together, nothing to divide them, every incident shared by them; why not? And yet why?

One Sunday morning Izz Huett returned from church, and spoke privately to Tess.

'You was not called home[1] this morning.'

'What?'

'It should ha' been the first time of asking to-day,' she answered, looking quietly at Tess. 'You meant to be married New Year's Eve, deary?'

The other returned a quick affirmative.

'And there must be three times of asking. And now there be only two Sundays left between.'

Tess felt her cheek paling; Izz was right; of course there must be three. Perhaps he had forgotten! If so, there must be a week's postponement, and that was unlucky. How could she remind her lover? She who had been so backward was suddenly fired with impatience and alarm lest she should lose her dear prize.

A natural incident relieved her anxiety. Izz mentioned the omission of the banns to Mrs. Crick, and Mrs. Crick assumed a matron's privilege of speaking to Angel on the point.

'Have ye forgot 'em, Mr. Clare? The banns, I mean.'

'No, I have not forgot 'em,' says Clare.

As soon as he caught Tess alone he assured her:

'Don't let them tease you about the banns. A licence° will be quieter for us, and I have decided on a licence without consulting you. So if you go to church on Sunday morning you will not hear your own name, if you wished to.'

'I didn't wish to hear it, dearest,' she said proudly.

But to know that things were in train was an immense relief to Tess notwithstanding, who had well-nigh feared that somebody would stand up and forbid the banns on the ground of her history. How events were favouring her!

'I don't quite feel easy,' she said to herself. 'All this good fortune may be scourged out of me afterwards by a lot of ill. That's how Heaven mostly does. I wish I could have had common banns!'

But everything went smoothly. She wondered whether he would like her to be married in her present best white frock, or if she ought

[1]'Called home' — local phrase for publication of banns [Hardy's note].
licence: Written permission from a bishop in place of banns.

to buy a new one. The question was set at rest by his forethought, disclosed by the arrival of some large packages addressed to her. Inside them she found a whole stock of clothing, from bonnet to shoes, including a perfect morning costume, such as would well suit the simple wedding they planned. He entered the house shortly after the arrival of the packages, and heard her upstairs undoing them.

A minute later she came down with a flush on her face and tears in her eyes.

'How thoughtful you've been!' she murmured, her cheek upon his shoulder. 'Even to the gloves and handkerchief! My own love — how good, how kind!'

'No, no, Tess; just an order to a tradeswoman in London — nothing more.'

And to divert her from thinking too highly of him he told her to go upstairs, and take her time, and see if it all fitted; and, if not, to get the village sempstress to make a few alterations.

She did return upstairs, and put on the gown. Alone, she stood for a moment before the glass looking at the effect of her silk attire; and then there came into her head her mother's ballad of the mystic robe° —

That never would become that wife
  That had once done amiss,

which Mrs. Durbeyfield had used to sing to her as a child, so blithely and so archly, her foot on the cradle, which she rocked to the tune. Suppose this robe should betray her by changing colour, as her robe had betrayed Queen Guénever. Since she had been at the dairy she had not once thought of the lines till now.

XXXIII

Angel felt that he would like to spend a day with her before the wedding, somewhere away from the dairy, as a last jaunt in her company while they were yet mere lover and mistress; a romantic day, in circumstances that would never be repeated; with that other and greater day beaming close ahead of them. During the preceding week, therefore, he suggested making a few purchases in the nearest town, and they started together.

her mother's ballad of the mystic robe: "The Boy and the Mantle," in which a robe betrays Queen Guénever, the wife of King Arthur.

Clare's life at the dairy had been that of a recluse in respect to the world of his own class. For months he had never gone near a town, and, requiring no vehicle, had never kept one, hiring the dairyman's cob or gig if he rode or drove. They went in the gig that day.

And then for the first time in their lives they shopped as partners in one concern. It was Christmas Eve, with its loads of holly and mistletoe, and the town was very full of strangers who had come in from all parts of the country on account of the day. Tess paid the penalty of walking about with happiness superadded to beauty on her countenance by being much stared at as she moved amid them on his arm.

In the evening they returned to the inn at which they had put up, and Tess waited in the entry while Angel went to see the horse and gig brought to the door. The general sitting-room was full of guests, who were continually going in and out. As the door opened and shut each time for the passage of these, the light within the parlour fell upon Tess's face. Two men came out and passed by her among the rest. One of them had stared her up and down in surprise, and she fancied he was a Traintridge man, though that village lay so many miles off that Trantridge folk were rarities here.

'A comely maid that,' said the other.

'True, comely enough. But unless I make a great mistake —— ' And he negatived the remainder of the definition forthwith.

Clare had just returned from the stable-yard, and, confronting the man on the threshold, heard the words, and saw the shrinking of Tess. The insult to her stung him to the quick, and before he had considered anything at all he struck the man on the chin with the full force of his fist, sending him staggering backwards into the passage.

The man recovered himself, and seemed inclined to come on, and Clare, stepping outside the door, put himself in a posture of defence. But his opponent began to think better of the matter. He looked anew at Tess as he passed her, and said to Clare —

'I beg pardon, sir; 'twas a complete mistake. I thought she was another woman, forty miles from here.'

Clare, feeling then that he had been too hasty, and that he was, moreover, to blame for leaving her standing in an inn-passage, did what he usually did in such cases, gave the man five shillings to plaster the blow; and thus they parted, bidding each other a pacific good-night. As soon as Clare had taken the reins from the ostler, and the young couple had driven off, the two men went in the other direction.

'And was it a mistake?' said the second one.

'Not a bit of it. But I didn't want to hurt the gentleman's feelings — not I.'

In the meantime the lovers were driving onward.

'Could we put off our wedding till a little later?' Tess asked in a dry dull voice. 'I mean if we wished?'

'No, my love. Calm yourself. Do you mean that the fellow may have time to summon me for assault?' he asked good-humouredly.

'No — I only meant — if it should have to be put off.'

What she meant was not very clear, and he directed her to dismiss such fancies from her mind, which she obediently did as well as she could. But she was grave, very grave, all the way home; till she thought, 'We shall go away, a very long distance, hundreds of miles from these parts, and such as this can never happen again, and no ghost of the past reach there.'

They parted tenderly that night on the landing, and Clare ascended to his attic. Tess sat up getting on with some little requisites, lest the few remaining days should not afford sufficient time. While she sat she head a noise in Angel's room overhead, a sound of thumping and struggling. Everybody else in the house was asleep, and in her anxiety lest Clare should be ill she ran up and knocked at his door, and asked him what was the matter.

'Oh, nothing, dear,' he said from within. 'I am so sorry I disturbed you! But the reason is rather an amusing one: I fell asleep and dreamt that I was fighting that fellow again who insulted you and the noise you heard was my pummeling away with my fists at my portmanteau, which I pulled out to-day for packing. I am occasionally liable to these freaks in my sleep. Go to bed and think of it no more.'

This was the last drachm required to turn the scale of her indecision. Declare the past to him by word of mouth she could not; but there was another way. She sat down and wrote on the four pages of a note-sheet a succinct narrative of those events of three or four years ago, put it into an envelope, and directed it to Clare. Then, lest the flesh should again be weak, she crept upstairs without any shoes and slipped the note under his door.

Her night was a broken one, as it well might be, and she listened for the first faint noise overhead. It came, as usual; he descended, as usual. She descended. He met her at the bottom of the stairs and kissed her. Surely it was as warmly as ever!

He looked a little disturbed and worn, she thought. But he said not a word to her about her revelation, even when they were alone.

Could he have had it? Unless he began the subject she felt that she could say nothing. So the day passed, and it was evident that whatever he thought he meant to keep to himself. Yet he was frank and affectionate as before. Could it be that her doubts were childish? that he forgave her; that he loved her for what she was, just as she was, and smiled at her disquiet as at a foolish nightmare? Had he really received her note? She glanced into his room, and could see nothing of it. It might be that he forgave her. But even if he had not received it she had a sudden enthusiastic trust that he surely would forgive her.

Every morning and night he was the same, and thus New Year's Eve broke — the wedding-day.

The lovers did not rise at milking-time, having through the whole of this last week of their sojourn at the dairy been accorded something of the position of guests, Tess being honoured with a room of her own. When they arrived downstairs at breakfast-time they were surprised to see what effects had been produced in the large kitchen for their glory since they had last beheld it. At some unnatural hour of the morning the dairyman had caused the yawning chimney-corner to be whitened, and the brick hearth reddened, and a blazing yellow damask blower to be hung across the arch in place of the old grimy blue cotton one with a black spring pattern which had formerly done duty here. This renovated aspect of what was the focus indeed of the room on a dull winter morning, threw a smiling demeanour over the whole apartment.

'I was determined to do summat in honour o't,' said the dairyman. 'And as you wouldn't hear of my gieing a rattling good randy wi' fiddles and bass-viols complete, as we should ha' done in old times, this was all I could think o' as a noiseless thing.'

Tess's friends lived so far off that none could conveniently have been present at the ceremony, even had any been asked; but as a fact nobody was invited from Marlott. As for Angel's family, he had written and duly informed them of the time, and assured them that he would be glad to see one at least of them there for the day if he would like to come. His brothers had not replied at all, seeming to be indignant with him; while his father and mother had written a rather sad letter, deploring his precipitancy in rushing into marriage, but making the best of the matter by saying that, though a dairywoman was the last daughter-in-law they could have expected, their son had arrived at an age at which he might be supposed to be the best judge.

This coolness in his relations distressed Clare less than it would have done had he been without the grand card with which he meant to surprise them ere long. To produce Tess, fresh from the dairy, as a d'Urberville and a lady, he had felt to be temerarious and risky; hence he had concealed her lineage till such time as, familiarized with worldly ways by a few months' travel and reading with him, he could take her on a visit to his parents, and impart the knowledge while triumphantly producing her as worthy of such an ancient line. It was a pretty lover's dream, if no more. Perhaps Tess's lineage had more value for himself than for anybody in the world besides.

Her perception that Angel's bearing towards her still remained in no whit altered by her own communication rendered Tess guiltily doubtful if he could have received it. She rose from breakfast before he had finished, and hastened upstairs. It had occurred to her to look once more into the queer gaunt room which had been Clare's den, or rather eyrie, for so long, and climbing the ladder she stood at the open door of the apartment, regarding and pondering. She stooped to the threshold of the doorway, where she had pushed in the note two or three days earlier in such excitement. The carpet reached close to the sill, and under the edge of the carpet she discerned the faint white margin of the envelope containing her letter to him, which he obviously had never seen, owing to her having in her haste thrust it beneath the carpet as well as beneath the door.

With a feeling of faintness she withdrew the letter. There it was — sealed up, just as it had left her hands. The mountain had not yet been removed. She could not let him read it now, the house being in full bustle of preparation; and descending to her own room she destroyed the letter there.

She was so pale when he saw her again that he felt quite anxious. The incident of the misplaced letter she had jumped at as if it prevented a confession; but she knew in her conscience that it need not; there was still time. Yet everything was in a stir; there was coming and going; all had to dress, the dairyman and Mrs. Crick having been asked to accompany them as witnesses; and reflection or deliberate talk was well-nigh impossible. The only minute Tess could get to be alone with Clare was when they met upon the landing.

'I am so anxious to talk to you — I want to confess all my faults and blunders!' she said with attempted lightness.

'No, no — we can't have faults talked of — you must be deemed perfect to-day at least, my Sweet!' he cried. 'We shall have plenty of time, hereafter, I hope, to talk over our failings. I will confess mine at the same time.'

'But it would be better for me to do it now, I think, so that you could not say —— '

'Well, my quixotic one, you shall tell me anything — say, as soon as we are settled in our lodging; not now. I, too, will tell you my faults then. But do not let us spoil the day with them; they will be excellent matter for a dull time.'

'Then you don't wish me to, dearest?'

'I do not, Tessy, really.'

The hurry of dressing and starting left no time for more than this. Those words of his seemed to reassure her on further reflection. She was whirled onward through the next couple of critical hours by the mastering tide of her devotion to him, which closed up further meditation. Her one desire, so long resisted, to make herself his, to call him her lord, her own — then, if necessary, to die — had at last lifted her up from her plodding reflective pathway. In dressing, she moved about in a mental cloud of many-coloured idealities, which eclipsed all sinister contingencies by its brightness.

The church was a long way off, and they were obliged to drive, particularly as it was winter. A close carriage was ordered from a roadside inn, a vehicle which had been kept there ever since the old days of post-chaise travelling. It had stout wheel-spokes, and heavy felloes,° a great curved bed, immense straps and springs, and a pole like a battering-ram. The postilion was a venerable 'boy' of sixty — a martyr to rheumatic gout, the result of excessive exposure in youth, counteracted by strong liquors — who had stood at inn-doors doing nothing for the whole five-and-twenty years that had elapsed since he had no longer been required to ride professionally, as if expecting the old times to come back again. He had a permanent running wound on the outside of his right leg, originated by the constant bruisings of aristocratic carriage-poles during the many years that he had been in regular employ at the King's Arms, Casterbridge.

Inside this cumbrous and creaking structure, and behind this decayed conductor, the *partie carrée*° took their seats — the bride and bridegroom and Mr. and Mrs. Crick. Angel would have liked one at least of his brothers to be present as groomsman, but their silence after his gentle hint to that affect by letter had signified that they did not care to come. They disapproved of the marriage, and could not be expected to countenance it. Perhaps it was as well that they could not be present. They were not worldly young fellows, but fraternizing with dairy-folk would have struck unpleasantly upon their biassed niceness, apart from their views of the match.

felloes: Sections of the wheels' rims. ***partie carrée:*** Party of four (Fr.).

Upheld by the momentum of the time Tess knew nothing of this; did not see anything; did not know the road they were taking to the church. She knew that Angel was close to her; all the rest was a luminous mist. She was a sort of celestial person, who owed her being to poetry — one of those classical divinities Clare was accustomed to talk to her about when they took their walks together.

The marriage being by licence there were only a dozen or so of people in the church; had there been a thousand they would have produced no more effect upon her. They were at stellar distances from her present world. In the ecstatic solemnity with which she swore her faith to him the ordinary sensibilities of sex seemed a flippancy. At a pause in the service, while they were kneeling together, she unconsciously inclined herself towards him, so that her shoulder touched his arm; she had been frightened by a passing thought, and the movement had been automatic, to assure herself that he was really there, and to fortify her belief that his fidelity would be proof against all things.

Clare knew that she loved him — every curve of her form showed that — but he did not know at that time the full depth of her devotion, its single-mindedness, its meekness; what long-suffering it guaranteed, what honesty, what endurance, what good faith.

As they came out of church the ringers swung the bells off their rests, and a modest peal of three notes broke forth — that limited amount of expression having been deemed sufficient by the church builders for the joys of such a small parish. Passing by the tower with her husband on the path to the gate she could feel the vibrant air humming round them from the louvered belfry in a circle of sound, and it matched the highly-charged mental atmosphere in which she was living.

This condition of mind, wherein she felt glorified by an irradiation not her own, like the angel whom St. John saw in the sun,° lasted till the sound of the church bells had died away, and the emotions of the wedding-service had calmed down. Her eyes could dwell upon details more clearly now, and Mr. and Mrs. Crick having directed their own gig to be sent for them, to leave the carriage to the young couple, she observed the build and character of that conveyance for the first time. Sitting in silence she regarded it long.

'I fancy you seem oppressed, Tessy,' said Clare.

'Yes,' she answered, putting her hand to her brow. 'I tremble at many things. It is all so serious, Angel. Among other things I seem to

the angel . . . : Revelation 19.17.

have seen this carriage before, to be very well acquainted with it. It is very odd — I must have seen it in a dream.'

'Oh — you have heard the legend of the d'Urberville Coach — that well-known superstition of this county about your family when they were very popular here; and this lumbering old thing reminds you of it.'

'I have never heard of it to my knowledge,' said she. 'What is the legend — may I know it?'

'Well — I would rather not tell it in detail just now. A certain d'Urberville of the sixteenth or seventeenth century committed a dreadful crime in his family coach; and since that time members of the family see or hear the old coach whenever —— But I'll tell you another day — it is rather gloomy. Evidently some dim knowledge of it has been brought back to your mind by the sight of this venerable caravan.'

'I don't remember hearing it before,' she murmured. 'Is it when we are going to die, Angel, that members of my family see it, or is it when we have committed a crime?'

'Now, Tess!'

He silenced her by a kiss.

By the time they reached home she was contrite and spiritless. She was Mrs. Angel Clare, indeed, but had she any moral right to the name? Was she not more truly Mrs. Alexander d'Urberville? Could intensity of love justify what might be considered in upright souls as culpable reticence? She knew not what was expected of women in such cases; and she had no counsellor.

However, when she found herself alone in her room for a few minutes — the last day this on which she was ever to enter it — she knelt down and prayed. She tried to pray to God, but it was her husband who really had her supplication. Her idolatry of this man was such that she herself almost feared it to be ill-omened. She was conscious of the notion expressed by Friar Laurence:° 'These violent delights have violent ends.' It might be too desperate for human conditions — too rank, too wild, too deadly.

'O my love, my love, why do I love you so!' she whispered there alone; 'for she you love is not my real self, but one in my image; the one I might have been!'

Afternoon came, and with it the hour for departure. They had decided to fulfil the plan of going for a few days to the lodgings in the old farmhouse near Wellbridge Mill, at which he meant to reside dur-

Friar Laurence: *Romeo and Juliet* 2.6.9.

ing his investigation of flour processes. At two o'clock there was nothing left to do but to start. All the servantry of the dairy were standing in the red-brick entry to see them go out, the dairyman and his wife following to the door. Tess saw her three chamber-mates in a row against the wall, pensively inclining their heads. She had much questioned if they would appear at the parting moment; but there they were, stoical and staunch to the last. She knew why the delicate Retty looked so fragile, and Izz so tragically sorrowful, and Marian so blank; and she forgot her own dogging shadow for a moment in contemplating theirs.

She impulsively whispered to him —

'Will you kiss 'em all, once, poor things, for the first and last time?'

Clare had not the least objection to such a farewell formality — which was all that it was to him — and as he passed them he kissed them in succession where they stood, saying 'Good-bye' to each as he did so. When they reached the door Tess femininely glanced back to discern the effect of that kiss of charity; there was no triumph in her glance, as there might have been. If there had it would have disappeared when she saw how moved the girls all were. The kiss had obviously done harm by awakening feelings they were trying to subdue.

Of all this Clare was unconscious. Passing on to the wicket-gate he shook hands with the dairyman and his wife, and expressed his last thanks to them for their attentions; after which there was a moment of silence before they had moved off. It was interrupted by the crowing of a cock. The white one with the rose comb had come and settled on the palings in front of the house, within a few yards of them, and his notes thrilled their ears through, dwindling away like echoes down a valley of rocks.

'Oh?' said Mrs. Crick. 'An afternoon crow!'

Two men were standing by the yard gate, holding it open.

'That's bad,' one murmured to the other, not thinking that the words could be heard by the group at the door-wicket.

The cock crew again — straight towards Clare.

'Well!' said the dairyman.

'I don't like to hear him!' said Tess to her husband. 'Tell the man to drive on. Good-bye, good-bye!'

The cock crew again.

'Hoosh! Just you be off, sir, or I'll twist your neck!' said the dairyman with some irritation, turning to the bird and driving him away. And to his wife as they went indoors: 'Now, to think o' that just today! I've not heard his crow of an afternoon all the year afore.'

'It only means a change in the weather,' said she; 'not what you think: 'tis impossible!'

XXXIV

They drove by the level road along the valley to a distance of a few miles, and, reaching Wellbridge, turned away from the village to the left, and over the great Elizabethan bridge which gives the place half its name. Immediately behind it stood the house wherein they had engaged lodgings, whose exterior features are so well known to all travellers through the Froom Valley; once portion of a fine manorial residence, and the property and seat of a d'Urberville, but since its partial demolition a farm-house.

'Welcome to one of your ancestral mansions!' said Clare as he handed her down. But he regretted the pleasantry; it was too near a satire.

On entering they found that, though they had only engaged a couple of rooms, the farmer had taken advantage of their proposed presence during the coming days to pay a New Year's visit to some friends, leaving a woman from a neighbouring cottage to minister to their few wants. The absoluteness of possession pleased them, and they realized it as the first moment of their experience under their own exclusive roof-tree.

But he found that the mouldy old habitation somewhat depressed his bride. When the carriage was gone they ascended the stairs to wash their hands, the charwoman showing the way. On the landing Tess stopped and started.

'What's the matter?' said he.

'Those horrid women!' she answered, with a smile. 'How they frightened me.'

He looked up, and perceived two life-size portraits on panels built into the masonry. As all visitors to the mansion are aware, these paintings represent women of middle age, of a date some two hundred years ago, whose lineaments once seen can never be forgotten. The long pointed features, narrow eye, and smirk of the one, so suggestive of merciless treachery; the bill-hook nose, large teeth, and bold eye of the other, suggesting arrogance to the point of ferocity, haunt the beholder afterwards in his dreams.

'Whose portraits are those?' asked Clare of the charwoman.

'I have been told by old folk that they were ladies of the

d'Urberville family, the ancient lords of this manor,' she said. 'Owing to their being builded into the wall they can't be moved away.'

The unpleasantness of the matter was that, in addition to their effect upon Tess, her fine features were unquestionably traceable in these exaggerated forms. He said nothing of this, however, and, regretting that he had gone out of his way to choose the house for their bridal time, went on into the adjoining room. The place having been rather hastily prepared for them they washed their hands in one basin. Clare touched hers under the water.

'Which are my fingers and which are yours?' he said, looking up. 'They are very much mixed.'

'They are all yours,' said she, very prettily, and endeavoured to be gayer than she was. He had not been displeased with her thoughtfulness on such an occasion; it was what every sensible woman would show: but Tess knew that she had been thoughtful to excess, and struggled against it.

The sun was so low on that short last afternoon of the year that it shone in through a small opening and formed a golden staff which stretched across to her skirt, where it made a spot like a paint-mark set upon her. They went into the ancient parlour to tea, and here they shared their first common meal alone. Such was their childishness, or rather his, that he found it interesting to use the same bread-and-butter plate as herself, and to brush crumbs from her lips with his own. He wondered a little that she did not enter into these frivolities with his own zest.

Looking at her silently for a long time; 'She is a dear dear Tess,' he thought to himself, as one deciding on the true construction of a difficult passage. 'Do I realize solemnly enough how utterly and irretrievably this little womanly thing is the creature of my good or bad faith and fortune? I think not. I think I could not, unless I were a woman myself. What I am in worldly estate, she is. What I become, she must become. What I cannot be, she cannot be. And shall I ever neglect her, or hurt her, or even forget to consider her? God forbid such a crime!'

They sat on over the tea-table waiting for their luggage, which the dairyman had promised to send before it grew dark. But evening began to close in, and the luggage did not arrive, and they had brought nothing more than they stood in. With the departure of the sun the calm mood of the winter day changed. Out of doors there began noises as of silk smartly rubbed; the restful dead leaves of the preceding autumn were stirred to irritated resurrection, and whirled about unwillingly, and tapped against the shutters. It soon began to rain.

'That cock knew the weather was going to change,' said Clare.

The woman who had attended upon them had gone home for the night, but she had placed candles upon the table, and now they lit them. Each candle-flame drew towards the fireplace.

'These old houses are so draughty,' continued Angel, looking at the flames, and at the grease guttering down the sides. 'I wonder where that luggage is. We haven't even a brush and comb.'

'I don't know,' she answered, absent-minded.

'Tess, you are not a bit cheerful this evening — not at all as you used to be. Those harridans on the panels upstairs have unsettled you. I am sorry I brought you here. I wonder if you really love me, after all?'

He knew that she did, and the words had no serious intent; but she was surcharged with emotion, and winced like a wounded animal. Though she tried not to shed tears she could not help showing one or two.

'I did not mean it!' said he, sorry. 'You are worried at not having your things, I know. I cannot think why old Jonathan has not come with them. Why, it is seven o'clock? Ah, there he is!'

A knock had come to the door, and, there being nobody else to answer it Clare went out. He returned to the room with a small package in his hand.

'It is not Jonathan, after all,' he said.

'How vexing!' said Tess.

The packet had been brought by a special messenger, who had arrived at Talbothays from Emminster Vicarage immediately after the departure of the married couple, and had followed them hither, being under injunction to deliver it into nobody's hands but theirs. Clare brought it to the light. It was less than a foot long, sewed up in canvas, sealed in red wax with his father's seal, and directed in his father's hand to 'Mrs. Angel Clare.'

'It is a little wedding-present for you, Tess,' said he, handing it to her. 'How thoughtful they are!'

Tess looked a little flustered as she took it.

'I think I would rather have you open it, dearest,' said she, turning over the parcel. 'I don't like to break those great seals; they look so serious. Please open it for me!'

He undid the parcel. Inside was a case of morocco leather, on the top of which lay a note and a key.

The note was for Clare, in the following words:

> My Dear Son, — Possibly you have forgotten that on the death of your godmother, Mrs. Pitney, when you were a lad, she — vain kind woman that she was — left to me a portion of the contents of her jewel-case in trust for your wife, if you should ever have one, as a mark of her affection for you and whomsoever you should choose. This trust I have fulfilled, and the diamonds have been locked up at my banker's ever since. Though I feel it to be a somewhat incongruous act in the circumstances, I am, as you will see, bound to hand over the articles to the woman to whom the use of them for her lifetime will now rightly belong, and they are therefore promptly sent. They become, I believe, heirlooms, strictly speaking, according to the terms of your godmother's will. The precise words of the clause that refers to this matter are enclosed.

'I do remember,' said Clare; 'but I had quite forgotten.'

Unlocking the case, they found it to contain a necklace, with pendant, bracelets, and ear-rings; and also some other small ornaments.

Tess seemed afraid to touch them at first, but her eyes sparkled for a moment as much as the stones when Clare spread out the set.

'Are they mine?' she asked incredulously.

'They are, certainly,' said he.

He looked into the fire. He remembered how, when he was a lad of fifteen, his godmother, the Squire's wife — the only rich person with whom he had ever come in contact — had pinned her faith to his success; had prophesied a wondrous career for him. There had seemed nothing at all out of keeping with such a conjectured career in the storing up of these showy ornaments for his wife and the wives of her descendants. They gleamed somewhat ironically now. 'Yet why?' he asked himself. It was but a question of vanity throughout; and if that were admitted into one side of the equation it should be admitted into the other. His wife was a d'Urberville: whom could they become better than her?

Suddenly he said with enthusiasm —

'Tess, put them on — put them on!' And he turned from the fire to help her.

But as if by magic she had already donned them — necklace, earrings, bracelets, and all.

'But the gown isn't right, Tess,' said Clare. 'It ought to be a low one for a set of brilliants like that.'

'Ought it?' said Tess.

'Yes,' said he.

He suggested to her how to tuck in the upper edge of her bodice, so as to make it roughly approximate to the cut for evening wear; and when she had done this, and the pendant to the necklace hung isolated amid the whiteness of her throat, as it was designed to do, he stepped back to survey her.

'My heavens,' said Clare, 'how beautiful you are!'

As everybody knows, fine feathers make fine birds; a peasant girl but very moderately prepossessing to the casual observer in her simple condition and attire, will bloom as an amazing beauty if clothed as a woman of fashion with the aids that Art can render; while the beauty of the midnight crush° would often cut but a sorry figure if placed inside the field-woman's wrapper upon a monotonous acreage of turnips on a dull day. He had never till now estimated the artistic excellence of Tess's limbs and features.

'If you were only to appear in a ball-room!' he said. 'But no — no, dearest; I think I love you best in the wing-bonnet and cotton-frock — yes, better than in this, well as you support these dignities.'

Tess's sense of her striking appearance had given her a flush of excitement, which was yet not happiness.

'I'll take them off,' she said, 'in case Jonathan should see me. They are not fit for me, are they? They must be sold I suppose?'

'Let them stay a few minutes longer. Sell them? Never. It would be a breach of faith.'

Influenced by a second thought she readily obeyed. She had something to tell, and there might be help in these. She sat down with the jewels upon her; and they again indulged in conjectures as to where Jonathan could possibly be with their baggage. The ale they had poured out for his consumption when he came had gone flat with long standing.

Shortly after this they began supper, which was already laid on a side-table. Ere they had finished there was a jerk in the fire-smoke, the rising skein of which bulged out into the room, as if some giant had laid his hand on the chimney-top for a moment. It had been caused by the opening of the outer door. A heavy step was now heard in the passage, and Angel went out.

crush: Crowded social gathering.

'I couldn' make nobody hear at all by knocking,' apologized Jonathan Kail, for it was he at last; 'and as't was raining out I opened the door. I've brought the things, sir.'

'I am very glad to see them. But you are very late.'

'Well, yes, sir.'

There was something subdued in Jonathan Kail's tone which had not been there in the day, and lines of concern were ploughed upon his forehead in addition to the lines of years. He continued —

'We've all been gallied at the dairy at what might ha' been a most terrible affliction since you and your Mis'ess — so — to name her now — left us this a'ternoon. Perhaps you ha'nt forgot the cock's afternoon crow?'

'Dear me; — what —— '

'Well, some says it do mane one thing, and some another; but what's happened is that poor little Retty Priddle hev tried to drown herself.'

'No! Really! Why, she bade us good-bye with the rest —— '

'Yes. Well, sir, when you and your Mis'ess — so to name what she lawful is — when you two drove away, as I say, Retty and Marian put on their bonnets and went out; and as there is not much doing now, being New Year's Eve, and folks mops and brooms from what's inside 'em, nobody took much notice. They went on to Lew-Everard, where they had summut to drink, and then on they vamped to Dree-armed Cross, and there they seemed to have parted, Retty striking across the water-meads as if for home, and Marian going on to the next village, where there's another public-house. Nothing more was zeed or heard o' Retty till the waterman,° on his way home, noticed something by the Great Pool; 'twas her bonnet and shawl packed up. In the water he found her. He and another man brought her home, thinking 'a was dead; but she fetched round by degrees.'

Angel, suddenly recollecting that Tess was overhearing this gloomy tale, went to shut the door between the passage and the ante-room to the inner parlour where she was; but his wife, flinging a shawl round her, had come to the outer room and was listening to the man's narrative, her eyes resting absently on the luggage and the drops of rain glistening upon it.

'And, more than this, there's Marian; she's been found dead drunk by the withy-bed° — a girl who hev never been known to touch

waterman: A man employed in the supply or distribution of water; e.g., a water-carrier (*OED*). **withy-bed:** Stand of willows.

anything before except shilling ale; though, to be sure, 'a was always a good trencher-woman,° as her face showed. It seems as if the maids had all gone out o' their minds!'

'And Izz?' asked Tess.

'Izz is about house as usual; but 'a do say 'a can guess how it happened; and she seems to be very low in mind about it, poor maid, as well she mid be. And so you see, sir, as all this happened just when we was packing your few traps and your Mis'ess's night-rail and dressing things into the cart, why, it belated me.'

'Yes. Well, Jonathan, will you get the trunks upstairs, and drink a cup of ale, and hasten back as soon as you can, in case you should be wanted?'

Tess had gone back to the inner parlour, and sat down by the fire, looking wistfully into it. She heard Jonathan Kail's heavy footsteps up and down the stairs till he had done placing the luggage, and heard him express his thanks for the ale her husband took out to him, and for the gratuity he received. Jonathan's footsteps then died from the door, and his cart creaked away.

Angel slid forward the massive oak bar which secured the door, and coming in to where she sat over the hearth, pressed her cheeks between his hands from behind. He expected her to jump up gaily and unpack the toilet-gear that she had been so anxious about, but as she did not rise he sat down with her in the firelight, the candles on the supper-table being too thin and glimmering to interfere with its glow.

'I am so sorry you should have heard this sad story about the girls,' he said. 'Still, don't let it depress you. Retty was naturally morbid, you know.'

'Without the least cause,' said Tess. 'While they who have cause to be, hide it, and pretend they are not.'

This incident had turned the scale for her. They were simple and innocent girls on whom the unhappiness of unrequited love had fallen; they had deserved better at the hands of Fate. She had deserved worse — yet she was the chosen one. It was wicked of her to take all without paying. She would pay to the uttermost farthing; she would tell, there and then. This final determination she came to when she looked into the fire, he holding her hand.

A steady glare from the now flameless embers painted the sides and back of the fireplace with its colour, and the well-polished andirons, and the old brass tongs that would not meet. The underside of the

trencher-woman: Woman with a good appetite.

mantel-shelf was flushed with the high-coloured light, and the legs of the table nearest the fire. Tess's face and neck reflected the same warmth, which each gem turned into an Aldebaran or a Sirius° — a constellation of white, red, and green flashes, that interchanged their hues with her every pulsation.

'Do you remember what we said to each other this morning about telling our faults?' he asked abruptly, finding that she still remained immovable. 'We spoke lightly perhaps, and you may well have done so. But for me it was no light promise. I want to make a confession to you, Love.'

This, from him, so unexpectedly apposite, had the effect upon her of a Providential interposition.

'You have to confess something?' she said quickly, and even with gladness and relief.

'You did not expect it? Ah — you thought too highly of me. Now listen. Put your head there, because I want you to forgive me, and not to be indignant with me for not telling you before, as perhaps I ought to have done.'

How strange it was! He seemed to be her double. She did not speak, and Clare went on —

'I did not mention it because I was afraid of endangering my chance of you, darling, the great prize of my life — my Fellowship I call you. My brother's Fellowship was won at his college, mine at Talbothays Dairy. Well, I would not risk it. I was going to tell you a month ago — at the time you agreed to be mine, but I could not; I thought it might frighten you away from me. I put it off; then I thought I would tell you yesterday, to give you a chance at least of escaping me. But I did not. And I did not this morning, when you proposed our confessing our faults on the landing — the sinner that I was! But I must, now I see you sitting there so solemnly. I wonder if you will forgive me?'

'O yes! I am sure that —— '

'Well, I hope so. But wait a minute. You don't know. To begin at the beginning. Though I imagine my poor father fears that I am one of the eternally lost for my doctrines, I am of course, a believer in good morals, Tess, as much as you. I used to wish to be a teacher of men, and it was a great disappointment to me when I found I could not enter the Church. I admired spotlessness, even though I could lay no claim to it, and hated impurity, as I hope I do now. Whatever one

an Aldebaran or a Sirius: Two of the brightest stars in the sky.

may think of plenary inspiration,° one must heartily subscribe to these words of Paul:° "Be thou an example — in word, in conversation, in charity, in spirit, in faith, in purity." It is the only safeguard for us poor human beings. "Integer vitae," says a Roman poet,° who is strange company for St. Paul —

> The man of upright life, from frailities free,
> Stands not in need of Moorish spear or bow.

Well, a certain place is paved with good intentions, and having felt all that so strongly, you will see what a terrible remorse it bred in me when, in the midst of my fine aims for other people, I myself fell.'

He then told her of that time of his life to which allusion has been made when, tossed about by doubts and difficulties in London, like a cork on the waves, he plunged into eight-and-forty hours' dissipation with a stranger.

'Happily I awoke almost immediately to a sense of my folly,' he continued. 'I would have no more to say to her, and I came home. I have never repeated the offence. But I felt I should like to treat you with perfect frankness and honour, and I could not do so without telling this. Do you forgive me?'

She pressed his hand tightly for an answer.

'Then we will dismiss it at once and for ever! — too painful as it is for the occasion — and talk of something lighter.'

'O, Angel — I am almost glad — because now *you* can forgive *me*! I have not made my confession. I have a confession, too — remember, I said so.'

'Ah, to be sure! Now then for it, wicked little one.'

'Perhaps, although you smile, it is as serious as yours, or more so.'

'It can hardly be more serious, dearest.'

'It cannot — O no, it cannot!' She jumped up joyfully at the hope. 'No, it cannot be more serious, certainly,' she cried, 'because 'tis just the same! I will tell you now.'

She sat down again.

Their hands were still joined. The ashes under the grate were lit by the fire vertically, like a torrid waste. Imagination might have beheld a Last Day luridness in this red-coaled glow, which fell on his face and hand, and on hers, peering into the loose hair about her brow, and fir-

plenary inspiration: The absolute truth of the Bible. **words of Paul:** 1 Timothy 4.12. **a Roman poet:** Horace, whose phrase, *Integer vitae,* in an ode is translated in the lines quoted as "upright life."

ing the delicate skin underneath. A large shadow of her shape rose upon the wall and ceiling. She bent forward, at which each diamond on her neck gave a sinister wink like a toad's; and pressing her forehead against his temple she entered on her story of her acquaintance with Alec d'Urberville and its results, murmuring the words without flinching, and with her eyelids drooping down.

End of Phase the Fourth

PHASE THE FIFTH. THE WOMAN PAYS

XXXV

Her narrative ended; even its re-assertions and secondary explanations were done. Tess's voice throughout had hardly risen higher than its opening tone; there had been no exculpatory phrase of any kind, and she had not wept.

But the complexion even of external things seemed to suffer transmutation as her announcement progressed. The fire in the grate looked impish — demoniacally funny, as if it did not care in the least about her strait. The fender grinned idly, as if it too did not care. The light from the water-bottle was merely engaged in a chromatic problem. All material objects around announced their irresponsibility with terrible iteration. And yet nothing had changed since the moments when he had been kissing her; or rather, nothing in the substance of things. But the essence of things had changed.

When she ceased the auricular impressions from their previous endearments seemed to hustle away into the corners of their brains, repeating themselves as echoes from a time of supremely purblind foolishness.

Clare performed the irrelevant act of stirring the fire; the intelligence had not even yet got to the bottom of him. After stirring the embers he rose to his feet; all the force of her disclosure had imparted itself now. His face had withered. In the strenuousness of his concentration he treadled fitfully on the floor. He could not, by any contrivance, think closely enough; that was the meaning of his vague movement. When he spoke it was in the most inadequate, commonplace voice of the many varied tones she had heard from him.

'Tess!'

'Yes, dearest.'

'Am I to believe this? From your manner I am to take it as true. O you cannot be out of your mind! You ought to be! Yet you are not. . . . My wife, my Tess — nothing in you warrants such a supposition as that?'

'I am not out of my mind,' she said.

'And yet —— ' He looked vacantly at her, to resume with dazed senses: 'Why didn't you tell me before? Ah, yes, you would have told me, in a way — but I hindered you, I remember!'

These and other of his words were nothing but the perfunctory babble of the surface while the depths remained paralyzed. He turned away, and bent over a chair. Tess followed him to the middle of the room where he was, and stood there staring at him with eyes that did not weep. Presently she slid down upon her knees beside his foot, and from this position she crouched in a heap.

'In the name of our love, forgive me!' she whispered with a dry mouth. 'I have forgiven you for the same!'

And, as he did not answer, she said again —

'Forgive me as you are forgiven! *I* forgive *you*, Angel.'

'You — yes, you do.'

'But you do not forgive me?'

'O Tess, forgiveness does not apply to the case! You were one person; now you are another. My God — how can forgiveness meet such a grotesque — prestidigitation as that!'

He paused, contemplating this definition; then suddenly broke into horrible laughter — as unnatural and ghastly as a laugh in hell.

'Don't — don't! It kills me quite, that!' she shrieked. 'O have mercy upon me — have mercy!'

He did not answer; and, sickly white, she jumped up.

'Angel, Angel! what do you mean by that laugh?' she cried out. 'Do you know what this is to me?'

He shook his head.

'I have been hoping, longing, praying, to make you happy! I have thought what joy it will be to do it, what an unworthy wife I shall be if I do not! That's what I have felt, Angel!'

'I know that.'

'I thought, Angel, that you loved me — me, my very self! If it is I you do love, O how can it be that you look and speak so? It frightens me! Having begun to love you, I love you for ever — in all changes, in all disgraces, because you are yourself. I ask no more. Then how can you, O my own husband, stop loving me?'

'I repeat, the woman I have been loving is not you.'

'But who?'

'Another woman in your shape.'

She perceived in his words the realization of her own apprehensive foreboding in former times. He looked upon her as a species of impostor; a guilty woman in the guise of an innocent one. Terror was upon her white face as she saw it; her cheek was flaccid, and her mouth had almost the aspect of a round little hole. The horrible sense of his view of her so deadened her that she staggered; and he stepped forward, thinking she was going to fall.

'Sit down, sit down,' he said gently. 'You are ill; and it is natural that you should be.'

She did sit down, without knowing where she was, that strained look still upon her face, and her eyes such as to make his flesh creep.

'I don't belong to you any more, then; do I, Angel?' she asked helplessly. 'It is not me, but another woman like me that he loved, he says.'

The image raised caused her to take pity upon herself as one who was ill-used. Her eyes filled as she regarded her position further; she turned round and burst into a flood of self-sympathetic tears.

Clare was relieved at this change, for the effect on her of what had happened was beginning to be a trouble to him only less than the woe of the disclosure itself. He waited patiently, apathetically, till the violence of her grief had worn itself out, and her rush of weeping had lessened to a catching gasp at intervals.

'Angel,' she said suddenly, in her natural tones, the insane, dry voice of terror having left her now. 'Angel, am I too wicked for you and me to live together?'

'I have not been able to think what we can do.'

'I shan't ask you to let me live with you, Angel, because I have no right to! I shall not write to mother and sisters to say we be married, as I said I would do; and I shan't finish the good-hussif' I cut out and meant to make while we were in lodgings.'

'Shan't you?'

'No I shan't do anything, unless you order me to; and if you go away from me I shall not follow 'ee; and if you never speak to me any more I shall not ask why, unless you tell me I may.'

'And if I do order you to do anything?'

'I will obey you like your wretched slave, even if it is to lie down and die.'

'You are very good. But it strikes me that there is a want of harmony between your present mood of self-sacrifice and your past mood of self-preservation.'

These were the first words of antagonism. To fling elaborate sarcasms at Tess, however, was much like flinging them at a dog or cat. The charms of their subtlety passed by her unappreciated, and she only received them as inimical sounds which meant that anger ruled. She remained mute, not knowing that he was smothering his affection for her. She hardly observed that a tear descended slowly upon his cheek, a tear so large that it magnified the pores of the skin over which it rolled, like the object lens of a microscope. Meanwhile reillumination as to the terrible and total change that her confession had wrought in his life, in his universe, returned to him, and he tried desperately to advance among the new conditions in which he stood. Some consequent action was necessary; yet what?

'Tess,' he said, as gently as he could speak, 'I cannot stay — in this room — just now. I will walk out a little way.'

He quietly left the room, and the two glasses of wine that he had poured out for their supper — one for her, one for him — remained on the table untasted. This was what their *Agape*° had come to. At tea, two or three hours earlier, they had, in the freakishness of affection, drunk from one cup.

The closing of the door behind him, gently as it had been pulled to, roused Tess from her stupor. He was gone; she could not stay. Hastily flinging her cloak around her she opened the door and followed, putting out the candles as if she were never coming back. The rain was over and the night was now clear.

She was soon close at his heels, for Clare walked slowly and without purpose. His form beside her light gray figure looked black, sinister, and forbidding, and she felt as sarcasm the touch of the jewels of which she had been momentarily so proud. Clare turned at hearing her footsteps, but his recognition of her presence seemed to make no difference in him, and he went on over the five yawning arches of the great bridge in front of the house.

The cow and horse tracks in the road were full of water, the rain having been enough to charge them, but not enough to wash them away. Across these minute pools the reflected stars flitted in a quick transit as she passed; she would not have known they were shining overhead if she had not seen them there — the vastest things of the universe imaged in objects so mean.

The place to which they had travelled to-day was in the same valley as Talbothays, but some miles lower down the river; and the surround-

Agape: Greek word meaning a highly spiritual love or a feast of love.

ings being open she kept easily in sight of him. Away from the house the road wound through the meads, and along these she followed Clare without any attempt to come up with him or to attract him, but with dumb and vacant fidelity.

At last, however, her listless walk brought her up alongside him, and still he said nothing. The cruelty of fooled honesty is often great after enlightenment, and it was mighty in Clare now. The outdoor air had apparently taken away from him all tendency to act on impulse; she knew that he saw her without irradiation — in all her bareness; that Time was chanting his satiric° psalm at her then —

> Behold, when thy face is made bare, he that loved thee shall hate;
> Thy face shall be no more fair at the fall of thy fate.
> For thy life shall fall as a leaf and be shed as the rain;
> And the veil of thine head shall be grief, and the crown shall be pain.

He was still intently thinking, and her companionship had now insufficient power to break or divert the strain of thought. What a weak thing her presence must have become to him! She could not help addressing Clare.

'What have I done — what *have* I done! I have not told of anything that interferes with or belies my love for you. You don't think I planned it, do you? It is in your own mind what you are angry at, Angel; it is not in me. O, it is not in me, and I am not that deceitful woman you think me!'

'H'm — well. Not deceitful, my wife; but not the same. No, not the same. But do not make me reproach you. I have sworn that I will not; and I will do everything to avoid it.'

But she went on pleading in her distraction; and perhaps said things that would have been better left to silence.

'Angel! — Angel! I was a child — a child when it happened! I knew nothing of men.'

'You were more sinned against than sinning,° that I admit.'

'Then will you not forgive me?'

'I do forgive you, but forgiveness is not all.'

'And love me?'

To this question he did not answer.

'O Angel — my mother says that it sometimes happens so! — she

satiric psalm: From A. C. Swinburne's *Atalanta in Calydon.* **more sinned against than sinning:** *King Lear* 3.2.60.

knows several cases where they were worse than I, and the husband has not minded it much — has got over it at least. And yet the woman has not loved him as I do you!'

'Don't, Tess; don't argue. Different societies, different manners. You almost make me say you are an unapprehending peasant woman, who have never been initiated into the proportions of social things. You don't know what you say.'

'I am only a peasant by position, not by nature!'

She spoke with an impulse to anger, but it went as it came.

'So much the worse for you. I think that parson who unearthed your pedigree would have done better if he had held his tongue. I cannot help associating your decline as a family with this other fact — of your want of firmness. Decrepit families imply decrepit wills, decrepit conduct. Heaven, why did you give me a handle for despising you more by informing me of your descent! Here was I thinking you a new-sprung child of nature; there were you, the belated seedling of an effete aristocracy!'

'Lots of families are as bad as mine in that! Retty's family were once large landowners, and so were Dairyman Billett's. And the Debbyhouses, who now are carters, were once the De Bayeux family. You find such as I everywhere; 'tis a feature of our county, and I can't help it.'

'So much the worse for the county.'

She took these reproaches in their bulk simply, not in their particulars; he did not love her as he had loved her hitherto, and to all else she was indifferent.

They wandered on again in silence. It was said afterwards that a cottager of Wellbridge, who went out late that night for a doctor, met two lovers in the pastures, walking very slowly, without converse, one behind the other, as in a funeral procession, and the glimpse that he obtained of their faces seemed to denote that they were anxious and sad. Returning later, he passed them again in the same field, progressing just as slowly, and as regardless of the hour and of the cheerless night as before. It was only on account of his preoccupation with his own affairs, and the illness in his house, that he did not bear in mind the curious incident, which, however, he recalled a long while after.

During the interval of the cottager's going and coming, she had said to her husband —

'I don't see how I can help being the cause of much misery to you all your life. The river is down there. I can put an end to myself in it. I am not afraid.'

'I don't wish to add murder to my other follies,' he said.

'I will leave something to show that I did it myself — on account of my shame. They will not blame you then.'

'Don't speak so absurdly — I wish not to hear it. It is nonsense to have such thoughts in this kind of case, which is rather one for satirical laughter than for tragedy. You don't in the least understand the quality of the mishap. It would be viewed in the light of a joke by nine-tenths of the world if it were known. Please oblige me by returning to the house, and going to bed.'

'I will,' said she dutifully.

They had rambled round by a road which led to the well-known ruins of the Cistercian abbey behind the mill, the latter having, in centuries past, been attached to the monastic establishment. The mill still worked on, food being a perennial necessity; the abbey had perished, creeds being transient. One continually sees the ministration of the temporary outlasting the ministration of the eternal. Their walk having been circuitous they were still not far from the house, and in obeying his direction she only had to reach the large stone bridge across the main river, and follow the road for a few yards. When she got back everything remained as she had left it, the fire being still burning. She did not stay downstairs for more than a minute, but proceeded to her chamber, whither the luggage had been taken. Here she sat down on the edge of the bed, looking blankly around, and presently began to undress. In removing the light towards the bedstead its rays fell upon the tester of white dimity; something was hanging beneath it, and she lifted the candle to see what it was. A bough of mistletoe. Angel had put it there; she knew that in an instant. This was the explanation of that mysterious parcel which it had been so difficult to pack and bring; whose contents he would not explain to her, saying that time would soon show her the purpose thereof. In his zest and his gaiety he had hung it there. How foolish and inopportune that mistletoe looked now.

Having nothing more to fear, having scarce anything to hope, for that he would relent there seemed no promise whatever, she lay down dully. When sorrow ceases to be speculative sleep sees her opportunity. Among so many happier moods which forbid repose this was a mood which welcomed it, and in a few minutes the lonely Tess forgot existence, surrounded by the aromatic stillness of the chamber that had once, possibly, been the bride-chamber of her own ancestry.

Later on that night Clare also retraced his steps to the house. Entering softly to the sitting-room he obtained a light, and with the manner of one who had considered his course he spread his rugs upon the old horse-hair sofa which stood there, and roughly shaped it to a sleeping-couch. Before lying down he crept shoeless upstairs, and listened at the door of her apartment. Her measured breathing told that she was sleeping profoundly.

'Thank God!' murmured Clare; and yet he was conscious of a pang of bitterness at the thought — approximately true, though not wholly so — that having shifted the burden of her life to his shoulders she was now reposing without care.

He turned away to descend; then, irresolute, faced round to her door again. In the act he caught sight of one of the d'Urberville dames, whose portrait was immediately over the entrance to Tess's bedchamber. In the candlelight the painting was more than unpleasant. Sinister design lurked in the woman's features, a concentrated purpose of revenge on the other sex — so it seemed to him then. The Caroline bodice of the portrait was low — precisely as Tess's had been when he tucked it in to show the necklace; and again he experienced the distressing sensation of a resemblance between them.

The check was sufficient. He resumed his retreat and descended.

His air remained calm and cold, his small compressed mouth indexing his powers of self-control; his face wearing still that terribly sterile expression which had spread thereon since her disclosure. It was the face of a man who was no longer passion's slave, yet who found no advantage in his enfranchisement. He was simply regarding the harrowing contingencies of human experience, the unexpectedness of things. Nothing so pure, so sweet, so virginal as Tess had seemed possible all the long while that he had adored her, up to an hour ago; but

> The little less, and what worlds away!°

He argued erroneously when he said to himself that her heart was not indexed in the honest freshness of her face; but Tess had no advocate to set him right. Could it be possible, he continued, that eyes which as they gazed never expressed any divergence from what the tongue was telling, were yet ever seeing another world behind her ostensible one, discordant and contrasting.

He reclined on his couch in the sitting-room, and extinguished the light. The night came in, and took up its place there, unconcerned and indifferent; the night which had already swallowed up his happiness, and was now digesting it listlessly; and was ready to swallow up the happiness of a thousand other people with as little disturbance or change of mien.

The little less, . . . : From stanza 39 of "By the Fire-Side" by Robert Browning (1812–1889).

XXXVI

Clare arose in the light of a dawn that was ashy and furtive, as though associated with crime. The fireplace confronted him with its extinct embers; the spread supper-table, whereon stood the two full glasses of untasted wine, now flat and filmy; her vacated seat and his own; the other articles of furniture, with their eternal look of not being able to help it, their intolerable inquiry what was to be done? From above there was no sound; but in a few minutes there came a knock at the door. He remembered that it would be the neighbouring cottager's wife, who was to minister to their wants while they remained here.

The presence of a third person in the house would be extremely awkward just now, and, being already dressed, he opened the window and informed her that they could manage to shift for themselves that morning. She had a milk-can in her hand, which he told her to leave at the door. When the dame had gone away he searched in the back quarters of the house for fuel, and speedily lit a fire. There was plenty of eggs, butter, bread, and so on in the larder, and Clare soon had breakfast laid, his experiences at the dairy having rendered him facile in domestic preparations. The smoke of the kindled wood rose from the chimney without like a lotus-headed column; local people who were passing by saw it, and thought of the newly-married couple, and envied their happiness.

Angel cast a final glance round, and then going to the foot of the stairs, called in a conventional voice —

'Breakfast is ready!'

He opened the front door, and took a few steps in the morning air. When, after a short space, he came back she was already in the sitting-room, mechanically readjusting the breakfast things. As she was fully attired, and the interval since his calling her had been but two or three minutes, she must have been dressed or nearly so before he went to summon her. Her hair was twisted up in a large round mass at the back of her head, and she had put on one of the new frocks — a pale blue woollen garment with neck-frillings of white. Her hands and face appeared to be cold, and she had possibly been sitting dressed in the bedroom a long time without any fire. The marked civility of Clare's tone in calling her seemed to have inspired her, for the moment, with a new glimmer of hope. But it soon died when she looked at him.

The pair were, in truth, but the ashes of their former fires. To the hot sorrow of the previous night had succeeded heaviness; it seemed as if nothing could kindle either of them to fervour of sensation any more.

He spoke gently to her, and she replied with a like undemonstrativeness. At last she came up to him, looking in his sharply-defined face as one who had no consciousness that her own formed a visible object also.

'Angel!' she said, and paused, touching him with her fingers lightly as a breeze, as though she could hardly believe to be there in the flesh the man who was once her lover. Her eyes were bright, her pale cheek still showed its wonted roundness, though half-dried tears had left glistening traces thereon; and the usually ripe red mouth was almost as pale as her cheek. Throbbingly alive as she was still, under the stress of her mental grief the life beat so brokenly, that a little further pull upon it would cause real illness, dull her characteristic eyes, and make her mouth thin.

She looked absolutely pure. Nature, in her fantastic trickery, had set such a seal of maidenhood upon Tess's countenance that he gazed at her with a stupefied air.

'Tess! Say it is not true! No, it is not true!'

'It is true.'

'Every word?'

'Every word.'

He looked at her imploringly, as if he would willingly have taken a lie from her lips, knowing it to be one, and have made of it, by some sort of sophistry, a valid denial. However, she only repeated —

'It is true.'

'Is he living?' Angel then asked.

'The baby died.'

'But the man?'

'He is alive.'

A last despair passed over Clare's face.

'Is he in England?'

'Yes.'

He took a few vague steps.

'My position — is this,' he said abruptly. 'I thought — any man would have thought — that by giving up all ambition to win a wife with social standing, with fortune, with knowledge of the world, I should secure rustic innocence as surely as I should secure pink cheeks; but —— However, I am no man to reproach you, and I will not.'

Tess felt his position so entirely that the remainder had not been needed. Therein lay just the distress of it; she saw that he had lost all round.

'Angel — I should not have let it go on to marriage with you if I had not known that, after all, there was a last way out of it for you; though I hoped you would never —— '

Her voice grew husky.

'A last way?'

'I mean, to get rid of me. You *can* get rid of me.'

'How?'

'By divorcing me.'

'Good heavens — how can you be so simple! How can I divorce you?'

'Can't you — now I have told you? I thought my confession would give you grounds for that.'

'O Tess — you are too, too — childish — unformed — crude, I suppose! I don't know what you are. You don't understand the law — you don't understand!'

'What — you cannot?'

'Indeed I cannot.'

A quick shame mixed with the misery upon his listener's face.

'I thought — I thought,' she whispered. 'O, now I see how wicked I seem to you! Believe me — believe me, on my soul, I never thought but that you could! I hoped you would not; yet I believed, without a doubt, that you could cast me off if you were determined, and didn't love me at — at — all!'

'You were mistaken,' he said.

'O, then I ought to have done it, to have done it last night! But I hadn't the courage. That's just like me!'

'The courage to do what?'

As she did not answer he took her by the hand.

'What were you thinking of doing?' he inquired.

'Of putting an end to myself.'

'When?'

She writhed under this inquisitorial manner of his. 'Last night,' she answered.

'Where?'

'Under your mistletoe.'

'My good — ! How?' he asked sternly.

'I'll tell you, if you won't be angry with me!' she said, shrinking. 'It was with the cord of my box. But I could not — do the last thing! I was afraid that it might cause a scandal to your name.'

The unexpected quality of this confession, wrung from her, and not volunteered, shook him perceptibly. But he still held her, and, letting his glance fall from her face downwards, he said,

'Now, listen to this. You must not dare to think of such a horrible thing! How could you! You will promise me as your husband to attempt that no more.'

'I am ready to promise. I saw how wicked it was.'

'Wicked! The idea was unworthy of you beyond description.'

'But, Angel,' she pleaded, enlarging her eyes in calm unconcern upon him, 'it was thought of entirely on your account — to set you free without the scandal of the divorce that I thought you would have to get. I should never have dreamt of doing it on mine. However, to do it with my own hand is too good for me, after all. It is you, my ruined husband, who ought to strike the blow. I think I should love you more, if that were possible, if you could bring yourself to do it, since there's no other way of escape for 'ee. I feel I am so utterly worthless! So very greatly in the way!'

'Ssh!'

'Well, since you say no, I won't. I have no wish opposed to yours.'

He knew this to be true enough. Since the desperation of the night her activities had dropped to zero, and there was no further rashness to be feared.

Tess tried to busy herself again over the breakfast-table with more or less success, and they sat down both on the same side, so that their glances did not meet. There was at first something awkward in hearing each other eat and drink, but this could not be escaped; moreover, the amount of eating done was small on both sides. Breakfast over he rose, and telling her the hour at which he might be expected to dinner, went off to the miller's in a mechanical pursuance of the plan of studying that business, which had been his only practical reason for coming here.

When he was gone Tess stood at the window, and presently saw his form crossing the great stone bridge which conducted to the mill premises. He sank behind it, crossed the railway beyond, and disappeared. Then, without a sigh, she turned her attention to the room, and began clearing the table and setting it in order.

The charwoman soon came. Her presence was at first a strain upon Tess, but afterwards an alleviation. At half-past twelve she left her assistant alone in the kitchen, and, returning to the sitting-room, waited for the reappearance of Angel's form behind the bridge.

About one he showed himself. Her face flushed, although he was a quarter of a mile off. She ran to the kitchen to get the dinner served by the time he should enter. He went first to the room where they had washed their hands together the day before, and as he entered the sitting-room the dish-covers rose from the dishes as if by his own motion.

'How punctual!' he said.

'Yes. I saw you coming over the bridge,' said she.

The meal was passed in commonplace talk of what he had been doing during the morning at the Abbey Mill, of the methods of bolting and the old-fashioned machinery, which he feared would not enlighten him greatly on modern improved methods, some of it seeming to have been in use ever since the days it ground for the monks in the adjoining conventual buildings — now a heap of ruins. He left the house again in the course of an hour, coming home at dusk, and occupying himself through the evening with his papers. She feared she was in the way, and, when the old woman was gone, retired to the kitchen, where she made herself busy as well as she could for more than an hour.

Clare's shape appeared at the door.

'You must not work like this,' he said. 'You are not my servant; you are my wife.'

She raised her eyes, and brightened somewhat. 'I may think myself that — indeed?' she murmured, in piteous raillery. 'You mean in name! Well, I don't want to be anything more.'

'You *may* think so, Tess! You are. What do you mean?'

'I don't know,' she said hastily, with tears in her accents. 'I thought I — because I am not respectable, I mean. I told you I thought I was not respectable enough long ago — and on that account I didn't want to marry you, only — only you urged me!'

She broke into sobs, and turned her back to him. It would almost have won round any man but Angel Clare. Within the remote depths of his constitution, so gentle and affectionate as he was in general, there lay hidden a hard logical deposit, like a vein of metal in a soft loam, which turned the edge of everything that attempted to traverse it. It had blocked his acceptance of the Church; it blocked his acceptance of Tess. Moreover, his affection itself was less fire than radiance, and, with regard to the other sex, when he ceased to believe he ceased to follow: contrasting in this with many impressionable natures, who remain sensuously infatuated with what they intellectually despise. He waited till her sobbing ceased.

'I wish half the women in England were as respectable as you,' he said, in an ebullition of bitterness against womankind in general. 'It isn't a question of respectability, but one of principle!'

He spoke such things as these and more of a kindred sort to her, being still swayed by the antipathetic wave which warps direct souls with such persistence when once their vision finds itself mocked by appearances. There was, it is true, underneath, a back current of sympathy through which a woman of the world might have conquered him. But Tess did not think of this; she took everything as her deserts, and hardly opened her mouth. The firmness of her devotion to him was indeed almost pitiful; quick-tempered as she naturally was, nothing that he could say made her unseemly; she sought not her own; was not provoked; thought no evil of his treatment of her. She might just now have been Apostolic Charity° herself returned to a self-seeking modern world.

This evening, night, and morning were passed precisely as the preceding ones had been passed. On one, and only one, occasion did she — the formerly free and independent Tess — venture to make any advances. It was on the third occasion of starting after a meal to go out to the flour-mill. As he was leaving the table he said 'Good-bye,' and she replied in the same words, at the same time inclining her mouth in the way of his. He did not avail himself of the invitation, saying, as he turned hastily aside —

'I shall be home punctually.'

Tess shrank into herself as if she had been struck. Often enough had he tried to reach those lips against her consent — often had he said gaily that her mouth and breath tasted of the butter and eggs and milk and honey on which she mainly lived, that he drew sustenance from them, and other follies of that sort. But he did not care for them now. He observed her sudden shrinking, and said gently —

'You know, I have to think of a course. It was imperative that we should stay together a little while, to avoid the scandal to you that would have resulted from our immediate parting. But you must see it is only for form's sake.'

'Yes,' said Tess absently.

He went out, and on his way to the mill stood still, and wished for a moment that he had responded yet more kindly, and kissed her once at least.

Thus they lived through this despairing day or two; in the same house, truly; but more widely apart than before they were lovers. It was evident to her that he was, as he had said, living with paralyzed activities, in his endeavour to think of a plan of procedure. She was awe-

Apostolic Charity: Charity as described by the Apostle Paul in 1 Corinthians 13.4–7.

stricken to discover such determination under such apparent flexibility. His consistency was, indeed, too cruel. She no longer expected forgiveness now. More than once she thought of going away from him during his absence at the mill; but she feared that this, instead of benefiting him, might be the means of hampering and humiliating him yet more if it should become known.

Meanwhile Clare was meditating, verily. His thought had been unsuspended; he was becoming ill with thinking; eaten out with thinking, withered by thinking; scourged out of all his former pulsating flexuous domesticity. He walked about saying to himself, 'What's to be done — what's to be done?' and by chance she overheard him. It caused her to break the reserve about their future which had hitherto prevailed.

'I suppose — you are not going to live with me — long, are you, Angel?' she asked, the sunk corners of her mouth betraying how purely mechanical were the means by which she retained that expression of chastened calm upon her face.

'I cannot,' he said, 'without despising myself, and what is worse, perhaps, despising you. I mean, of course, cannot live with you in the ordinary sense. At present, whatever I feel, I do not despise you. And, let me speak plainly, or you may not see all my difficulties. How can we live together while that man lives? — he being your husband in Nature, and not I. If he were dead it might be different. . . . Besides, that's not all the difficulty; it lies in another consideration — one bearing upon the future of other people than ourselves. Think of years to come, and children being born to us, and this past matter getting known — for it must get known. There is not an uttermost part of the earth but somebody comes from it or goes to it from elsewhere. Well, think of wretches of our flesh and blood growing up under a taunt which they will gradually get to feel the full force of with their expanding years. What an awakening for them! What a prospect! Can you honestly say Remain, after contemplating this contingency? Don't you think we had better endure the ills we have than fly to others?'

Her eyelids, weighted with trouble, continued drooping as before.

'I cannot say Remain,' she answered. 'I cannot; I had not thought so far.'

Tess's feminine hope — shall we confess it — had been so obstinately recuperative as to revive in her surreptitious visions of a domiciliary intimacy continued long enough to break down his coldness even against his judgment. Though unsophisticated in the usual sense, she was not incomplete; and it would have denoted deficiency of womanhood if she had not instinctively known what an argument lies in propinquity. Nothing else would serve her, she knew, if this failed. It was wrong to hope in what was of the nature of strategy, she said to herself: yet that sort of hope she could not extinguish. His last representation had now been made, and it was, as she said, a new view. She had truly never thought so far as that, and his lucid picture of possible offspring who would scorn her was one that brought deadly conviction to an honest heart which was humanitarian to its centre. Sheer experience had already taught her that, in some circumstances, there was one thing better than to lead a good life, and that was to be saved from leading any life whatever. Like all who have been previsioned by suffering, she could, in the words of M. Sully-Prudhomme,° hear a penal sentence in the fiat, 'You shall be born,' particularly if addressed to potential issue of hers.

Yet such is the vulpine slyness of Dame Nature, that, till now, Tess had been hoodwinked by her love for Clare into forgetting it might result in vitalizations that would inflict upon others what she had bewailed as a misfortune to herself.

She therefore could not withstand his argument. But with the self-combating proclivity of the super-sensitive, an answer thereto arose in Clare's own mind, and he almost feared it. It was based on her exceptional physical nature; and she might have used it promisingly. She might have added besides: 'On an Australian upland or Texan plain, who is to know or care about my misfortunes, or to reproach me or you?' Yet, like the majority of women, she accepted the momentary presentment as if it were the inevitable. And she may have been right. The intuitive heart of woman knoweth not only its own bitterness, but its husband's, and even if these assumed reproaches were not likely to be addressed to him or to his by strangers, they might have reached his ears from his own fastidious brain.

It was the third day of the estrangement. Some might risk the odd paradox that with more animalism he would have been the nobler man. We do not say it. Yet Clare's love was doubtless ethereal to a fault, imaginative to impracticability. With these natures, corporeal presence is sometimes less appealing than corporeal absence; the latter creating an ideal presence that conveniently drops the defects of the real. She found that her personality did not plead her cause so forcibly as she had anticipated. The figurative phrase was true: she was another woman than the one who had excited his desire.

M. Sully-Prudhomme: French poet and essayist (1839–1907).

'I have thought over what you say,' she remarked to him, moving her forefinger over the tablecloth, her other hand, which bore the ring that mocked them both, supporting her forehead. 'It is quite true all of it; it must be. You must go away from me.'

'But what can you do?'

'I can go home.'

Clare had not thought of that.

'Are you sure?' he inquired.

'Quite sure. We ought to part, and we may as well get it past and done. You once said that I was apt to win men against their better judgment; and if I am constantly before your eyes I may cause you to change your plans in opposition to your reason and wish; and afterwards your repentance and my sorrow will be terrible.'

'And you would like to go home?' he asked.

'I want to leave you, and go home.'

'Then it shall be so.'

Though she did not look up at him, she started. There was a difference between the proposition and the covenant, which she had felt only too quickly.

'I feared it would come to this,' she murmured, her countenance meekly fixed. 'I don't complain, Angel. I — I think it best. What you said has quite convinced me. Yes, though nobody else should reproach me if we should stay together, yet somewhen, years hence, you might get angry with me for any ordinary matter, and knowing what you do of my bygones you yourself might be tempted to say words, and they might be overheard, perhaps by my own children. O, what only hurts me now would torture and kill me then! I will go — to-morrow.'

'And I shall not stay here. Though I didn't like to initiate it, I have seen that it was advisable we should part — at least for a while, till I can better see the shape that things have taken, and can write to you.'

Tess stole a glance at her husband. He was pale, even tremulous; but, as before, she was appalled by the determination revealed in the depths of this gentle being she had married — the will to subdue the grosser to the subtler emotion, the substance to the conception, the flesh to the spirit. Propensities, tendencies, habits, were as dead leaves upon the tyrannous wind of his imaginative ascendency.

He may have observed her look, for he explained —

'I think of people more kindly when I am away from them;' adding cynically, 'God knows; perhaps we shall shake down together some day, for weariness; thousands have done it!'

That day he began to pack up, and she went upstairs and began to pack also. Both knew that it was in their two minds that they might part the next morning for ever, despite the gloss of assuaging conjectures thrown over their proceeding because they were of the sort to whom any parting which has an air of finality is a torture. He knew, and she knew, that, though the fascination which each had exercised over the other — on her part independently of accomplishments — would probably in the first days of their separation be even more potent than ever, time must attenuate that effect; the practical arguments against accepting her as a housemate might pronounce themselves more strongly in the boreal° light of a remoter view. Moreover, when two people are once parted — have abandoned a common domicile and a common environment — new growths insensibly bud upward to fill each vacated place; unforeseen accidents hinder intentions, and old plans are forgotten.

XXXVII

Midnight came and passed silently, for there was nothing to announce it in the Valley of the Froom.

Not long after one o'clock there was a slight creak in the darkened farmhouse once the mansion of the d'Urbervilles. Tess, who used the upper chamber, heard it and awoke. It had come from the corner step of the staircase, which, as usual, was loosely nailed. She saw the door of her bedroom open, and the figure of her husband crossed the stream of moonlight with a curiously careful tread. He was in his shirt and trousers only, and her first flush of joy died when she perceived that his eyes were fixed in an unnatural stare on vacancy. When he reached the middle of the room he stood still and murmured, in tones of indescribable sadness —

'Dead! dead! dead!'

Under the influence of any strongly-disturbing force Clare would occasionally walk in his sleep, and even perform strange feats, such as he had done on the night of their return from market just before their marriage, when he re-enacted in his bedroom his combat with the man who had insulted her. Tess saw that continued mental distress had wrought him into that somnambulistic state now.

Her loyal confidence in him lay so deep down in her heart that, awake or asleep, he inspired her with no sort of personal fear. If he had

boreal: Northern or arctic; that is, once his passions have cooled and he has some distance from the situation.

entered with a pistol in his hand he would scarcely have disturbed her trust in his protectiveness.

Clare came close, and bent over her. 'Dead, dead, dead!' he murmured.

After fixedly regarding her for some moments with the same gaze of unmeasurable woe he bent lower, enclosed her in his arms, and rolled her in the sheet as in a shroud. Then lifting her from the bed with as much respect as one would show to a dead body, he carried her across the room, murmuring —

'My poor, poor Tess — my dearest, darling Tess! So sweet, so good, so true!'

The words of endearment, withheld so severely in his waking hours, were inexpressibly sweet to her forlorn and hungry heart. If it had been to save her weary life she would not, by moving or struggling, have put an end to the position she found herself in. Thus she lay in absolute stillness, scarcely venturing to breathe, and, wondering what he was going to do with her, suffered herself to be borne out upon the landing.

'My wife — dead, dead!' he said.

He paused in his labours for a moment to lean with her against the banister. Was he going to throw her down? Self-solicitude was near extinction in her, and in the knowledge that he had planned to depart on the morrow, possibly for always, she lay in his arms in this precarious position with a sense rather of luxury than of terror. If they could only fall together, and both be dashed to pieces, how fit, how desirable.

However, he did not let her fall, but took advantage of the support of the handrail to imprint a kiss upon her lips — lips in the daytime scorned. Then he clasped her with a renewed firmness of hold, and descended the staircase. The creak of the loose stair did not awaken him, and they reached the ground-floor safely. Freeing one of his hands from his grasp of her for a moment, he slid back the door-bar and passed out, slightly striking his stockinged toe against the edge of the door. But this he seemed not to mind, and, having room for extension in the open air, he lifted her against his shoulder, so that he could carry her with ease, the absence of clothes taking much from his burden. Thus he bore her off the premises in the direction of the river a few yards distant.

His ultimate intention, if he had any, she had not yet divined; and she found herself conjecturing on the matter as a third person might have done. So easefully had she delivered her whole being up to him that it pleased her to think he was regarding her as his absolute possession, to dispose of as he should choose. It was consoling, under the hovering terror of tomorrow's separation, to feel that he really recognized her now as his wife Tess, and did not cast her off, even if in that recognition he went so far as to arrogate to himself the right of harming her.

Ah! now she knew what he was dreaming of — that Sunday morning when he had borne her along through the water with the other dairymaids, who had loved him nearly as much as she, if that were possible, which Tess could hardly admit. Clare did not cross the bridge with her, but proceeding several paces on the same side towards the adjoining mill, at length stood still on the brink of the river.

Its waters, in creeping down these miles of meadowland, frequently divided, serpentining in purposeless curves, looping themselves around little islands that had no name, returning and re-embodying themselves as a broad main stream further on. Opposite the spot to which he had brought her was such a general confluence, and the river was proportionately voluminous and deep. Across it was a narrow foot-bridge; but now the autumn flood had washed the handrail away, leaving the bare plank only, which, lying a few inches above the speeding current, formed a giddy pathway for even steady heads; and Tess had noticed from the window of the house in the daytime young men walking across upon it as a feat in balancing. Her husband had possibly observed the same performance; anyhow, he now mounted the plank, and, sliding one foot forward, advanced along it.

Was he going to drown her? Probably he was. The spot was lonely, the river deep and wide enough to make such a purpose easy of accomplishment. He might drown her if he would; it would be better than parting to-morrow to lead severed lives.

The swift stream raced and gyrated under them, tossing, distorting, and splitting the moon's reflected face. Spots of froth travelled past, and intercepted weeds waved behind the piles. If they could both fall together into the current now, their arms would be so tightly clasped together that they could not be saved; they would go out of the world almost painlessly, and there would be no more reproach to her, or to him for marrying her. His last half-hour with her would have been a loving one, while if they lived till he awoke his daytime aversion would return, and this hour would remain to be contemplated only as a transient dream.

The impulse stirred in her, yet she dared not indulge it, to make a movement that would have precipitated them both into the gulf. How she valued her own life had been proved; but his — she had no right to tamper with it. He reached the other side with her in safety.

Here they were within a plantation which formed the Abbey grounds, and taking a new hold of her he went onward a few steps till they reached the ruined choir of the Abbey-church. Against the north wall was the empty stone coffin of an abbot, in which every tourist with a turn for grim humour was accustomed to stretch himself. In this Clare carefully laid Tess. Having kissed her lips a second time he breathed deeply, as if a greatly desired end were attained. Clare then lay down on the ground alongside, when he immediately fell into the deep dead slumber of exhaustion, and remained motionless as a log. The spurt of mental excitement which had produced the effort was now over.

Tess sat up in the coffin. The night, though dry and mild for the season, was more than sufficiently cold to make it dangerous for him to remain here long, in his half-clothed state. If he were left to himself he would in all probability stay there till the morning, and be chilled to certain death. She had heard of such deaths after sleep-walking. But how could she dare to awaken him, and let him know what he had been doing, when it would mortify him to discover his folly in respect of her? Tess, however, stepping out of her stone confine, shook him slightly, but was unable to arouse him without being violent. It was indispensable to do something, for she was beginning to shiver, the sheet being but a poor protection. Her excitement had in a measure kept her warm during the few minutes' adventure; but that beatific interval was over.

It suddenly occurred to her to try persuasion; and accordingly she whispered in his ear, with as much firmness and decision as she could summon —

'Let us walk on, darling,' at the same time taking him suggestively by the arm. To her relief, he unresistingly acquiesced; her words had apparently thrown him back into his dream, which thenceforward seemed to enter on a new phase, wherein he fancied she had risen as a spirit, and was leading him to Heaven. Thus she conducted him by the arm to the stone bridge in front of their residence, crossing which they stood at the manor-house door. Tess's feet were quite bare, and the stones hurt her, and chilled her to the bone; but Clare was in his woollen stockings, and appeared to feel no discomfort.

There was no further difficulty. She induced him to lie down on his own sofa bed, and covered him up warmly, lighting a temporary fire of wood, to dry any dampness out of him. The noise of these attentions she thought might awaken him, and secretly wished that they might. But the exhaustion of his mind and body was such that he remained undisturbed.

As soon as they met the next morning Tess divined that Angel knew little or nothing of how far she had been concerned in the night's excursion, though, as regarded himself he may have been aware that he had not lain still. In truth, he had awakened that morning from a sleep deep as annihilation; and during those first few moments in which the brain, like a Samson shaking himself,° is trying its strength, he had some dim notion of an unusual nocturnal proceeding. But the realities of his situation soon displaced conjecture on the other subject.

He waited in expectancy to discern some mental pointing; he knew that if any intention of his, concluded over-night, did not vanish in the light of morning, it stood on a basis approximating to one of pure reason, even if initiated by impulse of feeling; that it was so far, therefore, to be trusted. He thus beheld in the pale morning light the resolve to separate from her; not as a hot and indignant instinct, but denuded of the passionateness which had made it scorch and burn; standing in its bones; nothing but a skeleton, but none the less there. Clare no longer hesitated.

At breakfast, and while they were packing the few remaining articles, he showed his weariness from the night's effort so unmistakably that Tess was on the point of revealing all that had happened; but the reflection that it would anger him, grieve him, stultify him, to know that he had instinctively manifested a fondness for her of which his common-sense did not approve; that his inclination had compromised his dignity when reason slept, again deterred her. It was too much like laughing at a man when sober for his erratic deeds during intoxication.

It just crossed her mind, too, that he might have a faint recollection of tender vagary, and was disinclined to allude to it from a conviction that she would take amatory advantage of the opportunity it gave her of appealing to him anew not to go.

He had ordered by letter a vehicle from the nearest town, and soon after breakfast it arrived. She saw in it the beginning of the end — the temporary end, at least, for the revelation of his tenderness by the incident of the night raised dreams of a possible future with him. The luggage was put on the top, and the man drove them off,

Samson shaking himself: The description alludes to Samson's misguided self-confidence in Judges 16.20 just before the Philistines capture him.

the miller and the old waiting-woman expressing some surprise at their precipitate departure, which Clare attributed to his discovery that the millwork was not of the modern kind which he wished to investigate, a statement that was true so far as it went. Beyond this there was nothing in the manner of their leaving to suggest a *fiasco*, or that they were not going together to visit friends.

Their route lay near the dairy from which they had started with such solemn joy in each other a few days back, and, as Clare wished to wind up his business with Mr. Crick, Tess could hardly avoid paying Mrs. Crick a call at the same time, unless she would excite suspicion of their unhappy state.

To make the call as unobtrusive as possible they left the carriage by the wicket leading down from the high road to the dairy-house, and descended the track on foot, side by side. The withy-bed had been cut, and they could see over the stumps the spot to which Clare had followed her when he pressed her to be his wife; to the left the enclosure in which she had been fascinated by his harp; and far away behind the cowstalls the mead which had been the scene of their first embrace. The gold of the summer picture was now gray, the colours mean, the rich soil mud, and the river cold.

Over the barton-gate the dairyman saw them, and came forward, throwing into his face the kind of jocularity deemed appropriate in Talbothays and its vicinity on the re-appearance of the newly-married. Then Mrs. Crick emerged from the house, and several others of their old acquaintance, though Marian and Retty did not seem to be there.

Tess valiantly bore their sly attacks and friendly humours, which affected her far otherwise than they supposed. In the tacit agreement of husband and wife to keep their estrangement a secret they behaved as would have been ordinary. And then, although she would rather there had been no word spoken on the subject, Tess had to hear in detail the story of Marian and Retty. The latter had gone home to her father's, and Marian had left to look for employment elsewhere. They feared she would come to no good.

To dissipate the sadness of this recital Tess went and bade all her favourite cows good-bye, touching each of them with her hand, and as she and Clare stood side by side at leaving, as if united body and soul, there would have been something peculiarly sorry in their aspect to one who should have seen it truly; two limbs of one life, as they outwardly were, his arm touching hers, her skirts touching him, facing one way, as against all the dairy facing the other, speaking in their adieux as 'we,' and yet sundered like the poles. Perhaps something unusually stiff and embarrassed in their attitude, some awkwardness in acting up to their profession of unity, different from the natural shyness of young couples, may have been apparent, for when they were gone Mrs. Crick said to her husband —

'How onnatural the brightness of her eyes did seem, and how they stood like waxen images and talked as if they were in a dream! Didn't it strike 'ee that 'twas so? Tess had always sommat strange in her, and she's not now quite like the proud young bride of a well-be-doing man.'

They re-entered the vehicle, and were driven along the roads towards Weatherbury and Stagfoot Lane, till they reached the Lane inn, where Clare dismissed the fly and man. They rested here a while, and entering the Vale were next driven onward towards her home by a stranger who did not know their relations. At a midway point, when Nuttlebury had been passed, and where there were cross-roads, Clare stopped the conveyance and said to Tess that if she meant to return to her mother's house it was here that he would leave her. As they could not talk with freedom in the driver's presence he asked her to accompany him for a few steps on foot along one of the branch roads; she assented, and directing the man to wait a few minutes they strolled away.

'Now, let us understand each other,' he said gently. 'There is no anger between us, though there is that which I cannot endure at present. I will try to bring myself to endure it. I will let you know where I go to as soon as I know myself. And if I can bring myself to bear it — if it is desirable, possible — I will come to you. But until I come to you it will be better that you should not try to come to me.'

The severity of the decree seemed deadly to Tess; she saw his view of her clearly enough; he could regard her in no other light than that of one who had practised gross deceit upon him. Yet could a woman who had done even what she had done deserve all this? But she could contest the point with him no further. She simply repeated after him his own words.

'Until you come to me I must not try to come to you?'

'Just so.'

'May I write to you?'

'O yes — if you are ill, or want anything at all. I hope that will not be the case; so that it may happen that I write first to you.'

'I agree to the conditions, Angel; because you know best what my punishment ought to be; only — only — don't make it more than I can bear!'

That was all she said on the matter. If Tess had been artful, had she made a scene, fainted, wept hysterically, in that lonely lane, notwithstanding the fury of fastidiousness with which he was possessed, he would probably not have withstood her. But her mood of long-suffering made his way easy for him, and she herself was his best advocate. Pride, too, entered into her submission — which perhaps was a symptom of that reckless acquiescence in chance too apparent in the whole d'Urberville family — and the many effective chords which she could have stirred by an appeal were left untouched.

The remainder of their discourse was on practical matters only. He now handed her a packet containing a fairly good sum of money, which he had obtained from his bankers for the purpose. The brilliants, the interest in which seemed to be Tess's for her life only (if he understood the wording of the will), he advised her to let him send to a bank for safety; and to this she readily agreed.

These things arranged he walked with Tess back to the carriage, and handed her in. The coachman was paid and told where to drive her. Taking next his own bag and umbrella — the sole articles he had brought with him hitherwards — he bade her good-bye; and they parted there and then.

The fly moved creepingly up a hill, and Clare watched it go with an unpremeditated hope that Tess would look out of the window for one moment. But that she never thought of doing, would not have ventured to do, lying in a half-dead faint inside. Thus he beheld her recede, and in the anguish of his heart quoted a line from a poet, with peculiar emendations of his own —

God's *not* in his heaven: all's *wrong* with the world!°

When Tess had passed over the crest of the hill he turned to go his own way, and hardly knew that he loved her still.

XXXVIII

As she drove on through Blackmoor Vale, and the landscape of her youth began to open around her, Tess aroused herself from her stupor. Her first thought was how would she be able to face her parents?

She reached a turnpike-gate which stood upon the highway to the village. It was thrown open by a stranger, not by the old man who had kept it for many years, and to whom she had been known; he had

God's *not* in his heaven . . . : A negation of Browning's well-known statement from *Pippa Passes*.

probably left on New Year's Day, the date when such changes were made. Having received no intelligence lately from her home, she asked the turnpike-keeper for news.

'Oh — nothing, miss,' he answered. 'Marlott is Marlott still. Folks have died and that. John Durbeyfield, too, hev had a daughter married this week to a gentleman-farmer; not from John's own house, you know; they was married elsewhere; the gentleman being of that high standing that John's own folk was not considered well-be-doing enough to have any part in it, the bridegroom seeming not to know how't have been discovered that John is a old and ancient nobleman himself by blood, with family skillentons in their own vaults to this day, but done out of his property in the time o' the Romans. However, Sir John, as we call 'n now, kept up the wedding-day as well as he could, and stood treat to everybody in the parish; and John's wife sung songs at The Pure Drop till past eleven o'clock.'

Hearing this, Tess felt so sick at heart that she could not decide to go home publicly in the fly with her luggage and belongings. She asked the turnpike-keeper if she might deposit her things at his house for a while, and, on his offering no objection, she dismissed her carriage, and went on to the village alone by a back lane.

At sight of her father's chimney she asked herself how she could possibly enter the house? Inside that cottage her relations were calmly supposing her far away on a wedding-tour with a comparatively rich man, who was to conduct her to bouncing prosperity; while here she was, friendless, creeping up to the old door quite by herself, with no better place to go to in the world.

She did not reach the house unobserved. Just by the garden-hedge she was met by a girl who knew her — one of the two or three with whom she had been intimate at school. After making a few inquiries as to how Tess came there, her friend, unheeding her tragic look, interrupted with —

'But where's thy gentleman, Tess?'

Tess hastily explained that he had been called away on business, and, leaving her interlocutor, clambered over the garden-hedge, and thus made her way to the house.

As she went up the garden-path she heard her mother singing by the back door, coming in sight of which she perceived Mrs. Durbeyfield on the doorstep in the act of wringing a sheet. Having performed this without observing Tess, she went indoors, and her daughter followed her.

The washing-tub stood in the same old place on the same old

quarter-hogshead, and her mother, having thrown the sheet aside, was about to plunge her arms in anew.

'Why — Tess! — my chil' — I thought you was married! — married really and truly this time — we sent the cider —— '

'Yes, mother; so I am.'

'Going to be?'

'No — I am married.'

'Married! Then where's thy husband?'

'Oh, he's gone away for a time.'

'Gone away! When was you married, then? The day you said?'

'Yes, Tuesday, mother.'

'And now 'tis on'y Saturday, and he gone away?'

'Yes; he's gone.'

'What's the meaning o' that? 'Nation seize such husbands as you seem to get, say I!'

'Mother!' Tess went across to Joan Durbeyfield, laid her face upon the matron's bosom, and burst into sobs. 'I don't know how to tell 'ee, mother! You said to me, and wrote to me, that I was not to tell him. But I did tell him — I couldn't help it — and he went away!'

'O you little fool — you little fool!' burst out Mrs. Durbeyfield, splashing Tess and herself in her agitation. 'My good God! that ever I should ha' lived to say it, but I say it again, you little fool!'

Tess was convulsed with weeping, the tension of so many days having relaxed at last.

'I know it — I know — I know!' she gasped through her sobs. 'But, O my mother, I could not help it! He was so good — and I felt the wickedness of trying to blind him as to what had happened! If — if — it were to be done again — I should do the same. I could not — I dared not — so sin — against him!'

'But you sinned enough to marry him first!'

'Yes, yes; that's where my misery do lie! But I thought he could get rid o' me by law if he were determined not to overlook it. And O, if you knew — if you could only half know how I loved him — how anxious I was to have him — and how wrung I was between caring so much for him and my wish to be fair to him!'

Tess was so shaken that she could get no further, and sank a helpless thing into a chair.

'Well, well; what's done can't be undone! I'm sure I don't know why children o' my bringing forth should all be bigger simpletons than other people's — not to know better than to blab such a thing as that, when he couldn't ha' found it out till too late!' Here Mrs.

Durbeyfield began shedding tears on her own account as a mother to be pitied. 'What your father will say I don't know,' she continued; 'for he's been talking about the wedding up at Rolliver's and The Pure Drop every day since, and about his family getting back to their rightful position through you — poor sill man! — and now you've made this mess of it! The Lord-a-Lord!'

As if to bring matters to a focus, Tess's father was heard approaching at that moment. He did not however, enter immediately, and Mrs. Durbeyfield said that she would break the bad news to him herself, Tess keeping out of sight for the present. After her first burst of disappointment Joan began to take the mishap as she had taken Tess's original trouble, as she would have taken a wet holiday or failure in the potato-crop; as a thing which had come upon them irrespective of desert or folly; a chance external impingement to be borne with; not a lesson.

Tess retreated upstairs, and beheld casually that the beds had been shifted, and new arrangements made. Her old bed had been adapted for two younger children. There was no place here for her now.

The room below being unceiled she could hear most of what went on there. Presently her father entered, apparently carrying a live hen. He was a foot-haggler° now, having been obliged to sell his second horse, and he travelled with his basket on his arm. The hen had been carried about this morning as it was often carried, to show people that he was in his work, though it had lain, with its legs tied, under the table at Rolliver's for more than an hour.

'We've just had up a story about —— ' Durbeyfield began, and thereupon related in detail to his wife a discussion which had arisen at the inn about the clergy, originated by the fact of his daughter having married into a clerical family. 'They was formerly styled "sir," like my own ancestry,' he said, 'though nowadays their true style, strictly speaking, is "clerk" only.' As Tess had wished that no great publicity should be given to the event, he had mentioned no particulars. He hoped she would remove that prohibition soon. He proposed that the couple should take Tess's own name, d'Urberville, as uncorrupted. It was better than her husband's. He asked if any letter had come from her that day.

Then Mrs. Durbeyfield informed him that no letter had come, but Tess unfortunately had come herself.

foot-haggler: Peddler.

When at last the collapse was explained to him a sullen mortification, not usual with Durbeyfield, overpowered the influence of the cheering glass. Yet the intrinsic quality of the event moved his touchy sensitiveness less than its conjectured effect upon the minds of others.

'To think, now, that this was to be the end o't!' said Sir John. 'And I with a family vault under that there church of Kingsbere as big as Squire Jollard's ale-cellar, and my folk lying there in sixes and sevens, as genuine county bones and marrow as any recorded in history. And now to be sure what they fellers at Rolliver's and The Pure Drop will say to me! How they'll squint and glane, and say, "This is yer mighty match is it; this is yer getting back to the true level of yer forefathers in King Norman's time!" I feel this is too much, Joan; I shall put an end to myself, title and all — I can bear it no longer! . . . But she can make him keep her if he's married her?'

'Why, yes. But she won't think o' doing that.'

'D'ye think he really have married her? — or is it like the first —— '

Poor Tess, who had heard as far as this, could not bear to hear more. The perception that her word could be doubted even here, in her own parental house, set her mind against the spot as nothing else could have done. How unexpected were the attacks of destiny! And if her father doubted her a little, would not neighbours and acquaintance doubt her much? O, she could not live long at home!

A few days, accordingly, were all that she allowed herself here, at the end of which time she received a short note from Clare, informing her that he had gone to the North of England to look at a farm. In her craving for the lustre of her true position as his wife, and to hide from her parents the vast extent of the division between them, she made use of this letter as her reason for again departing, leaving them under the impression that she was setting out to join him. Still further to screen her husband from any imputation of unkindness to her, she took twenty-five of the fifty pounds Clare had given her, and handed the sum over to her mother, as if the wife of a man like Angel Clare could well afford it, saying that it was a slight return for the trouble and humiliation she had brought upon them in years past. With this assertion of her dignity she bade them farewell; and after that there were lively doings in the Durbeyfield household for some time on the strength of Tess's bounty, her mother saying, and, indeed, believing, that the rupture which had arisen between the young husband and wife had adjusted itself under their strong feeling that they could not live apart from each other.

XXXIX

It was three weeks after the marriage that Clare found himself descending the hill which led to the well-known parsonage of his father. With his downward course the tower of the church rose into the evening sky in a manner of inquiry as to why he had come; and no living person in the twilighted town seemed to notice him, still less to expect him. He was arriving like a ghost, and the sound of his own footsteps was almost an encumbrance to be got rid of.

The picture of life had changed for him. Before this time he had known it but speculatively; now he thought he knew it as a practical man; though perhaps he did not, even yet. Nevertheless humanity stood before him no longer in the pensive sweetness of Italian art, but in the staring and ghastly attitudes of a Wiertz Museum,° and with the leer of a study by Van Beers.°

His conduct during these first weeks had been desultory beyond description. After mechanically attempting to pursue his agricultural plans as though nothing unusual had happened, in the manner recommended by the great and wise men of all ages, he concluded that very few of those great and wise men had ever gone so far outside themselves as to test the feasibility of their counsel. 'This is the chief thing: be not perturbed,' said the Pagan moralist.° That was just Clare's own opinion. But he was perturbed. 'Let not your heart be troubled, neither let it be afraid,' said the Nazarene.° Clare chimed in cordially; but his heart was troubled all the same. How he would have liked to confront those two great thinkers, and earnestly appeal to them as fellow-man to fellow-men, and ask them to tell him their method!

His mood transmuted itself into a dogged indifference till at length he fancied he was looking on his own existence with the passive interest of an outsider.

He was embittered by the conviction that all this desolation had been brought about by the accident of her being a d'Urberville. When he found that Tess came of that exhausted ancient line, and was not of the new tribes from below, as he had fondly dreamed, why had he not stoically abandoned her, in fidelity to his principles? This was what he had got by apostasy, and his punishment was deserved.

Wiertz Museum: Museum in Brussels containing the macabre works of the Flemish painter, Antoine Wiertz (1806–1865). **Van Beers:** Jan Van Beers (1852–1927), Flemish painter frequently compared to Wiertz. **Pagan moralist:** Marcus Aurelius Antoninus (A.D. 121–180), Roman emperor and stoic philosopher. **Nazarene:** Jesus, who says this at the Last Supper; John 14.27.

Then he became weary and anxious, and his anxiety increased. He wondered if he had treated her unfairly. He ate without knowing that he ate, and drank without tasting. As the hours dropped past, as the motive of each act in the long series of bygone days presented itself to his view, he perceived how intimately the notion of having Tess as a dear possession was mixed up with all his schemes and words and ways.

In going hither and thither he observed in the outskirts of a small town a red-and-blue placard setting forth the great advantages of the Empire of Brazil as a field for the emigrating agriculturist. Land was offered there on exceptionally advantageous terms. Brazil somewhat attracted him as a new idea. Tess could eventually join him there, and perhaps in that country of contrasting scenes and notions and habits the conventions would not be so operative which made life with her seem impracticable to him here. In brief he was strongly inclined to try Brazil, especially as the season for going thither was just at hand.

With this view he was returning to Emminster to disclose his plan to his parents, and to make the best explanation he could make of arriving without Tess, short of revealing what had actually separated them. As he reached the door the new moon shone upon his face, just as the old one had done in the small hours of that morning when he had carried his wife in his arms across the river to the graveyard of the monks; but his face was thinner now.

Clare had given his parents no warning of his visit, and his arrival stirred the atmosphere of the Vicarage as the dive of the kingfisher stirs a quiet pool. His father and mother were both in the drawing-room, but neither of his brothers was now at home. Angel entered, and closed the door quietly behind him.

'But — where's your wife, dear Angel?' cried his mother. 'How you surprise us!'

'She is at her mother's — temporarily. I have come home rather in a hurry because I've decided to go to Brazil.'

'Brazil! Why they are all Roman Catholics there surely!'

'Are they? I hadn't thought of that.'

But even the novelty and painfulness of his going to a Papistical land could not displace for long Mr. and Mrs. Clare's natural interest in their son's marriage.

'We had your brief note three weeks ago announcing that it had taken place,' said Mrs. Clare, 'and your father sent your godmother's gift to her, as you know. Of course it was best that none of us should be present, especially as you preferred to marry her from the dairy, and not at her home, wherever that may be. It would have embarrassed you, and given us no pleasure. Your brothers felt that very strongly. Now it is done we do not complain, particularly if she suits you for the business you have chosen to follow instead of the ministry of the Gospel. . . . Yet I wish I could have seen her first, Angel, or have known a little more about her. We sent her no present of our own, not knowing what would best give her pleasure, but you must suppose it only delayed. Angel, there is no irritation in my mind or your father's against you for this marriage; but we have thought it much better to reserve our liking for your wife till we could see her. And now you have not brought her. It seems strange. What has happened?'

He replied that it had been thought best by them that she should go to her parents' home for the present, whilst he came there.

'I don't mind telling you, dear mother,' he said, 'that I always meant to keep her away from this house till I should feel she could come with credit to you. But this idea of Brazil is quite a recent one. If I do go it will be unadvisable for me to take her on this my first journey. She will remain at her mother's till I come back.'

'And I shall not see her before you start?'

He was afraid they would not. His original plan had been, as he had said, to refrain from bringing her there for some little while — not to wound their prejudices — feelings — in any way; and for other reasons he had adhered to it. He would have to visit home in the course of a year, if he went out at once; and it would be possible for them to see her before he started a second time — with her.

A hastily prepared supper was brought in, and Clare made further exposition of his plans. His mother's disappointment at not seeing the bride still remained with her. Clare's late enthusiasm for Tess had infected her through her maternal sympathies, till she had almost fancied that a good thing could come out of Nazareth° — a charming woman out of Talbothays Dairy. She watched her son as he ate.

'Cannot you describe her? I am sure she is very pretty, Angel.'

'Of that there can be no question!' he said, with a zest which covered its bitterness.

'And that she is pure and virtuous goes without question?'

'Pure and virtuous, of course, she is.'

'I can see her quite distinctly. You said the other day that she was fine in figure; roundly built; had deep red lips like Cupid's bow; dark

a good thing could come out of Nazareth: John 1.46.

eyelashes and brows, an immense rope of hair like a ship's cable; and large eyes violety-bluey-blackish.'

'I did, mother.'

'I quite see her. And living in such seclusion she naturally had scarce ever seen any young man from the world without till she saw you.'

'Scarcely.'

'You were her first love?'

'Of course.'

'There are worse wives than these simple, rosy-mouthed, robust girls of the farm. Certainly I could have wished — well, since my son is to be an agriculturist, it is perhaps but proper that his wife should have been accustomed to an outdoor life.'

His father was less inquisitive; but when the time came for the chapter from the Bible which was always read before evening prayers, the Vicar observed to Mrs. Clare —

'I think, since Angel has come, that it will be more appropriate to read the thirty-first of Proverbs than the chapter which we should have had in the usual course of our reading?'

'Yes, certainly,' said Mrs. Clare. 'The words of King Lemuel' (she could cite chapter and verse as well as her husband). 'My dear son, your father has decided to read us the chapter in Proverbs in praise of a virtuous wife. We shall not need to be reminded to apply the words to the absent one. May Heaven shield her in all her ways!'

A lump rose in Clare's throat. The portable lectern was taken out from the corner and set in the middle of the fireplace, the two old servants came in, and Angel's father began to read at the tenth verse of the aforesaid chapter —

'"Who can find a virtuous woman? for her price is far above rubies. She riseth while it is yet night, and giveth meat to her household. She girdeth her loins with strength and strengtheneth her arms. She perceiveth that her merchandise is good; her candle goeth not out by night. She looketh well to the ways of her household, and eateth not the bread of idleness. Her children arise up and call her blessed; her husband also, and he praiseth her. Many daughters have done virtuously, but thou excellest them all."'

When prayers were over, his mother said —

'I could not help thinking how very aptly that chapter your dear father read applied, in some of its particulars, to the woman you have chosen. The perfect woman, you see, was a working woman; not an idler; not a fine lady; but one who used her hands and her head and her heart for the good of others. "Her children arise up and call her blessed; her husband also, and he praiseth her. Many daughters have done virtuously, but she excelleth them all." Well, I wish I could have seen her, Angel. Since she is pure and chaste she would have been refined enough for me.'

Clare could bear this no longer. His eyes were full of tears, which seemed like drops of molten lead. He bade a quick good-night to these sincere and simple souls whom he loved so well; who knew neither the world, the flesh, nor the devil° in their own hearts; only as something vague and external to themselves. He went to his own chamber.

His mother followed him, and tapped at his door. Clare opened it to discover her standing without, with anxious eyes.

"Angel,' she asked, 'is there something wrong that you go away so soon? I am quite sure you are not yourself.'

'I am not, quite, mother,' said he.

'About her? Now, my son, I know it is that — I know it is about her! Have you quarrelled in these three weeks?'

'We have not exactly quarrelled,' he said. 'But we have had a difference —— '

'Angel — is she a young woman whose history will bear investigation?'

With a mother's instinct Mrs. Clare had put her finger on the kind of trouble that would cause such a disquiet as seemed to agitate her son.

'She is spotless!' he replied; and felt that if it had sent him to eternal hell there and then he would have told that lie.

'Then never mind the rest. After all, there are few purer things in nature than an unsullied country maid. Any crudeness of manner which may offend your more educated sense at first, will, I am sure, disappear under the influence of your companionship and tuition.'

Such terrible sarcasm of blind magnanimity brought home to Clare the secondary perception that he had utterly wrecked his career by this marriage, which had not been among his early thoughts after the disclosure. True, on his own account he cared very little about his career; but he had wished to make it at least a respectable one on account of his parents and brothers. And now as he looked into the candle its flame dumbly expressed to him that it was made to shine on

the world, the flesh, nor the devil: "The world, the flesh, and the devil" are traditional temptations to sin mentioned in *The Book of Common Prayer*.

sensible people, and that it abhorred lighting the face of a dupe and a failure.

When his agitation had cooled he would be at moments incensed with his poor wife for causing a situation in which he was obliged to practise deception on his parents. He almost talked to her in his anger, as if she had been in the room. And then her cooing voice, plaintive in expostulation, disturbed the darkness, the velvet touch of her lips passed over his brow, and he could distinguish in the air the warmth of her breath.

This night the woman of his belittling deprecations was thinking how great and good her husband was. But over them both there hung a deeper shade than the shade which Angel Clare perceived, namely, the shade of his own limitations. With all his attempted independence of judgment this advanced and well-meaning young man, a sample product of the last five-and-twenty years, was yet the slave to custom and conventionality when surprised back into his early teachings. No prophet had told him, and he was not prophet enough to tell himself, that essentially this young wife of his was as deserving of the praise of King Lemuel as any other woman endowed with the same dislike of evil, her moral value having to be reckoned not by achievement but by tendency. Moreover, the figure near at hand suffers on such occasions, because it shows up its sorriness without shade; while vague figures afar off are honoured, in that their distance makes artistic virtues of their stains. In considering what Tess was not, he overlooked what she was, and forgot that the defective can be more than the entire.

XL

At breakfast Brazil was the topic, and all endeavoured to take a hopeful view of Clare's proposed experiment with that country's soil, notwithstanding the discouraging reports of some farm-labourers who had emigrated thither and returned home within the twelve months. After breakfast Clare went into the little town to wind up such trifling matters as he was concerned with there, and to get from the local bank all the money he possessed. On his way back he encountered Miss Mercy Chant by the church, from whose walls she seemed to be a sort of emanation. She was carrying an armful of Bibles for her class, and such was her view of life that events which produced heartache in others wrought beatific smiles upon her — an enviable result, although, in the opinion of Angel, it was obtained by a curiously unnatural sacrifice of humanity to mysticism.

She had learnt that he was about to leave England, and observed what an excellent and promising scheme it seemed to be.

'Yes; it is a likely scheme enough in a commercial sense, no doubt,' he replied. 'But, my dear Mercy, it snaps the continuity of existence. Perhaps a cloister would be preferable.'

'A cloister! O, Angel Clare!'

'Well?'

'Why, you wicked man, a cloister implies a monk, and a monk Roman Catholicism.'

'And Roman Catholicism sin, and sin damnation. Thou art in a parlous state, Angel Clare.'

'*I* glory in my Protestantism!' she said severely.

Then Clare, thrown by sheer misery into one of the demoniacal moods in which a man does despite to his true principles, called her close to him, and fiendishly whispered in her ear the most heterodox ideas he could think of. His momentary laughter at the horror which appeared on her fair face ceased when it merged in pain and anxiety for his welfare.

'Dear Mercy,' he said, 'you must forgive me. I think I am going crazy!'

She thought that he was; and thus the interview ended, and Clare re-entered the Vicarage. With the local banker he deposited the jewels till happier days should arise. He also paid into the bank thirty pounds — to be sent to Tess in a few months, as she might require; and wrote to her at her parents' home in Blackmoor Vale to inform her of what he had done. This amount, with the sum he had already placed in her hands — about fifty pounds — he hoped would be amply sufficient for her wants just at present, particularly as in an emergency she had been directed to apply to his father.

He deemed it best not to put his parents into communication with her by informing them of her address; and, being unaware of what had really happened to estrange the two, neither his father nor his mother suggested that he should do so. During the day he left the parsonage, for what he had to complete he wished to get done quickly.

As the last duty before leaving this part of England it was necessary for him to call at the Wellbridge farmhouse, in which he had spent with Tess the first three days of their marriage, the trifle of rent having to be paid, the key given up of the rooms they had occupied, and two or three small articles fetched away that they had left behind. It was under this roof that the deepest shadow ever thrown upon his life had stretched its gloom over him. Yet when he had unlocked the door of the sitting-room and looked into it, the memory which returned first upon him was that of their happy arrival on a similar afternoon, the first fresh sense of sharing a habitation conjointly, the first meal together, the chatting by the fire with joined hands.

The farmer and his wife were in the fields at the moment of his visit, and Clare was in the rooms alone for some time. Inwardly swollen with a renewal of sentiments that he had not quite reckoned with, he went upstairs to her chamber, which had never been his. The bed was smooth as she had made it with her own hands on the morning of leaving. The mistletoe hung under the tester just as he had placed it. Having been there three or four weeks it was turning colour, and the leaves and berries were wrinkled. Angel took it down and crushed it into the grate. Standing there he for the first time doubted whether his course in this conjuncture had been a wise, much less a generous, one. But had he not been cruelly blinded? In the incoherent multitude of his emotions he knelt down at the bedside wet-eyed. 'O Tess! If you had only told me sooner, I would have forgiven you!' he mourned.

Hearing a footstep below he rose and went to the top of the stairs. At the bottom of the flight he saw a woman standing, and on her turning up her face recognised the pale, dark-eyed Izz Huett.

'Mr. Clare,' she said, 'I've called to see you and Mrs. Clare, and to inquire if ye be well. I thought you might be back here again.'

This was a girl whose secret he had guessed, but who had not yet guessed his; an honest girl who loved him — one who would have made as good, or nearly as good, a practical farmer's wife as Tess.

'I am here alone,' he said; 'we are not living here now.' Explaining why he had come, he asked, 'Which way are you going home, Izz?'

'I have no home at Talbothays Dairy now, sir,' she said.

'Why is that?'

Izz looked down.

'It was so dismal there that I left! I am staying out this way.' She pointed in a contrary direction, the direction in which he was journeying.

'Well — are you going there now? I can take you if you wish for a lift.

Her olive complexion grew richer in hue.

'Thank 'ee, Mr. Clare,' she said.

He soon found the farmer, and settled the account for his rent and the few other items which had to be considered by reason of the sudden abandonment of the lodgings. On Clare's return to his horse and gig Izz jumped up beside him.

'I am going to leave England, Izz,' he said, as they drove on. 'Going to Brazil.'

'And do Mrs. Clare like the notion of such a journey?' she asked.

'She is not going at present — say for a year or so. I am going out to reconnoitre — to see what life there is like.'

They sped along eastward for some considerable distance, Izz making no observation.

'How are the others?' he inquired. 'How is Retty?'

'She was in a sort of nervous state when I zid her last; and so thin and hollow-cheeked that 'a do seem in a decline. Nobody will ever fall in love wi' her any more,' said Izz absently.

'And Marian?'

Izz lowered her voice.

'Marian drinks.'

'Indeed!'

'Yes. The dairyman has got rid of her.'

'And you!'

'I don't drink, and I bain't in a decline. But — I am no great things at singing afore breakfast now!'

'How is that? Do you remember how neatly you used to turn "'Twas down in Cupid's Gardens" and "The Tailor's Breeches" at morning milking?'

'Ah, yes! When you first came, sir, that was. Not when you had been there a bit.'

'Why was that falling-off?'

Her black eyes flashed up to his face for one moment by way of answer.

'Izz! — how weak of you — for such as I!' he said, and fell into reverie. 'Then — suppose I had asked *you* to marry me?'

'If you had I should have said "Yes," and you would have married a woman who loved 'ee!'

'Really!'

'Down to the ground!' she whispered vehemently. 'O my God! did you never guess it till now!'

By-and-by they reached a branch road to a village.

'I must get down. I live out there,' said Izz abruptly, never having spoken since her avowal.

Clare slowed the horse. He was incensed against his fate, bitterly disposed towards social ordinances; for they had cooped him up in a corner, out of which there was no legitimate pathway. Why not be revenged on society by shaping his future domesticities loosely, instead of kissing the pedagogic rod of convention in this ensnaring manner.

'I am going to Brazil alone, Izz,' said he. 'I have separated from my wife for personal, not voyaging, reasons. I may never live with her again. I may not be able to love you; but — will you go with me instead of her?'

'You truly wish me to go?'

'I do. I have been badly used enough to wish for relief. And you at least love me disinterestedly.'

'Yes — I will go,' said Izz, after a pause.

'You will? You know what it means, Izz?'

'It means that I shall live with you for the time you are over there — that's good enough for me.'

'Remember, you are not to trust me in morals now. But I ought to remind you that it will be wrong-doing in the eyes of civilization — Western civilization, that is to say.'

'I don't mind that; no woman do when it comes to agony-point, and there's no other way!'

'Then don't get down, but sit where you are.'

He drove past the cross-roads, one mile, two miles, without showing any signs of affection.

'You love me very, very much, Izz?' he suddenly asked.

'I do — I have said I do! I loved you all the time we was at the dairy together!'

'More than Tess?'

She shook her head.

'No,' she murmured, 'not more than she.'

'How's that?'

'Because nobody could love 'ee more than Tess did! . . . She would have laid down her life for 'ee. I could do no more.'

Like the prophet on the top of Peor° Izz Huett would fain have spoken perversely at such a moment, but the fascination exercised over her rougher nature by Tess's character compelled her to grace.

Clare was silent; his heart had risen at these straightforward words from such an unexpected unimpeachable quarter. In his throat was something as if a sob had solidified there. His ears repeated, '*She would have laid down her life for 'ee. I could do no more!*'

prophet on the top of Peor: Balaam, who refused to curse the Israelites; Numbers 23–24.

'Forget our idle talk, Izz,' he said, turning the horse's head suddenly. 'I don't know what I've been saying! I will now drive you back to where your lane branches off.'

'So much for honesty towards 'ee! O — how can I bear it — how can I — how can I!'

Izz Huett burst into wild tears, and beat her forehead as she saw what she had done.

'Do you regret that poor little act of justice to an absent one? O, Izz, don't spoil it by regret!'

She stilled herself by degrees.

'Very well, sir. Perhaps I didn't know what I was saying, either, wh — when I agreed to go! I wish — what cannot be!'

'Because I have a loving wife already.'

'Yes, yes! You have.'

They reached the corner of the lane which they had passed half an hour earlier and she hopped down.

'Izz — please, please forget my momentary levity!' he cried. 'It was so ill-considered, so ill-advised!'

'Forget it? Never, never! O, it was no levity to me!'

He felt how richly he deserved the reproach that the wounded cry conveyed, and, in a sorrow that was inexpressible, leapt down and took her hand.

'Well, but, Izz, we'll part friends, anyhow? You don't know what I've had to bear!'

She was a really generous girl, and allowed no further bitterness to mar their adieux.

'I forgive 'ee, sir!' she said.

'Now Izz,' he said, while she stood beside him there, forcing himself to the mentor's part he was far from feeling; 'I want you to tell Marian when you see her that she is to be a good woman, and not to give way to folly. Promise that, and tell Retty that there are more worthy men than I in the world, that for my sake she is to act wisely and well — remember the words — wisely and well — for my sake. I send this message to them as a dying man to the dying; for I shall never see them again. And you, Izzy, you have saved me by your honest words about my wife from an incredible impulse towards folly and treachery. Women may be bad, but they are not so bad as men in these things! On that one account I can never forget you. Be always the good and sincere girl you have hitherto been; and think of me as a worthless lover, but a faithful friend. Promise.'

She gave the promise.

'Heaven bless and keep you, sir. Good-bye!'

He drove on; but no sooner had Izz turned into the lane, and Clare was out of sight, than she flung herself down on the bank in a fit of racking anguish; and it was with a strained unnatural face that she entered her mother's cottage late that night. Nobody ever was told how Izz spent the dark hours that intervened between Angel Clare's parting from her and her arrival home.

Clare, too, after bidding the girl farewell, was wrought to aching thoughts and quivering lips. But his sorrow was not for Izz. That evening he was within a feather-weight's turn of abandoning his road to the nearest station, and driving across that elevated dorsal line of South Wessex which divided him from his Tess's home. It was neither a contempt for her nature, nor the probable state of her heart, which deterred him.

No; it was a sense that, despite her love, as corroborated by Izz's admission, the facts had not changed. If he was right at first, he was right now. And the momentum of the course on which he had embarked tended to keep him going in it, unless diverted by a stronger, more sustained force than had played upon him this afternoon. He could soon come back to her. He took the train that night for London, and five days after shook hands in farewell of his brothers at the port of embarkation.

XLI

From the foregoing events of the winter-time let us press on to an October day, more than eight months subsequent to the parting of Clare and Tess. We discover the latter in changed conditions; instead of a bride with boxes and trunks which others bore, we see her a lonely woman with a basket and a bundle in her own porterage, as at an earlier time when she was no bride; instead of the ample means that were projected by her husband for her comfort through this probationary period, she can produce only a flattened purse.

After again leaving Marlott, her home, she had got through the spring and summer without any great stress upon her physical powers, the time being mainly spent in rendering light irregular service at dairy-work near Port-Bredy to the west of the Blackmoor Valley, equally remote from her native place and from Talbothays. She preferred this to living on his allowance. Mentally she remained in utter stagnation, a condition which the mechanical occupation rather fostered than checked. Her consciousness was at that other dairy, at that other season, in the presence of the tender lover who had confronted her there — he who, the moment she had grasped him to keep for her own, had disappeared like a shape in a vision.

The dairy-work lasted only till the milk began to lessen, for she had not met with a second regular engagement as at Talbothays, but had done duty as a supernumerary only. However, as harvest was now beginning, she had simply to remove from the pasture to the stubble to find plenty of further occupation, and this continued till harvest was done.

Of the five-and-twenty pounds which had remained to her of Clare's allowance, after deducting the other half of the fifty as a contribution to her parents for the trouble and expense to which she had put them, she had as yet spent but little. But there now followed an unfortunate interval of wet weather, during which she was obliged to fall back upon her sovereigns.

She could not bear to let them go. Angel had put them into her hand, had obtained them bright and new from his bank for her; his touch had consecrated them to souvenirs of himself — they appeared to have had as yet no other history than such as was created by his and her own experiences — and to disperse them was like giving away relics. But she had to do it, and one by one they left her hands.

She had been compelled to send her mother her address from time to time, but she concealed her circumstances. When her money had almost gone a letter from her mother reached her. Joan stated that they were in dreadful difficulty; the autumn rains had gone through the thatch of the house, which required entire renewal; but this could not be done because the previous thatching had never been paid for. New rafters and a new ceiling upstairs also were required, which, with the previous bill, would amount to a sum of twenty pounds. As her husband was a man of means, and had doubtless returned by this time, could she not send them the money?

Tess had thirty pounds coming to her almost immediately from Angel's bankers, and, the case being so deplorable, as soon as the sum was received she sent the twenty as requested. Part of the remainder she was obliged to expend in winter clothing, leaving only a nominal sum for the whole inclement season at hand. When the last pound had gone, a remark of Angel's that whenever she required further resources she was to apply to his father, remained to be considered.

But the more Tess thought of the step the more reluctant was she to take it. The same delicacy, pride, false shame, whatever it may be called, on Clare's account, which had led her to hide from her own parents the prolongation of the estrangement, hindered her in owning to his that she was in want after the fair allowance he had left her. They probably despised her already; how much more they would despise her in the character of a mendicant! The consequence was that by no effort could the parson's daughter-in-law bring herself to let him know her state.

Her reluctance to communicate with her husband's parents might, she thought, lessen with the lapse of time; but with her own the reverse obtained. On her leaving their house after the short visit subsequent to her marriage they were under the impression that she was ultimately going to join her husband; and from that time to the present she had done nothing to disturb their belief that she was awaiting his return in comfort, hoping against hope that his journey to Brazil would result in a short stay only, after which he would come to fetch her, or that he would write for her to join him; in any case that they would soon present a united front to their families and the world. This hope she still fostered. To let her parents know that she was a deserted wife, dependent, now that she had relieved their necessities, on her own hands for a living, after the *éclat* of a marriage which was to nullify the collapse of the first attempt, would be too much indeed.

The set of brilliants returned to her mind. Where Clare had deposited them she did not know, and it mattered little, if it were true that she could only use and not sell them. Even were they absolutely hers it would be passing mean to enrich herself by a legal title to them which was not essentially hers at all.

Meanwhile her husband's days had been by no means free from trial. At this moment he was lying ill of fever in the clay lands near Curitiba in Brazil, having been drenched with thunder-storms and persecuted by other hardships, in common with all the English farmers and farm-labourers who, just at this time, were deluded into going thither by the promises of the Brazilian Government, and by the baseless assumption that those frames which, ploughing and sowing on English uplands, had resisted all the weathers to whose moods they had been born, could resist equally well all the weathers by which they were surprised on Brazilian plains.

To return. Thus it happened that when the last of Tess's sovereigns had been spent she was unprovided with others to take their place, while on account of the season she found it increasingly difficult to get employment. Not being aware of the rarity of intelligence, energy, health, and willingness in any sphere of life, she refrained from seeking an indoor occupation; fearing towns, large houses, people of means and social sophistication, and of manners other than rural. From that direction of gentility Black Care had come. Society might be better than she supposed from her slight experience of it. But she had no proof of this, and her instinct in the circumstances was to avoid its purlieus.

The small dairies to the west, beyond Port-Bredy, in which she had served as supernumerary milkmaid during the spring and summer required no further aid. Room would probably have been made for her at Talbothays, if only out of sheer compassion; but comfortable as her life had been there she could not go back. The anti-climax would be too intolerable; and her return might bring reproach upon her idolized husband. She could not have borne their pity, and their whispered remarks to one another upon her strange situation; though she would almost have faced a knowledge of her circumstances by every individual there, so long as her story had remained isolated in the mind of each. It was the interchange of ideas about her that made her sensitiveness wince. Tess could not account for this distinction; she simply knew that she felt it.

She was now on her way to an upland farm in the center of the county, to which she had been recommended by a wandering letter which had reached her from Marian. Marian had somehow heard that Tess was separated from her husband — probably through Izz Huett — and the good-natured and now tippling girl, deeming Tess in trouble, had hastened to notify to her former friend that she herself had gone to this upland spot after leaving the dairy, and would like to see her there, where there was room for other hands, if it was really true that she worked again as of old.

With the shortening of the days all hope of obtaining her husband's forgiveness began to leave her; and there was something of the habitude of the wild animal in the unreflecting instinct with which she rambled on — disconnecting herself by littles from her eventful past at every step, obliterating her identity, giving no thought to accidents or contingencies which might make a quick discovery of her whereabouts by others of importance to her own happiness, if not to theirs.

Among the difficulties of her lonely position not the least was the attention she excited by her appearance, a certain bearing of distinction, which she had caught from Clare, being superadded to her natural attractiveness. Whilst the clothes lasted which had been prepared for her marriage, these casual glances of interest caused her no inconvenience, but as soon as she was compelled to don the wrapper of a fieldwoman, rude words were addressed to her more than once; but nothing occurred to cause her bodily fear till a particular November afternoon.

She had preferred the country west of the River Brit to the upland farm for which she was now bound, because, for one thing, it was nearer to the home of her husband's father; and to hover about that region unrecognized, with the notion that she might decide to call at the Vicarage some day, gave her pleasure. But having once decided to try the higher and drier levels, she pressed back eastward, marching afoot towards the village of Chalk-Newton, where she meant to pass the night.

The lane was long and unvaried, and, owing to the rapid shortening of the days, dusk came upon her before she was aware. She had reached the top of a hill down which the lane stretched its serpentine length in glimpses, when she heard footsteps behind her back, and in a few moments she was overtaken by a man. He stepped up alongside Tess and said —

'Good-night, my pretty maid:' to which she civilly replied.

The light still remaining in the sky lit up her face, though the landscape was nearly dark. The man turned and stared hard at her.

'Why, surely, it is the young wench who was at Trantridge awhile — young Squire d'Urberville's friend? I was there at that time, though I don't live there now.'

She recognized in him the well-to-do boor whom Angel had knocked down at the inn for addressing her coarsely. A spasm of anguish shot through her, and she returned him no answer.

'Be honest enough to own it, and that what I said in the town was true, though your fancy-man° was so up about it — hey, my sly one? You ought to beg my pardon for that blow of his, considering.'

Still no answer came from Tess. There seemed only one escape for her hunted soul. She suddenly took to her heels with the speed of the wind, and, without looking behind her, ran along the road till she came to a gate which opened directly into a plantation. Into this she plunged, and did not pause till she was deep enough in its shade to be safe against any possibility of discovery.

Under foot the leaves were dry, and the foliage of some holly bushes which grew among the deciduous trees was dense enough to keep off draughts. She scraped together the dead leaves till she had formed them into a large heap, making a sort of nest in the middle. Into this Tess crept.

fancy-man: Sweetheart (slang); a man who lives on the earnings of a prostitute (*OED*). The *OED* cites this sentence in *Tess* as an example of the slang meaning.

Such sleep as she got was naturally fitful; she fancied she heard strange noises, but persuaded herself that they were caused by the breeze. She thought of her husband in some vague warm clime on the other side of the globe, while she was here in the cold. Was there another such a wretched being as she in the world? Tess asked herself; and, thinking of her wasted life, said, 'All is vanity.'° She repeated the words mechanically, till she reflected that this was a most inadequate thought for modern days. Solomon° had thought as far as that more than two thousand years ago; she herself, though not in the van of thinkers, had got much further. If all were only vanity, who would mind it? All was, alas, worse than vanity — injustice, punishment, exaction, death. The wife of Angel Clare put her hand to her brow, and felt its curve, and the edges of her eye-sockets perceptible under the soft skin, and thought as she did so that a time would come when that bone would be bare. 'I wish it were now,' she said.

In the midst of these whimsical fancies she heard a new strange sound among the leaves. It might be the wind; yet there was scarcely any wind. Sometimes it was a palpitation, sometimes a flutter; sometimes it was a sort of gasp or gurgle. Soon she was certain that the noises came from wild creatures of some kind, the more so when, originating in the boughs overhead, they were followed by the fall of a heavy body upon the ground. Had she been ensconced here under other and more pleasant conditions she would have been alarmed; but, outside humanity, she had at present no fear.

Day at length broke in the sky. When it had been day aloft for some little while it became day in the wood.

Directly the assuring and prosaic light of the world's active hours had grown strong, she crept from under her hillock of leaves, and looked around boldly. Then she perceived what had been going on to disturb her. The plantation wherein she had taken shelter ran down at this spot into a peak, which ended it hitherward, outside the hedge being arable ground. Under the trees several pheasants lay about, their rich plumage dabbled with blood; some were dead, some feebly twitching a wing, some staring up at the sky, some pulsating quickly, some contorted, some stretched out — all of them writhing in agony, except the fortunate ones whose tortures had ended during the night by the inability of nature to bear more.

'All is vanity.': Ecclesiastes 1.2. **Solomon:** Hebrew king noted for his wisdom. The opening chapters of Ecclesiastes are sometimes still associated with Solomon.

Tess guessed at once the meaning of this. The birds had been driven down into this corner the day before by some shooting-party; and while those that had dropped dead under the shot, or had died before nightfall, had been searched for and carried off, many badly wounded birds had escaped and hidden themselves away, or risen among the thick boughs, where they had maintained their position till they grew weaker with loss of blood in the night-time, when they had fallen one by one as she had heard them.

She had occasionally caught glimpses of these men in girlhood, looking over hedges, or peering through bushes, and pointing their guns, strangely accoutred, a bloodthirsty light in their eyes. She had been told that, rough and brutal as they seemed just then, they were not like this all the year round, but were, in fact, quite civil persons save during certain weeks of autumn and winter, when, like the inhabitants of the Malay Peninsula, they ran amuck, and made it their purpose to destroy life — in this case harmless feathered creatures, brought into being by artificial means solely to gratify these propensities — at once so unmannerly and so unchivalrous towards their weaker fellows in Nature's teeming family.

With the impulse of a soul who could feel for kindred sufferers as much as for herself, Tess's first thought was to put the still living birds out of their torture, and to this end with her own hands she broke the necks of as many as she could find, leaving them to lie where she had found them till the gamekeepers should come — as they probably would come — to look for them a second time.

'Poor darlings — to suppose myself the most miserable being on earth in the sight o' such misery as yours!' she exclaimed, her tears running down as she killed the birds tenderly. 'And not a twinge of bodily pain about me! I be not mangled, and I be not bleeding, and I have two hands to feed and clothe me.' She was ashamed of herself for her gloom of the night, based on nothing more tangible than a sense of condemnation under an arbitrary law of society which had no foundation in Nature.

XLII

It was now broad day, and she started again, emerging cautiously upon the highway. But there was no need for caution; not a soul was at hand, and Tess went onward with fortitude, her recollection of the birds' silent endurance of their night of agony impressing upon her the relativity of sorrows and the tolerable nature of her own, if she could once rise high enough to despise opinion. But that she could not do so long as it was held by Clare.

She reached Chalk-Newton, and breakfasted at an inn, where several young men were troublesomely complimentary to her good looks. Somehow she felt hopeful, for was it not possible that her husband also might say these same things to her even yet? She was bound to take care of herself on the chance of it, and keep off these casual lovers. To this end Tess resolved to run no further risks from her appearance. As soon as she got out of the village she entered a thicket and took from her basket one of the oldest field-gowns, which she had never put on even at the dairy — never since she had worked among the stubble at Marlott. She also, by a felicitous thought, took a handkerchief from her bundle and tied it round her face under her bonnet, covering her chin and half her cheeks and temples, as if she were suffering from toothache. Then with her little scissors, by the aid of a pocket looking-glass, she mercilessly nipped her eyebrows off, and thus insured against aggressive admiration she went on her uneven way.

'What a mommet° of a maid!' said the next man who met her to a companion.

Tears came into her eyes for very pity of herself as she heard him.

'But I don't care!' she said. 'O no — I don't care! I'll always be ugly now, because Angel is not here, and I have nobody to take care of me. My husband that was is gone away, and never will love me any more; but I love him just the same, and hate all other men, and like to make 'em think scornfully of me!'

Thus Tess walks on; a figure which is part of the landscape; a field-woman pure and simple, in winter guise; a gray serge cape, a red woollen cravat, a stuff skirt covered by a whitey-brown rough wrapper, and buff-leather gloves. Every thread of that old attire has become faded and thin under the stroke of raindrops, the burn of sunbeams, and the stress of winds. There is no sign of young passion in her now —

> The maiden's mouth is cold
> . . . .
> Fold over simple fold
> Binding her head.°

mommet: Variant of *maumet;* a term of abuse or contempt (dialect) (*OED*). **The maiden's mouth is cold . . . :** From "Fragoletta" by A. C. Swinburne.

Inside this exterior, over which the eye might have roved as over a thing scarcely percipient, almost inorganic, there was the record of a pulsing life which had learnt too well, for its years, of the dust and ashes° of things, of the cruelty of lust and the fragility of love.

Next day the weather was bad, but she trudged on, the honesty, directness, and impartiality of elemental enmity disconcerting her but little. Her object being a winter's occupation and a winter's home, there was no time to lose. Her experience of short hirings had been such that she was determined to accept no more.

Thus she went forward from farm to farm in the direction of the place whence Marian had written to her, which she determined to make use of as a last shift only, its rumoured stringencies being the reverse of tempting. First she inquired for the lighter kinds of employment, and, as acceptance in any variety of these grew hopeless, applied next for the less light, till, beginning with the dairy and poultry tendance that she liked best, she ended with the heavy and coarse pursuits which she liked least — work on arable land: work of such roughness, indeed, as she would never have deliberately volunteered for.

Towards the second evening she reached the irregular chalk tableland or plateau, bosomed with semi-globular tumuli — as if Cybele the Many-breasted° were supinely extended there — which stretched between the valley of her birth and the valley of her love.

Here the air was dry and cold, and the long cart-roads were blown white and dusty within a few hours after rain. There were few trees, or none, those that would have grown in the hedges being mercilessly plashed down with the quickset by the tenant-farmers, the natural enemies of tree, bush, and brake. In the middle distance ahead of her she could see the summits of Bulbarrow and of Nettlecombe Tout, and they seemed friendly. They had a low and unassuming aspect from this upland, though as approached on the other side from Blackmoor in her childhood they were as lofty bastions against the sky. Southerly, at many miles' distance, and over the hills and ridges coastward, she could discern a surface like polished steel: it was the English Channel at a point far out towards France.

Before her, in a slight depression, were the remains of a village. She had, in fact, reached Flintcomb-Ash, the place of Marian's sojourn. There seemed to be no help for it; hither she was doomed to

dust and ashes: Job 42.6. **Cybele the Many-breasted:** Phrygian fertility goddess who, in the form of a mother with many breasts, symbolizes nature.

come. The stubborn soil around her showed plainly enough that the kind of labour in demand here was of the roughest kind; but it was time to rest from searching, and she resolved to stay, particularly as it began to rain. At the entrance to the village was a cottage whose gable jutted into the road, and before applying for a lodging she stood under its shelter, and watched the evening close in.

'Who would think I was Mrs. Angel Clare!' she said.

The wall felt warm to her back and shoulders, and she found that immediately within the gable was the cottage fireplace, the heat of which came through the bricks. She warmed her hands upon them, and also put her cheek — red and moist with the drizzle — against their comforting surface. The wall seemed to be the only friend she had. She had so little wish to leave it that she could have stayed there all night.

Tess could hear the occupants of the cottage — gathered together after their day's labour — talking to each other within, and the rattle of their supper-plates was also audible. But in the village-street she had seen no soul as yet. The solitude was at last broken by the approach of one feminine figure, who, though the evening was cold, wore the print gown and the tilt-bonnet of summer time. Tess instinctively thought it might be Marian, and when she came near enough to be distinguishable in the gloom surely enough it was she. Marian was even stouter and redder in the face than formerly, and decidedly shabbier in attire. At any previous period of her existence Tess would hardly have cared to renew the acquaintance in such conditions; but her loneliness was excessive, and she responded readily to Marian's greeting.

Marian was quite respectful in her inquiries, but seemed much moved by the fact that Tess should still continue in no better condition than at first; though she had dimly heard of the separation.

'Tess — Mrs. Clare — the dear wife of dear he! And is it really so bad as this, my child? Why is your cwomely face tied up in such a way? Anybody been beating 'ee? Not *he*?'

'No, no, no! I merely did it not to be clipsed or colled,° Marian.'

She pulled off in disgust a bandage which could suggest such wild thoughts.

'And you've got no collar on' (Tess had been accustomed to wear a little white collar at the dairy).

'I know it, Marian.'

'You've lost it travelling.'

clipsed or colled: Embraced (dialect).

'I've not lost it. The truth is, I don't care anything about my looks; and so I didn't put it on.'

'And you don't wear your wedding-ring?'

'Yes, I do; but not in public. I wear it round my neck on a ribbon. I don't wish people to think who I am by marriage, or that I am married at all; it would be so awkward while I lead my present life.'

Marian paused.

'But you *be* a gentleman's wife; and it seems hardly fair that you should live like this!'

'O yes it is, quite fair; though I am very unhappy.'

'Well, well. *He* married you — and you can be unhappy!'

'Wives are unhappy sometimes; from no fault of their husbands — from their own.'

'You've no faults, deary; that I'm sure of. And he's none. So it must be something outside ye both.'

'Marian, dear Marian, will you do me a good turn without asking questions? My husband has gone abroad, and somehow I have overrun my allowance, so that I have to fall back upon my old work for a time. Do not call me Mrs. Clare, but Tess, as before. Do they want a hand here?'

'O yes; they'll take one always, because few care to come. 'Tis a starve-acre place. Corn and swedes are all they grow. Though I be here myself, I feel 'tis a pity for such as you to come.'

'But you used to be as good a dairywoman as I.'

'Yes; but I've got out o' that since I took to drink. Lord, that's the only comfort I've got now! If you engage, you'll be set swede-hacking.° That's what I be doing; but you won't like it.'

'O — anything! Will you speak for me?'

'You will do better by speaking for yourself.'

'Very well. Now, Marian, remember — nothing about *him,* if I get the place. I don't wish to bring his name down to the dirt.'

Marian, who was really a trustworthy girl though of coarser grain than Tess, promised anything she asked.

'This is pay-night,' she said, 'and if you were to come with me you would know at once. I be real sorry that you are not happy; but 'tis because he's away, I know. You couldn't be unhappy if he were here, even if he gie'd ye no money — even if he used you like a drudge.'

'That's true; I could not!'

They walked on together, and soon reached the farmhouse, which

swede-hacking: A swede is a Swedish turnip, or rutabaga.

was almost sublime in its dreariness. There was not a tree within sight; there was not, at this season, a green pasture — nothing but fallow and turnips everywhere; in large fields divided by hedges plashed to unrelieved levels.

Tess waited outside the door of the farmhouse till the group of workfolk had received their wages, and then Marian introduced her. The farmer himself, it appeared, was not at home, but his wife, who represented him this evening, made no objection to hiring Tess, on her agreeing to remain till Old Lady-Day.° Female field-labour was seldom offered now, and its cheapness made it profitable for tasks which women could perform as readily as men.

Having signed the agreement, there was nothing more for Tess to do at present than to get a lodging, and she found one in the house at whose gable-wall she had warmed herself. It was a poor subsistence that she had ensured, but it would afford a shelter for the winter at any rate.

That night she wrote to inform her parents of her new address, in case a letter should arrive at Marlott from her husband. But she did not tell them of the sorriness of her situation: it might have brought reproach upon him.

XLIII

There was no exaggeration in Marian's definition of Flintcomb-Ash farm as a starve-acre place. The single fat thing on the soil was Marian herself; and she was an importation. Of the three classes of village, the village cared for by its lord, the village cared for by itself, and the village uncared for either by itself or by its lord (in other words, the village of a resident squire's tenantry, the village of free or copyholders, and the absentee-owner's village, farmed with the land) this place, Flintcomb-Ash, was the third.

But Tess set to work. Patience, that blending of moral courage with physical timidity, was now no longer a minor feature in Mrs. Angel Clare; and it sustained her.

The swede-field in which she and her companion were set hacking was a stretch of a hundred odd acres, in one patch, on the highest ground of the farm, rising above stony lanchets or lynchets° — the

Old Lady-Day: When the calendar was changed in 1752, Lady-Day, or the Feast of the Annunciation, moved from April 6 to March 25, but April 6, or Old Lady-Day, continued to be used to set the beginning or the ending of employment. **lanchets or lynchets:** lanchet, or landshard (both dial.), is a synonym of lynchet, a "slope or terrace along the face of a chalk down" (*OED*).

outcrop of siliceous veins in the chalk formation, composed of myriads of loose white flints in bulbous, cusped, and phallic shapes. The upper half of each turnip had been eaten off by the live-stock, and it was the business of the two women to grub up the lower or earthy half of the root with a hooked fork called a hacker, that it might be eaten also. Every leaf of the vegetable having already been consumed, the whole field was in colour a desolate drab; it was a complexion without features, as if a face, from chin to brow, should be only an expanse of skin. The sky wore, in another colour, the same likeness; a white vacuity of countenance with the lineaments gone. So these two upper and nether visages confronted each other all day long, the white face looking down on the brown face, and the brown face looking up at the white face, without anything standing between them but the two girls crawling over the surface of the former like flies.

Nobody came near them, and their movements showed a mechanical regularity; their forms standing enshrouded in Hessian 'wroppers'° — sleeved brown pinafores, tied behind to the bottom, to keep their gowns from blowing about — scant skirts revealing boots that reached high up the ankles, and yellow sheepskin gloves with gauntlets. The pensive character which the curtained hood lent to their bent heads would have reminded the observer of some early Italian conception of the two Marys.°

They worked on hour after hour, unconscious of the forlorn aspect they bore in the landscape, not thinking of the justice or injustice of their lot. Even in such a position as theirs it was possible to exist in a dream. In the afternoon the rain came on again, and Marian said that they need not work any more. But if they did not work they would not be paid; so they worked on. It was so high a situation, this field, that the rain had no occasion to fall, but raced along horizontally upon the yelling wind, sticking into them like glass splinters till they were wet through. Tess had not known till now what was really meant by that. There are degrees of dampness, and a very little is called being wet through in common talk. But to stand working slowly in a field, and feel the creep of rain-water, first in legs and shoulders, then on hips and head, then at back, front, and sides, and yet to work on till the leaden light diminishes and marks that the sun is down, demands a distinct modicum of stoicism, even of valour.

'wroppers': Wrappers (dialect) (*OED*). **early Italian conception of the two Marys:** Because of their wrappings and pensive looks, they resemble painted representations from the Renaissance of Mary the mother of Christ and Mary Magdalen after the death of Jesus.

Yet they did not feel the wetness so much as might be supposed. They were both young, and they were talking of the time when they lived and loved together at Talbothays Dairy, that happy green tract of land where summer had been liberal in her gifts; in substance to all, emotionally to these. Tess would fain not have conversed with Marian of the man who was legally, if not actually, her husband; but the irresistible fascination of the subject betrayed her into reciprocating Marian's remarks. And thus, as has been said, though the damp curtains of their bonnets flapped smartly into their faces, and their wrappers clung about them to wearisomeness, they lived all this afternoon in memories of green, sunny, romantic Talbothays.

'You can see a gleam of a hill within a few miles o' Froom Valley from here when 'tis fine,' said Marian.

'Ah! Can you?' said Tess, awake to the new value of this locality.

So the two forces were at work here as everywhere, the inherent will to enjoy, and the circumstantial will against enjoyment. Marian's will had a method of assisting itself by taking from her pocket as the afternoon wore on a pint bottle corked with white rag, from which she invited Tess to drink. Tess's unassisted power of dreaming, however, being enough for her sublimation at present, she declined except the merest sip, and then Marian took a pull herself from the spirits.

'I've got used to it,' she said, 'and can't leave it off now. 'Tis my only comfort — You see I lost him: you didn't; and you can do without it perhaps.'

Tess thought her loss as great as Marian's, but upheld by the dignity of being Angel's wife, in the letter at least, she accepted Marian's differentiation.

Amid this scene Tess slaved in the morning frosts and in the afternoon rains. When it was not swede-grubbing it was swede-trimming, in which process they sliced off the earth and the fibres with a bill-hook before storing the roots for future use. At this occupation they could shelter themselves by a thatched hurdle if it rained; but if it was frosty even their thick leather gloves could not prevent the frozen masses they handled from biting their fingers. Still Tess hoped. She had a conviction that sooner or later the magnanimity which she persisted in reckoning as a chief ingredient of Clare's character would lead him to rejoin her.

Marian, primed to a humorous mood, would discover the queer-shaped flints aforesaid, and shriek with laughter, Tess remaining severely obtuse. They often looked across the country to where the Var or Froom was known to stretch, even though they might not be able to see it; and, fixing their eyes on the cloaking gray mist, imagined the old times they had spent out there.

'Ah,' said Marian, 'how I should like another or two of our old set to come here! Then we could bring up Talbothays every day here afield, and talk of he, and of what nice times we had there, and o' the old things we used to know, and make it all come back again a'most, in seeming!' Marian's eyes softened, and her voice grew vague as the visions returned. 'I'll write to Izz Huett,' she said. 'She's biding at home doing nothing now, I know, and I'll tell her we be here, and ask her to come; and perhaps Retty is well enough now.'

Tess had nothing to say against the proposal, and the next she heard of this plan for importing old Talbothays' joys was two or three days later, when Marian informed her that Izz had replied to her inquiry, and had promised to come if she could.

There had not been such a winter for years. It came on in stealthy and measured glides, like the moves of a chess-player.° One morning the few lonely trees and the thorns of the hedgerows appeared as if they had put off a vegetable for an animal integument. Every twig was covered with a white nap as of fur grown from the rind during the night, giving it four times its usual stoutness; the whole bush or tree forming a staring sketch in white lines on the mournful gray of the sky and horizon. Cobwebs revealed their presence on sheds and walls where none had ever been observed till brought out into visibility by the crystallizing atmosphere, hanging like loops of white worsted from salient points of the out-houses, posts, and gates.

After this season of congealed dampness came a spell of dry frost, when strange birds from behind the North Pole began to arrive silently on the upland of Flintcomb-Ash; gaunt spectral creatures with tragical eyes — eyes which had witnessed scenes of cataclysmal horror in inaccessible polar regions of a magnitude such as no human being had ever conceived, in curdling temperatures that no man could endure; which had beheld the crash of icebergs and the slide of snow-hills by the shooting light of the Aurora; been half blinded by the whirl of colossal storms and terraqueous distortions; and retained the expression of feature that such scenes had engendered. These nameless birds came quite near to Tess and Marian, but of all they had seen which humanity would never see, they brought no account. The traveller's ambition to tell was not theirs, and, with dumb impassivity, they

like the moves of a chess-player: Death is sometimes presented as a chess player, as in Ingmar Bergman's film, *The Seventh Seal.*

dismissed experiences which they did not value for the immediate incidents of this homely upland — the trivial movements of the two girls in disturbing the clods with their hackers so as to uncover something or other that these visitants relished as food.

Then one day a peculiar quality invaded the air of this open country. There came a moisture which was not of rain, and a cold which was not of frost. It chilled the eyeballs of the twain, made their brows ache, penetrated to their skeletons, affecting the surface of the body less than its core. They knew that it meant snow, and in the night the snow came. Tess, who continued to live at the cottage with the warm gable that cheered any lonely pedestrian who paused beside it, awoke in the night, and heard above the thatch noises which seemed to signify that the roof had turned itself into a gymnasium of all the winds. When she lit her lamp to get up in the morning she found that the snow had blown through a chink in the casement, forming a white cone of the finest powder against the inside, and had also come down the chimney, so that it lay sole-deep upon the floor, on which her shoes left tracks when she moved about. Without, the storm drove so fast as to create a snow-mist in the kitchen; but as yet it was too dark out-of-doors to see anything.

Tess knew that it was impossible to go on with the swedes; and by the time she had finished breakfast beside the solitary little lamp, Marian arrived to tell her that they were to join the rest of the women at reed-drawing° in the barn till the weather changed. As soon, therefore, as the uniform cloak of darkness without began to turn to a disordered medley of grays, they blew out the lamp, wrapped themselves up in their thickest pinners, tied their woollen cravats round their necks and across their chests, and started for the barn. The snow had followed the birds from the polar basin as a white pillar of a cloud,° and individual flakes could not be seen. The blast smelt of icebergs, arctic seas, whales, and white bears, carrying the snow so that it licked the land but did not deepen on it. They trudged onwards with slanted bodies through the flossy fields, keeping as well as they could in the shelter of hedges, which, however, acted as strainers rather than screens. The air, afflicted to pallor with the hoary multitudes that infested it, twisted and spun them eccentrically, suggesting an achromatic chaos of things. But both the young women were fairly cheerful; such weather on a dry upland is not in itself dispiriting.

reed-drawing: Preparing straw to be used as thatching material. **white pillar of a cloud:** God sent a pillar of cloud by day and a pillar of fire by night to enable Moses to lead the Israelites fleeing from Egypt safely through the wilderness (Exod. 13.21).

'Ha-ha! The cunning northern birds knew this was coming,' said Marian. 'Depend upon't, they keep just in front o't all the way from the North Star. Your husband, my dear, is, I make no doubt, having scorching weather all this time. Lord, if he could only see his pretty wife now! Not that this weather hurts your beauty at all — in fact, it rather does it good.'

'You mustn't talk about him to me, Marian,' said Tess severely.

'Well, but — surely you care for 'n! Do you?'

Instead of answering, Tess, with tears in her eyes, impulsively faced in the direction in which she imagined South America to lie, and, putting up her lips, blew out a passionate kiss upon the snowy wind.

'Well, well, I know you do. But 'pon my body, it is a rum life for a married couple! There — I won't say another word! Well, as for the weather, it won't hurt us in the wheat-barn; but reed-drawing is fearful hard work — worse than swede-hacking. I can stand it because I'm stout; but you be slimmer than I. I can't think why maister should have set 'ee at it.'

They reached the wheat-barn and entered it. One end of the long structure was full of corn; the middle was where the reed-drawing was carried on, and there had already been placed in the reed-press the evening before as many sheaves of wheat as would be sufficient for the women to draw from during the day.

'Why, here's Izz!" said Marian.

Izz it was, and she came forward. She had walked all the way from her mother's home on the previous afternoon, and, not deeming the distance so great, had been belated, arriving, however, just before the snow began, and sleeping at the ale-house. The farmer had agreed with her mother at market to take her on if she came to-day, and she had been afraid to disappoint him by delay.

In addition to Tess, Marian, and Izz, there were two women from a neighbouring village; two Amazonian sisters, whom Tess with a start remembered as Dark Car the Queen of Spades and her junior the Queen of Diamonds — those who had tried to fight with her in the midnight quarrel at Trantridge. They showed no recognition of her, and possibly had none, for they had been under the influence of liquor on that occasion, and were only temporary sojourners there as here. They did all kinds of men's work by preference, including well-sinking, hedging, ditching, and excavating, without any sense of fatigue. Noted reed-drawers were they too, and looked round upon the other three with some superciliousness.

Putting on their gloves all set to work in a row in front of the press, an erection formed of two posts connected by a cross-beam, under which the sheaves to be drawn from were laid ears outward, the beam being pegged down by pins in the uprights, and lowered as the sheaves diminished.

The day hardened in colour, the light coming in at the barn-doors upwards from the snow instead of downwards from the sky. The girls pulled handful after handful from the press; but by reason of the presence of the strange women, who were recounting scandals, Marian and Izz could not at first talk of old times as they wished to do. Presently they heard the muffled tread of a horse, and the farmer rode up to the barn-door. When he had dismounted he came close to Tess, and remained looking musingly at the side of her face. She had not turned at first, but his fixed attitude led her to look round, when she perceived that her employer was the native of Trantridge from whom she had taken flight on the high-road because of his allusion to her history.

He waited till she had carried the drawn bundles to the pile outside, when he said, 'So you be the young woman who took my civility in such ill part? Be drowned if I didn't think you might be as soon as I heard of your being hired! Well, you thought you had got the better of me the first time at the inn with your fancy-man, and the second time on the road, when you bolted; but now I think I've got the better of you.' He concluded with a hard laugh.

Tess, between the Amazons and the farmer like a bird caught in a clap-net, returned no answer, continuing to pull the straw. She could read character sufficiently well to know by this time that she had nothing to fear from her employer's gallantry; it was rather the tyranny induced by his mortification at Clare's treatment of him. Upon the whole she preferred that sentiment in man and felt brave enough to endure it.

'You thought I was in love with 'ee I suppose? Some women are such fools, to take every look as serious earnest. But there's nothing like a winter afield for taking that nonsense out o' young wenches' heads; and you've signed and agreed till Lady-Day. Now, are you going to beg my pardon?'

'I think you ought to beg mine.'

'Very well — as you like. But we'll see which is master here. Be they all the sheaves you've done to-day?'

'Yes, sir.'

''Tis a very poor show. Just see what they've done over there' (pointing to the two stalwart women). 'The rest too, have done better than you.'

'They've all practised it before, and I have not. And I thought it made no difference to you as it is task work, and we are only paid for what we do.'

'Oh, but it does. I want the barn cleared.'

'I am going to work all the afternoon instead of leaving at two as the others will do.'

He looked sullenly at her and went away. Tess felt that she could not have come to a much worse place; but anything was better than gallantry. When two o'clock arrived the professional reed-drawers tossed off the last half-pint in their flagon, put down their hooks, tied their last sheaves, and went away. Marian and Izz would have done likewise, but on hearing that Tess meant to stay, to make up by longer hours for her lack of skill, they would not leave her. Looking out at the snow, which still fell, Marian exclaimed, 'Now, we've got it all to ourselves.' And so at last the conversation turned to their old experiences at the dairy; and, of course, the incidents of their affection for Angel Clare.

'Izz and Marian,' said Mrs. Angel Clare, with a dignity which was extremely touching, seeing how very little of a wife she was: 'I can't join in talk with you now, as I used to do, about Mr. Clare; you will see that I cannot; because, although he is gone away from me for the present, he is my husband.'

Izz was by nature the sauciest and most caustic of all the four girls who had loved Clare. 'He was a very splendid lover, no doubt,' she said; 'but I don't think he is a too fond husband to go away from you so soon.'

'He had to go — he was obliged to go, to see about the land over there!' pleaded Tess.

'He might have tided 'ee over the winter.'

'Ah — that's owing to an accident — a misunderstanding; and we won't argue it,' Tess answered, with tearfulness in her words. 'Perhaps there's a good deal to be said for him! He did not go away, like some husbands, without telling me; and I can always find out where he is.'

After this they continued for some long time in a reverie, as they went on seizing the ears of corn, drawing out the straw, gathering it under their arms, and cutting off the ears with their bill-hooks, nothing sounding in the barn but the swish of the straw and the crunch of the hook. Then Tess suddenly flagged, and sank down upon the heap of wheat-ears at her feet.

'I knew you wouldn't be able to stand it!' cried Marian. 'It wants harder flesh than yours for this work.'

Just then the farmer entered. 'Oh, that's how you get on when I am away,' he said to her.

'But it is my own loss,' she pleaded. 'Not yours.'

'I want it finished,' he said doggedly, as he crossed the barn and went out at the other door.

'Don't 'ee mind him, there's a dear,' said Marian. 'I've worked here before. Now you go and lie down there, and Izz and I will make up your number.'

'I don't like to let you do that. I'm taller than you, too.'

However, she was so overcome that she consented to lie down awhile, and reclined on a heap of pull-tails — the refuse after the straight straw had been drawn — thrown up at the further side of the barn. Her succumbing had been as largely owing to agitation at reopening the subject of her separation from her husband as to the hard work. She lay in a state of percipience without volition, and the rustle of the straw and the cutting of the ears by the others had the weight of bodily touches.

She could hear from her corner, in addition to these noises, the murmur of their voices. She felt certain that they were continuing the subject already broached, but their voices were so low that she could not catch the words. At last Tess grew more and more anxious to know what they were saying, and, persuading herself that she felt better, she got up and resumed work.

Then Izz Huett broke down. She had walked more than a dozen miles the previous evening, had gone to bed at midnight, and had risen again at five o'clock. Marian alone, thanks to her bottle of liquor and her stoutness of build, stood the strain upon back and arms without suffering. Tess urged Izz to leave off, agreeing, as she felt better, to finish the day without her, and make equal division of the number of sheaves.

Izz accepted the offer gratefully, and disappeared through the great door into the snowy track to her lodging. Marian, as was the case every afternoon at this time on account of the bottle, began to feel in a romantic vein.

'I should not have thought it of him — never!' she said in a dreamy tone. 'And I loved him so! I didn't mind his having *you*. But this about Izz is too bad!'

Tess, in her start at the words, narrowly missed cutting off a finger with the bill-hook.

'Is it about my husband?' she stammered.

'Well, yes. Izz said, "Don't 'ee tell her;" but I am sure I can't help it! It was what he wanted Izz to do. He wanted her to go off to Brazil with him.'

Tess's face faded as white as the scene without, and its curves straightened. 'And did Izz refuse to go?' she asked.

'I don't know. Anyhow he changed his mind.'

'Pooh — then he didn't mean it! 'Twas just a man's jest!'

'Yes he did; for he drove her a good-ways towards the station.'

'He didn't take her!'

They pulled on in silence till Tess, without any premonitory symptoms, burst out crying.

'There!' said Marian. 'Now I wish I hadn't told 'ee!'

'No. It is a very good thing that you have done! I have been living on in a thirtover,° lackaday way, and have not seen what it may lead to! I ought to have sent him a letter oftener. He said I could not go to him, but he didn't say I was not to write as often as I liked. I won't dally like this any longer! I have been very wrong and neglectful in leaving everything to be done by him!'

The dim light in the barn grew dimmer, and they could see to work no longer. When Tess had reached home that evening, and had entered into the privacy of her little white-washed chamber, she began impetuously writing a letter to Clare. But falling into doubt she could not finish it. Afterwards she took the ring from the ribbon on which she wore it next her heart, and retained it on her finger all night, as if to fortify herself in the sensation that she was really the wife of this elusive lover of hers, who could propose that Izz should go with him abroad, so shortly after he had left her. Knowing that, how could she write entreaties to him, or show that she cared for him any more?

XLIV

By the disclosure in the barn her thoughts were led anew in the direction which they had taken more than once of late — to the distant Emminster Vicarage. It was through her husband's parents that she had been charged to send a letter to Clare if she desired; and to write to them direct if in difficulty. But that sense of her having morally no claim upon him had always led Tess to suspend her impulse to send these notes; and to the family at the Vicarage, therefore, as to her own parents since her marriage, she was virtually non-existent. This self-effacement in both directions had been quite in consonance with her

thirtover: Or thwart-over, meaning perverse (dialect) (*OED*).

independent character of desiring nothing by way of favour or pity to which she was not entitled on a fair consideration of her deserts. She had set herself to stand or fall by her qualities, and to waive such merely technical claims upon a strange family as had been established for her by the flimsy fact of a member of that family, in a season of impulse, writing his name in a church-book beside hers.

But now that she was stung to a fever by Izz's tale there was a limit to her powers of renunciation. Why had her husband not written to her? He had distinctly implied that he would at least let her know of the locality to which he had journeyed; but he had not sent a line to notify his address. Was he really indifferent? But was he ill? Was it for her to make some advance? Surely she might summon the courage of solicitude, call at the Vicarage for intelligence, and express her grief at his silence. If Angel's father were the good man she had heard him represented to be, he would be able to enter into her heart-starved situation. Her social hardships she could conceal.

To leave the farm on a week-day was not in her power; Sunday was the only possible opportunity. Flintcomb-Ash being in the middle of the cretaceous tableland over which no railway had climbed as yet, it would be necessary to walk. And the distance being fifteen miles each way she would have to allow herself a long day for the undertaking by rising early.

A fortnight later, when the snow had gone, and had been followed by a hard black frost, she took advantage of the state of the roads to try the experiment. At four o'clock that Sunday morning she came downstairs and stepped out into the starlight. The weather was still favourable, the ground ringing under her feet like an anvil.

Marian and Izz were much interested in her excursion, knowing that the journey concerned her husband. Their lodgings were in a cottage a little further along the lane, but they came and assisted Tess in her departure, and argued that she should dress up in her very prettiest guise to captivate the hearts of her parents-in-law; though she, knowing of the austere and Calvinistic tenets of old Mr. Clare, was indifferent, and even doubtful. A year had now elapsed since her sad marriage, but she had preserved sufficient draperies from the wreck of her then full wardrobe to clothe her very charmingly as a simple country girl with no pretensions to recent fashion; a soft gray woollen gown, with white crape quilling against the pink skin of her face and neck, and a black velvet jacket and hat.

''Tis a thousand pities your husband can't see 'ee now — you do look a real beauty!' said Izz Huett, regarding Tess as she stood on the threshold between the steely starlight without and the yellow candle-light within. Izz spoke with a magnanimous abandonment of herself to the situation; she could not be — no woman with a heart bigger than a hazel-nut could be — antagonistic to Tess in her presence, the influence which she exercised over those of her own sex being of a warmth and strength quite unusual, curiously overpowering the less worthy feminine feelings of spite and rivalry.

With a final tug and touch here, and a slight brush there, they let her go; and she was absorbed into the pearly air of the fore-dawn. They heard her footsteps tap along the hard road as she stepped out to her full pace. Even Izz hoped she would win, and, though without any particular respect for her own virtue, felt glad that she had been prevented wronging her friend when momentarily tempted by Clare.

It was a year ago, all but a day, that Clare had married Tess, and only a few days less than a year that he had been absent from her. Still, to start on a brisk walk, and on such an errand as hers, on a dry clear wintry morning, through the rarefied air of these chalky hogs'-backs, was not depressing; and there is no doubt that her dream at starting was to win the heart of her mother-in-law, tell her whole history to that lady, enlist her on her side, and so gain back the truant.

In time she reached the edge of the vast escarpment below which stretched the loamy Vale of Blackmoor, now lying misty and still in the dawn. Instead of the colourless air of the uplands the atmosphere down there was a deep blue. Instead of the great enclosures of a hundred acres in which she was now accustomed to toil there were little fields below her of less than half-a-dozen acres, so numerous that they looked from this height like the meshes of a net. Here the landscape was whitey-brown; down there, as in Froom Valley, it was always green. Yet it was in that vale that her sorrow had taken shape, and she did not love it as formerly. Beauty to her, as to all who have felt, lay not in the thing, but in what the thing symbolized.

Keeping the Vale on her right she steered steadily westward; passing above the Hintocks, crossing at right-angles the high-road from Sherton-Abbas to Casterbridge, and skirting Dogbury Hill and High-Stoy, with the dell between them called 'The Devil's Kitchen.' Still following the elevated way she reached Cross-in-Hand, where the stone pillar stands desolate and silent, to mark the site of a miracle, or murder, or both. Three miles further she cut across the straight and deserted Roman road called Long-Ash Lane; leaving which as soon as she reached it she dipped down a hill by a transverse lane into the small town or village of Evershead, being now about half-way over the distance. She made a halt here, and breakfasted a second time, heartily enough — not at the Sow-and-Acorn, for she avoided inns, but at a cottage by the church.

The second half of her journey was through a more gentle country, by way of Benvill Lane. But as the mileage lessened between her and the spot of her pilgrimage, so did Tess's confidence decrease, and her enterprise loom out more formidably. She saw her purpose in such staring lines, and the landscape so faintly, that she was sometimes in danger of losing her way. However, about noon she paused by a gate on the edge of the basin in which Emminster and its Vicarage lay.

The square tower, beneath which she knew that at that moment the Vicar and his congregation were gathered, had a severe look in her eyes. She wished that she had somehow contrived to come on a week-day. Such a good man might be prejudiced against a woman who had chosen Sunday, never realizing the necessities of her case. But it was incumbent upon her to go on now. She took off the thick boots in which she had walked thus far, put on her pretty thin ones of patent leather, and, stuffing the former into the hedge by the gate-post where she might readily find them again, descended the hill; the freshness of colour she had derived from the keen air thinning away in spite of her as she drew near the parsonage.

Tess hoped for some accident that might favour her, but nothing favoured her. The shrubs on the Vicarage lawn rustled uncomfortably in the frosty breeze; she could not feel by any stretch of imagination, dressed to her highest as she was, that the house was the residence of near relations; and yet nothing essential, in nature or emotion, divided her from them: in pains, pleasures, thoughts, birth, death, and after-death, they were the same.

She nerved herself by an effort, entered the swing-gate, and rang the door-bell. The thing was done; there could be no retreat. No; the thing was not done. Nobody answered to her ringing. The effort had to be risen to and made again. She rang a second time, and the agitation of the act, coupled with her weariness after the fifteen miles' walk, led her to support herself while she waited by resting her hand on her hip, and her elbow against the wall of the porch. The wind was so nipping that the ivy-leaves had become wizened and gray, each tapping incessantly upon its neighbour with a disquieting stir of her nerves. A piece of blood-stained paper, caught up from some meat-buyer's dust-heap, beat up and down the road without the gate; too flimsy to rest, too heavy to fly away; and a few straws kept it company.

The second peal had been louder, and still nobody came. Then she walked out of the porch, opened the gate, and passed through. And though she looked dubiously at the house-front as if inclined to return, it was with a breath of relief that she closed the gate. A feeling haunted her that she might have been recognized (though how she could not tell), and orders been given not to admit her.

Tess went as far as the corner. She had done all she could do; but determined not to escape present trepidation at the expense of future distress, she walked back again quite past the house, looking up at all the windows.

Ah — the explanation was that they were all at church, every one. She remembered her husband saying that his father always insisted upon the household, servants included, going to morning-service, and, as a consequence, eating cold food when they came home. It was, therefore, only necessary to wait till the service was over. She would not make herself conspicuous by waiting on the spot, and she started to get past the church into the lane. But as she reached the churchyard-gate the people began pouring out, and Tess found herself in the midst of them.

The Emminster congregation looked at her as only a congregation of small country-townsfolk walking home at its leisure can look at a woman out of the common whom it perceives to be a stranger. She quickened her pace, and ascended the road by which she had come, to find a retreat between its hedges till the Vicar's family should have lunched, and it might be convenient for them to receive her. She soon distanced the churchgoers, except two youngish men, who, linked arm-in-arm, were beating up behind her at a quick step.

As they drew nearer she could hear their voices engaged in earnest discourse, and, with the natural quickness of a woman in her situation, did not fail to recognize in those voices the quality of her husband's tones. The pedestrians were his two brothers. Forgetting all her plans, Tess's one dread was lest they should overtake her now, in her disorganized condition, before she was prepared to confront them; for though she felt that they could not identify her she instinctively dreaded their scrutiny. The more briskly they walked the more briskly walked she. They were plainly bent upon taking a sort quick stroll before going indoors to lunch or dinner, to restore warmth to limbs chilled with sitting through a long service.

Only one person had preceded Tess up the hill — a ladylike young woman, somewhat interesting, though, perhaps, a trifle *guindée*° and prudish. Tess had nearly overtaken her when the speed of her

guindée: Stiff, stilted, formal (Fr.); the narrator's word, rather than Tess's.

brothers-in-law brought them so nearly behind her back that she could hear every word of their conversation. They said nothing, however, which particularly interested her till, observing the young lady still further in front, one of them remarked, 'There is Mercy Chant. Let us overtake her.'

Tess knew the name. It was the woman who had been destined for Angel's life-companion by his and her parents, and whom he probably would have married but for her intrusive self. She would have known as much without previous information if she had waited a moment, for one of the brothers proceeded to say: 'Ah! Poor Angel, poor Angel! I never see that nice girl without more and more regretting his precipitancy in throwing himself away upon a dairy-maid, or whatever she may be. It is a queer business, apparently. Whether she has joined him yet or not I don't know; but she had not done so some months ago when I heard from him.'

'I can't say. He never tells me anything nowadays. His ill-considered marriage seems to have completed that estrangement from me which was begun by his extraordinary opinions.'

Tess beat up the long hill still faster; but she could not outwalk them without exciting notice. At last they outsped her altogether, and passed her by. The young lady still further ahead heard their footsteps and turned. Then there was a greeting and a shaking of hands, and the three went on together.

They soon reached the summit of the hill, and, evidently intending this point to be the limit of their promenade, slackened pace and turned all three aside to the gate whereat Tess had paused an hour before that time to reconnoitre the town before descending into it. During their discourse one of the clerical brothers probed the hedge carefully with his umbrella, and dragged something to light.

'Here's a pair of old boots,' he said. 'Thrown away, I suppose, by some tramp or other.'

'Some impostor who wished to come into the town barefoot, perhaps, and so excite our sympathies,' said Miss Chant. 'Yes, it must have been, for they are excellent walking-boots — by no means worn out. What a wicked thing to do! I'll carry them home for some poor person.'

Cuthbert Clare, who had been the one to find them, picked them up for her with the crook of his stick; and Tess's boots were appropriated.

She, who had heard this, walked past under the screen of her woollen veil, till, presently looking back, she perceived that the church party had left the gate with her boots and retreated down the hill.

Thereupon our heroine resumed her walk. Tears, blinding tears, were running down her face. She knew that it was all sentiment, all baseless impressibility, which had caused her to read the scene as her own condemnation; nevertheless she could not get over it; she could not contravene in her own defenceless person all these untoward omens. It was impossible to think of returning to the Vicarage. Angel's wife felt almost as if she had been hounded up that hill like a scorned thing by those — to her — super-fine clerics. Innocently as the slight had been inflicted, it was somewhat unfortunate that she had encountered the sons and not the father, who, despite his narrowness, was far less starched and ironed than they, and had to the full the gift of charity. As she again thought of her dusty boots she almost pitied those habiliments for the quizzing to which they had been subjected, and felt how hopeless life was for their owner.

'Ah!' she said, still sighing in pity of herself, '*they* didn't know that I wore those over the roughest part of the road to save these pretty ones *he* bought for me — no — they did not know it! And they didn't think that *he* chose the colour o' my pretty frock — no — how could they! If they had known perhaps they would not have cared, for they don't care much for him, poor thing!'

Then she grieved for the beloved man whose conventional standard of judgment had caused her all these latter sorrows; and she went her way without knowing that the greatest misfortune of her life was this feminine loss of courage at the last and critical moment through her estimating her father-in-law by his sons. Her present condition was precisely one which would have enlisted the sympathies of old Mr. and Mrs. Clare. Their hearts went out of them at a bound towards extreme cases, when the subtle mental troubles of the less desperate among mankind failed to win their interest or regard. In jumping at Publicans and Sinners they would forget that a word might be said for the worries of Scribes and Pharisees;° and this defect or limitation might have recommended their own daughter-in-law to them at this moment as a fairly choice sort of lost person for their love.

Thereupon she began to plod back along the road by which she had come not altogether full of hope, but full of a conviction that a crisis in her life was approaching. No crisis, apparently, had supervened; and there was nothing left for her to do but to continue upon that starve-acre farm till she could again summon courage to face the

Publicans and Sinners . . . Scribes and Pharisees: They were biased in favor of those who had fallen.

vicarage. She did, indeed, take sufficient interest in herself to throw up her veil on this return journey, as if to let the world see that she could at least exhibit a face such as Mercy Chant could not show. But it was done with a sorry shake of the head. 'It is nothing — it is nothing!' she said. 'Nobody loves it; nobody sees it. Who cares about the looks of a castaway like me!'

Her journey back was rather a meander than a march. It had no sprightliness, no purpose; only a tendency. Along the tedious length of Benvill Lane she began to grow tired, and she leant upon gates and paused by milestones.

She did not enter any house till, at the seventh or eighth mile, she descended the steep long hill below which lay the village or townlet of Evershead, where in the morning she had breakfasted with such contrasting expectations. The cottage by the church, in which she again sat down, was almost the first at that end of the village, and while the woman fetched her some milk from the pantry, Tess, looking down the street, perceived that the place seemed quite deserted.

'The people are gone to afternoon service, I suppose?' she said.

'No, my dear,' said the old woman. ''Tis too soon for that; the bells hain't strook out yet. They be all gone to hear the preaching in yonder barn. A ranter preaches there between the services — an excellent, fiery, Christian man, they say. But, Lord, I don't go to hear'n! What comes in the regular way over the pulpit is hot enough for I.'

Tess soon went onward into the village, her footsteps echoing against the houses as though it were a place of the dead. Nearing the central part her echoes were intruded on by other sounds; and seeing the barn not far off the road, she guessed these to be the utterances of the preacher.

His voice became so distinct in the still clear air that she could soon catch his sentences, though she was on the closed side of the barn. The sermon, as might be expected, was of the extremest antinomian type; on justification by faith, as expounded in the theology of St. Paul. This fixed idea of the rhapsodist was delivered with animated enthusiasm, in a manner entirely declamatory, for he had plainly no skill as a dialectician. Although Tess had not heard the beginning of the address, she learnt what the text had been from its constant iteration —

'O foolish Galatians, who hath bewitched you, that ye should not obey the truth, before whose eyes Jesus Christ hath been evidently set forth, crucified among you?'°

'O foolish Galatians, . . .': Galatians 3.1.

Tess was all the more interested, as she stood listening behind, in finding that the preacher's doctrine was a vehement form of the views of Angel's father, and her interest intensified when the speaker began to detail his own spiritual experiences of how he had come by those views. He had, he said, been the greatest of sinners. He had scoffed; he had wantonly associated with the reckless and the lewd. But a day of awakening had come, and, in a human sense, it had been brought about mainly by the influence of a certain clergyman, whom he had at first grossly insulted; but whose parting words had sunk into his heart, and had remained there, till by the grace of Heaven they had worked this change in him, and made him what they saw him.

But more startling to Tess than the doctrine had been the voice, which, impossible as it seemed, was precisely that of Alec d'Urberville. Her face fixed in painful suspense she came round to the front of the barn, and passed before it. The low winter sun beamed directly upon the great double-doored entrance on this side; one of the doors being open, so that the rays stretched far in over the threshing-floor to the preacher and his audience, all snugly sheltered from the northern breeze. The listeners were entirely villagers, among them being the man whom she had seen carrying the red paint-pot on a former memorable occasion. But her attention was given to the central figure, who stood upon some sacks of corn, facing the people and the door. The three o'clock sun shone full upon him, and the strange enervating conviction that her seducer confronted her, which had been gaining ground in Tess ever since she had heard his words distinctly, was at last established as a fact indeed.

End of Phase the Fifth

PHASE THE SIXTH. THE CONVERT

XLV

Till this moment she had never seen or heard from d'Urberville since her departure from Trantridge.

The rencounter came at a heavy moment, one of all moments calculated to permit its impact with the least emotional shock. But such was unreasoning memory that, though he stood there openly and palpably a converted man, who was sorrowing for his past irregularities, a fear overcame her, paralyzing her movement so that she neither retreated nor advanced.

To think of what emanated from that countenance when she saw it last, and to behold it now! . . . There was the same handsome unpleasantness of mien, but now he wore neatly trimmed, old-fashioned whiskers, the sable moustache having disappeared; and his dress was half-clerical, a modification which had changed his expression sufficiently to abstract the dandyism from his features, and to hinder for a second her belief in his identity.

To Tess's sense there was, just at first, a ghastly *bizarrerie,*° a grim incongruity, in the march of these solemn words of Scripture out of such a mouth. This too familiar intonation, less than four years earlier, had brought to her ears expressions of such divergent purpose that her heart became quite sick at the irony of the contrast.

It was less a reform than a transfiguration. The former curves of sensuousness were now modulated to lines of devotional passion. The lip-shapes that had meant seductiveness were now made to express supplication; the glow on the cheek that yesterday could be translated as riotousness was evangelized to-day into the splendour of pious rhetoric; animalism had become fanaticism; Paganism Paulinism; the bold rolling eye that had flashed upon her form in the old time with such mastery now beamed with the rude energy of a theolatry that was almost ferocious. Those black angularities which his face had used to put on when his wishes were thwarted now did duty in picturing the incorrigible backslider who would insist upon turning again to his wallowing in the mire.

The lineaments, as such, seemed to complain. They had been diverted from their hereditary connotation to signify impressions for which nature did not intend them. Strange that their very elevation was a misapplication, that to raise seemed to falsify.

Yet could it be so? She would admit the ungenerous sentiment no longer. D'Urberville was not the first wicked man who had turned away from his wickedness to save his soul alive, and why should she deem it unnatural in him? It was but the usage of thought which had been jarred in her at hearing good new words in bad old notes. The greater the sinner the greater the saint; it was not necessary to dive far into Christian history to discover that.

Such impressions as these moved her vaguely, and without strict definiteness. As soon as the nerveless pause of her surprise would allow

bizarrerie: Something strange, weird, singular, odd (Fr.).

her to stir, her impulse was to pass on out of his sight. He had obviously not discerned her yet in her position against the sun.

But the moment that she moved again he recognized her. The effect upon her old lover was electric, far stronger than the effect of his presence upon her. His fire, the tumultuous ring of his eloquence, seemed to go out of him. His lip struggled and trembled under the words that lay upon it; but deliver them it could not as long as she faced him. His eyes, after their first glance upon her face, hung confusedly in every other direction but hers, but came back in a desperate leap every few seconds. This paralysis lasted, however, but a short time; for Tess's energies returned with the atrophy of his, and she walked as fast as she was able past the barn and onward.

As soon as she could reflect it appalled her, this change in their relative platforms. He who had wrought her undoing was now on the side of the Spirit, while she remained unregenerate. And, as in the legend, it had resulted that her Cyprian image° had suddenly appeared upon his altar, whereby the fire of the priest had been wellnigh extinguished.

She went on without turning her head. Her back seemed to be endowed with a sensitiveness to ocular beams — even her clothing — so alive was she to a fancied gaze which might be resting upon her from the outside of that barn. All the way along to this point her heart had been heavy with an inactive sorrow; now there was a change in the quality of its trouble. That hunger for affection too long withheld was for the time displaced by an almost physical sense of an implacable past which still engirdled her. It intensified her consciousness of error to a practical despair; the break of continuity between her earlier and present existence, which she had hoped for, had not, after all, taken place. Bygones would never be complete bygones till she was a bygone herself.

Thus absorbed she recrossed the northern part of Long-Ash Lane at right angles, and presently saw before her the road ascending whitely to the upland along whose margin the remainder of her journey lay. Its dry pale surface stretched severely onward, unbroken by a single figure, vehicle, or mark, save some occasional brown horse-droppings which dotted its cold aridity here and there. While slowly breasting this ascent Tess became conscious of footsteps behind her, and turning she saw approaching that well-known form — so strangely

Cyprian image: The goddess of love in the ancient world, Venus or Aphrodite, was associated with Cyprus, but the legend mentioned has not been convincingly identified.

accoutred as the Methodist — the one personage in all the world she wished not to encounter alone on this side of the grave.

There was not much time, however, for thought or elusion, and she yielded as calmly as she could to the necessity of letting him overtake her. She saw that he was excited, less by the speed of his walk than by the feeling within him.

'Tess!' he said.

She slackened speed without looking round.

'Tess!' he repeated. 'It is I — Alec d'Urberville.'

She then looked back at him, and he came up.

'I see it is,' she answered coldly.

'Well — is that all? Yet I deserve no more! Of course,' he added, with a slight laugh, 'there is something of the ridiculous to your eyes in seeing me like this. But — I must put up with that. . . . I heard you had gone away, nobody knew where. Tess, you wonder why I have followed you?'

'I do, rather; and I would that you had not, with all my heart!'

'Yes — you may well say it,' he returned grimly, as they moved onward together, she with unwilling tread. 'But don't mistake me; I beg this because you may have been led to do so in noticing — if you did notice it — how your sudden appearance unnerved me down there. It was but a momentary faltering; and considering what you had been to me, it was natural enough. But will helped me through it — though perhaps you think me a humbug for saying it — and immediately afterwards I felt that, of all persons in the world whom it was my duty and desire to save from the wrath to come° — sneer if you like — the woman whom I had so grievously wronged was that person. I have come with that sole purpose in view — nothing more.'

There was the smallest vein of scorn in her words of rejoinder: 'Have you saved yourself? Charity begins at home, they say.'

'*I* have done nothing!' said he indifferently. 'Heaven, as I have been telling my hearers, has done all. No amount of contempt that you can pour upon me, Tess, will equal what I have poured upon myself — the old Adam of my former years! Well, it is a strange story; believe it or not; but I can tell you the means by which my conversion was brought about, and I hope you will be interested enough at least to listen. Have you ever heard the name of the parson of Emminster — you must have done so? — old Mr. Clare; one of the most earnest of his school; one of the few intense men left in the Church;

the wrath to come: An echo of Matthew 3.7.

not so intense as the extreme wing of Christian believers with which I have thrown in my lot, but quite an exception among the Established clergy, the younger of whom are gradually attenuating the true doctrines by their sophistries, till they are but the shadow of what they were. I only differ from him on the question of Church and State — the interpretation of the text, "Come out from among them and be ye separate, saith the Lord"° — that's all. He is one who, I firmly believe, has been the humble means of saving more souls in this country than any other man you can name. You have heard of him?'

'I have,' she said.

'He came to Trantridge two or three years ago to preach on behalf of some missionary society; and I, wretched fellow that I was, insulted him when, in his disinterestedness, he tried to reason with me and show me the way. He did not resent my conduct, he simply said that some day I should receive the first-fruits of the Spirit — that those who came to scoff sometimes remained to pray.° There was a strange magic in his words. They sank into my mind. But the loss of my mother hit me most; and by degrees I was brought to see daylight. Since then my one desire has been to hand on the true view to others, and that is what I was trying to do to-day; though it is only lately that I have preached hereabout. The first months of my ministry have been spent in the North of England among strangers, where I preferred to make my earliest clumsy attempts, so as to acquire courage before undergoing that severest of all tests of one's sincerity, addressing those who have known one, and have been one's companions in the days of darkness. If you could only know, Tess, the pleasure of having a good slap at yourself, I am sure —— '

'Don't go on with it!' she cried passionately, as she turned away from him to a stile by the wayside, on which she bent herself. 'I can't believe in such sudden things! I feel indignant with you for talking to me like this, when you know — when you know what harm you've done me! You, and those like you, take your fill of pleasure on earth by making the life of such as me bitter and black with sorrow; and then it is a fine thing, when you have had enough of that, to think of securing your pleasure in heaven by becoming converted! Out upon such — I don't believe in you — I hate it!'

'Come out from among them . . . : Paul paraphrasing in 2 Corinthians 6.17 the prophet Isaiah (Is. 52.11). **those who came to scoff . . . :** An echo of "The Deserted Village" (line 182), a poem by Oliver Goldsmith (1730?–1774), in which the village preacher is mentioned as having made unlikely converts.

'Tess,' he insisted; 'don't speak so! It came to me like a jolly new idea! And you don't believe me? What don't you believe?'

'Your conversion. Your scheme of religion.'

'Why?'

She dropped her voice. 'Because a better man than you does not believe in such.'

'What a woman's reason! Who is this better man?'

'I cannot tell you.'

'Well,' he declared, a resentment beneath his words seeming ready to spring out at a moment's notice, 'God forbid that I should say I am a good man — and you know I don't say any such thing. I am new to goodness, truly; but new comers see furthest sometimes.'

'Yes,' she replied sadly. 'But I cannot believe in your conversion to a new spirit. Such flashes as you feel, Alec, I fear don't last!'

Thus speaking she turned from the stile over which she had been leaning, and faced him; whereupon his eyes, falling casually upon the familiar countenance and form, remained contemplating her. The inferior man was quiet in him now; but it was surely not extracted nor even entirely subdued.

'Don't look at me like that!' he said abruptly.

Tess, who had been quite unconscious of her action and mien, instantly withdrew the large dark gaze of her eyes, stammering with a flush, 'I beg your pardon!' And there was revived in her the wretched sentiment which had often come to her before, that in inhabiting the fleshly tabernacle with which nature had endowed her she was somehow doing wrong.

'No, no! Don't beg my pardon. But since you wear a veil to hide your good looks, why don't you keep it down?'

She pulled down the veil, saying hastily, 'It was mostly to keep off the wind.'

'It may seem harsh of me to dictate like this,' he went on; 'but it is better that I should not look too often on you. It might be dangerous.'

'Ssh!' said Tess.

'Well, women's faces have had too much power over me already for me not to fear them! An evangelist has nothing to do with such as they; and it reminds me of the old times that I would forget!'

After this their conversation dwindled to a casual remark now and then as they rambled onward, Tess inwardly wondering how far he was going with her, and not liking to send him back by positive mandate. Frequently when they came to a gate or stile they found painted thereon in red or blue letters some text of Scripture, and she asked him if he knew who had been at the pains to blazon these announcements. He told her that the man was employed by himself and others who were working with him in that district, to paint these reminders that no means might be left untried which might move the hearts of a wicked generation.

At length the road touched the spot called 'Cross-in-Hand.' Of all spots on the bleached and desolate upland this was the most forlorn. It was so far removed from the charm which is sought in landscape by artists and view-lovers as to reach a new kind of beauty, a negative beauty of tragic tone. The place took its name from a stone pillar which stood there, a strange rude monolith, from a stratum unknown in any local quarry, on which was roughly carved a human hand. Differing accounts were given of its history and purport. Some authorities stated that a devotional cross had once formed the complete erection thereon, of which the present relic was but the stump; others that the stone as it stood was entire, and that it had been fixed there to mark a boundary or place of meeting. Anyhow, whatever the origin of the relic, there was and is something sinister, or solemn, according to mood, in the scene amid which it stands; something tending to impress the most phlegmatic passer-by.

'I think I must leave you now,' he remarked, as they drew near to this spot. 'I have to preach at Abbot's-Cernel at six this evening, and my way lies across to the right from here. And you upset me somewhat too, Tessy — I cannot, will not, say why. I must go away and get strength. . . . How is it that you speak so fluently now? Who has taught you such good English?'

'I have learnt things in my troubles,' she said evasively.

'What troubles have you had?'

She told him of the first one — the only one that related to him.

D'Urberville was struck mute. 'I knew nothing of this till now!' he next murmured. 'Why didn't you write to me when you felt your trouble coming on?'

She did not reply; and he broke the silence by adding: 'Well — you will see me again.'

'No,' she answered. 'Do not again come near me!'

'I will think. But before we part come here.' He stepped up to the pillar. 'This was once a Holy Cross. Relics are not in my creed; but I fear you at moments — far more than you need fear me at present; and to lessen my fear, put your hand upon that stone hand, and swear that you will never tempt me — by your charms or ways.'

'Good God — how can you ask what is so unnecessary! All this is furthest from my thought!'

'Yes — but swear it.'

Tess, half frightened, gave way to his importunity; placed her hand upon the stone and swore.

'I am sorry you are not a believer,' he continued; 'that some unbeliever should have got hold of you and unsettled your mind. But no more now. At home at least I can pray for you; and I will; and who knows what may not happen? I'm off. Good-bye!'

He turned to a hunting-gate in the hedge, and without letting his eyes again rest upon her leapt over, and struck out across the down in the direction of Abbot's-Cernel. As he walked his pace showed perturbation, and by-and-by, as if instigated by a former thought, he drew from his pocket a small book, between the leaves of which was folded a letter, worn and soiled, as from much re-reading. D'Urberville opened the letter. It was dated several months before this time, and was signed by Parson Clare.

The letter began by expressing the writer's unfeigned joy at d'Urberville's conversion, and thanked him for his kindness in communicating with the parson on the subject. It expressed Mr. Clare's warm assurance of forgiveness for d'Urberville's former conduct, and his interest in the young man's plans for the future. He, Mr. Clare, would much have liked to see d'Urberville in the Church to whose ministry he had devoted so many years of his own life, and would have helped him to enter a theological college to that end; but since his correspondent had possibly not cared to do this on account of the delay it would have entailed, he was not the man to insist upon its paramount importance. Every man must work as he could best work, and in the method towards which he felt impelled by the Spirit.

D'Urberville read and re-read this letter, and seemed to quiz himself cynically. He also read some passages from memoranda as he walked till his face assumed a calm, and apparently the image of Tess no longer troubled his mind.

She meanwhile had kept along the edge of the hill by which lay her nearest way home. Within the distance of a mile she met a solitary shepherd.

'What is the meaning of that old stone I have passed?' she asked of him. 'Was it ever a Holy Cross?'

'Cross — no; 'twer not a cross! 'Tis a thing of ill-omen, Miss. It was put up in wuld times by the relations of a malefactor who was tortured there by nailing his hand to a post and afterwards hung. The bones lie underneath. They say he sold his soul to the devil, and that he walks at times.'

She felt the *petite mort*° at this unexpectedly gruesome information, and left the solitary man behind her. It was dusk when she drew near to Flintcomb-Ash, and in the lane at the entrance to the hamlet she approached a girl and her lover without their observing her. They were talking no secrets, and the clear unconcerned voice of the young woman, in response to the warmer accents of the man, spread into the chilly air as the one soothing thing within the dusky horizon, full of a stagnant obscurity upon which nothing else intruded. For a moment the voices cheered the heart of Tess, till she reasoned that this interview had its origin, on one side or the other, in the same attraction which had been the prelude to her own tribulation. When she came close the girl turned serenely and recognized her, the young man walking off in embarrassment. The woman was Izz Huett, whose interest in Tess's excursion immediately superseded her own proceedings. Tess did not explain very clearly its results, and Izz, who was a girl of tact, began to speak of her own little affair, a phase of which Tess had just witnessed.

'He is Amby Seedling, the chap who used to sometimes come and help at Talbothays,' she explained indifferently. 'He actually inquired and found out that I had come here, and has followed me. He says he's been in love wi' me these two years. But I've hardly answered him.'

XLVI

Several days had passed since her futile journey, and Tess was afield. The dry winter wind still blew, but a screen of thatched hurdles erected in the eye of the blast kept its force away from her. On the sheltered side was a turnip-slicing machine, whose bright blue hue of new paint seemed almost vocal in the otherwise subdued scene. Opposite its front was a long mound or 'grave,' in which the roots had been preserved since early winter. Tess was standing at the uncovered end, chopping off with a bill-hook the fibres and earth from each root, and throwing it after the operation into the slicer. A man was turning the handle of the machine, and from its trough came the newly-cut swedes, the fresh smell of whose yellow chips was accompanied by the sounds of the snuffling wind, and the smart swish of the slicing-blades, and the choppings of the hook in Tess's leather-gloved hand.

petite mort: Shudder or chill; a premonition of death.

The wide acreage of blank agricultural brownness, apparent where the swedes had been pulled, was beginning to be striped in wales of darker brown, gradually broadening to ribands. Along the edge of each of these something crept upon ten legs, moving without haste and without rest up and down the whole length of the field; it was two horses and a man, the plough going between them, turning up the cleared ground for a spring sowing.

For hours nothing relieved the joyless monotony of things. Then, far beyond the ploughing-teams, a black speck was seen. It had come from the corner of a fence, where there was a gap, and its tendency was up the incline, towards the swede-cutters. From the proportions of a mere point it advanced to the shape of a ninepin, and was soon perceived to be a man in black, arriving from the direction of Flintcomb-Ash. The man at the slicer, having nothing else to do with his eyes, continually observed the comer, but Tess, who was occupied, did not perceive him till her companion directed her attention to his approach.

It was not her hard taskmaster, Farmer Groby; it was one in a semi-clerical costume, who now represented what had once been the free-and-easy Alec d'Urberville. Not being hot at his preaching there was less enthusiasm about him now, and the presence of the grinder seemed to embarrass him. A pale distress was already on Tess's face, and she pulled her curtained hood further over it.

D'Urberville came up and said, quietly —

'I want to speak to you, Tess.'

'You have refused my last request, not to come near me!' said she.

'Yes, but I have a good reason.'

'Well, tell it.'

'It is more serious than you may think.'

He glanced round to see if he were overheard. They were at some distance from the man who turned the slicer, and the movement of the machine, too, sufficiently prevented Alec's words reaching other ears. D'Urberville placed himself so as to screen Tess from the labourer, turning his back to the latter.

'It is this,' he continued, with capricious compunction. 'In thinking of your soul and mine when we last met, I neglected to inquire as to your worldly condition. You were well dressed, and I did not think of it. But I see now that it is hard — harder than it used to be when I — knew you — harder than you deserve. Perhaps a good deal of it is owing to me!'

She did not answer, and he watched her inquiringly, as, with bent head, her face completely screened by the hood, she resumed her trimming of the swedes. By going on with her work she felt better able to keep him outside her emotions.

'Tess,' he added, with a sigh of discontent, — 'yours was the very worst case I ever was concerned in! I had no idea of what had resulted till you told me. Scamp that I was to foul that innocent life! The whole blame was mine — the whole unconventional business of our time at Trantridge. You, too, the real blood of which I am but the base imitation, what a blind young thing you were as to possibilities! I say in all earnestness that it is a shame for parents to bring up their girls in such dangerous ignorance of the gins and the nets that the wicked may set for them, whether their motive be a good one or the result of simple indifference.'

Tess still did no more than listen, throwing down one globular root and taking up another with automatic regularity, the pensive contour of the mere fieldwoman alone marking her.

'But it is not that I came to say,' d'Urberville went on. 'My circumstances are these. I have lost my mother since you were at Trantridge, and the place is my own. But I intend to sell it, and devote myself to missionary work in Africa. A devil of a poor hand I shall make at the trade, no doubt. However, what I want to ask you is, will you put it in my power to do my duty — to make the only reparation I can make for the trick played you: that is, will you be my wife, and go with me? . . . I have already obtained this precious document. It was my old mother's dying wish.'

He drew a piece of parchment from his pocket, with a slight fumbling of embarrassment.

'What is it?' said she.

'A marriage licence.'

'O no, sir — no!' she said quickly, starting back.

'You will not? Why is that?'

And as he asked the question a disappointment which was not entirely the disappointment of thwarted duty crossed d'Urberville's face. It was unmistakably a symptom that something of his old passion for her had been revived; duty and desire ran hand-in-hand.

'Surely,' he began again, in more impetuous tones, and then looked round at the labourer who turned the slicer.

Tess, too, felt that the argument could not be ended there. Informing the man that a gentleman had come to see her, with whom she wished to walk a little way, she moved off with d'Urberville across the zebra-striped field. When they reached the first newly-ploughed section he held out his hand to help her over it; but she stepped forward on the summits of the earth-rolls as if she did not see him.

'You will not marry me, Tess, and make me a self-respecting man?' he repeated, as soon as they were over the furrows.

'I cannot.'

'But why?'

'You know I have no affection for you.'

'But you would get to feel that in time, perhaps — as soon as you really could forgive me?'

'Never!'

'Why so positive?'

'I love somebody else.'

The words seemed to astonish him.

'You do?' he cried. 'Somebody else? But has not a sense of what is morally right and proper any weight with you?'

'No, no, no — don't say that!'

'Anyhow, then, your love for this other man may be only a passing feeling which you will over-come —— '

'No — no.'

'Yes, yes! Why not?'

'I cannot tell you.'

'You must in honour!'

'Well then . . . I have married him.'

'Ah!' he exclaimed; and he stopped dead and gazed at her.

'I did not wish to tell — I did not mean to!' she pleaded. 'It is a secret here, or at any rate but dimly known. So will you, *please* will you, keep from questioning me? You must remember that we are now strangers.'

'Strangers — are we? Strangers!'

For a moment a flash of his old irony marked his face; but he determinedly chastened it down.

'Is that man your husband?' he asked mechanically, denoting by a sign the labourer who turned the machine.

'That man!' she said proudly. 'I should think not!'

'Who, then?'

'Do not ask what I do not wish to tell!' she begged, and flashed her appeal to him from her upturned face and lash-shadowed eyes.

D'Urberville was disturbed.

'But I only asked for your sake!' he retorted hotly. 'Angels of heaven! — God forgive me for such an expression — I came here, I swear, as I thought for your good. Tess — don't look at me so — I cannot stand your looks! There never were such eyes, surely, before Christianity or since! There — I won't lose my head; I dare not. I own that the sight of you has waked up my love for you, which, I believed, was extinguished with all such feelings. But I thought that our marriage might be a sanctification for us both. "The unbelieving husband is sanctified by the wife, and the unbelieving wife is sanctified by the husband,"° I said to myself. But my plan is dashed from me; and I must bear the disappointment!'

He moodily reflected with his eyes on the ground.

'Married. Married! . . . Well, that being so,' he added, quite calmly, tearing the licence slowly into halves and putting them in his pocket; 'that being prevented, I should like to do some good to you and your husband, whoever he may be. There are many questions that I am tempted to ask, but I will not do so, of course, in opposition to your wishes. Though, if I could know your husband, I might more easily benefit him and you. Is he on this farm?'

'No,' she murmured. 'He is far away.'

'Far away? From *you*? What sort of husband can he be?'

'O, do not speak against him! It was through you! He found out ——'

'Ah, is it so! . . . That's sad, Tess!'

'Yes.'

'But to stay away from you — to leave you to work like this!'

'He does not leave me to work!' she cried, springing to the defence of the absent one with all her fervour. 'He don't know it! It is by my own arrangement.'

'Then, does he write?'

'I — I cannot tell you. There are things which are private to ourselves.'

'Of course that means that he does not. You are a deserted wife, my fair Tess!'

In an impulse he turned suddenly to take her hand; the buff-glove was on it, and he seized only the rough leather fingers which did not express the life or shape of those within.

'You must not — you must not!' she cried fearfully, slipping her

"The unbelieving husband is sanctified by the wife, . . .": In 1 Corinthians, 7.13–14, Paul advises wives not to leave husbands who lack belief.

hand from the glove as from a pocket, and leaving it in his grasp. 'O, will you go away — for the sake of me and my husband — go, in the name of your own Christianity!'

'Yes, yes; I will,' he said abruptly, and thrusting the glove back to her turned to leave. Facing round, however, he said, 'Tess, as God is my judge, I meant no humbug in taking your hand!'

A pattering of hoofs on the soil of the field, which they had not noticed in their pre-occupation, ceased close behind them; and a voice reached her ear:

'What the devil are you doing away from your work at this time o' day?'

Farmer Groby had espied the two figures from the distance, and had inquisitively ridden across, to learn what was their business in his field.

'Don't speak like that to her!' said d'Urberville, his face blackening with something that was not Christianity.

'Indeed, Mister! And what mid Methodist pa'sons have to do with she?'

'Who is the fellow?' asked d'Urberville, turning to Tess.

She went close up to him.

'Go — I do beg you!' she said.

'What! And leave you to that tyrant? I can see in his face what a churl he is.'

'He won't hurt me. *He's* not in love with me. I can leave at Lady-Day.'

'Well, I have no right but to obey, I suppose. But — well, good-bye!'

Her defender, whom she dreaded more than her assailant, having reluctantly disappeared, the farmer continued his reprimand, which Tess took with the greatest coolness, that sort of attack being independent of sex. To have as a master this man of stone, who would have cuffed her if he had dared, was almost a relief after her former experiences. She silently walked back towards the summit of the field that was the scene of her labour, so absorbed in the interview which had just taken place that she was hardly aware that the nose of Groby's horse almost touched her shoulders.

'If so be you make an agreement to work for me till Lady-Day, I'll see that you carry it out,' he growled. ''Od rot the women — now 'tis one thing, and then 'tis another. But I'll put up with it no longer!'

Knowing very well that he did not harass the other women of the farm as he harassed her out of spite for the flooring he had once received, she did for one moment picture what might have been the result if she had been free to accept the offer just made her of being the monied Alec's wife. It would have lifted her completely out of subjection, not only to her present oppressive employer, but to a whole world who seemed to despise her. 'But no, no!' she said breathlessly; 'I could not have married him now! He is so unpleasant to me.'

That very night she began an appealing letter to Clare, concealing from him her hardships, and assuring him of her undying affection. Any one who had been in a position to read between the lines would have seen that at the back of her great love was some monstrous fear — almost a desperation — as to some secret contingencies which were not disclosed. But again she did not finish her effusion; he had asked Izz to go with him, and perhaps he did not care for her at all. She put the letter in her box, and wondered if it would ever reach Angel's hands.

After this her daily tasks were gone through heavily enough, and brought on the day which was of great import to agriculturists — the day of the Candlemas Fair. It was at this fair that new engagements were entered into for the twelve months following the ensuing Lady-Day, and those of the farming population who thought of changing their places duly attended at the county-town where the fair was held. Nearly all the labourers on Flintcomb-Ash Farm intended flight, and early in the morning there was a general exodus in the direction of the town, which lay at a distance of from ten to a dozen miles over hilly country. Though Tess also meant to leave at the quarter-day she was one of the few who did not go to the fair, having a vaguely-shaped hope that something would happen to render another outdoor engagement unnecessary.

It was a peaceful February day, of wonderful softness for the time, and one would almost have thought that winter was over. She had hardly finished her dinner when d'Urberville's figure darkened the window of the cottage wherein she was a lodger, which she had all to herself to-day.

Tess jumped up, but her visitor had knocked at the door, and she could hardly in reason run away. D'Urberville's knock, his walk up to the door, had some indescribable quality of difference from his air when she last saw him. They seemed to be acts of which the doer was ashamed. She thought that she would not open the door; but, as there was no sense in that either, she arose, and having lifted the latch stepped back quickly. He came in, saw her, and flung himself down into a chair before speaking.

'Tess — I couldn't help it!' he began desperately, as he wiped his heated face, which had also a superimposed flush of excitement. 'I felt that I must call at least to ask how you are. I assure you I had not been thinking of you at all till I saw you that Sunday; now I cannot get rid of your image, try how I may! It is hard that a good woman should do harm to a bad man; yet so it is. If you would only pray for me, Tess!'

The suppressed discontent of his manner was almost pitiable, and yet Tess did not pity him.

'How can I pray for you,' she said, 'when I am forbidden to believe that the great Power who moves the world would alter His plans on my account?'

'You really think that?'

'Yes. I have been cured of the presumption of thinking otherwise.'

'Cured? By whom?'

'By my husband, if I must tell.'

'Ah — your husband — your husband! How strange it seems! I remember you hinted something of the sort the other day. What do you really believe in these matters, Tess?' he asked. 'You seem to have no religion — perhaps owing to me.'

'But I have. Though I don't believe in anything supernatural.'

D'Urberville looked at her with misgiving.

'Then do you think that the line I take is all wrong?'

'A good deal of it.'

'H'm — and yet I've felt so sure about it,' he said uneasily.

'I believe in the *spirit* of the Sermon on the Mount,° and so did my dear husband. . . . But I don't believe —— '

Here she gave her negations.

'The fact is,' said d'Urberville drily, 'whatever your dear husband believed you accept, and whatever he rejected you reject, without the least inquiry or reasoning on your own part. That's just like you women. Your mind is enslaved to his.'

'Ah, because he knew everything!' said she, with a triumphant simplicity of faith in Angel Clare that the most perfect man could hardly have deserved, much less her husband.

'Yes, but you should not take negative opinions wholesale from another person like that. A pretty fellow he must be to teach you such scepticism!'

'He never forced my judgment! He would never argue on the subject with me! But I looked at it in this way; what he believed, after inquiring deep into doctrines, was much more likely to be right than what I might believe, who hadn't looked into doctrines at all.'

Sermon on the Mount: In which Jesus presents the Beatitudes; a crucial text of Christian belief (Matthew 5–7).

'What used he to say? He must have said something?'

She reflected; and with her acute memory for the letter of Angel Clare's remarks, even when she did not comprehend their spirit, she recalled a merciless polemical syllogism° that she had heard him use when, as it occasionally happened, he indulged in a species of thinking aloud with her at his side. In delivering it she gave also Clare's accent and manner with reverential faithfulness.

'Say that again,' asked d'Urberville, who had listened with the greatest attention.

She repeated the argument, and d'Urberville thoughtfully murmured the words after her.

'Anything else?' he presently asked.

'He said at another time something like this;' and she gave another, which might possibly have been paralleled in many a work of the pedigree ranging from the *Dictionnaire Philosophique* to Huxley's *Essays.*°

'Ah — ha How do you remember them?'

'I wanted to believe what he believed, though he didn't wish me to; and I managed to coax him to tell me a few of his thoughts. I can't say I quite understand that one; but I know it is right.'

'H'm. Fancy your being able to teach me what you don't know yourself!'

He fell into thought.

'And so I threw in my spiritual lot with his,' she resumed. 'I didn't wish it to be different. What's good enough for him is good enough for me.'

'Does he know that you are as big an infidel as he?'

'No — I never told him — if I am an infidel.'

'Well — you are better off to-day than I am, Tess, after all! You don't believe that you ought to preach my doctrine, and, therefore, do no despite to your conscience in abstaining. I do believe I ought to preach it, but like the devils I believe and tremble,° for I suddenly leave off preaching it, and give way to my passion for you.'

'How?'

'Why,' he said aridly; 'I have come all the way here to see you

a merciless polemical syllogism: The exact syllogism is not identifiable from the context. **from the *Dictionnaire Philosophique* to Huxley's *Essays:*** The *Dictionnaire* is a collection of essays published in the middle of the eighteenth century by Voltaire, who was antagonistic to Christianity; Thomas Henry Huxley (1825–1895), a respected scientist and supporter of Darwinian evolutionary theory, published many essays, including *Essays On Some Controverted Questions* (1892). **like the devils I believe and tremble:** An ironic allusion to James 2.19.

to-day! But I started from home to go to Casterbridge Fair, where I have undertaken to preach the Word from a waggon at half-past two this afternoon, and where all the brethren are expecting me this minute. Here's the announcement.'

He drew from his breast-pocket a poster whereon was printed the day, hour, and place of meeting, at which he, d'Urberville, would preach the Gospel as aforesaid.

'But how can you get there?' said Tess, looking at the clock.

'I cannot get there! I have come here.'

'What, you have really arranged to preach, and —— '

'I have arranged to preach, and I shall not be there — by reason of my burning desire to see a woman whom I once despised! — No, by my word and truth, I never despised you; if I had I should not love you now! Why I did not despise you was on account of your being unsmirched in spite of all; you withdrew yourself from me so quickly and resolutely when you saw the situation; you did not remain at my pleasure; so there was one petticoat in the world for whom I had no contempt, and you are she. But you may well despise me now! I thought I worshipped on the mountains, but I find I still serve in the groves!° Ha! ha!'

'O Alec d'Urberville! what does this mean? What have I done!'

'Done?' he said, with a soulless sneer in the word. 'Nothing intentionally. But you have been the means — the innocent means — of my backsliding, as they call it. I ask myself, am I, indeed, one of those "servants of corruption"° who, "after they have escaped the pollutions of the world, are again entangled therein and overcome" — whose latter end is worse than their beginning?' He laid his hand on her shoulder. 'Tess, my girl, I was on the way to, at least, social salvation till I saw you again!' he said freakishly shaking her, as if she were a child. 'And why then have you tempted me? I was firm as a man could be till I saw those eyes and that mouth again — surely there never was such a maddening mouth since Eve's!' His voice sank, and a hot archness shot from his own black eyes. 'You temptress, Tess; you dear damned witch of Babylon° — I could not resist you as soon as I met you again!'

'I couldn't help your seeing me again!' said Tess, recoiling.

'I know it — I repeat that I do not blame you. But the fact re-

I worshipped on the mountains . . . : The mountains were associated with worshipping Jehova; the groves, with worshipping Baal (2 Kings 17–23). **"servants of corruption":** This phrase and the remainder of Alec's question echo 2 Peter 2.19–20. **witch of Babylon:** In Revelation 17, there are references to the Whore of Babylon.

mains. When I saw you ill-used on the farm that day I was nearly mad to think that I had no legal right to protect you — that I could not have it; whilst he who has it seems to neglect you utterly!'

'Don't speak against him — he is absent!' she cried in much excitement. 'Treat him honourably — he has never wronged you! O leave his wife before any scandal spreads that may do harm to his honest name!'

'I will — I will,' he said, like a man awakening from a luring dream. 'I have broken my engagement to preach to those poor drunken boobies at the fair — it is the first time I have played such a practical joke. A month ago I should have been horrified at such a possibility. I'll go away — to swear — and — ah, can I! to keep away.' Then, suddenly: 'One clasp, Tessy — one! Only for old friendship —— '

'I am without defence, Alec! A good man's honour is in my keeping — think — be ashamed!'

'Pooh! Well yes — yes!'

He clenched his lips, mortified with himself for his weakness. His eyes were equally barren of worldly and religious faith. The corpses of those old fitful passions which had lain inanimate amid the lines of his face ever since his reformation seemed to wake and come together as in a resurrection. He went out indeterminately.

Though d'Urberville had declared that this breach of his engagement to-day was the simple backsliding of a believer, Tess's words, as echoed from Angel Clare, had made a deep impression upon him, and continued to do so after he had left her. He moved on in silence, as if his energies were benumbed by the hitherto undreamt-of possibility that his position was untenable. Reason had had nothing to do with his whimsical conversion, which was perhaps the mere freak of a careless man in search of a new sensation, and temporarily impressed by his mother's death.

The drops of logic Tess had let fall into the sea of his enthusiasm served to chill its effervescence to stagnation. He said to himself, as he pondered again and again over the crystallized phrases that she had handed on to him, 'That clever fellow little thought that, by telling her those things, he might be paving my way back to her!'

XLVII

It is the threshing of the last wheat-rick at Flintcomb-Ash Farm. The dawn of the March morning is singularly inexpressive, and there is nothing to show where the eastern horizon lies. Against the twilight rises the trapezoidal top of the stack, which has stood forlornly here through the washing and bleaching of the wintry weather.

When Izz Huett and Tess arrived at the scene of operations only a rustling denoted that others had preceded them; to which, as the light increased, there were presently added the silhouettes of two men on the summit. They were busily 'unhaling' the rick, that is, stripping off the thatch before beginning to throw down the sheaves; and while this was in progress Izz and Tess, with the other women-workers, in their whitey-brown pinners, stood waiting and shivering, Farmer Groby having insisted upon their being on the spot thus early to get the job over if possible by the end of the day. Close under the eaves of the stack, and as yet barely visible, was the red tyrant that the women had come to serve — a timber-framed construction, with straps and wheels appertaining — the threshing-machine which, whilst it was going, kept up a despotic demand upon the endurance of their muscles and nerves.

A little way off there was another indistinct figure; this one black, with a sustained hiss that spoke of strength very much in reserve. The long chimney running up beside an ash-tree, and the warmth which radiated from the spot, explained without the necessity of much daylight that here was the engine which was to act as the *primum mobile*° of this little world. By the engine stood a dark motionless being, a sooty and grimy embodiment of tallness, in a sort of trance, with a heap of coals by his side: it was the engine-man. The isolation of his manner and colour lent him the appearance of a creature from Tophet,° who had strayed into the pellucid smokelessness of this region of yellow grain and pale soil, with which he had nothing in common, to amaze and to discompose its aborigines.

What he looked he felt. He was in the agricultural world, but not of it. He served fire and smoke; these denizens of the fields served vegetation, weather, frost, and sun. He travelled with his engine from farm to farm, from county to county, for as yet the steam threshing-machine was itinerant in this part of Wessex. He spoke in a strange northern accent; his thoughts being turned inwards upon himself, his eye on his iron charge, hardly perceiving the scenes around him, and caring for them not at all: holding only strictly necessary intercourse

primum mobile: The outermost sphere of the world in Ptolemaic cosmography, which caused the movement of the heavens. **Tophet:** A place mentioned in the Bible where children were burned that became identified in Judaism with an underworld where wickedness was punished after death; a synonym for hell that came into Middle English from Hebrew.

with the natives, as if some ancient doom compelled him to wander here against his will in the service of his Plutonic master.° The long strap which ran from the driving-wheel of his engine to the red thresher under the rick was the sole tie-line between agriculture and him.

While they uncovered the sheaves he stood apathetic beside his portable repository of force, round whose hot blackness the morning air quivered. He had nothing to do with preparatory labour. His fire was waiting incandescent, his steam was at high pressure, in a few seconds he could make the long strap move at an invisible velocity. Beyond its extent the environment might be corn, straw, or chaos; it was all the same to him. If any of the autochthonous idlers asked him what he called himself, he replied shortly, 'an engineer.'

The rick was unhaled by full daylight; the men then took their places, the women mounted, and the work began. Farmer Groby — or, as they called him, 'he' — had arrived ere this, and by his orders Tess was placed on the platform of the machine, close to the man who fed it, her business being to untie every sheaf of corn handed on to her by Izz Huett, who stood next, but on the rick; so that the feeder could seize it and spread it over the revolving drum, which whisked out every grain in one moment.

They were soon in full progress, after a preparatory hitch or two, which rejoiced the hearts of those who hated machinery. The work sped on till breakfast-time, when the thresher was stopped for half an hour; and on starting again after the meal the whole supplementary strength of the farm was thrown into the labour of constructing the straw-rick, which began to grow beside the stack of corn. A hasty lunch was eaten as they stood, without leaving their positions, and then another couple of hours brought them near to dinner-time; the inexorable wheels continuing to spin, and the penetrating hum of the thresher to thrill to the very marrow all who were near the revolving wire-cage.

The old men on the rising straw-rick talked of the past days when they had been accustomed to thresh with flails on the oaken barn-floor; when everything, even to winnowing, was effected by hand-labour, which, to their thinking, though slow, produced better results. Those, too, on the corn-rick talked a little; but the perspiring ones at the machine, including Tess, could not lighten their duties by the

Plutonic master: Pluto, or Hades, god of the underworld, had the power to condemn people to hell.

exchange of many words. It was the ceaselessness of the work which tried her so severely, and began to make her wish that she had never come to Flintcomb-Ash. The women on the corn-rick — Marian, who was one of them, in particular — could stop to drink ale or cold tea from the flagon now and then, or to exchange a few gossiping remarks while they wiped their faces or cleared the fragments of straw and husk from their clothing; but for Tess there was no respite; for, as the drum never stopped, the man who fed it could not stop, and she, who had to supply the man with untied sheaves, could not stop either, unless Marian changed places with her, which she sometimes did for half an hour in spite of Groby's objection that she was too slow-handed for a feeder.

For some probably economical reason it was usually a woman who was chosen for this particular duty, and Groby gave as his motive in selecting Tess that she was one of those who best combined strength with quickness in untying, and both with staying power, and this may have been true. The hum of the thresher, which prevented speech, increased to a raving whenever the supply of corn fell short of the regular quantity. As Tess and the man who fed could never turn their heads she did not know that just before the dinner-hour a person had come silently into the field by the gate, and had been standing under a second rick watching the scene, and Tess in particular. He was dressed in a tweed suit of fashionable pattern, and he twirled a gay walking-cane.

'Who is that?' said Izz Huett to Marian. She had at first addressed the inquiry to Tess, but the latter could not hear it.

'Somebody's fancy-man, I s'pose,' said Marian laconically.

'I'll lay a guinea he's after Tess.'

'O no. 'Tis a ranter pa'son who's been sniffing after her lately; not a dandy like this.'

'Well — this is the same man.'

'The same man as the preacher? But he's quite different!'

'He hev left off his black coat and white neckercher, and hev cut off his whiskers; but he's the same man for all that.'

'D'ye really think so? Then I'll tell her,' said Marian.

'Don't. She'll see him soon enough, good-now.'

'Well, I don't think it at all right for him to join his preaching to courting a married woman, even though her husband mid be abroad, and she, in a sense, a widow.'

'Oh — he can do her no harm,' said Izz drily. 'Her mind can no more be heaved from that one place where it do bide than a stooded waggon° from the hole he's in. Lord love 'ee, neither court-paying, nor preaching, nor the seven thunders° themselves, can wean a woman when 'twould be better for her that she should be weaned.'

Dinner-time came, and the whirling ceased; whereupon Tess left her post, her knees trembling so wretchedly with the shaking of the machine that she could scarcely walk.

'You ought to het a quart o' drink into 'ee, as I've done,' said Marian. 'You wouldn't look so white then. Why, souls above us, your face is as if you'd been hagrode!'°

It occurred to the good-natured Marian that, as Tess was so tired, her discovery of her visitor's presence might have the bad effect of taking away her appetite; and Marian was thinking of inducing Tess to descend by a ladder on the further side of the stack when the gentleman came forward and looked up.

Tess uttered a short little 'Oh!' And a moment after she said, quickly, 'I shall eat my dinner here — right on the rick.'

Sometimes, when they were so far from their cottages, they all did this; but as there was rather a keen wind going to-day, Marian and the rest descended, and sat under the straw-stack.

The new-comer was, indeed, Alec d'Urberville, the late Evangelist, despite his changed attire and aspect. It was obvious at a glance that the original *Weltlust*° had come back; that he had restored himself, as nearly as a man could do who had grown three or four years older, to the old jaunty, slap-dash guise under which Tess had first known her admirer, and cousin so-called. Having decided to remain where she was, Tess sat down among the bundles, out of sight of the ground, and began her meal; till, by-and-by, she heard footsteps on the ladder, and immediately after Alec appeared upon the stack — now an oblong and level platform of sheaves. He strode across them, and sat down opposite to her without a word.

Tess continued to eat her modest dinner, a slice of thick pancake which she had brought with her. The other workfolk were by this time all gathered under the rick, where the loose straw formed a comfortable retreat.

'I am here again, as you see,' said d'Urberville.

'Why do you trouble me so!' she cried, reproach flashing from her very finger-ends.

'*I* trouble *you*? I think I may ask, why do you trouble me?'

stooded waggon: A wagon that is stuck (dialect). **the seven thunders:** Mentioned in Revelation 10.3–4. **hagrode:** Ridden by witches, troubled by nightmares (dialect). ***Weltlust:*** Desire for worldly things and pleasures (German).

'Sure, I don't trouble you any-when!'

'You say you don't? But you do! You haunt me. Those very eyes that you turned upon me with such a bitter flash a moment ago, they come to me just as you showed them then, in the night and in the day! Tess, ever since you told me of that child of ours, it is just as if my feelings, which have been flowing in a strong puritanical stream, had suddenly found a way open in the direction of you, and had all at once gushed through. The religious channel is left dry forthwith; and it is you who have done it!'

She gazed in silence.

'What — you have given up your preaching entirely?' she asked.

She had gathered from Angel sufficient of the incredulity of modern thought to despise flash enthusiasms; but, as a woman, she was somewhat appalled.

In affected severity d'Urberville continued —

'Entirely. I have broken every engagement since that afternoon I was to address the drunkards at Casterbridge Fair. The deuce only knows what I am thought of by the brethren. Ah-ha! The brethren! No doubt they pray for me — weep for me; for they are kind people in their way. But what do I care? How could I go on with the thing when I had lost my faith in it? — it would have been hypocrisy of the basest kind! Among them I should have stood like Hymenæus and Alexander,° who were delivered over to Satan that they might learn not to blaspheme. What a grand revenge you have taken! I saw you innocent, and I deceived you. Four years after, you find me a Christian enthusiast; you then work upon me, perhaps to my complete perdition! But Tess, my coz, as I used to call you, this is only my way of talking, and you must not look so horribly concerned. Of course you have done nothing except retain your pretty face and shapely figure. I saw it on the rick before you saw me — that tight pinafore-thing sets it off, and that wing-bonnet — you field-girls should never wear those bonnets if you wish to keep out of danger.' He regarded her silently for a few moments, and with a short cynical laugh resumed: 'I believe that if the bachelor-apostle,° whose deputy I thought I was, had been tempted by such a pretty face, he would have let go the plough for her sake as I do!'

Tess attempted to expostulate, but at this juncture all her fluency failed her, and without heeding he added:

Hymenæus and Alexander: In this sentence Alec is echoing Paul in 1 Timothy 1.18–20, where he mentions these figures as examples of those who have lost faith.
bachelor-apostle: St. Paul; Alec is echoing Luke 9.62.

'Well, this paradise that you supply is perhaps as good as any other, after all. But to speak seriously, Tess.' D'Urberville rose and came nearer, reclining sideways amid the sheaves, and resting upon his elbow. 'Since I last saw you, I have been thinking of what you said that *he* said. I have come to the conclusion that there does seem rather a want of commonsense in these threadbare old propositions; how I could have been so fired by poor Parson Clare's enthusiasm, and have gone so madly to work, transcending even him, I cannot make out! As for what you said last time, on the strength of your wonderful husband's intelligence — whose name you have never told me — about having what they call an ethical system without any dogma, I don't see my way to that at all.'

'Why, you can have the religion of loving-kindness and purity at least, if you can't have — what do you call it — dogma.'

'O no! I'm a different sort of fellow from that! If there's nobody to say, "Do this, and it will be a good thing for you after you are dead; do that, and it will be a bad thing for you," I can't warm up. Hang it, I am not going to feel responsible for my deeds and passions if there's nobody to be responsible to; and if I were you, my dear, I wouldn't either!'

She tried to argue, and tell him that he had mixed in his dull brain two matters, theology and morals, which in the primitive days of mankind had been quite distinct. But owing to Angel Clare's reticence, to her absolute want of training, and to her being a vessel of emotions rather than reasons, she could not get on.

'Well, never mind,' he resumed. 'Here I am, my love, as in the old times!'

'Not as then — never as then — 'tis different!' she entreated. 'And there was never warmth with me! O why didn't you keep your faith, if the loss of it has brought you to speak to me like this!'

'Because you've knocked it out of me; so the evil be upon your sweet head! Your husband little thought how his teaching would recoil upon him! Ha-ha — I'm awfuly glad you have made an apostate of me all the same! Tess, I am more taken with you than ever, and I pity you too. For all your closeness, I see you are in a bad way — neglected by one who ought to cherish you.'

She could not get her morsels of food down her throat; her lips were dry, and she was ready to choke. The voices and laughs of the workfolk eating and drinking under the rick came to her as if they were a quarter of a mile off.

'It is cruelty to me!' she said. 'How — how can you treat me to this talk, if you care ever so little for me?'

'True, true,' he said, wincing a little. 'I did not come to reproach you for my deeds. I came, Tess, to say that I don't like you to be working like this, and I have come on purpose for you. You say you have a husband who is not I. Well, perhaps you have; but I've never seen him, and you've not told me his name; and altogether he seems rather a mythological personage. However, even if you have one, I think I am nearer to you than he is. I, at any rate, try to help you out of trouble, but he does not, bless his invisible face! The words of the stern prophet Hosea that I used to read come back to me. Don't you know them, Tess? — "And she shall follow after her lover, but she shall not overtake him; and she shall seek him, but shall not find him; then shall she say, I will go and return to my first husband; for then was it better with me than now!"° . . . Tess, my trap is waiting just under the hill, and — darling mine, not his! — you know the rest.'

Her face had been rising to a dull crimson fire while he spoke; but she did not answer.

'You have been the cause of my backsliding,' he continued, stretching his arm towards her waist; 'you should be willing to share it, and leave that mule you call husband for ever.'

One of her leather gloves, which she had taken off to eat her skimmer-cake, lay in her lap, and without the slightest warning she passionately swung the glove by the gauntlet directly in his face. It was heavy and thick as a warrior's, and it struck him flat on the mouth. Fancy might have regarded the act as the recrudescence of a trick in which her armed progenitors were not unpractised. Alec fiercely started up from his reclining position. A scarlet oozing appeared where her blow had alighted, and in a moment the blood began dropping from his mouth upon the straw. But he soon controlled himself, calmly drew his handkerchief from his pocket, and mopped his bleeding lips.

She too had sprung up, but she sank down again.

'Now, punish me!' she said, turning up her eyes to him with the hopeless defiance of the sparrow's gaze before its captor twists its neck. 'Whip me, crush me; you need not mind those people under the rick! I shall not cry out. Once victim, always victim — that's the law!'

'O no, no, Tess,' he said blandly. 'I can make full allowance for this. Yet you most unjustly forget one thing, that I would have married you if you had not put it out of my power to do so. Did I not ask you flatly to be my wife — hey? Answer me.'

"And she shall follow after her lover, . . .": A similar statement occurs in Hosea 2.7.

'You did.'

'And you cannot be. But remember one thing!' His voice hardened as his temper got the better of him with the recollection of his sincerity in asking her and her present ingratitude, and he stepped across to her side and held her by the shoulders, so that she shook under his grasp. 'Remember, my lady, I was your master once! I will be your master again. If you are any man's wife you are mine!'

The threshers now began to stir below.

'So much for our quarrel,' he said, letting her go. 'Now I shall leave you, and shall come again for your answer during the afternoon. You don't know me yet! But I know you.'

She had not spoken again, remaining as if stunned. D'Urberville retreated over the sheaves, and descended the ladder, while the workers below rose and stretched their arms, and shook down the beer they had drunk. Then the threshing-machine started afresh; and amid the renewed rustle of the straw Tess resumed her position by the buzzing drum as one in a dream, untying sheaf after sheaf in endless succession.

XLVIII

In the afternoon the farmer made it known that the rick was to be finished that night, since there was a moon by which they could see to work, and the man with the engine was engaged for another farm on the morrow. Hence the twanging and humming and rustling proceeded with even less intermission than usual.

It was not till 'nammet'-time,° about three o'clock, that Tess raised her eyes and gave a momentary glance round. She felt but little surprise at seeing that Alec d'Urberville had come back, and was standing under the hedge by the gate. He had seen her lift her eyes, and waved his hand urbanely to her, while he blew her a kiss. It meant that their quarrel was over. Tess looked down again, and carefully abstained from gazing in that direction.

Thus the afternoon dragged on. The wheat-rick shrank lower, and the straw-rick grew higher, and the corn-sacks were carted away. At six o'clock the wheat-rick was about shoulder-high from the ground. But the unthreshed sheaves remaining untouched seemed countless still, notwithstanding the enormous numbers that had been gulped down by the insatiable swallower, fed by the man and Tess, through whose two young hands the greater part of them had passed. And the

'nammet'-time: Time for a snack at mid-morning or mid-afternoon (dialect).

immense stack of straw where in the morning there had been nothing, appeared as the *faeces* of the same buzzing red glutton. From the west sky a wrathful shine — all that wild March could afford in the way of sunset — had burst forth after the cloudy day, flooding the tired and sticky faces of the threshers, and dyeing them with a coppery light, as also the flapping garments of the women, which clung to them like dull flames.

A panting ache ran through the rick. The man who fed was weary, and Tess could see that the red nape of his neck was encrusted with dirt and husks. She still stood at her post, her flushed and perspiring face coated with the corn-dust, and her white bonnet embrowned by it. She was the only woman whose place was upon the machine so as to be shaken bodily by its spinning, and the decrease of the stack now separated her from Marian and Izz, and prevented their changing duties with her as they had done. The incessant quivering, in which every fibre of her frame participated, had thrown her into a stupefied reverie in which her arms worked on independently of her consciousness. She hardly knew where she was, and did not hear Izz Huett tell her from below that her hair was tumbling down.

By degrees the freshest among them began to grow cadaverous and saucer-eyed. Whenever Tess lifted her head she beheld always the great upgrown straw-stack, with the men in shirt-sleeves upon it, against the gray north sky; in front of it the long red elevator like a Jacob's ladder,° on which a perpetual stream of threshed straw ascended, a yellow river running up-hill, and spouting out on the top of the rick.

She knew that Alec d'Urberville was still on the scene, observing her from some point or other, though she could not say where. There was an excuse for his remaining, for when the threshed rick drew near its final sheaves a little ratting was always done, and men unconnected with the threshing sometimes dropped in for that performance — sporting characters of all descriptions, gents with terriers and facetious pipes, roughs with sticks and stones.

But there was another hour's work before the layer of live rats at the base of the stack would be reached; and as the evening light in the direction of the Giant's Hill by Abbot's-Cernel dissolved away, the white-faced moon of the season arose from the horizon that lay towards Middleton Abbey and Shottsford on the other side. For the last

Jacob's ladder: The ladder on which angels descend and ascend between heaven and earth, from Jacob's dream in Genesis 28.12.

hour or two Marian had felt uneasy about Tess, whom she could not get near enough to speak to, the other women having kept up their strength by drinking ale, and Tess having done without it through traditionary dread, owing to its results at her home in childhood. But Tess still kept going: if she could not fill her part she would have to leave; and this contingency, which she would have regarded with equanimity and even with relief a month or two earlier, had become a terror since d'Urberville had begun to hover round her.

The sheaf-pitchers and feeders had now worked the rick so low that people on the ground could talk to them. To Tess's surprise Farmer Groby came up on the machine to her, and said that if she desired to join her friend he did not wish her to keep on any longer, and would send somebody else to take her place. The 'friend' was d'Urberville, she knew, and also that this concession had been granted in obedience to the request of that friend, or enemy. She shook her head and toiled on.

The time for the rat-catching arrived at last, and the hunt began. The creatures had crept downwards with the subsidence of the rick till they were all together at the bottom, and being now uncovered from their last refuge they ran across the open ground in all directions, a loud shriek from the by-this-time half-tipsy Marian informing her companions that one of the rats had invaded her person — a terror which the rest of the women had guarded against by various schemes of skirt-tucking and self-elevation. The rat was at last dislodged, and, amid the barking of dogs, masculine shouts, feminine screams, oaths, stampings, and confusion as of Pandemonium, Tess untied her last sheaf; the drum slowed, the whizzing ceased, and she stepped from the machine to the ground.

Her lover, who had only looked on at the rat-catching, was promptly at her side.

'What — after all — my insulting slap, too!' said she in an underbreath. She was so utterly exhausted that she had not strength to speak louder.

'I should indeed be foolish to feel offended at anything you say or do,' he answered, in the seductive voice of the Trantridge time. 'How the little limbs tremble! You are as weak as a bled calf, you know you are; and yet you need have done nothing since I arrived. How could you be so obstinate? However, I have told the farmer that he has no right to employ women at steam-threshing. It is not proper work for them; and on all the better class of farms it has been given up, as he knows very well. I will walk with you as far as your home.'

'O yes,' she answered with a jaded gait. 'Walk wi' me if you will! I do bear in mind that you came to marry me before you knew o' my state. Perhaps — perhaps you are a little better and kinder than I have been thinking you were. Whatever is meant as kindness I am grateful for; whatever is meant in any other way I am angered at. I cannot sense your meaning sometimes.'

'If I cannot legitimize our former relations at least I can assist you. And I will do it with much more regard for your feelings than I formerly showed. My religious mania, or whatever it was, is over. But I retain a little good nature; I hope I do. Now Tess, by all that's tender and strong between man and woman, trust me! I have enough and more than enough to put you out of anxiety, both for yourself and your parents and sisters. I can make them all comfortable if you will only show confidence in me.'

'Have you seen 'em lately?' she quickly inquired.

'Yes. They didn't know where you were. It was only by chance that I found you here.'

The cold moon looked aslant upon Tess's fagged face between the twigs of the garden-hedge as she paused outside the cottage which was her temporary home, d'Urberville pausing beside her.

'Don't mention my little brothers and sisters — don't make me break down quite!' she said. 'If you want to help them — God knows they need it — do it without telling me. But no, no!' she cried. 'I will take nothing from you, either for them or for me!' He did not accompany her further, since, as she lived with the household, all was public indoors. No sooner had she herself entered, laved herself in a washing-tub, and shared supper with the family than she fell into thought, and withdrawing to the table under the wall, by the light of her own little lamp wrote in a passionate mood —

> MY OWN HUSBAND, — Let me call you so — I must — even if it makes you angry to think of such an unworthy wife as I. I must cry to you in my trouble — I have no one else! I am so exposed to temptation, Angel. I fear to say who it is, and I do not like to write about it at all. But I cling to you in a way you cannot think! Can you not come to me now, at once, before anything terrible happens? O, I know you cannot, because you are so far away! I think I must die if you do not come soon, or tell me to come to you. The punishment you have measured out to me is deserved — I do know that — well deserved — and you are right and just to be angry with me. But, Angel, please, please, not to be just — only a little kind to me, even if I do not deserve it, and come to

me! If you would come, I could die in your arms! I would be well content to do that if so be you had forgiven me!

Angel, I live entirely for you. I love you too much to blame you for going away, and I know it was necessary you should find a farm. Do not think I shall say a word of sting or bitterness. Only come back to me. I am desolate without you, my darling, O, so desolate! I do not mind having to work: but if you will send me one little line, and say, '*I am coming soon,*' I will bide on, Angel — O, so cheerfully!

It has been so much my religion ever since we were married to be faithful to you in every thought and look, that even when a man speaks a compliment to me before I am aware, it seems wronging you. Have you never felt one little bit of what you used to feel when we were at the dairy? If you have, how can you keep away from me? I am the same woman, Angel, as you fell in love with; yes, the very same! — not the one you disliked but never saw. What was the past to me as soon as I met you? It was a dead thing altogether. I became another woman, filled full of new life from you. How could I be the early one? Why do you not see this? Dear, if you would only be a little more conceited, and believe in yourself so far as to see that you were strong enough to work this change in me, you would perhaps be in a mind to come to me, your poor wife.

How silly I was in my happiness when I thought I could trust you always to love me! I ought to have known that such as that was not for poor me. But I am sick at heart, not only for old times, but for the present. Think — think how it do hurt my heart not to see you ever — ever! Ah, if I could only make your dear heart ache one little minute of each day as mine does every day and all day long, it might lead you to show pity to your poor lonely one.

People still say that I am rather pretty, Angel (handsome is the word they use, since I wish to be truthful). Perhaps I am what they say. But I do not value my good looks; I only like to have them because they belong to you, my dear, and that there may be at least one thing about me worth your having. So much have I felt this, that when I met with annoyance on account of the same I tied up my face in a bandage as long as people would believe in it. O Angel, I tell you all this not from vanity — you will certainly know I do not — but only that you may come to me!

If you really cannot come to me will you let me come to you! I am, as I say, worried, pressed to do what I will not do. It cannot be that I shall yield one inch, yet I am in terror as to what an accident might lead to, and I so defenceless on account of my first error. I cannot say more about this — it makes me too miserable. But if I break down by falling into some fearful snare, my last state will be worse than my first.° O God, I cannot think of it! Let me come at once, or at once come to me!

I would be content, ay, glad, to live with you as your servant, if I may not as your wife; so that I could only be near you, and get glimpses of you, and think of you as mine.

The daylight has nothing to show me, since you are not here, and I don't like to see the rooks and starlings in the fields, because I grieve and grieve to miss you who used to see them with me. I long for only one thing in heaven or earth or under the earth, to meet you, my own dear! Come to me — come to me, and save me from what threatens me! — Your faithful heartbroken

TESS.

XLIX

The appeal duly found its way to the breakfast-table of the quiet Vicarage to the westward, in that valley where the air is so soft and the soil so rich that the effort of growth requires but superficial aid by comparison with the tillage at Flintcomb-Ash, and where to Tess the human world seemed so different (though it was much the same). It was purely for security that she had been requested by Angel to send her communications through his father, whom he kept pretty well informed of his changing addresses in the country he had gone to exploit for himself with a heavy heart.

'Now,' said old Mr. Clare to his wife, when he had read the envelope, 'if Angel proposes leaving Rio for a visit home at the end of next month, as he told us that he hoped to do, I think this may hasten his plans; for I believe it to be from his wife.' He breathed deeply at the thought of her; and the letter was redirected to be promptly sent on to Angel.

'Dear fellow, I hope he will get home safely,' murmured Mrs. Clare. 'To my dying day I shall feel that he has been ill-used. You should have sent him to Cambridge in spite of his want of faith, and given him the same chance as the other boys had. He would have grown out of it under proper influence, and perhaps would have taken Orders after all. Church or no Church, it would have been fairer to him.'

my last state will be worse than my first: An echo of Alec's words near the end of chapter XLVI and of various biblical passages, including Matthew 12.45 and 2 Peter 2.20.

This was the only wail with which Mrs. Clare ever disturbed her husband's peace in respect of their sons. And she did not vent this often; for she was as considerate as she was devout, and knew that his mind too was troubled by doubts as to his justice in this matter. Only too often had she heard him lying awake at night, stifling sighs for Angel with prayers. But the uncompromising Evangelical did not even now hold that he would have been justified in giving his son, an unbeliever, the same academic advantages that he had given to the two others, when it was possible, if not probable, that those very advantages might have been used to decry the doctrines which he had made it his life's mission and desire to propagate, and the mission of his ordained sons likewise. To put with one hand a pedestal under the feet of the two faithful ones, and with the other to exalt the unfaithful by the same artificial means, he deemed to be alike inconsistent with his convictions, his position, and his hopes. Nevertheless, he loved his misnamed Angel, and in secret mourned over this treatment of him as Abraham° might have mourned over the doomed Isaac while they went up the hill together. His silent self-generated regrets were far bitterer than the reproaches which his wife rendered audible.

They blamed themselves for this unlucky marriage. If Angel had never been destined for a farmer he would never have been thrown with agricultural girls. They did not distinctly know what had separated him and his wife, nor the date on which the separation had taken place. At first they had supposed it must be something of the nature of a serious aversion. But in his later letters he occasionally alluded to the intention of coming home to fetch her; from which expressions they hoped the division might not owe its origin to anything so hopelessly permanent as that. He had told them that she was with her relatives, and in their doubts they had decided not to intrude into a situation which they knew no way of bettering.

The eyes for which Tess's letter was intended were gazing at this time on a limitless expanse of country from the back of a mule which was bearing him from the interior of the South-American Continent towards the coast. His experiences of this strange land had been sad. The severe illness from which he had suffered shortly after his arrival had never wholly left him, and he had by degrees almost decided to relinquish his hope of farming here, though, as long as the bare possibility existed of his remaining, he kept this change of view a secret from his parents.

Abraham: The story of Abraham's willingness to sacrifice his son Isaac is contained in Genesis 22.1–14.

The crowds of agricultural labourers who had come out to the country in his wake, dazzled by representations of easy independence, had suffered, died, and wasted away. He would see mothers from English farms trudging along with their infants in their arms, when the child would be stricken with fever and would die; the mother would pause to dig a hole in the loose earth with her bare hands, would bury the babe therein with the same natural grave-tools, shed one tear, and again trudge on.

Angel's original intention had not been emigration to Brazil, but a northern or eastern farm in his own country. He had come to this place in a fit of desperation, the Brazil movement among the English agriculturists having by chance coincided with his desire to escape from his past existence.

During this time of absence he had mentally aged a dozen years. What arrested him now as of value in life was less its beauty than its pathos. Having long discredited the old systems of mysticism, he now began to discredit the old appraisements of morality. He thought they wanted readjusting. Who was the moral man? Still more pertinently, who was the moral woman? The beauty or ugliness of a character lay not only in its achievements, but in its aims and impulses; its true history lay, not among things done, but among things willed.

How, then, about Tess?

Viewing her in these lights, a regret for his hasty judgment began to oppress him. Did he reject her eternally, or did he not? He could no longer say that he would always reject her, and not to say that was in spirit to accept her now.

This growing fondness for her memory coincided in point of time with her residence at Flintcomb-Ash, but it was before she had felt herself at liberty to trouble him with a word about her circumstances or her feelings. He was greatly perplexed; and in his perplexity as to her motives in withholding intelligence he did not inquire. Thus her silence of docility was misinterpreted. How much it really said if he had understood! — that she adhered with literal exactness to orders which he had given and forgotten; that despite her natural fearlessness she asserted no rights, admitted his judgment to be in every respect the true one, and bent her head dumbly thereto.

In the before-mentioned journey by mules through the interior of the country, another man rode beside him. Angel's companion was also an Englishman, bent on the same errand, though he came from another part of the island. They were both in a state of mental depression, and they spoke of home affairs. Confidence begat confidence.

With that curious tendency evinced by men, more especially when in distant lands, to entrust to strangers details of their lives which they would on no account mention to friends, Angel admitted to this man as they rode along the sorrowful facts of his marriage.

The stranger had sojourned in many more lands and among many more peoples than Angel; to his cosmopolitan mind such deviations from the social norm, so immense to domesticity, were no more than are the irregularities of vale and mountain-chain to the whole terrestrial curve. He viewed the matter in quite a different light from Angel; thought that what Tess had been was of no importance beside what she would be, and plainly told Clare that he was wrong in coming away from her.

The next day they were drenched in a thunderstorm. Angel's companion was struck down with fever, and died by the week's end. Clare waited a few hours to bury him, and then went on his way.

The cursory remarks of the large-minded stranger, of whom he knew absolutely nothing beyond a commonplace name, were sublimed by his death, and influenced Clare more than all the reasoned ethics of the philosophers. His own parochialism made him ashamed by its contrast. His inconsistencies rushed upon him in a flood. He had persistently elevated Hellenic Paganism at the expense of Christianity; yet in that civilization an illegal surrender was not certain dis-esteem. Surely then he might have regarded that abhorrence of the un-intact state, which he had inherited with the creed of mysticism, as at least open to correction when the result was due to treachery. A remorse struck into him. The words of Izz Huett, never quite stilled in his memory, came back to him. He had asked Izz if she loved him, and she had replied in the affirmative. Did she love him more than Tess did? No, she had replied; Tess would lay down her life for him, and she herself could do no more.

He thought of Tess as she had appeared on the day of the wedding. How her eyes had lingered upon him; how she had hung upon his words as if they were a god's! And during the terrible evening over the hearth, when her simple soul uncovered itself to his, how pitiful her face had looked by the rays of the fire, in her inability to realize that his love and protection could possibly be withdrawn.

Thus from being her critic he grew to be her advocate. Cynical things he had uttered to himself about her; but no man can be always a cynic and live; and he withdrew them. The mistake of expressing them had arisen from his allowing himself to be influenced by general principles to the disregard of the particular instance.

But the reasoning is somewhat musty; lovers and husbands have gone over the ground before to-day. Clare had been harsh towards her; there is no doubt of it. Men are too often harsh with women they love or have loved; women with men. And yet these harshnesses are tenderness itself when compared with the universal harshness out of which they grow; the harshness of the position towards the temperament, of the means towards the aims, of to-day towards yesterday, of hereafter towards to-day.

The historic interest of her family — that masterful line of d'Urbervilles — whom he had despised as a spent force, touched his sentiments now. Why had he not known the difference between the political value and the imaginative value of these things? In the latter aspect her d'Urberville descent was a fact of great dimensions; worthless to economics, it was a most useful ingredient to the dreamer, to the moralizer on declines and falls. It was a fact that would soon be forgotten — that bit of distinction in poor Tess's blood and name, and oblivion would fall upon her hereditary link with the marble monuments and leaded skeletons at Kingsbere. So does Time ruthlessly destroy his own romances. In recalling her face again and again, he thought now that he could see therein a flash of the dignity which must have graced her grand-dames; and the vision sent that *aura* through his veins which he had formerly felt, and which left behind it a sense of sickness.

Despite her not inviolate past, what still abode in such a woman as Tess outvalued the freshness of her fellows. Was not the gleaning of the grapes of Ephraim° better than the vintage of Abi-ezer?

So spoke love renascent, preparing the way for Tess's devoted outpouring, which was then just being forwarded to him by his father; though owing to his distance inland it was to be a long time in reaching him.

Meanwhile the writer's expectation that Angel would come in response to the entreaty was alternately great and small. What lessened it was that the facts of her life which had led to the parting had not changed — could never change; and that, if her presence had not attenuated them, her absence could not. Nevertheless she addressed her mind to the tender question of what she could do to please him best if he should arrive. Sighs were expended on the wish that she had taken more notice of the tunes he played on his harp, that she had inquired

grapes of Ephraim: In biblical history, the clan of Abiezer was rescued by the Ephraimites; the story is told in Judges 8.1–3, which the statement here echoes.

more curiously of him which were his favourite ballads among those the country-girls sang. She indirectly inquired of Amby Seedling, who had followed Izz from Talbothays, and by chance Amby remembered that, amongst the snatches of melody in which they had indulged at the dairyman's, to induce the cows to let down their milk, Clare had seemed to like 'Cupid's Gardens,' 'I have parks, I have hounds,' and 'The break o' the day;' and had seemed not to care for 'The Tailor's Breeches,' and 'Such a beauty I did grow,' excellent ditties as they were.

To perfect the ballads was now her whimsical desire. She practised them privately at odd moments, especially 'The break o' the day:'

Arise, arise, arise!
And pick your love a posy,
All o' the sweetest flowers
That in the garden grow.
The turtle doves and sma' birds
In every bough a-building,
So early in the May-time
At the break o' the day!

It would have melted the heart of a stone to hear her singing these ditties, whenever she worked apart from the rest of the girls in this cold dry time; the tears running down her cheeks all the while at the thought that perhaps he would not, after all, come to hear her, and the simple silly words of the songs resounding in painful mockery of the aching heart of the singer.

Tess was so wrapt up in this fanciful dream that she seemed not to know how the season was advancing; that the days had lengthened, that Lady-Day was at hand, and would soon be followed by Old Lady-Day, the end of her term here.

But before the quarter-day had quite come something happened which made Tess think of far different matters. She was at her lodging as usual one evening, sitting in the downstairs room with the rest of the family, when somebody knocked at the door and inquired for Tess. Through the doorway she saw against the declining light a figure with the height of a woman and the breadth of a child, a tall, thin, girlish creature whom she did not recognize in the twilight till the girl said 'Tess!'

'What — is it 'Liza-Lu?' asked Tess, in startled accents. Her sister, whom a little over a year ago she had left at home as a child, had sprung up by a sudden shoot to a form of this presentation, of which as yet Lu seemed herself scarce able to understand the meaning. Her thin legs, visible below her once long frock, now short by her growing, and her uncomfortable hands and arms, revealed her youth and inexperience.

'Yes, I have been traipsing about all day, Tess,' said Lu, with unemotional gravity, 'a-trying to find 'ee; and I'm very tired.'

'What is the matter at home?'

'Mother is took very bad, and the doctor says she's dying, and as father is not very well neither, and says 'tis wrong for a man of such a high family as his to slave and drave at common labouring work, we don't know what to do.'

Tess stood in reverie a long time before she thought of asking 'Liza-Lu to come in and sit down. When she had done so, and 'Liza-Lu was having some tea, she came to a decision. It was imperative that she should go home. Her agreement did not end till Old Lady-Day,° the sixth of April, but as the interval thereto was not a long one she resolved to run the risk of starting at once.

To go that night would be a gain of twelve hours; but her sister was too tired to undertake such a distance till the morrow. Tess ran down to where Marian and Izz lived, informed them of what had happened, and begged them to make the best of her case to the farmer. Returning, she got Lu a supper, and after that, having tucked the younger into her own bed, packed up as many of her belongings as would go into a withy basket, and started, directing Lu to follow her next morning.

L

She plunged into the chilly equinoctial darkness as the clock struck ten, for her fifteen miles' walk under the steely stars. In lonely districts night is a protection rather than a danger to a noiseless pedestrian, and knowing this Tess pursued the nearest course along by-lanes that she would almost have feared in the day time; but marauders were wanting now, and spectral fears were driven out of her mind by thoughts of her mother. Thus she proceeded mile after mile, ascending and descending till she came to Bulbarrow, and about midnight looked from that height into the abyss of chaotic shade which was all that revealed itself of the vale on whose further side she was born. Having already traversed about five miles on the upland she had now some ten or eleven

Old Lady-Day: When the calendar was changed in 1752, Lady-Day, or the Feast of the Annunciation, moved from April 6 to March 25, but April 6, or Old Lady-Day, continued to be used to set the beginning or the ending of employment.

in the lowland before her journey would be finished. The winding road downwards became just visible to her under the wan starlight as she followed it, and soon she paced a soil so contrasting with that above it that the difference was perceptible to the tread and to the smell. It was the heavy clay land of Blackmoor Vale, and a part of the Vale to which turnpike-roads had never penetrated. Superstitions linger longest on these heavy soils. Having once been forest, at this shadowy time it seemed to assert something of its old character, the far and the near being blended, and every tree and tall hedge making the most of its presence. The harts that had been hunted here, the witches that had been pricked and ducked,° the green-spangled fairies that 'whickered'° at you as you passed; — the place teemed with beliefs in them still, and they formed an impish multitude now.

At Nuttlebury she passed the village inn, whose sign creaked in response to the greeting of her footsteps, which not a human soul heard but herself. Under the thatched roofs her mind's eye beheld relaxed tendons and flaccid muscles, spread out in the darkness beneath coverlets made of little purple patchwork squares, and undergoing a bracing process at the hands of sleep for renewed labour on the morrow, as soon as a hint of pink nebulosity appeared on Hambledon Hill.

At three she turned the last corner of the maze of lanes she had threaded, and entered Marlott, passing the field in which, as a club-girl, she had first seen Angel Clare, when he had not danced with her; the sense of disappointment remained with her yet. In the direction of her mother's house she saw a light. It came from the bedroom window, and a branch waved in front of it and made it wink at her. As soon as she could discern the outline of the house — newly thatched with her money — it had all its old effect upon Tess's imagination. Part of her body and life it ever seemed to be; the slope of its dormers, the finish of its gables, the broken courses of brick which topped the chimney, all had something in common with her personal character. A stupefaction had come into these features, to her regard; it meant the illness of her mother.

She opened the door so softly as to disturb nobody; the lower room was vacant, but the neighbour who was sitting up with her mother came to the top of the stairs, and whispered that Mrs. Durbeyfield was no

pricked and ducked: The references are to ordeals used to identify witches, either by pricking them to see if they were insensitive or bled less than normal (in *The Return of the Native*, a neighbor, believing that Eustacia Vye is a witch, pricks her) or by ducking them to see if they sank (a sign of innocence) or floated (a sign of guilt) (*Enc. Brit.* 20: 175). **'whickered':** Snickered, giggled, tittered (dialect).

better, though she was sleeping just then. Tess prepared herself a breakfast, and then took her place as nurse in her mother's chamber.

In the morning, when she contemplated the children, they had all a curiously elongated look; although she had been away little more than a year their growth was astounding; and the necessity of applying herself heart and soul to their needs took her out of her own cares.

Her father's ill-health was of the same indefinite kind, and he sat in his chair as usual. But the day after her arrival he was unusually bright. He had a rational scheme for living, and Tess asked him what it was.

'I'm thinking of sending round to all the old anti-queerians in this part of England,' he said, 'asking them to subscribe to a fund to maintain me. I'm sure they'd see it as a romantical, artistical, and proper thing to do. They spend lots o' money in keeping up old ruins, and finding the bones o' things, and such like; and living remains must be more interesting to 'em still, if they only knowed of me. Would that somebody would go round and tell 'em what there is living among 'em, and they thinking nothing of him! If Pa'son Tringham, who discovered me, had lived, he'd ha' done it, I'm sure.'

Tess postponed her arguments on this high project till she had grappled with pressing matters in hand, which seemed little improved by her remittances. When indoor necessities had been eased she turned her attention to external things. It was now the season for planting and sowing; many gardens and allotments of the villagers had already received their spring tillage; but the garden and the allotment of the Durbeyfields were behindhand. She found, to her dismay, that this was owing to their having eaten all the seed potatoes, — that last lapse of the improvident. At the earliest moment she obtained what others she could procure, and in a few days her father was well enough to see to the garden, under Tess's persuasive efforts: while she herself undertook the allotment-plot which they rented in a field a couple of hundred yards out of the village.

She liked doing it after the confinement of the sick chamber, where she was not now required by reason of her mother's improvement. Violent motion relieved thought. The plot of ground was in a high, dry, open enclosure, where there were forty or fifty such pieces, and where labour was at its briskest when the hired labour of the day had ended. Digging began usually at six o'clock, and extended indefinitely into the dusk or moonlight. Just now heaps of dead weeds and refuse were burning on many of the plots, the dry weather favouring their combustion.

One fine day Tess and 'Liza-Lu worked on here with their neighbours till the last rays of the sun smote flat upon the white pegs that divided the plots. As soon as twilight succeeded to sunset the flare of the couch-grass and cabbage-stalk fires began to light up the allotments fitfully, their outlines appearing and disappearing under the dense smoke as wafted by the wind. When a fire glowed, banks of smoke, blown level along the ground, would themselves become illuminated to an opaque lustre, screening the workpeople from one another; and the meaning of the 'pillar of a cloud,'° which was a wall by day and a light by night, could be understood.

As evening thickened some of the gardening men and women gave over for the night, but the greater number remained to get their planting done, Tess being among them, though she sent her sister home. It was on one of the couch-burning plots that she laboured with her fork, its four shining prongs resounding against the stones and dry clods in little clicks. Sometimes she was completely involved in the smoke of her fire; then it would leave her figure free, irradiated by the brassy glare from the heap. She was oddly dressed to-night, and presented a somewhat staring aspect, her attire being a gown bleached by many washings, with a short black jacket over it, the effect of the whole being that of a wedding and funeral guest in one. The women further back wore white aprons, which, with their pale faces, were all that could be seen of them in the gloom, except when at moments they caught a flash from the flames.

Westward, the wiry boughs of the bare thorn hedge which formed the boundary of the field rose against the pale opalescence of the lower sky. Above, Jupiter hung like a full-blown jonquil, so bright as almost to throw a shade. A few small nondescript stars were appearing elsewhere. In the distance a dog barked, and wheels occasionally rattled along the dry road.

Still the prongs continued to click assiduously, for it was not late; and though the air was fresh and keen there was a whisper of spring in it that cheered the workers on. Something in the place, the hour, the crackling fires, the fantastic mysteries of light and shade, made others as well as Tess enjoy being there. Nightfall, which in the frost of winter comes as a fiend and in the warmth of summer as a lover, came as a tranquillizer on this March day.

'pillar of a cloud': God sent a pillar of cloud by day and a pillar of fire by night to enable Moses to lead the Israelites fleeing from Egypt safely through the wilderness (Exod. 13.21).

Nobody looked at his or her companions. The eyes of all were on the soil as its turned surface was revealed by the fires. Hence as Tess stirred the clods, and sang her foolish little songs with scarce now a hope that Clare would ever hear them, she did not for a long time notice the person who worked nearest to her — a man in a long smockfrock who, she found, was forking the same plot as herself, and whom she supposed her father had sent there to advance the work. She became more conscious of him when the direction of his digging brought him closer. Sometimes the smoke divided them; then it swerved, and the two were visible to each other but divided from all the rest.

Tess did not speak to her fellow-worker, nor did he speak to her. Nor did she think of him further than to recollect that he had not been there when it was broad daylight, and that she did not know him as any one of the Marlott labourers, which was no wonder, her absences having been so long and frequent of late years. By-and-by he dug so close to her that the fire-beams were reflected as distinctly from the steel prongs of his fork as from her own. On going up to the fire to throw a pitch of dead weeds upon it, she found that he did the same on the other side. The fire flared up, and she beheld the face of d'Urberville.

The unexpectedness of his presence, the grotesqueness of his appearance in a gathered smockfrock, such as was now worn only by the most old-fashioned of the labourers, had a ghastly comicality that chilled her as to its bearing. D'Urberville emitted a low long laugh.

'If I were inclined to joke I should say, How much this seems like Paradise!' he remarked whimsically, looking at her with an inclined head.

'What do you say?' she weakly asked.

'A jester might say this is just like Paradise. You are Eve, and I am the old Other One come to tempt you in the disguise of an inferior animal. I used to be quite up in that scene of Milton's,° when I was theological. Some of it goes —

"Empress, the way is ready, and not long,
Beyond a row of myrtles. . . .
. . . If thou accept
My conduct, I can bring thee thither soon."
"Lead then," said Eve.

that scene of Milton's: The scene is from *Paradise Lost,* and the passage quoted (Book IX: 626–631) is spoken to Eve by Satan in the form of the serpent.

And so on. My dear, dear Tess, I am only putting this to you as a thing that you might have supposed or said quite untruly, because you think so badly of me.'

'I never said you were Satan, or thought it. I don't think of you in that way at all. My thoughts of you are quite cold, except when you affront me. What, did you come digging here entirely because of me?'

'Entirely. To see you; nothing more. The smockfrock, which I saw hanging for sale as I came along, was an after-thought, that I mightn't be noticed. I come to protest against your working like this.'

'But I like doing it — it is for my father.'

'Your engagement at the other place is ended?'

'Yes.'

'Where are you going to next? To join your dear husband?'

She could not bear the humiliating reminder.

'O — I don't know!' she said bitterly. 'I have no husband!'

'It is quite true — in the sense you mean. But you have a friend, and I have determined that you shall be comfortable in spite of yourself. When you get down to your house you will see what I have sent there for you.'

'O, Alec, I wish you wouldn't give me anything at all! I cannot take it from you! I don't like — it is not right!'

'It *is* right!' he cried lightly. 'I am not going to see a woman whom I feel so tenderly for as I do for you, in trouble without trying to help her.'

'But I am very well off! I am only in trouble about — about — not about living at all!'

She turned, and desperately resumed her digging, tears dripping upon the fork-handle and upon the clods.

'About the children — your brothers and sisters,' he resumed. 'I've been thinking of them.'

Tess's heart quivered — he was touching her in a weak place. He had divined her chief anxiety. Since returning home her soul had gone out to those children with an affection that was passionate.

'If your mother does not recover, somebody ought to do something for them; since your father will not be able to do much, I suppose?'

'He can with my assistance. He must!'

'And with mine.'

'No, sir!'

'How damned foolish this is!' burst out d'Urberville. 'Why, he thinks we are the same family; and will be quite satisfied!'

'He don't. I've undeceived him.'

'The more fool you!'

D'Urberville in anger retreated from her to the hedge, where he pulled off the long smockfrock which had disguised him; and rolling it up and pushing it into the couch-fire, went away.

Tess could not get on with her digging after this; she felt restless; she wondered if he had gone back to her father's house; and taking the fork in her hand proceeded homewards.

Some twenty yards from the house she was met by one of her sisters.

'O, Tessy — what do you think! 'Liza-Lu is a-crying, and there's a lot of folk in the house, and mother is a good deal better, but they think father is dead!'

The child realized the grandeur of the news; but not as yet its sadness; and stood looking at Tess with round-eyed importance, till, beholding the effect produced upon her, she said —

'What, Tess, shan't we talk to father never no more?'

'But father was only a little bit ill!' exclaimed Tess distractedly.

'Liza-Lu came up.

'He dropped down just now, and the doctor who was there for mother said there was no chance for him, because his heart was growed in.'

Yes; the Durbeyfield couple had changed places; the dying one was out of danger, and the indisposed one was dead. The news meant even more than it sounded. Her father's life had a value apart from his personal achievements, or perhaps it would not have had much. It was the last of the three lives for whose duration the house and premises were held under a lease; and it had long been coveted by the tenant-farmer for his regular labourers, who were stinted in cottage accommodation. Moreover, 'liviers'° were disapproved of in villages almost as much as little freeholders, because of their independence of manner, and when a lease determined it was never renewed.

Thus the Durbeyfields, once d'Urbervilles, saw descending upon them the destiny which, no doubt, when they were among the Olympians of the county, they had caused to descend many a time, and severely enough, upon the heads of such landless ones as they themselves were now. So do flux and reflux — the rhythm of change — alternate and persist in everything under the sky.

'liviers': Lifeholders, that is, tenants whose lease ran the length of a specified number of lifetimes; by contrast, a freeholder's heirs could retain his lease in perpetuity.

LI

At length it was the eve of Old Lady-Day, and the agricultural world was in a fever of mobility such as only occurs at that particular date of the year. It is a day of fulfilment; agreements for outdoor service during the ensuing year, entered into at Candlemas, are to be now carried out. The labourers — or 'work-folk,' as they used to call themselves immemorially till the other word was introduced from without — who wish to remain no longer in old places are removing to the new farms.

These annual migrations from farm to farm were on the increase here. When Tess's mother was a child the majority of the field-folk about Marlott had remained all their lives on one farm, which had been the home also of their fathers and grandfathers; but latterly the desire for yearly removal had risen to a high pitch. With the younger families it was a pleasant excitement which might possibly be an advantage. The Egypt° of one family was the Land of Promise to the family who saw it from a distance, till by residence there it became in turn their Egypt also; and so they changed and changed.

However, all the mutations so increasingly discernible in village life did not originate entirely in the agricultural unrest. A depopulation was also going on. The village had formerly contained, side by side with the agricultural labourers, an interesting and better-informed class, ranking distinctly above the former — the class to which Tess's father and mother had belonged — and including the carpenter, the smith, the shoemaker, the huckster, together with nondescript workers other than farm-labourers; a set of people who owed a certain stability of aim and conduct to the fact of their being life-holders like Tess's father, or copyholders, or, occasionally, small freeholders. But as the long holdings fell in they were seldom again let to similar tenants, and were mostly pulled down, if not absolutely required by the farmer for his hands. Cottagers who were not directly employed on the land were looked upon with disfavour, and the banishment of some starved the trade of others, who were thus obliged to follow. These families, who had formed the backbone of the village life in the past, who were the depositaries of the village traditions, had to seek refuge in the large centres; the process, humorously designated by statisticians as 'the tendency of the rural population towards the large towns,' being really the tendency of water to flow uphill when forced by machinery.

Egypt: The land from which the Israelites fled in order to find the Promised Land.

The cottage accommodation at Marlott having been in this manner considerably curtailed by demolitions, every house which remained standing was required by the agriculturist for his work-people. Ever since the occurrence of the event which had cast such a shadow over Tess's life, the Durbeyfield family (whose descent was not credited) had been tacitly looked on as one which would have to go when their lease ended, if only in the interests of morality. It was, indeed, quite true that the household had not been shining examples either of temperance, soberness, or chastity. The father, and even the mother, had got drunk at times, the younger children seldom had gone to church, and the eldest daughter had made queer unions. By some means the village had to be kept pure. So on this, the first Lady-Day on which the Durbeyfields were expellable, the house, being roomy, was required for a carter with a large family; and Widow Joan, her daughters Tess and 'Liza-Lu, the boy Abraham and the younger children, had to go elsewhere.

On the evening preceding their removal it was getting dark betimes by reason of a drizzling rain which blurred the sky. As it was the last night they would spend in the village which had been their home and birthplace, Mrs. Durbeyfield, 'Liza-Lu, and Abraham had gone out to bid some friends good-bye, and Tess was keeping house till they should return.

She was kneeling in the window-bench, her face close to the casement, where an outer pane of rain-water was sliding down the inner pane of glass. Her eyes rested on the web of a spider, probably starved long ago, which had been mistakenly placed in a corner where no flies ever came, and shivered in the slight draught through the casement. Tess was reflecting on the position of the household, in which she perceived her own evil influence. Had she not come home her mother and the children might probably have been allowed to stay on as weekly tenants. But she had been observed almost immediately on her return by some people of scrupulous character and great influence: they had seen her idling in the churchyard, restoring as well as she could with a little trowel a baby's obliterated grave. By this means they had found that she was living here again; her mother was scolded for 'harbouring' her; sharp retorts had ensued from Joan, who had independently offered to leave at once; she had been taken at her word; and here was the result.

'I ought never to have come home,' said Tess to herself, bitterly.

She was so intent upon these thoughts that she hardly at first took note of a man in a white mackintosh whom she saw riding down the street. Possibly it was owing to her face being near to the pane that he saw her so quickly, and directed his horse so close to the cottage-front that his hoofs were almost upon the narrow border for plants growing under the wall. It was not till he touched the window with his riding-crop that she observed him. The rain had nearly ceased, and she opened the casement in obedience to his gesture.

'Didn't you see me?' asked d'Urberville.

'I was not attending,' she said. 'I heard you, I believe, though I fancied it was a carriage and horses. I was in a sort of dream.'

'Ah! you heard the d'Urberville Coach, perhaps. You know the legend, I suppose?'

'No. My — somebody was going to tell it me once, but didn't.'

'If you are a genuine d'Urberville I ought not to tell you either, I suppose. As for me, I'm a sham one, so it doesn't matter. It is rather dismal. It is that this sound of a non-existent coach can only be heard by one of d'Urberville blood, and it is held to be of ill-omen to the one who hears it. It has to do with a murder, committed by one of the family, centuries ago.'

'Now you have begun it, finish it.'

'Very well. One of the family is said to have abducted some beautiful woman, who tried to escape from the coach in which he was carrying her off, and in the struggle he killed her — or she killed him — I forget which. Such is one version of the tale. . . . I see that your tubs and buckets are packed. Going away, aren't you?'

'Yes, to-morrow — Old Lady-Day.'

'I heard you were, but could hardly believe it; it seems so sudden. Why is it?'

'Father's was the last life on the property, and when that dropped we had no further right to stay. Though we might, perhaps, have stayed as weekly tenants — if it had not been for me.'

'What about you?'

'I am not a — proper woman.'

D'Urberville's face flushed.

'What a blasted shame! Miserable snobs! May their dirty souls be burnt to cinders!' he exclaimed in tones of ironic resentment. 'That's why you are going, is it? Turned out?'

'We are not turned out exactly; but as they said we should have to go soon, it was best to go now everybody was moving, because there are better chances.'

'Where are you going to?'

'Kingsbere. We have taken rooms there. Mother is so foolish about father's people that she will go there.'

'But your mother's family are not fit for lodgings, and in a little hole of a town like that. Now why not come to my garden-house at Trantridge? There are hardly any poultry now, since my mother's death; but there's the house, as you know it, and the garden. It can be whitewashed in a day, and your mother can live there quite comfortably; and I will put the children to a good school. Really I ought to do something for you!'

'But we have already taken the rooms at Kingsbere!' she declared. 'And we can wait there —— '

'Wait — what for? For that nice husband, no doubt. Now look here, Tess, I know what men are, and, bearing in mind the *grounds* of your separation, I am quite positive he will never make it up with you. Now, though I have been your enemy, I am your friend, even if you won't believe it. Come to this cottage of mine. We'll get up a regular colony of fowls, and your mother can attend to them excellently; and the children can go to school.'

Tess breathed more and more quickly, and at length she said —

'How do I know that you would do all this? Your views may change — and then — we should be — my mother would be — homeless again.'

'O no — no. I would guarantee you against such as that in writing, if necessary. Think it over.'

Tess shook her head. But d'Urberville persisted; she had seldom seen him so determined; he would not take a negative.

'Please just tell your mother,' he said, in emphatic tones. 'It is her business to judge — not yours. I shall get the house swept out and whitened to-morrow morning, and fires lit; and it will be dry by the evening, so that you can come straight there. Now mind, I shall expect you.'

Tess again shook her head; her throat swelling with complicated emotion. She could not look up at d'Urberville.

'I owe you something for the past, you know,' he resumed. 'And you cured me, too, of that craze; so I am glad —— '

'I would rather you had kept the craze, so that you had kept the practice which went with it!'

'I am glad of this opportunity of repaying you a little. To-morrow I shall expect to hear your mother's goods unloading. . . . Give me your hand on it now — dear, beautiful Tess!'

With the last sentence he had dropped his voice to a murmur, and put his hand in at the half-open casement. With stormy eyes she pulled the stay-bar quickly, and, in doing so, caught his arm between the casement and the stone mullion.

'Damnation — you are very cruel!' he said, snatching out his arm. 'No, no! — I know you didn't do it on purpose. Well, I shall expect you, or your mother and the children at least.'

'I shall not come — I have plenty of money!' she cried.

'Where?'

'At my father-in-law's, if I ask for it.'

'*If* you ask for it. But you won't, Tess; I know you; you'll never ask for it — you'll starve first!'

With these words he rode off. Just at the corner of the street he met the man with the paint-pot, who asked him if he had deserted the brethren.

'You go to the devil!' said d'Urberville.

Tess remained where she was a long while, till a sudden rebellious sense of injustice caused the region of her eyes to swell with the rush of hot tears thither. Her husband, Angel Clare himself, had, like others, dealt out hard measure to her, surely he had! She had never before admitted such a thought; but he had surely! Never in her life — she could swear it from the bottom of her soul — had she ever intended to do wrong; yet these hard judgments had come. Whatever her sins, they were not sins of intention, but of inadvertence, and why should she have been punished so persistently?

She passionately seized the first piece of paper that came to hand, and scribbled the following lines:

> O why have you treated me so monstrously, Angel! I do not deserve it. I have thought it all over carefully, and I can never, never forgive you! You know that I did not intend to wrong you — why have you so wronged me? You are cruel, cruel indeed! I will try to forget you. It is all injustice I have received at your hands!
>
> T.

She watched till the postman passed by, ran out to him with her epistle, and then again took her listless place inside the window-panes.

It was just as well to write like that as to write tenderly. How could he give way to entreaty? The facts had not changed: there was no new event to alter his opinion.

It grew darker, the fire-light shining over the room. The two biggest of the younger children had gone out with their mother; the four smallest, their ages ranging from three-and-a-half years to eleven, all in black frocks, were gathered round the hearth babbling their own little subjects. Tess at length joined them, without lighting a candle.

'This is the last night that we shall sleep here, dears, in the house where we were born,' she said quickly. 'We ought to think of it, oughtn't we?'

They all became silent; with the impressibility of their age they were ready to burst into tears at the picture of finality she had conjured up, though all the day hitherto they had been rejoicing in the idea of a new place. Tess changed the subject.

'Sing to me, dears,' she said.

'What shall we sing?'

'Anything you know; I don't mind.'

There was a momentary pause; it was broken, first, by one little tentative note; then a second voice strengthened it, and a third and a fourth chimed in in unison, with words they had learnt at the Sunday-school —

Here we suffer grief and pain,
Here we meet to part again;
  In Heaven we part no more.°

The four sang on with the phlegmatic passivity of persons who had long ago settled the question, and there being no mistake about it, felt that further thought was not required. With features strained hard to enunciate the syllables they continued to regard the centre of the flickering fire, the notes of the youngest straying over into the pauses of the rest.

Tess turned from them, and went to the window again. Darkness had now fallen without, but she put her face to the pane as though to peer into the gloom. It was really to hide her tears. If she could only believe what the children were singing; if she were only sure, how different all would now be; how confidently she would leave them to Providence and their future kingdom! But, in default of that, it behoved her to do something; to be their Providence; for to Tess, as to not a few millions of others, there was ghastly satire in the poet's lines —

    Not in utter nakedness
But trailing clouds of glory do we come.°

Here we suffer grief and pain . . . : From the popular nineteenth-century hymn by Thomas Bilby known by various titles, including these words. **Not in utter nakedness . . . :** From stanza five of Wordsworth's "Ode: Intimations of Immortality from Recollections of Early Childhood."

To her and her like, birth itself was an ordeal of degrading personal compulsion, whose gratuitousness nothing in the result seemed to justify, and at best could only palliate.

In the shades of the wet road she soon discerned her mother with tall 'Liza-Lu and Abraham. Mrs. Durbeyfield's pattens° clicked up to the door, and Tess opened it.

'I see the tracks of a horse outside the window,' said Joan. 'Hev somebody called?'

'No,' said Tess.

The children by the fire looked gravely at her, and one murmured —

'Why, Tess, the gentleman a-horseback!'

'He didn't call,' said Tess. 'He spoke to me in passing.'

'Who was the gentleman?' asked her mother. 'Your husband?'

'No. He'll never, never come,' answered Tess in stony hopelessness.

'Then who was it?'

'Oh, you needn't ask. You've seen him before, and so have I.'

'Ah! What did he say?' said Joan curiously.

'I will tell you when we are settled in our lodgings at Kingsbere tomorrow — every word.'

It was not her husband, she had said. Yet a consciousness that in a physical sense this man alone was her husband seemed to weigh on her more and more.

LII

During the small hours of the next morning, while it was still dark, dwellers near the highways were conscious of a disturbance of their night's rest by rumbling noises, intermittently continuing till daylight — noises as certain to recur in this particular first week of the month as the voice of the cuckoo in the third week of the same. They were the preliminaries of the general removal, the passing of the empty waggons and teams to fetch the goods of the migrating families; for it was always by the vehicle of the farmer who required his services that the hired man was conveyed to his destination. That this might be accomplished within the day was the explanation of the reverberation occurring so soon after midnight, the aim of the carters being to reach the door of the outgoing households by six o'clock, when the loading of their movables at once began.

pattens: Elevated, wooden-soled shoes, often used for walking in mud and sometimes outfitted with an iron ring that can clink.

But to Tess and her mother's household no such anxious farmer sent his team. They were only women; they were not regular labourers; they were not particularly required anywhere; hence they had to hire a waggon at their own expense, and got nothing sent gratuitously.

It was a relief to Tess, when she looked out of the window that morning, to find that though the weather was windy and louring, it did not rain, and that the waggon had come. A wet Lady-Day was a spectre which removing families never forgot; damp furniture, damp bedding, damp clothing accompanied it, and left a train of ills.

Her mother, 'Liza-Lu, and Abraham were also awake, but the younger children were let sleep on. The four breakfasted by the thin light, and the 'house-ridding' was taken in hand.

It proceeded with some cheerfulness, a friendly neighbour or two assisting. When the large articles of furniture had been packed in position a circular nest was made of the beds and bedding, in which Joan Durbeyfield and the young children were to sit through the journey. After loading there was a long delay before the horses were brought, these having been unharnessed during the ridding; but at length, about two o'clock, the whole was under way, the cooking-pot swinging from the axle of the waggon, Mrs. Durbeyfield and family at the top, the matron having in her lap, to prevent injury to its works, the head of the clock, which, at any exceptional lurch of the waggon struck one, or one-and-a-half, in hurt tones. Tess and the next eldest girl walked alongside till they were out of the village.

They had called on a few neighbours that morning and the previous evening, and some came to see them off, all wishing them well, though, in their secret hearts, hardly expecting welfare possible to such a family, harmless as the Durbeyfields were to all except themselves. Soon the equipage began to ascend to higher ground, and the wind grew keener with the change of level and soil.

The day being the sixth of April, the Durbeyfield waggon met many other waggons with families on the summit of the load, which was built on a wellnigh unvarying principle, as peculiar, probably, to the rural labourer as the hexagon to the bee.° The groundwork of the arrangement was the family dresser, which, with its shining handles, and finger-marks, and domestic evidences thick upon it, stood importantly in front, over the tails of the shaft-horses, in its erect and natural position, like some Ark of the Covenant° that they were bound to carry reverently.

as the hexagon to the bee: The cells of honeycombs are hexagonal. **Ark of the Covenant:** The portable tabernacle containing the Ten Commandments that the Israelites carried into the wilderness with them on their way to the Promised Land (Exod. 25).

e them again, in case they should be still unsuccessful in their r shelter, of which he had just heard. When they had gone ille rode to the inn, and shortly after came out on foot.

e interim Tess, left with the children inside the bedstead, re- alking with them awhile, till, seeing that no more could be make them comfortable just then, she walked about the rd, now beginning to be embrowned by the shades of night- door of the church was unfastened, and she entered it for the in her life.

in the window under which the bedstead stood were the f the family, covering in their dates several centuries. They opied, altar-shaped, and plain; their carvings being defaced en; their brasses torn from the matrices, the rivet-holes re- like martin-holes in a sand-cliff. Of all the reminders that she received that her people were socially extinct there was none e as this spoliation.

lrew near to a dark stone on which was inscribed:

n sepulchri antiquae familiae d'Urberville.°

did not read Church-Latin like a Cardinal, but she knew that the door of her ancestral sepulchre, and that the tall knights of r father had chanted in his cups lay inside.

nusingly turned to withdraw, passing near an altar-tomb, the them all, on which was a recumbent figure. In the dusk she noticed it before, and would hardly have noticed it now but d fancy that the effigy moved. As soon as she drew close to it vered all in a moment that the figure was a living person; and to her sense of not having been alone was so violent that she overcome, and sank down nigh to fainting, not however till ecognized Alec d'Urberville in the form.

apt off the slab and supported her.

v you come in,' he said smiling, 'and got up there not to in- our meditations. A family gathering, is it not, with these old nder us here? Listen.'

tamped with his heel heavily on the floor; whereupon there ollow echo from below.

shook them a bit, I'll warrant!' he continued. 'And you I was the mere stone reproduction of one of them. But no. order changeth. The little finger of the sham d'Urberville can

pulchri . . . : Door of the tomb of the ancient family of d'Urberville.

Some of the households were lively, some mournful; some were stopping at the doors of wayside inns; where, in due time, the Durbeyfield menagerie also drew up to bait horses and refresh the travellers.

During the halt Tess's eyes fell upon a three-pint blue mug, which was ascending and descending through the air to and from the feminine section of a household, sitting on the summit of a load that had also drawn up at a little distance from the same inn. She followed one of the mug's journeys upward, and perceived it to be clasped by hands whose owner she well knew. Tess went towards the waggon.

'Marian and Izz!' she cried to the girls, for it was they, sitting with the moving family at whose house they had lodged. 'Are you house-ridding to-day, like everybody else?'

They were, they said. It had been too rough a life for them at Flintcomb-Ash, and they had come away, almost without notice, leaving Groby to prosecute them if he chose. They told Tess their destination, and Tess told them hers.

Marian leant over the load, and lowered her voice. 'Do you know that the gentleman who follows 'ee — you'll guess who I mean — came to ask for 'ee at Flintcomb after you had gone? We didn't tell'n where you was, knowing you wouldn't wish to see him.'

'Ah — but I did see him!' Tess murmured. 'He found me.'

'And do he know where you be going?'

'I think so.'

'Husband come back?'

'No.'

She bade her acquaintance good-bye — for the respective carters had now come out from the inn — and the two waggons resumed their journey in opposite directions; the vehicle whereon sat Marian, Izz, and the ploughman's family with whom they had thrown in their lot, being brightly painted, and drawn by three powerful horses with shining brass ornaments on their harness; while the waggon on which Mrs. Durbeyfield and her family rode was a creaking erection that would scarcely bear the weight of the superincumbent load; one which had known no paint since it was made, and drawn by two horses only. The contrast well marked the difference between being fetched by a thriving farmer and conveying oneself whither no hirer waited one's coming.

The distance was great — too great for a day's journey — and it was with the utmost difficulty that the horses performed it. Though they had started so early it was quite late in the afternoon when they turned the flank of an eminence which formed part of the upland called Greenhill. While the horses stood to stale° and breathe themselves Tess looked around. Under the hill, and just ahead of them, was the half-dead townlet of their pilgrimage, Kingsbere, where lay those ancestors of whom her father had spoken and sung to painfulness: Kingsbere, the spot of all spots in the world which could be considered the d'Urbervilles' home, since they had resided there for full five hundred years.

A man could be seen advancing from the outskirts towards them, and when he beheld the nature of their waggon-load he quickened his steps.

'You be the woman they call Mrs. Durbeyfield, I reckon?' he said to Tess's mother, who had descended to walk the remainder of the way.

She nodded. 'Though widow of the late Sir John d'Urberville, poor nobleman, if I cared for my rights; and returning to the domain of his forefathers.'

'Oh? Well, I know nothing about that; but if you be Mrs. Durbeyfield, I am sent to tell 'ee that the rooms you wanted be let. We didn't know you was coming till we got your letter this morning — when 'twas too late. But no doubt you can get other lodgings somewhere.'

The man had noticed the face of Tess, which had become ash-pale at his intelligence. Her mother looked hopelessly at fault. 'What shall we do now, Tess?' she said bitterly. 'Here's a welcome to your ancestors' lands! However, let's try further.'

They moved on into the town, and tried with all their might, Tess remaining with the waggon to take care of the children whilst her mother and 'Liza-Lu made inquiries. At the last return of Joan to the vehicle, an hour later, when her search for accommodation had still been fruitless, the driver of the waggon said the goods must be unloaded, as the horses were half-dead, and he was bound to return part of the way at least that night.

'Very well — unload it here,' said Joan recklessly. 'I'll get shelter somewhere.'

The waggon had drawn up under the churchyard wall, in a spot screened from view, and the driver, nothing loth, soon hauled down the poor heap of household goods. This done she paid him, reducing herself to almost her last shilling thereby, and he moved off and left them, only too glad to get out of further dealings with such a family. It was a dry night, and he guessed that they would come to no harm.

stale: Urinate (dialect).

Tess gazed desperately at the pile of furnitur this spring evening peered invidiously upon t upon the bunches of dried herbs shivering in brass handles of the dresser, upon the wicker-cr rocked in, and upon the well-rubbed clock-case the reproachful gleam of indoor articles abando of a roofless exposure for which they were neve were deparked° hills and slopes — now cut up and the green foundations that showed where sion once had stood; also an outlying stretch of always belonged to the estate. Hard by, the aisl the d'Urberville Aisle looked on imperturbably.

'Isn't your family vault your own freehold?' she returned from a reconnoitre of the church a course 'tis, and that's where we will camp, girls ancestors finds us a roof! Now Tess and 'Liza a me. We'll make a nest for these children, and t look round.'

Tess listlessly lent a hand, and in a quarter o post bedstead was dissociated from the heap under the south wall of the church, the part of the d'Urberville Aisle, beneath which the hug tester of the bedstead was a beautifully tracer lights, its date being the fifteenth centur d'Urberville Window, and in the upper par heraldic emblems like those on Durbeyfield's ol

Joan drew the curtains round the bed so a tent of it, and put the smaller children inside. 'I we can sleep there too, for one night,' she said on, and get something for the dears to eat! O, your playing at marrying gentlemen, if it leaves

Accompanied by 'Liza-Lu and the boy she a lane which secluded the church from the townl into the street they beheld a man on horsebac 'Ah — I'm looking for you!' he said, riding u deed a family gathering on the historic spot!'

It was Alec d'Urberville. 'Where is Tess?' he

Personally Joan had no liking for Alec. She direction of the church, and went on, d'Ur

deparked: Removed from their status as a park, that is, an the aristocracy through royal decree.

would search d'Urb In maine done churc fall. T first ti Wi tombs were and b mainir had ev so forc Sh

Os

Te this wa whom Sh oldest had nc for an she dis the sh was qu she ha He 'I s terrupt fellows He arose a 'T though The ol

Ostium

do more for you than the whole dynasty of the real underneath. . . . Now command me. What shall I do?'

'Go away!' she murmured.

'I will — I'll look for your mother,' said he blandly. But in passing her he whispered: 'Mind this; you'll be civil yet!'

When he was gone she bent down upon the entrance to the vaults, and said —

'Why am I on the wrong side of this door!'

In the meantime Marian and Izz Huett had journeyed onward with the chattels of the ploughman in the direction of their land of Canaan° — the Egypt of some other family who had left it only that morning. But the girls did not for a long time think of where they were going. Their talk was of Angel Clare and Tess, and Tess's persistent lover, whose connection with her previous history they had partly heard and partly guessed ere this.

''Tisn't as though she had never known him afore,' said Marian. 'His having won her once makes all the difference in the world. 'Twould be a thousand pities if he were to tole° her away again. Mr. Clare can never be anything to us, Izz; and why should we grudge him to her, and not try to mend this quarrel? If he could on'y know what straits she's put to, and what's hovering round, he might come to take care of his own.'

'Could we let him know?'

They thought of this all the way to their destination; but the bustle of re-establishment in their new place took up all their attention then. But when they were settled, a month later, they heard of Clare's approaching return, though they had learnt nothing more of Tess. Upon that, agitated anew by their attachment to him, yet honourably disposed to her, Marian uncorked the penny ink-bottle they shared, and a few lines were concocted between the two girls.

> HONOOR'D SIR — Look to your Wife if you do love her as much as she do love you. For she is sore put to by an Enemy in the shape of a Friend. Sir, there is one near her who ought to be Away. A woman should not be try'd beyond her Strength, and continual dropping will wear away a Stone — ay, more — a Diamond.
>
> FROM TWO WELL-WISHERS.

land of Canaan: The Promised Land. **tole:** Entice (dialect).

This they addressed to Angel Clare at the only place they had ever heard him to be connected with, Emminster Vicarage; after which they continued in a mood of emotional exaltation at their own generosity, which made them sing in hysterical snatches and weep at the same time.

End of Phase the Sixth

PHASE THE SEVENTH. FULFILMENT

LIII

It was evening at Emminster Vicarage. The two customary candles were burning under their green shades in the Vicar's study, but he had not been sitting there. Occasionally he came in, stirred the small fire which sufficed for the increasing mildness of the spring, and went out again; sometimes pausing at the front door, going on to the drawing-room, then returning again to the front door.

It faced westward, and though gloom prevailed inside, there was still light enough without to see with distinctness. Mrs. Clare, who had been sitting in the drawing-room, followed him hither.

'Plenty of time yet,' said the Vicar. 'He doesn't reach Chalk-Newton till six, even if the train should be punctual, and ten miles of country-road, five of them in Crimmercrock Lane, are not jogged over in a hurry by our old horse.'

'But he has done it in an hour with us, my dear.'

'Years ago.'

Thus they passed the minutes, each well knowing that this was only waste of breath, the one essential being simply to wait.

At length there was a slight noise in the lane, and the old pony-chaise appeared indeed outside the railings. They saw alight therefrom a form which they affected to recognize, but would actually have passed by in the street without identifying had he not got out of their carriage at the particular moment when a particular person was due.

Mrs. Clare rushed through the dark passage to the door, and her husband came more slowly after her.

The new arrival, who was just about to enter, saw their anxious faces in the doorway and the gleam of the west in their spectacles because they confronted the last rays of day; but they could only see his shape against the light.

'O, my boy, my boy — home again at last!' cried Mrs. Clare, who cared no more at that moment for the stains of heterodoxy which had caused all this separation than for the dust upon his clothes. What woman, indeed, among the most faithful adherents of the truth, believes the promises and threats of the Word in the sense in which she believes in her own children, or would not throw her theology to the wind if weighed against their happiness? As soon as they reached the room where the candles were lighted she looked at his face.

'O, it is not Angel — not my son — the Angel who went away!' she cried in all the irony of sorrow, as she turned herself aside.

His father, too, was shocked to see him, so reduced was that figure from its former contours by worry and the bad season that Clare had experienced, in the climate to which he had so rashly hurried in his first aversion to the mockery of events at home. You could see the skeleton behind the man, and almost the ghost behind the skeleton. He matched Crivelli's dead *Christus.*° His sunken eye-pits were of morbid hue, and the light in his eyes had waned. The angular hollows and lines of his aged ancestors had succeeded to their reign in his face twenty years before their time.

'I was ill over there, you know,' he said. 'I am all right now.'

As if, however, to falsify this assertion, his legs seemed to give way, and he suddenly sat down to save himself from falling. It was only a slight attack of faintness, resulting from the tedious day's journey, and the excitement of arrival.

'Has any letter come for me lately?' he asked. 'I received the last you sent on by the merest chance, and after considerable delay through being inland; or I might have come sooner.'

'It was from your wife, we supposed?'

'It was.'

Only one other had recently come. They had not sent it on to him, knowing he would start for home so soon.

He hastily opened the letter produced, and was much disturbed to read in Tess's handwriting the sentiments expressed in her last hurried scrawl to him.

> O why have you treated me so monstrously, Angel! I do not deserve it. I have thought it all over carefully, and I can never, never forgive you! You know that I did not intend to wrong you — why

Crivelli's dead *Christus:* Probably the Pietà by the fifteenth-century Italian painter, Carlo Crivelli (c. 1430–1495), in the National Gallery in London.

> have you so wronged me? You are cruel, cruel indeed! I will try to forget you. It is all injustice I have received at your hands.
>
> T.

'It is quite true!' said Angel, throwing down the letter. 'Perhaps she will never be reconciled to me!'

'Don't, Angel, be so anxious about a mere child of the soil!' said his mother.

'Child of the soil! Well, we all are children of the soil. I wish she were so in the sense you mean; but let me now explain to you what I have never explained before, that her father is a descendant in the male line of one of the oldest Norman houses, like a good many others who lead obscure agricultural lives in our villages, and are dubbed "sons of the soil."'

He soon retired to bed; and the next morning, feeling exceedingly unwell, he remained in his room pondering. The circumstances amid which he had left Tess were such that though, while on the south of the Equator and just in receipt of her loving epistle, it had seemed the easiest thing in the world to rush back into her arms the moment he chose to forgive her, now that he had arrived it was not so easy as it had seemed. She was passionate, and her present letter, showing that her estimate of him had changed under his delay — too justly changed, he sadly owned, — made him ask himself if it would be wise to confront her unannounced in the presence of her parents. Supposing that her love had indeed turned to dislike during the last weeks of separation, a sudden meeting might lead to bitter words.

Clare therefore thought it would be best to prepare Tess and her family by sending a line to Marlott announcing his return, and his hope that she was still living with them there, as he had arranged for her to do when he left England. He despatched the inquiry that very day, and before the week was out there came a short reply from Mrs. Durbeyfield which did not remove his embarrassment, for it bore no address, though to his surprise it was not written from Marlott.

> SIR — J write these few lines to say that my Daughter is away from me at present, and J am not sure when she will return, but J will let you know as Soon as she do. J do not feel at liberty to tell you Where she is temperly biding. J should say that me and my Family have left Marlott for some Time. — Yours,
>
> J. DURBEYFIELD.

It was such a relief to Clare to learn that Tess was at least apparently well that her mother's stiff reticence as to her whereabouts did not long distress him. They were all angry with him, evidently. He would wait till Mrs. Durbeyfield could inform him of Tess's return, which her letter implied to be soon. He deserved no more. His had been a love 'which alters when it alteration finds.'° He had undergone some strange experiences in his absence; he had seen the virtual Faustina° in the literal Cornelia,° a spiritual Lucretia° in a corporeal Phryne;° he had thought of the woman taken and set in the midst as one deserving to be stoned,° and of the wife of Uriah° being made a queen; and he had asked himself why he had not judged Tess constructively rather than biographically, by the will rather than by the deed?

A day or two passed while he waited at his father's house for the promised second note from Joan Durbeyfield, and indirectly to recover a little more strength. The strength showed signs of coming back, but there was no sign of Joan's letter. Then he hunted up the old letter sent on to him in Brazil, which Tess had written from Flintcomb-Ash, and re-read it. The sentences touched him now as much as when he had first perused them.

> I must cry to you in my trouble — I have no one else. . . . I think I must die if you do not come soon, or tell me to come to you. . . . Please, please not to be just; only a little kind to me! . . . If you would come I could die in your arms! I would be well content to do that if so be you had forgiven me! . . . If you will send me one little line and say, *I am coming soon,* I will bide on, Angel, O so cheerfully! . . . Think how it do hurt my heart not to see you ever, ever! Ah, if I could only make your dear heart ache one little minute of each day as mine does every day and all day long, it might lead you to show pity to your poor lonely one. . . . I would be content, ay, glad, to live with you as your servant, if I may not as your wife; so that I could only be near you, and get glimpses of you, and think of you as mine. . . . I long for only one thing in heaven, or earth, or under the earth, to meet you, my own dear! Come to me, come to me, and save me from what threatens me.

'which alters when it alteration finds': From Shakespeare's Sonnet 116. **Faustina:** Wife of Roman Emperor and philosopher Marcus Aurelius; she was widely reputed to be unfaithful. **Cornelia:** Wife of Scipio Africanus the Younger (second century B.C.), who devoted herself to raising her twelve children and refused offers of marriage after she was widowed (*Enc. Brit.,* 7: 167). **Lucretia:** Or Lucrece, wife of Collatinus, known for her virtue, who killed herself after being raped by Lucius Tarquinius. See note to chapter XII. **Phryne:** Athenian courtesan who was the model and lover of Praxiteles, the sculptor. **one deserving to be stoned:** In John 8.3–11, instead of encouraging her stoning, Jesus forgives a woman brought to him as an adulteress by Scribes and Pharisees. **wife of Uriah:** Bathsheba, whom King David committed adultery with and then married after sending Uriah to his death in battle (2 Samuel 11).

Clare determined that he would no longer believe in her more recent and severer regard of him; but would go and find her immediately. He asked his father if she had applied for any money during his absence. His father returned a negative, and then for the first time it occurred to Angel that her pride had stood in her way, and that she had suffered privation. From his remarks his parents now gathered the real reason of the separation; and their Christianity was such that, reprobates being their especial care, the tenderness towards Tess which her blood, her simplicity, even her poverty, had not engendered, was instantly excited by her sin.

Whilst he was hastily packing together a few articles for his journey he glanced over a poor plain missive also lately come to hand — the one from Marian and Izz Huett, beginning —

'HONOUR'D SIR — Look to your wife if you do love her as much as she do you,' and signed, 'FROM TWO WELL-WISHERS.'

LIV

In a quarter of an hour Clare was leaving the house, whence his mother watched his thin figure as it disappeared into the street. He had declined to borrow his father's old mare, well knowing of its necessity to the household. He went to the inn, where he hired a trap, and could hardly wait during the harnessing. In a very few minutes after he was driving up the hill out of the town which, three or four months earlier in the year, Tess had descended with such hopes and ascended with such shattered purposes.

Benvill Lane soon stretched before him, its hedges and trees purple with buds; but he was looking at other things, and only recalled himself to the scene sufficiently to enable him to keep the way. In something less than an hour-and-a-half he had skirted the south of the King's Hintock estates and ascended to the untoward solitude of Cross-in-Hand, the unholy stone whereon Tess had been compelled by Alec d'Urberville, in his whim of reformation, to swear the strange oath that she would never wilfully tempt him again. The pale and blasted nettle-stems of the preceding year even now lingered nakedly in the banks, young green nettles of the present spring growing from their roots.

Thence he went along the verge of the upland overhanging the other Hintocks, and, turning to the right, plunged into the bracing calcareous region of Flintcomb-Ash, the address from which she had written to him in one of the letters, and which he supposed to be the place of sojourn referred to by her mother. Here, of course, he did not find her; and what added to his depression was the discovery that no 'Mrs. Clare' had ever been heard of by the cottagers or by the farmer himself, though Tess was remembered well enough by her Christian name. His name she had obviously never used during their separation, and her dignified sense of their total severance was shown not much less by this abstention than by the hardships she had chosen to undergo (of which he now learnt for the first time) rather than apply to his father for more funds.

From this place they told him Tess Durbeyfield had gone, without due notice, to the home of her parents on the other side of Blackmoor, and it therefore became necessary to find Mrs. Durbeyfield. She had told him she was not now at Marlott, but had been curiously reticent as to her actual address, and the only course was to go to Marlott and inquire for it. The farmer who had been so churlish with Tess was quite smooth-tongued to Clare, and lent him a horse and man to drive him towards Marlott, the gig he had arrived in being sent back to Emminster; for the limit of a day's journey with that horse was reached.

Clare would not accept the loan of the farmer's vehicle for a further distance than to the outskirts of the Vale, and, sending it back with the man who had driven him, he put up at an inn, and next day entered on foot the region wherein was the spot of his dear Tess's birth. It was as yet too early in the year for much colour to appear in the gardens and foliage; the so-called spring was but winter over-laid with a thin coat of greenness, and it was of a parcel with his expectations.

The house in which Tess had passed the years of her childhood was now inhabited by another family who had never known her. The new residents were in the garden, taking as much interest in their own doings as if the homestead had never passed its primal time in conjunction with the histories of others, beside which the histories of these were but as a tale told by an idiot.° They walked about the garden paths with thoughts of their own concerns entirely uppermost, bringing their actions at every moment into jarring collision with the dim ghosts behind them, talking as though the time when Tess lived there were not one whit intenser in story than now. Even the spring birds sang over their heads as if they thought there was nobody missing in particular.

On inquiry of these precious innocents, to whom even the name of their predecessors was a failing memory, Clare learned that John

tale told by an idiot: *Macbeth* 5.5.26–27.

Durbeyfield was dead; that his widow and children had left Marlott, declaring that they were going to live at Kingsbere, but instead of doing so had gone on to another place they mentioned. By this time Clare abhorred the house for ceasing to contain Tess, and hastened away from its hated presence without once looking back.

His way was by the field in which he had first beheld her at the dance. It was as bad as the house — even worse. He passed on through the churchyard, where, amongst the new headstones, he saw one of a somewhat superior design to the rest. The inscription ran thus:

> In memory of John Durbeyfield, rightly d'Urberville, of the once powerful family of that Name, and Direct Descendant through an Illustrious Line from Sir Pagan d'Urberville, one of the Knights of the Conqueror. Died March 10th, 18 ——
>
> How are the Mighty Fallen.°

Some man, apparently the sexton, had observed Clare standing there, and drew nigh. 'Ah, sir, now that's a man who didn't want to lie here, but wished to be carried to Kingsbere, where his ancestors be.'

'And why didn't they respect his wish?'

'Oh — no money. Bless your soul, sir, why — there, I wouldn't wish to say it everywhere, but — even this headstone, for all the flourish wrote upon en, is not paid for.'

'Ah, who put it up?'

The man told the name of a mason in the village, and, on leaving the churchyard, Clare called at the mason's house. He found that the statement was true, and paid the bill. This done he turned in the direction of the migrants.

The distance was too long for a walk, but Clare felt such a strong desire for isolation that at first he would neither hire a conveyance nor go to a circuitous line of railway by which he might eventually reach the place. At Shaston, however, he found he must hire; but the way was such that he did not enter Joan's place till about seven o'clock in the evening, having traversed a distance of over twenty miles since leaving Marlott.

The village being small he had little difficulty in finding Mrs. Durbeyfield's tenement, which was a house in a walled garden, remote from the main road, where she had stowed away her clumsy old furniture as best she could. It was plain that for some reason or other she had not wished him to visit her, and he felt his call to be somewhat of

How are the Mighty Fallen: 2 Samuel 1.19. See note to chapter 1.

an intrusion. She came to the door herself, and the light from the evening sky fell upon her face.

This was the first time that Clare had ever met her, but he was too preoccupied to observe more than that she was still a handsome woman, in the garb of a respectable widow. He was obliged to explain that he was Tess's husband, and his object in coming there, and he did it awkwardly enough. 'I want to see her at once,' he added. 'You said you would write to me again, but you have not done so.'

'Because she've not come home,' said Joan.

'Do you know if she is well?'

'I don't. But you ought to, sir,' said she.

'I admit it. Where is she staying?'

From the beginning of the interview Joan had disclosed her embarrassment by keeping her hand to the side of her cheek.

'I — don't know exactly where she is staying,' she answered. 'She was — but —— '

'Where was she?'

'Well, she is not there now.'

In her evasiveness she paused again, and the younger children had by this time crept to the door, where, pulling at his mother's skirts, the youngest murmured —

'Is this the gentleman who is going to marry Tess?'

'He has married her,' Joan whispered. 'Go inside.'

Clare saw her efforts for reticence, and asked —

'Do you think Tess would wish me to try and find her? If not, of course —— '

'I don't think she would.'

'Are you sure?'

'I am sure she wouldn't.'

He was turning away; and then he thought of Tess's tender letter.

'I am sure she would!' he retorted passionately. 'I know her better than you do.'

'That's very likely, sir; for I have never really known her.'

'Please tell me her address, Mrs. Durbeyfield, in kindness to a lonely wretched man!'

Tess's mother again restlessly swept her cheek with her vertical hand, and seeing that he suffered, she at last said, in a low voice —

'She is at Sandbourne.'

'Ah — where there? Sandbourne has become a large place, they say.'

'I don't know more particularly than I have said — Sandbourne. For myself, I was never there.'

It was apparent that Joan spoke the truth in this, and he pressed her no further.

'Are you in want of anything?' he said gently.

'No, sir,' she replied. 'We are fairly well provided for.'

Without entering the house Clare turned away. There was a station three miles ahead, and paying off his coachman, he walked thither. The last train to Sandbourne left shortly after, and it bore Clare on its wheels.

LV

At eleven o'clock that night, having secured a bed at one of the hotels and telegraphed his address to his father immediately on his arrival, he walked out into the streets of Sandbourne. It was too late to call on or inquire for any one, and he reluctantly postponed his purpose till the morning. But he could not retire to rest just yet.

This fashionable watering-place, with its eastern and its western stations, its piers, its groves of pines, its promenades, and its covered gardens, was, to Angel Clare, like a fairy place suddenly created by the stroke of a wand, and allowed to get a little dusty. An outlying eastern tract of the enormous Egdon Waste was close at hand, yet on the very verge of that tawny piece of antiquity such a glittering novelty as this pleasure city had chosen to spring up. Within the space of a mile from its outskirts every irregularity of the soil was prehistoric, every channel an undisturbed British trackway; not a sod having been turned there since the days of the Cæsars. Yet the exotic had grown here, suddenly as the prophet's gourd;° and had drawn hither Tess.

By the midnight lamps he went up and down the winding ways of this new world in an old one, and could discern between the trees and against the stars the lofty roofs, chimneys, gazebos, and towers of the numerous fanciful residences of which the place was composed. It was a city of detached mansions; a Mediterranean lounging-place on the English Channel; and as seen now by night it seemed even more imposing that it was.

The sea was near at hand, but not intrusive; it murmured, and he thought it was the pines; the pines murmured in precisely the same tones, and he thought they were the sea.

Where could Tess possibly be, a cottage-girl, his young wife, amidst all this wealth and fashion? The more he pondered the more

prophet's gourd: In the Bible (Jon. 4.5–10), a gourd springs up overnight to give shade to Jonah.

was he puzzled. Were there any cows to milk here? There certainly were no fields to till. She was most probably engaged to do something in one of these large houses; and he sauntered along, looking at the chamber-windows and their lights going out one by one; and wondered which of them might be hers.

Conjecture was useless, and just after twelve o'clock he entered and went to bed. Before putting out his light he re-read Tess's impassioned letter. Sleep, however, he could not, — so near her, yet so far from her — and he continually lifted the window-blind and regarded the backs of the opposite houses, and wondered behind which of the sashes she reposed at that moment.

He might almost as well have sat up all night. In the morning he arose at seven, and shortly after went out, taking the direction of the chief post-office. At the door he met an intelligent postman coming out with letters for the morning delivery.

'Do you know the address of a Mrs. Clare?' asked Angel.

The postman shook his head.

Then, remembering that she would have been likely to continue the use of her maiden name, Clare said —

'Or a Miss Durbeyfield?'

'Durbeyfield?'

This also was strange to the postman addressed.

'There's visitors coming and going every day, as you know, sir,' he said; 'and without the name of the house 'tis impossible to find 'em.'

One of his comrades hastening out at that moment, the name was repeated to him.

'I know no name of Durbeyfield; but there is the name of d'Urberville at The Herons,' said the second.

'That's it!' cried Clare, pleased to think that she had reverted to the real pronunciation. 'What place is The Herons?'

'A stylish lodging-house. 'Tis all lodging-houses here, bless 'ee.'

Clare received directions how to find the house, and hastened thither, arriving with the milkman. The Herons, though an ordinary villa, stood in its own grounds, and was certainly the last place in which one would have expected to find lodgings, so private was its appearance. If poor Tess was a servant here, as he feared, she would go to the back-door to that milkman, and he was inclined to go thither also. However, in his doubts he turned to the front, and rang.

The hour being early the landlady herself opened the door. Clare inquired for Teresa d'Urberville or Durbeyfield.

'Mrs. d'Urberville?'

'Yes.'

Tess, then, passed as a married woman, and he felt glad, even though she had not adopted his name.

'Will you kindly tell her that a relative is anxious to see her?'

'It is rather early. What name shall I give, sir?'

'Angel.'

'Mr. Angel?'

'No; Angel. It is my Christian name. She'll understand.'

'I'll see if she is awake.'

He was shown into the front room — the dining-room — and looked out through the spring curtains at the little lawn, and the rhododendrons and other shrubs upon it. Obviously her position was by no means so bad as he had feared, and it crossed his mind that she must somehow have claimed and sold the jewels to attain it. He did not blame her for one moment. Soon his sharpened ear detected footsteps upon the stairs, at which his heart thumped so painfully that he could hardly stand firm. 'Dear me! what will she think of me, so altered as I am!' he said to himself; and the door opened.

Tess appeared on the threshold — not at all as he had expected to see her — bewilderingly otherwise, indeed. Her great natural beauty was, if not heightened, rendered more obvious by her attire. She was loosely wrapped in a cashmere dressing-gown of gray-white, embroidered in half-mourning tints, and she wore slippers of the same hue. Her neck rose out of a frill of down, and her well-remembered cable of dark-brown hair was partially coiled up in a mass at the back of her head and partly hanging on her shoulder — the evident result of haste.

He had held out his arms, but they had fallen again to his side; for she had not come forward, remaining still in the opening of the doorway. Mere yellow skeleton that he was now he felt the contrast between them, and thought his appearance distasteful to her.

'Tess!' he said huskily, 'can you forgive me for going away? Can't you — come to me? How do you get to be — like this?'

'It is too late,' said she, her voice sounding hard through the room, her eyes shining unnaturally.

'I did not think rightly of you — I did not see you as you were!' he continued to plead. 'I have learnt to since, dearest Tessy mine!'

'Too late, too late!' she said, waving her hand in the impatience of a person whose tortures cause every instant to seem an hour. 'Don't come close to me, Angel! No — you must not. Keep away.'

'But don't you love me, my dear wife, because I have been so pulled down by illness? You are not so fickle — I am come on purpose for you — my mother and father will welcome you now!'

'Yes — O, yes, yes! But I say, I say it is too late.'

She seemed to feel like a fugitive in a dream, who tries to move away, but cannot. 'Don't you know all — don't you know it? Yet how do you come here if you do not know?'

'I inquired here and there, and I found the way.'

'I waited and waited for you,' she went on, her tones suddenly resuming their old fluty pathos. 'But you did not come! And I wrote to you, and you did not come! He kept on saying you would never come any more, and that I was a foolish woman. He was very kind to me, and to mother, and to all of us after father's death. He —— '

'I don't understand.'

'He has won me back to him.'

Clare looked at her keenly, then, gathering her meaning, flagged like one plague-stricken, and his glance sank; it fell on her hands, which, once rosy, were now white and more delicate.

She continued —

'He is upstairs. I hate him now, because he told me a lie — that you would not come again; and you *have* come! These clothes are what he's put upon me: I didn't care what he did wi' me! But — will you go away, Angel, please, and never come any more?'

They stood fixed, their baffled hearts looking out of their eyes with a joylessness pitiful to see. Both seemed to implore something to shelter them from reality.

'Ah — it is my fault!' said Clare.

But he could not get on. Speech was as inexpressive as silence. But he had a vague consciousness of one thing, though it was not clear to him till later; that his original Tess had spiritually ceased to recognize the body before him as hers — allowing it to drift, like a corpse upon the current, in a direction dissociated from its living will.

A few instants passed, and he found that Tess was gone. His face grew colder and more shrunken as he stood concentrated on the moment, and a minute or two after he found himself in the street, walking along he did not know whither.

LVI

Mrs. Brooks, the lady who was the householder at The Herons, and owner of all the handsome furniture, was not a person of an unusually curious turn of mind. She was too deeply materialized, poor woman, by her long and enforced bondage to that arithmetical demon Profit-and-Loss, to retain much curiosity for its own sake, and apart from possible lodgers' pockets. Nevertheless, the visit of Angel Clare to her well-paying tenants, Mr. and Mrs. d'Urberville, as she deemed them, was sufficiently exceptional in point of time and manner to reinvigorate the feminine proclivity which had been stifled down as useless save in its bearings on the letting trade.

Tess had spoken to her husband from the doorway, without entering the dining-room, and Mrs. Brooks, who stood within the partly-closed door of her own sitting-room at the back of the passage, could hear fragments of the conversation — if conversation it could be called — between those two wretched souls. She heard Tess re-ascend the stairs to the first floor, and the departure of Clare, and the closing of the front door behind him. Then the door of the room above was shut, and Mrs. Brooks knew that Tess had re-entered her apartment. As the young lady was not fully dressed Mrs. Brooks knew that she would not emerge again for some time.

She accordingly ascended the stairs softly, and stood at the door of the front room — a drawing-room, connected with the room immediately behind it (which was a bedroom) by folding-doors in the common manner. This first floor, containing Mrs. Brooks's best apartments, had been taken by the week by the d'Urbervilles. The back room was now in silence; but from the drawing-room there came sounds.

All that she could at first distinguish of them was one syllable, continually repeated in a low note of moaning, as if it came from a soul bound to some Ixionian wheel — °

'O — O — O!'

Then a silence, then a heavy sigh, and again —

'O — O — O!'

The landlady looked through the keyhole. Only a small space of the room inside was visible, but within that space came a corner of the breakfast table, which was already spread for the meal, and also a chair beside. Over the seat of the chair Tess's face was bowed, her posture being a kneeling one in front of it; her hands were clasped over her head, the skirts of her dressing-gown and the embroidery of her night-gown flowed upon the floor behind her, and her stockingless feet, from which the slippers had fallen, protruded upon the carpet. It was from her lips that came the murmur of unspeakable despair.

Ixionian wheel: In Greek mythology, Ixion's eternal punishment was to be bound to a revolving wheel of fire.

Then a man's voice from the adjoining bedroom —

'What's the matter?'

She did not answer, but went on, in a tone which was a soliloquy rather than an exclamation, and a dirge rather than a soliloquy. Mrs. Brooks could only catch a portion:

'And then my dear, dear husband came home to me . . . and I did not know it! . . . And you had used your cruel persuasion upon me . . . you did not stop using it — no — you did not stop! My little sisters and brothers and my mother's needs — they were the things you moved me by . . . and you said my husband would never come back — never; and you taunted me, and said what a simpleton I was to expect him! . . . And at last I believed you and gave way! . . . And then he came back! Now he is gone. Gone a second time, and I have lost him now for ever . . . and he will not love me the littlest bit ever any more — only hate me! . . . O yes, I have lost him now — again because of — you!' In writhing, with her head on the chair, she turned her face towards the door, and Mrs. Brooks could see the pain upon it; and that her lips were bleeding from the clench of her teeth upon them, and that the long lashes of her closed eyes stuck in wet tags on her cheeks. She continued: 'And he is dying — he looks as if he is dying! . . . And my sin will kill him and not kill me! . . . O, you have torn my life all to pieces . . . made me be what I prayed you in pity not to make me be again! . . . My own true husband will never, never — O God — I can't bear this! — I cannot!'

There were more and sharper words from the man; then a sudden rustle; she had sprung to her feet. Mrs. Brooks, thinking that the speaker was coming to rush out of the door, hastily retreated down the stairs.

She need not have done so, however, for the door of the sitting-room was not opened. But Mrs. Brooks felt it unsafe to watch on the landing again, and entered her own parlour below.

She could hear nothing through the floor, although she listened intently, and thereupon went to the kitchen to finish her interrupted breakfast. Coming up presently to the front room on the ground floor she took up some sewing, waiting for her lodgers to ring that she might take away the breakfast, which she meant to do herself, to discover what was the matter if possible. Overhead, as she sat, she could now hear the floorboards slightly creak, as if some one were walking about, and presently the movement was explained by the rustle of garments against the banisters, the opening and the closing of the front door, and the form of Tess passing to the gate on her way into the street. She was fully dressed now in the walking costume of a well-to-do young lady in which she had arrived, with the sole addition that over her hat and black feathers a veil was drawn.

Mrs. Brooks had not been able to catch any word of farewell, temporary or otherwise, between her tenants at the door above. They might have quarrelled, or Mr. d'Urberville might still be asleep, for he was not an early riser.

She went into the back room which was more especially her own apartment, and continued her sewing there. The lady lodger did not return, nor did the gentleman ring his bell. Mrs. Brooks pondered on the delay, and on what probable relation the visitor who had called so early bore to the couple upstairs. In reflecting she leant back in her chair.

As she did so her eyes glanced casually over the ceiling till they were arrested by a spot in the middle of its white surface which she had never noticed there before. It was about the size of a wafer when she first observed it, but it speedily grew as large as the palm of her hand, and then she could perceive that it was red. The oblong white ceiling, with this scarlet blot in the midst, had the appearance of a gigantic ace of hearts.

Mrs. Brooks had strange qualms of misgiving. She got upon the table, and touched the spot in the ceiling with her fingers. It was damp, and she fancied that it was a blood stain.

Descending from the table, she left the parlour, and went upstairs, intending to enter the room overhead, which was the bedchamber at the back of the drawing-room. But, nerveless woman as she had now become, she could not bring herself to attempt the handle. She listened. The dead silence within was broken only by a regular beat.

Drip, drip, drip.

Mrs. Brooks hastened downstairs, opened the front door, and ran into the street. A man she knew, one of the workmen employed at an adjoining villa, was passing by, and she begged him to come in and go upstairs with her; she feared something had happened to one of her lodgers. The workman assented, and followed her to the landing.

She opened the door of the drawing-room, and stood back for him to pass in, entering herself behind him. The room was empty; the breakfast — a substantial repast of coffee, eggs, and a cold ham — lay spread upon the table untouched, as when she had taken it up, excepting that the carving knife was missing. She asked the man to go through the folding-doors into the adjoining room.

He opened the doors, entered a step or two, and came back almost instantly with a rigid face. 'My good God, the gentleman in bed is dead! I think he has been hurt with a knife — a lot of blood has run down upon the floor!'

The alarm was soon given, and the house which had lately been so quiet resounded with a tramp of many footsteps, a surgeon among the rest. The wound was small, but the point of the blade had touched the heart of the victim, who lay on his back, pale, fixed, dead, as if he had scarcely moved after the infliction of the blow. In a quarter of an hour the news that a gentleman who was a temporary visitor to the town had been stabbed in his bed, spread through every street and villa of the popular watering-place.

LVII

Meanwhile Angel Clare had walked automatically along the way by which he had come, and, entering his hotel, sat down over the breakfast, staring at nothingness. He went on eating and drinking unconsciously till on a sudden he demanded his bill; having paid which he took his dressing-bag in his hand, the only luggage he had brought with him, and went out.

At the moment of his departure a telegram was handed to him — a few words from his mother, stating that they were glad to know his address, and informing him that his brother Cuthbert had proposed to and been accepted by Mercy Chant.

Clare crumpled up the paper, and followed the route to the station; reaching it, he found that there would be no train leaving for an hour and more. He sat down to wait, and having waited a quarter of an hour felt that he could wait there no longer. Broken in heart and numbed, he had nothing to hurry for; but he wished to get out of a town which had been the scene of such an experience, and turned to walk to the first station onward, and let the train pick him up there.

The highway that he followed was open, and at a little distance dipped into a valley, across which it could be seen running from edge to edge. He had traversed the greater part of this depression, and was climbing the western acclivity, when, pausing for breath, he unconsciously looked back. Why he did so he could not say, but something seemed to impel him to the act. The tape-like surface of the road diminished in his rear as far as he could see, and as he gazed a moving spot intruded on the white vacuity of its perspective.

It was a human figure running. Clare waited, with a dim sense that somebody was trying to overtake him.

The form descending the incline was a woman's, yet so entirely was his mind blinded to the idea of his wife's following him that even when she came nearer he did not recognize her under the totally changed attire in which he now beheld her. It was not till she was quite close that he could believe her to be Tess.

'I saw you — turn away from the station — just before I got there — and I have been following you all this way!'

She was so pale, so breathless, so quivering in every muscle, that he did not ask her a single question, but seizing her hand, and pulling it within his arm, he led her along. To avoid meeting any possible wayfarers he left the high road, and took a footpath under some fir-trees. When they were deep among the moaning boughs he stopped and looked at her inquiringly.

'Angel,' she said, as if waiting for this, 'do you know what I have been running after you for? To tell you that I have killed him!' A pitiful white smile lit her face as she spoke.

'What!' said he, thinking from the strangeness of her manner that she was in some delirium.

'I have done it — I don't know how,' she continued. 'Still, I owed it to you, and to myself, Angel. I feared long ago, when I struck him on the mouth with my glove, that I might do it some day for the trap he set for me in my simple youth, and his wrong to you through me. He has come between us and ruined us, and now he can never do it any more. I never loved him at all, Angel, as I loved you. You know it, don't you? You believe it? You didn't come back to me, and I was obliged to go back to him. Why did you go away — why did you — when I loved you so? I can't think why you did it. But I don't blame you; only, Angel, will you forgive me my sin against you, now I have killed him? I thought as I ran along that you would be sure to forgive me now I have done that. It came to me as a shining light that I should get you back that way. I could not bear the loss of you any longer — you don't know how entirely I was unable to bear your not loving me! Say you do now, dear, dear husband; say you do, now I have killed him!'

'I do love you, Tess — O, I do — it is all come back!' he said, tightening his arms round her with fervid pressure. 'But how do you mean — you have killed him?'

'I mean that I have,' she murmured in a reverie.

'What, bodily? Is he dead?'

'Yes. He heard me crying about you, and he bitterly taunted me; and called you by a foul name; and then I did it. My heart could not bear it. He had nagged me about you before. And then I dressed myself and came away to find you.'

By degrees he was inclined to believe that she had faintly attempted, at least, what she said she had done; and his horror at her impulse was mixed with amazement at the strength of her affection for himself, and at the strangeness of its quality, which had apparently extinguished her moral sense altogether. Unable to realize the gravity of her conduct she seemed at last content; and he looked at her as she lay upon his shoulder, weeping with happiness, and wondered what obscure strain in the d'Urberville blood had led to this aberration — if it were an aberration. There momentarily flashed through his mind that the family tradition of the coach and murder might have arisen because the d'Urbervilles had been known to do these things. As well as his confused and excited ideas could reason, he supposed that in the moment of mad grief of which she spoke her mind had lost its balance, and plunged her into this abyss.

It was very terrible if true; if a temporary hallucination, sad. But, anyhow, here was this deserted wife of his, this passionately-fond woman, clinging to him without a suspicion that he would be anything to her but a protector. He saw that for him to be otherwise was not, in her mind, within the region of the possible. Tenderness was absolutely dominant in Clare at last. He kissed her endlessly with his white lips, and held her hand, and said —

'I will not desert you! I will protect you by every means in my power, dearest love, whatever you may have done or not have done!'

They then walked on under the trees, Tess turning her head every now and then to look at him. Worn and unhandsome as he had become, it was plain that she did not discern the least fault in his appearance. To her he was, as of old, all that was perfection, personally and mentally. He was still her Antinous, her Apollo° even; his sickly face was beautiful as the morning to her affectionate regard on this day no less than when she first beheld him; for was it not the face of the one man on earth who had loved her purely, and who had believed in her as pure.

With an instinct as to possibilities he did not now, as he had intended, make for the first station beyond the town, but plunged still farther under the firs, which here abounded for miles. Each clasping

her Antinous . . . : A favorite of the Roman Emperor Hadrian; like Apollo, the Greek god of the sun and of music, Antinous was a figure of male beauty.

the other round the waist they promenaded over the dry bed of fir-needles, thrown into a vague intoxicating atmosphere at the consciousness of being together at last, with no living soul between them; ignoring that there was a corpse. Thus they proceeded for several miles till Tess, arousing herself, looked about her, and said, timidly — 'Are we going anywhere in particular?'

'I don't know, dearest. Why?'

'I don't know.'

'Well, we might walk a few miles further, and when it is evening find lodgings somewhere or other — in a lonely cottage, perhaps. Can you walk well, Tessy?'

'O yes! I could walk for ever and ever with your arm round me!'

Upon the whole it seemed a good thing to do. Thereupon they quickened their pace, avoiding high roads, and following obscure paths tending more or less northward. But there was an unpractical vagueness in their movements throughout the day; neither one of them seemed to consider any question of effectual escape, disguise, or long concealment. Their every idea was temporary and unforefending, like the plans of two children.

At mid-day they drew near to a roadside inn, and Tess would have entered it with him to get something to eat, but he persuaded her to remain among the trees and bushes of this half-woodland, half-moorland part of the country, till he should come back. Her clothes were of recent fashion; even the ivory-handled parasol that she carried was of a shape unknown in the retired spot to which they had now wandered; and the cut of such articles would have attracted attention in the settle of a tavern. He soon returned, with food enough for half-a-dozen people and two bottles of wine — enough to last them for a day or more, should any emergency arise.

They sat down upon some dead boughs and shared their meal. Between one and two o'clock they packed up the remainder and went on again.

'I feel strong enough to walk any distance,' said she.

'I think we may as well steer in a general way towards the interior of the country, where we can hide for a time, and are less likely to be looked for than anywhere near the coast,' Clare remarked. 'Later on, when they have forgotten us, we can make for some port.'

She made no reply to this beyond that of grasping him more tightly, and straight inland they went. Though the season was an English May the weather was serenely bright, and during the afternoon it was quite warm. Through the latter miles of their walk their footpath had taken them into the depths of the New Forest, and towards evening, turning the corner of a lane, they perceived behind a brook and bridge a large board on which was painted in white letters, 'This desirable Mansion to be Let Furnished;' particulars following, with directions to apply to some London agents. Passing through the gate they could see the house, an old brick building of regular design and large accommodation.

'I know it,' said Clare. 'It is Bramshurst Court. You can see that it is shut up, and grass is growing on the drive.'

'Some of the windows are open,' said Tess.

'Just to air the rooms, I suppose.'

'All these rooms empty, and we without a roof to our heads!'

'You are getting tired, my Tess!' he said. 'We'll stop soon.' And kissing her sad mouth he again led her onwards.

He was growing weary likewise, for they had wandered a dozen or fifteen miles, and it became necessary to consider what they should do for rest. They looked from afar at isolated cottages and little inns, and were inclined to approach one of the latter, when their hearts failed them, and they sheered off. At length their gait dragged, and they stood still.

'Could we sleep under the trees?' she asked.

He thought the season insufficiently advanced.

'I have been thinking of that empty mansion we passed,' he said. 'Let us go back towards it again.'

They retraced their steps, but it was half an hour before they stood without the entrance-gate as earlier. He then requested her to stay where she was, whilst he went to see who was within.

She sat down among the bushes within the gate, and Clare crept towards the house. His absence lasted some considerable time, and when he returned Tess was wildly anxious, not for herself, but for him. He had found out from a boy that there was only an old woman in charge as caretaker, and she only came there on fine days, from the hamlet near, to open and shut the windows. She would come to shut them at sunset. 'Now, we can get in through one of the lower windows, and rest there,' said he.

Under his escort she went tardily forward to the main front, whose shuttered windows, like sightless eyeballs, excluded the possibility of watchers. The door was reached a few steps further, and one of the windows beside it was open. Clare clambered in, and pulled Tess in after him.

Except the hall the rooms were all in darkness, and they ascended the staircase. Up here also the shutters were tightly closed, the ventilation being perfunctorily done, for this day at least, by opening the hall-window in front and an upper window behind. Clare unlatched the door of a large chamber, felt his way across it, and parted the shutters to the width of two or three inches. A shaft of dazzling sunlight glanced into the room, revealing heavy, old-fashioned furniture, crimson damask hangings, and an enormous four-post bedstead, along the head of which were carved running figures, apparently Atalanta's race.°

'Rest at last!' said he, setting down his bag and the parcel of viands.

They remained in great quietness till the caretaker should have come to shut the windows: as a precaution, putting themselves in total darkness by barring the shutters as before, lest the woman should open the door of their chamber for any casual reason. Between six and seven o'clock she came, but did not approach the wing they were in. They heard her close the windows, fasten them, lock the door, and go away. Then Clare again stole a chink of light from the window, and they shared another meal, till by-and-by they were enveloped in the shades of night which they had no candle to disperse.

LVIII

The night was strangely solemn and still. In the small hours she whispered to him the whole story of how he had walked in his sleep with her in his arms across the Froom stream, at the imminent risk of both their lives, and laid her down in the stone coffin at the ruined abbey. He had never known of that till now.

'Why didn't you tell me next day?' he said. 'It might have prevented much misunderstanding and woe.'

'Don't think of what's past!' said she. 'I am not going to think outside of now. Why should we! Who knows what to-morrow has in store?'

But it apparently had no sorrow. The morning was wet and foggy, and Clare, rightly informed that the caretaker only opened the windows on fine days, ventured to creep out of their chamber, and explore the house, leaving Tess asleep. There was no food on the premises, but there was water, and he took advantage of the fog to emerge from the mansion, and fetch tea, bread, and butter from a

Atalanta's race: Atalanta was a Grecian huntress who refused to marry any suitor who could not outrun her; the penalty for those who lost was death.

shop in a little place two miles beyond, as also a small tin kettle and spirit-lamp, that they might get fire without smoke. His re-entry awoke her; and they breakfasted on what he had brought.

They were indisposed to stir abroad, and the day passed, and the night following, and the next, and next; till, almost without their being aware, five days had slipped by in absolute seclusion, not a sight or sound of a human being disturbing their peacefulness, such as it was. The changes of the weather were their only events, the birds of the New Forest their only company. By tacit consent they hardly once spoke of any incident of the past subsequent to their wedding-day. The gloomy intervening time seemed to sink into chaos, over which the present and prior times closed as if it never had been. Whenever he suggested that they should leave their shelter, and go forwards towards Southampton or London, she showed a strange unwillingness to move.

'Why should we put an end to all that's sweet and lovely!' she deprecated. 'What must come will come.' And, looking through the shutter-chink: 'All is trouble outside there; inside here content.'

He peeped out also. It was quite true; within was affection, union, error forgiven: outside was the inexorable.

'And — and,' she said, pressing her cheek against his; 'I fear that what you think of me now may not last. I do not wish to outlive your present feeling for me. I would rather not. I would rather be dead and buried when the time comes for you to despise me, so that it may never be known to me that you despised me.'

'I cannot ever despise you.'

'I also hope that. But considering what my life has been I cannot see why any man should, sooner or later, be able to help despising me. . . . How wickedly mad I was! Yet formerly I never could bear to hurt a fly or a worm, and the sight of a bird in a cage used often to make me cry.'

They remained yet another day. In the night the dull sky cleared, and the result was that the old caretaker at the cottage awoke early. The brilliant sunrise made her unusually brisk; she decided to open the contiguous mansion immediately, and to air it thoroughly on such a day. Thus it occurred that, having arrived and opened the lower rooms before six o'clock, she ascended to the bedchambers, and was about to turn the handle of the one wherein they lay. At that moment she fancied she could hear the breathing of persons within. Her slippers and her antiquity had rendered her progress a noiseless one so far, and she made for instant retreat; then, deeming that her hearing might have deceived her, she turned anew to the door and softly tried the handle. The lock was out of order, but a piece of furniture had been moved forward on the inside, which prevented her opening the door more than an inch or two. A stream of morning light through the shutter-chink fell upon the faces of the pair, wrapped in profound slumber, Tess's lips being parted like a half-opened flower near his cheek. The caretaker was so struck with their innocent appearance, and with the elegance of Tess's gown hanging across a chair, her silk stockings beside it, the pretty parasol, and the other habits in which she had arrived because she had none else, that her first indignation at the effrontery of tramps and vagabonds gave way to a momentary sentimentality over this genteel elopement, as it seemed. She closed the door, and withdrew as softly as she had come, to go and consult with her neighbours on the odd discovery.

Not more than a minute had elapsed after her withdrawal when Tess woke, and then Clare. Both had a sense that something had disturbed them, though they could not say what; and the uneasy feeling which it engendered grew stronger. As soon as he was dressed he narrowly scanned the lawn through the two or three inches of shutter-chink.

'I think we will leave at once,' said he. 'It is a fine day. And I cannot help fancying somebody is about the house. At any rate, the woman will be sure to come to-day.'

She passively assented, and putting the room in order they took up the few articles that belonged to them, and departed noiselessly. When they had got into the Forest she turned to take a last look at the house.

'Ah, happy house — good-bye!' she said. 'My life can only be a question of a few weeks. Why should we not have stayed there?'

'Don't say it, Tess! We shall soon get out of this district altogether. We'll continue our course as we've begun it, and keep straight north. Nobody will think of looking for us there. We shall be looked for at the Wessex ports if we are sought at all. When we are in the north we will get to a port and away.'

Having thus persuaded her the plan was pursued, and they kept a bee line northward. Their long repose at the manor-house lent them walking power now; and towards mid-day they found that they were approaching the steepled city of Melchester, which lay directly in their way. He decided to rest her in a clump of trees during the afternoon, and push onward under cover of darkness. At dusk Clare purchased food as usual, and their night march began, the boundary between Upper and Mid-Wessex being crossed about eight o'clock.

To walk across country without much regard to roads was not new to Tess, and she showed her old agility in the performance. The intercepting city, ancient Melchester, they were obliged to pass through in order to take advantage of the town bridge for crossing a large river that obstructed them. It was about midnight when they went along the deserted streets, lighted fitfully by the few lamps, keeping off the pavement that it might not echo their footsteps. The graceful pile of cathedral architecture rose dimly on their left hand, but it was lost upon them now. Once out of the town they followed the turnpike-road, which after a few miles plunged across an open plain.

Though the sky was dense with cloud a diffused light from some fragment of a moon had hitherto helped them a little. But the moon had now sunk, the clouds seemed to settle almost on their heads, and the night grew as dark as a cave. However, they found their way along, keeping as much on the turf as possible that their tread might not resound, which it was easy to do, there being no hedge or fence of any kind. All around was open loneliness and black solitude, over which a stiff breeze blew.

They had proceeded thus gropingly two or three miles further when on a sudden Clare became conscious of some vast erection close in his front, rising sheer from the grass. They had almost struck themselves against it.

'What monstrous place is this?' said Angel.

'It hums,' said she. 'Hearken!'

He listened. The wind, playing upon the edifice, produced a booming tune, like the note of some gigantic one-stringed harp. No other sound came from it, and lifting his hand and advancing a step or two, Clare felt the vertical surface of the structure. It seemed to be of solid stone, without joint or moulding. Carrying his fingers onward he found that what he had come in contact with was a colossal rectangular pillar; by stretching out his left hand he could feel a similar one adjoining. At an indefinite height overhead something made the black sky blacker, which had the semblance of a vast architrave uniting the pillars horizontally. They carefully entered beneath and between; the surfaces echoed their soft rustle; but they seemed to be still out of doors. The place was roofless. Tess drew her breath fearfully, and Angel, perplexed, said —

'What can it be?'

Feeling sideways they encountered another tower-like pillar, square and uncompromising as the first; beyond it another and another. The place was all doors and pillars, some connected above by continuous architraves.

'A very Temple of the Winds,'° he said.

The next pillar was isolated; others composed a trilithon; others were prostrate, their flanks forming a causeway wide enough for a carriage; and it was soon obvious that they made up a forest of monoliths grouped upon the grassy expanse of the plain. The couple advanced further into this pavillion of the night till they stood in its midst.

'It is Stonehenge!'° said Clare.

'The heathen temple, you mean?'

'Yes. Older than the centuries; older than the d'Urbervilles! Well, what shall we do, darling? We may find shelter further on.'

But Tess, really tired by this time, flung herself upon an oblong slab that lay close at hand, and was sheltered from the wind by a pillar. Owing to the action of the sun during the preceding day the stone was warm and dry, in comforting contrast to the rough and chill grass around, which had damped her skirts and shoes.

'I don't want to go any further, Angel,' she said stretching out her hand for his. 'Can't we bide here?'

'I fear not. This spot is visible for miles by day, although it does not seem so now.'

'One of my mother's people was a shepherd here-abouts, now I think of it. And you used to say at Talbothays that I was a heathen. So now I am at home.'

He knelt down beside her outstretched form, and put his lips upon hers.

'Sleepy are you, dear? I think you are lying on an altar.'

'I like very much to be here,' she murmured. 'It is so solemn and lonely — after my great happiness — with nothing but the sky above my face. It seems as if there were no folk in the world but we two; and I wish there were not — except 'Liza-Lu.'

Clare thought she might as well rest here till it should get a little lighter, and he flung his overcoat upon her, and sat down by her side.

Temple of the Winds: Also known as the "tower of the winds," an octagonal tower in Athens for telling time, built in the first century B.C., decorated with representations of the winds (*Enc. Brit.* 1: 976; 2: 839). **Stonehenge:** Prehistoric stone structure near Salisbury in Wiltshire, whose origin and purpose have been the subject of debate; the name, which means "hanging stones," refers to the trilithons that compose part of the structure.

'Angel, if anything happens to me, will you watch over 'Liza-Lu for my sake?' she asked, when they had listened a long time to the wind among the pillars.

'I will.'

'She is so good and simple and pure. O, Angel — I wish you would marry her if you lose me, as you will do shortly. O, if you would!'

'If I lose you I lose all! And she is my sister-in-law.'

'That's nothing, dearest. People marry sister-laws continually about Marlott; and 'Liza-Lu is so gentle and sweet, and she is growing so beautiful. O I could share you with her willingly when we are spirits! If you would train her and teach her, Angel, and bring her up for your own self! . . . She has all the best of me without the bad of me; and if she were to become yours it would almost seem as if death had not divided us. . . . Well, I have said it. I won't mention it again.'

She ceased, and he fell into thought. In the far north-east sky he could see between the pillars a level streak of light. The uniform concavity of black cloud was lifting bodily like the lid of a pot, letting in at the earth's edge the coming day, against which the towering monoliths and trilithons began to be blackly defined.

'Did they sacrifice to God here?' asked she.

'No,' said he.

'Who to?'

'I believe to the sun. That lofty stone set away by itself is in the direction of the sun, which will presently rise behind it.'

'This reminds me, dear,' she said. 'You remember you never would interfere with any belief of mine before we were married? But I knew your mind all the same, and I thought as you thought — not from any reasons of my own, but because you thought so. Tell me now, Angel, do you think we shall meet again after we are dead? I want to know.'

He kissed her to avoid a reply at such a time.

'O, Angel — I fear that means no!' said she, with a suppressed sob. 'And I wanted so to see you again — so much, so much! What — not even you and I, Angel, who love each other so well?'

Like a greater than himself,° to the critical question at the critical time he did not answer; and they were again silent. In a minute or two her breathing became more regular, her clasp of his hand relaxed, and she fell asleep. The band of silver paleness along the east horizon made

a greater than himself: When asked if he claimed to be the Son of God or the King of the Jews, Jesus either remained silent or spoke in ways that did not provide direct answers (Matthew 26.63–64, 27.11–14).

even the distant parts of the Great Plain appear dark and near; and the whole enormous landscape bore that impress of reserve, taciturnity, and hesitation which is usual just before day. The eastward pillars and their architraves stood up blackly against the light, and the great flame-shaped Sun-stone beyond them; and the Stone of Sacrifice midway. Presently the night wind died out, and the quivering little pools in the cup-like hollows of the stones lay still. At the same time something seemed to move on the verge of the dip eastward — a mere dot. It was the head of a man approaching them from the hollow beyond the Sun-stone. Clare wished they had gone onward, but in the circumstances decided to remain quiet. The figure came straight towards the circle of pillars in which they were.

He heard something behind him, the brush of feet. Turning, he saw over the prostrate columns another figure; then before he was aware, another was at hand on the right, under a trilithon, and another on the left. The dawn shone full on the front of the man westward, and Clare could discern from this that he was tall, and walked as if trained. They all closed in with evident purpose. Her story then was true! Springing to his feet, he looked around for a weapon, loose stone, means of escape, anything. By this time the nearest man was upon him.

'It is no use, sir,' he said. 'There are sixteen of us on the Plain, and the whole country is reared.'

'Let her finish her sleep!' he implored in a whisper of the men as they gathered round.

When they saw where she lay, which they had not done till then, they showed no objection, and stood watching her, as still as the pillars around. He went to the stone and bent over her, holding one poor little hand; her breathing now was quick and small, like that of a lesser creature than a woman. All waited in the growing light, their faces and hands as if they were silvered, the remainder of their figures dark, the stones glistening green-gray, the Plain still a mass of shade. Soon the light was strong, and a ray shone upon her unconscious form, peering under her eyelids and waking her.

'What is it, Angel?' she said, starting up. 'Have they come for me?'

'Yes, dearest,' he said. 'They have come.'

'It is as it should be,' she murmured. 'Angel, I am almost glad — yes, glad! This happiness could not have lasted. It was too much. I have had enough; and now I shall not live for you to despise me!'

She stood up, shook herself, and went forward, neither of the men having moved.

'I am ready,' she said quietly.

LIX

The city of Wintoncester, that fine old city, aforetime capital of Wessex, lay amidst its convex and concave downlands in all the brightness and warmth of a July morning. The gabled brick, tile, and freestone houses had almost dried off for the season their integument of lichen, the streams in the meadows were low, and in the sloping High Street, from the West Gateway to the mediæval cross, and from the mediæval cross to the bridge, that leisurely dusting and sweeping was in progress which usually ushers in an old-fashioned market-day.

From the western gate aforesaid the highway, as every Wintoncestrian knows, ascends a long and regular incline of the exact length of a measured mile, leaving the houses gradually behind. Up this road from the precincts of the city two persons were walking rapidly, as if unconscious of the trying ascent — unconscious through preoccupation and not through buoyancy. They had emerged upon this road through a narrow barred wicket in a high wall a little lower down. They seemed anxious to get out of the sight of the houses and of their kind, and this road appeared to offer the quickest means of doing so. Though they were young they walked with bowed heads, which gait of grief the sun's rays smiled on pitilessly.

One of the pair was Angel Clare, the other a tall budding creature — half girl, half woman — a spiritualized image of Tess, slighter than she, but with the same beautiful eyes — Clare's sister-in-law, 'Liza-Lu. Their pale faces seemed to have shrunk to half their natural size. They moved on hand in hand, and never spoke a word, the drooping of their heads being that of Giotto's 'Two Apostles.'°

When they had nearly reached the top of the great West Hill the clocks in the town struck eight. Each gave a start at the notes, and, walking onward yet a few steps, they reached the first milestone, standing whitely on the green margin of the grass, and backed by the down, which here was open to the road. They entered upon the turf, and, impelled by a force that seemed to overrule their will, suddenly stood still, turned, and waited in paralyzed suspense beside the stone.

The prospect from this summit was almost unlimited. In the valley beneath lay the city they had just left, its more prominent buildings showing as in an isometric drawing — among them the broad cathedral tower, with its Norman windows and immense length of aisle and nave, the spires of St. Thomas's, the pinnacled tower of the College,

Giotto's 'Two Apostles': Hardy probably had in mind the fresco in the National Gallery in London that is now attributed to Spinello Aretino (active 1371–1410).

and, more to the right, the tower and gables of the ancient hospice, where to this day the pilgrim may receive his dole of bread and ale. Behind the city swept the rotund upland of St. Catherine's Hill; further off, landscape beyond landscape, till the horizon was lost in the radiance of the sun hanging above it.

Against these far stretches of country rose, in front of the other city edifices, a large red-brick building, with level gray roofs, and rows of short barred windows bespeaking captivity, the whole contrasting greatly by its formalism with the quaint irregularities of the Gothic erections. It was somewhat disguised from the road in passing it by yews and evergreen oaks, but it was visible enough up here. The wicket from which the pair had lately emerged was in the wall of this structure. From the middle of the building an ugly flat-topped octagonal tower ascended against the east horizon, and viewed from this spot, on its shady side and against the light, it seemed the one blot on the city's beauty. Yet it was with this blot, and not with the beauty, that the two gazers were concerned.

Upon the cornice of the tower a tall staff was fixed. Their eyes were riveted on it. A few minutes after the hour had struck something moved slowly up the staff, and extended itself upon the breeze. It was a black flag.

'Justice' was done, and the President of the Immortals, in Æschylean phrase,° had ended his sport with Tess. And the d'Urberville knights and dames slept on in their tombs unknowing. The two speechless gazers bent themselves down to the earth, as if in prayer, and remained thus a long time, absolutely motionless: the flag continued to wave silently. As soon as they had strength they arose, joined hands again, and went on.

The End

Æschylean phrase: "President of the Immortals" translates a phrase from *Prometheus Bound* (1.169), by Aeschylus; Hardy here brings the novel full circle (see the quotation from *King Lear* in the "Preface to the Fifth and Later Editions," p. 27), by suggesting that the highest power in the universe uses human beings for "sport."

PART TWO

Tess of the d'Urbervilles: A Case Study in Contemporary Criticism

A Critical History of *Tess of the d'Urbervilles*

Although the voluminous critical response to *Tess* by its readers resists brief presentation, the main elements of the book's reception are clear. The abundant commentary on the novel in the past hundred years has emphasized in varying combinations Hardy's life and ideas, the book's publication history, its aesthetic form, and, most insistently, its representations of characters and their society.[1] The emphasis on character and context is consonant with Hardy's own grouping of *Tess,* in the General Preface to the Wessex Edition of 1912, among his "Novels of Character and Environment," the works that he seems to have valued most highly.

[1]In *Tess of the d'Urbervilles* (1987), a monograph on critical views of the novel that deals almost exclusively with material published before 1970, Terence Wright provides an alternative scheme for classifying discussions of *Tess.* He identifies five approaches: social, character, ideas, formal or structural, and genetic. By "genetic" Wright means the study of the book's coming into being — the history of Hardy's revisions, insofar as there is evidence about them — and *Tess*'s publication in various forms during Hardy's lifetime. In the introduction and the annotated "Further Reading" section of his edition of theoretically informed essays on *Tess, 'Tess of the d'Urbervilles': Thomas Hardy* (1993), Peter Widdowson provides a sketch of the critical literature that focuses primarily on work published since 1970. Widdowson takes exception to most studies that appeared before 1980 and praises work that understands Hardy as an antirealist author who is relevant to postmodernism.

As is the case with some other novels that are frequently taught in colleges and universities, in the past decade several critics have written monographs about *Tess.* These include: Peter J. Casagrande's *'Tess of the d'Urbervilles': Unorthodox Beauty* (1992), Graham Handley's *Thomas Hardy: 'Tess of the d'Urbervilles'* (1991), and Dale Kramer's *Thomas Hardy: 'Tess of the d'Urbervilles'* (1991). Readers interested in extended, well-informed recent commentary on *Tess* will find it in these volumes. Kramer's monograph provides particularly thoughtful, suggestive discussions of important topics concerning the novel, including social and literary backgrounds, characters, plot, tragedy, and influences on Hardy.

The hundred years of popularity and critical scrutiny, including the recent monographs, collections of essays, critical editions, and casebooks focusing on *Tess,* indicate that Hardy's novel has become a central, highly valued document for understanding the late nineteenth-century attitudes, social practices, and literary styles that remain a significant element of our heritage. This development would surely have surprised some of the novel's first readers, including some editors and reviewers. Hardy had difficulty arranging for the initial serial publication of *Tess.* Although the novel received much critical acclaim and sold well when it appeared in book form, there were also sharply negative reviews that Hardy refers to in the Preface to the Fifth Edition (July 1892). The attacks focused on Hardy's pessimism, mockingly called his "Tessimism," on his questionable morality, and on his awkward style.[2] Hardy's attitudes continue to disturb many readers, who find them gloomy or pessimistic, but his skepticism about religious truths and Victorian moral conventions do not offend readers now as they did in the 1890s. The charge of immorality is also no longer an important issue, as most readers today readily accept stories that mention premarital sexuality and the birth of children out of wedlock. Hardy's style is still a matter that is debated because of its sometimes exaggerated qualities and its frequent changes of register.

The intensity of our institutionalized interest in *Tess* suggests that the passion evident in Hardy's own stance toward the novel and in the initial responses to it has not abated. Despite complaints expressed by critics and writers of stature, including the novelist and critic E. M. Forster, the importance of *Tess of the d'Urbervilles* has been generally

[2]Michael Millgate sketches the initial response to *Tess* in *Thomas Hardy: A Biography* (319–21). Early responses are reprinted in R. G. Cox's *Thomas Hardy: The Critical Heritage* (1970) and in Lerner and Holstrom's *Thomas Hardy and His Readers* (1968).

accepted. Hardy himself placed it at the head of his collected works, though it comes late chronologically in his fiction-writing career, and many critics have judged *Tess* to be his most compelling novel. *Tess* has been a significant stimulus to thinking about cultural values, both moral and aesthetic.

HARDY'S LIFE AND IDEAS

Critical writing focusing on Hardy the man in relation to his works, including *Tess,* has taken various forms, including biographies, commentaries influenced by the biographies, interpretations that stress Hardy's attitudes of a philosophical kind as defining elements, and studies of the novel's publication history. While not, strictly speaking, works of literary criticism, biographies of Hardy always include some explicit and much implicit interpretation of the relation between the life and the work. The sometimes speculative perspective they bring to Hardy's life can provide useful background and context for understanding his writing. There is, of course, ample reason why the interpreting of Hardy's novels overlaps with the documenting and interpreting of his life. What sort of individual, we may well ask, could have produced a novel such as *Tess,* which includes so many changes in stylistic register and ends with a bitter statement, containing an allusion to Greek tragedy, about human beings as the playthings of the gods? And does some knowledge of that individual's life help explain the work's meanings?

It is no surprise in this regard that one of the best commentaries on Hardy's fiction, *Thomas Hardy: His Career as a Novelist* (1971), was written by one of his biographers, Michael Millgate, who argues that *Tess* is Hardy's greatest novel. Although his book was published more than twenty-five years ago, Millgate's carefully formulated, sensitive chapter on *Tess* still offers an illuminating general commentary. Millgate combines and elaborates to excellent advantage several elements of importance in the critical history of *Tess.* He focuses primarily on Hardy's advocacy of Tess, the limited significance of the narrator's philosophical statements, the presentation of Tess's mental states, the novel's aesthetic dimension (realism and expressionism, tragedy, and the technique of multiple juxtaposition), the burdens placed on the reader, and Tess's evasion of restrictive social classifications despite her constricting experiences.

The major biographies are Robert Gittings's two volumes, *Young Thomas Hardy* (1975) and *Thomas Hardy's Later Years* (1978),

Michael Millgate's *Thomas Hardy: A Biography* (1982), and, most recently, Martin Seymour-Smith's highly opinionated, pugnacious *Hardy: A Biography* (1994). Seymour-Smith engages more fully with critics' interpretations of *Tess* than do either of the other biographers. Gittings's two-volume biography provides examples of ways in which biographical speculation can give rise to interpretive readings of Hardy's fiction. But it should also make us aware of the difficulties involved in moving convincingly from representations about the life to readings of the work. By contrast, Millgate's more detailed biography is circumspect in its interpretive claims about the fiction, which Millgate presents separately in his book on Hardy as novelist.

In the last chapter of *Young Thomas Hardy,* Gittings prepares for the direction he will pursue in the second volume of his biography by stressing Hardy's tendency to speak about Tess as if she were a real person, though one composed of elements he took from various people he had seen briefly or known. Gittings describes Hardy's interest in the deaths of women, particularly the impression Hardy took from witnessing at close range when he was sixteen years old the hanging of a woman, Martha Brown, who had murdered her husband. After attempting to document that impression in his fourth chapter, Gittings asserts that Hardy's engagement with the scene was voyeuristic and sexually charged, that it "remained powerfully in his thoughts," and, further, that "it supplied at least part of the emotional power" (34) of *Tess.* In making this assertion, Gittings does not stake out a clear position, for he does not specify how large that "part" is and what the other parts might be. His phrasing, especially the use of "powerfully" and "power," blurs the distinction between something coming from the author's emotions and something that we feel as an effect of the book on us that the author may not have intended. Gittings never explains how or whether a particular emotion in the author results in a text that somehow carries the same emotional charge for the reader to recognize, experience, and accept. By begging important questions concerning authorial intention, the character of textual details, and their effect on the reader, Gittings leaves the impression that *Tess* contains, conveys, and perhaps even fosters an antifeminist perspective attributable to Hardy. As a consequence, Gittings's biography presents a conflicted reading of *Tess.* Even though Gittings judges *Tess* to be Hardy's "finest work" (*Later Years* 65), he gives us obvious reasons to distance ourselves morally from its "emotional power."

We need not accept Gittings's conclusions, particularly his vague assertion that "in a sense, the fictional Tess was doomed by her creator" (*Young* 216); that is, that Hardy participated in and enjoyed killing her. Still, his claims do provide a biographical dimension for the critical question of what Hardy intended by presenting Tess as a woman who attracts the gaze of men and dies by hanging. This is necessarily an issue of concern to critics, especially those sensitive to feminist issues. It is worth pointing out that Hardy's interest in dead women emerges as well in his poetry, and not in an antifeminist way. In the poem "Not Only I," for example, the speaker, who is a dead woman, is clearly a more vital, admirable presence than the living who are left behind to misunderstand her. The same can be said of Tess.

By contrast with Gittings, without insisting on a close association with *Tess,* Michael Millgate reports the incident of the hanging (*Biography* 63), including the sexual overtones in Hardy's description of the scene and its aftermath. In one of his infrequent interpretive comments in the biography, Millgate suggests that standing behind *Tess* is not abnormal sexual interest but "the surging and almost uncontrollable movement of human compassion," which is evident in the narrator's "advocacy of the heroine's case" and in Hardy's belated addition of the subtitle, which insists on Tess's purity (*Biography* 296). As I have already mentioned, Millgate pursues this interpretation in *Thomas Hardy: His Career as a Novelist.* Seymour-Smith goes further in countering Gittings's view by claiming that in *Tess* Hardy "identified with its protagonist" more than he did with the central characters of some of his other novels specifically because she was "a woman rather than a man." In Seymour-Smith's view, Hardy presents with great hostility a "malignantly male" world that victimizes Tess (433). The divergent views of Gittings and the other two biographers define starkly alternative perspectives for understanding the novel. Does the novel compassionately object to Tess's sufferings by revealing the morally indefensible, avoidable causes of her destruction, or does it invite the reader to participate in Tess's exploitation?

In *Thomas Hardy's Later Years,* Gittings devotes parts of chapters five and six to early versions of *Tess* and to its final form. By speculating on possible models for Tess and other characters in the novel who may have inspired some of Hardy's short stories as well, Gittings provides a basis for interpreting *Tess* in relation to these other tales. He also presents Hardy's interests outside literature while he was writing *Tess,* including his admiration for the paintings of J. M. W. Turner, as a way to understand some aspects of the novel that emphasize the spiritual over the material. He accounts as well for revisions Hardy made in writing *Tess* as arising from what Gittings sees as a kind of Darwinian attitude toward the inevitable that Hardy may have derived not only from a reading of Darwin but from a sense of doom in his own family. Hardy's revisions, his interests beyond literature, and his attitude toward fate have been important for other critics.

From the beginning of the critical response to *Tess,* reflection on Hardy's intellectual beliefs and ideas, as they appear to be embodied in his writing, has been a recurring element. Lionel Johnson's early study, *The Art of Thomas Hardy* (1894; new edition 1928), for example, complains about Hardy's lack of consistency in his presentation of "nature" in his fiction. Hardy would have encountered much discussion about nature as he read works by Thomas Henry Huxley, Herbert Spencer, and Charles Darwin, among other widely discussed intellectuals of his time. It is not surprising, then, that some, even many, nineteenth-century attitudes toward nature would appear in Hardy's writings. Johnson's complaint, however, applies too strict a standard of intellectual consistency to Hardy, who wrote fiction, not philosophy.

Several other critics have complained about Hardy's apparent emphasis on fate and his neglect of the importance of human agency and free will in the lives of his characters. In *Aspects of the Novel* (1927), for example, E. M. Forster claims that Hardy's emphasis on causality, that is, on determinism, is a flaw. The complaint focuses on Hardy's pessimism. A particularly clear example of the critical focus on determinism is John Holloway's *The Victorian Sage* (1953). Holloway argues that Hardy's deterministic views arise from his attitude toward nature as a rigid system of law. According to Holloway, Hardy transfers this view to a conception of society as modeled on nature. This reading accuses Hardy of a mistake like that made by Social Darwinists, who assume that society can be understood in the same terms as the natural world. In *Tess,* Holloway finds determining, anticipatory images, such as caged or injured birds and the dairyman's gallows-like fork, that communicate, according to his interpretation, the inevitable, unalterable character of Tess's fate. The deterministic reading has met resistance from other critics. In his critical study of Hardy's fiction, for instance, Millgate argues against Holloway's position by interpreting the narrator's philosophical statements in *Tess* as having local meanings rather than the global significance that Holloway claims for them (*Career* 271–72). J. Hillis Miller's essay on repetition in *Tess,* mentioned below, presents a view of Hardy's imagery that refuses to give defining significance to the comparatively isolated examples on which Holloway bases his argument.

In *Thomas Hardy: The Will and the Way* (1965), Roy Morrell presents at length an effective challenge and corrective to Holloway's deterministic reading. According to Morrell, for Hardy character is fate. His characters have sufficient choice and freedom to determine their own fate within limits, and those limits are not divinely legislated but socially imposed. Morrell proposes an original reading of the final paragraph of *Tess,* concerning the President of the Immortals, as an example of Hardy's irony. In Morrell's view, Hardy expects the reader to object because the narrative has revealed not the hand of a malevolent deity but the morally indefensible, socially encouraged behavior of other characters toward Tess. Morrell also tends to stress Tess's own contribution to her ultimate end, a contribution that he overstates.

Critics besides Holloway have produced illuminating discussions of the influence of Hardy's beliefs and knowledge on *Tess,* commentaries that deal with matters other than fate. In "Psychic Evolution: Darwinism and Initiation in *Tess of the d'Urbervilles,*" Elliott B. Gose, Jr., examines Hardy's knowledge of contemporary anthropology and the use to which Hardy puts it by including symbolic initiations in his novel. He cites, for example, the death of Prince, the Durbeyfield horse, as a result of which Tess is smeared with blood like a participant in a ritual sacrifice. In David DeLaura's "'The Ache of Modernism' in Hardy's Later Novels" (1967), DeLaura presents a suggestive reading of *Tess* that focuses on the phrase from chapter nineteen, quoted in his essay's title, in relation to Hardy's debt to Matthew Arnold and Hardy's attitude toward Christianity. Of special note concerning Hardy and nineteenth-century intellectual developments is Gillian Beer's nuanced work in *Darwin's Plots: Evolutionary Narrative in Darwin, George Eliot, and Nineteenth-Century Fiction* (1983) concerning Hardy's complex relation to Darwin and evolutionary thought.

PUBLICATION HISTORY

Studies of the novel's publication history provide a different type of background or contextual information relevant to interpreting *Tess.* These commentaries and editions have a more minute textual emphasis than personally or intellectually oriented biographical criticism that takes the novels into account. Because they describe the author's life as a writer, the commentaries that focus on revisions often include or imply critical positions. The issue for critics with an interest in establishing the best text of Hardy's writings is regularly Hardy's intentions, and those intentions have implications for the way we make sense of details in the text.

Hardy has been well served by scholars who have turned their attention to the publication history of *Tess.* The novel provides a thoroughly documented instance of a major text that was restored and revised by its author after originally being published in installments in altered form to meet audience and editorial expectations. J. T. Laird's *The Shaping of 'Tess of the d'Urbervilles'* (1975) traces in careful detail the development of *Tess* from its original conception through serial publication under editorial pressure to the version printed in the Wessex Edition of 1912 (accepted and reprinted in this casebook edition as the most accurate text produced in Hardy's lifetime). As part of his study, Laird argues convincingly that Hardy intended in some important decisions and revisions to stress Tess's purity, both through details that he modified or added (as in the case of the subtitle) and in his reticence about presenting some events directly, including Tess's violation (190–91). Laird also argues that Hardy's sometimes awkward and bitter authorial comments can be read as unequivocal protests against "the prevailing ethos of his time" (191), an ethos that Hardy holds responsible for Tess's downfall.

An indispensable textual study for the criticism of *Tess* is the scholarly, critical edition of the novel produced by Juliet Grindle and Simon Gatrell (1983), which provides in accessible form both a text of the novel and variant readings from the whole range of published and manuscript versions. In their introduction, Grindle and Gatrell argue, as does Laird in his study, for the implications of Hardy's revisions, including especially his changes that emphasize Tess's purity and her victimization by Alec (46–48). The scholarly focus on textual history yields further interpretive results in two books published by Simon Gatrell, *Hardy the Creator: A Textual Biography* (1988) and *Thomas Hardy and the Proper Study of Mankind* (1993). In his comments on Hardy's revisions to *Tess* in *Hardy the Creator,* Gatrell provides details and interpretive commentary that help clarify our understanding of passages that Hardy revised by contrast with earlier versions. He argues persuasively that Hardy's changes contributed to embodying "in his narrator the representative of his class," a rural "artisan-craftsman class" that has been "displaced and oppressed" (104), like Tess herself. By contrast with critics who complain about Hardy's awkwardly intrusive narrator, Gatrell argues for "the remarkable flexibility of the narrative voice in *Tess*" (106). Some of the details that he considers lead

Gatrell to conclude that Hardy intended to present Tess as sensitively self-aware about her actions and feelings. He emphasizes Hardy's addition of material to make it evident that Angel's rejection of Tess is based on a double standard that is self-serving and self-deceiving.

Gatrell takes even fuller interpretive advantage of his knowledge of Hardy's revisions in *Thomas Hardy and the Proper Study of Mankind*. The second of the two pieces on *Tess* published there, an example of fiction as literary criticism entitled "Angel Clare's Story," is a tour de force. In it Gatrell adopts the fictional first-person voice of "Michael James," the putative real-life model for the central male character in the novel, in order to retell Angel's story from James's perspective. By having the fictional James write during World War I, Gatrell is able to attribute to him knowledge of all the major published versions of the novel during Hardy's lifetime, as well as knowledge of the prepublication materials in the British Museum. James's comments on various decisions that Hardy made in writing *Tess* enable us to understand what is distinctive about the novel by presenting what it might have been by contrast with what it finally became. Gatrell frames *Tess* within the realistic writing that is James's fictional autobiographical statement. In so doing, he establishes by implication the book's antirealistic character, specifically the obstacles it presents to being understood primarily with reference to events in a real life. Unlike a biographical critic, such as Gittings, who sees events in a life as important keys to our reading, Gatrell emphasizes, through a meditation on revisions, how resistant *Tess* is to referential interpretation and how essential its aesthetic form is to our understanding. In an unusual, unexpected way, textual criticism gives rise here to an antibiographical, antirealistic vision of *Tess*.

AESTHETIC FORM

The question of Hardy's place in the realistic tradition of English fiction has been frequently addressed, though often implicitly, by critics who focus on aspects of his style. Important work on the style and structure of *Tess* began in the 1960s with essays by David Lodge and Tony Tanner, which were followed by books and essays written by Jean R. Brooks and J. Hillis Miller, among others. In his chapter on *Tess*, "Tess, Nature, and the Voices of Hardy," in *The Language of Fiction* (1966), David Lodge, the English novelist and critic, argues that the inconsistencies in tone and style present the conundrum of multiple voices. The argument effectively displaces Hardy from the realistic tradition, which depends on consistency of voice in the narration and in the presentation of character. In a nearly contemporaneous essay, "Colour and Movement in Hardy's *Tess of the d'Urbervilles*" (1968), Tony Tanner links sometimes widely separated moments in the novel through common imagery. But that imagery, rather than providing consistency or stability, reveals contradictions or the linking of apparent opposites. In Tanner's reading, nature turns against itself in the destruction of Tess, whose association with the color red in the ribbon she wears links her to sexual passion and birth, on the one hand, and to murder and death on the other.

Both Jean R. Brooks in *Thomas Hardy: The Poetic Structure* (1971) and J. Hillis Miller in *Thomas Hardy: Distance and Desire* (1970) argue for Hardy's connection not to a nineteenth-century literary tradition that is Romantic or realistic but to the more disturbing, unconventional works of Kafka and Beckett in the twentieth century. The asserted connection forcefully shifts Hardy into a new interpretive context in which the distinction between genres in his writing career is ignored. For these critics, the writings of Hardy the poet and Hardy the novelist can be merged for interpretation. Both Brooks and Miller rely on mid-twentieth-century developments in European thought to enable a kind of reading that foreshadows attempts by later critics, such as Peter Widdowson, to generate commentaries informed by European-inspired literary theory. Brooks draws on existential writers, especially Camus; Miller, in *Distance and Desire,* is influenced by the work of the Swiss phenomenological critic, Georges Poulet. Miller's method, derived from Poulet, of linking for discussion aspects of different texts by Hardy, precludes an emphasis on plot, character, or realistic detail.

Miller's later deconstructive commentary on *Tess,* entitled "Repetition as Immanent Design" (1982), extends Miller's earlier antirealistic reading of Hardy; it is, in effect, an intensified extrapolation of some of Tanner's views on *Tess.* Miller collects in a more systematic way than Tanner the images of red in the novel as a basis for arguing that the chain of linkages leads to no central instance and no determinate explanation. Because of Hardy's style of repetition, according to Miller, the reader is invited into "a lateral dance of interpretation" that provides an antihierarchical experience of indeterminacy. In this poststructuralist reading, the text supports a proliferating series of interpretations rather than inviting primarily a determinate, referential understanding.

Other studies of lasting value that emphasize formal or structural elements include Dale Kramer's *Thomas Hardy: The Forms of Tragedy* (1975), which deals with form in relation to genre, and Ian Gregor's *The Great Web: The Form of Hardy's Major Fiction* (1974), which emphasizes process and the reader's position. Kramer reads *Tess* as a late stage in the development of Hardy's tragic vision, a state in which the form is open-ended but consciousness is the central aesthetic element. He emphasizes the "organic" form of Hardy's fiction and argues for the relation between form and tragic effect. For Kramer, the tragedy of *Tess* is a tragedy of the individual that Hardy explores through experiments in point of view as part of a democratizing of tragedy in his late fiction. In *The Great Web,* Gregor also sees the form of Hardy's fiction as open, and his figure of the "web" suggests the cumulative result of a series of movements and shifts. He stresses the degree to which Hardy's narratives provide an alternative to the expectations for form created by Henry James's novels. For Gregor, Hardy's stories unfold gradually to create the reader's experience, which is open because of central, ambiguous elements, including Tess's violation, which may be a rape or a seduction.

CHARACTERS AND SOCIETY

Despite the importance of style and aesthetic form in understanding Hardy's writing, because of the evident effect of society on the individual in *Tess,* substantial critical commentary about the novel has dealt not primarily with style but with characters, often in relation to a limiting social context. One of the most distinctive and memorable commentaries on characters is D. H. Lawrence's "Study of Thomas Hardy" (1936). Lawrence does not discuss the novel as an example of psychological realism. He claims instead that unconscious or subconscious forces are primarily at work in the interactions among the characters in *Tess.* As in Hardy's other important novels, according to Lawrence, in *Tess* the most passionate character must die for being unconventional. She becomes the victim of men who are both attracted by her depths and unable to respond to them in ways that recognize her right to exist.

Despite the obvious importance of characters in the narrative of *Tess,* the novel tends not to invite treatment as an example of psychological realism, since Tess's internal states are often presented indirectly. In his chapter on the novel, Millgate claims that there is a link between style and character in this regard, because the disturbances of style reflect Tess's intense inner life (*Career* 272). Other critics have argued for psychologized landscapes or a nearly allegorical use of locales in *Tess* as primary for the presentation of character. In "The Novel as Moral Protest" (1962), Ian Gregor argues for the correlation between landscapes and Tess's inner life. Irving Howe, in *Thomas Hardy* (1967), presents a related reading. He argues that "nothing finally matters in the novel nearly so much as Tess herself: not the other characters, not the philosophic underlay, not the social setting" (110). For Howe, Tess is not a fully psychological presence but a partially allegorized one. He claims Hardy for the tradition of Bunyan's *Pilgrim's Progress,* as Hardy presents a journey in which each important locale includes a test for the central figure.

Studies that emphasize the role of society in *Tess* from a Marxist, materialist, or feminist orientation are more concerned with the structures of power that determine characters' lives than they are with characters considered as comparatively independent psychological presences. The most influential Marxist and materialist readings are contained in Arnold Kettle's *An Introduction to the English Novel* (1951–53), Raymond Williams's *The English Novel from Dickens to Lawrence* (1970), and George Wotton's more recent *Thomas Hardy: Towards a Materialist Criticism* (1985). Kettle reads *Tess* as a fable about the destruction of England's peasantry. He allegorizes Tess's seduction into the sacrificing of the peasantry to a new era overseen by a class, represented by Alec, whose money was made from manufacturing, not from the land. In this interpretation, Tess eventually experiences the dehumanizing work of tending a steam threshing machine because she is part of a historical process, not because of her individual character or the history of her family.

Williams, another Marxist critic, modifies these claims by presenting a more complex sense of English history as reflected in *Tess,* in which country people, rather than peasants narrowly conceived, face difficulties that are not simply imposed by events that impinge on them from afar. Williams allows more room for the individual within history, but, like Kettle, he gives historical and economic factors primary attention. Less distinguished than Williams's work, George Wotton's post-Marxist, materialist study carries forward the project of presenting Tess's fate as part of a historical process by linking issues of class with issues of gender. He rightly suggests that Hardy's focus on working folk, particularly on women, requires explanations that take historical and political elements centrally into account. Wotton is more successful at identifying ideological biases of traditional critics than at establishing his own extended convincing reading of any of Hardy's novels.

One virtue of Wotton's study is his attempt to connect issues of social class with issues involving the social position of women in Hardy's fiction. A related, but more satisfying, attempt to combine matters of class and gender occurs in a poststructuralist mode in the final chapter of Peter Widdowson's fast-paced, suggestive *Hardy in History: A Study in Literary Sociology* (1989). Although Widdowson refers to Wotton's work admiringly, his own, more penetrating materialist study is poststructuralist rather than post-Marxist. In his closing chapter, Widdowson moves around freely among a number of Hardy's novels, but *Tess* receives considerable attention. Widdowson emphasizes in thoughtfully insistent ways the degree to which Hardy's characters are not so much individuals as instances of class consciousness in an unstable social situation. The instability is complicated for Widdowson by the sexual politics of Hardy's narratives, in which Widdowson identifies an unresolved contradiction between liberating and patriarchal tendencies. The contradiction and instability manifest themselves, according to Widdowson, in Hardy's "antirealism," which takes Hardy out of the reach of conventional readings that refuse to deal with class, gender, and style.

At the end of his book, Widdowson introduces those elements as intertwined in *Tess,* though he does so to suggest energetically a direction for further work, not as part of a sustained interpretation of the novel. The particular fusion of critical issues evident in Widdowson's approach is typical of a poststructuralist criticism overtly focused on politics. The large ambition and critical promise of this type of approach remain to be achieved, as Widdowson himself indicates. That Widdowson is intent on achieving that ambition and promise is evident from his publications since *Hardy in History.* These include his essay, "'Moments of Vision': Postmodernising *Tess of the d'Urbervilles;* or, *Tess of the d'Urbervilles* Faithfully Presented by Peter Widdowson" (1994), and his edited volume, *'Tess of the d'Urbervilles': Thomas Hardy* (1993), a casebook containing thirteen critical essays that merge theoretical perspectives with textual interpretation.

The further work that Widdowson rightly calls for at the end of his book will have to take into account the numerous commentaries on Hardy that have appeared in the past two decades dealing with questions of concern to feminists. These include Mary Jacobus's "Tess: The Making of a Pure Woman" (1978), Patricia Stubbs's

Women and Fiction: Feminism and the Novel 1880–1920 (1979), Adrian Poole's "'Men's Words' and Hardy's Women" (1981), Penny Boumelha's *Thomas Hardy and Women: Sexual Ideology and Narrative Form* (1982), Kaja Silverman's "History, Figuration and Female Subjectivity in *Tess of the d'Urbervilles*" (1984), Rosemarie Morgan's *Women and Sexuality in the Novels of Thomas Hardy* (1988), Patricia Ingham's *Thomas Hardy* (1990), Marjorie Garson's *Hardy's Fables of Integrity: Woman, Body, Text* (1991), and essays in two collections published in the 1990s, one edited by Linda M. Shires, *Rewriting the Victorians: Theory, History, and the Politics of Gender* (1992), the other edited by Margaret R. Higonnet, *The Sense of Sex: Feminist Perspectives on Hardy* (1993). As this long list suggests, intense energy has gone into feminist interpretations of Hardy, including centrally *Tess.* It is unlikely that any other male author writing in English has attracted more attention from feminist critics, a great deal of it thoughtful and positive.

Feminist criticism has largely moved away from the antagonistic, denigratory position taken by Ellen Moers, who argues in "Hardy Perennial" (1967) that "Tess is a fantasy of almost pornographic dimensions, manipulated with clearly sadistic affection" (100). There are critics who still hold to this attitude, including some who have been influenced by feminist film theory concerning the manipulating, dehumanizing effects of the male gaze on women. In "*Tess,* Tourism, and the Spectacle of the Woman" (Shires 70–86), for example, Jeff Nunokawa claims that Hardy makes a spectacle of Tess to delight a reader cast in the role of a tourist. In Nunokawa's reading, Hardy's narration is a guidebook that encourages the consuming of the spectacle. But much of the criticism concerned with feminism avoids this kind of reductive interpretation. Even critics who raise objections to Hardy's handling of female characters often recognize a critique of gender injustices in his writing. Patricia Stubbs, for example, identifies a contradiction in Hardy, suggesting that his sense of the injustices suffered by women is coupled with his own patriarchal attitudes, which are at base prejudiced against women.

In her influential study, *Thomas Hardy and Women,* Penny Boumelha presents a sensitive evaluation of Hardy's feminism by connecting Hardy's experiments as a writer with the subversive presentation of relations between the genders. On the one hand, Boumelha asserts that Hardy attempts to achieve through an androgynous mode of narration an inside view of Tess that is also an outside view. She finds evidence of Hardy's desire to possess and exhibit Tess in his attempt to represent her as both subject and object through a male narrative voice that evokes the female. But in Boumelha's view, Hardy's swerves from realism suggest that he abandons his frame for controlling Tess. The mixture of modes and the discontinuities that develop in the style of *Tess* indicate, in Boumelha's reading, that Hardy has encountered a limit in his attempt to know and explain his central female character from within and from without. By remaining "unknowable and unrepresentable" (Boumelha 121), Tess's sexuality eludes Hardy's efforts. The style, then, is a mark of Tess's autonomy, her resistance to being controlled by anyone, including Thomas Hardy's narrator. As I mentioned near the beginning of this critical history, Michael Millgate argues, on a different basis from Boumelha, that Tess evades reduction to restrictive social classifications despite her constricting experiences. Boumelha extends Tess's evasion to include Hardy's rendering of her through aesthetic forms. These related positions deserve the elaboration and reconsideration they will undoubtedly receive in the continuing response to Thomas Hardy's *Tess.*

John Paul Riquelme

WORKS CITED

Beer, Gillian. *Darwin's Plots: Evolutionary Narrative in Darwin, George Eliot, and Nineteenth-Century Fiction.* London: Routledge, 1983.

Boumelha, Penny. *Thomas Hardy and Women: Sexual Ideology and Narrative Form.* Totowa: Barnes, 1982.

Brooks, Jean R. *Thomas Hardy: The Poetic Structure.* Ithaca: Cornell UP, 1971.

Casagrande, Peter J. *'Tess of the d'Urbervilles': Unorthodox Beauty.* New York: Twayne, 1992.

Cox, R. G., ed. *Thomas Hardy, The Critical Heritage.* New York: Barnes, 1970.

DeLaura, David J. "'The Ache of Modernism' in Hardy's Later Novels." *ELH* 34 (1967): 380–99.

Forster, E. M. *Aspects of the Novel.* New York: Harcourt, 1927.

Garson, Marjorie. *Hardy's Fables of Integrity: Woman, Body, Text.* Oxford: Clarendon, 1991.

Gatrell, Simon. *Hardy the Creator: A Textual Biography.* Oxford: Clarendon, 1988.

———. *Thomas Hardy and the Proper Study of Mankind.* Charlottesville: UP of Virginia, 1993.

Gittings, Robert. *Thomas Hardy's Later Years.* Boston: Little, 1978.

———. *Young Thomas Hardy.* Boston: Little, 1975.

Gose, Elliott B., Jr. "Psychic Evolution: Darwinism and Initiation in *Tess of the d'Urbervilles.*" *Nineteenth-Century Fiction* 18 (1963): 261–72.

Gregor, Ian. *The Great Web: The Form of Hardy's Major Fiction.* Boston: Faber, 1974.

———. "The Novel as Moral Protest." *The Moral and the Story.* Ian Gregor and Brian Nicholas. London: Faber, 1962. 126–50.

Grindle, Juliet, and Simon Gatrell, eds. *Tess of the d'Urbervilles* by Thomas Hardy. Oxford: Clarendon, 1983.

Handley, Graham. *Thomas Hardy: 'Tess of the d'Urbervilles'.* London: Penguin, 1991.

Higgonet, Margaret R., ed. *The Sense of Sex: Feminist Perspectives on Hardy.* Urbana: U of Illinois P, 1993.

Holloway, John. *The Victorian Sage.* London: Macmillan, 1953.

Howe, Irving. *Thomas Hardy.* New York: Macmillan, 1967.

Ingham, Patricia. *Thomas Hardy.* Atlantic Highlands: Humanities, 1990.

Jacobus, Mary. "Tess: The Making of a Pure Woman." *Tearing the Veil: Essays on Femininity.* Ed. Susan Lipshitz. Boston: Routledge, 1978. 77–92.

Johnson, Lionel. *The Art of Thomas Hardy.* 1894; Revised ed., 1928. New York: Russell, 1965.

Kettle, Arnold. *An Introduction to the English Novel.* Vol. II. *Henry James to the Present Day.* London: Hutchinson's University Library, 1951–1953.

Kramer, Dale. *Thomas Hardy: The Forms of Tragedy.* Detroit: Wayne State UP, 1975.

———. *Thomas Hardy: Tess of the d'Urbervilles.* Cambridge: Cambridge UP, 1991.

Laird, J. T. *The Shaping of 'Tess of the d'Urbervilles'.* Oxford: Clarendon, 1975.

Lawrence, D. H. "Study of Thomas Hardy." *Phoenix: The Posthumous Papers of D. H. Lawrence.* Ed. Edward D. McDonald. 1936. New York: Viking, 1968. 398–516.

Lerner, Laurence, and John Holstrom, eds. *Thomas Hardy and His Readers.* New York: Barnes, 1968.

Lodge, David. "Tess, Nature, and the Voices of Hardy." *The Language of Fiction.* London: Routledge, 1966. 164–88.

Miller, J. Hillis. "*Tess of the d'Urbervilles:* Repetition as Immanent Design." *Fiction and Repetition.* Oxford: Basil Blackwell, 1982. 116–46.

———. *Thomas Hardy: Distance and Desire.* Cambridge: Harvard UP, 1970.

Millgate, Michael. *Thomas Hardy: A Biography.* New York: Random, 1982.

———. *Thomas Hardy: His Career as a Novelist.* New York: Random, 1971.

Moers, Ellen. "Hardy Perennial." *The New York Review of Books* 9 Nov. 1967: 31–33.

Morgan, Rosemarie. *Women and Sexuality in the Novels of Thomas Hardy.* London: Routledge, 1988.

Morrell, Roy. *Thomas Hardy: The Will and the Way.* Kuala Lumpur: U of Malaya P, 1965.

Nunokawa, Jeff. "*Tess,* Tourism, and the Spectacle of the Woman." Shires 70–86.

Poole, Adrian. "'Men's Words' and Hardy's Women." *Essays in Criticism* 31 (1981): 328–44.

Seymour-Smith, Martin. *Hardy: A Biography.* New York: St. Martin's, 1994.

Shires, Linda M., ed. *Rewriting the Victorians: Theory, History, and the Politics of Gender.* New York: Routledge, 1992.

Silverman, Kaja. "History, Figuration and Female Subjectivity in *Tess of the d'Urbervilles.*" *Novel* 18 (1984): 5–28.

Stubbs, Patricia. *Women and Fiction: Feminism and the Novel 1880–1920.* New York: Barnes, 1979.

Tanner, Tony. "Colour and Movement in Hardy's *Tess of the d'Urbervilles.*" *Critical Quarterly* 10 (1968): 219–39.

Widdowson, Peter. *Hardy in History: A Study in Literary Sociology.* London: Routledge, 1989.

———. "'Moments of Vision': Postmodernising *Tess of the d'Urbervilles;* or, *Tess of the d'Urbervilles* Faithfully Presented by Peter Widdowson." *New Perspectives on Thomas Hardy.* Ed. Charles P. C. Pettit. New York: St. Martin's, 1994. 80–100.

———, ed. '*Tess of the d'Urbervilles*': *Thomas Hardy.* New York: St. Martin's, 1993.

Williams, Raymond. *The English Novel from Dickens to Lawrence.* New York: Oxford UP, 1970.

Wotton, George. *Thomas Hardy: Towards a Materialist Criticism.* Totowa: Barnes, 1985.

Wright, Terence. *Tess of the d'Urbervilles.* Atlantic Highlands: Humanities, 1987.

The New Historicism and *Tess of the d'Urbervilles*

WHAT IS THE NEW HISTORICISM?

The title of Brook Thomas's *The New Historicism and Other Old-Fashioned Topics* (1991) is telling. Whenever an emergent theory, movement, method, approach, or group gets labeled with the adjective "new," trouble is bound to ensue, for what is new today is either established, old, or forgotten tomorrow. Few of you will have heard of the band called "The New Kids on the Block." New Age bookshops and jewelry may seem "old hat" by the time this introduction is published. The New Criticism, or formalism, is just about the oldest approach to literature and literary study currently being practiced. The new historicism, by contrast, is *not* as old-fashioned as formalism, but it is hardly new, either. The term "new" eventually and inevitably requires some explanation. In the case of the new historicism, the best explanation is historical.

Although a number of influential critics working between 1920 and 1950 wrote about literature from a psychoanalytic perspective, the majority took what might generally be referred to as the historical approach. With the advent of the New Criticism, however, historically oriented critics almost seemed to disappear from the face of the earth. The dominant New Critics, or formalists, tended to treat literary works as if they were self-contained, self-referential objects. Rather than basing their interpretations on parallels between the text and historical contexts (such as the author's life or stated intentions in writing the work), these critics concentrated on the relationships *within* the text that give it its form and meaning. During the heyday of the New Criticism, concern about the interplay between literature and history virtually disappeared from literary discourse. In its place was a concern about intratextual repetition, particularly of images or symbols but also of rhythms and sound effect.

About 1970 the New Criticism came under attack by reader-response critics (who believe that the meaning of a work is not inherent in its internal form but rather is cooperatively produced by the reader and the text) and poststructuralists (who, following the philosophy of Jacques Derrida, argue that texts are inevitably self-contradictory and that we can find form in them only by ignoring or suppressing conflicting details or elements). In retrospect it is clear that, their outspoken opposition to the New Criticism notwithstanding, the reader-response critics and poststructuralists of the 1970s were very much *like* their formalist predecessors in two important respects: for the most part, they ignored the world beyond the text and its reader, and, for the most part, they ignored the historical contexts within which literary works are written and read.

Jerome McGann first articulated this retrospective insight in 1985, writing that "a text-only approach has been so vigorously promoted during the last thirty-five years that most historical critics have been driven from the field, and have raised the flag of their surrender by yielding the title 'critic,' and accepting the title 'scholar' for themselves" (*Inflections* 17). Most, but not all. The American Marxist Fredric Jameson had begun his 1981 book *The Political Unconscious* with the following two-word challenge: "Always historicize!" (9). Beginning about 1980, a form of historical criticism practiced by Louis Montrose and Stephen Greenblatt had transformed the field of Renaissance studies and begun to influence the study of American and English Romantic literature as well. And by the mid-1980s, Brook Thomas was working on an essay in which he suggests that classroom discussions of Keats's "Ode on a Grecian Urn" might begin with questions such as the following: Where would Keats have seen such an urn? How did a Grecian urn end up in a museum in England? Some very important historical and political realities, Thomas suggests, lie behind and inform Keats's definitions of art, truth, beauty, the past, and timelessness.

When McGann lamented the surrender of "most historical critics," he no doubt realized what is now clear to everyone involved in the study of literature. Those who had *not* yet surrendered — had not yet "yield[ed] the title 'critic'" to the formalist, reader-response, and poststructuralist "victors" — were armed with powerful new arguments and intent on winning back long-lost ground. Indeed, at about the same time that McGann was deploring the near-complete dominance of critics advocating the text-only approach, Herbert Lindenberger was sounding a more hopeful note: "It comes as something of a surprise," he wrote in 1984, "to find that history is making a powerful comeback" ("New History" 16).

We now know that history was indeed making a powerful comeback in the 1980s, although the word is misleading if it causes us to imagine that the historical criticism being practiced in the 1980s by Greenblatt and Montrose, McGann and Thomas, was the same as the historical criticism that had been practiced in the 1930s and 1940s. Indeed, if the word "new" still serves any useful purpose in defining the historical criticism of today, it is in distinguishing it from the old historicism. The new historicism is informed by the poststructuralist and reader-response theory of the 1970s, plus the thinking of feminist, cultural, and Marxist critics whose work was also "new" in the 1980s. New historicist critics are less fact- and event-oriented than historical critics used to be, perhaps because they have come to wonder whether the truth about what really happened can ever be purely and objectively known. They are less likely to see history as linear and progressive, as something developing toward the present or the future ("teleological"), and they are also less likely to think of it in terms of specific eras, each with a definite, persistent, and consistent *Zeitgeist* ("spirit of the times"). Consequently, they are unlikely to suggest that a literary text has a single or easily identifiable historical context.

New historicist critics also tend to define the discipline of history more broadly than it was defined before the advent of formalism. They view history as a social science and the social sciences as being properly historical. In *Historical Studies and Literary Criticism* (1985), McGann speaks of the need to make "sociohistorical" subjects and methods central to literary studies; in *The Beauty of Inflections: Literary Investigations in Historical Method and Theory* (1985), he links sociology and the future of historical criticism. "A sociological poetics," he writes, "must be recognized not only as relevant to the analysis of poetry, but in fact as central to the analysis" (62). Lindenberger cites anthropology as particularly useful in the new historical analysis of literature, especially anthropology as practiced by Victor Turner and Clifford Geertz.

Geertz, who has related theatrical traditions in nineteenth-century Bali to forms of political organization that developed during the same period, has influenced some of the most important critics writing the new kind of historical criticism. Due in large part to Geertz's anthropological influence, new historicists such as Greenblatt have asserted that literature is not a sphere apart or distinct from the history that is relevant to it. That is what the old criticism tended to do: present the background information you needed to know before you could fully appreciate the separate world of art. The new historicists have used what Geertz would call "thick description" to blur distinctions, not only between history and the other social sciences but also between background and foreground, historical and literary materials, political and poetical events. They have erased the old boundary line dividing historical and literary materials, showing that the production of one of Shakespeare's historical plays was a political act and historical event, while at the same time showing that the coronation of Elizabeth I was carried out with the same care for staging and symbol lavished on works of dramatic art.

In addition to breaking down barriers that separate literature and history, history and the social sciences, new historicists have reminded us that it is treacherously difficult to reconstruct the past as it really was, rather than as we have been conditioned by our own place and time to believe that it was. And they know that the job is utterly impossible for those who are unaware of that difficulty and insensitive to the bent or bias of their own historical vantage point. Historical criticism must be "conscious of its status as interpretation," Greenblatt has written (*Renaissance* 4). McGann obviously concurs, writing that "historical criticism can no longer make any part of [its] sweeping picture unselfconsciously, or treat any of its details in an untheorized way" (*Studies* 11).

Unselfconsciously and *untheorized* are the key words in McGann's statement. When new historicist critics of literature describe a historical change, they are highly conscious of, and even likely to discuss, the *theory* of historical change that informs their account. They know that the changes they happen to see and describe are the ones that their theory of change allows or helps them to see and describe. And they know, too, that their theory of change is historically determined. They seek to minimize the distortion inherent in their perceptions and representations by admitting that they see through preconceived notions; in other words, they learn to reveal the color of the lenses in the glasses that they wear.

Nearly everyone who wrote on the new historicism during the 1980s cited the importance of the late Michel Foucault. A French philosophical historian who liked to think of himself as an archaeologist of human knowledge, Foucault brought together incidents and phenomena from areas of inquiry and orders of life that we normally regard as being unconnected. As much as anyone, he encouraged the new historicist critic of literature to redefine the boundaries of historical inquiry.

Foucault's views of history were influenced by the philosopher Friedrich Nietzsche's concept of a *wirkliche* ("real" or "true") history that is neither melioristic (that is, "getting better all the time") nor metaphysical. Like Nietzsche, Foucault didn't see history in terms of a continuous development toward the present. Neither did he view it as an abstraction, idea, or ideal, as something that began "In the beginning" and that will come to THE END, a moment of definite closure, a Day of Judgment. In his own words, Foucault "abandoned [the old history's] attempts to understand events in terms of . . . some great evolutionary process" (*Discipline and Punish* 129). He warned a new generation of historians to be aware of the fact that investigators are themselves "situated." It is difficult, he reminded them, to see present cultural practices critically from within them, and because of the same cultural practices, it is extremely difficult to enter bygone ages. In *Discipline and Punish: The Birth of the Prison* (1975), Foucault admitted that his own interest in the past was fueled by a passion to write the history of the present.

Like Marx, Foucault saw history in terms of power, but his view of power probably owed more to Nietzsche than to Marx. Foucault seldom viewed power as a repressive force. He certainly did not view it as a tool of conspiracy used by one specific individual or institution against another. Rather, power represents a whole web or complex of forces; it is that which produces what happens. Not even a tyrannical aristocrat simply wields power, for the aristocrat is himself formed and empowered by a network of discourses and practices that constitute power. Viewed by Foucault, power is "positive and productive," not "repressive" and "prohibitive" (Smart 63). Furthermore, no historical event, according to Foucault, has a single cause; rather, it is intricately connected with a vast web of economic, social, and political factors.

A brief sketch of one of Foucault's major works may help clarify some of his ideas. *Discipline and Punish* begins with a shocking but accurate description of the public drawing and quartering of a Frenchman who had botched his attempt to assassinate King Louis XV in 1757. Foucault proceeds by describing rules governing the daily life of modern Parisian felons. What happened to torture, to punishment as public spectacle? he asks. What complex network of forces made it disappear? In working toward a picture of this "power," Foucault turns up many interesting puzzle pieces, such as the fact that in the early years of the nineteenth century, crowds would sometimes identify with the prisoner and treat the executioner as if *he* were the guilty party. But Foucault sets forth a related reason for keeping prisoners alive, moving punishment indoors, and changing discipline from physical torture into mental rehabilitation: colonization. In this historical period, people were needed to establish colonies and trade, and prisoners could be used for that purpose. Also, because these were politically unsettled times, governments needed infiltrators and informers. Who better to fill those roles than prisoners pardoned or released early for showing a willingness to be rehabilitated? As for rehabilitation itself, Foucault compares it to the old form of punishment, which began with a torturer extracting a confession. In more modern, "reasonable" times, psychologists probe the minds of prisoners with a scientific rigor that Foucault sees as a different kind of torture, a kind that our modern perspective does not allow us to see as such.

Thus, a change took place, but perhaps not as great a change as we generally assume. It may have been for the better or for the worse; the point is that agents of power didn't make the change because mankind is evolving and, therefore, more prone to perform good-hearted deeds. Rather, different objectives arose, including those of a new class of doctors and scientists bent on studying aberrant examples of the human mind. And where do we stand vis-à-vis the history Foucault tells? We are implicated by it, for the evolution of discipline as punishment into the study of the human mind includes the evolution of the "disciplines" as we now understand that word, including the discipline of history, the discipline of literary study, and now a discipline that is neither and both, a form of historical criticism that from the vantage point of the 1980s looked "new."

Foucault's type of analysis has been practiced by a number of literary critics at the vanguard of the back-to-history movement. One of them is Greenblatt, who along with Montrose was to a great extent re-

sponsible for transforming Renaissance studies in the early 1980s and revitalizing historical criticism in the process. Greenblatt follows Foucault's lead in interpreting literary devices as if they were continuous with all other representational devices in a culture; he therefore turns to scholars in other fields in order to better understand the workings of literature. "We wall off literary symbolism from the symbolic structures operative elsewhere," he writes, "as if art alone were a human creation, as if humans themselves were not, in Clifford Geertz's phrase, cultural artifacts" (*Renaissance* 4).

Greenblatt's name, more than anyone else's, is synonymous with the new historicism; his essay entitled "Invisible Bullets" (1981) has been said by Patrick Brantlinger to be "perhaps the most frequently cited example of New Historicist work" ("Cultural Studies" 45). An English professor at the University of California, Berkeley — the early academic home of the new historicism — Greenblatt was a founding editor of *Representations*, a journal published by the University of California Press that is still considered today to be *the* mouthpiece of the new historicism.

In *Learning to Curse* (1990), Greenblatt cites as central to his own intellectual development his decision to interrupt his literary education at Yale University by accepting a Fulbright fellowship to study in England at Cambridge University. There he came under the influence of the great Marxist cultural critic Raymond Williams, who made Greenblatt realize how much — and what — was missing from his Yale education. "In Williams' lectures," Greenblatt writes, "all that had been carefully excluded from the literary criticism in which I had been trained — who controlled access to the printing press, who owned the land and the factories, whose voices were being repressed as well as represented in literary texts, what social strategies were being served by the aesthetic values we constructed — came pressing back in upon the act of interpretation" (2).

Greenblatt returned to the United States determined not to exclude such matters from his own literary investigations. Blending what he had learned from Williams with poststructuralist thought about the indeterminacy or "undecidability" of meaning, he eventually developed a critical method that he now calls "cultural poetics." More tentative and less overtly political than cultural criticism, it involves what Thomas calls "the technique of montage. Starting with the analysis of a particular historical event, it cuts to the analysis of a particular literary text. The point is not to show that the literary text reflects the historical event but to create a field of energy between the two so that we come to see the event as a social text and the literary text as a social event" ("New Literary Historicism" 490). Alluding to deconstructor Jacques Derrida's assertion that "there is nothing outside the text," Montrose explains that the goal of this new historicist criticism is to show the "historicity of texts and the textuality of history" (Veeser 20).

The relationship between the cultural poetics practiced by a number of new historicists and the cultural criticism associated with Marxism is important, not only because of the proximity of the two approaches but also because one must recognize the difference between the two to understand the new historicism. Still very much a part of the contemporary critical scene, cultural criticism (sometimes called "cultural studies" or "cultural critique") nonetheless involves several tendencies more compatible with the old historicism than with the thinking of new historicists such as Greenblatt. These include the tendency to believe that history is driven by economics; that it is determinable even as it determines the lives of individuals; and that it is progressive, its dialectic one that will bring about justice and equality.

Greenblatt does not privilege economics in his analyses and views individuals as agents possessing considerable productive power. (He says that "the work of art is the product of a negotiation between a creator or class of creators . . . and the institutions and practices of a society" [*Learning* 158]: he also acknowledges that artistic productions are "intensely marked by the private obsessions of individuals," however much they may result from "collective negotiation and exchange" [*Negotiations* vii].) His optimism about the individual, however, should not be confused with optimism about either history's direction or any historian's capacity to foretell it. Like a work of art, a work of history is the negotiated product of a private creator and the public practices of a given society.

This does not mean that Greenblatt does not discern historical change, or that he is uninterested in describing it. Indeed, in works from *Renaissance Self-Fashioning* (1980) to *Shakespearean Negotiations* (1988), he has written about Renaissance changes in the development of both literary characters and real people. But his view of change — like his view of the individual — is more Foucauldian than Marxist. That is to say, it is not melioristic or teleological. And, like Foucault, Greenblatt is careful to point out that any one change is connected with a host of others, no one of which may simply be identified as cause or effect, progressive or regressive, repressive or enabling.

Not all of the critics trying to lead students of literature back to history are as Foucauldian as Greenblatt. Some even owe more to

Marx than to Foucault. Others, like Thomas, have clearly been more influenced by Walter Benjamin, best known for essays such as "Theses on the Philosophy of History" and "The Work of Art in the Age of Mechanical Reproduction." Still others — McGann, for example — have followed the lead of Soviet critic M. M. Bakhtin, who viewed literary works in terms of discourses and dialogues between the official, legitimate voices of a society and other, more challenging or critical voices echoing popular or traditional culture. In the "polyphonic" writings of Rabelais, for instance, Bakhtin found that the profane language of Carnival and other popular festivals offsets and parodies the "legitimate" discourses representing the outlook of the king, church, and socially powerful intellectuals of the day.

Moreover, there are other reasons not to consider Foucault the single or even central influence on the new historicism. First, he critiqued the old-style historicism to such an extent that he ended up being antihistorical, or at least ahistorical, in the view of a number of new historicists. Second, his commitment to a radical remapping of the relations of power and influence, cause and effect, may have led him to adopt too cavalier an attitude toward chronology and facts. Finally, the very act of identifying and labeling *any* primary influence goes against the grain of the new historicism. Its practitioners have sought to "decenter" the study of literature, not only by overlapping it with historical studies (broadly defined to include anthropology and sociology) but also by struggling to see history from a decentered perspective. That struggle has involved recognizing (1) that the historian's cultural and historical position may not afford the best purview of a given set of events and (2) that events seldom have any single or central cause. In keeping with these principles, it may be appropriate to acknowledge Foucault as just one of several powerful, interactive intellectual forces rather than to declare him the single, master influence.

Throughout the 1980s it seemed to many that the ongoing debates about the sources of the new historicist movement, the importance of Marx or Foucault, Walter Benjamin or Mikhail Bakhtin, and the exact locations of all the complex boundaries between the new historicism and other "isms" (Marxism and poststructuralism, to name only two) were historically contingent functions of the new historicism *newness.* In the initial stages of their development, new intellectual movements are difficult to outline clearly because, like partially developed photographic images, they are themselves fuzzy and lacking in definition. They respond to disparate influences and include thinkers who represent a wide range of backgrounds; like movements that are disintegrating, they inevitably include a broad spectrum of opinions and positions.

From the vantage point of the 1990s, however, it seems that the inchoate quality of the new historicism is characteristic rather than a function of newness. The boundaries around the new historicism remain fuzzy, not because it hasn't reached its full maturity but because, if it is to live up to its name, it must always be subject to revision and redefinition as historical circumstances change. The fact that so many critics we label new historicist are working right at the border of Marxist, poststructuralist, cultural, postcolonial, feminist, and now even a new form of reader-response (or at least reader-oriented) criticism is evidence of the new historicism's multiple interests and motivations, rather than of its embryonic state.

New historicists themselves advocate and even stress the need to perpetually redefine categories and boundaries — whether they be disciplinary, generic, national, or racial — not because definitions are unimportant but because they are historically constructed and thus subject to revision. If new historicists like Thomas and reader-oriented critics like Steven Mailloux and Peter Rabinowitz seem to spend most of their time talking over the low wall separating their respective fields, then maybe the wall is in the wrong place. As Catherine Gallagher has suggested, the boundary between new historicists and feminists studying "people and phenomena that once seemed insignificant, indeed outside of history: women, criminals, the insane" often turns out to be shifting or even nonexistent (Veeser 43).

If the fact that new historicists all seem to be working on the border of another school should not be viewed as a symptom of the new historicism's newness (or disintegration), neither should it be viewed as evidence that new historicists are intellectual loners or divisive outriders who enjoy talking over walls to people in other fields but who share no common views among themselves. Greenblatt, McGann, and Thomas all started with the assumption that works of literature are simultaneously influenced by and influencing reality, broadly defined. Whatever their disagreements, they share a belief in referentiality — a belief that literature refers to and is referred to by things outside itself — stronger than that found in the works of formalist, poststructuralist, and even reader-response critics. They believe with Greenblatt that the "central concerns" of criticism "should prevent it from permanently sealing off one type of discourse from another or decisively separating works of art from the minds and lives of their creators and their audiences" (*Renaissance* 5).

McGann, in his introduction to *Historical Studies and Literary Criticism*, turns referentiality into a rallying cry:

> What will not be found in these essays . . . is the assumption, so common in text-centered studies of every type, that literary works are self-enclosed verbal constructs, or looped intertextual fields of autonomous signifiers and signifieds. In these essays, the question of referentiality is once again brought to the fore. (3)

In "Keats and the Historical Method in Literary Criticism," he suggests a set of basic, scholarly procedures to be followed by those who have rallied to the cry. These procedures, which he claims are "practical derivatives of the Bakhtin school," assume that historicist critics will study a literary work's "point of origin" by studying biography and bibliography. The critic must then consider the expressed intentions of the author, because, if printed, these intentions have also modified the developing history of the work. Next, the new historicist must learn the history of the work's reception, as that body of opinion has become part of the platform on which we are situated when we study the work at our own particular "point of reception." Finally, McGann urges the new historicist critic to point toward the future, toward his or her *own* audience, defining for its members the aims and limits of the critical project and injecting the analysis with a degree of self-consciousness that alone can give it credibility (*Inflections* 62).

In his introduction to a collection of new historical writings on *The New Historicism* (1989), H. Aram Veeser stresses the unity among new historicists, not by focusing on common critical procedures but, rather, by outlining five "key assumptions" that "continually reappear and bind together the avowed practitioners and even some of their critics":

> 1. that every expressive act is embedded in a network of material practices;
> 2. that every act of unmasking, critique, and opposition uses the tools it condemns and risks falling prey to the practice it exposes;
> 3. that literary and non-literary texts circulate inseparably;
> 4. that no discourse, imaginative or archival, gives access to unchanging truths nor expresses inalterable human nature;
> 5. finally, . . . that a critical method and a language adequate to describe culture under capitalism participate in the economy they describe. (xi)

These same assumptions are shared by a group of historians practicing what is now commonly referred to as "the new cultural history."

Influenced by *Annales*-school historians in France, post-Althusserian Marxists, and Foucault, these historians share with their new historicist counterparts not only many of the same influences and assumptions but also the following: an interest in anthropological and sociological subjects and methods; a creative way of weaving stories and anecdotes about the past into revealing thick descriptions; a tendency to focus on nontraditional, noncanonical subjects and relations (historian Thomas Laqueur is best known for *Making Sex: Body and Gender from the Greeks to Freud* [1990]); and some of the same journals and projects.

Thus, in addition to being significantly unified by their own interests, assumptions, and procedures, new historicist literary critics have participated in a broader, interdisciplinary movement toward unification virtually unprecedented within and across academic disciplines. Their tendency to work along disciplinary borderlines, far from being evidence of their factious or fractious tendencies, has been precisely what has allowed them to engage historians in a conversation certain to revolutionize the way in which we understand the past, present, and future.

In the essay that follows, Catherine Gallagher begins her new historicist approach to *Tess of the d'Urbervilles* by discussing the work of the mid-nineteenth-century philologist Max Müller. According to Müller, the Western world first viewed divinity as pure, transcendent spirit; with the advent of a Greek culture grounded in Indic sources, however, a "mythic language" at once "concrete and metaphoric" was developed, causing "prelinguistic" spiritual impulses and essences to be personified, sensualized, and sexualized. As a result, Müller argues, the earliest Western "concept of a spiritual divinity" was obscured by anthropomorphic myths involving an amorous Sun God.

By 1890, however, early Western myths were being viewed in an entirely new light. Philologists such as William Robertson Smith and J. G. Frazer opposed the idea that myths personified older, purely spiritual divinities. They instead viewed myths as "sublimations of ritual practices" that involved worship of the earth rather than of the sun. Most important, they rejected the earlier view that these practices were meant to achieve union with a supernatural deity; rather, as Gallagher puts it, they were aimed "at something far more mundane: something called 'fertility.'" Frazer's work *The Golden Bough* (1890), Gallagher argues, was particularly innovative in suggesting that ancient rituals combined "eroticism and sacrifice" in the interest of promoting fertility.

The ideas of Smith and Frazer were paralleled by those of early British anthropologists including Andrew Lang and Edward Burnett

Tylor, who according to Gallagher "posited a uniform and universal pattern of human cultural development, and then argued that the contemporary world provided examples of societies at various stages of the progress from savagery toward civilization." As a result of this theory, Westerners began looking for "survivals" — attitudes and practices extinct in the civilized world — not only in "uncivilized" corners of the earth but also in "primitive" pockets of modern civilization. "Descriptions of the archaic, both at home and abroad," seemed to indicate that culture began with rites through which primitive man sought to ensure that his land, his animals, and his women would prove fertile.

Dismissed as "risible" (laughable) in some quarters of Victorian society, these anthropological theories complemented both the Malthusian views of political economists preoccupied with the relationship between reproduction, food supply, and economic conditions and the emerging philosophical notion that "the highest expressions of human intellectual ambition evolved out of our basic biological dilemmas." This idea, Gallagher maintains, was expressed in various ways by Darwin, Comte, and Spencer, nineteenth-century thinkers by whom Hardy was undeniably influenced.

Having provided this deep background, Gallagher proceeds to read Hardy's *Tess* not as a response to anthropological and philosophical theory but, rather, as a text that parallels, crosses, and recrosses the discourses of philosophy, anthropology, political economy, and literary criticism. Gallagher argues that, from its reference to the May-Day procession as a "Cerealia" to its image of Tess on a sacrificial altar, Hardy's text bristles with "allusions, metaphors, descriptions, dialogues, interpolated stories, and explicit narratorial comments identify[ing] Tess as a sacrificial victim set apart by virtue of her desirability and potential fecundity." In working out this argument, Gallagher focuses on critically important scenes (the scene in The Chase, for instance), but her real purpose is not to offer close readings or formal analyses of scenes or characters. Rather, it is to provide us with a multilayered, interdisciplinary account not only of Hardy, his "self-anthropologizing text," and several critical, contemporary contexts but also of Hardy's readers, for their shared understanding of the Bible caused their response to a novel urging its audience to "honor and identify with" its eroticized, sacrificial victim to be different from our own. Gallagher accomplishes her goals impressively, the result being a "thick description" of a novelist, a text, and an era "at cross-purposes with itself."

Ross C Murfin

THE NEW HISTORICISM: A SELECTED BIBLIOGRAPHY

The New Historicism: Further Reading

Brantlinger, Patrick. "Cultural Studies vs. the New Historicism." *English Studies/Cultural Studies: Institutionalizing Dissent.* Ed. Isaiah Smithson and Nancy Ruff. Urbana: U of Illinois P, 1994. 43–58.

Cox, Jeffrey N., and Larry J. Reynolds, eds. *New Historical Literary Study.* Princeton: Princeton UP, 1993.

Dimock, Wai-Chee. "Feminism, New Historicism, and the Reader." *American Literature* 63 (1991): 601–22.

Howard, Jean. "The New Historicism in Renaissance Studies." *English Literary Renaissance* 16 (1986): 13–43.

Lindenberger, Herbert. *The History in Literature: On Value, Genre, Institutions.* New York: Columbia UP, 1990.

———. "Toward a New History in Literary Study." *Profession: Selected Articles from the Bulletins of the Association of Departments of English and the Association of the Departments of Foreign Languages.* New York: MLA, 1984. 16–23.

Liu, Alan. "The Power of Formalism: The New Historicism." *English Literary History* 56 (1989): 721–71.

McGann, Jerome. *The Beauty of Inflections: Literary Investigations in Historical Method and Theory.* Oxford: Clarendon–Oxford UP, 1985.

———. *Historical Studies and Literary Criticism.* Madison: U of Wisconsin P, 1985. See especially the introduction and the essays in the following sections: "Historical Methods and Literary Interpretations" and "Biographical Contexts and the Critical Object."

Montrose, Louis Adrian. "Renaissance Literary Studies and the Subject of History." *English Literary Renaissance* 16 (1986): 5–12.

Morris, Wesley. *Toward a New Historicism.* Princeton: Princeton UP, 1972.

New Literary History 21 (1990). "History and . . ." (special issue). See especially the essays by Carolyn Porter, Rena Fraden, Clifford Geertz, and Renato Rosaldo.

Representations. This quarterly journal, printed by the University of California Press, regularly publishes new historicist studies and cultural criticism.

Thomas, Brook. "The Historical Necessity for — and Difficulties with — New Historical Analysis in Introductory Courses." *College English* 49 (1987): 509–22.

———. *The New Historicism and Other Old-Fashioned Topics.* Princeton: Princeton UP, 1991.

———. "The New Literary Historicism." *A Companion to American Thought.* Ed. Richard Wightman Fox and James T. Klappenberg. New York: Basil Blackwell, 1995.

———. "Walter Benn Michaels and the New Historicism: Where's the Difference?" *Boundary 2* 18 (1991): 118–59.

Veeser, H. Aram, ed. *The New Historicism.* New York: Routledge, 1989. See especially Veeser's introduction, Louis Montrose's "Professing the Renaissance," Catherine Gallagher's "Marxism and the New Historicism," and Frank Lentricchia's "Foucault's Legacy: A New Historicism?"

Wayne, Don E. "Power, Politics and the Shakespearean Text: Recent Criticism in England and the United States." *Shakespeare Reproduced: The Text in History and Ideology.* Ed. Jean Howard and Marion O'Connor. New York: Methuen, 1987. 47–67.

Winn, James A. "An Old Historian Looks at the New Historicism." *Comparative Studies in Society and History* 35 (1993): 859–70.

The New Historicism: Influential Examples

The new historicism has taken its present form less through the elaboration of basic theoretical postulates and more through certain influential examples. The works listed represent some of the most important contributions guiding research in this area.

Bercovitch, Sacvan. *The Rites of Assent: Transformations in the Symbolic Construction of America.* New York: Routledge, 1993.

Brown, Gillian. *Domestic Individualism: Imagining Self in Nineteenth-Century America.* Berkeley: U of California P, 1990.

Dollimore, Jonathan. *Radical Tragedy: Religion, Ideology and Power in the Drama of Shakespeare and His Contemporaries.* Brighton, Eng.: Harvester, 1984.

Dollimore, Jonathan, and Alan Sinfield, eds. *Political Shakespeare: New Essays in Cultural Materialism.* Manchester, Eng.: Manchester UP, 1985. This volume occupies the borderline between new historicist and cultural criticism. See especially the essays by Dollimore, Greenblatt, and Tennenhouse.

Gallagher, Catherine. *The Industrial Reformation of English Fiction.* Chicago: U of Chicago P, 1985.

Goldberg, Jonathan. *James I and the Politics of Literature.* Baltimore: Johns Hopkins UP, 1983.

Greenblatt, Stephen J. *Learning to Curse: Essays in Early Modern Culture.* New York: Routledge, 1990.

———. *Marvelous Possessions: The Wonder of the New World.* Chicago: U of Chicago P, 1991.

———. *Renaissance Self-Fashioning from More to Shakespeare.* Chicago: U of Chicago P, 1980. See chapter 1 and the chapter on *Othello* titled "The Improvisation of Power."

———. *Shakespearean Negotiations: The Circulation of Social Energy in Renaissance England.* Berkeley: U of California P, 1988. See especially "The Circulation of Social Energy" and "Invisible Bullets."

Liu, Alan. *Wordsworth, the Sense of History.* Stanford: Stanford UP, 1989.

Marcus, Leah. *Puzzling Shakespeare: Local Reading and Its Discontents.* Berkeley: U of California P, 1988.

McGann, Jerome. *The Romantic Ideology.* Chicago: U of Chicago P, 1983.

Michaels, Walter Benn. *The Gold Standard and the Logic of Naturalism: American Literature at the Turn of the Century.* Berkeley: U of California P, 1987.

Montrose, Louis Adrian. "'Shaping Fantasies': Figurations of Gender and Power in Elizabethan Culture." *Representations* 2 (1983): 61–94. One of the most influential early new historicist essays.

Mullaney, Steven. *The Place of the Stage: License, Play, and Power in Renaissance England.* Chicago: U of Chicago P, 1987.

Orgel, Stephen. *The Illusion of Power: Political Theater in the English Renaissance.* Berkeley: U of California P, 1975.

Sinfield, Alan. *Literature, Politics, and Culture in Postwar Britain.* Berkeley: U of California P, 1989.

Tennenhouse, Leonard. *Power on Display: The Politics of Shakespeare's Genres.* New York: Methuen, 1986.

Foucault and His Influence

As I point out in the introduction to the new historicism, some new historicists would question the "privileging" of Foucault implicit in this section heading ("Foucault and His Influence") and the following one ("Other Writers and Works"). They might cite the greater importance of one of those other writers or point out that to cite a central influence or a definitive cause runs against the very spirit of the movement.

Dreyfus, Hubert L., and Paul Rabinow. *Michel Foucault: Beyond Structuralism and Hermeneutics.* Chicago: U of Chicago P, 1983.

Foucault, Michel. *The Archaeology of Knowledge.* Trans. A. M. Sheridan Smith. New York: Harper, 1972.

———. *Discipline and Punish: The Birth of the Prison.* 1975. Trans. Alan Sheridan. New York: Pantheon, 1978.

———. *The History of Sexuality.* Trans. Robert Hurley. Vol. 1. New York: Pantheon, 1978.

———. *Language, Counter-Memory, Practice.* Ed. Donald F. Bouchard. Trans. Donald F. Bouchard and Sherry Simon. Ithaca: Cornell UP, 1977.

———. *The Order of Things: An Archaeology of the Human Sciences.* New York: Vintage, 1973.

———. *Politics, Philosophy, Culture.* Ed. Lawrence D. Kritzman. Trans. Alan Sheridan et al. New York: Routledge, 1988.

———. *Power/Knowledge.* Ed. Colin Gordon. Trans. Colin Gordon et al. New York: Pantheon, 1980.

———. *Technologies of the Self.* Ed. Luther H. Martin, Huck Gutman, and Patrick H. Hutton. Amherst: U of Massachusetts P, 1988.

Sheridan, Alan. *Michel Foucault: The Will to Truth.* New York: Tavistock, 1980.

Smart, Barry. *Michel Foucault.* New York: Ellis Horwood and Tavistock, 1985.

Other Writers and Works of Interest to New Historicist Critics

Bakhtin, M. M. *The Dialogic Imagination: Four Essays.* Ed. Michael Holquist. Trans. Caryl Emerson. Austin: U of Texas P, 1981. Bakhtin wrote many influential studies on subjects as varied as Dostoyevsky, Rabelais, and formalist criticism. But this book, in part due to Holquist's helpful introduction, is probably the best place to begin reading Bakhtin.

Benjamin, Walter. "The Work of Art in the Age of Mechanical Reproduction." 1936. *Illuminations.* Ed. Hannah Arendt. Trans. Harry Zohn. New York: Harcourt, 1968.

Fried, Michael. *Absorption and Theatricality: Painting and Beholder in the Works of Diderot.* Berkeley: U of California P, 1980.

Geertz, Clifford. *The Interpretation of Cultures.* New York: Basic, 1973.

———. *Negara: The Theatre State in Nineteenth-Century Bali.* Princeton: Princeton UP, 1980.

Goffman, Erving. *Frame Analysis.* New York: Harper, 1974.

Jameson, Fredric. *The Political Unconscious.* Ithaca: Cornell UP, 1981.

Koselleck, Reinhart. *Futures Past.* Trans. Keith Tribe. Cambridge: MIT P, 1985.

Said, Edward. *Orientalism.* New York: Columbia UP, 1978.

Turner, Victor. *The Ritual Process: Structure and Anti-Structure.* Chicago: Aldine, 1969.

Young, Robert. *White Mythologies: Writing History and the West.* New York: Routledge, 1990.

New Historicist Criticism of *Tess*

Kucich, John. "Moral Authority in the Late Novels: The Gendering of Art." *The Sense of Sex: Feminist Perspectives on Hardy.* Ed. Margaret R. Higonnet. Urbana: U of Illinois P, 1993. 221–41.

Nunokawa, Jeff. "*Tess,* Tourism, and the Spectacle of the Woman." *Rewriting the Victorians: Theory, History, and the Politics of Gender.* Ed. Linda M. Shires. New York: Routledge, 1992.

A NEW HISTORICIST PERSPECTIVE

CATHERINE GALLAGHER

Tess of the d'Urbervilles: Hardy's Anthropology of the Novel

In the 1880s, a few otherwise inoffensive Oxbridge dons were busy sexing the archē.[1] The process that was to culminate in such modernist milestones as Sigmund Freud's *Totem and Taboo*, Virginia Woolf's *Mrs. Dalloway* (1925), T. S. Eliot's *The Waste Land* (1922), and James Joyce's *Ulysses* (1922) was then a fairly modest debate between comparative mythologists. From 1860 to 1880, the philologist Max Müller had dominated the study of prehistorical European civilization, promulgating the idea that the shadowy tribal Aryans were the originators of Western myths. Greek culture, he claimed, had its

[1]By "archē" Gallagher means the beginning (*arkhē* in Greek) of culture. "Sexing the archē" means finding an origin that is sexual in character.

roots in Indic ancestors, especially in solar myths, behind which could be discerned the worship of a transcendent power that manifests itself in nature. The mythopoeic age, Müller thought, was one in which the concept of a spiritual divinity was extant but was betrayed by the overly concrete and metaphoric nature of primitive language. Mythic language, he claimed, defeated an impulse toward pure spirit, and the sun, to Müller a potential emblem of an immaterial god, was weighted down with personification. "Words were heavy and unwieldy," Müller wrote.

> They said more than they ought to say. . . . Where we speak of the sun following the dawn, the ancient poets could only speak and think of the Sun loving and embracing the Dawn. Our sunrise was to them the Night giving birth to a beautiful child; and in the Spring they really saw the Sun or the Sky embracing the earth with a warm embrace, and showering treasures into the lap of nature (qtd. in Ackerman 27–28).

Müller imagined an earlier disembodied, prelinguistic idea trying to escape from inside the sensuousness of both classical myths and their Indic originals. One cannot deny that Müller dwelt lovingly on the sensual, indeed — as in the above examples — on the explicitly sexual metaphors of the myths, but he nevertheless held that these were merely the linguistic trappings of transcendent spiritual longings.

By 1889, when William Robertson Smith published his *Lectures on the Religion of the Semites,* J. G. Frazer finished the first version of *The Golden Bough,* and Thomas Hardy was revising *Tess of the d'Urbervilles,* most of Müller's terms had been reversed. The earth, not the sun, seemed the center of the prehistoric universe; myths were no longer thought to be personifications of prior ideas, but were instead viewed as sublimations of ritual practices; and those ritual practices were aimed not at transcendent spirit, but at something far more mundane: something called "fertility." In the writings of Robertson Smith and Frazer, the myths that spoke incessantly of breeding did not, as Müller had believed, "say more than they ought" but instead provided the key to the fertility rites that were their true originals.

Robertson Smith and Frazer didn't sex the archē all by themselves. They had quite a bit of help from outside the discipline of philology, especially from Andrew Lang and Edward Burnett Tylor, whom we now think of as the first English anthropologists. I will indicate briefly what Lang and Tylor contributed to the project I am describing. They assimilated comparative mythology to evolutionary social science. That is, they posited a uniform and universal pattern of human cultural development, and then argued that the contemporary world provided examples of societies at various stages of the progress from savagery to civilization. This claim allowed them to draw evidence about prehistoric peoples from contemporary folklore and from the reports of travelers to so-called primitive societies. They littered their own society, too, with shards of the archaic, for they adapted the evolutionary doctrine of "survivals" to fit their cultural progressivist model. By "survivals" they meant objects, attitudes, or practices that had been preserved from one stage of development to another, in which they were no longer functional, through mere cultural conservatism. Hence, every degree of modern civilization contains remnants of the archaic. Briefly, comparative mythology as a branch of anthropology became less dependent on texts, less limited to language groups, and more apt to look for the archaic in the contemporary: in nineteenth-century societies designated "primitive," in European folkways, and even in literary texts.

When the philologists Robertson Smith and Frazer began writing, the anthropological evolutionary movement was in full force. Robertson Smith, a Semiticist, and Frazer, a classicist, not only collaborated but also drew on a vast reservoir of travelers' reports and folklorists' investigations. Frazer, especially, tapped into a sea of amateur Victorian descriptions of the archaic, both at home and abroad. Hence, to read him is not to read simply an individual thinker but to survey the deeps of Victorian primitivistic fantasies. The category that organizes and explains this material is, as I said earlier, "fertility," and by virtue of this category comparative anthropology took its place, demurely, off to the side of the more ostentatiously sexual sciences of the period.

Overflowing with recondite evidence, mired in endless and not always relevant detail, and seemingly obsessed with vegetables, *The Golden Bough* was not greeted as a bold and scandalous book, but readers found there an argument putting human sexuality at the origin of culture. This was an enormous innovation. To claim that culture began not in intimations of immortality, nor in narrative explanations of the mysterious movements of heavenly bodies, but rather in *rites of fertility* was to posit a startlingly ignominious lineage. These rites, according to Frazer, were pre-ideational. They existed long before explanatory myths, mere second-order intellectual elaborations, appeared. The rituals were closely bound up with daily life, and through them primitive man "tried to get his fields, his flocks, his women to bear."[2]

Indeed, even before he had fields and flocks (but not women), primitive man tried to fertilize the world by imitating the life-spirit of trees, enacting a ritual cycle of violent death, burial, and rebirth, not only to keep the vegetation alive but also to renew the potency of the human group. The dying and reviving god, the central figure of *The Golden Bough,* was both an archetypical representation of the natural cycle and an attempt to control it: first, by the literal or simulated coupling of representatives of the gods in the rituals; second, by slaying the figure representing divinity before he or she grew old and feeble, thereby preserving his or her potency by transferring it to a younger body; and third, often in the interim between death and rebirth, through the group's orgiastic behavior. Hence, Frazer speculates, eroticism and sacrifice were probably inseparable in the rites of the vegetation gods — such as Baal, Adonis, Osiris, Dionysius, Artemis, Ceres, and Persephone — and the sexual and sacred were similarly linked in the rites of the "corn spirits" and the "sacrament of first fruits." Dubbed the Covent Garden School of anthropology, Frazer and his followers seemed more risible than outrageous to some Victorians, but certainly we should remind ourselves that vegetables were not the only things sold at Covent Garden, which was a notorious haunt of prostitutes.

I do not, however, want to give the impression that *The Golden Bough* was merely a channel for the expression of late-Victorian sexual fantasies, for the book's emphasis on sexuality proceeds from its deepest intellectual commitments. *The Golden Bough,* I believe, demonstrates that the political economists' Malthusian preoccupation — that is, the preoccupation with human reproduction in relation to the food supply — had taken over the study not only of sexual and economic behavior but also of religion and artistic expression by the 1880s. Darwin, Comte, and Spencer (the three nineteenth-century thinkers to whom Hardy was most indebted) had all implied that the highest expressions of human intellectual ambition evolved out of our basic biological dilemmas. And at the end of the eighteenth century, Malthus had articulated the most fundamental quandary of all: if we indulge our sexual passions, we will either overpopulate and starve or be forced

[2]Much of the description of the background to Frazer's work is taken from Ackerman, 1–45.

into "vicious" practices (abortion, birth control, infanticide) to limit our numbers; if we don't indulge them, we'll be miserable. In Frazer's descriptions, primitive religions always implore the gods to increase humans and their food supply, so to speak, *proportionally*. To Malthus, such proportional increase, unless accomplished through misery or vice, was an unattainable goal. We might think of Frazer's primitive man as a creature trying to overcome the Malthusian dilemma through sympathetic magic. For the fornication that brings overpopulation, primitive rituals, in Frazer's account, substituted a magical sexuality that supposedly augmented the food supply. To avoid the dearth and starvation that should follow upon unrestrained sexual activity, primitive religions ritually killed an individual who represented both the human group and its food supply, ensuring the rebirth of both.

In other words, the rituals Frazer describes might be said both symbolically to express the Malthusian version of things and magically to invert it. Primitive people did not think *like* Malthusians, but they did think *about* the same things. However ineffectual their solutions, what is striking about Frazer's primitive religions is that they so thoroughly inhabit the Malthusian predicament. As the reviewer for the *Edinburgh Review* put it, in Frazer's world, "even the gods are only respected as agencies for the control of the blind natural forces against which man is constantly striving" ("Review" 552). By turning every god into a fertility god, by finding a fertility ritual at the core of every myth, Frazer creates a primitive human being who is as obsessed with fecundity as any nineteenth-century social scientist who had read Malthus and Spencer. Frazer's primitive is, to paraphrase E. B. Tylor, a savage political economist and therefore immersed in the topic of sexuality.[3]

When I say that Frazer's sources were full of primitivist sexual fantasies, therefore, I am not suggesting that these were the products of repressed Victorian libidos. Sexing the archē was a profoundly disciplined endeavor, a composite of economic and evolutionary thought with comparative religion, philological classicism, and the Higher Criticism of the Bible, itself a legacy of German Romanticism. I want to stress the disciplines Frazer drew on because they are the same disciplines that provided the furniture of Hardy's mind, and the following argument relies on certain congruences as well as certain divergences between Frazer's enterprise and Hardy's. Although Hardy read Frazer

[3]John B. Vickery discusses Frazer's relation to Utilitarian thinkers in general and mentions Malthus in particular (7–16).

while he was working on *Tess of the d'Urbervilles* and that reading led to some significant revisions, I will not be treating *The Golden Bough* as the source of Hardy's anthropological imagination. Rather, I will read Frazer, as well as Robertson Smith and Walter Pater, as writers whose works parallel, rather than precede, *Tess*.

We first see Tess Durbeyfield in a May-Day procession, which the learned narrator calls a "Cerealia"[4], and we last see her stretched out on what Angel describes as the sacrificial altar of Stonehenge. Between these initial and ultimate images, dozens of allusions, metaphors, descriptions, dialogues, interpolated stories, and explicit narratorial comments identify Tess as a sacrificial victim set apart by virtue of her desirability and potential fecundity. That *Tess of the d'Urbervilles* fully participates in the primitivizing of the ancient and the sexualizing of the primitive is, I believe, easy to demonstrate. I say this despite the fact that twentieth-century critics have uniformly failed to notice that *Tess*'s classical and biblical allusions have anything to do with its primitivism. Some have even had the temerity to suggest that Hardy used allusions to ancient texts, especially the classics, to upgrade the pedigree of his story.[5] In a book obsessed with the ironies of pedigree, however, no such cheap recourses to establishing "literary" lineage can be taken at face value. We cannot really credit a Hardy who goes about the literary neighborhood claiming kin with more august relations, as if he were an intellectual version of Joan Durbeyfield. Such a view is, moreover, quite inattentive to the actual uses of ancient prototypes in this novel. The narrator of *Tess,* far from decking his story in learned allusions as a form of social climbing, relentlessly strips decorum from the classics and shakes the venerable cloak of monotheism off of the Hebrew Bible. He is intent on making us see that our literary heritage, like Tess's aristocratic ancestor Sir Pagan d'Urberville, is full of savagery. If we mistake these exposures for garden-variety literary allusions, we diminish the primitive to the merely prim.

The novel itself, indeed, mockingly comments on the myopia of those who idealize and domesticate ancient culture by giving us a

[4]J. T. Laird argues that the substitution of the word "Cerealia" for the word "Vestal" (which appears in an earlier draft of the novel) was probably inspired by Hardy's reading of *The Golden Bough* in 1891. He also points out that "Cerealia" is in the spirit of Frazer because it emphasizes that Tess is celebrating a fertility ritual. Frazer's book "may well have opened Hardy's eyes to or reminded him of" the primitive worship of Diana, not as a goddess of virginity, but as a goddess of fertility (Laird 425–28). On Hardy's use of solar myths, see J. B. Bullen.

[5]See, for example, Millgate, 131 and passim.

would-be hero, Angel Clare, whose devotion to J. J. Winckelman's version of the formal perfection, poise, and luminosity of Greek art misleads him into thinking that the pagan world excluded the bloody, agonistic tumult of the primitive. The text merges Angel's misunderstanding of the ancients with his misprision of Tess herself. Through his veneration of a conventionally *innocent,* nonviolent, and Hellenic paganism, he perceives the archetypal dimensions of Tess but nevertheless imagines that she could be virginal and harmless. In the hazy light of dawn, the narrator tells us,

> She was no longer [in Clare's eyes] the milkmaid, but a visionary essence of woman — a whole sex condensed into one typical form. He called her Artemis, Demeter, and other fanciful names half teasingly, which she did not like because she did not understand them.
>
> 'Call me Tess,' she would say askance; and he did. (146)

Annotators are typically as blind to the passage's irony as Angel himself, blandly asserting that Artemis was the Greek goddess of hunting and chastity. This may be a fair representation of Angel's understanding, but it entirely ignores the resonances that "Artemis" had taken on by the late 1880s. Anthropologizers of the classics had thoroughly blasted Artemis's modesty.

Walter Pater, for example, represented Artemis's Roman equivalent, Diana, not as a symbol of maidenly control, but as an embodiment of human kinship with — and therefore competitive antagonism against — wild animals. She could be kind, but her rites were frequently bloody. In the classical world, Pater tells us, she was increasingly worshipped "as a Deity of Slaughter — the Taurian goddess who demands the sacrifice" of strangers, "the cruel, moonstruck, huntress, who brings . . . sudden death" (136). The blood sports and sadistic executions of the Roman decadence, Pater argues, were late instances of the rites of Artemis.

In a later edition of *The Golden Bough,* Frazer synthesizes the views of his time by depicting an Artemis, originally goddess of the woodlands, who eventually "developed into a personification of the teeming life of nature, both animal and vegetable" (162). In short, like all other deities in *The Golden Bough,* Artemis was a fertility goddess. Since a fertility goddess must herself be fertile, Frazer reasons, a human embodiment of Artemis probably ritually mated every year with a representative of Virbius, the King of the Wood at

Nemi.[6] So much for her virginity. Her sexuality, moreover, was a prelude to sacrifice, for the king of the wood had to be ritually slaughtered, and, according to Frazer, "the great goddess Artemis herself appears to have been annually hanged in effigy in her sacred grove of Condylea among the Arcadian hills, and there accordingly she went by the name of the Hanged One."[7] If you are beginning to recognize in these rituals the main events of Tess Durbeyfield's destiny — sex in the primeval forest, murder by stabbing of the priest-husband, and the execution of the goddess herself — I hope you will also be willing to agree with me that the Artemis whose rites are exacted in this novel is a lurid, anthropologized goddess bearing little resemblance to the fastidious virgin of Angel Clare's anemic imagination.

Hardy, then, was one of a group of authors who undertook in those years to primitivize the ancient and sexualize the primitive. If Hardy was not alone in sexualizing the archē, he may nevertheless have been the first to explore the narrative implications of this activity. As a figure, Tess not only resonates against a background of archaic prototypes but also is imagined to contain organic memory traces of ritual behavior antedating all stories. In other words, drawing on contemporary theories of organic memory, Hardy locates the sexualized archē not only in the culture but also in the individual.[8] By installing a substratum of primeval sexual and aggressive urges beneath the superstructure of individual personality, Hardy at first seems just to be laying a different foundation for narrative. I am about to argue, though, that the lost rituals and their partial survival as ur-memories[9] and "instincts" in Tess and other characters are made to stand aloof from the plot, not just from this specific plot, but from plots in general. Sexing the archē in *Tess* leads to dissociations of event from plot and of plot from narrative. After discussing these dissociations, I will end by

[6]Frazer's description of the relation between Virbius and Diana as newer (male) and older (female) vegetation deities has an ironic parallel in Alec's appropriation of Tess's ancient lineage. Here Frazer describes the mating of the deities in the sacred grove as a continuity of power from old to new: "On the present hypothesis [Virbius] was the newer tree-spirit, whose relation to the old tree-spirit (Diana) was explained by representing him as her favourite or lover" (362).

[7]This particular quotation is from the third edition of *The Golden Bough* (see Frazer 413), but the first edition contains numerous instances of the mock executions of female fertility symbols (see Frazer 213–77).

[8]Laura Otis argues that Hardy uses the idea of organic memory in *Tess* even though his narrator never commits himself to the theory (158–72).

[9]The prefix "ur," taken from German, suggests something originary or primitive.

arguing not only that *Tess*'s formal disconnections register the presence of comparative anthropology *in* the novel but also that they point us toward an anthropology *of* the novel: in the acts of reading and writing novels, they imply, archaic sacrificial urges survive.

As I have already argued, those who sexed the archē concentrated on ritual action and interpreted the mythic stories of ancient religions as mere second-order explanations. We might say, then, that emphasizing isolated, repetitive, agonistic moments at the expense of an explanatory plot is a structural feature of this discourse. Hardy's narrative technique is a variation on this feature; it does not deemphasize the plot, the series of represented actions linked in a causal chain; rather, it questions the plot's explanatory adequacy by covering certain moments with multiple explanations or failed explanations that conjure ritual possibilities without naming them. These moments in *Tess* — such as the incidents from the Artemis rituals that I identified earlier — are, moreover, barely narrated, and the implication is that they are barely narratable. They acquire their power from the fact that they seem to exist at the vanishing point of representation, as if they were naturally occult. The narrator does not explicate the archetypal import of these events, as Frazer or Robertson Smith would; rather, he indicates the *hiddenness* of the ritual necessity, exploiting the *cache* of the primitive. Consider, for example, the non-narration of Tess's defloration:

> Darkness and silence ruled everywhere around. Above them rose the primeval yews and oaks of The Chase, in which were poised gentle roosting birds in their last nap; and about them stole the hopping rabbits and hares. But, might some say, where was Tess's guardian angel? where was the providence of her simple faith? Perhaps, like that other god of whom the ironical Tishbite spoke, he was talking, or he was pursuing, or he was in a journey, or he was sleeping and not to be awaked.
>
> Why it was that upon this beautiful feminine tissue, sensitive as gossamer, and practically blank as snow as yet, there should have been traced such a coarse pattern as it was doomed to receive; why so often the coarse appropriates the finer thus . . . , many thousand years of analytical philosophy have failed to explain to our sense of order. One may, indeed, admit the possibility of a retribution lurking in the present catastrophe. Doubtless some of Tess d'Urberville's mailed ancestors rollicking home from a fray had dealt the same measure even more ruthlessly towards peasant girls at their time. But though to visit the sins of the fathers upon the children may be a morality good enough for divinities, it is

scorned by average human nature; and it therefore does not mend the matter.

As Tess's own people down in those retreats are never tired of saying among each other in their fatalistic way: 'It was to be.' (94–95)

Perhaps the first thing we notice in coming to this passage from the preceding paragraphs is an abrupt shift in narrative point of view. In the earlier paragraphs, focalized through Alec d'Urberville, the scene became less and less visible as a dense fog shrouded the forest, Tess herself appearing merely a "pale nebulousness" (94) at Alec's feet, and the sight of her face requiring cheek-to-cheek proximity. But we begin these paragraphs with preternaturally sharp vision, despite the "darkness" that introduces them. Because we can see animals in the tops of trees and on the forest floor, we know we inhabit the point of view of no character. For a prolonged moment, we have the unimpeded vision of gods, but we choose, it seems, to avert our gaze from Tess and Alec. Their coitus is occurring tacitly. It would seem that this tacitness would be sufficient to meet Victorian demands for propriety, but in the middle of this first paragraph, a screen of biblical allusion comes sliding across the scene. The allusion follows the question "Where was Tess's guardian angel?", which recalls earlier incidents of the plot — we've been introduced to a character named Angel who disappeared — and foreshadows later ones. But this little flash of plot is soon blotted out by an emphatic intertextuality, for the biblical allusion that ends the paragraph is not blended into Hardy's prose. We find ourselves confronted with the uncolloquial, archaic, and noneuphonius language of 1 Kings 18 in the King James version: "Tishbite" (why not the more familiar "Elijah"?), "in a journey" instead of "on a journey." This is not an instance of the novel's language resonating, as it so often does, with biblical overtones. The allusion, rather, insists on the difficult particularity of a certain biblical passage, cuing the reader to look beneath it, as it were, for a level of explanation that is not in the story we are reading.

Let's imagine what a nineteenth-century reader, familiar with the allusion and used to engaging in biblical hermeneutics, might have made of this passage on reflection. She would probably have been surprised to find not only Tess's "angel" but also the "providence" of the heroine's simple faith unexpectedly likened here to the pagan god Baal, object of Elijah the Tishbite's scorn. She would also have recognized that the narrator takes up Elijah's tone of mockery, and she might have felt some tension between the suddenly "ironical" tone and the pathos of Tess's situation. She could not have failed to notice that the passage is flagrantly irreligious: Christian faith in benevolent providence, it explicitly says, is as ill-founded as that of Baal's priests, for at times of crisis all deities tend to abscond. Hence, by aligning himself with Elijah, Jehovah's faithful prophet, the skeptical narrator exposes Christian providentialism as just another untenable superstition.

Our nineteenth-century reader would have understood all of this and would also have known that the scene from which the sentence is taken in 1 Kings is one of the sacrifice; indeed, it is a contest between sacrifices: the failed sacrifice to Baal and Elijah's successful sacrifice to Jehovah, both imploring rain to fertilize the earth. Baal's priests cut themselves in the course of their sacrifice, letting their own blood flow as well as that of the sacrificial animals. Elijah cuts only the animal, implying the superior humanity of the Israelites' religion. In *Tess,* however, the narrator introduces the allusion to sacrifice in such a way as to imply that Tess's defloration could be located in either the pagan or the Hebrew tradition: it may be the bloodletting demanded of Baal's devotees; or it may be an act of revenge. Because Tess's guardian Baal has absconded, she is left to the tender mercies of the retributive god of the Israelites, who allows, we are reminded in the next paragraph, "the sins of the fathers [to be visited] upon the children." Thus, as other critics have noted, the narrator inverts the usual reading of 1 Kings. Baal definitely seems the kinder god here, and the putatively higher morality of biblical monotheism is only a crueler exaction of blood; crueler because it turns sacrifice into punishment. What carries over from ancient Semitic religion into monotheism, these allusions indicate, is not some common *story,* some comprehensible context for the event, but merely the imperative of sacrifice. They further imply, though, that if sacrifice is the common bedrock of humanity, its humane accomplishment and sympathetic understanding may have declined since pagan times.

Let me sum up what I have so far argued about this passage: first, that it is set off from the plot by an abrupt shift in point of view, removing us from the characters' experience; second, that another abrupt shift obscures the scene altogether and replaces it with an exercise in biblical hermeneutics, which the dutiful nineteenth-century reader undertakes.[10] In that exercise our reader moves further from the

[10]J. Hillis Miller makes several of these points in his reading of the passage, noting especially the ironic inversion of biblical values and the hint that Tess may be a sacrificial victim (129–35).

immediate plot and into speculations about the nature and necessity of blood sacrifice in the ancient world. Third, those speculations might conclude that Tess's defloration is not only an instance of a primitive prototype but also best understood in terms of its oldest, pagan significance. Tess's sacrifice, in other words, can be seen as radically misunderstood by the world she inhabits and hence at odds with the plot that organizes it.

This much a reflective nineteenth-century reader might have been able to glean from a fairly common understanding of the Bible. I would now like to suggest that some readers, noting the way the biblical passage sticks out from Hardy's prose like the top of an ancient burial mound that seems to say "dig here," would have been drawn to what lay even further beneath the biblical language. That is, they would have moved on from the hermeneutic exercise to the anthropologizing of the Bible encouraged by the German Higher Criticism. What is hidden beneath the Bible is the world explored by Hardy's fellow primitivizers, and what they have to say about Baal and his rites only increases the felt tension between the pagan ritual moment and its organization into a biblical plot of retribution. You will probably not be surprised to hear that Frazer and Robertson Smith tell us that Baal was the name applied to numerous local fertility deities. Indeed, Frazer sees them as versions of Adonis and therefore also as manifestations of the same reproductive processes worshipped in the form of Artemis. "Baal," we also learn, is the word for "husband" in several Semitic languages, he who fertilizes or "tills" his wife (Smith 109).

Even more apposite lore about Baal, however, comes from Robertson Smith's account of the same ritual described in 1 Kings. When Elijah mocks the priests of Baal, they are engaged in a blood sacrifice, cutting, as I have already pointed out, their own arms. This sacrifice, according to Robertson Smith, has been misunderstood as a self-inflicted punishment, a form of atonement. In fact, he claims, the shedding of blood in this way is an act of communion with, rather than subjection to, the fertility god. Among other forms of nonfatal blood sacrifice that create bonds of identification between the bleeder and the deity, Robertson Smith (329) mentions two that are particularly relevant to the Hardy passage: first, the sacrifice of the maidenhead (demanded by some cults of Adonis) and second, tattooing, a practice suggested by the opening image of the second paragraph, in which a pattern is traced on Tess's "beautiful feminine tissue."

In the pagan context that unfurls in this lore as the obscured background to Elijah's mean-spirited mockery, Tess's agon in the primeval grove would have been an ennobling initiation, a rite of renewal and marriage to the godhead. But under the monotheistic regime initiated by the Hebrews and made even more pernicious by a Christianity that insists the ultimate sacrifice — Christ's — has already been made, Tess's sacrificial tattoo can only become a stain of blood on her flimsy, white frock, the coarse pattern of a plot that will be increasingly obsessed with sin and punishment.

The narrator, I should add, uses other devices as well to make this event resist the plot, the story of Tess the individual. For example, the reference to Tess's "mailed ancestors" stretches the moment into a repeated series of forcible deflowering and then later retracts it into the most minimal formulation of fatedness — "It was to be." The necessity of the event is stressed, but it is explicitly not simply an exigency of this particular plot alone. For what might, in some other novel, seem the usual outcome of circumstances in which an unprincipled man finds himself alone in an isolated place with an innocent, sleeping girl, Hardy's narrator turns into an elaborate mystery bristling with unanswerable questions: "Where . . . Why . . . why . . . ?" I've been arguing that the biblical allusions invite us to desacralize scripture and search the occulted and sexualized primitive for the answers, and that those answers make it all the harder to fit the event neatly back into the plot.

If we recognize this distinction between the catastrophic events and the story that attempts to contain them, we can begin to understand why the narrator's tone swings from fatalistic acceptance to outraged indignation. The main actions of Tess's life, it is hinted, are rooted deep in archaic universals and cannot be altered. However, their organization into a plot of sin and punishment, of wrongdoing and retribution, that culminates in the abjection, rather than the honoring, of the sacrificial figure — this plot denies and perverts the potential archetypal significance of the events.

The story of retribution is not, to be sure, the only one the novel makes available. Indeed, plot becomes an explicit topic in the novel because different versions of the sequence of events are assigned to different consciousnesses. The country people, for example, observe the action through the fatalism and supernaturalism of the ballad, while Tess often thinks in terms of the spiritual progress or romance quest, with its emphasis on testing and proving one's fidelity. Aeschylean dramatic tragedy, which stresses the paradoxical identity of chance and fate, putting the linear plot under constant pressure, is obviously the narrator's choice. But this very interpretive multiplicity indicates the inadequacy of all the genres as well as the dissimilarities between the plots they generate. In other words, as J. Hillis Miller has noted, the plot in *Tess* is problematic not because events are underexplained but because they are multiply explained.[11]

This peculiar narrative technique in *Tess* produces, however, more than undecidability; it contributes to the sense of concealed realities achieving only momentary manifestations, of something occulted that will breach the surface and then disappear again no matter what conventions order the story. Consider, for example, another of the sacrificial catastrophes that I earlier associated with the rites of Artemis: the stabbing of Alec d'Urberville. Like Tess's deflowering, this second bloodletting is narratively obscured: this time, though, point of view is carefully controlled through the eyes of a stranger, the landlady who knows nothing of the plot. She tries to see Tess and Alec through the keyhole, but cannot really get, or give us, a comprehensive vantage point. The event is purposely hidden, and our first inkling of it recalls the image of a spot on a white fabric:

> [The landlady's] eyes glanced casually over the ceiling till they were arrested by a spot in the middle of its white surface which she had never noticed there before. It was about the size of a wafer when she first observed it, but it speedily grew as large as the palm of her hand, and then she could perceive that it was red. The oblong white ceiling, with this scarlet blot in the midst, had the appearance of a gigantic ace of hearts. (370)

The growth of the spot into a full heart implies some sort of "fulfillment," as the title of this section of the novel indicates; but what, exactly, is fulfilled, or completed here? There are several possibilities: the ballad expectation that the wronged woman will avenge herself; the Aeschylean revelation that chance and destiny are one, as the figure of the playing card implies; or the proof of Tess's love. The gigantic ace of hearts, we should note, also looks like an enormous valentine, a big red heart on a white background.

But the threads of plots are both gathered and obliterated in this passage. As the "wafer," an obvious allusion to the bloodless sacrifice of Christian communion, turns into a bloody heart, it implies that atavistic urges survive all new dispensations. As the blood from the pierced heart traces an image of itself on the ceiling, it converts

[11]For Miller, repetition is always at odds with narration, as iteration always both creates intelligibility and problematizes it (129–35). Late-nineteenth-century ritualists made a particular use of the idea of repetition that emphasized its antinarrative dimension.

murder into eros, revenge into caritas, the particular organic into the generally symbolic. As the heart, we learn in the next paragraph, continues to beat even while it bleeds — "The dead silence within was broken only by a regular beat. Drip, drip, drip." (370) — a ritual aura gathers about the scene of what is no longer just a crime. By the time we visualize the corpse, its individual identity has been dissolved. "The victim" (371), we're told, lies on his back, and there is no sign of a struggle, just a neat, slender puncture that goes straight to the heart. Questions of justice and motivation are at least temporarily lost in the unfathomable.

Hardy, I have been arguing, seeks not to excavate primitive sacrificial impulses in *Tess* but to activate them. In this aspiration, I would now like to argue, the novel implicitly anthropologizes itself. At this point, I will turn from an investigation of the tension between archetype and plot, the ritual moment and the story of Tess, to a different tension: that between the ritual impulse and the anthropological understanding of it. By the time Hardy wrote *Tess,* the idea that novels contain modern survivals of the bloody rites of the ancient world had already been articulated by Walter Pater in *Marius the Epicurean.* The human sacrifices of very early times, he explains, had later become the popular amusements of the Roman amphitheaters; and these amusements, in turn, were

> the novel-reading of that age — a current help provided for sluggish imaginations, in regard, for instance, to grisly accidents, such as might happen to one's self; but with every facility for comfortable inspection. . . . If the part of Marsyas was called for, there was a criminal condemned to lose his skin. It might be almost edifying to study minutely the expression of his face, while the assistants corded and pegged him to the bench, cunningly; the servant of the law waiting by, who, after one short cut with his knife, would slip the man's leg from his skin, as neatly as if it were a stocking . . . (137)

Pater's comparison of the novel with the Roman long shows and of both with earlier human sacrifices rests on the vicariousness of suffering in all three and on the representational nature of the victims. That is, the Romans did not turn out simply to see criminals executed; they wanted to see criminals executed in the guise of mythical persons, just as humans were earlier sacrificed, not as themselves but as representatives of gods. Simultaneously, though, the victim also represents the viewer, who can experience the suffering and still remain unhurt. In 1888, when he was beginning *Tess,* Hardy echoed the opinion that reading a novel is like watching someone being flayed and skinned. In novels like *Tess* that display the passions in a state of turmoil, he claimed, "the nerves and muscles of [the] figures . . . can be seen as in an *écorché*" (Hardy 124–25).

The implicit anthropological account of the novel that emerges in *Tess,* however, differs substantially from Pater's. For Pater, the novel's connection to human sacrifice implied its degeneracy, whereas the buried link in *Tess* seems to feed the genre's vitality even as it undermines its intelligibility. The difference is partly due to the fact that Pater imagined an ultimately indifferent reader, motivated by idle curiosity, whereas Hardy imagines a reader in love with the victim. Furthermore, whereas Pater discloses that the sacrificial victim is really a criminal, Hardy reverses this procedure in *Tess* and reveals that the putative criminal is really a victim. The anthropology of *Tess,* therefore, implies a universal need not only to sacrifice someone distinguished by virtue and beauty but also to honor and identify with the victim. The novel fulfills this need by denying the retributive logic that it also requires to bring about its final, unrepresented, transformation of Tess into The Hanged One in the last of the novel's arcane references to the rites of Artemis.

In these remaining pages, I cannot outline all of the problems we would encounter if we examined the novel's self-anthropologization closely. The most obvious is implied in Pater's association of condemned criminals and fictional characters; what links them is their shared expendability. The criminal, according to Pater, will die anyway, so he might as well be put to death in such a way as to achieve the efficacy of human sacrifice. Similarly Tess's life, never having been actual, is a very cheap price to pay for sacrificial satisfactions. Even if one were to insist that what is really expended in the novel is the life of the reader, both the reader's time and the concern she has lavished on a nonexistent fellow creature whose loss she must suffer in the end, such a formulation would apply to any novel, no matter how happy the outcome. If, as Robertson Smith tells us, the essential thing about the ancient sacrificial victim was its literal *embodiment* of the sacred life of the human group united to the godhead (Smith 361), then the substitution of a fictional character is obviously cheating.

To press this ontological objection, however, would be to dismiss out of hand what dozens of writers thought they were proving in the late nineteenth and early twentieth centuries: that, however muted and modified, sacrificial impulses had been preserved through the progressive sublimations that produced not only modern religion but also art. The logic of this claim seems to rest on the assumption that, since ritual sacrifice was always representational, the change from synecdochal to metaphoric representation was not fatal. To gain a sympathetic understanding of the primitivizing modernists, then, we must suppress the ontological problem for the time being.

In the case of *Tess,* however, another, related problem immediately emerges in its stead: Can a literary work both preserve the ritual nugget and suggest, using the anthropologists' comparative method, its own status as a modern "survival" of ritual practice? That is, even if we were willing to grant that tragic drama, for example, has been a survival of the rites of Dionysius and that it could have sacrificial efficacy for its audience, can we grant the endurance of those emotions in a work that self-consciously designates itself as a survival? Or, to put the question differently, what is the *affect* of this comparative method, this self-anthropologization of the novel?

We have noted throughout this analysis that the sacrificial is encrypted in *Tess,* that the narrator conjures it as the inaccessible, implying that its power survives by virtue of being buried. And yet the artifice of this concealment bespeaks its prior revelation, indeed, a conceptual understanding of how it works. And such an understanding, I would argue, constantly threatens to drain Tess's agon of its immediacy and power. Indeed, an important exchange between Tess and Angel calls attention to this very problem. Angel offers to teach Tess history, and she construes this as an invitation to contemplate, not the linear development of civilization, but the repetition of catastrophic events. Having correctly identified the dimension of time to which this novel consigns her, Tess refuses to engage in the comparative method herself: "'Because what's the use of learning that I am one of a long row only — finding out that there is set down in some old book somebody just like me, and to know that I shall only act her part; making me sad, that's all'" (142). And indeed, the novel is not content, cannot be content, to make Tess "sad, that's all." The impulses that make Tess a sacrificial heroine push beyond sadness to agony, and she dimly recognizes here that they would be stilled by the very comparative method that reveals their archetypal significance to us.

The novel, in other words, registers some uncertainty about its own anthropological technique when it points to a yawning gap between Tess's mentality, which is truly agonistic, and the mere "sadness" — or pessimism — produced by the historically minded paganizers of the late nineteenth century. When, for example, Angel glosses Tess's alarmed apprehension of her destiny, her closeness to death, as an expression of "feelings which might almost have been called those of the age — the *ache* of modernism" (140; emphasis added), he misreads her agon as a mere ache. Angel is partly misled by Tess's apparent inexperience; he cannot guess that she feels, as we soon learn, that, like Job, "'My soul chooseth strangling and death rather than my life'" (140). But even if he did know the story, the perception of its archetypal resonances (here echoing back through Bunyan) would depend on an anthropological method that the passage juxtaposes against the ritual emotions. To make the ritual intelligible as a heightened moment when the "supreme fact in nature" reveals itself to be "the eternal succession of birth and death, of verdure and decay, of reaping and sowing, of destruction for the purpose of reproduction" ("Review" 552) is to learn from it only what was already known.

Hence, *Tess* seems to be at cross-purposes with itself, striving, on the one hand, to perform a ritual and, on the other, to reveal the ritual's essence as nothing more than a particularly intense instant in a rather dismal reproductive cycle. In his travels, Angel briefly encounters a "stranger" who "had sojourned in many more lands and among many more peoples than Angel; to his cosmopolitan mind such deviations [as Tess's] from the social norm . . . were no more than are the irregularities of vale and mountain-chain to the whole terrestrial curve" (333). This comparative thinker is able to fold Tess's experience into the global round and convince Angel to go home to her. But the image of rounding out, of loosing the mountainous rocks in the regular curve of the earth, signals the loss of an encounter with the sacrificial outcropping itself, so forcefully figured in the novel's penultimate chapter as the sensation of coming abruptly upon Stonehenge in the dark:

> They had proceeded thus gropingly two or three miles further when on a sudden Clare became conscious of some vast erection close in his front, rising sheer from the grass. They had almost struck themselves against it. (379)

The universal archē, the novel seems to warn, can survive anything with the possible exception of the very comparative anthropological procedures that had recently discovered it.

WORKS CITED

Ackerman, Robert. *The Myth and Ritual School: J. G. Frazer and the Cambridge Ritualists.* New York: Garland, 1991.

Bullen, J. B. "Thomas Hardy and Mythology." *The Sun Is God: Painting, Literature, and Mythology in the Nineteenth Century.* Ed. J. B. Bullen. Oxford: Clarendon, 1989.

Frazer, J. G. *The Golden Bough: A Study in Magic and Religion.* Vol. I. Abr. ed. New York: Macmillan, 1960.

Hardy, Thomas. "The Profitable Reading of Fiction." *Thomas Hardy's Personal Writings: Prefaces, Literary Opinions, Reminiscences.* Ed. Harold Orel. Lawrence: U of Kansas P, 1966. 110–25.

Laird, J. T. "New Light on the Evolution of *Tess of the d'Urbervilles.*" *R. E. S., New Series* 31 (1980): 425–28.

Miller, J. Hillis. "Tess of the d'Urbervilles: Repetition as Immanent Design." *Fiction and Repetition: Seven English Novels.* Cambridge: Harvard UP, 1982. 116–46.

Millgate, Michael. *Thomas Hardy: His Career as a Novelist.* New York: Random, 1971.

Müller, Max. *Chips from a German Workshop.* Vol. II. New York: Scribner, 1869.

Otis, Laura. *Organic Memory: History and the Body in the Late Nineteenth and Early Twentieth Centuries.* Lincoln: U of Nebraska P, 1994.

Pater, Walter. *Marius the Epicurean: His Sensations and Ideas.* Ed. Ian Small. 2nd ed, 1885. New York: Oxford UP, 1986.

"Review of *The Golden Bough.*" *Edinburgh Review* 172 (1890): 552.

Smith, W. Robertson. *Lectures on the Religion of the Semites. First Series, The Fundamental Institutions.* London: Adam and Charles Black, 1901.

Vickery, John B. *The Literary Impact of the Golden Bough.* Princeton: Princeton UP, 1973.

Feminist and Gender Criticism and *Tess of the d'Urbervilles*

WHAT ARE FEMINIST AND GENDER CRITICISM?

Among the most exciting and influential developments in the field of literary studies, feminist and gender criticism participate in a broad philosophical discourse that extends far beyond literature, far beyond the arts in general. The critical *practices* of those who explore the representation of women and men in works by male or female, lesbian or gay writers inevitably grow out of and contribute to a larger and more generally applicable *theoretical* discussion of how gender and sexuality are constantly shaped by and shaping institutional structures and attitudes, artifacts, and behaviors.

Feminist criticism was accorded academic legitimacy in American universities "around 1981," Jane Gallop claims in her book *Around 1981: Academic Feminist Literary Theory* (1992). With Gallop's title and approximation in mind, Naomi Schor has since estimated that "around 1985, feminism began to give way to what has come to be called gender studies" (275). Some would argue that feminist criticism became academically legitimate well before 1981. Others would take issue with the notion that feminist criticism and women's studies have been giving way to gender criticism and gender studies, and with the either/or distinction that such a claim implies. Taken together, however, Gallop and Schor provide us with a useful fact — that of feminist criticism's historical precedence — and a chronological focus on the early to mid-1980s, a period during which the feminist approach was unquestionably influential and during which new interests emerged, not all of which were woman centered.

During the early 1980s, three discrete strains of feminist theory and practice — commonly categorized as French, North American, and British — seemed to be developing. French feminists tended to focus their attention on language. Drawing on the ideas of the psychoanalytic philosopher Jacques Lacan, they argued that language as we commonly think of it — as public discourse — is decidedly phallocentric, privileging what is valued by the patriarchal culture. They also spoke of the possibility of an alternative, feminine language and of *l'écriture féminine:* women's writing. Julia Kristeva, who is generally seen as a pioneer of French feminist thought, even though she dislikes the feminist label, suggested that feminine language is associated with the maternal and derived from the pre-oedipal fusion between mother and child. Like Kristeva, Hélène Cixous and Luce Irigaray associated feminine writing with the female body. Both drew an analogy between women's writing and women's sexual pleasure, Irigaray arguing that just as a woman's "*jouissance*" is more diffuse and complex than a man's unitary phallic pleasure ("woman has sex organs just about everywhere"), so "feminine" language is more diffuse and less obviously coherent than its "masculine" counterpart (*This Sex* 101–03).

Kristeva, who helped develop the concept of *l'écriture féminine,* nonetheless urged caution in its use and advocacy. Feminine or feminist writing that resists or refuses participation in "masculine" discourse, she warned, risks political marginalization, relegation to the outskirts (pun intended) of what is considered socially and politically significant. Kristeva's concerns were not unfounded: the concept of *l'écriture féminine* did prove controversial, eliciting different kinds of criticism from different kinds of feminist and gender critics. To some, the concept appears to give writing a biological basis, thereby suggesting that there is an *essential* femininity, and/or that women are *essentially* different from men. To others, it seems to suggest that men can write as women, so long as they abdicate authority, sense, and logic in favor of diffusiveness, playfulness, even nonsense.

While French feminists of the 1970s and early 1980s focused on language and writing from a psychoanalytic perspective, North American critics generally practiced a different sort of criticism.

Characterized by close textual reading and historical scholarship, it generally took one of two forms. Critics like Kate Millett, Carolyn Heilbrun, and Judith Fetterley developed what Elaine Showalter called the "feminist critique" of "male constructed literary history" by closely examining canonical works by male writers, exposing the patriarchal ideology implicit in such works, and arguing that traditions of systematic masculine dominance are indelibly inscribed in our literary tradition. Fetterley urged women to become "resisting readers" — to notice how biased most of the classic texts by male authors are in their language, subjects, and attitudes and to actively reject that bias as they read, thereby making reading a different, less "immasculating" experience. Meanwhile, another group of North American feminists, including Showalter, Sandra Gilbert, Susan Gubar, and Patricia Meyer Spacks, developed a different feminist critical model — one that Showalter referred to as "gynocriticism." These critics analyzed great books by women from a feminist perspective, discovered neglected or forgotten women writers, and attempted to recover women's culture and history, especially the history of women's communities that nurtured female creativity.

The North American endeavor to recover women's history — for example, by emphasizing that women developed their own strategies to gain power within their sphere — was seen by British feminists like Judith Newton and Deborah Rosenfelt as an endeavor that "mystifies" male oppression, disguising it as something that has created a special world of opportunities for women. More important from the British standpoint, the universalizing and "essentializing" tendencies of French theory and a great deal of North American practice disguised women's oppression by highlighting sexual difference, thereby seeming to suggest that the dominant system may be impervious to change. As for the North American critique of male stereotypes that denigrate women, British feminists maintained that it led to counterstereotypes of female virtue that ignore real differences of race, class, and culture among women.

By now, the French, North American, and British approaches have so thoroughly critiqued, influenced, and assimilated one another that the work of most Western practitioners is no longer easily identifiable along national boundary lines. Instead, it tends to be characterized according to whether the category of *woman* is the major focus in the exploration of gender and gender oppression or, alternatively, whether the interest in sexual difference encompasses an interest in other differences that also define identity. The latter paradigm encompasses the work of feminists of color, Third World (preferably called post-colonial) feminists, and lesbian feminists, many of whom have asked whether the universal category of woman constructed by certain French and North American predecessors is appropriate to describe women in minority groups or non-Western cultures.

These feminists stress that, while all women are female, they are something else as well (such as African American, lesbian, Muslim Pakistani). This "something else" is precisely what makes them — including their problems and their goals — different from other women. As Armit Wilson has pointed out, Asian women living in Great Britain are expected by their families and communities to preserve Asian cultural traditions; thus, the expression of personal identity through clothing involves a much more serious infraction of cultural rules than it does for a Western woman. Gloria Anzaldúa has spoken personally and eloquently about the experience of many women on the margins of Eurocentric North American culture. "I am a border woman," she writes in *Borderlands: La Frontera = The New Mestiza* (1987). "I grew up between two cultures, the Mexican (with a heavy Indian influence) and the Anglo. . . . Living on the borders and in margins, keeping intact one's shifting and multiple identity and integrity is like trying to swim in a new element, an 'alien' element" (i).

Instead of being divisive and isolating, this evolution of feminism into femin*isms* has fostered a more inclusive, global perspective. The era of recovering women's texts, especially texts by white Western women, has been succeeded by a new era in which the goal is to recover entire cultures of women. Two important figures of this new era are Trinh T. Minh-ha and Gayatri Spivak. Spivak, in works such as *In Other Worlds: Essays in Cultural Politics* (1987) and *Outside in the Teaching Machine* (1993), has shown how political independence (generally looked upon by metropolitan Westerners as a simple and beneficial historical and political reversal) has complex implications for "subaltern" or subproletarian women.

The understanding of woman not as a single, deterministic category but rather as the nexus of diverse experiences has led some white, Western, "majority" feminists like Jane Tompkins and Nancy K. Miller to advocate and practice "personal" or "autobiographical" criticism. Once reluctant to reveal themselves in their analyses for fear of being labeled idiosyncratic, impressionistic, and subjective by men, some feminists are now openly skeptical of the claims to reason, logic, and objectivity that male critics have made in the past. With the advent of more personal feminist critical styles has come a powerful new interest in women's autobiographical writings, manifested in essays such as "Authorizing the Autobiographical" by Shari Benstock, which first appeared in her influential collection *The Private Self: Theory and Practice of Women's Autobiographical Writings* (1988).

Traditional autobiography, some feminists have argued, is a gendered, "masculinist" genre; its established conventions call for a life-plot that turns on action, triumph through conflict, intellectual self-discovery, and often public renown. The body, reproduction, children, and intimate interpersonal relationships are generally well in the background and often absent. Arguing that the lived experiences of women and men differ — women's lives, for instance, are often characterized by interruption and deferral — Leigh Gilmore has developed a theory of women's self-representation in her book *Autobiographics: A Feminist Theory of Self-Representation.*

Autobiographics was published in 1994, well after the chronological divide that, according to Schor, separates the heyday of feminist criticism and the rise of gender studies. Does that mean that Gilmore's book is a feminist throwback? Is she practicing gender criticism instead, the use of the word "feminist" in her book's subtitle notwithstanding? Or are both of these questions overly reductive? As implied earlier, many knowledgeable commentators on the contemporary critical scene are skeptical of the feminst/gender distinction, arguing that feminist criticism is by definition gender criticism and pointing out that one critic whose work *everyone* associates with feminism (Julia Kristeva) has problems with the feminist label while another critic whose name is continually linked with the gender approach (Teresa de Lauretis) continues to refer to herself and her work as feminist.

Certainly, feminist and gender criticism are not polar opposites but, rather, exist along a continuum of attitudes toward sex and sexism, sexuality and gender, language and the literary canon. There are, however, a few distinctions to be made between those critics whose writings are inevitably identified as being toward one end of the continuum or the other.

One distinction is based on focus: as the word implies, "feminists" have concentrated their efforts on the study of women and women's issues. Gender criticism, by contrast, has not been woman centered. It has tended to view the male and female sexes — and the masculine and feminine genders — in terms of a complicated continuum, much as we are viewing feminist and gender criticism. Critics like Diane K.

Lewis have raised the possibility that black women may be more like white men in terms of familial and economic roles, like black men in terms of their relationships with whites, and like white women in terms of their relationships with men. Lesbian gender critics have asked whether lesbian women are really more like straight women than they are like gay (or for that matter straight) men. That we refer to gay and lesbian studies as gender studies has led some to suggest that gender studies is a misnomer; after all, homosexuality is not a gender. This objection may easily be answered once we realize that one purpose of gender criticism is to criticize gender as we commonly conceive of it, to expose its insufficiency and inadequacy as a category.

Another distinction between feminist and gender criticism is based on the terms "gender" and "sex." As de Lauretis suggests in *Technologies of Gender* (1987), feminists of the 1970s tended to equate gender with sex, gender difference with sexual difference. But that equation doesn't help us explain "the differences among women, . . . the differences *within women*." After positing that "we need a notion of gender that is not so bound up with sexual difference," de Lauretis provides just such a notion by arguing that "gender is not a property of bodies or something originally existent in human beings"; rather, it is "the product of various social technologies, such as cinema" (2). Gender is, in other words, a construct, an effect of language, culture, and its institutions. It is gender, not sex, that causes a weak old man to open a door for an athletic young woman. And it is gender, not sex, that may cause one young woman to expect old men to behave in this way, another to view this kind of behavior as chauvinistic and insulting, and still another to have mixed feelings (hence de Lauretis's phrase "differences *within women*") about "gentlemanly gallantry."

Still another related distinction between feminist and gender criticism is based on the *essentialist* views of many feminist critics and the *constructionist* views of many gender critics (both those who would call themselves feminists and those who would not). Stated simply and perhaps too reductively, the term "essentialist" refers to the view that women are essentially different from men. "Constructionist," by contrast, refers to the view that most of those differences are characteristics not of the male and female sex (nature) but, rather, of the masculine and feminine genders (nurture). Because of its essentialist tendencies, "radical feminism," according to the influential gender critic Eve Kosofsky Sedgwick, "tends to deny that the meaning of gender or sexuality has ever significantly changed; and more damagingly, it can make future change appear impossible" (*Between Men* 13).

Most obviously essentialist would be those feminists who emphasize the female body, its difference, and the manifold implications of that difference. The equation made by some avant-garde French feminists between the female body and the *maternal* body has proved especially troubling to some gender critics, who worry that it may paradoxically play into the hands of extreme conservatives and fundamentalists seeking to reestablish patriarchal family values. In her book *The Reproduction of Mothering* (1978), Nancy Chodorow, a sociologist of gender, admits that what we call "mothering" — not having or nursing babies but mothering more broadly conceived — is commonly associated not just with the feminine gender but also with the female sex, often considered nurturing by nature. But she critically interrogates the common assumption that it is in women's nature or biological destiny to "mother" in this broader sense, arguing that the separation of home and workplace brought about by the development of capitalism and the ensuing industrial revolution made mothering *appear* to be essentially a woman's job in modern Western society.

If sex turns out to be gender where mothering is concerned, what differences *are* grounded in sex — that is, nature? *Are* there *essential* differences between men and women — other than those that are purely anatomical and anatomically determined (for example, a man can exclusively take on the job of feeding an infant milk, but he may not do so from his own breast)? A growing number of gender critics would answer the question in the negative. Sometimes referred to as "extreme constructionists" and "postfeminists," these critics have adopted the viewpoint of philosopher Judith Butler, who in her book *Gender Trouble* (1990) predicts that "sex, by definition, will be shown to have been gender all along" (8). As Naomi Schor explains their position, "there is nothing outside or before culture, no nature that is not always and already enculturated" (278).

Whereas a number of feminists celebrate women's difference, postfeminist gender critics would agree with Chodorow's statement that men have an "investment in difference that women do not have" (Eisenstein and Jardine 14). They see difference as a symptom of oppression, not a cause for celebration, and would abolish it by dismantling gender categories and, ultimately, destroying gender itself. Since gender categories and distinctions are embedded in and perpetuated through language, gender critics like Monique Wittig have called for the wholesale transformation of language into a nonsexist, and nonheterosexist, medium.

Language has proved the site of important debates between feminist and gender critics, essentialists and constructionists. Gender critics have taken issue with those French feminists who have spoken of a feminine language and writing and who have grounded differences in language and writing in the female body.[1] For much the same reason, they have disagreed with those French-influenced Anglo-American critics who, like Toril Moi and Nancy K. Miller, have posited an essential relationship between sexuality and textuality. (In an essentialist sense, such critics have suggested that when women write, they tend to break the rules of plausibility and verisimilitude that men have created to evaluate fiction.) Gender critics like Peggy Kamuf posit a relationship only between *gender* and textuality, between what most men and women *become* after they are born and the way in which they write. They are therefore less interested in the author's sexual "signature" — in whether the author was a woman writing — than in whether the author was (to borrow from Kamuf) "Writing like a Woman."

Feminists like Miller have suggested that no man could write the "female anger, desire, and selfhood" that Emily Brontë, for instance, inscribed in her poetry and in *Wuthering Heights* (*Subject* 72). In the view of gender critics, it is and has been possible for a man to write like a woman, a woman to write like a man. Shari Benstock, a noted feminist critic whose investigations into psychoanalytic and poststructuralist theory have led her increasingly to adopt the gender approach, poses the following question to herself in *Textualizing the Feminine* (1991): "Isn't it precisely 'the feminine' in Joyce's writings and Derrida's that carries me along?" (45). In an essay entitled "Unsexing Language: Pronomial Protest in Emily Dickinson's 'Lay this Laurel,'" Anna Shannon Elfenbein has argued that "like Walt Whitman, Emily Dickinson crossed the gender barrier in some remarkable poems," such as "We learned to like the Fire / By playing Glaciers — when a Boy — " (Berg 215).

It is also possible, in the view of most gender critics, for women to read as men, men as women. The view that women can, and indeed have been forced to, read as men has been fairly noncontroversial.

[1]Because feminist/gender studies, not unlike sex/gender, should be thought of as existing along a continuum of attitudes and not in terms of simple opposition, attempts to highlight the difference between feminist and gender criticism are inevitably prone to reductive overgeneralization and occasional distortion. Here, for instance, French feminism is made out to be more monolithic than it actually is. Hélène Cixous has said that a few men (such as Jean Genet) have produced "feminine writing," although she suggests that these are exceptional men who have acknowledged their own bisexuality.

Everyone agrees that the literary canon is largely "androcentric" and that writings by men have tended to "immasculate" women, forcing them to see the world from a masculine viewpoint. But the question of whether men can read as women has proved to be yet another issue dividing feminist and gender critics. Some feminists suggest that men and women have some essentially different reading strategies and outcomes, while gender critics maintain that such differences arise entirely out of social training and cultural norms. One interesting outcome of recent attention to gender and reading is Elizabeth A. Flynn's argument that women in fact make the best interpreters of imaginative literature. Based on a study of how male and female students read works of fiction, she concludes that women come up with more imaginative, open-ended readings of stories. Quite possibly the imputed hedging and tentativeness of women's speech, often seen by men as disadvantages, are transformed into useful interpretive strategies — receptivity combined with critical assessment of the text — in the act of reading (Flynn and Schweickart 286).

In singling out a catalyst of the gender approach, many historians of criticism have pointed to Michel Foucault. In his *History of Sexuality* (1976, tr. 1978), Foucault distinguished sexuality (that is, sexual behavior or practice) from sex, calling the former a "technology of sex." De Lauretis, who has deliberately developed her theory of gender "along the lines of . . . Foucault's theory of sexuality," explains his use of "technology" this way: "Sexuality, commonly thought to be a natural as well as a private matter, is in fact completely constructed in culture according to the political aims of the society's dominant class" (*Technologies* 2, 12). Foucault suggests that homosexuality as we now think of it was to a great extent an invention of the nineteenth century. In earlier periods there had been "acts of sodomy" and individuals who committed them, but the "sodomite" was, according to Foucault, "a temporary aberration," not the "species" he became with the advent of the modern concept of homosexuality (42–43). By historicizing sexuality, Foucault made it possible for his successors to consider the possibility that all of the categories and assumptions that currently come to mind when we think about sex, sexual difference, gender, and sexuality are social artifacts, the products of cultural discourses.

In explaining her reason for saying that feminism began to give way to gender studies "around 1985," Schor says that she chose that date "in part because it marks the publication of *Between Men*," a seminal book in which Eve Kosofsky Sedgwick "articulates the insights of feminist criticism onto those of gay-male studies, which had up to then pursued often parallel but separate courses (affirming the existence of a homosexual or female imagination, recovering lost traditions, decoding the cryptic discourse of works already in the canon by homosexual or feminist authors)" (276). Today, gay and lesbian criticism is so much a part of gender criticism that some people equate it with the gender approach, while others have begun to prefer the phrase "sexualities criticism" to "gender criticism."

Following Foucault's lead, some gay and lesbian gender critics have argued that the heterosexual/homosexual distinction is as much a cultural construct as is the masculine/feminine dichotomy. Arguing that sexuality is a continuum, not a fixed and static set of binary oppositions, a number of gay and lesbian critics have critiqued heterosexuality as a norm, arguing that it has been an enforced corollary and consequence of what Gayle Rubin has referred to as the "sex/gender system." (Those subscribing to this system assume that persons of the male sex should be masculine, that masculine men are attracted to women, and therefore that it is natural for masculine men to be attracted to women and unnatural for them to be attracted to men.) Lesbian gender critics have also taken issue with their feminist counterparts on the grounds that they proceed from fundamentally heterosexual and even heterosexist assumptions. Particularly offensive to lesbians like the poet-critic Adrienne Rich have been those feminists who, following Doris Lessing, have implied that to make the lesbian choice is to make a statement, to act out feminist hostility against men. Rich has called heterosexuality "a beachhead of male dominance" that, "like motherhood, needs to be recognized and studied as a political institution" ("Compulsory Heterosexuality" 143, 145).

If there is such a thing as reading like a woman and such a thing as reading like a man, how then do lesbians read? Are there gay and lesbian ways of reading? Many would say that there are. Rich, by reading Emily Dickinson's poetry as a lesbian — by not assuming that "heterosexual romance is the key to a woman's life and work" — has introduced us to a poet somewhat different from the one heterosexual critics have made familiar (*Lies* 158). As for gay reading, Wayne Koestenbaum has defined "the (male twentieth-century first world) gay reader" as one who "reads resistantly for inscriptions of his condition, for texts that will confirm a social and private identity founded on a desire for other men. . . . Reading becomes a hunt for histories that deliberately foreknow or unwittingly trace a desire felt not by author but by reader, who is most acute when searching for signs of himself" (Boone and Cadden 176–77).

Lesbian critics have produced a number of compelling reinterpretations, or in-scriptions, of works by authors as diverse as Emily Dickinson, Virginia Woolf, and Toni Morrison. As a result of these provocative readings, significant disagreements have arisen between straight and lesbian critics and among lesbian critics as well. Perhaps the most famous and interesting example of this kind of interpretive controversy involves the claim by Barbara Smith and Adrienne Rich that Morrison's novel *Sula* can be read as a lesbian text — and author Toni Morrison's counterclaim that it cannot.

Gay male critics have produced a body of readings no less revisionist and controversial, focusing on writers as staidly classic as Henry James and Wallace Stevens. In Melville's *Billy Budd* and *Moby-Dick,* Robert K. Martin suggests, a triangle of homosexual desire exists. In the latter novel, the hero must choose between a captain who represents "the imposition of the male on the female" and a "Dark Stranger" (Queequeg) who "offers the possibility of an alternate sexuality, one that is less dependent upon performance and conquest" (5).

Masculinity as a complex construct producing and reproducing a constellation of behaviors and goals, many of them destructive (like performance and conquest) and most of them injurious to women, has become the object of an unprecedented number of gender studies. A 1983 issue of *Feminist Review* contained an essay entitled "Anti-Porn: Soft Issue, Hard World," in which B. Ruby Rich suggested that the "legions of feminist men" who examine and deplore the effects of pornography on women might better "undertake the analysis that can tell us why men like porn (not, piously, why this or that exceptional man does *not*)" (Berg 185). The advent of gender criticism makes precisely that kind of analysis possible. Stephen H. Clark, who alludes to Ruby Rich's challenge, reads T. S. Eliot "as a man." Responding to "Eliot's implicit appeal to a specifically masculine audience — "'You! hypocrite lecteur! — mon semblable, — mon *frère!*'" — Clark concludes that poems like "Sweeney Among the Nightingales" and "Gerontion," rather than offering what they are usually said to offer — "a social critique into which a misogynistic language accidentally seeps" — instead articulate a masculine "psychology of sexual fear and desired retaliation" (Berg 173).

Some gender critics focusing on masculinity have analyzed "the anthropology of boyhood," a phrase coined by Mark Seltzer in an article in which he comparatively reads, among other things, Stephen

Crane's *Red Badge of Courage*, Jack London's *White Fang*, and the first *Boy Scouts of America* handbook (Boone and Cadden 150). Others have examined the fear men have that artistry is unmasculine, a guilty worry that surfaces perhaps most obviously in "The Custom-House," Hawthorne's lengthy preface to *The Scarlet Letter*. Still others have studied the representation in literature of subtly erotic disciple-patron relationships, relationships like the ones between Nick Carraway and Jay Gatsby, Charlie Marlow and Lord Jim, Doctor Watson and Sherlock Holmes, and any number of characters in Henry James's stories. Not all of these studies have focused on literary texts. Because the movies have played a primary role in gender construction during our lifetimes, gender critics have analyzed the dynamics of masculinity (vis-à-vis femininity and androgyny) in films from *Rebel Without a Cause* to *Tootsie* to last year's Best Picture. One of the "social technologies" most influential in (re)constructing gender, film is one of the media in which today's sexual politics is most evident.

Necessary as it is, in an introduction such as this one, to define the difference between feminist and gender criticism, it is equally necessary to conclude by unmaking the distinction, at least partially. The two topics just discussed (film theory and so-called queer theory) give us grounds for undertaking that necessary deconstruction. The alliance I have been creating between gay and lesbian criticism on one hand and gender criticism on the other is complicated greatly by the fact that not all gay and lesbian critics are constructionists. Indeed, a number of them (Robert K. Martin included) share with many feminists the *essentialist* point of view; that is to say, they believe homosexuals and heterosexuals to be essentially different, different by nature, just as a number of feminists believe men and women to be different.

In film theory and criticism, feminist and gender critics have so influenced one another that their differences would be difficult to define based on any available criteria, including the ones outlined above. Cinema has been of special interest to contemporary feminists like Minh-ha (herself a filmmaker) and Spivak (whose critical eye has focused on movies including *My Beautiful Laundrette* and *Sammie and Rosie Get Laid*). Teresa de Lauretis, whose *Technologies of Gender* (1987) has proved influential in the area of gender studies, continues to publish film criticism consistent with earlier, unambiguously feminist works in which she argued that "the representation of woman as spectacle — body to be looked at, place of sexuality, and object of desire — so pervasive in our culture, finds in narrative cinema its most complex expression and widest circulation" (*Alice* 4).

Feminist film theory has developed alongside a feminist performance theory grounded in Joan Riviere's recently rediscovered essay "Womanliness as a Masquerade" (1929), in which the author argues that there is no femininity that is *not* masquerade. Marjorie Garber, a contemporary cultural critic with an interest in gender, has analyzed the constructed nature of femininity by focusing on men who have apparently achieved it — through the transvestism, transsexualism, and other forms of "cross-dressing" evident in cultural productions from Shakespeare to Elvis, from "Little Red Riding Hood" to *La Cage aux Folles*. The future of feminist and gender criticism, it would seem, is not one of further bifurcation but one involving a refocusing on femininity, masculinity, and related sexualities, not only as represented in poems, novels, and films but also as manifested and developed in video, on television, and along the almost infinite number of waystations rapidly being developed on the information highways running through an exponentially expanding cyberspace.

In her headnote to the essay that follows, Ellen Rooney summarizes Catharine A. MacKinnon's argument that, although society distinguishes between rape and seduction, the distinction is not as clear as the law makes it appear to be; sometimes, perhaps often, a woman honestly *feels* she has been raped by a man who honestly *feels* that his sexual partner consented to intercourse. Rooney subsequently views Hardy's *Tess of the d'Urbervilles* in light of MacKinnon's theory, pointing out that Hardy makes the "seemingly contradictory argument" that Tess is on one hand "pure" because she has "been raped against her will" and, on the other hand, pure "despite her seduction." If Hardy's argument had been successfully made, Rooney claims, it would have "anticipate[d] MacKinnon's claim that in many contested [sexual] interactions 'reality is split,'" that is, perceived to mean different things according to the gender of the person who has lived through the experience.

But Hardy did not succeed, according to Rooney, either in overturning the patriarchal mindset or in representing a "desiring," "speaking," truly "female subject," because he in fact reinforces "the opposition between rape and seduction" and becomes embroiled in the traditional "problematics of consent." Rather than representing the sex act that dooms Tess from her own point of view, he "consigns his heroine" to "passivity and silence, and so . . . cannot articulate the *meaning* of the ambiguous encounter in The Chase as Tess . . . sees it."

Hardy is constantly in a double bind, or, as Rooney puts it, "blocked in both directions." To the extent that he wants to thumb his nose at conventional assumptions about gender and sexuality, he makes Tess a "seductive woman." But that seductiveness threatens to turn her into a *seductress,* which, in turn, threatens to moot the question of whether she was raped or seduced.

To the extent that Hardy understands conventional thinking, he knows Tess must be represented as passive and silent if she is to be believably pure. "Yet a figure with no potential as a desiring subject can only formally be said to refuse desire." Can it, then, be formally said that Tess only formally refused Alec? If so, can it then also be said that in *some sense* this apparently seductive but libido-less woman consented — or that Alec might have thought she did?

Rooney develops her argument by "thematizing" the "problem of judging Tess." She does so by discussing Hardy's revision of the rape/seduction scene between editions — and by examining Hardy's representation of Tess's physical being (via animal imagery and in scenes that seem to equate *body* and *self*). But to summarize fully the development of her argument would be to spoil the intellectual pleasure of watching it unfold. Suffice it to say that, in "Tess and the Subject of Sexual Violence: Reading, Rape, Seduction," Rooney reflects on most of the issues and problems being raised by contemporary feminist thinkers, including feminist literary critics. Her essay engages the contemporary debate between those feminists who argue that rape is a crime of violence, not of sex, and those others who "acknowledge the violence *within* sexuality in our culture," pointing out that erotic heterosexual relations tend to be defined in terms of "male power and female submission."

Rooney's essay also exemplifies contemporary feminist criticism insofar as it explores the relationship between gendered *subjectivity* on one hand and gendered *representation* on the other; that is, Rooney posits a relationship between what Tess experiences and what she would say or write if she were allowed to represent the meaning of her experiences from her own point of view. And, because Tess is a character created by a man who imbues her with seductiveness and subsequently silences her sexuality, Rooney implicitly raises contemporary questions about whether a nineteenth-century man could — or a twentieth-century man can — represent, let alone write like, a woman.

Ross C Murfin

FEMINIST AND GENDER CRITICISM: A SELECTED BIBLIOGRAPHY

French Feminist Theory

Cixous, Hélène. "The Laugh of the Medusa." Trans. Keith Cohen and Paula Cohen. *Signs* 1 (1976): 875–93.

Cixous, Hélène, and Catherine Clément. *The Newly Born Woman.* Trans. Betsy Wing. Minneapolis: U of Minnesota P, 1986.

Irigaray, Luce. *An Ethics of Sexual Difference.* Trans. Carolyn Burke and Gillian C. Gill. Ithaca: Cornell UP, 1993.

———. *This Sex Which Is Not One.* Trans. Catherine Porter. Ithaca: Cornell UP, 1985.

Jones, Ann Rosalind. "Inscribing Femininity: French Theories of the Feminine." *Making a Difference: Feminist Literary Criticism.* Ed. Gayle Green and Coppélia Kahn. London: Methuen, 1985. 80–112.

———. "Writing the Body: Toward an Understanding of *L'Écriture féminine.*" Showalter, *The New Feminist Criticism* 361–77.

Kristeva, Julia. *Desire in Language: A Semiotic Approach to Literature and Art.* Ed. Leon S. Roudiez. Trans. Thomas Gora, Alice Jardine, and Roudiez. New York: Columbia UP, 1980.

Marks, Elaine, and Isabelle de Courtivron, eds. *New French Feminisms: An Anthology.* Amherst: U of Massachusetts P, 1980.

Moi, Toril, ed. *French Feminist Thought: A Reader.* Oxford: Basil Blackwell, 1987.

Feminist Theory: Classic Texts, General Approaches, Collections

Abel, Elizabeth, and Emily K. Abel, eds. *The "Signs" Reader: Women, Gender, and Scholarship.* Chicago: U of Chicago P, 1983.

Barrett, Michèle, and Anne Phillips. *Destabilizing Theory: Contemporary Feminist Debates.* Stanford: Stanford UP, 1992.

Beauvoir, Simone de. *The Second Sex.* 1953. Trans. and ed. H. M. Parshley. New York: Bantam, 1961.

Benstock, Shari. *Textualizing the Feminine: On the Limits of Genre.* Norman: U of Oklahoma P, 1991.

Butler, Judith. *Gender Trouble: Feminism and the Subversion of Identity.* New York: Routledge, 1990.

de Lauretis, Teresa, ed. *Feminist Studies/Critical Studies.* Bloomington: Indiana UP, 1986.

Felman, Shoshana. "Women and Madness: The Critical Phallacy." *Diacritics* 5 (1975): 2–10.

Fetterley, Judith. *The Resisting Reader: A Feminist Approach to American Fiction*. Bloomington: Indiana UP, 1978.

Fuss, Diana. *Essentially Speaking: Feminist, Nature and Difference*. New York: Routledge, 1989.

Gallop, Jane. *Around 1981: Academic Feminist Literary Theory*. New York: Routledge, 1992.

———. *The Daughter's Seduction: Feminism and Psychoanalysis*. Ithaca: Cornell UP, 1982.

hooks, bell. *Feminist Theory: From Margin to Center*. Boston: South End, 1984.

Kolodny, Annette. "Dancing Through the Minefield: Some Observations on the Theory, Practice, and Politics of a Feminist Literary Criticism." Showalter, *The New Feminist Criticism* 144–67.

———. "Some Notes on Defining a 'Feminist Literary Criticism.'" *Critical Inquiry* 2 (1975): 78.

Lovell, Terry, ed. *British Feminist Thought: A Reader*. Oxford: Basil Blackwell, 1990.

Meese, Elizabeth, and Alice Parker, eds. *The Difference Within: Feminism and Critical Theory*. Philadelphia: John Benjamins, 1989.

Miller, Nancy K., ed. *The Poetics of Gender*. New York: Columbia UP, 1986.

Millett, Kate. *Sexual Politics*. Garden City: Doubleday, 1970.

Rich, Adrienne. *On Lies, Secrets, and Silence: Selected Prose, 1966–1979*. New York: Norton, 1979.

Showalter, Elaine. "Toward a Feminist Poetics." Showalter, *The New Feminist Criticism* 125–43.

———, ed. *The New Feminist Criticism: Essays on Women, Literature, and Theory*. New York: Pantheon, 1985.

Stimpson, Catherine R. "Feminist Criticism." *Redrawing the Boundaries: The Transformation of English and American Literary Studies*. Ed. Stephen Greenblatt and Giles Gunn. New York: MLA, 1992. 251–70.

Warhol, Robyn, and Diane Price Herndl, eds. *Feminisms: An Anthology of Literary Theory and Criticism*. New Brunswick: Rutgers UP, 1991.

Weed, Elizabeth, ed. *Coming to Terms: Feminism, Theory, Politics*. New York: Routledge, 1989.

Woolf, Virginia. *A Room of One's Own*. New York: Harcourt, 1929.

Women's Writing and Creativity

Abel, Elizabeth, ed. *Writing and Sexual Difference.* Chicago: U of Chicago P, 1982.

Berg, Temma F., ed. *Engendering the Word: Feminist Essays in Psychosexual Poetics.* Co-ed. Anna Shannon Elfenbein, Jeanne Larsen, and Elisa Kay Sparks. Urbana: U of Illinois P, 1989.

DuPlessis, Rachel Blau. *The Pink Guitar: Writing as Feminist Practice.* New York: Routledge, 1990.

Finke, Laurie. *Feminist Theory, Women's Writing.* Ithaca: Cornell UP, 1992.

Gilbert, Sandra M., and Susan Gubar. *The Madwoman in the Attic: The Woman Writer and the Nineteenth-Century Literary Imagination.* New Haven: Yale UP, 1979.

Homans, Margaret. *Bearing the Word: Language and Female Experience in Nineteenth-Century Women's Writing.* Chicago: U of Chicago P, 1986.

Jacobus, Mary, ed. *Women Writing and Writing about Women.* New York: Barnes, 1979.

Miller, Nancy K. *Subject to Change: Reading Feminist Writing.* New York: Columbia UP, 1988.

Newton, Judith Lowder. *Women, Power and Subversion: Social Strategies in British Fiction, 1778–1860.* Athens: U of Georgia P, 1981.

Poovey, Mary. *The Proper Lady and the Woman Writer: Ideology as Style in the Works of Mary Wollstonecraft, Mary Shelley, and Jane Austen.* Chicago: U of Chicago P, 1984.

Showalter, Elaine. *A Literature of Their Own: British Women Novelists from Brontë to Lessing.* Princeton: Princeton UP, 1977.

Spacks, Patricia Meyer. *The Female Imagination.* New York: Knopf, 1975.

Feminism, Race, Class, and Nationality

Anzaldúa, Gloria. *Borderlands: La Frontera = The New Mestiza.* San Francisco: Spinsters/Aunt Lute, 1987.

Christian, Barbara. *Black Feminist Criticism: Perspectives on Black Women Writers.* New York: Pergamon, 1985.

hooks, bell. *Ain't I a Woman?: Black Women and Feminism.* Boston: South End, 1981.

———. *Black Looks: Race and Representation.* Boston: South End, 1992.

Kaplan, Cora. *Sea Changes: Essays on Culture and Feminism*. London: Verso, 1986.

Moraga, Cherrie, and Gloria Anzaldúa. *This Bridge Called My Back: Writings by Radical Women of Color*. New York: Kitchen Table, 1981.

Newton, Judith, and Deborah Rosenfelt, eds. *Feminist Criticism and Social Change: Sex, Class, and Race in Literature and Culture*. New York: Methuen, 1985.

Pryse, Marjorie, and Hortense Spillers, eds. *Conjuring: Black Women, Fiction, and Literary Tradition*. Bloomington: Indiana UP, 1985.

Robinson, Lillian S. *Sex, Class, and Culture*. 1978. New York: Methuen, 1986.

Smith, Barbara. "Towards a Black Feminist Criticism." Showalter, *The New Feminist Criticism* 168–85.

Feminism and Postcoloniality

Emberley, Julia. *Thresholds of Difference: Feminist Critique, Native Women's Writings, Postcolonial Theory*. Toronto: U of Toronto P, 1993.

Mohanty, Chandra Talpade, Ann Russo, and Lourdes Torres, eds. *Third World Women and the Politics of Feminism*. Bloomington: Indiana UP, 1991.

Schipper, Mineke, ed. *Unheard Words: Women and Literature in Africa, the Arab World, Asia, the Caribbean, and Latin America*. London: Allison, 1985.

Spivak, Gayatri Chakravorty. *In Other Worlds: Essays in Cultural Politics*. New York: Methuen, 1987.

———. *Outside in the Teaching Machine*. New York: Routledge, 1993.

Trinh T. Minh-ha. *Woman, Native, Other: Writing Postcoloniality and Feminism*. Bloomington: Indiana UP, 1989.

Wilson, Armit. *Finding a Voice: Asian Women in Britain*. 1979. London: Virago, 1980.

Women's Self-Representation and Personal Criticism

Benstock, Shari, ed. *The Private Self: Theory and Practice of Women's Autobiographical Writings*. Chapel Hill: U of North Carolina P, 1988.

Gilmore, Leigh. *Autobiographics: A Feminist Theory of Self-Representation*. Ithaca: Cornell UP, 1994.

Martin, Biddy, and Chandra Talpade Mohanty. "Feminist Politics: What's Home Got to Do with It?" *Life/Lines: Theorizing Women's Autobiography*. Ed. Bella Brodski and Celeste Schenck. Ithaca: Cornell UP, 1988.

Miller, Nancy K. *Getting Personal: Feminist Occasions and Other Autobiographical Acts*. New York: Routledge, 1991.

Smith, Sidonie. *A Poetics of Women's Autobiography: Marginality and the Fictions of Self-Representation*. Bloomington: Indiana UP, 1988.

Feminist Film Theory

de Lauretis, Teresa. *Alice Doesn't: Feminism, Semiotics, Cinema*. Bloomington: Indiana UP, 1986.

Doane, Mary Ann. *Re-vision: Essays in Feminist Film Criticism*. Frederick: U Publications of America, 1984.

Modleski, Tania. *Feminism without Women: Culture and Criticism in a "Postfeminist" Age*. New York: Routledge, 1991.

Mulvey, Laura. *Visual and Other Pleasures*. Bloomington: Indiana UP, 1989.

Penley, Constance, ed. *Feminism and Film Theory*. New York: Routledge, 1988.

Studies of Gender and Sexuality

Boone, Joseph A., and Michael Cadden, eds. *Engendering Men: The Question of Male Feminist Criticism*. New York: Routledge, 1990.

Butler, Judith. *Gender Trouble: Feminism and the Subversion of Identity*. New York: Routledge, 1990.

Chodorow, Nancy. *The Reproduction of Mothering: Psychoanalysis and the Sociology of Gender*. Berkeley: U of California P, 1978.

Claridge, Laura, and Elizabeth Langland, eds. *Out of Bounds: Male Writing and Gender(ed) Criticism*. Amherst: U of Massachusetts P, 1990.

de Lauretis, Teresa. *Technologies of Gender: Essays on Theory, Film, and Fiction*. Bloomington: Indiana UP, 1987.

Doane, Mary Ann. "Masquerade Reconsidered: Further Thoughts on the Female Spectator." *Discourse* 11 (1988–89): 42–54.

Eisenstein, Hester, and Alice Jardine, eds. *The Future of Difference*. Boston: G. K. Hall, 1980.

Flynn, Elizabeth A., and Patrocinio P. Schweickart, eds. *Gender and Reading: Essays on Readers, Texts, and Contexts*. Baltimore: Johns Hopkins UP, 1986.

Foucault, Michel. *The History of Sexuality: Volume I: An Introduction.* Trans. Robert Hurley. New York: Random, 1978.

Kamuf, Peggy. "Writing Like a Woman." *Women and Language in Literature and Society.* New York: Praeger, 1980. 284–99.

Laqueur, Thomas. *Making Sex: Body and Gender from the Greeks to Freud.* Cambridge: Harvard UP, 1990.

Riviere, Joan. "Womanliness as a Masquerade." 1929. Rpt. in *Formations of Fantasy.* Ed. Victor Burgin, James Donald, and Cora Kaplan. London: Methuen, 1986. 35–44.

Rubin, Gayle. "Thinking Sex: Notes for a Radical Theory of the Politics of Sexuality." Abelove et al., *The Lesbian and Gay Reader* 3–44.

———. "The Traffic in Women: Notes on the 'Political Economy' of Sex." *Toward an Anthropology of Women.* Ed. Rayna R. Reiter. New York: Monthly Review, 1975. 157–210.

Schor, Naomi. "Feminist and Gender Studies." *Introduction to Scholarship in Modern Languages and Literatures.* Ed. Joseph Gibaldi. New York: MLA, 1992. 262–87.

Sedgwick, Eve Kosofsky. *Between Men: English Literature and Male Homosocial Desire.* New York: Columbia UP, 1988.

———. "Gender Criticism." *Redrawing the Boundaries: The Transformation of English and American Literary Studies.* Ed. Stephen Greenblatt and Giles Gunn. New York: MLA, 1992. 271–302.

Lesbian and Gay Criticism

Abelove, Henry, Michèle Aina Barale, and David Halperin, eds. *The Lesbian and Gay Studies Reader.* New York: Routledge, 1993.

Butters, Ronald, John M. Clum, and Michael Moon, eds. *Displacing Homophobia: Gay Male Perspectives in Literature and Culture.* Durham: Duke UP, 1989.

Craft, Christopher. *Another Kind of Love: Male Homosexual Desire in English Discourse, 1850–1920.* Berkeley: U of California P, 1994.

de Lauretis, Teresa. *The Practice of Love: Lesbian Sexuality and Perverse Desire.* Bloomington: Indiana UP, 1994.

Dollimore, Jonathan. *Sexual Dissidence: Augustine to Wilde, Freud to Foucault.* Oxford: Clarendon, 1991.

Fuss, Diana, ed. *Inside/Out: Lesbian Theories, Gay Theories.* New York: Routledge, 1991.

Garber, Marjorie. *Vested Interests: Cross-Dressing and Cultural Anxiety.* New York: Routledge, 1992.

Halperin, David M. *One Hundred Years of Homosexuality and Other Essays on Greek Love.* New York: Routledge, 1990.

The Lesbian Issue. Special issue, *Signs* 9 (1984).

Martin, Robert K. *Hero, Captain, and Stranger: Male Friendship, Social Critique, and Literary Form in the Sea Novels of Herman Melville.* Chapel Hill: U of North Carolina P, 1986.

Munt, Sally, ed. *New Lesbian Criticism: Literary and Cultural Readings.* New York: Harvester Wheatsheaf, 1992.

Rich, Adrienne. "Compulsory Heterosexuality and Lesbian Existence." Ed. Elizabeth Abel and Emily K. Abel, *The "Signs" Reader,* 139–68.

Stimpson, Catherine R. "Zero Degree Deviancy: The Lesbian Novel in English." *Critical Inquiry* 8 (1981): 363–79.

Weeks, Jeffrey. *Sexuality and Its Discontents: Meanings, Myths, and Modern Sexualities.* London: Routledge, 1985.

Wittig, Monique. "The Mark of Gender." Miller, *The Poetics of Gender,* 63–73.

———. "One Is Not Born a Woman." *Feminist Issues* 1.2 (1981): 47–54.

———. *The Straight Mind and Other Essays.* Boston: Beacon, 1992.

Queer Theory

Butler, Judith. *Bodies That Matter: On the Discursive Limits of "Sex."* New York: Routledge, 1993.

Cohen, Ed. *Talk on the Wilde Side: Towards a Genealogy of Discourse on Male Sexualities.* New York: Routledge, 1993.

de Lauretis, Teresa, ed. Issue on Queer Theory, *differences* 3.2 (1991).

Sedgwick, Eve Kosofsky. *Epistemology of the Closet.* Berkeley: U of California P, 1991.

———. *Tendencies.* Durham: Duke UP, 1993.

Sinfield, Alan. *Cultural Politics — Queer Reading.* Philadelphia: U of Pennsylvania P, 1994.

———. *The Wilde Century: Effeminacy, Oscar Wilde, and the Queer Moment.* New York: Columbia UP, 1994.

Warner, Michael, ed. *Fear of a Queer Planet: Queer Politics and Social Theory.* Minneapolis: U of Minnesota P, 1993.

Feminist Criticism of *Tess*

Boumelha, Penny. *Thomas Hardy and Women*. Totowa: Barnes, 1982.

Jacobus, Mary. "Tess: The Making of a Pure Woman." *Tearing the Veil: Essays on Femininity*. Ed. Susan Lipshitz. Boston: Routledge, 1978. 77–92.

Poole, Adrian. "'Men's Words' and Hardy's Women." *Essays in Criticism* 31 (1981): 328–44.

Silverman, Kaja. "History, Figuration and Female Subjectivity in *Tess of the d'Urbervilles. Novel* 18 (1984): 5–28.

A FEMINIST AND GENDER PERSPECTIVE

ELLEN ROONEY

Tess and the Subject of Sexual Violence: Reading, Rape, Seduction

> The law distinguishes rape from intercourse by the woman's lack of consent coupled with the man's (usually) knowing disregard of it. A feminist distinction between rape and intercourse, to hazard a beginning approach, lies instead in the *meaning* of the act from women's point of view.
>
> –CATHARINE A. MACKINNON

The original version of this essay was published in Rape and Representation, *Brenda Silver and Lynn Higgins's 1991 feminist collection on the problematics of sexual violence. My focus there was on Catharine MacKinnon's argument that "meaning" is a crucial question for rape law: "whether [or not] a contested interaction is rape comes down to whose meaning wins" (652). MacKinnon's work speaks to literary critics in part because of this hermeneutic emphasis; its importance for readers of* Tess, *however, has to do with the emergence, in both MacKinnon and the critical history of* Tess, *of a hermeneutically powerful opposition between seduction and rape. In MacKinnon's work, the fact that "rape is a sex crime that is not a crime when it looks like sex," means that reality is both split and gendered; the "problem is the rape law's assumption that a single, objective state of affairs existed, one which merely needs to be determined by evidence, when many (maybe even most) rapes involve honest men and violated women. When reality is split — a woman is raped but not by a rapist? — the law tends to conclude that a rape did not happen . . . [The] subjectivity [that] becomes the objectivity of 'what happened' is a matter of . . . sexual politics" (654). The impossibility of objectivity means that the opposition rape/seduction finally collapses for MacKinnon; she proposes that the question "what is the violation of rape?" be replaced by another: "what is the non-violation of intercourse?" (667).*

"Violation" and an unstable opposition between rape and seduction also characterize the critical history of Tess of the d'Urbervilles, *beginning with the reviewers who speak of "violation" to acknowledge Tess's injury while blurring the distinction between seduction and rape (see Cox, Gregor, Miller). The oxymoron "violent seduction" displaces the configuration of power and desire that defines rape as seduction. In this essay, I argue that Hardy's effort to distinguish rape from seduction repeatedly falls short, its terms collapsing into one another, in part because these seemingly opposed terms both assume a passive female figure, a female subject barred from desire, left only with the task of consenting to (or refusing) another's desire. What is ultimately at stake in any attempt to read the scene of sexual violence is the place and status of this female subject. In the case of Hardy's* Tess, *the overwhelming imperative to establish that Tess is a "Pure Woman" leads ineluctably toward the reinscription within seduction and within rape of the problematic of consent and the very patriarchal dichotomies Hardy hoped to escape.*[1]

Faithfully Presented

The polemic of *Tess of the d'Urbervilles* has always been controversial. In the *Quarterly Review* (April 1892), Mowbray Morris complained, "we are *required* to read the story of Tess (or Theresa) Durbeyfield as the story of 'A pure woman faithfully presented by Thomas Hardy.' Compliance with this request entails something of a strain upon the English language" (Lerner 85). Hardy's later insistence in his Preface that the book was "intended to be neither didactic nor aggressive" because "a novel is an impression, not an argument" (25) only lends support to Penny Boumelha's observation that with the publication of *Tess,* Hardy came to be thought of as a writer with an ax to grind.[2] The novel clearly contains a brief for Tess as the "Pure Woman" of the subtitle, and some of the contradictions in the text

[1]See MacKinnon ("Agenda" and "Jurisprudence") and Rooney.
[2]Hardy's disclaimer first appeared in the Fifth Edition.

result from revisions intended not to satisfy various censorious editors but to strengthen Tess's case. But Hardy's defense argument, as argument, is internally contradictory: it seeks both "to exonerate Tess and to secure forgiveness" for her (Boumelha 129).[3] This is an obvious contradiction, but it just as obviously does not transform the defense into an indictment. Hardy asks his reader not to blame Tess too much and to believe in her innocence, but all of his arguments bend toward a single theme: Tess is a pure woman.[4]

The difficulty for readers persists. What, in this novel is a pure woman? How ironic is Hardy's subtitle, "appended," as he eventually claimed, "at the last moment, after reading the final proofs" (28)? Mary Jacobus and Boumelha agree that the effort to exonerate Tess is an obvious "attempt to rescue her for a conventionally realized purity" (Boumelha 129). Yet, in his 1892 Preface, Hardy criticizes the "artificial and derivative meaning" of the word and chastises those who "ignore the meaning of the word in Nature, together with all aesthetic claims upon it, not to mention the spiritual interpretation afforded by the finest side of their own Christianity" (26). Finally, he characterizes the subtitle "as being the estimate left in a candid mind of the heroine's character — an estimate that nobody would be likely to dispute. It was disputed more than anything else in the book. *Melius fuerat non scribere*. But there it stands" (28). This disclaimer seems disingenuous. The use of Latin for the confession of error testifies to a certain reluctance to withdraw from the dispute unambiguously, in plain English, and, in the case of a book as heavily revised as *Tess,* Hardy's hint that fidelity to the text requires him to allow the subtitle to "stand" strains credulity.

If we read *Tess* in light of Catharine MacKinnon's emphasis on *meaning* as the essential issue in a "contested interaction" such as a scene of sexual violence, Hardy's apparent "confusion of many standards" (see Paris) takes on a new significance. His seemingly contradictory argument — Tess is pure because she "had been made to break an accepted social law" (105), that is, been raped against her will, *and* Tess is pure because she remains "unsmirched," despite her seduction — anticipates

[3]Numerous scholars have noted the apparent self-contradictions, discontinuities, multiplicity, and even confusion of too many explanations in the text, though some have defended them in the name of literariness or as the truths of fiction. See Bayley, Boumelha, Cox, Miller, Paris, and Schweik for a range of views.

[4]Jacobus details the "sustained campaign of rehabilitation" in "Tess: A Pure Woman," and Claridge revisits the polemic in "Tess: A Less than Pure Woman Ambivalently Presented." Claridge's sympathies lie with Mowbray. Yet defenses like Hardy's are sometimes heard in courtrooms.

MacKinnon's claim that in many contested interactions "reality is split" and a single, objective state of affairs cannot be determined by the evidence (or even said to exist). But Hardy's effort simultaneously to assert Tess's purity and to revise the meaning of purity itself traps him in the opposition between rape and seduction, between the unambiguous violence that would guarantee Tess's purity in even the most rigid patriarchal codes and the ambiguous and thus less pure space of complicity, desire, and reading, where a female subject might emerge. Once he selects the opposition between rape and seduction as the mechanism for articulating Tess's purity, Hardy's text is constrained by the problematics of consent. Ultimately, the meaning of purity hinges on the relation between seduction and rape; as Hardy attempts, without success, to clarify that relation, Tess's body is textualized, "converted into evidence" (Ferguson 91), and the relation between her body and her desire becomes the focus of intense representational anxiety. The impossibility of resolving that anxiety while preserving her purity is the impossibility of representing Tess as a desiring or speaking subject.

The figure of the seductive woman is thus enormously important for any reading of *Tess*. "Seductive" is a word Hardy uses sparingly in the final, 1912 edition of the novel. He deletes it in a number of places: "the *seductive* Tess," for example, becomes "the *soft and silent* Tess" (161; emphasis added). The "seductive Tess" is in fact the hinge of the novel, but seductiveness and seduction are two terms Hardy cannot articulate clearly. Rape is the third term that smooths over the aporia of the pure, seductive woman.

Given his commitment to her purity, Hardy's figuration of Tess as a seductive woman seems counterintuitive, a red flag to critics like Mowbray. Hardy overlooks what MacKinnon's analysis emphasizes: the problematic of consent consigns his heroine to passivity and silence, and so he cannot articulate the *meaning* of the ambiguous encounter in The Chase as Tess — one of the *subjects* of sexual violence — sees it. This is, in part, because the status of Tess's subjectivity is what is at stake in The Chase, indeed in the whole novel. *Tess* critics generally discuss the heroine's "violated subjectivity" without considering how that subjectivity is first constituted or the degree to which Hardy's novel is about the production of a female subject.[5] (I stress female because, as we shall see, Tess's efforts to escape the [strictly] feminine are harshly rebuffed: the subject exists here only in sexual difference.) Hardy believed at one point

[5]Boumelha's very interesting work is an exception; another is Silverman's "History, Figuration and Female Subjectivity in *Tess of the d'Urbervilles*," which focuses on issues very similar to these.

that the most "suitable" title for his novel would be "The Body and Soul of Sue," and, while the heroine's name was changed, for Tess subjectivity remains a question of embodiment. Her subjectivity is structured as her flesh is structured: female, over and against (and for) the male. This construction fundamentally disrupts Hardy's effort to represent the scene of sexual violence from Tess's point of view, to make her a subject of the encounter in The Chase, even as his inscription of her subjectivity through her flesh is an effect of this failure of representation.

Hardy is unable to represent the *meaning* of the encounter in The Chase from Tess's point of view because to present Tess as a speaking subject is to risk the possibility that she may appear as the subject of desire.[6] Yet a figure with no potential as a desiring subject can only formally be said to refuse desire, to testify to the absence of her desire; the possibilities of action all lie elsewhere. Hardy is blocked in both directions. To preserve Tess's purity, he must insist on her passivity, situating her firmly in the problematic of consent: a "subject" who does not speak, her silence guarantees our sympathy. Thus at three crucial moments in the plot, we find elisions in the text: the sexual encounter in The Chase, Tess's misplaced letter, and her confession to Angel. Hardy's exclusion of Tess's narrative on her wedding night repeats his exclusion of her representation of the events in The Chase. And the impossibility of presenting Tess as a speaking or desiring subject forces Hardy to figure her as the "seductive woman," a victim of her "own" mute sexuality, which is summed up in her seductive appeal. Tess embodies rather than acts desire, but in the problematic of the seductive woman, all feminine behavior is seductive. As we shall see, Tess never finally escapes the "risks" her own appearance constitutes (278).

Tess's seductiveness is ultimately troped as the essential form of sexual violence: silent and still, she is nonetheless an overpowering temptress who ravishes men. The impossibility and the necessity of representing the events in The Chase from her point of view impose a fundamental equivocation on the novel, and this contradiction produces Hardy's apparent muddle on the topic of Tess's body: his insistence that her flesh *can* be read, that her soul appears to the eye, *and* that her body and soul, exterior and interior, depart from one another, that her body is not "her very self" (232). In the end, the scene of sexual violence, Tess and the female subject all remain radically unreadable figures.

[6]This is also a problem for MacKinnon, though from the other side. As Haraway has argued, for MacKinnon, woman "in a deep sense does not exist as a subject, or even potential subject, since she owes her existence as a woman to sexual appropriation" (77).

"A Little More Than Persuading": Rape and Seduction

Hardy thematizes the problem of judging Tess, within his plot and for his readers, and is immediately ensnared in the opposition of rape and seduction. The title of this section cites an emendation Hardy made to the first bound edition of *Tess* that appeared in September 1892. In Phase the Second ("Maiden No More"), two field-women observe the young mother as she nurses Sorrow and then covers him with kisses, which, the narrator remarks, "strangely combined passionateness with contempt" (109). The women then begin to discuss Tess's feelings for the child.[7] The entire passage reads as follows, with the revision in italics.

> 'She's fond of that there child, though she mid pretend *to hate en,* and say she wishes the baby and her too were in the churchyard,' observed the woman in the red petticoat.
>
> 'She'll soon leave off saying that,' replied the one in buff. 'Lord, 'tis wonderful what a body can get used to *o' that sort* in time!'
>
> *'A little more than persuading had to do wi' the coming o't, I reckon. There were they that heard a sobbing one night last year in The Chase; and it mid ha' gone hard wi' a certain party if folks had come along.'*
>
> *'Well, a little more, or a little less,* 'twas a thousand pities that it should have happened to she, of all others. But 'tis always the comeliest! The plain ones be as safe as churches — hey, Jenny?' The speaker turned to one of the group who certainly was not ill-defined as plain. (109)

Tess's passionate contempt for her child hints at Hardy's plans for the infant. Sorrow dies by the chapter's end; Hardy refuses to redeem Tess by means of a heroic, self-sacrificing motherhood. The allusions to Tess's beauty and to Jenny's plainness as a source of protection are chilling, and they form a persistent pattern of observation in the novel: Tess's sexuality — figured by her beauty/body — is a temptation to men that places her in almost constant danger. As this scene opens, the narrator speculates: "Perhaps one reason why she seduces casual attention is that she never courts it, though the other women often gaze

[7]This scene and all of chapter XIV were deleted from the original serialization of the text, which ran in the *Graphic* from July to December 1891; the chapter appeared alone as "The Midnight Baptism: A Study in Christianity" in *Fortnightly Review* (May 1891); it was restored to the novel in the three-volume edition of 1891.

around them" (107). The seductive woman is a paradoxical figure who seduces (casual) attention precisely because she never "courts" or *actively* seeks it. In this phrase, Hardy captures the absolute divergence of Tess's experience (or practice) of her body and its effects on others; her seductiveness — where seductive describes her embodiment of sexuality — is here determined by her lack of seductiveness — the absence of the seducer's active courting. This peculiarly inactive embodiment is at the heart of Tess's quandary as a potential subject of desire or discourse: her passion is to suffer the effects of her body on others.

This spoken exchange strengthens the reader's impression that the contested interaction in The Chase was a rape: sexual violence, not seduction. Some evidence is adduced ("the sobbing") but vaguely, without attribution ("they that heard"). Nevertheless, the speakers are clearly in sympathy with Tess and place the guilt or blame for her sorrow elsewhere. Hardy offers his readers these local judges as models; their sympathy for Tess and contempt for Alec is plain, although any anger they might feel is tempered by their apparent fatalism: "'tis always the comeliest."

Yet, the expressions "a little more than persuading" and "a little more, a little less" expose the contradictions that haunt the opposition of rape and seduction. They also disclose the degree to which Hardy's efforts to clarify the nature of Tess's "violation" are hindered by the rhetoric that links rape to seduction. The observation that "a little more than persuading had to do wi' the coming o't" defines sexual violence as something added to persuading, persuading and then some; seduction tips over into rape when force appears, when ineffective words give way to "irresistible" actions. Thus, rape is an extension of seduction, of courting, in the direction of violence; rather than a radical break distinguishing rape from seduction, we have a continuity and an implied narrative of the movement from seduction to rape.

This blurring of the boundary between seduction and rape contradicts some feminist positions developed in the wake of Susan Brownmiller's *Against Our Will* (1975). If rape is defined as "pure" violence, violence is necessarily barred from discussions of seduction, that is, of sexuality. (The emphasis on the "purity" of violence curiously repeats the passion for the "pure" victim.) This position can lead to judgments, like Terry Eagleton's, that rape is a "virulently anti-sexual act" (63). This characterization is essential to any diagnosis of misogyny, both in literature and in law. But it elides the eroticization of dominance and submission in favor of articulating feminism's ethical project. The radical edge of recent feminist work on sexuality is produced by the broad range of feminist thinkers (from Susan Griffin to Jane Gallop to MacKinnon herself) who acknowledge the violence *within* sexuality in our culture.[8] The term "rape culture" expresses the view that in our patriarchy "eroticism is wedded to power" and romantic "love finds erotic expression through male dominance and female submission" (Griffin 7, 8).

Hardy seems to share this more ambivalent view. But the words "a little more, a little less" complicate this reading. In one register, they sound skeptical about the nature of the events in The Chase, weighing the possibilities, implying that perhaps there was more than persuading, but then again, perhaps not. Yet, this same remark can suggest that rape should be defined as *less* than persuading; rape falls short of persuasion, is perhaps wholly distinct from the question of persuasion — violence, not sex. In this reading, the bond between rape and seduction is broken. Rape and seduction might then appear as independent phenomena, with seduction at play in the realm of the sexual and rape relegated to the sphere of violence.

The final turn of the interpretation reads these lines with (or as) a shrug. The question of whether a "certain party" bothered (or even attempted) to persuade Tess is not compelling: the difference between rape and seduction is really no difference. No matter, it is a pity in any case, and the sorrow is the same. In this reading, the "little more" that is added to seduction is too trivial to bear mention; it is no longer a question of the violence within sexuality. Rape and seduction collapse into each other — at best, the project of distinguishing them clearly is a fruitless one.

Hardy repeats this ambiguous inscription of the couple rape/seduction in revising the critical passages at the end of Phase the First. In the pages leading to the notorious elision, from which Tess emerges "Maiden No More," Alec is the lover-seducer. The "master" is a wheedling servant, who pouts, pleads, bribes, and tries to persuade:

> 'Will you, I ask once more, show your belief in me by letting me clasp you with my arm? Come, between us two and nobody else, now. We know each other well; and you know that I love you, and think you the prettiest girl in the world, which you are. Mayn't I treat you as a lover?' (91)

Alec complains in a mode that is almost Petrarchan: "'For near three mortal months have you trifled with my feelings, eluded me, and

[8]See Eagleton, Gallop, Griffin, MacKinnon, and Marcus for a range of positions vis à vis the relation of violence to sexuality.

snubbed me'" (91), and he insists that Tess is "devilish unkind" (91). His bribes include gifts for her family, and Hardy reports that he "steals" a "cursory kiss." When Tess dismounts, he makes her a "sort of couch or nest" and covers her "tenderly" with his overcoat, asking, "'Tessy — don't you love me ever so little now?'" (93). A little more, or a little less?

These attentions produce tears and embarrassed denials, but also more equivocal tones: "'How could you be so treacherous!' said Tess, between archness and real dismay" (92). The scene rehearses Tess's paralysis as a speaking subject and the strange "between"-ness that Hardy's equivocations produce as defining her subjectivity. In response to Alec's request to treat her as a lover, she stutters, "writhing uneasily on her seat": "'I don't know — I wish — how can I say yes or no, when ——'" (91). Hardy reports that Alec slipped his arm around her and "Tess expressed no further negative" (91). This failure to express a negative — a practical negation of Tess's refusal — is her last reported gesture in this phase of Maidenhood. Although she has managed "reluctantly [to] admit" that as for loving Alec, even a little, "'But I fear I do not ——'" (93); when he nearly stumbles over her sleeping form and calls her name, Hardy reports: "There was no answer" (94). At the crucial moment, Tess fails to answer "yes or no." The final passages of this Phase read:

> Darkness and silence ruled everywhere around. Above them rose the primeval yews and oaks of The Chase, in which were poised gentle roosting birds in their last nap; and about them stole the hopping rabbits and hares. But, might some say, where was Tess's guardian angel? where was the providence of her simple faith? Perhaps, like that other god of whom the ironical Tishbite spoke, he was talking, or he was pursuing, or he was in a journey, or he was sleeping and not to be awaked.
>
> *Why it was that upon this beautiful feminine tissue, sensitive as gossamer, and practically blank as snow as yet, there should have been traced such a coarse pattern as it was doomed to receive; why so often the coarse appropriates the finer thus, the wrong man the woman, the wrong woman the man, many thousand years of analytical philosophy have failed to explain to our sense of order. One may, indeed, admit the possibility of a retribution lurking in the present catastrophe. Doubtless some of Tess d'Urberville's mailed ancestors rollicking home from a fray had dealt the same measure even more ruthlessly towards peasant girls of their time. But though to visit the sins of the fathers upon the children may be a morality good enough for divinities, it is scorned by average human nature; and it therefore does not mend the matter.*

> As Tess's own people down in those retreats are never tired of saying among each other in their fatalistic way: 'It was to be.' There lay the pity of it. *An immeasurable social chasm was to divide our heroine's personality thereafter from that previous self of hers who stepped from her mother's door to try her fortune at Trantridge poultry-farm.* (94–95)

From "why it was . . ." on, the passage is heavily revised, with most of it (italicized here) added after the serialization in the *Graphic*. Again, the revision's overall effect is to strengthen the argument that what is *not* represented *is* a rape, even while — almost compulsively — introducing certain ambiguities into the opposition between rape and seduction. Tess's "ancestors" as they are presented here, were definitely rapists; the analogy paints Alec as an assailant, ruthless and sinning: rape is unambiguous, large-scale violence. But the passage and the chapter as a whole also present the same *continuity* between seduction and rape that we saw assumed by the gossip in the fields. Alec first appears as a too-ardent lover, then as a latter-day d'Urberville. And, of course, we do not see him act the second role, or act at all after kneeling at Tess's side and putting his cheek to hers — a gesture singular in its lack of aggression and implicit equality.

Hardy's invocation of the brutal and "more ruthless" rapes committed by bands of armed lords ironically works to reopen the distance between the ancient d'Urbervilles and the imposter Alec, between rape and seduction. At one level, Alec is the antithesis of these "mailed" and "rollicking" knights, even as he is cited as their contemporary incarnation, revenging their violence. His "violation" of Tess is both radically different from the spectacular violence of knights in armor, that is, a seduction, and no different from the more obvious forms of rape, "the same measure." The parallel construction in Hardy's description of the "appropriation" in The Chase further complicates matters. When Hardy asks "why so often the coarse appropriates the finer thus, the wrong man the woman, the wrong woman the man," he sets Tess and Alec in rough equivalence, each appropriating the other against the odds, each mistaken or "wrong." His elision then opens a space for the double reading that represents sexuality as an irremediably "split reality." If there is no single "meaning" of the events in The Chase, Tess is in a position to have a story, to construe the interaction from her point of view. Ironically, Hardy's elision is also the first sign that his narrative will make it impossible for her to do so.

Rape and seduction reappear in similarly tangled relations throughout the novel: sometimes presented as continuous, sometimes as radically distinct or opposed, sometimes as practical equivalents. But they are invariably invoked in tandem, as if the opposition could not finally be broken. Their coupling ensures Tess's violation and thus her purity: she cannot be condemned as impure; the possibility of rape is too firmly articulated, too pervasive. But at the same time, the intimate pairing of rape and seduction confines her in a problematic of consent, to a passivity that renders her purity as constraining and silent as it is sure.

The Same Old Story: Word for Word

Hardy evokes Tess's concern that she have the opportunity to tell "her story" repeatedly in the novel. She tells Angel that he must know her "'history. I want you to know it — you must let me tell'" (196). Tess's commitment to the importance of "a woman telling her story," (190) and her desire to tell "'my experiences — all about myself — all!'" (187) provoke Angel to a "loving satire" on her inexperience. "Looking into her face," he agrees: "'Your experiences, dear; yes, certainly; any number . . . My Tess has, no doubt, almost as many experiences as that wild convolvulus out there on the garden hedge, that opened itself this morning for the first time'" (187). His reading of Tess's face permits Angel to laugh at her insistence on "this precious history" and to dictate its predictable form and unremarkable content: "'Yes, I was born at so and so, Anno Domini ——'" (196). As the wedding approaches, Tess's anxiety grows: "She resolved, with a bursting heart, to tell all her history to Angel Clare, despite her mother's command" (207) that "on no account do you say a word of your Bygone Trouble to him" (199).

Tess finds the courage to offer her narrative in an intuition of equality that flares on her wedding night when Angel confesses his sexual adventure and asks forgiveness for his faults: "How strange it was! He seemed to be her double" (229). His excuses and fears about admitting his past before the ceremony mirror her own, and after his confession, she celebrates her story's similarity, indeed, identity to his own: "'O Angel — I am almost glad. . . . [It] cannot be more serious, certainly, . . . because 'tis just the *same!*'" (230; emphasis added). Tess's resolve to tell her story is predicated on her (mis)perception that a woman's story may be the same as a man's; she begins to narrate in *imitation* of Angel. The reader is not in a position to agree with her, quite. Indeed, the scene of "a woman telling her story" is completely erased, like the scene of sexual violence itself, and for the same reason:

its meaning cannot be represented from Tess's point of view. That point of view is emphatically excluded.

> 'Say it is not true! No, it is not true!'
> 'It is true.'
> 'Every word?'
> 'Every word.' (240)

Hardy all but mocks his readers' exclusion from the text of Tess's confession. "Every word" is missing from the scene. We learn only that "there had been no exculpatory phrase of any kind" in her speech and no tears (231).[9] Who speaks thus?

When Tess finishes what she mistakenly thinks is the "same" story Angel has told, she asks him for equal treatment: "Forgive me as you are forgiven," she argues. "I have forgiven you for the same. *I* forgive *you,* Angel" (232). This effort to speak as a subject is to no effect. Angel enforces difference on every level. Tess is "not the same. No, not the same" (235). With breathtaking self-righteousness, he asserts both that the "same" experience has rendered them hopelessly different and that she is no longer the same woman, literally no longer herself: "'You were one person; now you are another. My God — how can forgiveness meet such a grotesque — prestidigitation as that!'" "'The woman I have been loving is not you.'" "But who?" she asks. (233). 'Another woman in your shape,'" he replies (233). Here, the potential discontinuity between the flesh and the self, which operates throughout the novel as the mechanism that guarantees Tess's purity despite her seductiveness, is revealed to a masculine reader with devastating effect. The consequences for Tess are grave.

"Your shape" is perhaps a poor figure for what remains of Tess in Angel's eyes, as it is precisely knowledge of an alteration in her body itself that alienates Angel: only her shape is altered. Yet his charge is originally one Tess levels at herself: "'O my love, my love, why do I love you so!' . . . 'for she you love is *not my real self,* but one in my *image;* the one I might have been!'" (220; emphasis added). Tess voices a similar anxiety about the status of what she calls her "self" at other points in the novel. She asks the Vicar to speak not "as saint to

[9]Silverman notes that in this scene Tess is subjected to overwhelming representational pressure: "At perhaps no other point in the novel is figural meaning so explicitly circumscribed by sexual difference. Angel is partly in the scene, on the side of the spectacle, as well as partly outside the scene, on the other side of vision, but the narrator's gaze slides quickly past him . . . it turns a searchlight on Tess, who remains all the time unseeing" (20).

sinner, but as you yourself to me myself — poor me" (115). At the moment of crisis, she says, "'I thought, Angel, that you loved me — me, my very self! If it is I you do love, O how can it be that you look and speak so!'" (232). Tess struggles to believe her body and this self are not identical, that she possesses a "very self," who survives "all changes," "all disgraces," but she never asserts the meaning of that self for Angel in a way that eludes the mark that Alec has left on her flesh, or indeed, the seductiveness that the narrator presents as an integral quality of that flesh. Angel insists that he loved "another woman" in Tess's seductive "shape," but actually it is "soft and silent" Tess in another shape, intact rather than "un-intact" (333), whole rather than broken (into), the Pure Tess, whom Angel loves.

Hardy insists on Angel's refusal to see the *meaning* of the events in The Chase as Tess sees them, that is, to see them as forgivable in part because Angel's mode of reading has been Hardy's as well. Angel, like the narrator, persistently reads Tess's flesh, even after her confession, when he might have begun to suspect the limits if not the complete inadequacy of his method: "She looked absolutely pure. Nature, in her fantastic trickery, had set such a seal of maidenhood upon Tess's countenance that he gazed at her with a stupefied air" (240). The narrator intervenes to berate Angel for lacking confidence in his reading of Tess's body: "[Angel] argued erroneously when he said to himself that her heart was not indexed in the honest freshness of her face; but Tess had no advocate to set him right" (238). The narrator so prizes the indexical quality of Tess's body that her effort to *speak* as her own advocate is dismissed, even as it is elided in the text. Tess's words do not disrupt Angel's vision, but only the trust he has in his own reading of the form before him. The narrator comments that the "essence of things had changed" (231) rather than their substance. The story that Tess had hoped would bring her subjectivity out into Angel's view, has only convinced him of the trickery of nature. "Her personality did not plead her cause so forcibly as she had anticipated" (246); following Angel's interpretation with "dumb and vacant fidelity" (235), she agrees that "the figurative phrase was true: she was another woman than the one who had excited his desire" (246).

Hardy all but parodies his consistent elisions of Tess's narrative in the episode of her letter, written in defiance of her mother's command, but accidentally slipped beneath the carpet and thus unread on the eve of the wedding. The triple exclusion of Tess's story is spectacular, even grandiose; the lack her silences engender is filled only by Sorrow. His presence, brief as it is, is the material guarantee of Tess's sexual experience, and thus an essential condition of the plot, given both her silence and the narrator's elisions. The problem Hardy finally presents us is thus uniquely a problem of reading, of locating in external form, in the "substance" or letter of one's text, its true meaning. The ambiguity of the scene of sexual violence refigured both as an ambiguity *within* Tess, a mind-body problem, and as a fatal discontinuity that separates the appearance from the reality, the external from the internal, leaves the reader hopelessly dependent on his own desire to ground his reading. MacKinnon's account of reality as split applies to Angel and Tess as it does to Alec and Tess, and in the end, to Tess herself: the meaning of the contested interaction from Tess's point of view is radically unavailable, and so we too face the problem of reading the silent, seductive Tess as a text, confined by the limits that mark every reading of the scene of sexual violence.

A Portion of the Field: "A Lesser Creature Than a Woman"

It has frequently been remarked that Tess is the least human of Hardy's protagonists. She is repeatedly compared to animals: birds, cats, snakes, a leopard, a fly (e.g., 137, 138, 234). "Creature" (117) is also a term used to describe her. At Talbothays in the dawn light, when Angel sees Tess as the "visionary essence of woman" and is most "impressed," he describes her as "ghostly, as if she were merely a soul at large" (146). By the novel's end, her breathing is "quick and small, like that of a lesser creature than a woman" (382). An animal, a ghost, a vision: a shadow of subjectivity, not quite human.

Tess is also persistently engulfed by the vegetation of the natural world she inhabits. The "social chasm" that divides the heroine's personality (not just her body from her mind) — and thus differentiates her sexual experience from Angel's — is partially defined by this well-known passage: "a field man is a *personality* afield; a field-woman is a portion of the field; she has somehow lost her own margin, imbibed the essence of her surrounding, and assimilated herself with it" (107; emphasis added). This potential for the loss of personality is specifically feminine in *Tess of the d'Urbervilles,* and Tess recognizes herself in these terms at times. As Hardy puts it,

> her quiescent glide was of a piece with the element she moved in. Her flexuous and stealthy figure became an integral part of the scene. At times her whimsical fancy would intensify natural processes around her till they seemed a part of her own story.

> Rather they became a part of it; for the world is only a psychological phenomenon, and what they seemed they were. (104–05)

The metaphors assimilating Tess to the natural world suggest the physical problem — which is ultimately a sexual problem — she faces throughout the novel. Losing her margin, seeming and therefore apparently becoming a creature less than human, Tess inhabits a foreign body. The "problem" of Tess's body is the most powerful figure by which Hardy distances her from ordinary (masculine) humanity and thus marks her peculiar lack of subjectivity as feminine.

Tess's body is a particular burden to her. And the status of that body — after her sexual experience and the birth of her child — is constantly in question. She herself wonders if lost chastity is forever lost. Joan Durbeyfield regards the "Bygone Trouble" as a "passing accident." Hardy's narrator is of two minds on the matter. As many readers have observed, he insists on Tess's purity, but he is obsessed with that "immeasurable social chasm" that divides her *personality* — and not only her flesh — on that night in The Chase. He shifts from one view to the other, depending on his antagonist within the plot. Thus the narrator suggests that "Tess Durbeyfield, otherwise d'Urberville, [is] somewhat changed — the same, but not the same" (108). At another point, he compares her experience to the acquisition of a "liberal education":

> Almost at a leap Tess thus changed from simple girl to complex woman. Symbols of reflectiveness passed into her face, and a note of tragedy at times into her voice. Her eyes grew larger and more *eloquent.* (117; emphasis added)

Clearly the change in Tess is not simply a matter of the world's opinion. This reading of her body is in fact a paradigm for Angel's reading in the aftermath of her confession. Hardy's aestheticization of her is complete; he makes her intensely literary — symbolic, tragic, eloquent — in her flesh, her eyes, her voice, her face. Furthermore, he makes it clear that sexual experience is to a woman what literature (and looking at Tess) is to a man. Her body directly expresses all of the "changes" her "liberal education" has produced in her. The truth of her inner life is vivid in her appearance. Her body is plain text, a transparent notation of her essential self.

"True correspondence" between inner and outer is essential to Hardy's effort to represent Tess without taking the risk of allowing her to tell her own story. But this essential correspondence breaks down when Hardy approaches Tess's sexuality in a context where he cannot code it as beauty. We have seen that she is seductive, provocative, without even trying, without courting our attention. Insofar as this provocative quality is equated with her sexuality, it is a wholly external condition, an imposition. Tess cannot function as a subject of the discourse of desire. This was clear to Mowbray Morris, who in rejecting the book for *Macmillan's Magazine* observed that

> even Angel Clare . . . has not yet got beyond a purely sensuous admiration for her person. Tess herself does not appear to have any feelings of this sort about her; but her capacity for stirring and by implication for gratifying these feelings for others is pressed rather more frequently and elaborately than strikes me as altogether convenient, at any rate for my magazine.[10]

Tess's sexuality is this tempting quality, this unconscious, indeed, unwanted seductiveness. Alec sees her as a temptress and a witch, but admits she has "done" nothing; she is the innocent means of his backsliding. Tess herself reminds Angel, "'You once said that I was apt to win men against their better judgment; and if I am constantly before your eyes I may cause you to change your plans in opposition to your reason and wish'" (247). The meaning of Tess's sexuality is consistently determined elsewhere. Indeed, her sexuality has no "meaning" for her per se; this is the price of her purity. The narrator defends her from at least some of those meanings, from those that would challenge her purity, for example, but as he is unable to represent the meaning of her sexuality from her point of view without risking the emergence of her active desire, he is in fact the most persistent of the readers of Tess's body.

Hardy naturally has some difficulty negotiating the question of Tess's consciousness of her seductive beauty. He obviously cannot portray her as manipulating it; on the other hand, her "tragedy" depends on it, and he can hardly leave her ignorant of the account men give of her effect on them, especially after her experience with Alec. I have referred to this effect as unwanted and unconscious, but it can only be unwanted to the degree that some consciousness of it is forced on Tess as a subject. The awkwardness of Hardy's position is obvious in his commentary on Tess and Angel's discussion of their future after their twin "confessions":

[10]Manuscript held at Dorset County Museum, to Thomas Hardy, 25 November 1889; cited in Laird.

> Tess's feminine hope — shall we confess it — had been so obstinately recuperative as to revive in her surreptitious visions of a domiciliary intimacy continued long enough to break down his coldness even against his judgment. Though *unsophisticated* in the usual sense, she was not *incomplete;* and it would have denoted *deficiency of womanhood* if she had not *instinctively* known what an argument lies in propinquity. Nothing else would serve her, she knew, if this failed. It was wrong to hope in what was of the nature of *strategy,* she said to herself: yet that sort of hope she could not extinguish. (245–46; emphasis added)

Hardy argues that Tess's *completeness* depends not on her physical or emotional purity, but on her properly feminine awareness of her seductive power. To seduce may be "to break down . . . coldness even against [another's] judgment." Alec hoped (at first) to wear Tess down by a combination of his proximity and bullying; Tess hopes, in the nature of a strategy, to weaken Angel's resolve by the argument of her seductive presence. Hardy balances this confession of Tess's capacity for stratagems with the assurance that her knowledge is inherent in her femininity, her "womanhood." She knows the force of her sexual appeal "instinctively," not as a subject of knowledge. Instinct here is opposed to "sophistication," as the natural is opposed to the social. The latter is culpable: man-made and articulate, like the verbal persuasions of seduction. The former remains pure: animal, feminine, and dumb, like "soft, silent Tess."

Hardy's fear of the possibility that Tess might appear as a desiring subject — and so seem impure — is so intense that he explicitly posits her consciousness of her sexuality only in the context of sexual violence. As a victim of her sexuality, which is her seductiveness, she can remain pure. The encounter in The Chase is elided, but we do see Tess "assaulted" once. Hardy tells us "there was something of the habitude of the wild animal in the unreflecting instinct with which she rambled on" after Angel's departure, "obliterating her identity" (274) as she roams. He adds that "among the difficulties of her lonely position not the least was the attention she excited by her appearance" (274). Appearance is not here a reference to a mere "seeming," but to Tess's body, which is her identity. Strangers address her with "rude words" more than once, but she feels no "bodily fear" until the farmer who eventually employs her accosts her, demanding she admit the truth about her past with Alec and suggesting that she "ought to beg [his] pardon for that blow of" Angel's (275). Tess flees into the woods and sleeps, again in a nest of leaves. She then "resolve[s] to run no further risks from her appearance";

she undoes her physical beauty to protect herself from "aggressive admiration" (278). She dresses in her oldest clothing, wraps her jaw in a bandage, and cuts away her eyebrows. This disfiguration secures her a certain peace and the comfort of insults from passersby. Hardy remarks that she "walks on; a figure which is part of the landscape; a fieldwoman pure and simple. . . . There is no sign of young passion in her now" (278). Tess remakes her body into a surface "over which the eye might have roved as over a thing scarcely percipient, almost inorganic" (279); she has completely "lost her own margin" now and is nothing more than "a portion of the field" (107).

"Obliterating her identity" by mutilating her face, Tess is no longer a "sign" to attract the aggressive admiration of others. She is safe, though shrunken, and she does not really fear the farmer (as she had Alec): "*He's* not in love with me" (312). But she has recovered, that is to say, grown beautiful again, before she travels to visit Angel's father. After Mercy Chant and Angel's smug brothers take her boots, Tess angrily throws back her veil — "take[s] sufficient interest in herself" is how the narrator describes the gesture — "as if to let the world see she could at least exhibit a face such as Mercy Chant could not show" (298). Yet, without Angel's desire, Tess insists, "'It is nothing — it is nothing! . . . Nobody loves it; nobody sees it. Who cares about the looks of a castaway like me!'" (298).

This return to "self-interest," to the only subjectivity Tess is granted, a subjectivity that is an immediate extension of her flesh, leads to the renewed acquaintance with Alec. Many circumstances conspire to drive Tess back to Alec, not least among them her final acquiescence to the view that a physical change, the loss of virginity, is the definitive experience, in effect, the meaning of her life. Tess is the first character in the novel to wonder if the meaning of her encounter with Alec is not equal to the meaning of marriage. She harbors "a religious sense of a certain moral validity in the previous union" (191) and wonders: "She was Mrs. Angel Clare, indeed, but had she any moral right to the name? Was she not more truly Mrs. Alexander d'Urberville?" (220). When Angel asks "'How can we live together while that man lives? — he being your husband in Nature, and not I,'" (245), and Alec claims, "'If you are any man's wife you are mine!'" (325), they merely echo Tess. And even as she rebuffs Alec, "a consciousness that in a physical sense this man alone was her husband seemed to weigh on her more and more" (349).

When Tess accepts this "physical sense" as *the* meaning of her experience, it is at the price of no longer imagining herself as possessing any order of subjectivity.[11] She muses at Flintcomb-Ash that to have married Alec's wealth and position "would have lifted her completely out of subjection, not only to her present oppressive employer, but to a whole world who seemed to despise her" (313). When Angel returns, he finds her "lifted out of subjection" in another sense: "His original Tess had spiritually ceased to recognize the body before him as hers — allowing it to drift, like a corpse upon the current, in a direction dissociated from its living will" (367). There is an irony, of course, in the word "original." Given his view that the original Tess ceased to exist once she had told her story and revealed her bodily history, Angel's remark is ambiguous in its referent: where might we locate the "original Tess"?

Angel's account of Tess in this passage has an unexpected resonance with an earlier description of her, a passage in which Hardy comes close to representing Tess as a desiring rather than only a desired/desirable subject.

> Tess flung herself down upon the rustling undergrowth of spear-grass, as upon a bed, and remained crouching in palpitating misery broken by momentary shoots of joy, which her fears about the ending could not altogether suppress.
>
> In reality, she was drifting into acquiescence. Every see-saw of her breath, every wave of her blood, every pulse singing in her ears, was a voice that joined with nature in revolt against her scrupulousness. Reckless, inconsiderate acceptance of him; to close with him at the altar, revealing nothing, and chancing discovery; to snatch ripe pleasure before the iron teeth of pain could have time to shut upon her: that was what love counseled; and in almost a terror of ecstasy Tess divined that, despite her many months of lonely self-chastisement, wrestlings, communings, schemes to lead a future of austere isolation, love's counsel would prevail. . . .
>
> 'I shall give way — I shall say yes — I shall let myself marry him — I cannot help it!' (187–88)

"Drifting," just as she is in her final relation to Alec, Tess is here at the mercy of currents and waves, and of her rebellious blood, succumbing

[11]This defeat contrasts with what Frances Ferguson sees as Clarissa's resistance in Samuel Richardson's *Clarissa* (1748) to "recogniz[ing] herself in a new form as a result of [her] rape." Clarissa insists on the "inability of a form to carry mental states in anything but excessively capacious (that is, ambiguous) or potentially self-contradictory stipulated forms. . . . When Clarissa begins dying and Lovelace begins longing for her consent, the novel is literally haunted by the specter of psychology, in which mental states do not so much appear as register the improbability of their appearing" (106).

to "love's counsel," giving way despite her chastisements and "better judgment." The context, of course, is radically different, and Hardy emphasizes Tess's joy and her sense of snatching pleasure. But her terrified subjection to external force — here Hardy names it nature — is intensely realized. Tess's "desire," like her sexuality, is an imposition she ultimately consents to, moving in its currents, adrift.

Angel's remark echoes Tess's claim "'that our souls can be made to go outside our bodies when we are alive'" (136). She encourages her listeners at Talbothays to lie in a field and stare up at the stars: "You will soon find that you are hundreds and hundreds o' miles away from your body, which *you don't seem to want at all*" (136; emphasis added). That Tess should finally not want her body is a consequence of her inability to make her reading of it more potent in her world. Part of the interpretative difficulty Hardy creates in his double view of Tess and her relation to her body is captured by the contradiction in Angel's suggestion that the corpse before him — Tess — is "dissociated from its living will." Tess's body has never been granted the force of will; indeed, only by abandoning her seductive flesh can she hope to escape its tormenting effects.

Dissociation thus follows inexorably from Hardy's insistence in reading Tess as a body and his inability to allow her to speak as a subject; ironically, we might say that Tess dies when she accepts the complete association or identification of her body and her will, which has the same result as their dissociation — the death of the subject. This is the moment of complete purification, the point at which Tess abandons her struggle to distinguish her body from her "very self," to construct a subjectivity that speaks or desires in an idiom other than that of her flesh. As a subject, she finally has no experience to speak of; only her body is experienced, and her silence requires that we project meaning upon it. Alec's murder does not allow her to go on living, but it enables Tess to give over that body to the judges, utterly silenced and purified, not by Hardy's failure to see that she might speak, but by his unflinching description of the inexorable forces that produce her as the seductive object of the discourses of man.

WORKS CITED

Bayley, John. *An Essay on Hardy*. Cambridge: Cambridge UP, 1978.

Boumelha, Penny. *Thomas Hardy and Women: Sexual Ideology and Narrative Form*. Totowa: Barnes, 1982.

Brownmiller, Susan. *Against Our Will: Men, Women and Rape*. New York: Simon, 1975.

Claridge, Laura. "Tess: A Less than Pure Woman Ambivalently Presented." *Texas Studies in Language and Literature* 28 (1986): 324–38.

Cox, R. G., ed. *Thomas Hardy: The Critical Heritage*. New York: Barnes, 1970.

Eagleton, Terry. *The Rape of Clarissa*. Minneapolis: U of Minnesota P, 1982.

Estrich, Susan. *Real Rape*. Cambridge: Harvard UP, 1987.

Ferguson, Frances. "Rape and the Rise of the Novel." *Representations* 20 (1987): 88–112.

Gallop, Jane. *The Daughter's Seduction*. Ithaca: Cornell UP, 1982.

Gregor, Ian. *The Great Web*. Totowa: Rowman and Littlefield, 1974.

Griffin, Susan. *Rape: The Power of Consciousness*. San Francisco: Harper, 1979.

Haraway, Donna. "A Manifesto for Cyborgs: Science, Technology, and Socialist Feminism in the 1980s." *Socialist Review* 15 (1985): 65–107.

Hardwick, Elizabeth. *Seduction and Betrayal*. New York: Vintage, 1975.

Jacobus, Mary. "Tess: A Pure Woman." *Tearing the Veil: Essays on Femininity*. Ed. Susan Lipshitz. London: Routledge and Kegan Paul, 1978. 75–92.

Laird, J. T. *The Shaping of Tess of the d'Urbervilles*. Oxford: Oxford UP, 1975.

Lerner, Laurence, and Holmstrom, John. *Thomas Hardy and His Readers*. London: Bodley Head, 1968.

MacKinnon, Catharine A. "Feminism, Marxism, Method and the State: An Agenda for Theory." *Signs* 7 (1982): 515–44.

———. "Feminism, Marxism, Method and the State: Towards Feminist Jurisprudence." *Signs* 8 (1983): 635–58.

Marcus, Sharon. "Fighting Bodies, Fighting Words: A Theory and Politics of Rape Prevention." *Feminists Theorize the Political*. Eds. Judith Butler and Joan W. Scott. London: Routledge, 1992. 385–403.

Miller, J. Hillis. *Fiction and Repetition*. Cambridge: Harvard UP, 1981.

Paris, Bernard. "A Confusion of Many Standards: Conflicting Value Systems in *Tess of the d'Urbervilles*." *Nineteenth Century Fiction* 24 (1969): 57–79.

Rooney, Ellen. "'A Little More Than Persuading': Tess and the Subject of Sexual Violence." *Rape and Representation*. Eds. Brenda R. Silver and Lynn A. Higgins. New York: Columbia UP, 1992. 87–114.

Schweik. Robert C. "Moral Perspectives in *Tess of the d'Urbervilles.*" *College English* 24 (1962): 14–18.

Silverman, Kaja. "History, Figuration and Female Subjectivity in *Tess of the d'Urbervilles.*" *Novel* 18 (1984): 5–28.

Deconstruction and *Tess of the d'Urbervilles*

WHAT IS DECONSTRUCTION?

Deconstruction has a reputation for being the most complex and forbidding of contemporary critical approaches to literature, but in fact almost all of us have, at one time, either deconstructed a text or badly wanted to deconstruct one. Sometimes when we hear a lecturer effectively marshal evidence to show that a book means primarily one thing, we long to interrupt and ask what he or she would make of other, conveniently overlooked passages that seem to contradict the lecturer's thesis. Sometimes, after reading a provocative critical article that *almost* convinces us that a familiar work means the opposite of what we assumed it meant, we may wish to make an equally convincing case for our former reading of the text. We may not think that the poem or novel in question better supports our interpretation, but we may recognize that the text can be used to support *both* readings. And sometimes we simply want to make that point: texts can be used to support seemingly irreconcilable positions.

To reach this conclusion is to feel the deconstructive itch. J. Hillis Miller, the preeminent American deconstructor, puts it this way: "Deconstruction is not a dismantling of the structure of a text, but a demonstration that it has already dismantled itself. Its apparently solid ground is no rock but thin air" ("Stevens' Rock" 341). To deconstruct a text isn't to show that all the high old themes aren't there to be found in it. Rather, it is to show that a text — not unlike DNA with its double helix — can have intertwined, opposite "discourses" — strands of narrative, threads of meaning.

Ultimately, of course, deconstruction refers to a larger and more complex enterprise than the practice of demonstrating that a text can have contradictory meanings. The term refers to a way of reading texts practiced by critics who have been influenced by the writings of the French philosopher Jacques Derrida. It is important to gain some understanding of Derrida's project and of the historical backgrounds of his work before reading the deconstruction that follows, let alone attempting to deconstruct a text.

Derrida, a philosopher of language who coined the term *deconstruction,* argues that we tend to think and express our thoughts in terms of opposites. Something is black but not white, masculine and therefore not feminine, a cause rather than an effect, and so forth. These mutually exclusive pairs or dichotomies are too numerous to list but would include beginning/end, conscious/unconscious, presence/absence, and speech/writing. If we think hard about these dichotomies, Derrida suggests, we will realize that they are not simply oppositions; they are also hierarchies in miniature. In other words, they contain one term that our culture views as being superior and one term viewed as negative or inferior. Sometimes the superior term seems only subtly superior (*speech, cause*), but at other times we know immediately which term is culturally preferable (*presence, beginning,* and *consciousness* are easy choices). But the hierarchy always exists.

Of particular interest to Derrida, perhaps because it involves the language in which all the other dichotomies are expressed, is the hierarchical opposition "speech/writing." Derrida argues that the "privileging" of speech, that is, the tendency to regard speech in positive terms and writing in negative terms, cannot be disentangled from the privileging of presence. (Postcards are written by absent friends; we read Plato because he cannot speak from beyond the grave.) Furthermore, according to Derrida, the tendency to privilege both speech and presence is part of the Western tradition of *logocentrism,* the belief that in some ideal beginning were creative *spoken* words, such as "Let there be light," spoken by an ideal, *present* God.[1] According to logocentric

[1]Derrida sometimes uses the word *phallogocentrism* to indicate that there is "a certain indissociability" between logocentrism and the "phallocentrism" (*Acts* 57) of a culture whose God created light, the world, and man before creating woman — from Adam's rib. "Phallocentrism" is another name for patriarchy. The role that deconstruction has played in feminist analysis will be discussed later.

tradition, these words can now be represented only in unoriginal speech or writing (such as the written phrase in quotation marks above). Derrida doesn't seek to reverse the hierarchized opposition between speech and writing, or presence and absence, or early and late, for to do so would be to fall into a trap of perpetuating the same forms of thought and expression that he seeks to deconstruct. Rather, his goal is to erase the boundary between oppositions such as speech and writing, and to do so in such a way as to throw the order and values implied by the opposition into question.

Returning to the theories of Ferdinand de Saussure, who invented the modern science of linguistics, Derrida reminds us that the association of speech with present, obvious, and ideal meaning — and writing with absent, merely pictured, and therefore less reliable meaning — is suspect, to say the least. As Saussure demonstrated, words are *not* the things they name and, indeed, they are only arbitrarily associated with those things. A word, like any sign, is what Derrida has called a "deferred presence"; that is to say, "the signified concept is never present in itself," and "every concept is necessarily . . . inscribed in a chain or system, within which it refers to another and to other concepts" ("Différance" 138, 140). Neither spoken nor written words have present, positive, identifiable attributes themselves. They have meaning only by virtue of their difference from other words (*red, read, reed*) and, at the same time, their contextual relationship to those words. Take *read* as an example. To know whether it is the present or past tense of the verb — whether it rhymes with *red* or *reed* — we need to see it in relation to some other words (for example, *yesterday*).

Because the meanings of words lie in the differences between them and in the differences between them and the things they name, Derrida suggests that all language is constituted by *différance,* a word he has coined that puns on two French words meaning "to differ" and "to defer": words are the deferred presences of the things they "mean," and their meaning is grounded in difference. Derrida, by the way, changes the *e* in the French word *différence* to an *a* in his neologism *différance;* the change, which can be seen in writing but cannot be heard in spoken French, is itself a playful, witty challenge to the notion that writing is inferior or "fallen" speech.

In *Dissemination* (1972) and *De la grammatologie* [*Of Grammatology*] (1967), Derrida begins to redefine writing by deconstructing some old definitions. In *Dissemination,* he traces logocentrism back to Plato, who in the *Phaedrus* has Socrates condemn writing and who, in all the great dialogues, powerfully postulates that metaphysical longing for origins and ideals that permeates Western thought. "What Derrida does in his reading of Plato," Barbara Johnson points out in her translator's introduction to *Dissemination,* "is to unfold dimensions of Plato's *text* that work against the grain of (Plato's own) Platonism" (xxiv). Remember: that is what deconstruction does, according to Miller; it shows a text dismantling itself.

In *Of Grammatology,* Derrida turns to the *Confessions* of Jean-Jacques Rousseau and exposes a grain running against the grain. Rousseau — who has often been seen as another great Western idealist and believer in innocent, noble origins — on one hand condemned writing as mere representation, a corruption of the more natural, childlike, direct, and therefore undevious speech. On the other hand, Rousseau acknowledged his own tendency to lose self-presence and blurt out exactly the wrong thing in public. He confesses that, by writing at a distance from his audience, he often expressed himself better: "If I were present, one would never know what I was worth," Rousseau admitted (Derrida, *Of Grammatology* 142). Thus, Derrida shows that one strand of Rousseau's discourse made writing seem a secondary, even treacherous supplement, while another made it seem necessary to communication.

Have Derrida's deconstructions of *Confessions* and the *Phaedrus* explained these texts, interpreted them, opened them up and shown us what they mean? Not in any traditional sense. Derrida would say that anyone attempting to find a single, homogeneous or universal meaning in a text is simply imprisoned by the structure of thought that would oppose two readings and declare one to be right and not wrong, correct rather than incorrect. In fact, any work of literature that we interpret defies the laws of Western logic, the laws of opposition and noncontradiction. From deconstruction's point of view, texts don't say "A and not B." They say "A and not-A." "Instead of a simple 'either/or' structure," Johnson explains, "deconstruction attempts to elaborate a discourse that says *neither* 'either/or' *nor* 'both/and' nor even 'neither/nor,' while at the same time not totally abandoning these logics either. The word deconstruction is meant to undermine the either/or logic of the opposition 'construction/destruction.' Deconstruction is both, it is neither, and it reveals the way in which both construction and destruction are themselves not what they appear to be" (Johnson, *World* 12–13).

Although its ultimate aim may be to criticize Western idealism and logic, deconstruction began as a response to structuralism and to formalism, another structure-oriented theory of reading. Using Saussure's theory as Derrida was to do later, European structuralists attempted to create a *semiology,* or science of signs, that would give humankind at once a scientific and a holistic way of studying the world and its human inhabitants. Roland Barthes, a structuralist who later shifted toward poststructuralism, hoped to recover literary language from the isolation in which it had been studied and to show that the laws that govern it govern all signs, from road signs to articles of clothing. Claude Lévi-Strauss, a structural anthropologist who studied everything from village structure to the structure of myths, found in myths what he called *mythemes,* or building blocks, such as basic plot elements. Recognizing that the same mythemes occur in similar myths from different cultures, he suggested that all myths may be elements of one great myth being written by the collective human mind.

Derrida did not believe that structuralists had the concepts that would someday explain the laws governing human signification and thus provide the key to understanding the form and meaning of everything from an African village to Greek myth to Rousseau's *Confessions.* In his view, the scientific search by structural anthropologists for what unifies humankind amounts to a new version of the old search for the lost ideal, whether that ideal be Plato's bright realm of the Idea or the Paradise of Genesis or Rousseau's unspoiled Nature. As for the structuralist belief that texts have "centers" of meaning, in Derrida's view that derives from the logocentric belief that there is a reading of the text that accords with "the book as seen by God." Jonathan Culler, who thus translates a difficult phrase from Derrida's *L'Écriture et la différence* [*Writing and Difference*] (1967) in his book *Structuralist Poetics* (1975), goes on to explain what Derrida objects to in structuralist literary criticism:

> [When] one speaks of the structure of a literary work, one does so from a certain vantage point: one starts with notions of the meaning or effects of a poem and tries to identify the structures responsible for those effects. Possible configurations or patterns that make no contribution are rejected as irrelevant. That is to say, an intuitive understanding of the poem functions as the "centre". . . : it is both a starting point and a limiting principle. (244)

Deconstruction calls into question assumptions made about literature by formalist, as well as by structuralist, critics. Formalism, or the New Criticism as it was once commonly called, assumes a work of literature to be a freestanding, self-contained object, its meanings found in the complex network of relations that constitute its parts (images, sounds, rhythms, allusions, and so on). To be sure, deconstruction is somewhat like formalism in several ways. Both formalism and deconstruction are text-oriented approaches whose practitioners pay a great deal of attention to rhetorical *tropes* (forms of figurative language including allegory, symbol, metaphor, and metonymy). And formalists, long before deconstructors, discovered counterpatterns of meaning in the same text. Formalists find ambiguity: deconstructors find undecidability. On close inspection, however, the formalist understanding of rhetorical tropes or figures is quite different from that of deconstruction, and undecidability turns out to be different from the ambiguity formalists find in texts.

Formalists, who associated literary with figurative language, made qualitative distinctions between types of figures of speech; for instance, they valued symbols and metaphors over metonyms. (A metonym is a term standing for something with which it is commonly associated or contiguous; we use metonymy when we say we had "the cold plate" for lunch.) From the formalist perspective, metaphors and symbols are less arbitrary figures than metonyms and thus rank more highly in the hierarchy of tropes: a metaphor ("I'm feeling blue") supposedly involves a special, intrinsic, nonarbitrary relationship between its two terms (the feeling of melancholy and the color blue); a symbol ("the river of life") allegedly involves a unique fusion of image and idea.

From the perspective of deconstruction, however, these distinctions are suspect. In "The Rhetoric of Temporality" Paul de Man deconstructs the distinction between symbol and allegory; elsewhere, he, Derrida, and Miller have similarly questioned the metaphor/metonymy distinction, arguing that all figuration is a process of linguistic substitution. In the case of a metaphor (or symbol), they claim, we have forgotten that juxtaposition or contiguity gave rise to the association that now seems mysteriously special. Derrida, in "White Mythology," and de Man, in "Metaphor (*Second Discourse*)," have also challenged the priority of literal over figurative language, and Miller has gone so far as to deny the validity of the literal/figurative distinction, arguing that all words are figures because all language involves *catachresis,* "the violent, forced, or abusive importation of a term from another realm to name something which has no proper name" (Miller, *Ariadne* 21).

The difference between the formalist concept of literary ambiguity and the deconstructive concept of undecidability is as significant as the gap between formalist and deconstructive understandings of figurative language. Undecidability, as de Man came to define it, is a complex notion easily misunderstood. There is a tendency to assume it refers to readers who, when forced to decide between two or more equally plausible and conflicting readings, throw up their hands and decide that the choice can't be made. But undecidability in fact debunks this whole notion of reading as a decision-making process carried out on texts by readers. To say we are forced to choose or decide, or that we are unable to do so, is to locate the problem of undecidability falsely within ourselves, rather than recognizing that it is an intrinsic feature of the text.

Undecidability is thus different from ambiguity, as understood by formalists. Formalists believed that a complete understanding of a literary work is possible, an understanding in which ambiguities will be resolved objectively by the reader, even if only in the sense that they will be shown to have definite, meaningful functions. Deconstructors do not share that belief. They do not accept the formalist view that a work of literary art is demonstrably unified from beginning to end, in one certain way, or that it is organized around a single center that ultimately can be identified and defined. Neither do they accept the concept of irony as simply saying one thing and meaning another thing that will be understood with certainty by the reader. As a result, deconstructors tend to see texts as more radically heterogeneous than do formalists. The formalist critic ultimately makes sense of ambiguity; undecidability, by contrast, is never reduced, let alone mastered by deconstructive reading, although the incompatible possibilities between which it is impossible to decide can be identified with certainty.

For critics practicing deconstruction, a literary text is neither a sphere with a center nor an unbroken line with a definite beginning and end. In fact, many assumptions about the nature of texts have been put in question by deconstruction, which in Derrida's words "dislocates the borders, the framing of texts, everything which should preserve their immanence and make possible an internal reading or merely reading in the classical sense of the term" ("Some Statements" 86). A text consists of words inscribed in and inextricable from the myriad discourses that inform it; from the point of view of deconstruction, the boundaries between any given text and that larger text we call language are always shifting.

It was that larger text that Derrida was referring to when he made his famous statement "*there is nothing outside the text*" (*Grammatology* 158). To understand what Derrida meant by that statement, consider the following: we know the world through language, and the acts and practices that constitute that "real world" (the Oklahoma City bombing, the decision to marry) are inseparable from the discourses out of which they arise and as open to interpretation as any work of literature. Derrida is not alone in deconstructing the world/text opposition. De Man viewed language as something that has great power in individual, social, and political life. Geoffrey Hartman, who was closely associated with deconstruction during the 1970s, wrote that "nothing can lift us out of language" (xii).

Once we understand deconstruction's view of the literary text — as words that are part of and that resonate with an immense linguistic structure in which we live and move and have our being — we are in a better position to understand why deconstructors reach points in their readings at which they reveal, but cannot decide between, incompatible interpretive possibilities. A text is not a unique, hermetically sealed space. Perpetually open to being seen in the light of new contexts, any given text has the potential to be different each time it is read. Furthermore, as Miller has shown in *Ariadne's Thread: Story Lines* (1992), the various "terms" and "famil[ies] of terms" we use in performing our readings invariably affect the results. Whether we choose to focus on a novel's characters or its realism, for instance, leads us to different views of the same text. "No one thread," Miller asserts, "can be followed to a central point where it provides a means of overseeing, controlling, and understanding the whole" (21).

Complicating matters still further is the fact that the individual words making up narratives — the words out of which we make our mental picture of a character or place — usually have several (and often have conflicting) meanings due to the complex histories of their usage. (If your professor tells the class that you have written a "fulsome report" and you look up the word *fulsome* in a contemporary dictionary, you will learn that it can mean either "elaborate" or "offensive"; if, for some reason, you don't know what *offensive* means, you will find out that it can equally well describe your favorite quarterback and a racist joke.) "Each word," as Miller puts it, "inheres in a labyrinth of branching interverbal relationships"; often there are "forks in the etymological line leading to bifurcated or trifurcated roots." Deconstructors often turn to etymology, not to help them decide whether a statement means this or that, but rather as a way of revealing the coincidence of several meanings in the same text. "The effect of etymological retracing," Miller writes, "is not to ground the work solidly but to render it unstable, equivocal, wavering, groundless" (*Ariadne* 19).

Deconstruction is not really interpretation, the act of choosing between or among possible meanings. Derrida has glossed de Man's statement that "there is no need to deconstruct Rousseau" by saying that "this was another way of saying: there is always already deconstruction, at work *in* works, especially *literary* works. It cannot be applied, after the fact and from outside, as a technical instrument. Texts deconstruct *themselves* by themselves" (*Memoires* 123). If deconstruction is not interpretation, then what is it? Deconstruction may be defined as reading, as long as reading is defined as de Man defined it — as a process involving moments of what he called *aporia* or terminal uncertainty, and as an act performed with full knowledge of the fact that all texts are ultimately unreadable (if reading means reducing a text to a single, homogeneous meaning). Miller explains unreadability by saying that although there are moments of great lucidity in reading, each "lucidity will in principle contain its own blind spot requiring a further elucidation and exposure of error, and so on, ad infinitum. . . . One should not underestimate, however, the productive illumination produced as one moves through these various stages of reading" (*Ethics* 42, 44).

Miller's point is important because, in a sense, it deconstructs or erases the boundary between the readings of deconstructors and the interpretations of more traditional critics. It suggests that all kinds of critics have had their moments of lucidity; it also suggests that critics practicing deconstruction know that their *own* insights — even their insights into what is or isn't contradictory, undecidable, or unreadable in a text — are hardly the last word. As Art Berman writes,

> In *Blindness and Insight* de Man demonstrates that the apparently well-reasoned arguments of literary critics contain contradiction at their core; yet there is no alternative path to insight. . . . The readers of criticism recognize the blindness of their predecessors, reorganize it, and thereby gain both the insight of the critics and a knowledge of the contradiction that brings forth insight. Each reader, of course, has his own blindness; and the criticism of criticism is not a matter of rectifying someone else's mistakes (239–40).

When de Man spoke of the resistance to theory he referred generally to the antitheoretical bias in literary studies. But he might as well have been speaking specifically of the resistance to deconstruction, as expressed not only in academic books and journals but also in popular magazines such as *Newsweek*. Attacks on deconstruction became more common and more personal some four years after de Man's death in 1983. That was the year that a Belgian scholar working on a doctoral thesis discovered ninety-two articles that de Man had written during World War II for the Brussels newspaper *Le Soir,* a widely read French-language daily that had fallen under Nazi control during the German occupation of Belgium. Ultimately, one hundred and seventy articles by de Man were found in *Le Soir;* another ten were discovered in *Het Vlaamsche Land,* a collaborationist newspaper published in Flemish. These writings, which date from 1941 (when de Man was twenty-one years old), ceased to appear before 1943, by which time it had become clear to most Belgians that Jews were being shipped to death camps such as Auschwitz.

De Man's wartime journalism consists mainly, but not entirely, of inoffensive literary pieces. In one article de Man takes Germany's triumph in World War II as a given, places the German people at the center of Western civilization, and foresees a mystical era involving suffering but also faith, exaltation, and rapture. In another article, entitled "*Les Juifs dans la littérature actuelle*" ["Jews in Present-day Literature"], de Man scoffs at the notion that Jewish writers have significantly influenced the literature of his day and, worse, considers the merits of creating a separate Jewish colony that would be isolated from Europe.

No one who had known de Man since his immigration to the United States in 1948 had found him to be illiberal or anti-Semitic. Furthermore, de Man had spent his career in the United States demystifying or, as he would have said, "debunking" the kind of ideological assumptions (about the relationship between aesthetics and national cultures) that lie behind his most offensive Belgian newspaper writings. The critic who in *The Resistance to Theory* (1986) argued that literature must not become "a substitute for theology, ethics, etc." (de Man 24) had either changed radically since writing of the magical integrity and wholeness of the German nation and its culture or had not deeply believed what he had written as a young journalist.

These points have been made in various ways by de Man's former friends and colleagues. Geoffrey Hartman has said that de Man's later work, the work we associate with deconstruction, "looks like a belated, but still powerful, act of conscience" (26–31). Derrida, who like Hartman is a Jew, has read carefully de Man's wartime discourse, showing it to be "split, disjointed, engaged in incessant conflicts" (Hamacher, Hertz, and Keenan 135). "On the one hand," Derrida finds "*unpardonable*" de Man's suggestion that a separate Jewish colony be set up; "on the other hand," he notes that of the four writers de Man praises in the same article (André Gide, Franz Kafka, D. H. Lawrence, and Ernest Hemingway), not one was German, one (Kafka) *was* Jewish, and all four "represent everything that Nazism . . . would have liked to extirpate from history and the great tradition" (Hamacher, Hertz, and Keenan 145).

While friends asserted that some of de Man's statements were unpardonable, deconstruction's severest critics tried to use a young man's sometimes deplorable statements as evidence that a whole critical movement was somehow morally as well as intellectually flawed. As Andrej Warminski summed it up, "the 'discovery' of the 1941–42 writings is being used to perpetuate the old myths about so-called 'deconstruction'" (Hamacher, Hertz, and Keenan 389). Knowing what some of those myths are — and why, in fact, they *are* myths — aids our understanding in an indirect, contrapuntal way that is in keeping with the spirit of deconstruction.

In his book *The Ethics of Reading* (1987), Miller refutes two notions commonly repeated by deconstruction's detractors. One is the idea that deconstructors believe a text means nothing in the sense that it means whatever the playful reader *wants* it to mean. The other is the idea that deconstruction is "immoral" insofar as it refuses to view literature in the way it has traditionally been viewed, namely, "as the foundation and embodiment, the means of preserving and transmitting, the basic humanistic values of our culture" (9). Responding to the first notion, Miller points out that neither Derrida nor de Man "has ever asserted the freedom of the reader to make the text mean anything he or she wants it to mean. Each has in fact asserted the reverse" (10). As for the second notion — that deconstructors are guilty of shirking an ethical responsibility because their purpose is not to (re)discover and (re)assert the transcendent and timeless values contained in great books — Miller argues that "this line of thought" rests "on a basic misunderstanding of the way the ethical moment enters into the act of reading" (9). That "ethical moment," Miller goes on to argue, "is not a matter of response to a thematic content asserting this or that idea about morality. It is a much more fundamental 'I must' responding to the language of literature in itself. . . . Deconstruction is nothing more or less than good reading as such" (9–10). Reading itself, in other words, is an act that leads to further ethical acts, decisions, and behaviors in a real world involving relations to other people and to society at large. For these, the reader must take responsibility, as for any other ethical act.

A third commonly voiced objection to deconstruction is to its playfulness, to the evident pleasure its practitioners take in teasing out all the contradictory interpretive possibilities generated by the words in a text, their complex etymologies and contexts, and their potential to be read figuratively or even ironically. Certainly, playfulness and pleasure are aspects of deconstruction. In his book *The Post Card* (1987), Derrida specifically associates deconstruction with pleasure; in an interview published in a collection of his essays entitled *Acts of Literature* (1992), he speculates that "it is perhaps this *jouissance* which most irritates the all-out adversaries of deconstruction" (56). But such adversaries misread deconstruction's "jouissance," its pleasurable playfulness. Whereas they see it as evidence that deconstructors view texts as tightly enclosed fields on which they can play delightfully useless little word games, Derrida has said that the "subtle and intense pleasure" of deconstruction arises from the "dismantl[ing]" of repressive assumptions, representations, and ideas — in short, from the "lifting of repression" (*Acts* 56–57). As Gregory S. Jay explains in his book *America the Scrivener: Deconstruction and the Subject of Literary History* (1990), "Deconstruction has been not only a matter of reversing binary oppositions but also a matter of disabling the hierarchy of values they enable and of speculating on alternative modes of knowing and of acting" (xii).

Far from viewing literature as a word-playground, Derrida, in Derek Attridge's words, "emphasizes . . . literature as an institution," one "not given in nature or the brain but brought into being by processes that are social, legal, and political, and that can be mapped historically and geographically" (*Acts* 23). By thus characterizing Derrida's emphasis, Attridge counters the commonest of the charges that have been leveled at deconstructors, namely, that they divorce literary texts from historical, political, and legal institutions.

In *Memoires for Paul de Man* (1986), Derrida argues that, where history is concerned, "deconstructive discourses" have pointedly and effectively questioned "the classical assurances of history, the genealogical narrative, and periodizations of all sorts" (15) — in other words, the tendency of historians to view the past as the source of (lost) truth and value, to look for explanations in origins, and to view as unified epochs (for example, the Victorian period, 1837–1901) what are in fact complex and heterogeneous times in history. As for politics, Derrida points out that de Man invariably "says something about institutional structures and the political stakes of hermeneutic conflicts," which is to say that de Man's commentaries acknowledge that conflicting interpretations reflect and are reflected in the politics of institutions (such as the North American university).

In addition to history and politics, the law has been a subject on which deconstruction has had much to say of late. In an essay on Franz Kafka's story "Before the Law," Derrida has shown that for Kafka the law as such exists but can never be confronted by those who would do so and fulfill its commands. Miller has pointed out that the law "may only be confronted in its delegates or representatives or by its effects on us or others" (*Ethics* 20). What or where, then, is the law itself? The law's presence, Miller suggests, is continually deferred by narrative, that is, writing about or on the law which constantly reinterprets the law in the attempt to reveal what it really is and means. This very act of (re)interpretation, however, serves to "defer" or distance the law even further from the case at hand, since the (re)interpretation takes precedence (and assumes prominence) over the law itself. (As Miller defines it, narrative would include everything from a Victorian novel that promises to reveal moral law to the opinion of a Supreme Court justice regarding the constitutionality of a given action, however different these two documents are in the conventions they follow and the uses to which they are put.) Miller likens the law to a promise, "the validity of [which] does not lie in itself but in its future fulfillment," and to a story "divided against itself" that in the end "leaves its readers . . . still in expectation" (*Ethics* 33).

Because the facts about deconstruction are very different from the myth of its playful irreverence and irrelevance, a number of contemporary thinkers have found it useful to adapt and apply deconstruction in their work. For instance, a deconstructive theology has been developed. Architects have designed and built buildings grounded, as it were, in deconstructive architectural theory. In the area of law, the Critical Legal Studies movement has, in Christopher Norris's words, effectively used "deconstructive thinking" of the kind de Man used in analyzing Rousseau's *Social Contract* "to point up the blind spots, conflicts, and antinomies that plague the discourse of received legal wisdom." Critical legal theorists have debunked "the formalist view of law," that is, the "view which holds law to be a system of neutral precepts and principles," showing instead how the law "gives rise to various disabling contradictions," such as "the problematic distinction between 'private' and 'public' domains." They have turned deconstruction into "a sophisticated means of making the point that all legal discourse is performative in character, i.e., designed to secure assent through its rhetorical power to convince or persuade" (Norris, *Deconstruction and the Interests* 17). Courtroom persuasion, Gerald

Lopez has argued in a 1989 article in the *Michigan Law Review*, consists of storytelling as much as argument (Clayton 13).

In the field of literary studies, the influence of deconstruction may be seen in the work of critics ostensibly taking some other, more political approach. Barbara Johnson has put deconstruction to work for the feminist cause. She and Shoshana Felman have argued that chief among those binary oppositions "based on repression of differences with entities" is the opposition man/woman (Johnson, *Critical* x). In a reading of the "undecidability" of "femininity" in Balzac's story "The Girl with the Golden Eyes," Felman puts it this way: "the rhetorical hierarchization of the . . . opposition between the sexes is . . . such that woman's *difference* is suppressed, being totally subsumed by the reference of the feminine to masculine identity" ("Rereading" 25).

Elsewhere, Johnson, Felman, and Gayatri Spivak have combined Derrida's theories with the psychoanalytic theory of Jacques Lacan to analyze the way in which gender and sexuality are ultimately textual, grounded in language and rhetoric. In an essay on Edmund Wilson's reading of Henry James's story *The Turn of the Screw,* Felman has treated sexuality as a form of rhetoric that can be deconstructed, shown to contain contradictions and ambiguities that more traditional readings of sexuality have masked. Gay and lesbian critics have seen the positive implications of this kind of analysis, hence Eve Kosofsky Sedgwick's admission in the early pages of her book *Epistemology of the Closet* (1990): "One main strand of argument in this book is deconstructive, in a fairly specific sense. The analytic move it makes is to demonstrate that categories presented in a culture as symmetrical binary oppositions . . . actually subsist in a more unsettled and dynamic tacit relation" (9–10).

In telling "The Story of Deconstruction" in his book on contemporary American literature and theory, Jay Clayton assesses the current status of this unique approach. Although he notes how frequently deconstructive critics have been cited for their lack of political engagement, he concludes that deconstruction, "a movement accused of formalism and arid intellectualism, participates in the political turn of contemporary culture" (34). He suggests that what began as theory in the late 1960s and 1970s has, over time, developed into a method employed by critics taking a wide range of approaches to literature — ethnic, feminist, new historicist, Marxist — in addition to critics outside of literary studies per se who are involved in such areas as Critical Legal Studies and Critical

Race Theory, which seeks to "sustain a complementary relationship between the deconstructive energies of Critical Legal Studies and the constructive energies of civil rights activism" (58).

Clayton cites the work of Edward Said as a case in point. Through 1975, the year that his *Beginnings: Intention and Method* was published, Said was employing a form of deconstructive criticism that, in Clayton's words, emphasized the "power" of texts "to initiate projects in the real world" (45–46). Said became identified with cultural and postcolonial criticism, however, beginning in 1978 with the publication of his book *Orientalism,* in which he deconstructs the East/West, Orient/Occident opposition. Said argues that Eastern and Middle Eastern peoples have for centuries been stereotyped by the Western discourses of "orientalism," a textuality that in no way reflects the diversity and differences that exist among the peoples it claims to represent. According to Said, that stereotyping not only facilitated the colonization of vast areas of the globe by the so-called West but also still governs, to a great extent, relations with the Arab and the so-called Eastern world. The expansion of Said's field of vision to include not just literary texts but international relations is powerfully indicative of the expanding role that deconstruction currently plays in developing contemporary understandings of politics and culture, as well as in active attempts to intervene in these fields.

John Paul Riquelme begins the deconstructive essay that follows by pointing out that many people view Thomas Hardy as a writer in the nineteenth-century realistic tradition. The "apparent correspondence" between the places in which his stories are set and real places in the South of England leads them to think that Hardy's novels represent a "determinate" (fixed and reliable) reality through a text whose meaning is itself "determinable" (capable of being determined). But appearances can be deceiving, as Riquelme shows in his analysis of the "antirealistic aspects" of Hardy's *Tess of the d'Urbervilles.* Riquelme uses Hardy's depiction of Stonehenge as an example of what he is talking about. Stonehenge, admittedly a "real place" that would seem to invoke literally a "rocklike determinacy," is not only "presented by the story's language . . . as indeterminate and obscure" but was also, in Hardy's time, the source of endless speculation with regard to origin and purpose.

Riquelme identifies several ways in which Hardy swerves from the realistic tradition in *Tess.* For instance, Hardy seems to forfeit credibility deliberately by naming his protagonist's husband "Angel"; he even has Angel play the harp at a key point in the plot! Riquelme asserts that "Hardy could easily have simplified the reader's response in the direction of realism and determinacy by . . . giving Angel Clare a more ordinary name"; he "contributes to the narrative's strangeness" by doing otherwise. Hardy also creates characters that combine contradictory or antithetical elements, according to Riquelme. (Tess, who is portrayed as innocent despite her experience, speaks both dialect and standard English in a way that "blurs the class distinctions" that are so relevant to the story.) Riquelme maintains that such contradictory or antithetical elements do not result from "an unintended failure of realism" but, rather, serve as "a carefully crafted deviation from realism."

The language of *Tess,* Riquelme goes on to demonstrate, is characterized by "a controlled style that announces his refusal to present a smooth, undistracting surface for his narrative" — the kind of surface that readers of realistic novels had come to expect. Among the more subtly antirealistic elements of Hardy's style is his regular use of chiasmus, a rhetorical figure of speech in which terms are presented and then repeated in reverse order. A short though imperfect example of chiasmus would be Hardy's phrase "if *you* [Angel] do love *her* [Tess] as much as *she* [Tess] do love *you* [Angel]." (This particular chiasmus, to which italics and bracketed identifications have been added for the sake of clarity, is imperfect because its second and third terms — "her" and "she," both of which signify Tess rather than Angel — are not the same, even though they are both pronouns referring to Tess.) Riquelme argues that chiastic structure, which suggests "self-undoing" insofar as it is a structure of repetition and reversal simultaneously, underlies Hardy's larger worldview. (What Tess's aristocratic male ancestors did to peasant women, the male descendants of those peasants now do to Tess.) But even as he identifies plot reversals. Riquelme also shows how they simultaneously manifest continuity, just as the reversals of chiasmus simultaneously involve repetition. (Tess is always the true aristocrat; she physically resembles her aristocratic ancestors and even perpetuates her family's violent history by murdering Alec.)

At times, Riquelme performs close readings that point out the antirealistic, because unauthoritative and undecidable, nature of certain chiastic passages from *Tess.* In one such passage, the narrator reports Angel's thought processes by saying that "The *sea* was near at hand, but not intrusive; it *murmured,* and he thought it was the *pines;* the *pines murmured* in precisely the same tones, and he thought they were the *sea.*" The sentence is "odd," Riquelme points out, when "considered as realistic report." Angel

> hears something that seems to him to be multiple (the pines) but that the narrator has told us is singular (the sea); then the character hears something that seems to him to be singular (the sea) but that the narrator has told us is multiple (the pines). And to complicate matters, the narrator states that the tones were, in fact, *precisely* the same. If the tones were literally identical, whatever that may mean exactly, then neither the character's views nor the narrator's are authoritative in an unambiguous way. The passage creates uncertainty, not the impression of a determinate scene. Questions arise for us, but no answers are forthcoming. Where are we to find confirmation or explanation for what is stated in the passage?

At other points in his analysis, Riquelme points out the chiastic nature of larger structures, that is, whole chapters or even clusters of chapters. Toward the end of his essay, for instance, he argues that the two closing chapters of *Tess* "constitute together a structural chiasmus in which centripetal is matched and reversed by centrifugal." In the penultimate — second to the last — chapter, Tess and Angel "are the centripetal focus of advancing police who have come to apprehend Tess"; in the last chapter, "Angel and Tess's sister Liza-Lu, who has replaced Tess as Angel's companion," become observers, going to a hill from which they see the black flag indicating Tess's execution and, past that, "landscape beyond landscape, till the horizon was lost."

Throughout his essay, Riquelme focuses on Hardy's tendency to echo himself in odd ways. (Chiasmus is itself an odd sort of echo, one that causes us to hear the same terms but in reverse order.) Hardy's echoes, instead of re-presenting what preceded them in a way that confirms what we thought we heard, richly complicate or confuse matters. "By means of an echoic tendency that regularly turns away from determinate representations, conventional attitudes, and stable views," Riquelme argues, "Hardy enables us to desire and imagine an unhierarchical context for freedom in which male and female, aristocrat and laborer, standard English and dialect could change places, mingle or merge without destructive violence."

Insofar as it is legitimate to speak of "typical" aspects of deconstruction (which, after all, seeks to erase the boundaries that define "type"), one can say that Riquelme's essay exhibits several features of deconstruction as it has been practiced since the 1970s. These include his tendency to use close reading to show that apparently "determinate" (fixed and reliable) language is instead treacherously indeterminate, his interest in figurative and rhetorical devices that complicate reading more than clarify meaning, his exposition of the contradictory nature of seemingly unified statements or characters, and his focus on echoes or repetitions that would seem to make meaning more "determinable" but that instead contribute to a text's undecidability. But to the extent that Riquelme suggests that we may glimpse, through the strangeness of literary language, the possibility of a revolution in relationships and values — to the extent that he views Hardy not as a realist but instead as a kind of proto-deconstructor pointing out the contradictory nature of "conventional attitudes" and "stable views" — he practices the kind of deconstruction that has emerged in recent years, the kind that views privileges associated with gender, class, and race as being as suspect as those that "privilege" presence over absence, speech over writing.

Ross C Murfin

DECONSTRUCTION: A SELECTED BIBLIOGRAPHY

Writings on Deconstruction

Arac, Jonathan, Wlad Godzich, and Wallace Martin, eds. *The Yale Critics: Deconstruction in America.* Minneapolis: U of Minnesota P, 1983. See especially the essays by Bové, Godzich, Pease, and Corngold.

Berman, Art. *From the New Criticism to Deconstruction: The Reception of Structuralism and Post-Structuralism.* Urbana: U of Illinois P, 1988.

Butler, Christopher. *Interpretation, Deconstruction, and Ideology: An Introduction to Some Current Issues in Literary Theory.* Oxford: Oxford UP, 1984.

Clayton, Jay. *The Pleasure of Babel: Contemporary American Literature and Theory.* New York: Oxford UP, 1993.

Culler, Jonathan. *On Deconstruction: Theory and Criticism After Structuralism.* Ithaca: Cornell UP, 1982.

———. *Structuralist Poetics: Structuralism, Linguistics, and the Study of Literature.* Ithaca: Cornell UP, 1975. See especially ch. 10.

Esch, Deborah. "Deconstruction." *Redrawing the Boundaries: The Transformation of English and American Literary Studies.* Ed. Stephen Greenblatt and Giles Gunn. New York: MLA, 1992. 374–91.

Feminist Studies 14 (1988). Special issue on deconstruction and feminism.

Hamacher, Werner, Neil Hertz, and Thomas Keenan. *Responses: On Paul de Man's Wartime Journalism.* Lincoln: U of Nebraska P, 1989.

Hartman, Geoffrey. "Blindness and Insight." *The New Republic,* 7 Mar. 1988.

Jay, Gregory S. *America the Scrivener: Deconstruction and the Subject of Literary History.* Ithaca: Cornell UP, 1990.

Leitch, Vincent B. *American Literary Criticism from the Thirties to the Eighties.* New York: Columbia UP, 1988. See especially ch. 10, "Deconstructive Criticism."

———. *Cultural Criticism, Literary Theory, Poststructuralism.* New York: Columbia UP, 1992.

Loesberg, Jonathan. *Aestheticism and Deconstruction: Pater, Derrida, and de Man.* Princeton: Princeton UP, 1991.

Melville, Stephen W. *Philosophy Beside Itself: On Deconstruction and Modernism.* Theory and History of Lit. 27. Minneapolis: U of Minnesota P, 1986.

Norris, Christopher. *Deconstruction and the Interests of Theory.* Oklahoma Project for Discourse and Theory 4. Norman: U of Oklahoma P, 1989.

———. *Deconstruction: Theory and Practice.* London: Methuen, 1982. Rev. ed. London: Routledge, 1991.

———. *Paul de Man, Deconstruction and the Critique of Aesthetic Ideology.* New York: Routledge, 1988.

Weber, Samuel. *Institution and Interpretation.* Minneapolis: U of Minnesota P, 1987.

Works by de Man, Derrida, and Miller

de Man, Paul. *Allegories of Reading.* New Haven: Yale UP, 1979. See especially ch. 1, "Semiology and Rhetoric," and ch. 7, "Metaphor (*Second Discourse*)."

———. *Blindness and Insight.* New York: Oxford UP, 1971. Minneapolis: U of Minnesota P, 1983. The 1983 edition contains important essays not included in the original edition.

———. "Phenomenality and Materiality in Kant." *Hermeneutics: Questions and Prospects.* Ed. Gary Shapiro and Alan Sica. Amherst: U of Massachusetts P, 1984. 121–44.

———. *The Resistance to Theory.* Minneapolis: U of Minnesota P, 1986.

———. *Romanticism and Contemporary Culture*. Ed. E. S. Burt, Kevin Newmarkj, and Andrzej Warminski. Baltimore: Johns Hopkins UP, 1993.

———. *Wartime Journalism, 1939–1943*. Lincoln: U of Nebraska P, 1989.

Derrida, Jacques. *Acts of Literature*. Ed. Derek Attridge. New York: Routledge, 1992.

———. "Différance." *Speech and Phenomena*. Trans. David B. Alison. Evanston: Northwestern UP, 1973.

———. *Dissemination*. 1972. Trans. Barbara Johnson. Chicago: U of Chicago P, 1981. See especially the concise, incisive "Translator's Introduction," which provides a useful point of entry into this work and others by Derrida.

———. "Force of Law: The 'Mystical Foundation of Authority.'" Trans. Mary Quaintance. *Deconstruction and the Possibility of Justice*. Ed. Drucilla Cornell, Michel Rosenfeld, and David Gray Carlson. New York: Routledge, 1992. 3–67.

———. *Given Time. 1, Counterfeit Money*. Trans. Peggy Kamuf. Chicago: U of Chicago P, 1992.

———. *Margins of Philosophy*. Trans. Alan Bass. Chicago: U of Chicago P, 1982. Contains the essay "White Mythology: Metaphor in the Text of Philosophy."

———. *Memoires for Paul de Man*. Wellek Library Lectures. Trans. Cecile Lindsay, Jonathan Culler, and Eduardo Cadava. New York: Columbia UP, 1986.

———. *Of Grammatology*. 1967. Trans. Gayatri C. Spivak. Baltimore: Johns Hopkins UP, 1976. Trans. of *De la grammatologie*. 1967.

———. "Passions." *Derrida: A Critical Reader*. Ed. David Wood. Cambridge: Basil Blackwell, 1992.

———. *The Post Card: From Socrates to Freud and Beyond*. Trans. with intro. Alan Bass. Chicago: U of Chicago P, 1987.

———. "Some Statements and Truisms about Neo-logisms, Newisms, Postisms, and Other Small Seisisms." *The States of "Theory."* New York: Columbia UP, 1990. 63–94.

———. *Specters of Marx*. Trans. Peggy Kamuf. New York: Routledge, 1994.

———. *Writing and Difference*. 1967. Trans. Alan Bass. Chicago: U of Chicago P, 1978.

Miller, J. Hillis. *Ariadne's Thread: Story Lines*. New Haven: Yale UP, 1992.

———. *The Ethics of Reading: Kant, de Man, Eliot, Trollope, James, and Benjamin*. New York: Columbia UP, 1987.

———. *Fiction and Repetition: Seven English Novels.* Cambridge: Harvard UP, 1982.

———. *Hawthorne and History: Defacing It.* Cambridge: Basil Blackwell, 1991. Contains a bibliography of Miller's work from 1955 to 1990.

———. *Illustrations.* Cambridge: Harvard UP, 1992.

———. "Stevens' Rock and Criticism as Cure." *Georgia Review* 30 (1976): 3–31, 330–48.

———. *Typographies.* Stanford: Stanford UP, 1994.

———. *Versions of Pygmalion.* Cambridge: Harvard UP, 1990.

Essays on Deconstruction and Poststructuralism

Barthes, Roland. *S/Z.* Trans. Richard Miller. New York: Hill, 1974. In this influential work, Barthes turns from a structuralist to a poststructuralist approach.

Benstock, Shari. *Textualizing the Feminine: On the Limits of Genre.* Norman: U of Oklahoma P, 1991.

Bloom, Harold, et al., eds. *Deconstruction and Criticism.* New York: Seabury, 1979. Includes essays by Bloom, de Man, Derrida, Miller, and Hartman.

Chase, Cynthia. *Decomposing Figures.* Baltimore: Johns Hopkins UP, 1986.

Cohen, Tom. *Anti-Mimesis: From Plato to Hitchcock.* Cambridge: Cambridge UP, 1994.

Elam, Diane. *Feminism and Deconstruction: Ms. en Abyme.* New York: Routledge, 1994.

Felman, Shoshana. "Rereading Femininity." Special Issue on "Feminist Readings: French Texts/American Contexts," *Yale French Studies* 62 (1981).

———. "Turning the Screw of Interpretation." *Literature and Psychoanalysis: The Question of Reading: Otherwise.* Special issue, *Yale French Studies* 55–56 (1978): 3–508. Baltimore: Johns Hopkins UP, 1982.

Harari, Josué, ed. *Textual Strategies: Perspectives in Post-Structuralist Criticism.* Ithaca: Cornell UP, 1979.

Johnson, Barbara. *The Critical Difference: Essays in the Contemporary Rhetoric of Reading.* Baltimore: Johns Hopkins UP, 1980.

———. *A World of Difference.* Baltimore: Johns Hopkins UP, 1987.

Krupnick, Mark, ed. *Displacement: Derrida and After.* Bloomington: Indiana UP, 1987.

Meese, Elizabeth, and Alice Parker, eds. *The Difference Within: Feminism and Critical Theory.* Philadelphia: John Benjamins, 1989.

Sedgwick, Eve Kosofsky. *Epistemology of the Closet.* Berkeley: U of California P, 1990.

Ulmer, Gregory L. *Applied Grammatology.* Baltimore: Johns Hopkins UP, 1985.

———. *Teletheory: Grammatology in the Age of Video.* New York: Routledge, 1989.

Deconstructive Criticism of *Tess*

Lecercle, Jean Jacques. "The Violence of Style in *Tess of the d'Urbervilles.*" In *Alternative Hardy.* Ed. Lance St. John Butler. New York: St. Martin's, 1989. 1–25.

Miller, J. Hillis. "*Tess of the d'Urbervilles:* Repetition as Immanent Design." In *Fiction and Repetition.* Oxford: Basil Blackwell, 1982. 116–46.

Widdowson, Peter. "'Moments of Vision': Postmodernising *Tess of the d'Urbervilles;* or, *Tess of the d'Urbervilles* Faithfully Presented by Peter Widdowson." In *New Perspectives on Thomas Hardy.* Ed. Charles P. C. Pettit. New York: St. Martin's, 1994. 80–100.

A DECONSTRUCTIVE PERSPECTIVE

JOHN PAUL RIQUELME

Echoic Language, Uncertainty, and Freedom in *Tess of the d'Urbervilles*

> Art is a disproportioning — (i.e., distorting, throwing out of proportion) — of realities, to show more clearly the features that matter in those realities, which, if merely copied or reported inventorially, might possibly be observed, but would more probably be overlooked. Hence 'realism' is not Art.
>
> – THOMAS HARDY, *The Life and Work of Thomas Hardy*

As a novelist Thomas Hardy appears to belong firmly in the line of realistic writing that stretches back in the nineteenth century through George Eliot to Jane Austen. Hardy's attention to details of character, plot, and scene invite us to group him with these realistic writers rather than with the Joyce of *Ulysses* (1922). Many of his characters are presented in psychologically convincing detail, their actions are often believable, and the descriptions of setting and locale regularly suggest the reality of place. With regard to the locales. Hardy ascribed alternative, invented names to many places in his fictional Wessex that appear to correspond to real places in the South of England. The apparent correspondence to real places has led many readers to imagine a determinate reality in his fiction beneath a thin, nearly transparent veneer. Hardy nurtured this response by providing maps in his novels identical in many regards to maps of England and by mentioning in prefaces various identifications that readers had made or attempted. Some of the places he included in his narratives do seem identical to real places, even in name, as in the case of Stonehenge in the penultimate chapter of *Tess*. Like the stones of that prehistoric structure, numerous details in Hardy's fiction encourage us to recognize apparently determinate material and social realities undergirding his stories.

Although it would be foolish to deny that Hardy's novels concern characters and events that might have existed in a recognizable social and physical world, prominent aspects of style and story in his writings warrant our reading Hardy's works as other than realistic. Among his novels, *Tess*, in particular, is and is not realistic. As Hardy says in his third-person autobiography, "'realism' is not Art" (entry for 5 August

1890) (239). Hardy's importance as a novelist is in significant measure a matter of the distinctive aesthetic form that he created, including especially the antirealistic styles and structures of his narratives. Hardy's departures from realism need to be taken into account in any interpretation of what his narratives represent and imply. *Tess* is not *Ulysses,* a book that is filled with stylistic excesses that cannot be easily overlooked. But *Tess* does swerve from the tradition of realism in English fiction, and it is the character and the implications of that swerve that I focus on in my commentary.

The antirealistic aspects of *Tess* include the presentation of characters, the handling of places, and the style and structure of the story. Often, the antirealistic elements involve a doubling and a reversal that resembles literally or conceptually the rhetorical figure of chiasmus. In this echoic figure of speech, elements are presented first in one order and then in a reversed arrangement. Chiastic language and structurally chiastic plots are inherently double and antithetical because of repetition and reversal. Chiasmus provides a rhetorical device for calling up apparently distinct, and sometimes antithetical, elements that are also linked, as in Karl Marx's frequent use of the figure to formulate his attitude toward history. For example, the well-known definition of history from Marx and Engels's *The German Ideology* involves chiasmus rhetorically and conceptually to present continuity and rupture, repetition and reversal: "History is nothing but the succession of the separate generations, each of which exploits the materials . . . handed down to it . . . and thus, on the one hand, continues the *traditional activity* in *completely changed circumstances* and, on the other, modifies the *old circumstances* with a *completely changed activity*" (172; emphasis added). The chiasmus of "activity . . . circumstances . . . circumstances . . . activity" is complicated and doubled by reversed predication when "circumstances" reappears modified by "old," meaning "traditional," and "activity," instead of "circumstances," is "completely changed."

Chiasmus often points to a destructive or self-destructive situation, as when Marx characterizes bourgeois society as proceeding in ways that will have an effect opposite to what was intended. Chiasmus in this form suggests self-undoing because of unresolved contradictory tendencies. Chiasmus, however, can also be used in an apparently antithetical way to express renewal and the possibility of creating something new, as in the case of a revolution that dismantles the elements of an old order and reconfigures them into something not just different but preferable. Although in *Tess* chiasmus presents destruction and self-destruction in emphatic ways, it also opens alternative possibilities. It does so because chiasmus in *Tess* evokes uncertainty through a suspension of elements that, like destruction and renewal in a period of political revolution, can at times not be clearly distinguished. Rather than expressing necessarily outcomes that are determined by clear relations between causes and effects, chiasmus can and often does express surprising reversals. The blurring of determinate distinctions through style and action involving chiasmus, doubling, and reversal goes against the grain of realism. In *Tess,* the displacing of determinacies by doubling and uncertainty offers a challenge to views of human experience as fated, determined, prescribed, or narrowly limited in advance, even while the story confirms those views in some important regards.

Hardy's presentation of characters in *Tess* provides obvious examples of his antirealistic tendencies, some of which emerge through doublings and reversals. The naming of Tess's eventual husband "Angel" stretches the credibility of the story, especially when Hardy has Angel play a harp in the crucial chapter XIX. Angel, the man who studies farming, has a double, inevitably called up by our traditional conception of a harp-playing, divine creature. Because of her name and family background, Tess herself illustrates history as a process in which traditional and new actions and circumstances have mingled in ways that emerge as doublings and reversals. She is simultaneously Tess Durbeyfield, the daughter of an agricultural worker, and Tess d'Urberville, both because she is a child in the ancient d'Urberville line and because of her illicit alliance early and late in the narrative with Alec d'Urberville. History has worked a reversal on the fortunes of Tess's family, a fall in class standing that is indicated in the corruption of the d'Urberville name into Durbeyfield. The narrative presents the reversal again when Tess becomes the mate of a modern d'Urberville whose family has been able to take over the name because of their commercially earned wealth. The reality for Tess is that changed circumstances have reversed her class position and placed in ascendancy over her a man who lacks her aristocratic background. But there is continuity as well as change in her story. Tess repeats and continues her aristocratic past because of her looks and her temperament. She resembles the portraits of her female ancestors hanging in the lodgings that Angel secures for their wedding night. And the violent history of her family continues in the murder of Alec d'Urberville, as if it were her unavoidable fate to commit such an act.

Tess, then, stands in at least two places at once, since her quite different family past has contributed to making her what she is in a present that has contributed in equal measure to her situation. She is neither singular nor determinate. Angel, for example, thinks of her in antithetical ways. On the one hand, she is a natural, pure creature, as if generated spontaneously from the landscape. At the end of chapter XVIII, he thinks of her as "a fresh and virginal daughter of Nature" (137). On the other hand, as he discovers to his chagrin, she is a woman with a history that to him is as ugly as she is attractive. He considers her innocent and naive, yet in their conversation in chapter XIX, he discovers a knowledge and a depth of experience in Tess that belies his continuing sense of her simplicity. Her mixed nature emerges as well in her relation to her parents and in her upbringing. She combines in her family origins her father's distant aristocratic heritage and her mother's peasant background. The source of her beauty is, in this regard, ambiguous. It comes from Tess's d'Urberville heritage, but, as her mother implies at the end of chapter VII, her good looks come from her mother.

In a way that contributes to the book's mixed style, Tess is her own double in her speech. On the one hand, she speaks the dialect that her parents use; on the other, because of her education, she speaks standard English. Her ability with language is sufficiently developed to enable her to repeat her husband's theological arguments in convincing ways to Alec d'Urberville in chapter XLVI. Along with other aspects of her speech and history, this mimicry helps make Tess a figure that resembles Echo, the mythological counterpart of Narcissus. Like a physical echo, Tess's reverberating quality is composed of overlapping elements whose origin and end are difficult, if not impossible, to identify. As in the contemporary discussion of ebonics, or black English, in the United States, Hardy's inclusion of dialect raises issues of class that, along with other hierarchical factors, are central to Tess's story. Tess's fluency in a regional dialect used by agricultural laborers and in standard English blurs the class distinctions that are regularly reflected by accent, pronunciation, and diction. That blurring of differences embodied in Tess's linguistic ability subtly presents a challenge to the conventional structures of social value that ensure her demise. Like some black American novelists, including Zora Neale Hurston, Hardy expresses in his style a mastery of two sides of the English language that are often kept distinct by class boundaries. By attributing a related mastery to Tess, Hardy aligns her, among the characters in the novel, most closely with himself. She occupies an unusual position in that regard. Only Angel Clare, through his experiences on the land studying farming, moves toward Tess's bilingualism within English. His movement in her direction linguistically, indicated by the change in his speech, noted with surprise by his brothers at the end of chapter XXV, indicates his openness to a leveling of hierarchical relations. But that openness is not sufficiently strong soon enough in the narrative to prevent Tess's downfall. Even so, through her double character, Tess continues to represent, in spite of her death, a potential for leveling that is never adequately realized in the details of her life.

Doubling and uncertainty, or indeterminacy, also characterize Hardy's handling of locales, both the recognizable places renamed as locations in Wessex and the places, such as Stonehenge, that bear their ordinary names. By mapping Wessex as a kind of overlay for the normal map of England, Hardy asks us not merely to see through the overlay but to acknowledge his act of remapping the landscape, an act that opens up new possibilities by not conforming to conventions. That act involves a refusal to create in any straightforward manner the illusion that his characters inhabit the real world. It also suggests that other remappings are possible. As with the allegorical naming of Angel, Hardy's use of Wessex names emphasizes the fictive nature of his narratives rather than their direct correspondence to reality. By means of a doubling, the creating of a second name, what might otherwise have seemed singular and readily understood announces its position in a fictive world that is and is not the world of nineteenth-century England. Hardy could easily have simplified the reader's response in the direction of realism and determinacy by using conventional place names and by giving Angel Clare a more ordinary name. That he does neither contributes to the narrative's strangeness. Like other doublings in *Tess,* the doubling of place can be disconcerting for the reader who expects Hardy to maintain the illusions of realism.

Even some of the places whose everyday names Hardy retains make it difficult for us to orient ourselves in ways that seem secure or singular. Stonehenge provides an apt example, particularly considering its prominence within the narrative. It is, in fact, one of the narrative's two ultimate locations, an end toward which the action's trajectory tends, and this particular end, as we shall see, is full of uncertainty. On the one hand, Stonehenge evokes literally a rocklike determinacy. Etymologically, the name, which means "hanging stones," refers to the literal arrangement into uprights and crosspieces of the stones that compose the site. In the context of Tess's story, however, "hanging" refers not only to the elevated position of the crosspieces but to the sun overlooking the landscape of the final chapter and to Tess's eventual death. Hardy had no need to rename Stonehenge to give it a dual character, since its name in the context of Tess's story has a double referent.

We can find Stonehenge on real maps of Salisbury Plain in Wiltshire, and we can visit it by traveling to a spot about seven miles north of Salisbury. But this "monstrous place" (379), as Angel calls it, is vividly presented by the story's language, including Angel's, as indeterminate and obscure. Hardy uses it to evoke an uncertainty, if not a darkness, at the heart of apparently determinate realities. That uncertainty and others in the novel create difficulties for making sense of Tess's story and for rendering moral judgments about her actions. Hardy would have been aware, as we should be, that Stonehenge's history, its purpose and origins, were and continue to be shrouded in the obscurity of the distant past.[1] The eleventh edition of *The Encyclopaedia Britannica* (1910), which represents authoritatively the state of knowledge in the English-speaking world around the turn of the century, tells us that "no prehistoric monument in Great Britain has given rise to more speculation as to its origin, date and purpose." The author of the encyclopedia entry concludes unambiguously that

> notwithstanding the many attempts, both by excavations and speculative writings, to elucidate the history of this unique monument, the archaeological data available are insufficient to decide definitely between the conflicting opinions held with regard to the date of its construction and the purpose for which it was originally intended.

The uncertainty that Stonehenge represents in *Tess* provides an important counter to the kinds of rigid certainties, such as those held to by Angel Clare, that contribute significantly to Tess's downfall. As the novel undoes Angel's certainties, it proceeds stylistically and structurally in ways that do not rely primarily on maintaining the illusion of realistic determinacy.

Part of the difficulty in classifying Hardy as a realist has to do with changes of register in his style, particularly his inclusion from time to time of figurative language and rhetorical patterns that draw attention to themselves, while the language at the same time seems to be presenting a believable scene, action, or person. In *Tess* the stylized character of language is especially marked, most prominently in Phase the Seventh, the phase in which Stonehenge plays an important role.

[1]For a discussion of Stonehenge's history and possible uses by an astronomer that includes suggestive photographs and drawings, see Gerald S. Hawkins, *Stonehenge Decoded* (Garden City: Doubleday, 1965).

Critics have also often remarked on the sometimes awkward or uneven character of Hardy's style. The roughness tends to distract some readers into blaming Hardy for being an inept stylist, yet despite this they find him a powerful storyteller. This response portrays Hardy as a realist who does not succeed entirely in his handling of narrative language because of unintended blemishes that ruffle the surface of the presentation. In this view, the fact that we sometimes notice the style as much as what it represents is a failure of realistic effect. However, the actual effect is not an unintended failure of realism but a carefully crafted deviation from realism.

Complaints about Hardy's style do an injustice to his skill as an artist and to his accomplishment. Hardy's uneven style, sometimes rough and sometimes complexly refined, is also a controlled style that announces his refusal to present a smooth, undistracting surface for his narrative. That aesthetic refusal is cognate with a rejection of conventional attitudes that are not simply aesthetic. Like his creation of Wessex place names, Hardy's style invites us to see his language as stylized and fictive, not to see through it, as if it were a transparent medium. We can discern in the style of *Tess,* at times arrestingly, a chiastic pattern of doubling and reversal that provides a structure for the overarching narrative, for some elements as small as sentences and parts of sentences, and for our oscillating, unstable position as observers.

Hardy's mannered, echoic style begins bringing Tess's story into a culminating focus in Phase the Seventh when Angel returns ill and chastened from his abortive attempt to make a fortune by farming in Brazil. The book's realism, which is fractured in various ways throughout, becomes even more visibly fractured with Angel's return, as if the lesson he learns, through his experiences in Brazil, about what it means to be human warrants a further loosening of realistic constraints. The stylistic change reflects Angel's movement toward a reassessment of values that reverses attitudes that held him fast earlier in the narrative. The structure of this experience, which involves doubling and reversal, as when we gaze in a mirror, is chiastic.

Through an intensification, the distinctive rhetoric of Phase the Seventh, particularly its repetitions and echoes, amplifies the echoes and repetitions that have been present less obviously all along. Even the book's title and Tess's ancestral name contain an echo: Ur-ber. This would be a trivial matter were the verb the narrator employs most often to indicate speech not "murmur." Hardy uses "murmur" more than fifty times, and in almost every case the verb is predicated of Tess. She murmurs. Tess d'*Ur*b*er*ville m*ur*m*ur*s: ur ur ur ur. According to one prominent theorist, Julia Kristeva, echoic language, or echolalia, embodies a basic human tendency from early childhood that is retained in literary language, especially poetry, as a way to break up and challenge the conventional structures of adult understanding, including grammar and logic.[2] The frequent use of echoic language can disturb those structures and through repetition can prevent a narrative style from being realistic.

Hardy clusters and compresses some of the echoes in Phase the Seventh into instances of chiasmus. The first instance is only apparent as a chiasmus upon close examination, but it is important because it occurs in the phase's first chapter (LIII), specifically when the narrator is presenting Angel's thoughts in the wake of his having undergone the "strange experiences" of Brazil: "He had seen the virtual Faustina in the literal Cornelia, a spiritual Lucretia in a corporeal Phryne" (359). The passage calls attention to itself for its mannered, allusive eccentricity, which, on the one hand, is Angel Clare's eccentricity but on the other is the narrator's. This kind of narration, an intimate report of consciousness, ia precisely what Joyce develops into antirealistic styles of writing in *A Portrait of the Artist as a Young Man* (1916) and *Ulysses*. When it is unclear whether the language of the narration originates with the character or the narrator, the nagging question "who speaks?" distracts us from the realistic surface. In realism, uncertainty about who speaks is rarely an issue. Prescribed, denotative meanings to be found in dictionaries are not sufficient to interpret the words in this passage, which require our active, modifying engagement to bring to light their connotations.

The chiastic aspects of Angel's thoughts are, in fact, multiple. They occur in the order of the proper names but also in smaller units and in ways that affect our sense of what the adjectives mean. The most evident repetition and reversal occurs in the names: "Faustina *[bad woman]* . . . Cornelia *[good woman]* . . . Lucretia *[good woman]* . . . Phryne *[bad woman]*." As in the case of Marx and Engels on history, the effect created by the sequence of adjectives contributes to the complexity of the reversal's specific implications: virtual . . . literal . . . spiritual . . . corporeal. In this sequence there are parallels as well as

[2]For a brief, accessible discussion of the ways in which the semiotic disrupts the symbolic by means of echolalia, see Julia Kristeva, "The Speaking Subject," *On Signs*, ed. Marshall Blonsky (Baltimore: Johns Hopkins UP, 1985) 210–20. A lengthier account, which focuses on French poetry of the nineteenth century, can be found in Kristeva's *Revolution in Poetic Language*, trans. Margaret Waller (New York: Columbia UP, 1984).

contrasts. *Virtual,* which suggests that something is not wholly the case but is so in effect or nearly, stands in initial opposition to *literal,* meaning actual. *Spiritual* and *corporeal* repeat the opposition but are predicated now of different kinds of women than are their counterparts in the first half of the sequence. Because of the reversed implications of the names, the adjectives lose part of their parallel character. They could not, for example, be substituted for each other, even though *spiritual* can stand in opposition to *literal* in the way that the spirit differs from the letter. As a result, the apparently determinate differences between virtual and literal, spiritual and corporeal, spirit and letter soften. Despite the ostensible parallelism, it would not make sense to speak of a spiritual Faustina or a corporeal Cornelia; through the crossing over of the chiasmus, a slippage has taken place that puts the precise meanings and relations of words at issue.

The rhymes among the adjectives add another layer of complexity to the structure, which turns out to be multiply chiastic: virtu*al,* liter*al,* spiritu*al,* corpore*al.* The rhyming both links all the words and differentiates them into pairs, the words that end in *-tual* and those that end in *-al* only. On the phonemic level, the pairs that rhyme most closely also contain reversed, opposing elements that immediately precede the rhyming elements:

v*ir*-tual/spi*ri*-tual: ir . . . ri
lit*er*-al/corpo*re*-al: er . . . re.

Restored to the sequence of the sentence, this yields "-ir- . . . -er- . . . -ri- . . . -re-," a small series of reversals in sound that nests within the larger parallelisms and reversals of the sentence. We have here a poetic fragment embedded in a would-be realistic report.

Such a close reading would seem unjustified except that the transformation of realism in *Tess* regularly involves the coalescence of apparent opposites and the emergence of a difference where there appeared to be unity. Such coalescence and emergence occur emphatically in Phase the Seventh. In addition, the number, variety, and vivid peculiarities of the chiastic structures late in the novel invite us to attend to them closely as persistent, symptomatic stylistic devices. Attention to details of plot is not sufficient for interpreting the story's oddly presented characters and events.

At chapter's end, there is a simpler example of chiasmus that comes neither from Angel's new way of thinking nor from the narrator's independent perspective. It is contained rather in the warning that Tess's two friends send to Angel: "Look to your wife if *you do love her* as much as *she do you*" (360; emphasis added). Another obvious but more extended use of the figure occurs early in chapter LV. When Angel reaches Sandbourne, the town where he will find Tess, the narrator reports his thoughts again in language that combines ambiguously the narrator's language and Angel's. The combination helps shape the observer's position, that is, our position, into a chiastic form that ambiguously links aspects of Angel Clare and the narrator. That the alignment and the merger appear as chiasmus at this point and earlier in the phase while Angel is moving physically and emotionally closer to Tess suggests that chiasmus and related echoic forms provide a defining shape for the events, for the language in which they are rendered, and for their implications. Clare and the narrator experience and express the following:

> The sea was near at hand, but not intrusive; it murmured, and he thought it was the pines; the pines murmured in precisely the same tones, and he thought they were the sea. (364)

Or, schematically presented as repetitions and reversals, we have:

> sea . . . it murmured . . . it was the pines // the pines murmured . . . they were the sea.

Considered as realistic report, this is exceedingly odd. The character hears something that seems to be multiple (the pines) but that the narrator has already presented as singular (the sea); then the character hears something that seems to him to be singular (the sea) but that the narrator has told us is multiple (the pines). And to complicate matters, the narrator states that the tones were, in fact, *precisely* the same. If the tones were literally identical, whatever that may mean exactly, then neither the character's views nor the narrator's are authoritative in an unambiguous way. The passage creates uncertainty, not the impression of a determinate scene. Questions arise for us, but no answers are forthcoming. Where are we to find confirmation or explanation for what is stated in the passage?

Murmured may be the most significant word in this peculiar passage in which the sea and the pines speak in the same way but are heard by two observers who make distinctions that seem difficult if not impossible to maintain, accept, or explain. In *Tess,* distinctions blur or reversals occur through an echoic process of murmur. Since *murmur* is associated with Tess throughout the novel, what Angel hears is a version of Tess's double character, in which apparent opposites, like the singular sea and the multiple pines, are the same *virtually* if not *literally.* The word "tones" also occurs again in the chapter when Angel speaks with Tess and her voice changes dramatically, "her tones suddenly resuming their old fluty pathos" (367). But what her tones say is as echoic as the murmur of the chiastic passages: "Too late, too late!" . . . "'Yes — O yes, yes! But I say, I say, it is too late.'" . . . "'I waited and waited'" (367).

Curiously, in the next chapter, "tone" is replaced by "note," in an orthographic inversion that is chiastic (*tone* . . . *note*), and Tess's echoic language continues: "'O — O — O!' . . . 'O — O — O!' . . . 'you did not stop . . . you did not stop! . . . never . . . never . . . gone. Gone . . . never never'" (368–69). "Note" occurs again in chapter LVIII in the eerie scene in which Angel and Tess unknowingly stumble onto Stonehenge, whose name contains within it "tone," the word used earlier to evoke the confusing, confounding murmur of different things that actually sound the same. This "note" produced by the wind and the stones is, we learn, like the sound of "some gigantic one-stringed harp" (379), as if the music came from a weird version of Angel's own musical instrument. The comparison to the harp suggests that the fate Tess meets at Stonehenge, her apprehension by the law and her ultimate execution, is in some sense a product of Angel's actions or that Angel's behavior is part of a process antagonistic to her that includes Stonehenge as well. These implications, which are closer to questions than answers, are carried by the figurative language, not by realistic descriptions or direct statements.

Stonehenge, a structure whose height is "indefinite," hums and echoes with a "soft rustle" and makes "the black sky blacker" (379). It is "a forest of monoliths" (380) but also a "pavilion of the night" (380), though without a roof. This pavilion of the night seems also to be associated with the sun, which as it begins to rise makes the distant parts of the Plain "appear dark and near" (382). Whether by night or by day, uncanny, inexplicable, unexpected, contrary occurrences happen here. Stonehenge is a real place, but it is not presented primarily in determinate, easily intelligible ways.

The sun rules the next chapter, the book's final one, but so does the blackness of the flag that goes up at Tess's hanging. Light and dark have become one in their dominance. The book is simultaneously expanding and contracting as it comes to an end. It provides that doubled but contrary status for us as observers when the two final chapters mirror each other structurally in the presentation of observation within the action. At Stonehenge, as the sun comes up, the objects of observation (Tess and Angel) are the centripetal focus of advancing police who have come to apprehend Tess. The officers stand around and look at her until she awakes. In the final chapter, Angel and Tess's sister Liza-Lu, who has replaced Tess as Angel's companion, have taken the position of the observers in the scene, rather than those observed, on a hill that provides a vantage point for looking at the black signal for Tess's hanging. But the only hanging literally mentioned in the chapter is done by the sun. The landscape visible from this point of vantage sweeps "further off, landscape beyond landscape, till the horizon was lost in the radiance of the sun hanging above it" (384). In opposition to the movement in the previous chapter, which was in toward a center, here the direction is out toward the periphery.

The two closing chapters constitute together a structural chiasmus in which centripetal is matched and reversed by centrifugal; the object of intense concentrated observation has an antithetical counterpart in the unnoticed landscapes that expand and dissolve in the distance; observer and observed within the scenes change places, with Angel playing both roles. This structural chiasmus provides, in embedded form, a coda that reflects not only the shape of some of the novel's sentences but the larger structural chiasmus of the entire novel, which connects two violent turning points: Alec's violation of Tess and Tess's murder of Alec. At the conclusion of Phase the First, Alec violates Tess's body by penetrating it and draws the blood of her virginity through a violent act on the floor of the forest that is their marriage bed. In Phase the Seventh, in an act that repeats and reverses what Alec has done to her but that does not undo his earlier action, Tess violates her seducer's body by penetrating it and draws blood through a violent act on their shared bed.

The reversal that Tess effects involves centrally the changing of places by the man and the woman. This kind of reversal has been building in Phase the Sixth. There, Tess's encounters with Alec indicate they have changed positions. The shifts in this phase move toward Tess's retribution by reversal for her violation, itself presented earlier in terms of reversals.

At the end of Phase the First, the narrator's comments on Tess's violation are literally and conceptually chiastic. He meditates on the way in which "the wrong man [appropriates] the woman, the wrong woman the man" (94). He mentions in addition the reversal of retribution: "Doubtless some of Tess d'Urberville's mailed ancestors . . . had dealt the same measure . . . toward peasant girls of their time" (94). That is, what Tess's aristocratic male ancestors did to peasant women, the male descendant of peasants has now done to Tess, in a reversal of positions between classes and genders. This is also the moment in the narration in which the narrator identifies Tess as "d'Urberville" rather than Durbeyfield. While asserting a continuity, the narrator announces a rupture by claiming that "an immeasurable social chasm was to divide our heroine's personality thereafter from that previous self of hers" (95). The book's stylized narration reflects the difficulty of measuring what has happened to Tess, its aftermath, and its potential antidotes.

The change for Tess includes eventually Alec's transformed behavior toward her. In chapters XLV and XLVI of Phase the Sixth, he asks that she not look at him, whereas earlier his aggressive pursuit of her was an attempt to see and possess all of her. The shifting of positions between man and woman occurs as well between Tess's parents in this phase. When her father dies in chapter L, we learn that "Yes: the Durbeyfield couple had changed places: the dying one was out of danger, and the indisposed one was dead" (342). Alec's ambiguous rendition of the tale of the d'Urberville coach in the next chapter suggests the shift again: "he killed her — or she killed him" (345). The sequel for these multiple preambles occurs when Tess physically realizes the reversal of positions and fulfills one version of the tale.

She has taken over what was the man's role and repaid him for having dominated her as a woman. His actions and her ultimate response could have been the basis for a realistic story. Because of the oddness of Hardy's narration, it is instead the scaffolding for something more complex and more resistant to determinate interpretations. The complexity and the resistance come in part from the coalescence of opposites and the emergence of difference in unexpected ways. By means of repetitions and reversals, in the structure and the style of *Tess,* Hardy suggests the identity of ostensible opposites. He does so in ways that leave us not with closure and determinate representations but with instances of folding back and reversing that are themselves symptoms of something not entirely determinate or not yet brought into being. And with that puzzling swerve from determinate representations to representing the indeterminate or immeasurable in rhetorically arresting ways, a sharply antirealistic style emerges out of what at times appears to be realistic writing.

When a woman can take the man's role, a leveling occurs that contravenes the hierarchical conventions that rule Angel's thinking and behavior for much of the novel. At the end of chapter XXXVI, Tess is "appalled by the determination" and "the will to subdue" that she senses in him, which the narrator renders as "the tyrannous wind of his

imaginative ascendency" (247). Angel's decision to be a farmer suggests that mastery of the earth by technological means is cognate with the social hierarchy that he accepts, in which men think and behave in certain prescribed ways and women are expected to think and behave in their different determined and subordinate ways. The result of the attitudes supporting such a hierarchy in Tess's case include a destructive coalescence of opposites and a separation of what should be joined. When Angel finds Tess at Sandbourne in chapter LV, we learn that speech and silence have become oddly one: "Speech was as inexpressive as silence" (367). We learn as well, in a curious folding back of temporal perspectives, that in the future Angel will understand that Tess has become double in a kind of living death: "Tess had spiritually ceased to recognize the body before him as hers — allowing it to drift, like a corpse upon the current, in a direction dissociated from its living will" (367). This doubling realizes in one way the difference between *spiritual* and *corporeal* from the earlier chiasmus concerning good and bad women. What could be, and in Angel's view once was, singular has become dissociated.

The narrative provides no consoling overcoming of this division, no restoration of the living dead to long life and continuing happiness. We are left instead with perplexities expressed through echoic styles and structures that create uncertainties for us. These include the moral dilemma in which, like Tess, we stand in at least two places at once, on the one hand condemning her act of murder and, on the other, accepting the justice of her action and rejecting the punishment she receives. We may even condone an act that we simultaneously deplore. The issue here is the extent to which Tess becomes our double, the extent to which we forgive, accept, and perhaps even applaud what she has done.

By means of an echoic tendency that regularly turns away from determinate representations, conventional attitudes, and stable views, Hardy enables us to desire and imagine an unhierarchical context for freedom in which male and female, aristocrat and laborer, standard English and dialect could change places, mingle, or merge without destructive violence. In such a context, Tess's recognition at the end of Phase the Fourth that her husband is her "double" (229), because he has just admitted his sexual activity before their marriage, would be accepted rather than challenged. In the next chapter, her plea for mutuality, which takes the form of chiasmus, would be granted rather than refused: "'Forgive me as you are forgiven. *I* forgive *you,* Angel'" (232). By refusing to admit their equality, Angel contributes to the dissociation that turns Tess eventually into one of the living dead: "'You were one person; now you are another'" (232). Near the opening of chapter XXXIV, Angel himself articulates what is necessary when he considers whether he could understand adequately Tess's dependence on him: "'I think I could not, unless I were a woman myself'" (223). Hardy invites us to see the apparent stability of Angel's conventional views of selfhood, moral purity, and relations between the genders as in fact rigid, restrictive, hierarchical, destructive, and self-destructive. They prevent him from understanding, honoring, and helping his partner until it is too late.

The freedom of mutuality is not attainable for Tess or for Angel in any lasting way within the limits of the story's social world. The place in which such freedom can flourish lies beyond the horizon of Hardy's Wessex. Even so, the echoic language of his style evokes the possibility of bringing that utopian space into view up over the horizon. Through the narration's style and structure, the aesthetic restrictions and limits of realism are exceeded because an echoic, oscillating instability emerges. Such instability can be a prelude for freedom. When we experience the instability by standing simultaneously in different places, the unlikely, unconventional coexistence of opposites comes virtually, spiritually, and imaginatively, though not yet literally and corporeally, within our grasp.

WORKS CITED

Hardy, Thomas. *The Life and Work of Thomas Hardy*. Ed. Michael Millgate. Athens: U of Georgia P, 1985.

Marx, Karl, and Friedrich Engels. *The German Ideology*. Tucker, Robert C., ed. *The Marx-Engels Reader*. 2nd ed. New York: Norton, 1978.

"Stonehenge." *The Encyclopaedia Britannica*. 11th ed. 1910.

Reader-Response Criticism and *Tess of the d'Urbervilles*

WHAT IS READER-RESPONSE CRITICISM?

Students are routinely asked in English courses for their reactions to the texts they are reading. Sometimes there are so many different reactions that we may wonder whether everyone has read the same text. And some students respond so idiosyncratically to what they read that we say their responses are "totally off the wall." This variety of response interests reader-response critics, who raise theoretical questions about whether our responses to a work are the same as its meanings, whether a work can have as many meanings as we have responses to it, and whether some responses are more valid than others. They ask what determines what is and what isn't "off the wall." What, in other words, is the wall, and what standards help us define it?

In addition to posing provocative questions, reader-response criticism provides us with models that aid our understanding of texts and the reading process. Adena Rosmarin has suggested that a literary text may be likened to an incomplete work of sculpture: to see it fully, we must complete it imaginatively, taking care to do so in a way that responsibly takes into account what exists. Other reader-response critics have suggested other models, for reader-response criticism is not a monolithic school of thought but, rather, an umbrella term covering a variety of approaches to literature.

Nonetheless, as Steven Mailloux has shown, reader-response critics *do* share not only questions but also goals and strategies. Two of the basic goals are to show that a work gives readers something to do and to describe what the reader does by way of response. To achieve those goals, the critic may make any of a number of what Mailloux calls "moves." For instance, a reader-response critic might typically (1) cite direct references to reading in the text being analyzed, in order to justify the focus on reading and show that the world of the text is continuous with the one in which the reader reads; (2) show how other nonreading situations in the text nonetheless mirror the situation the reader is in ("Fish shows how in *Paradise Lost* Michael's teaching of Adam in Book XI resembles Milton's teaching of the reader throughout the poem"); and (3) show, therefore, that the reader's response is, or is analogous to, the story's action or conflict. For instance, Stephen Booth calls *Hamlet* the tragic story of "an audience that cannot make up its mind" (Mailloux, "Learning" 103).

Although reader-response criticism is often said to have emerged in the United States in the 1970s, it is in one respect as old as the foundations of Western culture. The ancient Greeks and Romans tended to view literature as rhetoric, a means of making an audience react in a certain way. Although their focus was more on rhetorical strategies and devices than on the reader's (or listener's) response to those methods, the ancients by no means left the audience out of the literary equation. Aristotle thought, for instance, that the greatness of tragedy lay in its "cathartic" power to cleanse or purify the emotions of audience members. Plato, by contrast, worried about the effects of artistic productions, so much so that he advocated evicting poets from the Republic on the grounds that their words "feed and water" the passions!

In our own century, long before 1970, there were critics whose concerns and attitudes anticipated those of reader-response critics. One of these, I. A. Richards, is usually associated with formalism, a supposedly objective, text-centered approach to literature that reader-response critics of the 1970s roundly attacked. And yet in 1929 Richards managed to sound surprisingly *like* a 1970s-vintage reader-response critic, writing in *Practical Criticism* that "the personal situation of the reader inevitably (and within limits rightly) affects his reading, and many more are drawn to poetry in quest of some reflection of their latest emotional crisis than would admit it" (575). Rather than deploring this fact, as many of his formalist contemporaries would have done, Richards argued that the reader's feelings and experiences provide a kind of reality check, a way of testing the authenticity of emotions and events represented in literary works.

Approximately a decade after Richards wrote *Practical Criticism,* an American named Louise M. Rosenblatt published *Literature as Exploration* (1938). In that seminal book, now in its fourth edition (1983), Rosenblatt began developing a theory of reading that blurs the boundary between reader and text, subject and object. In a 1969 article entitled "Towards a Transactional Theory of Reading," she sums up her position by writing that "a poem is what the reader lives through under the guidance of the text and experiences as relevant to the text" (127). Rosenblatt knew her definition would be difficult for many to accept: "The idea that a *poem* presupposes a *reader* actively involved with a *text,*" she wrote, "is particularly shocking to those seeking to emphasize the objectivity of their interpretations" ("Transactional" 127).

Rosenblatt implicitly and generally refers to formalists (also called the "New Critics") when she speaks of supposedly objective interpreters shocked by the notion that a "poem" is something cooperatively produced by a "reader" and a "text." Formalists spoke of "the poem itself," the "concrete work of art," the "real poem." They had no interest in what a work of literature makes a reader "live through." In fact, in *The Verbal Icon* (1954), William K. Wimsatt and Monroe C. Beardsley defined as fallacious the very notion that a reader's response is relevant to the meaning of a literary work:

> The Affective Fallacy is a confusion between the poem and its *results* (what it *is* and what it *does*). . . . It begins by trying to derive the standards of criticism from the psychological effects of a poem and ends in impressionism and relativism. The outcome . . . is that the poem itself, as an object of specifically critical judgment, tends to disappear. (21)

Reader-response critics have taken issue with their formalist predecessors. Particularly influential has been Stanley Fish, whose early work is seen by some as marking the true beginning of contemporary reader-response criticism. In "Literature in the Reader: Affective Stylistics" (1970), Fish took on the formalist hegemony, the New Critical establishment, by arguing that any school of criticism that would see a work of literature as an object, claiming to describe what it *is* and never what it *does,* is guilty of misconstruing the very essence of literature and reading. Literature exists when it is read, Fish suggests, and its force is an affective force. Furthermore, reading is a temporal process. Formalists assume it is a spatial one as they step back and survey the literary work as if it were an object spread out before them. They may find elegant patterns in the texts they examine and reexamine, but they fail to take into account that the work is quite different to a reader who is turning the pages and being moved, or affected, by lines that appear and disappear as the reader reads.

In a discussion of the effect that a sentence penned by the seventeenth-century physician Thomas Browne has on a reader reading, Fish pauses to say this about his analysis and also, by extension, about his critical strategy: "Whatever is persuasive and illuminating about [it] is the result of my substituting for one question — what does this sentence mean? — another, more operational question — what does this sentence do?" He then quotes a line from John Milton's *Paradise Lost,* a line that refers to Satan and the other fallen angels: "Nor did they not perceive their evil plight." Whereas more traditional critics might say that the "meaning" of the line is "They did perceive their evil plight," Fish relates the uncertain movement of the reader's mind *to* that half-satisfying interpretation. Furthermore, he declares that "the reader's inability to tell whether or not 'they' do perceive and his involuntary question . . . are part of the line's *meaning,* even though they take place in the mind, not on the page" (*Text* 26).

The stress on what pages *do* to minds (and what minds do in response) pervades the writings of most, if not all, reader-response critics. Stephen Booth, whose book *An Essay on Shakespeare's Sonnets* (1969) greatly influenced Fish, sets out to describe the "reading experience that results" from a "multiplicity of organizations" in a sonnet by Shakespeare (*Essay* ix). Sometimes these organizations don't make complete sense, Booth points out, and sometimes they even seem curiously contradictory. But that is precisely what interests reader-response critics, who, unlike formalists, are at least as interested in fragmentary, inconclusive, and even unfinished texts as in polished, unified works. For it is the reader's struggle to *make sense* of a challenging work that reader-response critics seek to describe.

The German critic Wolfgang Iser has described that sense-making struggle in his books *The Implied Reader* (1974) and *The Act of Reading: A Theory of Aesthetic Response* (1978). Iser argues that texts are full of "gaps" (or "blanks," as he sometimes calls them). These gaps powerfully affect the reader, who is forced to explain them, to connect what they separate, to create in his or her mind aspects of a poem or novel or play that aren't *in* the text but that the text incites. As Iser puts it in *The Implied Reader,* the "unwritten aspects" of a story "draw the reader into the action" and "lead him to shade in the many outlines suggested by the given situations, so that these take on a reality of their own." These "outlines" that "the reader's imagination animates" in turn "influence" the way in which "the written part of the text" is subsequently read (276).

In *Self-Consuming Artifacts: The Experience of Seventeenth-Century Literature* (1972), Fish reveals his preference for literature that makes readers work at making meaning. He contrasts two kinds of literary presentation. By the phrase "rhetorical presentation," he describes literature that reflects and reinforces opinions that readers already hold; by "dialectical presentation," he refers to works that prod and provoke. A dialectical text, rather than presenting an opinion as if it were truth, challenges readers to discover truths on their own. Such a text may not even have the kind of symmetry that formalist critics seek. Instead of offering a "single, sustained argument," a dialectical text, or self-consuming artifact, may be "so arranged that to enter into the spirit and assumptions of any one of [its] . . . units is implicitly to reject the spirit and assumptions of the unit immediately preceding" (*Artifacts* 9). Whereas a critic of another school might try to force an explanation as to why the units are fundamentally coherent, the reader-response critic proceeds by describing how the reader deals with the sudden twists and turns that characterize the dialectical text, returning to earlier passages and seeing them in an entirely new light.

"The value of such a procedure," Fish has written, "is predicated on the idea of meaning as *an event,*" not as something "located (presumed to be embedded) *in* the utterance" or "verbal object as a thing in itself" (*Text* 28). By redefining meaning as an event rather than as something inherent in the text, the reader-response critic once again locates meaning in time: the reader's time. A text exists and signifies while it is being read, and what it signifies or means will depend, to no small extent, on *when* it is read. (*Paradise Lost* had some meanings for a seventeenth-century Puritan that it would not have for a twentieth-century atheist.)

With the redefinition of literature as something that exists meaningfully only in the mind of the reader, with the redefinition of the literary work as a catalyst of mental events, comes a concurrent redefinition of the reader. No longer is the reader the passive recipient of those ideas that an author has planted in a text. "The reader is *active,*" Rosenblatt insists ("Transactional" 123). Fish begins "Literature in the Reader" with a similar observation: "If at this moment someone were to ask, 'what are you doing,' you might reply, 'I am reading,' and thereby acknowledge that reading is . . . something *you do*" (*Text* 22). Iser, in focusing critical interest on the gaps in texts, on what is not expressed, similarly redefines the reader as an active maker.

Amid all this talk of "the reader," it is tempting and natural to ask, "Just who *is* the reader?" (Or, to place the emphasis differently, "Just who is *the* reader?") Are reader-response critics simply sharing their own idiosyncratic responses when they describe what a line from *Paradise Lost* does in and to the reader's mind? "What about my responses?" you may want to ask. "What if they're different? Would reader-response critics be willing to say that my responses are equally valid?"

Fish defines "the reader" in this way: "*the* reader is the *informed* reader." The informed reader (whom Fish sometimes calls "the *intended* reader") is someone who is "sufficiently experienced as a reader to have internalized the properties of literary discourses, including everything from the most local of devices (figures of speech, etc.) to whole genres." And, of course, the informed reader is in full possession of the "semantic knowledge" (knowledge of idioms, for instance) assumed by the text (*Artifacts* 406).

Other reader-response critics define "*the* reader" differently. Wayne C. Booth, in *A Rhetoric of Irony* (1974), uses the phrase "the implied reader" to mean the reader "created by the work." (Only "by agreeing to play the role of this created audience," Susan Suleiman explains, "can an actual reader correctly understand and appreciate the work" [8].) Gerard Genette and Gerald Prince prefer to speak of "the narratee, . . . the necessary counterpart of a given narrator, that is, the person or figure who receives a narrative" (Suleiman 13). Like Booth, Iser employs the term "the implied reader," but he also uses "the educated reader" when he refers to what Fish called the "informed reader."

Jonathan Culler, who in 1981 criticized Fish for his sketchy definition of the informed reader, set out in *Structuralist Poetics* (1975) to describe the educated or "competent" reader's education by elaborating those reading conventions that make possible the understanding of poems and novels. In retrospect, however, Culler's definitions seem sketchy as well. By "competent reader," Culler meant competent reader of "literature." By "literature," he meant what schools and colleges mean when they speak of literature as being part of the curriculum. Culler, like his contemporaries, was not concerned with the fact that curricular content is politically and economically motivated. And "he did not," in Mailloux's words, "emphasize how the literary competence he described was embedded within larger formations and traversed by political ideologies extending beyond the academy" ("Turns" 49). It remained for a later generation of reader-oriented critics to do those things.

The fact that Fish, following Rosenblatt's lead, defined reader-response criticism in terms of its difference from and opposition to the New Criticism or formalism should not obscure the fact that the formalism of the 1950s and early 1960s had a great deal in common with the reader-response criticism of the late 1960s and early 1970s. This has become increasingly obvious with the rise of subsequent critical approaches whose practitioners have proved less interested in the close reading of texts than in the way literature represents, reproduces, and/or resists prevailing ideologies concerning gender, class, and race. In a retrospective essay entitled "The Turns of Reader-Response Criticism" (1990), Mailloux suggests that, from the perspective of hindsight, the "close reading" of formalists and "Fish's early 'affective stylistics'" seem surprisingly similar. Indeed, Mailloux argues, the early "reader talk of . . . Iser and Fish enabled the continuation of the formalist practice of close reading. Through a vocabulary focused on a text's manipulation of readers, Fish was especially effective in extending and diversifying the formalist practices that continued business as usual within literary criticism" (48).

Since the mid-1970s, however, reader-response criticism (once commonly referred to as the "School of Fish") has diversified and taken on a variety of new forms, some of which truly *are* incommensurate with formalism, with its considerable respect for the integrity and power of the text. For instance, "subjectivists" like David Bleich, Norman Holland, and Robert Crosman have assumed what Mailloux calls the "absolute priority of individual selves as creators of texts" (*Conventions* 31). In other words, these critics do not see the reader's response as one "guided" by the text but rather as one motivated by deep-seated, personal, psychological needs. What they find in texts is, in Holland's phrase, their own "identity theme." Holland has argued that as readers we use "the literary work to symbolize and finally to replicate ourselves. We work out through the text our own characteristic patterns of desire" ("UNITY" 816). Subjective critics, as you may already have guessed, often find themselves confronted with the following question: If all interpretation is a function of private, psychological identity, then why have so many readers interpreted, say,

Shakespeare's *Hamlet* in the same way? Different subjective critics have answered the question differently. Holland simply has said that common identity themes exist, such as that involving an oedipal fantasy.

Meanwhile, Fish, who in the late 1970s moved away from reader-response criticism as he had initially helped define it, came up with a different answer to the question of why different readers tend to read the same works the same way. His answer, rather than involving common individual identity themes, involved common *cultural* identity. In "Interpreting the *Variorum*" (1976), he argues that the "stability of interpretation among readers" is a function of shared "interpretive strategies." These strategies, which "exist prior to the act of reading and therefore determine the shape of what is read," are held in common by "interpretive communities" such as the one constituted by American college students reading a novel as a class assignment (*Text* 167, 171). In developing the model of interpretive communities, Fish truly has made the break with formalist or New Critical predecessors, becoming in the process something of a social, structuralist, reader-response critic. Recently, he has been engaged in studying reading communities and their interpretive conventions in order to understand the conditions that give rise to a work's intelligibility.

Fish's shift in focus is in many ways typical of changes that have taken place within the field of reader-response criticism — a field that, because of those changes, is increasingly being referred to as "reader-*oriented*" criticism. Less and less common are critical analyses examining the transactional interface between the text and its individual reader. Increasingly, reader-oriented critics are investigating reading communities, as the reader-oriented cultural critic Janice A. Radway has done in her study of female readers of romance paperbacks (*Reading the Romance,* 1984). They are also studying the changing reception of literary works across time; see, for example, Mailloux in his "pragmatic readings" of American literature in *Interpretive Conventions* (1982) and *Rhetorical Power* (1989).

An important catalyst of this gradual change was the work of Hans Robert Jauss, a colleague of Iser's whose historically oriented reception theory (unlike Iser's theory of the implied reader) was not available in English book form until the early 1980s. Rather than focusing on the implied, informed, or intended reader, Jauss examined actual past readers. In *Toward an Aesthetic of Reception* (1982), he argued that the reception of a work or author tends to depend upon the reading public's "horizons of expectations." He noted that, in the morally conservative climate of mid-nineteenth-century France, *Madame Bo-*

vary was literally put on trial, its author Flaubert accused of glorifying adultery in passages representing the protagonist's fevered delirium via free indirect discourse, a mode of narration in which a third-person narrator tells us in an unfiltered way what a character is thinking and feeling.

As readers have become more sophisticated and tolerant, the popularity and reputation of *Madame Bovary* have soared. Sometimes, of course, changes in a reading public's horizons of expectations cause a work to be *less* well received over time. As American reception theorists influenced by Jauss have shown, Mark Twain's *Adventures of Huckleberry Finn* has elicited an increasingly ambivalent reaction from a reading public increasingly sensitive to demeaning racial stereotypes and racist language. The rise of feminism has prompted a downward revaluation of everything from Andrew Marvell's "To His Coy Mistress" to D. H. Lawrence's *Women in Love.*

Some reader-oriented feminists, such as Judith Fetterley, Patrocinio Schweickart, and Monique Wittig, have challenged the reader to become what Fetterley calls "the resisting reader." Arguing that literature written by men tends, in Schweickart's terms, to "immasculate" women, they have advocated strategies of reading that involve substituting masculine for feminine pronouns and male for female characters in order to expose the sexism inscribed in patriarchal texts. Other feminists, such as Nancy K. Miller in *Subject to Change* (1988), have suggested that there may be essential differences between the way women and men read and write.

That suggestion, however, has prompted considerable disagreement. A number of gender critics whose work is oriented toward readers and reading have admitted that there is such a thing as "reading like a woman" (or man), but they have also tended to agree with Peggy Kamuf that such forms of reading, like gender itself, are cultural rather than natural constructs. Gay and lesbian critics, arguing that sexualities have been similarly constructed within and by social discourse, have argued that there is a homosexual way of reading; Wayne Koestenbaum has defined "the (male twentieth-century first world) gay reader" as one who "reads resistantly for inscriptions of his condition, for texts that will confirm a social and private identity founded on a desire for other men. . . . Reading becomes a hunt for histories that deliberately foreknow or unwittingly trace a desire felt not by author but by reader, who is most acute when searching for signs of himself" (Boone and Cadden 176–77).

Given this kind of renewed interest in the reader and reading, some students of contemporary critical practice have been tempted to conclude that reader-oriented theory has been taken over by feminist, gender, gay, and lesbian theory. Others, like Elizabeth Freund, have suggested that it is deconstruction with which the reader-oriented approach has mixed and merged. Certainly, all of these approaches have informed and been informed by reader-response or reader-oriented theory. The case can be made, however, that there is in fact still a distinct reader-oriented approach to literature, one whose points of tangency are neither with deconstruction nor with feminist, gender, and so-called queer theory but, rather, with the new historicism and cultural criticism.

This relatively distinct form of reader theory is practiced by a number of critics but is perhaps best exemplified by the work of scholars like Mailloux and Peter J. Rabinowitz. In *Before Reading: Narrative Conventions and the Politics of Interpretation* (1987), Rabinowitz sets forth four conventions or rules of reading, which he calls the rules of "notice," "signification," "configuration," and "coherence" — rules telling us which parts of a narrative are important, which details have a reliable secondary or special meaning, which fit into which familiar patterns, and how stories fit together as a whole. He then proceeds to analyze the misreadings and misjudgments of critics and to show that politics governs the way in which those rules are applied and broken. ("The strategies employed by critics when they read [Raymond Chandler's] *The Big Sleep,*" Rabinowitz writes, "can teach us something about the structure of misogyny, not the misogyny of the novel itself, but the misogyny of the world outside it" [195].) In subsequent critical essays, Rabinowitz proceeds similarly, showing how a society's ideological assumptions about gender, race, and class determine the way in which artistic works are perceived and evaluated.

Mailloux, who calls his approach "rhetorical reception theory" or "rhetorical hermeneutics," takes a similar tack, insofar as he describes the political contexts of (mis)interpretation. In a recent essay on "Misreading as a Historical Act" (1993), he shows that a mid-nineteenth-century review of Frederick Douglass's slave *Narrative* by protofeminist Margaret Fuller seems to be a misreading until we situate it "within the cultural conversation of the 'Bible politics' of 1845" (Machor 9). Woven through Mailloux's essay on Douglas and Fuller are philosophical pauses in which we are reminded, in various subtle ways, that all reading (including Mailloux's and our own) is culturally situated and likely to seem like *mis*reading someday. One such reflective pause, however, accomplishes more; in it, Mailloux reads the map of where reader-oriented criticism is today, affords a rationale for its being there, and plots its likely future direction. "However we have arrived at our present juncture," Mailloux writes,

> the current talk about historical acts of reading provides a welcome opportunity for more explicit consideration of how reading is historically contingent, politically situated, institutionally embedded, and materially conditioned; of how reading any text, literary or nonliterary, relates to a larger cultural politics that goes well beyond some hypothetical private interaction between an autonomous reader and an independent text; and of how our particular views of reading relate to the liberatory potential of literacy and the transformative power of education. (5)

In the essay that follows, Garrett Stewart begins his reader-response approach to *Tess of the d'Urbervilles* by telling us that Hardy complained about the "too genteel reader" in his Preface to the First Edition of the novel and that, in his Preface to the Fifth Edition, he praised those more receptive readers who "have repaired my defects of narration by their own imaginative intuition." The work Hardy thereby associated with reading — repair — is, Stewart suggests, not unlike the gap-closing work described by Wolfgang Iser in *The Implied Reader.* (Stewart, however, prefers the term "implicated reader," given his view of *Tess* as a story that provides its reader with an "emotional charge" as the heroine's "erotic vitality" is steadily drained away.)

In the course of his analysis, Stewart makes a number of moves typical of contemporary reader-response criticism. He pays close attention to the language of the novel, revealing the effects that it has on our experience of and response to the work and its steadily ground-down protagonist. He shows us, for instance, how the text's myriad allusions and foreshadowings cause us to view ironically Tess's constant struggle *not* to read significance into words, pictures, and events more generally. For example, Stewart reminds us that after Tess loses her "walking boots in a failed visit to Angel's parents," she "upbraids herself about the 'baseless impressibility' that 'had caused her to read the scene as her own condemnation.' We know better." We also think we know better, Stewart suggests, when Tess "resists" the notion "'that there is set down in some old book somebody just like me, and . . . that I shall only act her part."

Stewart also follows the lead of reader-response critics from Fish to Mailloux by focusing on passages in which characters are presented or see themselves as readers. Such scenes foreground the process — reading — that we ourselves experience, thereby better allowing us to "read reading" in the text, that is, to reflect critically on the view of interpretation that the text implies. Stewart follows this practice when he quotes the passage in which Tess scolds herself for the "impressibility" that caused her to "read" a scene "as her own condemnation" and, even more effectively, when *he* reads a scene in which Tess and the reader read words painted by an evangelistic sign-painter: "THY, DAMNATION, SLUMBERETH, NOT" and "THOU, SHALT, NOT, COMMIT — ." Unlike Tess, Stewart suggests, the reader reads the dash at the end of the second sign as a suggestive foreshadowing of Tess's life-plot, predictively filling in the blanks not with one but, rather with both of the cardinal sins anticipated by the verb "commit," namely, adultery and murder. At a later point in his essay, Stewart reflects on another passage: "The eyes for which Tess's letter was intended were gazing . . . on . . . the interior of the South-American continent." Here, while reading the text of *Tess,* we do the work — reading Tess's letter — intended by the letter's author (Tess) and have the positive response its intended reader (Angel) was intended to have; in the process, we come to realize the tragic significance of his failure to read the letter positively.

Stewart's argument ultimately concerns the gap between Tess's will to believe in organic, stable identity (as seen in her passionate denial of Angel's claim that she was "one person" and is now "another") and the view that readers arrive at in response to the text, namely, the view of the self as "schismatic, ruptural, discontinuous, self-alienating." In developing this argument, Stewart effectively synthesizes the methods of reader-response criticism and the theories of deconstructor Paul de Man, whose radical writings on the relationship between allegory and irony, plot and figurative language, and interpretive "blindness" and "insight" have been a shaping force in the development of deconstruction, another contemporary approach to literature represented in this volume.

Ross C Murfin

READER-RESPONSE CRITICISM: A SELECTED BIBLIOGRAPHY

Some Introductions to Reader-Response Criticism

Beach, Richard. *A Teacher's Introduction to Reader-Response Theories.* Urbana: NCTE, 1993.

Fish, Stanley E. "Literature in the Reader: Affective Stylistics." *New Literary History* 2 (1970): 123–61. Rpt. in Fish, *Text* 21–67, and in Primeau 154–79.

Freund, Elizabeth. *The Return of the Reader: Reader-Response Criticism.* London: Methuen, 1987.

Holub, Robert C. *Reception Theory: A Critical Introduction.* New York: Methuen, 1984.

Leitch, Vincent B. *American Literary Criticism from the Thirties to the Eighties.* New York: Columbia UP, 1988.

Mailloux, Steven. "Learning to Read: Interpretation and Reader-Response Criticism." *Studies in the Literary Imagination* 12 (1979): 93–108.

———. "Reader-Response Criticism?" *Genre* 10 (1977): 413–31.

———. "The Turns of Reader-Response Criticism." *Conversations: Contemporary Critical Theory and the Teaching of Literature.* Ed. Charles Moran and Elizabeth F. Penfield. Urbana: NCTE, 1990. 38–54.

Rabinowitz, Peter J. "Whirl Without End: Audience-Oriented Criticism." *Contemporary Literary Theory.* Ed. G. Douglas Atkins and Laura Morrow. Amherst: U of Massachusetts P, 1989. 81–100.

Rosenblatt, Louise M. "Towards a Transactional Theory of Reading." *Journal of Reading Behavior* 1 (1969): 31–47. Rpt. in Primeau 121–46.

Suleiman, Susan R. "Introduction: Varieties of Audience-Oriented Criticism." Suleiman and Crosman 3–45.

Tompkins, Jane P. "An Introduction to Reader-Response Criticism." Tompkins ix–xxiv.

Reader-Response Criticism in Anthologies and Collections

Flynn, Elizabeth A., and Patrocinio P. Schweickart, eds. *Gender and Reading: Essays on Readers, Texts, and Contexts.* Baltimore: Johns Hopkins UP, 1986.

Garvin, Harry R., ed. *Theories of Reading, Looking, and Listening.* Lewisburg: Bucknell UP, 1981. Essays by Cain and Rosenblatt.

Machor, James L., ed. *Readers in History: Nineteenth-Century American Literature and the Contexts of Response.* Baltimore: Johns Hopkins UP, 1993. Contains Mailloux essay "Misreading as a Historical Act: Cultural Rhetoric, Bible Politics, and Fuller's 1845 Review of Douglass's *Narrative.*"

Primeau, Ronald, ed. *Influx: Essays on Literary Influence.* Port Washington: Kennikat, 1977. Essays by Fish, Holland, and Rosenblatt.

Suleiman, Susan R., and Inge Crosman, eds. *The Reader in the Text: Essays on Audience and Interpretation.* Princeton: Princeton UP, 1980. See especially the essays by Culler, Iser, and Todorov.

Tompkins, Jane P., ed. *Reader-Response Criticism: From Formalism to Post-Structuralism.* Baltimore: Johns Hopkins UP, 1980. See especially the essays by Bleich, Fish, Holland, Prince, and Tompkins.

Reader-Response Criticism: Some Major Works

Bleich, David. *Subjective Criticism.* Baltimore: Johns Hopkins UP, 1978.

Booth, Stephen. *An Essay on Shakespeare's Sonnets.* New Haven: Yale UP, 1969.

Booth, Wayne C. *A Rhetoric of Irony.* Chicago: U of Chicago P, 1974.

Eco, Umberto. *The Role of the Reader: Explorations in the Semiotics of Texts.* Bloomington: Indiana UP, 1979.

Fish, Stanley Eugene. *Doing What Comes Naturally: Change, Rhetoric, and the Practice of Theory in Literary and Legal Studies.* Durham: Duke UP, 1989.

———. *Is There a Text in This Class? The Authority of Interpretive Communities.* Cambridge: Harvard UP, 1980. This volume contains most of Fish's most influential essays, including "Literature in the Reader: Affective Stylistics," "What It's Like to Read *L'Allegro* and *Il Penseroso,*" "Interpreting the *Variorum,*" "Is There a Text in This Class?" "How to Recognize a Poem When You See One," and "What Makes an Interpretation Acceptable?"

———. *Self-Consuming Artifacts: The Experience of Seventeenth-Century Literature.* Berkeley: U of California P, 1972.

———. *Surprised by Sin: The Reader in "Paradise Lost."* 2nd ed. Berkeley: U of California P, 1971.

Holland, Norman N. *5 Readers Reading.* New Haven: Yale UP, 1975.

———. "UNITY IDENTITY TEXT SELF." *PMLA* 90 (1975): 813–22.

Iser, Wolfgang. *The Act of Reading: A Theory of Aesthetic Response.* Baltimore: Johns Hopkins UP, 1978.

———. *The Implied Reader: Patterns of Communication in Prose Fiction from Bunyan to Beckett.* Baltimore: Johns Hopkins UP, 1974.

Jauss, Hans Robert. *Toward an Aesthetic of Reception.* Trans. Timothy Bahti. Intro. Paul de Man. Brighton, Eng.: Harvester, 1982.

Mailloux, Steven. *Interpretive Conventions: The Reader in the Study of American Fiction.* Ithaca: Cornell UP, 1982.

———. *Rhetorical Power.* Ithaca: Cornell UP, 1989.

Messent, Peter. *New Readings of the American Novel: Narrative Theory and Its Application.* New York: Macmillan, 1991.

Prince, Gerald. *Narratology.* New York: Mouton, 1982.

Rabinowitz, Peter J. *Before Reading: Narrative Conventions and the Politics of Interpretation.* Ithaca: Cornell UP, 1987.

Radway, Janice A. *Reading the Romance: Women, Patriarchy, and Popular Literature.* Chapel Hill: U of North Carolina P, 1984.

Rosenblatt, Louise M. *Literature as Exploration.* 4th ed. New York: MLA, 1983.

———. *The Reader, the Text, the Poem: The Transactional Theory of the Literary Work.* Carbondale: Southern Illinois UP, 1978.

Slatoff, Walter J. *With Respect to Readers: Dimensions of Literary Response.* Ithaca: Cornell UP, 1970.

Steig, Michael. *Stories of Reading: Subjectivity and Literary Understanding.* Baltimore: Johns Hopkins UP, 1989.

Exemplary Short Readings of Major Texts

Anderson, Howard. "*Tristram Shandy* and the Reader's Imagination." *PMLA* 86 (1971): 966–73.

Berger, Carole. "The Rake and the Reader in Jane Austen's Novels." *Studies in English Literature, 1500–1900* 15 (1975): 531–44.

Booth, Stephen. "On the Value of *Hamlet.*" *Reinterpretations of English Drama: Selected Papers from the English Institute.* Ed. Norman Rabkin. New York: Columbia UP, 1969. 137–76.

Easson, Robert R. "William Blake and His Reader in *Jerusalem.*" *Blake's Sublime Allegory.* Ed. Stuart Curran and Joseph A. Wittreich. Madison: U of Wisconsin P, 1973. 309–28.

Kirk, Carey H. "*Moby-Dick:* The Challenge of Response." *Papers on Language and Literature* 13 (1977): 383–90.

Leverenz, David. "Mrs. Hawthorne's Headache: Reading *The Scarlet Letter.*" *Nathaniel Hawthorne, "The Scarlet Letter."* Ed. Ross C Murfin. Case Studies in Contemporary Criticism. Boston: Bedford–St. Martin's, 1991. 263–74.

Lowe-Evans, Mary. "Reading with a 'Nicer Eye': Responding to *Frankenstein.*" *Mary Shelley, "Frankenstein."* Ed. Johanna M. Smith. Case Studies in Contemporary Criticism. Boston: Bedford–St. Martin's, 1992. 215–29.

Rabinowitz, Peter J. "'A Symbol of Something': Interpretive Vertigo in 'The Dead.'" *James Joyce, "The Dead."* Ed. Daniel R. Schwarz. Case Studies in Contemporary Criticism. Boston: Bedford–St. Martin's, 1994. 137–49.

Treichler, Paula. "The Construction of Ambiguity in *The Awakening.*" *Kate Chopin, "The Awakening."* Ed. Nancy A. Walker. Case Studies in Contemporary Criticism. Boston: Bedford–St. Martin's, 1993. 308–28.

Other Works Referred to in "What Is Reader-Response Criticism?"

Booth, Wayne C. *A Rhetoric of Irony.* Chicago: U of Chicago P, 1974.

Culler, Jonathan. *Structural Poetics: Structuralism, Linguistics, and the Study of Literature.* Ithaca: Cornell UP, 1975.

Koestenbaum, Wayne. "Wilde's Hard Labor and the Birth of Gay Reading." *Engendering Men: The Question of Male Feminist Criticism.* Ed. Joseph A. Boone and Michael Cadden. New York: Routledge, 1990.

Richards, I. A. *Practical Criticism.* New York: Harcourt, 1929. Rpt. in *Criticism: The Major Texts.* Ed. Walter Jackson Bate. Rev. ed. New York: Harcourt, 1970. 575.

Wimsatt, William K., and Monroe C. Beardsley. *The Verbal Icon.* Lexington: U of Kentucky P, 1954. See especially the discussion of "The Affective Fallacy," with which reader-response critics have so sharply disagreed.

Reader-Oriented Criticism of Hardy's Fiction

Brown, Suzanne Hunter. "'Tess' and *Tess*: An Experiment in Genre." *Modern Fiction Studies* 28.1 (Spring 1982): 25–44.

Gregor, Ian. *The Great Web: The Form of Hardy's Major Fiction.* Boston: Faber, 1974.

Stewart, Garrett. *Dear Reader: The Conscripted Audience in Nineteenth-Century British Fiction.* Baltimore: Johns Hopkins UP, 1996.

A READER-RESPONSE PERSPECTIVE

GARRETT STEWART

"Driven Well Home to the Reader's Heart": *Tess*'s Implicated Audience

The most controversial major novelist of the Victorian period, Thomas Hardy regularly stood in an embattled relation to the "too genteel reader" (25) whom he dismisses in his explanatory note to the First Edition of *Tess of the d'Urbervilles* (following its illustrated weekly serialization, to whose pages we will return). This is the reader dramatically squeamish and morally fastidious. Yet Hardy's note also suggests another relation to what later criticism would call "reader response" or "response aesthetics," a compact by which the audience collaborates with and completes a text. Hardy puts it modestly in the Preface to the Fifth Edition when he mentions those receptive readers who "have only too largely repaired my defects of narration by their own imaginative intuition" (25). The larger ramifications are clear: not just bridging over the gaps in continuity by their construction of a credible story space, readers round out the narrative by sympathetic participation. But Hardy's deliberate modesty may also be a cover for an "imaginative intuition" that verges on voyeuristic titillation — and is calculated to do so. It is at such a point that the aesthetics of response shifts over into its ethics via the trials — both the labor and the testing — of reader psychology.

Wolfgang Iser's influential subject in *The Implied Reader* (1974) is the inferred deciphering agency necessary to the generation of a text as cogent narrative representation. Hardy's narrative reminds us that the enlisted reading of a novel may complicate this work ethic with a pleasure principle by no means always calculated to flatter the reader's motives in helping to motor the plot. By speaking of the *implicated* rather than merely the implied reader, I mean to highlight the enacted energies of reading not only called upon but called out by a text like Hardy's — including the darker shading of the term, as when one is implicated by being suspected of a transgression. Few nineteenth-century novels are in fact so often commented on in regard to the guilty pleasures of their reading as is *Tess of the d'Urbervilles,* where a combination of the prurient and the lurid locates much of the text's emotional charge in the steady draining of the heroine's erotic vitality.[1] Catharsis becomes vampirism. But this is not enough to notice. The suspect pleasures of narrative reading in *Tess* involve a more pointed guilt by association — an association not just with the manipulative sexual urges of the characters within the plot but with the mechanisms of narrative itself, its underlying schema for the graduated staging of a life story.

Implicated, then, rather than merely implied, tactically cornered rather than merely tacit, you as reader of *Tess* find your own function repeatedly doubled or undone by narrative event. Y/ours is a function either performed by proxy in a scene of reading or turned inside out when denied to a character of deficient literacy. In one way or another, by enactment or evacuation, the reader function is displaced but also replayed. This involves far more than a thematics of textual encounter, where the experience of fiction can be debated by a text through its delegation to character psychology. Let me call what results a *systemics* rather than a thematics of reading, one in which every level of textual processing, from turns of figurative phrase to the turning points of plot, is intermeshed in a manifold circuit of directed energy and subjected attention. In ways that cannot avoid calling into question the narrative's own design, the novel becomes one long reading lesson — and not wholly an improving one. You may even come to share the heroine's explicit view, from the midst of her tragic diminishment, that reading lessens. This is why it is not enough to say of Hardy's novel that form infiltrates content — not even when the symmetries and escalations of plot seem internalized by characters as a chafing fate; not even when omniscient purview invades their world in the voyeuristic form of coercive prurience. Your narrative reading has even more to answer for, and all the more so the more closely you do it.

To begin with, from its Shakespearean epigraph forward, the novel is itself a reading of other texts. The allusive field is by turns internal and external, with books either mentioned by characters or recruited by the narrator on their behalf. The novel's first two embedded texts

[1]Writes Harold Bloom: "Hardy's pragmatic version of the aesthetic vision in this novel is essentially sado-masochistic, and the sufferings of poor Tess give an equivocal pleasure of repetition to the reader" (7). The point is made even more strongly by James Kincaid: "*Tess* becomes . . a titillating snuff movie we run in our own minds" (29).

(or at least titles) are *The Counterblast to Agnosticism,* read offstage by the Clare brothers, and *The Compleat Fortune-Teller,* scanned just before we meet her by Tess's mother after hearing about the family's d'Urberville lineage. With the latter grimy book soon returned by Tess herself to its usual resting place in the outhouse, this is hardly a propitious site for the novel's first stand-in as prophetic volume. Together, then, these first two infratexts collide to tell a larger tale. For Hardy's novel is nothing if not an agnostic blast that repeatedly drops omens in the form of antiprovidential exempla.

The novel further mocks the providential, even while restaging it, in the very texture of its figurative, turned prefigurative, language. Diction becomes prediction. In this way do the most nuanced satisfactions of reading derive from ironies operating at the expense of the heroine's own vulnerability. No dead metaphor, for instance, could be more abortively revived than when news of the Durbeyfield's aristocratic ancestry, whose last issue will be Tess's doomed child, "seemed to have impregnated the whole family" (54). But Tess herself is denied the right to that superstitious overreading that is an important interpretive credential of Hardy's reader, the tendency to sense foreboding in the least detail. After she has lost her walking boots in a failed visit to Angel's parents, Tess upbraids herself about the "baseless impressibility" that "had caused her to read the scene as her own condemnation" (297). We know better. But this is also a way of knowing that the tax on the hermeneutic pleasure we take from structural as well as figurative anticipation is levied in the long run against the novel's own characters.

Just as the far horizon of *Tess*'s plot lies with the reader in the impure security of reception, so does its other vanishing point reach back behind the story to those textual prototypes from which it — along with much of the reader's intellectual invigoration, and none of the heroine's — derives. This is why both the precedents for narrative action generated by textual allusion and the premonitory dramatic ironies "read" by characters or audience are two halves of the same fateful, ensnaring tale: Hardy's novel not just as processed in reading but as a parable of reading and, at key moments, its scene. Here is Tess in sudden confrontation with the sign-painter's blood-red inscription from Peter, "THY, DAMNATION, SLUMBERETH, NOT" (99), its words separated by commas in order to be "driven well home to the reader's heart" (99) — yours as well as that of any passerby within the scene. Again, the dead metaphor of this message seems itself proleptic, for it is just when a physically exhausted and spiritually somnolent Tess nods off in the predawn forest with Alec that the tireless vigilance of damnation catches up with her by way of sexual violation.

Compounding this seeded dramatic irony, the sign-painter's second inscription breaks off at a moment of fundamental undecidability, requiring the participatory energies of its reader, here Tess in our place (whose thoughts go unrecorded), to fill in the admonitory blank: "THOU, SHALT, NOT, COMMIT —— ." (100) In general idiomatic terms, there are of course two cardinal sins that take the verb "commit," and the bulk of Hardy's plot lies latent in that ominous ellipsis. Between any unchaste behavior in a broad theological understanding of "adultery" (in Tess's case more like rape) and a renewal of the liaison with Alec in the stricter form of marital adultery (Tess by then wed to Angel) is a space virtually coterminous with the collapsed distance between sexual transgression and that other sin of "commission" for which the punishment is mortal: namely, murder. Thus does the sign-painter's script offer an inlaid and counter-set text fitting flush with the surface of Hardy's own narrative. With the sign's arrested clause as plot matrix, the heroine's foundational scene of reading thereby brackets the whole arc of narrative across the divided grammatical objects of a single *accusative* case. To triple the irony, we come to realize that it all could have been avoided if Tess had succumbed to the *letter of the law* — a governing idiom behind the methodical sign-painting scene — and made no emotional or marital "commitment" whatever.

It is scarcely an accident that Tess's later scene of reading in the novel is again the decipherment of a public inscription — when, that is, she manages to decode the Church Latin on the door of the d'Urberville tomb. Classical languages are not otherwise Tess's strength, to say nothing of modern literatures. Even as Hardy's reader is at once flattered and edified by the book's range of allusions, the dead language of Western high culture remains unavailable as solace for its half-literate heroine — and undesirable as precedent. Yet she is besieged from all sides. Allusions even appear by negation in her own reported consciousness, the phantom other of her half-formed intuitions, as when Tess "might have ironically said to God with Saint Augustine: 'Thou hast counselled a better course than Thou hast permitted'" (116). Or: "She had Jeremy Taylor's thought that some time in the future those who had known her would say: 'It is the — th, the day that poor Tess Durbeyfield died'" (117). Whereas Angel is hedged round by self-consciously *received* opinion, Tess has the thoughts of others without knowing it.

What is more, she wants it this way. She resents allusions for two good reasons, first because they escape her, but also because they would efface her, rob her of her coveted originality. When offering her some high-toned reading lessons, Angel is met with her overt fears of belatedness. She resists the idea of "learning that I am one of a long row only — finding out that there is set down in some old book somebody just like me, and to know that I shall only act her part" (142). At this point she seems to have forgotten the cautionary function of fictional narrative, whose absence from her life she has earlier regretted in connection with Alec's seduction: "'Ladies know what to fend hands against, because they read novels that tell them of these tricks; but I never had the chance o' learning in that way'" (102). Yet this is to say that novels, like history, would only expose the derivative nature of her predicament. Once again, and this time as admonitory fable rather than eroticized spectacle, the novel promotes its very reception at the expense of its heroine. For Tess might well object not only to finding herself a statistical deduction from antecedent patterns of human behavior but, just as strenuously, to being offered up as narrative object lesson — and aesthetic scapegoat — for generations of readers to come.

Indeed, Tess's biggest problem is not the books she hasn't read, the omen-reading she is prey to, or the textual parallels she superstitiously resists, but, above all, the self-serving banality with which she herself is read by others — which is to say narrativized. Angel's view of her existence as "actualized poetry" (175) is a superficially benign form of the syndrome, but even there one senses trouble coming. Within a "poetics" of tragic melodrama, the novel's advancing of its own narrative agenda ultimately takes a correlative toll on the sacrificed heroine, with all the negative ramifications one might imagine for the implicated — and now openly complicit — reader. We think we are appalled by what our acquiescence has actually paved the way for. A single scene detonates the crisis: a crisis both of plot and of plotting. This is the moment of blistering human rejection in *Tess* that must be the most shocking and at the same time predictable turn of its story, activating as it does not only the figurative cliche of the two-faced woman but the novel's own template for character transformation. "Her narrative ended" (231) begins "Phase the Fifth. The Woman Pays," with the term "narrative" referring back to her honeymoon confession, by means of which Angel has been briefly moved into alignment with the reader by becoming the recipient of the very story we have all along been reading. The alignment grows contaminating. As he is elevated to our degree of knowledge, we may at last realize how we have long ago been lowered to his level of schematic response. To her bridal admission, he reacts with the mutilating cruelty of "'You were one person; now you are another'" (232). Even our immediate recoil from his self-blinding repudiation cannot shake the sense that he is only mobilizing with perverse and defensive venom the narrative's own view of character development — character not as multifaceted but as schismatic, ruptural, discontinuous, self-alienating. As far as possible from Romanticism's organic continuum of the self, Hardy's novel has all along tracked psychological transformation as a series of defaults and fractures. It has *narrativized* development not as unfolding maturation but as the wrenchingly undergone gaps — barely overcome — of emotional dislocation, not just separate "phases" (the part headings) but punishingly disjunct stages in life's aggravated, broken plotline.

Listen, for example, to the language that topples over into the yawning gulf, typographic and psychological both, between "Phase the First. The Maiden" and its wholesale negation in "Phase the Second. Maiden No More." The former section pitches the heroine forward on a note of psychic closure and traumatic rebirth, so that mere recap becomes epitaphic: "An immeasurable social chasm was to divide our heroine's personality thereafter from that previous self of hers who stepped from her mother's door to try her fortune at Trantridge poultry-farm" (95). Even that overstressed phrasing "previous self of hers" suggests the strained fragility of so-called self-possession by which such a fate is even to be owned to by her. Only once before, near the end of the preceding chapter, has Tess been referred to as "our heroine" (88), as she will later be when the tragic plot thickens. The earliest such tag has been used to flag the almost mock-epic confrontation between Tess and the jealous working-girls after the local dance. A chapter later, though, in the distancing overview of her life made instrumental for storytelling, the renewed inclusion of the reader within the scope of the editorial plural may seem suddenly insidious. If we accept this proffered claim on her, we concede that she is performing for us, that the "chasm" demarcating a new phase of her tragedy gives shape to our own ready comprehension and so to our pleasure. Death by hanging arrives as only one more fissure of psychic incommensurability and narrative fit — and does so under the rubric of "Phase the Seventh. Fulfilment," so-called in an unnerving blend of bitter irony and the narrative self-congratulation of tragic catharsis.

Yet the novel's irony scores less against its own structural machinations (though they cannot pass unscathed) than against the tendency toward overplotting in any sense of a life story. When Angel Clare, upon meeting Tess, decides that, rather than closet himself with lifeless texts, he "preferred to read human nature" (134), the eros of such study does not preclude its schematic bias. Tess's "actualized poetry" scarcely escapes his view of a human subject sequentially redefined by its social subjections. And we do unto ourselves what we do unto others. This is the far edge of Hardy's point. As soon as we convert our life to a story, our duration to a plot, as of course we always do, it runs the risks brought to the forefront in *Tess*. We become multiple, staggered, and irreversible. Since you the reader have already subscribed to — or been conscripted by — such formats for characterization, you stand to be doubly shocked when the potentially sadistic reductiveness of these models shows up so implacably in Angel's view of Tess. Narrative psychology does not produce in her the "split subject" of postmodern theory. Rather, Hardy's heroine instances — and comes almost paradoxically to embody — the nonsimultaneously rent subject of one Tess then, another now. Worse yet, Tess too, under duress, ends up thinking this way for and of herself.

The process begins in a state of shock and gets converted only later to an amorous strategy. In the immediate aftermath of Angel's rejection, narrative discourse in the next chapter — hovering ambivalently between authorial commentary and Tess's own internal monologue — explicitly recalls Angel's exaggerated sense of her two selves: "The figurative phrase was true: she was another woman than the one who had excited his desire" (246). Here it is Tess herself who seems to internalize his hyperbole as proof of her own difference in his eyes. And this from the woman who, just a chapter before, has tried to opt out of the novel's whole program by insisting on a nondisjunctive selfhood: "'I love you for ever — in all changes, in all disgraces, because *you are yourself*'" (232; emphasis added). By contrast with Tess as the temporary champion of irrevocable continuity, a genuinely disquieting force of the novel's ironic disjunctions remains the global self-inclusion of that irony, the text laying the ethical traps into which its own form cannot help but fall. This is the way readers grow implicated in the cruel de/gradations of Tess's overplotted story even when those same readers think they are distancing themselves in every way possible from the unfeeling self-interest of the male characters.

Poetic justice cannot entirely mitigate such an ironic ricochet — neither when a desperate Tess manipulates this model of riven personality to woo Angel back nor when, once returned, he is confronted with the narrative materialization of his own blunt and brutal logic. He has said on their wedding night, in effect, that a former Tess has come out of hiding to usurp the place of his virginal bride. In order to meet his mystified sense of transfigured identity on its own terms, Tess's final letter to him marks her complete internalization of a plotted rather than integrated sense of self. Pleading for his return, she insists: "I am the same woman, Angel, as you fell in love with; yes, the very same! — not the one you disliked but never saw" (329). All that precedes their meeting is personified as a corpse: "What was the past to me as soon as I met you? It was a dead thing altogether," and this because "I became another woman" — as if born by impregnation from his chaste love, "filled full of new life from you" (329). In her view, if still on his model, the point is strictly logical: "How could I be the early one? Why do you not see this?" (329). This is Hardy's "immeasurable chasm" again in his heroine's own words, words meant for other eyes than the reader's. Sent to Angel's parents as he had instructed, and forwarded unopened by them to South America, the letter is never portrayed in receipt by Angel. Instead, the reader has interceded at the point of its composition, and your privileged view of its contents is insinuated in the next chapter by an elaborate circumlocution: "*The eyes for which Tess's letter was intended* were gazing at this time on a limitless expanse of country from the back of a mule which was bearing him from the interior of the South-American Continent towards the coast" (331); emphasis added). With the long-lost protagonist already homeward bound, the only eyes that by this point have read the letter serve to bear the plot, rather than speed the characters, toward conclusion — still under the sign of the self as a post-Romantic figure of sequential deaths and rebirths.

Returning too late, Angel realizes from Tess's second confession about yet a second liaison with Alec that "*his* original Tess had spiritually ceased to recognize the body before him as *hers*" (367; emphasis added). Once again Hardy appears as the syntactician of the cleft subject. In this further ironic grammar of possession, unwanted carnal knowledge results in carnal nonrecognition when Tess's body does not even seem *hers,* let alone herself. By a final knife-twist of dramatic irony, just such a detachment of spiritual and bodily determinants derails Angel's own comprehension in the next chapter. After Tess has three times declared that she has "killed" Alec, and then reiterated again under direct questioning that she means what she says, Angel still needs to ask, "'What, bodily? Is he dead?'"(372). In a novel where selves are metaphorically (because metamorphically) expendable — and especially for Angel the honeymoon sleepwalker who once, having eight times called Tess "Dead!" (248–49) in a midnight bout of somnambulism, laid his dream bride to rest in the symbolic coffin of her virginity at a nearby abbey — in such a novel and for such a character, the difference between metaphorical and bodily murder, figurative and literal extermination, must indeed be laboriously spelled out. (You see, Angel, Alec was one person, now he is another — a dead person.)

It might well seem too easy to say of this whole pattern that the revolving door of selfhood in Hardy's novel works to "deconstruct" any sense of stable identity. What it does do is expose the vulnerable dependence of identity on the language one uses for it, a language in this case relational and wholly relative. It is just here that one of the most influential essays of American deconstruction, Paul de Man's "The Rhetoric of Temporality" (1971), can shed light on the literary-historical register of Hardy's novel. For de Man, narrative after Romanticism owes its ironic structure to the nature of figurative language itself, the space opened between signifier and signified. We might return for illustration to a heavily marked example in Hardy, another early and ominous dead metaphor like "impregnated": the sign-painter's warnings (with their hint of murder as well as sexual license) "driven well home to the reader's heart" — as, just for instance, Tess's knife will later be driven well home to the heart of the novel's most culpable adulterer. Highlighted by such loaded phrasing is the affiliation, the unholy bond, discussed by de Man (with other texts than Hardy's in mind) between irony and allegory, trope and plot. Ironic disjunction in *Tess* is frequently mapped as a vector of narrative discontinuity: de Man's *rhetoric of temporality* by any other name, where the allegory of sequential self-alienation is the novelistic form of irony's tensed double vantage. The signifier that says one thing and means another becomes the narrative logic that repeats events with a signifying difference — the accidental stabbing to death, say, of a beast named Prince (the family horse) followed much later by the stabbing of a beastly false aristocrat. Tess suffers in other words — but often in almost the same words — for the pangs of ironic rhetoric when stretched on the rack of duration. Her true lapse is the primal fall into plot.

For the reader garnering aesthetic gratification from that plot, the ethical balancing act is delicate indeed. And you are by no means let off the hook simply by recognizing this. Why you care at all about Tess is under suspicion in the first place, or in other words from the first chapter forward. That the prolonged torture of Tess services the reader's sense of drastic reversal and violent transformation, taunted as she is by proleptic hints and battered by the patterns of narrative's own phased demarcations, at once burdened by plot and spurned by Angel as a *serial* self — all this makes for a pervading irony that extends the novel's initial image of her as our heavily invested construction: an image of rural girlhood for which the text gives only the slightest excuse (and the slimmest clues). Criticism, as mentioned, has not failed to recognize the reader's more than ordinary tendency to imagine Tess, and luxuriate over her, as the carnal embodiment of all she means, the vessel but also the flesh of suffering, where ripeness is all. What has been insufficiently stressed is the way this visualization of her charms depends upon a detour around writing whose very willfulness, on the reader's part, Hardy's text renders unevadably ironic.

Here is how *Tess* finds words for Tess that deliberately keep her from coming to view — or tease us with the need to incarnate our own version of her. By a redundantly emphatic phrasing that says less rather than more, Tess is first sketched as "fine and handsome" (38). As if to specify this effect, "her mobile peony mouth and large innocent eyes added *eloquence* to *colour* and *shape*" (38; emphasis added). To what? Dislodged even slightly from its immediate context, this phrasing arrives like nothing so much as a description of figurative rhetoric itself, where all three key terms are bywords for the shapeliness of a colorful passage, an eloquent piece of verbal evocation. Against all the dictates of realism, then, the novel would seem to be setting its own rhetorical standards in the deconstruction of its title figure as sheer figuration. Yet it does so only to saddle its frustrated readers with a further burden: the queasy acknowledgment of your own desire to find Tess fleshed in her essence in order to sustain your fascination with her destiny.

If there is "eloquence" to be had from her flowerlike mouth (a displaced site of her eventual defloration), it is only through the reader's bodily contribution as silent enunciator. To voice even subvocally the "*m*obile *p*eony" shape of her "*p*outed-u*p* dee*p* red *m*outh" is to amass labials in a burst of silently pursed lips. For Tess, the scapegoat, this is our most tangible locus of identification and our kiss of death. So, too, with the "characteristic intonation" of the "dialect for this district" that was so palpably "on her tongue" — namely, the "voicing approximately rendered by the syllable UR, probably as rich an utterance as any to be found in human speech" (39). A mere five words away from that offhand phonetic analysis, the pivotal syllable of "utterance" itself opens out to an overarching irony of plot: the supposed enriching of Tess Durbeyfield by the reverbed UR of "d'*Ur*b*er*ville." This name is the one truly striking instance of the "UR" sound that we ever hear in connection with Tess or her voice — and then only by producing it ourselves as we read. The phonetic microdrama of this opening passage is thus a microcosm of positioned reading in the overall experience — or execution — of the novel, its "actualized" prose, where it is up to us to perform the seductive lushness that by projective investment we seek to find in a heroine like Tess.

If this is the implicated reading position fostered by the mere verbal texture of the novel's opening chapters, then it might seem inevitably undercut by the visual overdetermination of any specific pictorial illustration. Yet in the illustrations for the original serial publication of the novel — in a weekly magazine entitled the *Graphic*, no less — the reader is given to see Tess in a way that does not in fact eliminate the irony of libidinal projection but instead tampers with the stage directions of the novel just enough to enforce it in an unexpected fashion. In so doing, even this illustration confirms what the ironized narrative structure of sequential selfhood in the plot has implied: that fictional characters regularly stand arrested before the reader for analytic scrutiny at major turning points of the plot, often victimized unknowingly by the schemata through which their life stories get partitioned and paced off.

As we turn the large format page of the *Graphic* from chapter II into chapter III, Tess's at best sketchy physical description in the prose is followed suddenly by her emergence into visual image for us — and others within the scene. Yet the lines of sight are reversed from the novel's. In Hardy's version, Tess has torn herself away from the evening dance for a too familiar setting that "struck upon the girl's senses with an unspeakable dreariness" (43). These are her domestic confines impinging once again upon her, a realm whose threshold she crosses like a self-caged animal. In the illustration, however, her glance is abstracted rather than concentrated to a careworn knot — the proverbial faraway look. No longer the optical anchor of the assaulting impressions, she is gazed upon rather than gazing, the entered doorway becoming the proscenium arch for the costumed theater of her vernal apotheosis: the farmhand as May-Day goddess. She is the cynosure of the familial space, its denizens arrayed before her, backs to the reader, now viewer, like a second, mediating audience. The serial form of the novel has in this way further deferred our identification with the heroine's subjectivity, giving us a second exterior view of Tess even from within her own domestic interior. What Tess has been for the idle onlooker at the dance, she is now for her own family as spectatorial tribe. Just where the prose suddenly plummets into the constraints of her interior landscape in collision with the reduced scope of her domestic drudgery, the illustration sustains a glamorized view of the heroine as performing self, a body on display.

This is the least of it. It does so across the turn of the page to an outsized illustration whose very mechanics of page-turned disclosure enhance the largest composite suggestion of the plate: the visual hint that Tess's advent on the domestic threshold tacitly reduplicates the very scene of reading. On the right half of the wide-format text, the half on which the eye falls first in flipping the page, there is an immediate association between the reader's — suddenly viewer's — line of sight and that of the young boy at the right margin (Tess's brother Abraham, named in this scene but undescribed in his actions or position by Hardy), leaning into the frame to stare at his sister. Other details from the illustration are there in the prose: the rocked cradle, the washbasin in which Tess's white gown had yesterday been scrubbed clean. But Abraham's place as stand-in for the viewer is an illustrator's invention, a canny interpretive act in its own right, especially as regards the unidentifiable, lecternlike stand on which he rests, its surface glowing as if from the reflected light of the opened door — or as if it held an illuminated page from which he has just looked up.

The first thing we see when we turn our page, then, the male spectator leaning forward to stare at a radiant feminine presence, brings focus to the entire interior space as the scene not of Tess's entrapment but of her prolonged objectification as a fine and handsome "shape."

Reversing, if only by deferring briefly, all emphasis on Tess's own narrowed field of vision and action, the precinematic "reverse shot" of this illustration thus captures and holds our attention as an image of just that attention. It transfigures the squalor of Tess's home — transvalues the space of her most intimate and wearying relations — into the zone of surrogate spectacle routinely occasioned by the domestic scene of reading, at least in households having more access than Tess's to the compensatory excitement of novels.

A critical debate that happens to have sprung up around this illustration is enlightening here for precisely the way it skirts the issue of erotic investment while nonetheless stressing the importance of the picture in transfixing readerly participation. In one account, Arlene M. Jackson understands the richly rendered domestic scene as what can only amount to an instance of tactical false advertising, meant to lure in the Victorian family reader before the luridness of the plot has tipped its hand.[2] From a different perspective associated with a Marxist or materialist analysis, and yet coming to much the same point, this solicitation of the reader is seen to depend not on the inviting pictorial surface but on the stare of the baby out into the field of the reader, a reader who is thereby "interpellated" (Althusser's term) into the "class" ideology of the popular commodity text (Feltes 70–71). My own point is that the reader's invoked interest rests at least as much with the deflected stare of the heroine, out past your gaze but entirely available to it. It is this very availability that inscribes — or conscribes — your reading, right from the start, within the complex literary ideology of character as embodiment, selfhood as carnal localization, and hence spiritual change as serial reincarnation, including the varieties of psychic damage entailed along the way by such prototypes for anything ordinarily called "identity."

One astute reader of this early image even finds in its ironic "figuration" another prophetic clue to the plot's tragic close, a kind of visual dead metaphor. Later to emerge, on execution day, as "a tall budding creature — half girl, half woman — a spiritualized image of Tess" (383), Liza-Lu here faces the bloom of young womanhood in the decked-out person of her older sister with a no-doubt unconscious instinct of threat; she seems to reach for her own neck not only in a relieving stretch after the strain of her chores, as they contrast with Tess's holiday, but in a tacit anticipation of the gallows noose to which all her

[2]Jackson discusses the engraving by Hubert Herkomer for its place in the "domestic theme" as well as its hospitality to domestic readers, "a calculated appeal to an audience looking for a 'family' novel" (Jackson 106).

sister's expectant freshness will eventually lead.[3] To notice any such irony in glancing back over the illustrations with the plot in mind — to decode this pictorial configuration, that is to say, according to the rhetoric of temporality — would only be to superimpose a later Tess upon the early one. This later figure would be that very Tess who, just in time for the ultimate abjection of her physical being in violent death, "had spiritually ceased to recognize the body before her as hers." Like Tess herself, we too, though always imagining that body even when no illustration does our work for us, are nonetheless spared the brunt of this final execution scene. The respite seems to come as a reward for having learned to think, in Tess's own way, that it must be some other self — no longer our heroine — who has had any renewed relationship with Alec at all, she and only she who can now be found going to the scaffold over its outcome.

In that first and typifying illustration, then, Tess's abstracted look is averted from the very gaze that her good looks provoke: looks that, nevertheless, everything in the staging of the allegorical tableau reminds you your usual reading works to produce rather than strains to glimpse. As with ordinary narrative effects, what you see is what you beget. For Tess is never more than, in the rhetorical sense, a fine figure of a woman. As with her inscribed person, so with her plot. It is in the nature of her fame and, within the story, of her infamy that Tess the woman, like *Tess* the book, exists to be read, now by omen and prolepsis, now by prototype and intertext, now by abrupt but steadily measurable transformations of her social and psychological status. To understand the process as well as the product, there is no way for the implicated reader to stand outside. You stand, instead, sutured into and skewered by it — nailed by the very fascination through which the novel's appeal to sympathy has both drawn and taken you in. Appearances to the contrary, it is not an altogether pretty picture.

WORKS CITED

Bloom, Harold. *Thomas Hardy's "Tess of the D'Urbervilles."* Modern Critical Interpretations. New York: Chelsea House, 1987.

de Man, Paul. "The Rhetoric of Temporality." *Blindness and Insight.* Minneapolis: U of Minnesota P, 1971. 187–228.

[3]I am indebted to Hilary Schor for this observation, in response to an earlier version of this essay delivered at the 1995 International Conference on Narrative.

Reversing, if only by deferring bri
rowed field of vision and act
this illustration thus captures
just that attention. It transfigures
values the space of her most intim
the zone of surrogate spectacle routi
scene of reading, at least in households
to the compensatory excitement of novels.

A critical debate that happens to have spru
tion is enlightening here for precisely the way it s
investment while nonetheless stressing the importan
transfixing readerly participation. In one account, Arlen
derstands the richly rendered domestic scene as what can
an instance of tactical false advertising, meant to lure in t
family reader before the luridness of the plot has tipped its han
a different perspective associated with a Marxist or materialist a
and yet coming to much the same point, this solicitation of the rea
seen to depend not on the getting pictorial surface but on the stare
the baby out into the field of the reader, a reader who is thereby "inter-pellated" (Althusser's term) to the "class" ideology of the popular commodity text (Feltes 70). My own point is that the reader's invoked interest rests at least as much with the deflected stare of the heroine, out past your gaze but barely available to it. It is this very availability that inscribes — or conscribes — your reading, right from the start, within the complex literary ideology of character as embodiment, selfhood as carnal localization, and hence spiritual change as serial reincarnation, including the variety of psychic damage entailed along the way by such prototypes for anything ordinarily called "identity."

One astute reader of the early image even finds in its ironic "figuration" another prophetic cue to the plot's tragic close, a kind of visual dead metaphor. Later to emerge, on execution day, as "a tall budding creature — half girl, half woman — a spiritualized image of Tess" (383), Liza-Lu here fixes the bloom of young womanhood in the decked-out person of her older sister with a no-doubt unconscious instinct of threat; she seems to reach for her own neck not only in a relieving stretch after the strain of her chores, as they contrast with Tess's holiday, but in a tacit anticipation of the gallows noose to which all her

[2]Jackson discusses the engraving by Hubert Herkomer for its place in the "domestic theme" as well as its hospitality to domestic readers, "a calculated appeal to an audience looking for a 'family' novel" (Jackson 106).

ant freshness will eventually lead.[3] To notice any such ing back over the illustrations with the plot in mind — to pictorial configuration, that is to say, according to the temporality — would only be to superimpose a later Tess early one. This later figure would be that very Tess who, just in the ultimate abjection of her physical being in violent death, piritually ceased to recognize the body before her as hers." Like erself, we too, though always imagining that body even when no ation does our work for us, are nonetheless spared the brunt of this execution scene. The respite seems to come as a reward for having rned to think, in Tess's own way, that must be some other self — no nger our heroine — who has had any newed relationship with Alec t all, she and only she who can now be nd going to the scaffold over its outcome.

In that first and typifying illustrat then, Tess's abstracted look is averted from the very gaze that her d looks provoke: looks that, nevertheless, everything in the stag if the allegorical tableau reminds you your usual reading works roduce rather than strains to glimpse. As with ordinary narrative es, what you see is what you beget. For Tess is never more than, in rhetorical sense, a fine figure of a woman. As with her inscribed per so with her plot. It is in the nature of her fame and, within the st of her infamy that Tess the woman, like *Tess* the book, exists to b d, now by omen and prolepsis, now by prototype and intertext, n by abrupt but steadily measurable transformations of her social psychological status. To understand the process as well as the p uct, there is no way for the implicated reader to stand outside. Y stand, instead, sutured into and skewered by it — nailed by the ve scination through which the novel's appeal to sympathy has both d n and taken you in. Appearances to the contrary, it is not an altog er pretty picture.

WORKS CITED

Bloom, Harold. *Thomas Hardy's "Tess of the D'Urbervilles."* Modern Critical Interpretations. New York: Chelsea House, 1987.

de Man, Paul. "The Rhetoric of Temporality." *Blindness and Insight.* Minneapolis: U of Minnesota P, 1971. 187–228.

[3] I am indebted to Hilary Schor for this observation, in response to an earlier version of this essay delivered at the 1995 International Conference on Narrative.

Feltes, N. N. *Modes of Production of Victorian Fiction.* Chicago: U of Chicago P, 1986.

Iser, Wolfgang. *The Implied Reader: Patterns of Communication in Prose Fiction from Bunyan to Beckett.* Baltimore: Johns Hopkins UP, 1974.

Jackson, Arlene M. *Illustration and the Novels of Thomas Hardy.* Totowa: Rowman and Littlefield, 1981.

Kincaid, James. "'You Did Not Come': Absence, Death and Eroticism in *Tess.*" *Sex and Death in Victorian Literature.* Ed. Regina Barreca. London: Macmillan, 1990.

Cultural Criticism and *Tess of the d'Urbervilles*

WHAT IS CULTURAL CRITICISM?

What do you think of when you think of culture? The opera or ballet? A performance of a Mozart symphony at Lincoln Center or a Rembrandt show at the De Young Museum in San Francisco? Does the phrase "cultural event" conjure up images of young people in jeans and T-shirts — or of people in their sixties dressed formally? Most people hear "culture" and think "high culture." Consequently, when they first hear of cultural criticism, most people assume it is more formal than, well, say, formalism. They suspect it is "highbrow," in both subject and style.

Nothing could be further from the truth. Cultural critics oppose the view that culture refers exclusively to high culture, Culture with a capital C. Cultural critics want to make the term refer to popular, folk, urban, and mass (mass-produced, -disseminated, -mediated, and -consumed) culture, as well as to that culture we associate with the so-called classics. Raymond Williams, an early British cultural critic whose ideas will later be described at greater length, suggested that "art and culture are ordinary"; he did so not to "pull art down" but rather to point out that there is "creativity in all our living. . . . We create our human world as we have thought of art being created" (*Revolution* 37).

Cultural critics have consequently placed a great deal of emphasis on what Michel de Certeau has called "the practice of everyday life." Rather than approaching literature in the elitist way that academic literary critics have traditionally approached it, cultural critics view it more as an anthropologist would. They ask how it emerges from and competes with other forms of discourse within a given culture (science, for instance, or television). They seek to understand the social contexts in which a given text was written, and under what conditions it was — and is — produced, disseminated, read, and used.

Contemporary cultural critics are as willing to write about *Star Trek* as they are to analyze James Joyce's *Ulysses,* a modern literary classic full of allusions to Homer's *Odyssey.* And when they write about *Ulysses,* they are likely to view it as a collage reflecting and representing cultural forms common to Joyce's Dublin, such as advertising, journalism, film, and pub life. Cultural critics typically show how the boundary we tend to envision between high and low forms of culture — forms thought of as important on one hand and relatively trivial on the other — is transgressed in all sorts of exciting ways within works on both sides of the putative cultural divide.

A cultural critic writing about a revered classic might contrast it with a movie, or even a comic-strip version produced during a later period. Alternatively, the literary classic might be seen in a variety of other ways: in light of some more common form of reading material (a novel by Jane Austen might be viewed in light of Gothic romances or ladies' conduct manuals); as the reflection of some common cultural myths or concerns (*Adventures of Huckleberry Finn* might be shown to reflect and shape American myths about race and concerns about juvenile delinquency); or as an example of how texts move back and forth across the alleged boundary between "low" and "high" culture. For instance, one group of cultural critics has pointed out that although Shakespeare's history plays probably started off as popular works enjoyed by working people, they were later considered "highbrow" plays that only the privileged and educated could appreciate. That view of them changed, however, due to later film productions geared toward a national audience. A film version of *Henry V* produced during World War II, for example, made a powerful, popular, patriotic statement about England's greatness during wartime (Humm, Stigant, and Widdowson 6–7). More recently, cultural critics have analyzed the "cultural work" accomplished cooperatively by Shakespeare and Kenneth Branagh in the latter's 1992 film production of *Henry V.*

In combating old definitions of what constitutes culture, of course, cultural critics sometimes end up contesting old definitions of what constitutes the literary canon, that is, the once-agreed-upon honor roll of Great Books. They tend to do so, however, neither by adding books (and movies and television sitcoms) *to* the old list of texts that every "culturally literate" person should supposedly know nor by substituting some kind of counterculture canon. Instead, they tend to critique the very *idea* of canon.

Cultural critics want to get us away from thinking about certain works as the "best" ones produced by a given culture. They seek to be more descriptive and less evaluative, more interested in relating than in rating cultural products and events. They also aim to discover the (often political) reasons *why* a certain kind of aesthetic or cultural product is more valued than others. This is particularly true when the product in question is one produced since 1945, for most cultural critics follow Jean Baudrillard (*Simulations,* 1981) and Andreas Huyssen (*The Great Divide,* 1986) in thinking that any distinctions that may once have existed between high, popular, and mass culture collapsed after the end of World War II. Their discoveries have led them beyond the literary canon, prompting them to interrogate many other value hierarchies. For instance, Pierre Bourdieu in *Distinction: A Social Critique of the Judgment of Taste* (1984 [1979]) and Dick Hebdige in *Hiding the Light: On Images and Things* (1988) have argued that definitions of "good taste" — which are instrumental in fostering and reinforcing cultural discrimination — tell us at least as much about prevailing social, economic, and political conditions as they do about artistic quality and value.

In an article entitled "The Need for Cultural Studies," four groundbreaking cultural critics have written that "Cultural Studies should . . . abandon the goal of giving students access to that which represents a culture." A literary work, they go on to suggest, should be seen in relation to other works, to economic conditions, or to broad social discourses (about childbirth, women's education, rural decay, and so on) within whose contexts it makes sense. Perhaps most important, critics practicing cultural studies should counter the prevalent notion of culture as some preformed whole. Rather than being static or monolithic, culture is really a set of interactive *cultures,* alive and changing, and cultural critics should be present- and even future-oriented. They should be "resisting intellectuals," and cultural studies should be "an emancipatory project" (Giroux et al. 478–80).

The paragraphs above are peppered with words like *oppose, counter, deny, resist, combat, abandon,* and *emancipatory.* What such words quite accurately suggest is that a number of cultural critics view themselves in political, even oppositional, terms. Not only are they likely to take on the literary canon, they are also likely to oppose the institution of the university, for that is where the old definitions of culture as high culture (and as something formed, finished, and canonized) have been most vigorously preserved, defended, and reinforced.

Cultural critics have been especially critical of the departmental structure of universities, which, perhaps more than anything else, has kept the study of the "arts" relatively distinct from the study of history, not to mention from the study of such things as television, film, advertising, journalism, popular photography, folklore, current affairs, shoptalk, and gossip. By maintaining artificial boundaries, universities have tended to reassert the high/low culture distinction, implying that all the latter subjects are best left to historians, sociologists, anthropologists, and communication theorists. Cultural critics have taken issue with this implication, arguing that the way of thinking reinforced by the departmentalized structure of universities keeps us from seeing the aesthetics of an advertisement as well as the propagandistic elements of a work of literature. Cultural critics have consequently mixed and matched the analytical procedures developed in a variety of disciplines. They have formed — and encouraged other scholars to form — networks and centers, often outside of those enforced departmentally.

Some initially loose interdisciplinary networks have, over time, solidified to become cultural studies programs and majors. As this has happened, a significant if subtle danger has arisen. Richard Johnson, who along with Hebdige, Stuart Hall, and Richard Hoggart was instrumental in developing the Center for Contemporary Cultural Studies at Birmingham University in England, has warned that cultural studies must not be allowed to turn into yet another traditional academic discipline — one in which students encounter a canon replete with soap operas and cartoons, one in which belief in the importance of such popular forms has become an "orthodoxy" (39). The only principles that critics doing cultural studies can doctrinally espouse, Johnson suggests, are the two that have thus far been introduced: the principle that "culture" has been an "inegalitarian" concept, a "tool" of "condescension," and the belief that a new, "interdisciplinary (and even antidisciplinary)" approach to *true* culture (that is, to the forms in which culture currently lives) is required now that history, art, and the communications media are so complex and interrelated (42).

> The object of cultural study should not be a body of works assumed to comprise or reflect a given culture. Rather, it should be human consciousness, and the goal of that critical analysis should be to understand and show how that consciousness is itself forged and formed, to a great extent, by cultural forces. "Subjectivities," as Johnson has put it, are "produced, not given, and are . . . objects of inquiry" inevitably related to "social practices," whether those involve factory rules, supermarket behavior patterns, reading habits, advertisements, myths, or languages and other signs to which people are exposed (44–45).

Although the United States has probably contributed more than any other nation to the *media* through which culture is currently expressed, and although many if not most contemporary practitioners of cultural criticism are North American, the evolution of cultural criticism and, more broadly, cultural studies has to a great extent been influenced by theories developed in Great Britain and on the European continent.

Among the Continental thinkers whose work allowed for the development of cultural studies are those whose writings we associate with structuralism and poststructuralism. Using the linguistic theory of Ferdinand de Saussure, structuralists suggested that the structures of language lie behind all human organization. They attempted to create a *semiology* — a science of signs — that would give humankind at once a scientific and holistic way of studying the world and its human inhabitants. Roland Barthes, a structuralist who later shifted toward poststructuralism, attempted to recover literary language from the isolation in which it had been studied and to show that the laws that govern it govern all signs, from road signs to articles of clothing. Claude Lévi-Strauss, an anthropologist who studied the structures of everything from cuisine to villages to myths, looked for and found recurring, common elements that transcended the differences within and between cultures.

Of the structuralist and poststructuralist thinkers who have had an impact on the evolution of cultural studies, Jacques Lacan is one of three whose work has been particularly influential. A structuralist psychoanalytic theorist, Lacan posited that the human unconscious is structured like a language and treated dreams not as revealing symptoms of repression but, rather, as forms of discourse. Lacan also argued that the ego, subject, or self that we think of as being natural (our individual human nature) is in fact a product of the social order and its symbolic systems (especially, but not exclusively, language). Lacan's thought has served as the theoretical underpinning for cultural critics seeking to show the way in which subjectivities are produced by social discourses and practices.

Jacques Derrida, a French philosopher whose name has become synonymous with poststructuralism, has had an influence on cultural criticism at least as great as that of Lacan. The linguistic focus of structuralist thought has by no means been abandoned by poststructuralists, despite their opposition to structuralism's tendency to find universal patterns instead of textual and cultural contradictions. Indeed, Derrida has provocatively asserted that "*there is nothing outside the text*" (*Grammatology* 158), by which he means something like the following: we come to know the world through language, and even our most worldly actions and practices (the Gulf War, the wearing of condoms) are dependent upon discourses (even if they deliberately contravene those discourses). Derrida's "deconstruction" of the world/text distinction, like his deconstruction of so many of the hierarchical oppositions we habitually use to interpret and evaluate reality, has allowed cultural critics to erase the boundaries between high and low culture, classic and popular literary texts, and literature and other cultural discourses that, following Derrida, may be seen as manifestations of the same textuality.

Michel Foucault is the third Continental thinker associated with structuralism and/or poststructuralism who has had a particularly powerful impact on the evolution of cultural studies — and perhaps *the* strongest influence on American cultural criticism and the so-called new historicism, an interdisciplinary form of cultural criticism whose evolution has often paralleled that of cultural criticism. Although Foucault broke with Marxism after the French student uprisings of 1968, he was influenced enough by Marxist thought to study cultures in terms of power relationships. Unlike Marxists, however, Foucault refused to see power as something exercised by a dominant class over a subservient class. Indeed, he emphasized that power is not just repressive power, that is, a tool of conspiracy by one individual or institution against another. Power, rather, is a whole complex of forces; it is that which produces what happens.

Thus even a tyrannical aristocrat does not simply wield power but is empowered by "discourses" — accepted ways of thinking, writing, and speaking — and practices that embody, exercise, and amount to power. Foucault tried to view all things, from punishment to sexuality, in terms of the widest possible variety of discourses. As a result, he traced what he called the "genealogy" of topics he studied through texts that more traditional historians and literary critics would have overlooked, examining (in Lynn Hunt's words) "memoirs of deviants, diaries, political treatises, architectural blueprints, court records, doctors' reports — appl[ying] consistent principles of analysis in search of moments of reversal in discourse, in search of events as loci of the conflict where social practices were transformed" (Hunt 39). Foucault tended not only to build interdisciplinary bridges but also, in the process, to bring into the study of culture the "histories of women, homosexuals, and minorities" — groups seldom studied by those interested in Culture with a capital C (Hunt 45).

Of the British influences on cultural studies and criticism, two stand out prominently. One, the Marxist historian E. P. Thompson, revolutionized the study of the industrial revolution by writing about its impact on human attitudes, even consciousness. He showed how a shared cultural view, specifically that of what constitutes a fair or just price, influenced crowd behavior and caused such things as the "food riots" of the eighteenth and nineteenth centuries (during which the women of Nottingham repriced breads in the shops of local bakers, paid for the goods they needed, and carried them away). The other, even more important early British influence on contemporary cultural criticism and cultural studies was Raymond Williams, who coined the phrase "culture is ordinary." In works like *Culture and Society: 1780–1950* (1958) and *The Long Revolution* (1961) Williams demonstrated that culture is not fixed and finished but, rather, living and evolving. One of the changes he called for was the development of a common socialist culture.

Although Williams dissociated himself from Marxism during the period 1945–58, he always followed the Marxist practice of viewing culture in relation to ideologies, which he defined as the "residual," "dominant," or "emerging" ways of viewing the world held by classes or individuals holding power in a given social group. He avoided dwelling on class conflict and class oppression, however, tending instead to focus on people as people, on how they experience the conditions in which they find themselves and creatively respond to those conditions through their social practices. A believer in the resiliency of the individual, Williams produced a body of criticism notable for what Stuart Hall has called its "humanism" (63).

As is clearly suggested in several of the preceding paragraphs, Marxism is the background to the background of cultural criticism.

What isn't as clear is that some contemporary cultural critics consider themselves Marxist critics as well. It is important, therefore, to have some familiarity with certain Marxist concepts — those that would have been familiar to Foucault, Thompson, and Williams, plus those espoused by contemporary cultural critics who self-identify with Marxism. That familiarity can be gained from an introduction to the works of four important Marxist thinkers: Mikhail Bakhtin, Walter Benjamin, Antonio Gramsci, and Louis Althusser.

Bakhtin was a Russian, later a Soviet, critic so original in his thinking and wide-ranging in his influence that some would say he was never a Marxist at all. He viewed literary works in terms of discourses and dialogues *between* discourses. The narrative of a novel written in a society in flux, for instance, may include an official, legitimate discourse, plus others that challenge its viewpoint and even its authority. In a 1929 book on Dostoyevsky and the 1940 study *Rabelais and His World,* Bakhtin examined what he calls "polyphonic" novels, each characterized by a multiplicity of voices or discourses. In Dostoyevsky the independent status of a given character is marked by the difference of his or her language from that of the narrator. (The narrator's language may itself involve a dialogue involving opposed points of view.) In works by Rabelais, Bakhtin finds that the (profane) languages of Carnival and of other popular festivities play against and parody the more official discourses of the magistrates and the church. Bakhtin's relevance to cultural criticism lies in his suggestion that the dialogue involving high and low culture takes place not only between classic and popular texts but also between the "dialogic" voices that exist within all great books.

Walter Benjamin was a German Marxist who, during roughly the same period, attacked fascism and questioned the superior value placed on certain traditional literary forms that he felt conveyed a stultifying "aura" of culture. He took this position in part because so many previous Marxist critics (and, in his own day, Georg Lukács) had seemed to prefer nineteenth-century realistic novels to the modernist works of their own time. Benjamin not only praised modernist movements, such as dadaism, but also saw as promising the development of new art forms utilizing mechanical production and reproduction. These forms, including photography, radio, and film, promised that the arts would become a more democratic, less exclusive, domain. Anticipating by decades the work of those cultural critics interested in mass-produced, mass-mediated, and mass-consumed culture, Benjamin analyzed the meanings and (defensive) motivations behind words like *unique* and *authentic* when used in conjunction with mechanically reproduced art.

Antonio Gramsci, an Italian Marxist best known for his *Prison Notebooks* (first published in 1947), critiqued the very concept of literature and, beyond that, of culture in the old sense, stressing the importance of culture more broadly defined and the need for nurturing and developing proletarian, or working-class, culture. He argued that all intellectual or cultural work is fundamentally political and expressed the need for what he called "radical organic" intellectuals. Today's cultural critics urging colleagues to "legitimate the notion of writing reviews and books for the general public," to "become involved in the political reading of popular culture," and more generally to "repoliticize" scholarship have viewed Gramsci as an early precursor (Giroux et al. 482).

Gramsci related literature to the ideologies — the prevailing ideas, beliefs, values, and prejudices — of the culture in which it was produced. He developed the concept of "hegemony," which refers at once to the process of consensus-formation and to the authority of the ideologies so formed, that is to say, their power to shape the way things look, what they would seem to mean, and, therefore, what reality *is* for the majority of people. But Gramsci did not see people, even poor people, as the helpless victims of hegemony, as ideology's pathetic robots. Rather, he believed that people have the freedom and power to struggle against and shape ideology, to alter hegemony, to break out of the weblike system of prevailing assumptions and to form a new consensus. As Patrick Brantlinger has suggested in *Crusoe's Footprints: Cultural Studies in Britain and America* (1990), Gramsci rejected the "intellectual arrogance that views the vast majority of people as deluded zombies, the victims or creatures of ideology" (100).

Of those Marxists who, after Gramsci, explored the complex relationship between literature and ideology, the French Marxist Louis Althusser had a significant impact on cultural criticism. Unlike Gramsci, Althusser tended to portray ideology as being in control of people, and not vice versa. He argued that the main function of ideology is to reproduce the society's existing relations of production, and that that function is even carried out in literary texts. In many ways, though, Althusser is as good an example of how Marxism and cultural criticism part company as he is of how cultural criticism is indebted to Marxists and their ideas. For although Althusser did argue that literature is relatively autonomous — more independent of ideology than, say, church, press, or state — he meant literature in the high cultural sense, certainly not the variety of works that present-day cultural critics routinely examine alongside those of Tolstoy and Joyce, Eliot and Brecht. Popular fictions, Althusser assumed, were mere packhorses designed (however unconsciously) to carry the baggage of a culture's ideology, or mere brood mares destined to reproduce it.

Thus, while a number of cultural critics would agree both with Althusser's notion that works of literature reflect certain ideological formations and with his notion that, at the same time, literary works may be relatively distant from or even resistant to ideology, they have rejected the narrow limits within which Althusser and some other Marxists (such as Georg Lukács) have defined literature. In "Marxism and Popular Fiction" (1986), Tony Bennett uses *Monty Python's Flying Circus* and another British television show, *Not the 9 o'clock News,* to argue that the Althusserian notion that all forms of culture belong "among [all those] many material forms which ideology takes . . . under capitalism" is "simply not true." The "entire field" of "popular fiction" — which Bennett takes to include films and television shows as well as books — is said to be "replete with instances" of works that do what Bennett calls the "work" of "distancing." That is, they have the effect of separating the audience from, not rebinding the audience to, prevailing ideologies (249).

Although Marxist cultural critics exist (Bennett himself is one, carrying on through his writings what may be described as a lovers' quarrel with Marxism), most cultural critics are not Marxists in any strict sense. Anne Beezer, in writing about such things as advertisements and women's magazines, contests the "Althusserian view of ideology as the construction of the subject" (qtd. in Punter 103). That is, she gives both the media she is concerned with and their audiences more credit than Althusserian Marxists presumably would. Whereas they might argue that such media make people what they are, she points out that the same magazines that, admittedly, tell women how to please their men may, at the same time, offer liberating advice to women about how to preserve their independence by not getting too serious romantically. And, she suggests, many advertisements advertise their status as ads, just as many people who view or read them see advertising as advertising and interpret it accordingly.

The complex sort of analysis that Beezer has brought to bear on women's magazines and advertisements has been focused on paperback romance novels by Tania Modleski and Janice A. Radway in *Loving with a Vengeance* (1982) and *Reading the Romance* (1984), respectively. Radway, a feminist cultural critic who uses but ultimately goes beyond Marxism, points out that many women who read romances do so in order to carve out a time and space that is wholly their own, not to be intruded upon by husbands or children. Although many such novels end in marriage, the marriage is usually between a feisty and independent heroine and a powerful man she has "tamed," that is, made sensitive and caring. And why do so many of these stories involve such heroines and end as they do? Because, as Radway demonstrates through painstaking research into publishing houses, bookstores, and reading communities, their consumers *want* them to. They don't buy — or, if they buy they don't recommend — romances in which, for example, a heroine is raped: thus, in time, fewer and fewer such plots find their way onto the racks by the supermarket checkout.

Radway's reading is typical of feminist cultural criticism in that it is *political,* but not exclusively about oppression. The subjectivities of women may be "produced" by romances — the thinking of romance readers may be governed by what is read — but the same women also govern, to a great extent, what gets written or produced, thus performing "cultural work" of their own. Rather than seeing all forms of popular culture as manifestations of ideology, soon to be remanifested in the minds of victimized audiences, cultural critics tend to see a sometimes disheartening but always dynamic synergy between cultural forms and the culture's consumers. Their observations have increasingly led to an analysis of consumerism, from a feminist but also from a more general point of view. This analysis owes a great deal to the work of de Certeau, Hall, and, especially, Hebdige, whose 1979 book *Subculture: The Meaning of Style* paved the way for critics like John Fiske (*Television Culture,* 1987), Greil Marcus (*Dead Elvis,* 1991), and Rachel Bowlby (*Shopping with Freud,* 1993). These later critics have analyzed everything from the resistance tactics employed by television audiences to the influence of consumers on rock music styles to the psychology of consumer choice.

The overlap between feminist and cultural criticism is hardly surprising, especially given the recent evolution of feminism into various femin*isms,* some of which remain focused on "majority" women of European descent, others of which have focused instead on the lives and writings of minority women in Western culture and of women living in Third World (now preferably called postcolonial) societies. The culturalist analysis of value hierarchies within and between cultures has inevitably focused on categories that include class, race, national origin, gender, and sexualities; the terms of its critique have proved useful to contemporary feminists, many of whom differ from their predecessors insofar as they see *woman* not as a universal category but, rather, as one of several that play a role in identity- or subject-formation. The influence of cultural criticism (and, in some cases, Marxist class analysis) can be seen in the work of contemporary feminist critics such as Gayatri Spivak, Trinh T. Minh-ha, and Gloria Anzaldúa, each of whom has stressed that while all women are female, they are something else as well (such as working-class, lesbian, Native American, Muslim Pakistani) and that that something else must be taken into account when their writings are read and studied.

The expansion of feminism and feminist literary criticism to include multicultural analysis, of course, parallels a transformation of education in general. On college campuses across North America, the field of African-American studies has grown and flourished. African-American critics have been influenced by and have contributed to the cultural approach by pointing out that the white cultural elite of North America has tended to view the oral-musical traditions of African Americans (traditions that include jazz, the blues, sermons, and folktales) as entertaining, but nonetheless inferior. Black writers, in order not to be similarly marginalized, have produced texts that, as Henry Louis Gates has pointed out, fuse the language and traditions of the white Western canon with a black vernacular and traditions derived from African and Caribbean cultures. The resulting "hybridity" (to use Homi K. Bhabha's word), although deplored by a handful of black separatist critics, has proved both rich and complex — fertile ground for many cultural critics practicing African-American criticism.

Interest in race and ethnicity at home has gone hand in hand with a new, interdisciplinary focus on colonial and postcolonial societies abroad, in which issues of race, class, and ethnicity also loom large. Edward Said's book *Orientalism* (1978) is generally said to have inaugurated postcolonial studies, which in Bhabha's words "bears witness to the unequal and uneven forces of cultural representation involved in the contest for political and social authority within the modern world order" ("Postcolonial Criticism" 437). *Orientalism* showed how Eastern and Middle Eastern peoples have for centuries been systematically stereotyped by the West, and how that stereotyping facilitated the colonization of vast areas of the East and Middle East by Westerners. Said's more recent books, along with postcolonial studies by Bhabha and Patrick Brantlinger, are among the most widely read and discussed works of literary scholarship. Brantlinger focuses on British literature of the Victorian period, examining representations of the colonies in works written during an era of imperialist expansion. Bhabha complements Brantlinger by suggesting that modern Western culture is best understood from the postcolonial perspective.

Thanks to the work of scholars like Brantlinger, Bhabha, Said, Gates, Anzaldúa, and Spivak, education in general and literary study in particular is becoming more democratic, decentered (less patriarchal and Eurocentric), and multicultural. The future of literary criticism will owe a great deal indeed to those early cultural critics who demonstrated that the boundaries between high and low culture are at once repressive and permeable, that culture is common and therefore includes all forms of popular culture, that cultural definitions are inevitably political, and that the world we see is seen through society's ideology. In a very real sense, the future of education *is* cultural studies.

Jennifer Wicke begins the essay that follows with her own brief synopsis of cultural criticism. "A major premise" of the approach, she asserts, "is that a literary work . . . is a focal point for the study of culture." She views the "language" of a literary text — "in other words its linguistic complexities on the large scale of plot and narrative and the smaller scale of image, scene, passage, or word" — as "a cultural concentrator." As such, literature is no mere "static reflection" of culture; rather, a literary work is "part of culture in the making" and, consequently, an important clue to discovering what the significant cultural issues were at the time the text was written.

What Hardy's *Tess of the d'Urbervilles* reveals, Wicke argues, is the "complexity and uncertainty" of the new, large-scale, impersonal "market society" that had emerged in nineteenth-century Europe:

> The tragedies that hover over Tess throughout the novel have everything to do with the loss of a neighborhood "market," where eggs and horses can be bartered for wood or clothing, to an anonymous and abstract market that chews up and spits out workers like Tess in imitation of the threshing machine.

In a novel, which is a "marketable commodity," about a young woman who is *herself* a marketable commodity, Wicke argues that Hardy poses the following question: "What about people, finally: if people are inevitably evaluated as goods on the market, how will they be categorized? As standard, substandard, better than standard?" Before approaching Hardy's answer to that question, however, Wicke offers a brief history of the modern notion of "standards" — a notion inextricably intertwined with the demise of local markets, the growth of manufacturing, and the end of the world as Tess's ancestors knew it.

Wicke then examines the language of the novel, which is "bursting with the phenomenon and the language of standards, trademarks, and brands — whether [Hardy] intended this to be the case or not." In a description of Tess, Hardy says that her eyes were "neither black nor blue nor gray nor violet; rather all those shades together, and a hundred others, . . . an almost standard woman, but for the slight incautiousness of character inherited from her race." When Tess baptizes the child Sorrow, it is with water from a "Keelwell's Marmalade" jar. ("What strikes one as peculiar," Wicke asserts, "is that the Durbeyfields would not make their own jam.") Alec d'Urberville is a self-described "sham d'Urberville," who appears to be a "reproduction."

Tess, Wicke maintains, is a novel of incipient standardization that does not itself fully comprehend standardization's cost; it is a work produced by a culture "before it had become clear to the culture that the new phenomenon of standards would bear a human price." Like Coca-Cola, Tess may in some sense be "the real thing" as well as an "almost standard woman"; in many important ways, though, she is "an ultimately unstandardizable type, a perfect anomaly, a standardizing oxymoron." According to Wicke, the novel even asks its readers *who* is "responsible for setting the standards such that Tess will end up on the gallows." From the vantage point of cultural criticism, the answer is a *what,* namely, "Standards" themselves. "The force that drives poor Tess to her end is that mysterious cultural force of Standards, not the gods or God."

Wicke's essay exhibits most of the characteristics of the best contemporary cultural criticism. It sees the language of the novel as a web of interpenetrating discourses continuous with those of the culture that produced it. Wicke views that culture as a network of "sites" at which interrelated forms of work (writing novels, milking, manufacturing, advertising) get done. She also notes that differing human practices within these sites can be and are described using the same concepts and terminology. (For instance, "reproduction" outside of wedlock renders a previously "pure woman," "damaged goods.") Finally, Wicke's essay typifies contemporary criticism insofar as it relates the questions and issues of Hardy's day to those still prevalent in our own world of consumerism, brand names, branded individuals, and questionable standards of purity.

Ross C Murfin

CULTURAL CRITICISM: A SELECTED BIBLIOGRAPHY

General Introductions to Cultural Criticism, Cultural Studies

Bathrick, David. "Cultural Studies." *Introduction to Scholarship in Modern Languages and Literatures.* Ed. Joseph Gibaldi. New York: MLA, 1992.

Brantlinger, Patrick. *Crusoe's Footprints: Cultural Studies in Britain and America.* New York: Routledge, 1990.

———. "Cultural Studies vs. the New Historicism." *English Studies/ Cultural Studies: Institutionalizing Dissent.* Ed. Isaiah Smithson and Nancy Ruff. Urbana: U of Illinois P, 1994. 43–58.

Brantlinger, Patrick, and James Naremore, eds. *Modernity and Mass Culture.* Bloomington: Indiana UP, 1991.

Brummett, Barry. *Rhetoric in Popular Culture.* New York: St. Martin's, 1994.

Desan, Philippe, Priscilla Parkhurst Ferguson, and Wendy Griswold. "Editors' Introduction: Mirrors, Frames, and Demons: Reflections on the Sociology of Literature." *Literature and Social Practice.* Ed. Desan, Ferguson, and Griswold. Chicago: U of Chicago P, 1989. 1–10.

During, Simon, ed. *The Cultural Studies Reader.* New York: Routledge, 1993.

Eagleton, Terry. "Two Approaches in the Sociology of Literature." *Critical Inquiry* 14 (1988): 469–76.

Easthope, Antony. *Literary into Cultural Studies.* New York: Routledge, 1991.

Fisher, Philip. "American Literary and Cultural Studies since the Civil War." *Redrawing the Boundaries: The Transformation of English and American Literary Studies.* Ed. Stephen Greenblatt and Giles Gunn. New York: MLA, 1992. 232–50.

Giroux, Henry, David Shumway, Paul Smith, and James Sosnoski. "The Need for Cultural Studies: Resisting Intellectuals and Oppositional Public Spheres." *Dalhousie Review* 64.2 (1984): 472–86.

Graff, Gerald, and Bruce Robbins. "Cultural Criticism." *Redrawing the Boundaries: The Transformation of English and American Literary Studies.* Ed. Stephen Greenblatt and Giles Gunn. New York: MLA, 1992. 419–36.

Grossberg, Lawrence, Cary Nelson, and Paula A. Treichler, eds. *Cultural Studies.* New York: Routledge, 1992.

Gunn, Giles. *The Culture of Criticism and the Criticism of Culture.* New York: Oxford UP, 1987.

Hall, Stuart. "Cultural Studies: Two Paradigms." *Media, Culture and Society* 2 (1980): 57–72.

Humm, Peter, Paul Stigant, and Peter Widdowson, eds. *Popular Fictions: Essays in Literature and History.* New York: Methuen, 1986.

Hunt, Lynn, ed. *The New Cultural History: Essays.* Berkeley: U of California P, 1989.

Johnson, Richard. "What Is Cultural Studies Anyway?" *Social Text: Theory/Culture/Ideology* 16 (1986–87): 38–80.

Pfister, Joel. "The Americanization of Cultural Studies." *Yale Journal of Criticism* 4 (1991): 199–229.

Punter, David, ed. *Introduction to Contemporary Critical Studies.* New York: Longman, 1986. See especially Punter's "Introduction: Culture and Change" 1–18, Tony Dunn's "The Evolution of Cultural Studies" 71–91, and the essay "Methods for Cultural Studies Students" by Anne Beezer, Jean Grimshaw, and Martin Barker 95–118.

Storey, John. *An Introductory Guide to Cultural Theory and Popular Culture.* Athens: U of Georgia P, 1993.

Turner, Graeme. *British Cultural Studies: An Introduction.* Boston: Unwin Hyman, 1990.

Cultural Studies:
Some Early British Examples

Hoggart, Richard. *Speaking to Each Other.* 2 vols. London: Chatto, 1970.

———. *The Uses of Literacy: Changing Patterns in English Mass Culture.* Boston: Beacon, 1961.

Thompson, E. P. *The Making of the English Working Class.* New York: Harper, 1958.

———. *William Morris: Romantic to Revolutionary.* New York: Pantheon, 1977.

Williams, Raymond. *Culture and Society, 1780–1950.* 1958. New York: Harper, 1966.

———. *The Long Revolution.* New York: Columbia UP, 1961.

Cultural Studies: Continental and Marxist Influences

Althusser, Louis. *For Marx.* Trans. Ben Brewster. New York: Pantheon, 1969.

———. "Ideology and Ideological State Apparatuses." *Lenin and Philosophy.* Trans. Ben Brewster. New York: Monthly Review P, 1971. 127–86.

Althusser, Louis, and Étienne Balibar. *Reading Capital.* Trans. Ben Brewster. New York: Pantheon, 1971.

Bakhtin, Mikhail. *The Dialogic Imagination: Four Essays.* Ed. Michael Holquist. Trans. Caryl Emerson. Austin: U of Texas P, 1981.

———. *Rabelais and His World.* Trans. Hélène Iswolsky. Cambridge: MIT P, 1968.

Baudrillard, Jean. *Simulations.* Trans. Paul Foss, Paul Patton, and Philip Beitchnan. 1981. New York: Semiotext(e), 1983.

Benjamin, Walter. *Illuminations.* Ed. with intro. Hannah Arendt. Trans. Harry H. Zohn. New York: Harcourt, 1968.

Bennett, Tony. "Marxism and Popular Fiction." Humm, Stigant, and Widdowson 237–65.

Bourdieu, Pierre. *Distinction: A Social Critique of the Judgment of Taste.* Trans. Richard Nice. Cambridge: Harvard UP, 1984.

de Certeau, Michel. *The Practice of Everyday Life.* Trans. Steven F. Rendall. Berkeley: U of California P, 1984.

Foucault, Michel. *Discipline and Punish: The Birth of the Prison.* Trans. Alan Sheridan. New York: Pantheon, 1978.

———. *The History of Sexuality.* Trans. Robert Hurley. Vol. 1. New York: Pantheon, 1978.

Gramsci, Antonio. *Selections from the Prison Notebooks.* Ed. Quintin Hoare and Geoffrey Nowell Smith. New York: International, 1971.

Modern Cultural Studies: Selected British and American Examples

Bagdikian, Ben H. *The Media Monopoly.* Boston: Beacon, 1983.

Bowlby, Rachel. *Shopping with Freud.* New York: Routledge, 1993.

Chambers, Iain. *Popular Culture: The Metropolitan Experience.* New York: Methuen, 1986.

Colls, Robert, and Philip Dodd, eds. *Englishness: Politics and Culture, 1880–1920.* London: Croom Helm, 1986.

Denning, Michael. *Mechanic Accents: Dime Novels and Working-Class Culture in America*. New York: Verso, 1987.

Fiske, John. "British Cultural Studies and Television." *Channels of Discourse: Television and Contemporary Criticism*. Ed. Robert C. Allen. Chapel Hill: U of North Carolina P, 1987.

———. *Television Culture*. New York: Methuen, 1987.

Hebdige, Dick. *Hiding the Light: On Images and Things*. New York: Routledge, 1988.

———. *Subculture: The Meaning of Style*. London: Methuen, 1979.

Huyssen, Andreas. *After the Great Divide: Modernism, Mass Culture, Postmodernism*. Bloomington: Indiana UP, 1986.

Marcus, Greil. *Dead Elvis: A Chronicle of a Cultural Obsession*. New York: Doubleday, 1991.

———. *Lipstick Traces: A Secret History of the Twentieth Century*. Cambridge: Harvard UP, 1989.

Modleski, Tania. *Loving with a Vengeance: Mass-Produced Fantasies for Women*. Hamden: Archon, 1982.

Poovey, Mary. *Uneven Developments: The Ideological Work of Gender in Mid-Victorian England*. Chicago: U of Chicago P, 1988.

Radway, Janice A. *Reading the Romance: Women, Patriarchy, and Popular Literature*. Chapel Hill: U of North Carolina P, 1984.

Reed, T. V. *Fifteen Jugglers, Five Believers: Literary Politics and the Poetics of American Social Movements*. Berkeley: U of California P, 1992.

Ethnic and Minority Criticism, Postcolonial Studies

Anzaldúa, Gloria. *Borderlands: La Frontera = The New Mestiza*. San Francisco: Spinsters/Aunt Lute, 1987.

Baker, Houston. *Blues, Ideology, and Afro-American Literature: A Vernacular Theory*. Chicago: U of Chicago P, 1984.

———. *The Journey Back: Issues in Black Literature and Criticism*. Chicago: U of Chicago P, 1980.

Bhabha, Homi K. *The Location of Culture*. New York: Routledge, 1994.

———, ed. *Nation and Narration*. New York: Routledge, 1990.

———. "Postcolonial Criticism." *Redrawing the Boundaries: The Transformation of English and American Literary Studies*. Ed. Stephen Greenblatt and Giles Gunn. New York: MLA, 1992. 437–65.

Brantlinger, Patrick. *Rule of Darkness: British Literature and Imperialism, 1830–1914.* Ithaca: Cornell UP, 1988.

Gates, Henry Louis, Jr. *Black Literature and Literary Theory.* New York: Methuen, 1984.

———, ed. *"Race," Writing, and Difference.* Chicago: U of Chicago P, 1986.

Gayle, Addison. *The Black Aesthetic.* Garden City: Doubleday, 1971.

———. *The Way of the New World: The Black Novel in America.* Garden City: Doubleday, 1975.

JanMohamed, Abdul. *Manichean Aesthetics: The Politics of Literature in Colonial Africa.* Amherst: U of Massachusetts P, 1983.

JanMohamed, Abdul, and David Lloyd, eds. *The Nature and Context of Minority Discourse.* New York: Oxford UP, 1991.

Kaplan, Amy, and Donald E. Pease, eds. *Cultures of United States Imperialism.* Durham: Duke UP, 1983.

Neocolonialism. Special issue, *Oxford Literary Review* 13 (1991).

Said, Edward. *After the Last Sky: Palestinian Lives.* New York: Pantheon, 1986.

———. *Culture and Imperialism.* New York: Knopf, 1993.

———. *Orientalism.* New York: Pantheon, 1978.

———. *The World, the Text, and the Critic.* Cambridge: Harvard UP, 1983.

Spivak, Gayatri Chakravorty. *In Other Worlds: Essays in Cultural Politics.* New York: Methuen, 1987.

Stepto, Robert B. *From Behind the Veil: A Study of Afro-American Narrative.* Urbana: U of Illinois P, 1979.

Young, Robert. *White Mythologies: Writing, History, and the West.* London: Routledge, 1990.

Cultural Criticism of Hardy's Fiction

Widdowson, Peter. *Hardy in History: A Study in Literary Sociology.* London: Routledge, 1989.

A CULTURAL PERSPECTIVE

JENNIFER WICKE

The Same and the Different: Standards and Standardization in Thomas Hardy's *Tess of the d'Urbervilles*

The Wessex universe of *Tess of the d'Urbervilles* is numinous, charged with particles of opalescence and phosphorescence, refractive, prismatic, or vaporous. In that sense it is atmospheric and spectral, color-washed and color-flecked, seen through a late nineteenth-century Claude glass — but darkly. The flecks, spots, gleams, penumbra, and, above all, the drops that spatter and dapple the rhetorical surface so portentously in *Tess* could be said to be specific to a cultural style emphasizing discretion — an emphasis on what is discrete, separable, or even synecdochic: the part standing in for the whole. By the myriad frecklings of its own ontologies, *Tess* shows it is bound up in a cultural dialectic between the same and the different, the type and the sport, the mass and the individual, whose oscillations stud the narrative path. And when we connect the drops, or the dots, often a face appears, a gleaming face whose lineaments either are tragically the same or rapturously different — or both at once.

A major premise of cultural criticism is that a literary work, viewed as a dynamic site of language, is a focal point for the study of a culture. According to this theory, a literary text acts a bit like the magnifying glass children hold over a sidewalk on sunny days, where the lens so concentrates the sun's light that it is capable of setting something — let's hope it's a piece of paper — on fire. The language of a literary work, in other words its linguistic complexities on the large scale of plot or narrative and the smaller scale of image, scene, passage, or word, is a cultural concentrator. Because language is always social and shared, however personally significant or aesthetically beautiful, literature as a heightened form of language crystallizes the social, shared meanings rocketing about in a culture, bringing what is a more diffuse force in the cultural realm — like sunlight — to a point of fiery intensity. What may have been invisible before, because of its dispersion over the cultural field, becomes apparent, becomes visible.

The one problem with the magnifying glass analogy is that it suggests the literary work is a static, finished product, polished to a high gloss like the glassy lens. Cultural criticism would argue, however, that language is a dynamic, active substance, even in the form of a completed literary work. Things are still happening in that piece of language, as words rub up against one another, as different voices or levels fight for claim of the linguistic turf, as plots double or fall apart or fail to conclude. Literature is language heightened, yes, but not language frozen — or dead. In the sense of language in action, literature is a part of culture in the making, not a static reflection of it. Cultural criticism seeks out the sites of maximum cultural activity in a text, the places where the lens of language is making things hot. Reading a literary text in this way assumes that readers of literature can discover cultural preoccupations, issues, or conflicts there that might not be accessible to that culture itself, except in literary form. Cultural criticism of literature doesn't "boil down" the rich textures of literary language to any one cultural cause, either. It is the very richness of literary textuality — its metaphors, its narratives, its descriptions, its figures of speech — that give the clues to how a cultural problem is being activated and enacted, that allow for the discovery of something new, unanticipated, or even now confusing.

Tess of the d'Urbervilles burnishes the literary language of the novel genre to a high sheen. The extravagance of Hardy's vocabulary, the convolutions of Tess's life journey, and the proliferating subplots and image clusters put language under a wonderful pressure. In this foray into cultural criticism of the novel, I will argue that a specific cultural question is responsible for some of the pyrotechnics of the language used by Hardy (but not, of course, all), and furthermore, that Hardy's novel explores a cultural problem much larger than its theme or the characters alone. What *Tess of the d'Urbervilles* reveals culturally is the complexity and the uncertainty of the market — the market being the imaginary place where all exchanges between people are transacted in society. The exchanges may be monetary, but they can also be educational, erotic, familial, political, and so on. The market is so elastic it embraces nearly every social relation — including reading.

The market is a huge challenge to cultural understanding and cultural behavior, because while everyone in a given society will participate in the market, how and why they participate remains obscure. In a market society of the sort established by the end of the nineteenth century in Britain, for example, "the market" is largely invisible, consisting as it does of the phantom circulation of stocks, of global finance, and of exchanges among people for goods, wages, services, and labor. The market is where people get their living, but also where they are described and identified — as employed or unemployable, for instance. Not only goods are in circulation on the market, human beings are too, and Tess's migrant labors are one index of what that means. She circulates throughout her section of England trying to find farm labor, completely unaware of the fluctuations of price in world and local markets that make her sometimes desirable, mostly not. The tragedies that hover over Tess throughout the novel have everything to do with the loss of a neighborhood "market," where eggs and horses can be bartered for wood or clothing, to an anonymous and abstract market that chews up and spits out workers like Tess in imitation of the threshing machine. The term "market" was of course extended from the earlier meaning of market, which was a literal place people came together for the exchange of goods. In England, this would involve urban marketplaces, like London's Covent Garden, and regional markets, or market fairs, that happened at set times of year and drew together people from far-flung rural areas. Market fairs were definitely the primary place where goods were exchanged, sometimes for other goods, sometimes for money; since they were special occasions, aspects of festival or carnival clung to them, and they involved entertainment, preaching, refreshment, sport, and gambling. The market fair created a momentary social space complete with all its levels, services, and amusements. It was the place to go to conduct business, and thereby to live, and it could also be a place for political organization, marriage markets, child and indentured servant auctions, dancing, drinking, praying, protesting, and parading.

The industrialized, capitalized market I refer to had been forming since the eighteenth-century alongside the older tradition of the market fair. Literary works as diverse as Charlotte Brontë's *Shirley* (1849), Jane Austen's *Emma* (1816), and any work of Dickens captured the shock waves of these changes. The argument about Hardy and *Tess of the d'Urbervilles* I am making is much more specific to the latter half of the century and to a new concern brought about by market society during this period. The abstract, invisible market had replaced the market fair as the engine of the economy and of social change, although market fairs did continue to exist, primarily in rural areas. Vestiges of the market fair still survive now in such practices as the tag sale, the county fair, the flea market, or the country auction, but there is no question that market society has usurped earlier forms of market. While there were no explicit rules governing the market as it developed over the course of the two centuries, keeping so much money and so many goods, services and so forth in circulation began to be staggeringly complicated, and needless to say, beyond individual human comprehension — statistics, formulae, and economic "projections" filled in for the limitations of one mind to contain all the concomitant levels.

Toward the end of the century a cultural concept gradually developed in response to the perceived chaos of the market and its multiple facets: the notion of "standards." Standards meant many things in relation to the perplexity of a whirling, swirling, invisible marketplace; standards applied to goods themselves, to how goods could be made, and how, when, and where they could go on the market; standards established practices for manufacture, sale, and advertising; and standards, as in "standard of living," became a way of evaluating human performance and human experience. No one person or group came up with the notion of a standard; this happened haphazardly and accidentally across many arenas of social life, from economics and education to science, politics, art, and religion. *Tess of the d'Urbervilles* is a novel, a work of literature, and its language has an especially heightened concern for the world of the market — where the novel, like its heroine Tess, is every bit as much a marketable commodity as the items for sale in a shop. Beyond this, I'll try to show, is a uniquely relevant investigation of standards and the standardization brought about by the market place: Tess lives and embodies that investigation.

We still have an echo in English of the original meaning of standard — "high standards" are noble ideals that approximate the glorious height of the medieval nobleman's flag of arms, or his "standard." When standards get mixed up with economics and statistics, as well as science and technology, ethics and aesthetics, we start to see perturbations in the cultural field. The standard becomes a problem — what constitutes "a" or "the" standard, anyway, and by whose reckoning or whose authority does it get designated as standard? And does this necessarily imply standardization? Is the standard a maximum or a minimum, the ideal or the lowest common denominator? What about people, finally: If people are inevitably evaluated as goods on the market, how will they be categorized? As standard, substandard, better than standard? In part, the problem could be treated as an offshoot of the Darwinism so pervasive in Hardy's work and so pervasively remarked: Darwinian theory concentrates on the type, the genus, the species, and then the changes that are wrought within these categories. The issue in *Tess* and in late nineteenth-century culture is much broader, though, and less a matter of intellectual history than a material watershed. *Tess* is set within a moment — let's say a twenty-year moment, a Rip van Winkle moment from 1881, when the International Prototype Meter was installed in Paris, to 1891 and *Tess*'s publication, to 1901 and the establishment of the British Standards Institute — a moment wherein the notion of a standard is being crystallized in disparate cultural practices and concretized as a cultural concept.

The narrative of Tess Durbeyfield begins slightly obliquely with reference to a market-day past, one on which Parson Tringham had first greeted John Durbeyfield with the honorific "Sir John" (31), and ends on market day in the city of Wintoncester, where "that leisurely dusting and sweeping was in progress which usually ushers in an old-fashioned market-day" (383) and in this case, too, an execution. I hope I can be forgiven for seeing a fearful symmetry in this bracketing with market fairs and market days, which rites also stipple the rest of the text, as in the Candlemas market day and fair that signal the general disencampment of all the tenants who rent in the area, and the many market-day excursions that involve the "Amazonian" sisters and cheerfully drunken co-workers of Tess. Tess "runs into" both Alec and Angel, coincidentally, at market booths, or walking away in the evening from the market fair. The premarket market fair is the site of coalescence, of exchange, and of narrative confluence in *Tess.*

The significance I would want to read into this is its allusion to *Tess* as a story of going to market. The "old-fashioned" market day is just that — an older fashion or custom, whose routes and routines are being reshaped in the narrative unfolding of *Tess.* To have a market day requires that you have a literal market — a place people come to for the exchange, barter, or sale of goods, and for the social performance and symbolic exchange to be found there. What had begun the book as a ritual fact of life, going to market, even if fraught with perils like having your horse killed on the way there, is by the end of the book viewed retrospectively as an old-fashioned event, and the "market" something else altogether. In the space of a few years of narrative time, one is no longer hailed by name at the market — even if by a new and rather bewildering name like "Sir John" — but one's hanging is a pendant to a quaint market festival, and even the text doesn't mention your name. Tess ruptures the tradition of the market as she signals the takeover of a newer, invisible market, one where damaged goods like Tess are not on display.

In speaking of the market abstractly, I draw on the vocabulary Hardy invents and invests with market significance in *Tess of the d'Urbervilles.*[1] This varies widely and wildly across the narrative but finds special energy in the notions of sameness, difference, and distinction, which correspondingly energize the new discourse of standards. Standards could be seen as the spread of modern bureaucracy, another name for the process of rationalization Max Weber charted as the path of modernity. While standards in some sense do emanate from the bureaucratization and capital atomization characteristic of middle-aged capitalism, they are a mysterious development whose special mysteries temporarily dumbfounded the individual citizen — with the exception of works like *Tess,* which narrativize the peculiarities of standards as they emerge and claim their place. This is not to say that Thomas Hardy had a privileged insight into market structures; cultural criticism would claim that Hardy's book is bursting with the phenomenon and the language of standards, whether he intended for this to be the case or not.

Standards first appeared in modern Western societies as an explicit topic when Eli Whitney, called "the Father of Standardization," created in 1793 a set of standards in his Connecticut rifle factory such that the pieces of all the guns manufactured were uniform and interchangeable. The rifles were no longer made as unique, individual wholes, but as a composite of standardized parts. Standardization of parts caught on as the basis for factory manufacture; standards were self-imposed units of measure, weight, and materials. The sea-change in standardization came about when regulatory bodies decided to set up standards of quality for consumer goods, and when manufacturers and advertisers began to label and trademark products to identify them by "brand." Brand names involved declaring a standard — for soap powder, say — which the brand-name product met, and establishing a standard to make the brand unique: "Ivory is the Queen of powdered soap flakes." A further feature of the changing universe of standards came from science and technology; the protocols for a chemical reaction, for instance, came to be known as the "standards" for that reaction. The chemical and engineering technologies of so much manufacture required a "science" of standardization. Legal issues came into play as "standards" had to be defined to protect producers from unfair competition, and consumers from fraud or injury. The circulation of

[1]A wonderful glimpse at this vocabulary as employed by a leading economist of the time, rather than by a novelist, is provided in the classic work *Principles of Economics,* by the British neoclassical economist Alfred Marshall. The first edition of the book came out in 1890, and it went through nine editions all told. "Standards" of all kinds pervade the analysis.

commodities on the market had to be controlled at every point, and standards were issued to cover all the transactions and exchanges. In short, the market brought about standards and standardization as an attempt to make sense of itself, not that this was possible.

A sample inventory of new standards codified as law in Britain in the year 1907 takes us into the interstices between commodity and practice, where generally angels fear to tread. Each product or commodity is followed by the specific type of "standard" that had been devised for it in that year:

> Clinical thermometers (performance)
> Mopsticks (types)
> Porcelain plumbing fixtures (grading)
> Fuel oils (physical and chemical)
> Red cedar closet lining (labeling)
> Knit underwear (symbols for models)
> Mohair pile fabrics (construction)
> Mattresses for institutions (size)
> Articles made of silver in combination with gold (quality marks, exemptions)
> Elastic overall webbing (testing)
> Automatic mechanical oil draft burners for domestic installations (certification).[2]

A delirious array: Who knew that there were standards for types of knit underwear, or that mattresses for institutions had different standards than those for home use, or that red cedar closets have to be labeled in particular ways, or that separate standards for testing the elasticity of webbing in overalls, as opposed to skirt waists, must be drafted into law? This assemblage of disparate goods and rarefied features — labeling, testing, certification — refigures the world as a vast collection of objects all in some strange standardized relation to one another, summoned into being by language, circulated by standards, and consumed with standardized relish. The highly abstracted nature of these standards is utterly unsuited to the earlier form of the market — whether it be market fair or marketplace. Just as there are no trademarks, no tests, no certifications, no special uses in the market fair, it seems no object can go on the modern market unadorned by standards. It is hard to know what to make of these skeins of production, distribution, and consumption when the objects or commodities are translated into standards. A hard ball of language encompasses even the most meager

[2]As cited in Edwards 87.

and simple of products — the mopstick or porcelain toilet fixtures. It becomes even harder to know what kind of object one's self is — if every other good on the market is surrounded by a wed of standards, what sort of standards obtain for human beings, and who supplies the specifications?

An early director of the National Bureau of Standards took a retrospective glance back at standards in 1939 with revealingly metaphysical language. Lyman J. Briggs writes:

> The more the mysteries of nature are dispelled by knowledge, the more is standardization revealed, as in the geometrical arrangement of crystal formation, predicted discoveries of new chemical elements, or the coming of a comet. We depend upon the meticulous regularity of the sun's appearance, the recurring phases of the moon, and the perfectly timed rotation of the planets. We accept as indisputable facts the definitely established freezing and boiling points, the peculiar behavior of certain materials and the changeless normal properties of elasticity, strength, hardness, ductility, viscosity, refractivity, electric conductivity, permeability, and other properties of the elemental things of nature which man is constantly appropriating for his use. . . . The variations of color available to the painter are composed of parts of a narrow band of spectral wave lengths and all of the artistry of music is conveyed through another small group of frequencies. And yet we hear no complaints that nature has carried standardization to extremes, that life is dull, drab or dreary as a result of standardized chemical elements, standardized crystalline growth, or wave lengths.

The Parmenidean problems of the one and the many, the same and the different, haunt standardization. Plato took this matter up as the crux of philosophy, and in his dialogue "Parmenides," he entertains the problem of whether Being is one unified whole, or many composite things. In addition, the question of identity is key. Is something what it is because it is the same as itself? Do you have to have "many" — at least two things — for there to be one same thing, identical to itself? If it is not one, but many, does "it" lose originality, uniqueness, beauty, difference? If things are the same and not troublingly, unmanageably different, at what point does the reassurance of order give way to stultifying monotony? When the philosophical problem turns into a cultural problem of standards, the logic remains perplexing: How can standards imbricate objects without making them lose their aura, their freshness, their novelty or desirability? The metaphysical decisions of advertising campaigns rest on the Platonic issues of one and many, same and different. Advertisers face the problem of whether it is better to make their product seem different, and so to stand out, or whether that may be dangerous in losing the impact of sameness, or the One. "New and improved" is the cultural label for this dilemma. If a product is genuinely new, then it is not the same as itself, and it is not the One; if it is improved, then it is different, and it is Many, and the old One did not meet Standards. From such a metaphysics spring bizarre social events, such as creating New Coke, finding no one liked it, and having to return with chagrin to Old Coke under the new rubric Classic Coke. The "It's the Real Thing" slogan for Coca-Cola is not just an advertising ploy but an almost inevitably philosophical solution to the nagging problem of standardizing goods. If Coke is a Real Thing, then its standard is set by itself; since it is *the* real thing, it is also different from other beverages that might want to compete for real thing-ness. The oddly Kantian title for Coke becomes a way out of the philosophical fly-bottle of the One and the Many, the Same and the Different, advertising-style.

The new cultural obsession with standards is imported back into the natural world in Lyman Briggs's rhetoric, thereby obviating the problems of standardization, that is, its monadology, its regimentation, its "disenchantment of the world," in Schiller's phrase as borrowed by Max Weber.[3] A structure of standards underlies the wonders of nature and of the cultural realm — art itself is a matter of the manipulation of standards. Thomas Hardy is no Lyman J. Briggs (or perhaps it's the other way around), but the perils of standardization *for* art and standardization *as* art are profoundly manifest in the rhetorical whorls and flights of *Tess*. After all, standards imply uniformity, but an initial perfection that is then uniformly reproduced or copied. In the context of standards, we are truly back in the metaphysical realm of Plato's forms, where the bed is the copy of the Form (or, may I say, the Standard) of the Bed.

What does this make Tess, and what does this make *Tess*? The Standard is, then, both the original and the copy, the representation and the thing, and the implications for art-making are staggering. As Angel Clare has it:

> But he could not get on. Speech was as inexpressive as silence. But he had a vague consciousness of one thing, though it was not

[3]See especially Max Weber's essay "Science as a Vocation," 1918, as collected in *From Max Weber*.

> clear to him till later; that his original Tess had spiritually ceased to recognize the body before him as hers. (367)

Originals, copies, products, reproductions, difference: Hardy will have to push his words through a new linguistic mesh — the social grid of standards — in order to silk-screen the spatter-drops that then read as *Tess.*

When Alice L. Edwards, a theorist of standardization, contemplates these wonders (in her book *Product Standards and Labeling for Consumers*), she is moved to write:

> The story of the contribution of standards and their employment in industrial progress and mass production resembles a tale of wonderland — a wonderland in which men are impatiently seeking to release its potential bounties to enrich all groups, be they producers, distributors, or consumers. (38)

Now Alice is on to something in this Wonderland she describes. First, there is her incisive naming of the possible groups into which people can and must fall, three and only three possibilities. Moreover, Edwards shows us that standards themselves fall into five categories, those of measurement, quality, nomenclature, performance, and practice. Like quarks, standards have two valences that subtend all five categories, not charm or flavor but the valences of voluntary and mandatory compliance. Lest one think that standards are simply commodity specifications or grades of manufacture, Edwards declares that "in their earlier forms, standards and standardization were most frequently manifest in social customs and religious symbols and ceremonies, slowly evolved over countless years. . . ." (38). At some point, standards become standards of quality, either relative or practical. In Edwards's view, relative quality is determined by words like good, better, and best, and practical quality by

> a composite of many characteristics, such as dimension, composition, performance, construction, texture, finish, color, flavor, odor, and freedom from imperfections. These characteristics which contribute to the determination of quality often make up a motley and seemingly incongruous array but, in one way or another, each usually contributes its own peculiar significance of the product to the user. (38)

The motley array of qualities that make up quality or value are ever so reminiscent of the bedazzled surfaces of Tess herself, the girl with the *je ne sais quoi* quality. Both relative and practical standards are continually invoked by Hardy's text to position her, to deliver her to us not as a species of goods but a Standard — a "Tess" with relative (the best) and practical ("flexuous" etc.) Tess-ness. Tess Durbeyfield makes her mad dashes through vale and dale as a species of unstandardized goods, as an "ultimate consumer" in Alice L. Edwards's felicitous phrase, and an ultimate consumed. If we were to supply a narrative analogy, it might be vivid to compare her to a billiard ball being knocked very effectively into the pocket, only to be taken out and knocked soundly in the other direction. The charged inexorability of her orbit is, of course, gendered and classed and ruralized and all that. But what is happening to the grassy green table top as Tess careens across it is an invasion of standards and practices, practices and standards. These are shot through with symbolic import and incongruity, just like the novel is.

Most often this is textually played out through physiognomy. Unlike the concentration on faces of a slightly earlier period of literature (as discussed by Christopher Rivers in *Face Value*) where facial lineaments are a guide to traits and qualities, Hardy manages to describe Tess's face innumerable times without stabilizing it, often giving a negative or abstract cast, as in finding it "unknightly, unhistorical" (43), or tracing in it "symbols of reflectiveness" (117), or:

> . . . it was impossible for even an enemy to feel otherwise on looking at Tess as she sat there, with her flower-like mouth and large tender eyes, neither black nor blue nor gray nor violet; rather all those shades together, and a hundred others, which could be seen if one looked into their irises — shade behind shade — tint beyond tint — around pupils that had no bottom; an almost *standard* woman, but for the slight incautiousness of character inherited from her race. (109; emphasis added)

An abyss of undescribed colors, like the proliferation of paint-chip samples marking newly standardized paints and their very colors, a bottomless black void, a near-miss "standard" woman who yet cannot be described. Tess's mother Joan refers to the former's face as her "trump card" because it is a blazon of odd prettiness, not a reflection of old "blood" (73). Faciality becomes akin to the newest practices of standardization, which involve labeling, in some ways the equivalent of putting a "face" on a commodity, and thus naming and branding and trademarking in a trinitarian gesture of simultaneity. To put it to advertising's music — it's three, three, three steps in one. As even the title of Edwards's book reveals, the elaboration of the "label" as both a site of description and information for the ultimate consumer was central to standardization as a process. In the market sense, Tess's predicament could be apostrophized as one of old blood (d'Urberville brand) in new bottles (Durbeyfield nonstandard or off-brand), the reverse of the New Testament's new wine in old bottles. Current practices of standardization don't recognize the old label, and anyway Tess's father decides to sell the label — the title — for twenty pounds.

As is obvious by now, words have a privileged position in the determination of standards and in the act of standardization. Some features of standardization are quantifiable, as in prescribed temperature limits or degree of dye saturation. Overall, though, standards are a numinous cloud of words, conferring via language and rhetoric the quality of being Standard, something like the haze or halo of "vegeto-human pollen" (84) Hardy floats over one agricultural scene. Words "mark" the object, product, or practice so it can be taken up into the realm of the standard and then *trademark* the universal as a sign of the particular. A label, mark, trademark, and then advertisement need to be confected out of language to place something in the horizon of Standardization and to keep it there. Thus follows the extraordinary fascination with marks, labels, spots, drops, and finally stains in the novel: discrete pieces and bits of language that mark out and magically bestow the sameness *and* difference of the standard. For example, Alec d'Urberville has a poster period in his truncated career as an evangelist, where signs spring up everywhere announcing his arrival. He becomes a label, a mark, in his own right. Alec is "the same" in that he professes to be a mere conduit for the Lord's word, but he is "different" in that his preaching is described as something unusual or special. Christianity is a difficult area for standards, as *the* Standard is presumably Christ crucified. However, in Hardy's world as in ours, religion is in every way tied up with the market, and Alec must market his own standard brand of fine preaching, the proof of which would be the conversion of his audience.

Signs, ads, marks, and standards appear everywhere. Angel Clare is led to his doomed venture as a farmer in Brazil by seeing a billboard advertising farm plots in that exotic region that crops up incongruously by a country roadside. Alice Edwards actually traces Great Britain's primacy in the development of the cultural episteme of standardization, which she calls a *practice,* to its far-flung empire. Imperialism was the mother of standards, in that the "opening up of far-off markets was followed by long-distance selling, which immediately revealed the need of standards by which to describe commodities so that reliable information about goods could be furnished to the prospective purchaser" (Edwards 126). This bland language goes far to make us feel pity for the otherwise infuriatingly obtuse Angel Clare, who became, in the instance of his blighted imperial enterprise at least, what Tess always was, defrauded ultimate consumer and ultimately the consumed. The land he went to was unfarmable, and he was far below the human standards for living and working in that climate. The incongruous billboard in the English countryside misled the prospective purchaser, Angel, not only by an erroneous description of the commodity for sale, but by imposing a false standard — the sturdy, all-conquering Englishman stereotype — on him.

Our heroine Tess comes across marks, trademarks, and signs with frightening regularity, as in the ominous signboards that take biblical language and convert it to what Hardy happily, for my purposes, calls advertising: "THY, DAMNATION, SLUMBERETH, NOT" (99) is written in "large square letters" (99), with commas between each word to drive it "well home to the reader's heart." "The old gray wall began to *advertise* a similar fiery lettering to the first, with a strange and unwonted mien, as if distressed at duties it had never before been called upon to perform" (100; emphasis added). The wall is a face, the writing or sign is a face, the face is a sign or label, and none more so than Tess, who is a face, a sign, *and* a label.

Her face as a market token has a plausible relation to the new bottle she places on her own baby Sorrow's grave (in a scene so full of pathos it puts little Nell out to pasture): the grieving mother places flowers in honor of the baby into a marmalade jar. "What matter was it that on the outside of the jar the eye of mere observation noted the words 'Keelwell's Marmalade'?" (116) The marmalade jar becomes another sort of vessel altogether, a transfiguration of the product by the inner eye of consumption, and all the aspects of standardization symbolized by the incised labeling on the jar, its *trademarking,* fall away. "Keelwell's Marmalade" is a tracery on the glass surface of the jar itself; it names the product (marmalade), it gives it a brand (Keelwell's), it establishes a standard (this jar contains only that marmalade that falls within the specifications set for something to be legitimately called marmalade, i.e., a viscous compound of fruitstuffs and rind with a specific purity level and wholesomeness of preparation), and it trademarks the product (thou shalt eat no other marmalade before me, Keelwell's, it is the Best, no other marmalades may so designate themselves). Two simple words take on such a density and richness of cultural signification and practice as to be literally transfiguring and transmogrifying. What strikes one as peculiar in the scenario is that the Durbeyfields would not make their own jam. Like the popular ballads so beloved of Joan Durbeyfield, those new songs that mysteriously arrive through the air on a weekly basis from the unknown "outside" world of mass culture, so too Keelwell's Marmalade has insinuated itself, a homely yet transfigured icon of the Standard.

This transfiguration never happens to Tess herself, unless, perhaps, at the moment of her fall from the gallows, when she has fallen out of the market with a vengeance. Her crime is detected by the spreading bloodstain or advertising placard of murder that spreads on the ceiling of the room below that where Alec d'Urberville lies dying, a label witnessed by Mrs. Brooks, a "deeply materialized" (367) woman who otherwise reads only the signs of commercial arithmetic. Tess has to be kept out of sight by Angel Clare in his futile attempt to hide her after the murder, because Tess has become a sign, a label, a placard for fashion, something she never had been before:

> Her clothes were of recent fashion; even the ivory-handled parasol that she carried was of a shape unknown in the retired spot to which they had not wandered; and the cut of such articles would have attracted attention in the settle of a tavern. (374)

Heretofore in the narrative Tess was free of any claims to fashion, and indeed this was her distinction, that whether in the body-wropper of wheat-threshing costume, in her white country dancing dress, or dressed for traveling, she was a "simple country girl with no pretensions to recent fashion; a soft gray woollen gown, with white crape quilling against the pink skin of her face and neck, and a black velvet jacket and hat" (292). Tess ordinarily doesn't bear the marks of fashion, which paradoxically makes her different and thus less standard, but then when dressed fashionably, she is different and thus less standard — and a murderess. The paradoxes of standardization enter the aesthetic realm no less than the zone of fashion, where same and different must coalesce as rapidly as possible. To be "fashionable" means to be wearing the latest, newest thing, but not so new that it is not being worn by multitudes of other fashionable people. Fashion purports to be about novelty and uniqueness, but it relies on uniformity and a Standard to point to its own fashionability. Tess is fashion's victim, if we can allow fashion to be seen as at the extreme end of a gradient of standardization.

Tess of the d'Urbervilles is one of the saddest books ever written and that one ever has to read. Is standardization part of its fabric of sadness? I would find the automatic equation of standardization with what the literary theorist Georg Lukács called *reification*, meaning the treatment of human beings as if they were things, producing the inevitable social and psychic alienation of modernity, too quick a move.[4] Equating the two would become another way of cheaply lamenting the pre-Industrial Age, sentimentally disposing of Tess and her tribe as the predestined victims of capitalism. It is by no means clear that nostalgia for rural England is the intention of the book, nor that Tess and those like her, especially women, would have found rural life a paradise at any time. What we may be left with is that standardization is a reality, for good and for ill, and Hardy dramatizes this by putting Tess through the bodily inscription of society's standards.

Standardization is so complex, pervasive, and intricate as a cultural, social, economic, and psychic practice that it alters the texture of narrative itself. Narrative, in other words, participates in standardization and infuses it, as standardization practices help to transform it. Slightly facetiously, I introduce an over-the-top discussion of standardization and happiness by one Charles Carpenter, a writer at another pole from Hardy, to put it mildly, in order to highlight in relief the tragic etching of *Tess*. Carpenter, in his *Dollars and Sense* (1928) is impatient with those who would condemn standardization out of hand, or who would see it as the only refuge of consumers otherwise beset by the corruptions of consumption. In a variation of King Lear's "Oh, reason not the need!" speech in Shakespeare's tragedy (2.4.266), Carpenter vehemently opines:

> To go into a well-furnished drug store, to be waited upon by a courteous clerk, to select a particular brand of tooth paste put up in an attractive package, and then go home to enjoy the taste or odor in the use of that paste makes for happiness. To go into a dingy store like those of fifty years ago — where there were fewer brands and goods just in bulk — and buy an ounce of chalk without odor and taste and then go home to apply it with a cloth adds nothing whatever to happiness. To contend that none of these dentifrices possess any merit over chalk is silly rot. (220–21)

King Lear had argued that human beings need more than the barest necessities of food, shelter, and clothing to truly rise to human stature. Among the things they need "more" of to distinguish themselves from other animals are art, aesthetic pleasure, and personal creativity. To accomplish these things, human beings will often need

[4]See the essay "Reification" in Lukács's *History and Class Consciousness.*

props. Carpenter is underscoring the aesthetic experience and the personal happiness standardization can bring into being — true, in light of a dentifrice. However, *Tess* makes similarly clear the exigencies of the old-fashioned market along with the depredations of the newer market. One can starve at a rural market-fair just as surely as outside a factory. Hardy's *Tess* voices the agonizing flip side of Carpenter's blast; yes, standardization can give new life and happiness, but it also takes it away. Tess is the very "hieroglyphic" of this conundrum. The letter she writes to Angel Clare while he is incommunicado in Brazil, and she is virtually starving for food and for love, establishes in a most tragic register the predicament of standardization, and the figuring of it:

> I am the same woman, Angel, as you fell in love with; yes, the very same! — not the one you disliked but never saw. What was the past to me as soon as I met you? It was a dead thing altogether. I became another woman, filled full of new life from you. (329)

Tess is a surd social element, a Standard who cannot be standardized and thus made safe for consumption. Why not say it: *Tess* is standardization *avant la lettre,* before it had become clear to the culture that the new phenomenon of standards would bear a human price. The textual prescience of *Tess* is to be a "tex" (in the dialect of Wessex) that questions and furthers the aesthetic and cultural dimension of standardization, while inscribing its exactions. *All* products in the age of labeling, trademarking, and standardization are copies of a standard, copies of themselves — even narratives and novels like *Tess.* They duplicate themselves, they reproduce in acts of virtual parthenogenesis. Alec d'Urberville at one point calls himself a "sham d'Urberville" who has the appearance of a mere stone reproduction (354). Standardization is production as reproduction and as resurrection. The Christianizing vocabulary of *Tess* is thoroughly intertwined with the vocabulary of standardization as transubstantiation. But such "new life" eludes Tess. They broke the mold when they made her; they made it impossible to have her be both the same — because she was so much the same, so much a Woman — and different — because she was so different, so distinctive, so untrademarkable. *Her* past molds are the d'Urberville ancestors, skeletons asleep in moldy and damaged coffins, incapable of being reproduced or recycled in the lively and macabre market of 1891. Even their "labels" have dropped off over time; they rest unremarked and untrademarked in their vandalized crypt.

The drops of whey, milk, and blood that have peppered Tess's body, face, and mind throughout the novel give way to a more inscrutable and abstract form of discrete drops at novel's end. Her friends write an anonymous note to Angel Clare telling him that "continual dropping will wear away a Stone — ay, more — a Diamond" (355). By the end Tess has become as crystal-hard as that diamond, and she delivers herself of, of all things, "drops of logic" (317). Difficult to envision or picture, and falling in any event on the deaf ears of Angel Clare, logic drops are somehow appropriate to the social logic of the impersonal They of standardization. No one knows who gives the orders to standardize, who sets the standards, and then who enforces the penalty — it's all done by "bureaus" or "institutes" without a human face. Standards are a faceless product of culture, or at least They would like us to think so. A tag on a pillow I purchased recently indicates that this They is still in force. The pillow tag first warns that it must not be removed, "by law," and then adds "except by consumer." The inner contents of the pillow are attested to be "All new material consisting of 100% polyester fiber." Then the label pulls out its authority: "This article is made in compliance with an Act of Dist. of Col. Approved July 3,1926; Kansas approved March 1923; Minnesota approved April 24, 1929; New Jersey revised status 26, 10-18 to 18. Certification is made by the manufacturer that the materials in this article are described in accordance with Law." One wonders: polyester had not been invented in 1923, so whatever standards then existed for pillows had to involve down or feathers or stuffing. Who is this claim meant to reassure? What kind of speech act is this written label — a promise, a ritual gesture, a boast, a legal regulation? The They of standards makes it very hard to read the tag, to comprehend its human message, if there is one. Behind it would seem to be the invisible gods of Standards, Olympian and eternal, who finally have decided to let the consumers tear off the tag if they absolutely must.

Tess of the d'Urbervilles asks its readers who is responsible for setting the standards such that Tess will end up on the gallows. Providence, or God, does not watch out for Tess; the market would seem to be the anonymous force that sets her tortured life in motion and takes it away. Hardy suggests that the invisible narrative tormentors of Tess, her They, are the gods in their wanton sport with humankind: "The President of the Immortals, in Æschylean phrase, had ended his sport with Tess" (384), Hardy writes ironically as Tess's body sags from the gallows in the book's final paragraph. The uncaring and mischievous gods of Greek myth and Greek tragedy are back to do their worst: in the words of Shakespeare's *Lear,* which Hardy quotes in his preface, "as flies to wanton boys are we to the gods." But Tess was herself a "sport," a word that means the accidental outcome of a genetic mutation. She was an ultimately unstandardizable type, a perfect anomaly, a standardizing oxymoron. The force that drives poor Tess to her end is that mysterious cultural force of Standards, not the gods or God. Thomas Hardy brings Tess into a market world where she has no place; all he can do, like a deus ex machina, is to remove her from the market world. She becomes the Standard, the fictional standard-bearer, for a real human predicament, one that has no ready answer. Tess is the answer to the question They never bothered to ask.

The book ends with the calligraphy of Tess's death marked on the horizon by what Hardy calls the "blot" (384) of the prison tower and the black flag run up as a sign of her death, both marks seen from afar. In the gazes of Angel Clare and Liza-Lu, the cultural referent of the blotted, black mark against the sky, which they and we know to signify the death by execution of Tess Durbeyfield Clare, is to the visual mark of Jesus's dead, bent figure hanging on the cross. Tess is Christlike in her sacrifice and suffering, and her mourners "bent themselves down to the earth, as if in prayer, and remained thus a long time, absolutely motionless: the flag continued to wave silently" (384). Her passing is momentous; it has deep import akin to the crucifixion of Christ in his innocence, but the lines are very peculiar. Angel and Liza-Lu bend down to earth, not up to sky, "as if" but not definitely in prayer.

The flag, or standard, waves in the wind, its silence not surprising given the distance between its flapping cloth and the viewers, and causing us to think it signals Tess, that Tess is now the dark extended flag. The silent black flag and the tower's blot are akin to the marks and signs of the page, to the printed letters of written literature. Tess at the end of the novel no longer appears in bodily form, but is a visual apostrophe hanging in the sky, a piece of punctuation, a label for the novel that bears her name. The anything-but-faceless Tess of the rest of the book has become an abstract, anonymous mark on a standard-sized, standardly white page. She's not going anywhere, least of all to her resurrection. Her punctuation point sends us back in a circulating movement to the beginning of the novel, back to the book, which is where the indescribable Tess, Tess with a Standard and not at all a merely standard or average face, moves and has her being. In the concluding grief of the last page, we might also look to see the sardonic smile on the face of Standards, the tears hovering in Standardization's eyes.

WORKS CITED

Briggs, Lyman J. *Commercial Standards and Their Value to Business.* Washington, DC: Government Printing Office, 1939.

Carpenter, Charles E. *Dollars and Sense.* Garden City, NY: Doubleday, 1928.

Edwards, Alice L. *Product Standards and Labeling for Consumers.* New York: The Ronald Press Company, 1940.

Lukács, Georg. *History and Class Consciousness.* London: Verso, 1979.

Marshall, Alfred. *Principles of Economics.* London and New York: Macmillan, 1890.

Rivers, Christopher. *Face Value: Physiognomical Thought and the Legible Body in Marivaux, Lavater, Balzac, Gautier, and Zola.* Madison: U of Wisconsin, 1994.

Weber, Max. *From Max Weber: Essays in Sociology.* Ed. and trans. H. H. Gerth and C. Wright Mills. New York: Oxford UP, 1946.

Glossary of Critical and Theoretical Terms

Most terms have been glossed parenthetically where they first appear in the text. Mainly, the glossary lists terms that are too complex to define in a phrase or a sentence or two. A few of the terms listed are discussed at greater length elsewhere (*feminist criticism*, for instance); these terms are defined succinctly, and a page reference to the longer discussion is provided.

AFFECTIVE FALLACY First used by William K. Wimsatt and Monroe C. Beardsley to refer to what they regarded as the erroneous practice of interpreting texts according to the psychological responses of readers. "The Affective Fallacy," they wrote in a 1946 essay later republished in *The Verbal Icon* (1954), "is a confusion between the poem and its *results* (what it *is* and what it *does*). . . . It begins by trying to derive the standards of criticism from the psychological effects of a poem and ends in impressionism and relativism." The affective fallacy, like the intentional fallacy (confusing the meaning of a work with the author's expressly intended meaning), was one of the main tenets of the New Criticism, or formalism. The affective fallacy has been contested by reader-response critics, who have deliberately dedicated their efforts to describing the way individual readers and "interpretive communities" go about "making sense" of texts.

See also: Authorial Intention, Formalism, Reader-Response Criticism.

AUTHORIAL INTENTION Defined narrowly, an author's intention in writing a work, as expressed in letters, diaries, interviews, and conversations. Defined more broadly, "intentionality" involves unexpressed motivations, designs, and purposes, some of which may have remained unconscious.

The debate over whether critics should try to discern an author's intentions (conscious or otherwise) is an old one. William K. Wimsatt and Monroe C. Beardsley, in an essay first published in the 1940s, coined the term "intentional fallacy" to refer to the practice of basing interpretations on the expressed or implied intentions of authors, a practice they judged to be erroneous. As proponents of the New Criticism, or formalism, they argued that a work of literature is an object in itself and should be studied as such. They believed that it is sometimes helpful to learn what an author intended, but the critic's real purpose is to show what is actually in the text, not what an author intended to put there.

See also: Affective Fallacy, Formalism.

BASE *See* Marxist Criticism.

BINARY OPPOSITIONS *See* Oppositions.

BLANKS *See* Gaps.

CANON Since the fourth century, used to refer to those books of the Bible that the Christian church accepts as being Holy Scripture. The term has come to be applied more generally to those literary works given special status, or "privileged," by a culture. Works we tend to think of as "classics" or the "Great Books" produced by Western culture—texts that are found in every anthology of American, British, and world literature—would be among those that constitute the canon.

Recently, Marxist, feminist, minority, and postcolonial critics have argued that, for political reasons, many excellent works never enter the canon. Canonized works, they claim, are those that reflect—and respect—the culture's dominant ideology and/or perform some socially acceptable or even necessary form of "cultural work." Attempts have been made to broaden or redefine the canon by discovering valuable texts, or versions of texts, that were repressed or ignored for political reasons. These have been published both in traditional and in nontraditional anthologies. The most outspoken critics of the canon, especially radical critics practicing cultural criticism, have called into question the whole concept of canon or "canonicity." Privileging no form of artistic expression that reflects and revises the culture, these critics treat cartoons, comics, and soap operas with the same cogency and respect they accord novels, poems, and plays.

See also: Cultural Criticism, Feminist Criticism, Ideology, Marxist Criticism.

CONFLICTS, CONTRADICTIONS *See* Gaps.

CULTURAL CRITICISM A critical approach that is sometimes referred to as "cultural studies" or "cultural critique." Practitioners of cultural criticism oppose "high" definitions of culture and take seriously popular cultural forms. Grounded in a variety of continental European influences, cultural criticism nonetheless gained institutional force in England, in 1964, with the founding of the Centre for Contemporary Cultural Studies at Birmingham University. Broadly interdisciplinary in its scope and approach, cultural criticism views the text as the locus and catalyst of a complex network of political and economic discourses. Cultural critics share with Marxist critics an interest in the ideological contexts of cultural forms. *See* "What Is Cultural Criticism?" pp. 552–70.

DECONSTRUCTION A poststructuralist approach to literature that is strongly influenced by the writings of the French philosopher Jacques Derrida. Deconstruction, partly in response to structuralism and formalism, posits the undecidability of meaning for all texts. In fact, as the deconstructionist critic J. Hillis Miller points out, "deconstruction is not a dismantling of the structure of a text but a demonstration that it has already dismantled itself." *See* "What Is Deconstruction?" pp. 484–505.

DIALECTIC Originally developed by Greek philosophers, mainly Socrates and Plato, as a form and method of logical argumentation; the term later came to denote a philosophical notion of evolution. The German philosopher G. W. F. Hegel described dialectic as a process whereby a thesis, when countered by an antithesis, leads to the synthesis of a new idea. Karl Marx and Friedrich Engels, adapting Hegel's idealist theory, used the phrase "dialectical materialism" to discuss the way in which a revolutionary class war might lead to the synthesis of a new social economic order. The American Marxist critic Fredric Jameson has coined the phrase "dialectical criticism" to refer to a Marxist critical approach that synthesizes structuralist and poststructuralist methodologies.

See also: Marxist Criticism, Poststructuralism, Structuralism.

DIALOGIC *See* Discourse.

DISCOURSE Used specifically, can refer to (1) spoken or written discussion of a subject or area of knowledge; (2) the words in, or text of, a narrative as opposed to its story line; or (3) a "strand" within a given narrative that argues a certain point or defends a given value system.

More generally, "discourse" refers to the language in which a subject or area of knowledge is discussed or a certain kind of business is transacted. Human knowledge is collected and structured in discourses. Theology and medicine are defined by their discourses, as are politics, sexuality, and literary criticism.

A society is generally made up of a number of different discourses or "discourse communities," one or more of which may be dominant or serve the dominant ideology. Each discourse has its own vocabulary, concepts, and rules, knowledge of which constitutes power. The psychoanalyst and psychoanalytic critic Jacques Lacan has treated the unconscious as a form of discourse, the patterns of which are repeated in literature. Cultural critics, following Mikhail Bakhtin, use the word "dialogic" to discuss the dialogue *between* discourses that takes place within language or, more specifically, a literary text.

See also: Cultural Criticism, Ideology, Narrative, Psychoanalytic Criticism.

FEMINIST CRITICISM An aspect of the feminist movement whose primary goals include critiquing masculine-dominated language and literature by showing how they reflect a masculine ideology; writing the history of unknown or undervalued women writers, thereby earning them their rightful place in the literary canon; and helping create a climate in which women's creativity may be fully realized and appreciated. *See* "What Are Feminist and Gender Criticism?" pp. 441–62.

FIGURE *See* Metaphor, Metonymy, Symbol.

FORMALISM Also referred to as the New Criticism, formalism reached its height during the 1940s and 1950s, but it is still practiced today.

Formalists treat a work of literary art as if it were a self-contained, self-referential object. Rather than basing their interpretations of a text on the reader's response, the author's stated intentions, or parallels between the text and historical contexts (such as the author's life), formalists concentrate on the relationships *within* the text that give it its own distinctive character or form. Special attention is paid to repetition, particularly of images or symbols, but also of sound effects and rhythms in poetry.

Because of the importance placed on close analysis and the stress on the text as a carefully crafted, orderly object containing observable formal patterns, formalism has often been seen as an attack on Romanticism and impressionism, particularly impressionistic criticism. It has sometimes even been called an "objective" approach to literature. Formalists are more likely than certain other critics to believe and say that the meaning of a text can be known objectively. For instance, reader-response critics see meaning as a function either of each reader's experience or of the norms that govern a particular "interpretive community," and deconstructors argue that texts mean opposite things at the same time.

Formalism was originally based on essays written during the 1920s and 1930s by T. S. Eliot, I. A. Richards, and William Empson. It was significantly developed later by a group of American poets and critics, including R. P. Blackmur, Cleanth Brooks, John Crowe Ransom, Allen Tate, Robert Penn Warren, and William K. Wimsatt. Although we associate formalism with certain principles and terms (such as the "affective fallacy" and the "intentional fallacy" as defined by Wimsatt and Monroe C. Beardsley), formalists were trying to make a cultural statement rather than establish a critical dogma. Generally southern, religious, and culturally conservative, they advocated the inherent value of literary works (particularly of literary works regarded as beautiful art objects) because they were sick of the growing ugliness of modern life and contemporary events. Some recent theorists even suggest that the rising popularity of formalism after World War II was a feature of American isolationism, the formalist tendency to isolate literature from biography and history being a manifestation of the American fatigue with wider involvements.

See also: Affective Fallacy, Authorial Intention, Deconstruction, Reader-Response Criticism, Symbol.

GAPS When used by reader-response critics familiar with the theories of Wolfgang Iser, refers to "blanks" in texts that must be filled in by readers. A gap may be said to exist whenever and wherever a reader perceives something to be missing between words, sentences, paragraphs, stanzas, or chapters. Readers respond to gaps actively and creatively, explaining apparent inconsistencies in point of view, accounting for jumps in chronology, speculatively supplying information missing from plots, and resolving problems or issues left ambiguous or "indeterminate" in the text.

Reader-response critics sometimes speak as if a gap actually exists in a text; a gap is, of course, to some extent a product of readers' perceptions. Different readers may find gaps in different texts, and different gaps in the same text. Furthermore, they may fill these gaps in different ways, which is why, a reader-response critic might argue, works are interpreted in different ways.

Although the concept of the gap has been used mainly by reader-response critics, it has also been used by critics taking other theoretical approaches.

Practitioners of deconstruction might use "gap" when speaking of the radical contradictoriness of a text. Marxists have used the term to speak of everything from the gap that opens up between economic base and cultural superstructure to the two kinds of conflicts or contradictions to be found in literary texts. The first of these, they would argue, results from the fact that texts reflect ideology, within which certain subjects cannot be covered, things cannot be said, contradictory views cannot be recognized as contradictory. The second kind of conflict, contradiction, or gap within a text results from the fact that works don't just reflect ideology: they are also fictions that, consciously or unconsciously, distance themselves from the same ideology.

See also: Deconstruction, Ideology, Marxist Criticism, Reader-Response Criticism.

GENDER CRITICISM Developing out of feminist criticism in the mid-1980s, this fluid and inclusive movement by its nature defies neat definition. Its practitioners include, but are not limited to, self-identified feminists, gay and lesbian critics, queer and performance theorists, and poststructuralists interested in deconstructing oppositions such as masculine/feminine, heterosexual/homosexual. This diverse group of critics shares an interest in interrogating categories of gender and sexuality and exploring the relationships between them, though it does not necessarily share any central assumptions about the nature of these categories. For example, some gender critics insist that all gender identities are cultural constructions, but others have maintained a belief in essential gender identity. Often gender critics are more interested in examining gender issues through a literary text than a literary text through gender issues. *See* "What Are Feminist and Gender Criticism?" pp. 441–83.

GENRE A French word referring to a kind or type of literature. Individual works within a genre may exhibit a distinctive form, be governed by certain conventions, and/or represent characteristic subjects. Tragedy, epic, and romance are all genres.

Perhaps inevitably, the term *genre* is used loosely. Lyric poetry is a genre, but so are characteristic *types* of the lyric, such as the sonnet, the ode, and the elegy. Fiction is a genre, as are detective fiction and science fiction. The list of genres grows constantly as critics establish new lines of connection between individual works and discern new categories of works with common characteristics. Moreover, some writers form hybrid genres by combining the characteristics of several in a single work. Knowledge of genres helps critics to understand and explain what is conventional and unconventional, borrowed and original, in a work.

HEGEMONY Given intellectual currency by the Italian communist Antonio Gramsci, the word (a translation of *egemonia*) refers to the pervasive system of assumptions, meanings, and values—the web of ideologies, in other words—that shapes the way things look, what they mean, and therefore what reality *is* for the majority of people within a given culture.

See also: Ideology, Marxist Criticism.

IDEOLOGY A set of beliefs underlying the customs, habits, and/or practices common to a given social group. To members of that group, the beliefs seem obviously true, natural, and even universally applicable. They may seem just as obviously arbitrary, idiosyncratic, and even false to outsiders or members of another group who adhere to another ideology. Within a society, several ideologies may coexist, or one or more may be dominant.

Ideologies may be forcibly imposed or willingly subscribed to. Their component beliefs may be held consciously or unconsciously. In either case, they come to form what Johanna M. Smith has called "the unexamined ground of our experience." Ideology governs our perceptions, judgments, and prejudices —our sense of what is acceptable, normal, and deviant. Ideology may cause a revolution; it may also allow discrimination and even exploitation.

Ideologies are of special interest to sociologically oriented critics of literature because of the way in which authors reflect or resist prevailing views in their texts. Some Marxist critics have argued that literary texts reflect and reproduce the ideologies that produced them; most, however, have shown how ideologies are riven with contradictions that works of literature manage to expose and widen. Still other Marxists have focused on the way in which texts themselves are characterized by gaps, conflicts, and contradictions between their ideological and anti-ideological functions.

Feminist critics have addressed the question of ideology by seeking to expose (and thereby call into question) the patriarchal ideology mirrored or inscribed in works written by men—even men who have sought to counter sexism and break down sexual stereotypes. New historicists have been interested in demonstrating the ideological underpinnings not only of literary representations but also of our interpretations of them. Fredric Jameson, an American Marxist critic, argues that all thought is ideological, but that ideological thought that knows itself as such stands the chance of seeing through and transcending ideology.

See also: Cultural Criticism, Feminist Criticism, Marxist Criticism, New Historicism.

IMAGINARY ORDER One of the three essential orders of the psychoanalytic field (*see* Real and Symbolic Order), it is most closely associated with the senses (sight, sound, touch, taste, and smell). The infant, who by comparison to other animals is born premature and thus is wholly dependent on others for a prolonged period, enters the Imaginary order when it begins to experience a unity of body parts and motor control that is empowering. This usually occurs between six and eighteen months, and is called by Lacan the "mirror stage" or "mirror phase," in which the child anticipates mastery of its body. It does so by identifying with the *image* of wholeness (that is, seeing its own image in the mirror, experiencing its mother as a whole body, and so on). This sense of oneness, and also difference from others (especially the mother or primary caretaker), is established through an image or a vision of harmony that is both a mirroring and a "mirage of maturation" or false sense of individuality and independence. The Imaginary is a metaphor for unity, is related to the visual order, and is always part of human subjectivity. Because the subject is fundamentally separate from others and also internally divided (conscious/unconscious), the apparent coherence of the Imaginary, its fullness and grandiosity, is always false, a *mis*recognition that the ego (or "me") tries to deny by imagining itself as coherent and empowered. The Imaginary operates in conjunction with the Real and Symbolic and is not a "stage" of development equivalent to Freud's "pre-oedipal stage," nor is it prelinguistic.

See also: Psychoanalytic Criticism, Real, Symbolic Order.

IMPLIED READER A phrase used by some reader-response critics in place of the phrase "the reader." Whereas "the reader" could refer to any idiosyncratic individual who happens to have read or to be reading the text, "the implied reader" is *the* reader intended, even created, by the text. Other reader-response critics seeking to describe this more generally conceived reader have spoken of the "informed reader" or the "narratee," who is "the necessary counterpart of a given narrator."

See also: Reader-Response Criticism.

INTENTIONAL FALLACY *See* Authorial Intention.

INTENTIONALITY *See* Authorial Intention.

INTERTEXTUALITY The condition of interconnectedness among texts. Every author has been influenced by others, and every work contains explicit and implicit references to other works. Writers may consciously or unconsciously echo a predecessor or precursor; they may also consciously or unconsciously disguise their indebtedness, making intertextual relationships difficult for the critic to trace.

Reacting against the formalist tendency to view each work as a freestanding object, some poststructuralist critics suggested that the meaning of a work emerges only intertextually, that is, within the context provided by other works. But there has been a reaction, too, against this type of intertextual criticism. Some new historicist critics suggest that literary history is itself too narrow a context and that works should be interpreted in light of a larger set of cultural contexts.

There is, however, a broader definition of intertextuality, one that refers to the relationship between works of literature and a wide range of narratives and discourses that we don't usually consider literary. Thus defined, intertextuality could be used by a new historicist to refer to the significant interconnectedness between a literary text and nonliterary discussions of or discourses about contemporary culture. Or it could be used by a poststructuralist to suggest that a work can only be recognized and read within a vast field of signs and tropes that is *like* a text and that makes any single text self-contradictory and "undecidable."

See also: Discourse, Formalism, Narrative, New Historicism, Poststructuralism, Trope.

MARXIST CRITICISM An approach that treats literary texts as material products, describing them in broadly historical terms. In Marxist criticism, the text is viewed in terms of its production and consumption, as a product *of* work that does identifiable cultural work of its own. Following Karl Marx, the founder of communism, Marxist critics have used the terms *base* to refer to economic reality and *superstructure* to refer to the corresponding or "homologous" infrastructure consisting of politics, law, philosophy, religion, and the arts. Also following Marx, they have used the word *ideology* to refer to that set of cultural beliefs that literary works at once reproduce, resist, and revise.

METAPHOR The representation of one thing by another related or similar thing. The image (or activity or concept) used to represent or "figure" something else is known as the "vehicle" of the metaphor; the thing represented is called the "tenor." In other words, the vehicle is what we substitute for the tenor. The relationship between vehicle and tenor can provide much additional meaning. Thus, instead of saying, "Last night I read a book," we might say, "Last night I plowed through a book." "Plowed through" (or the activity of plowing) is the vehicle of our metaphor; "read" (or the act of reading) is the tenor, the thing being figured. The increment in meaning through metaphor is fairly obvious. Our audience knows not only *that* we read but also *how* we read, because to read a book in the way that a plow rips through earth is surely to read in a relentless, unreflective way. Note that in the sentence above, a new metaphor—"rips through"—has been used to explain an old one. This serves (which is a metaphor) as an example of just how thick (another metaphor) language is with metaphors!

Metaphor is a kind of "trope" (literally, a "turning," that is, a figure of speech that alters or "turns" the meaning of a word or phrase). Other tropes include allegory, conceit, metonymy, personification, simile, symbol, and synecdoche. Traditionally, metaphor and symbol have been viewed as the principal tropes; minor tropes have been categorized as *types* of these two major ones. Similes, for instance, are usually defined as simple metaphors that usually employ *like* or *as* and state the tenor outright, as in "My love is like a red, red rose." Synecdoche involves a vehicle that is a *part* of the tenor, as in "I see a sail" meaning "I see a boat." Metonymy is viewed as a metaphor involving two terms commonly if arbitrarily associated with (but not fundamentally or intrinsically related to) each other. Recently, however, deconstructors such as Paul de Man and J. Hillis Miller have questioned the "privilege" granted to metaphor and the metaphor/metonymy distinction or "opposition." They have suggested that all metaphors are really metonyms and that all figuration is arbitrary.

See also: Deconstruction, Metonymy, Oppositions, Symbol.

METONYMY The representation of one thing by another that is commonly and often physically associated with it. To refer to a writer's handwriting as his or her "hand" is to use a metonymic "figure" or "trope." The image or thing used to represent something else is known as the "vehicle" of the metonym; the thing represented is called the "tenor."

Like other tropes (such as metaphor), metonymy involves the replacement of one word or phrase by another. Liquor may be referred to as "the bottle," a monarch as "the crown." Narrowly defined, the vehicle of a metonym is arbitrarily, not intrinsically, associated with the tenor. In other words, the bottle just happens to be what liquor is stored in and poured from in our culture. The hand may be involved in the production of handwriting, but so are the brain and the pen. There is no special, intrinsic likeness between a crown and a monarch; it's just that crowns traditionally sit on monarchs' heads and not on the heads of university professors. More broadly, *metonym* and *metonymy* have been used by recent critics to refer to a wide range of figures and tropes. Deconstructors have questioned the distinction between metaphor and metonymy.

See also: Deconstruction, Metaphor, Trope.

NARRATIVE A story or a telling of a story, or an account of a situation or of events. A novel and a biography of a novelist are both narratives, as are Freud's case histories.

Some critics use the word "narrative" even more generally; Brook Thomas, a new historicist, has critiqued "narratives of human history that neglect the role human labor has played."

NEW CRITICISM *See* Formalism.

NEW HISTORICISM First practiced and articulated in the late 1970s and early 1980s in the work of critics such as Stephen Greenblatt—who named this movement in contemporary critical theory—and Louis Montrose, its practitioners share certain convictions, primarily that literary critics need to develop a high degree of historical consciousness and that literature should not be viewed apart from other human creations, artistic or otherwise. They share a belief in referentiality—a belief that literature refers to and is referred to by things outside itself—that is fainter in the works of formalist, poststructuralist, and even reader-response critics. Discarding old distinctions between literature, history, and the social sciences, new historicists agree with Greenblatt that the "central concerns" of criticism "should prevent it from permanently sealing off one type of discourse from another, or decisively separating works of art from the minds and lives of their creators and their audiences." *See,* "What Is the New Historicism?" pp. 405–22.

See also: Authorial Intention, Deconstruction, Formalism, Ideology, Poststructuralism, Psychoanalytic Criticism.

OPPOSITIONS A concept highly relevant to linguistics, inasmuch as linguists maintain that words (such as *black* and *death*) have meaning not in themselves but in relation to other words (*white* and *life*). Jacques Derrida, a poststructuralist philosopher of language, has suggested that in the West we think in terms of these "binary oppositions" or dichotomies, which on examination turn out to be evaluative hierarchies. In other words, each opposition—beginning/end, presence/absence, or consciousness/unconsciousness—contains one term that our culture views as superior and one term that we view as negative or inferior.

Derrida has "deconstructed" a number of these binary oppositions, including two—speech/writing and signifier/signified—that he believes to be central to linguistics in particular and Western culture in general. He has concurrently critiqued the "law" of noncontradiction, which is fundamental to Western logic. He and other deconstructors have argued that a text can contain opposed strands of discourse and, therefore, mean opposite things: reason *and* passion, life *and* death, hope *and* despair, black *and* white. Traditionally, criticism has involved choosing between opposed or contradictory meanings and arguing that one is present in the text and the other absent.

French feminists have adopted the ideas of Derrida and other deconstructors, showing not only that we think in terms of such binary oppositions as male/female, reason/emotion, and active/passive, but that we also associate reason and activity with masculinity and emotion and passivity with femininity. Because of this, they have concluded that language is "phallocentric," or masculine-dominated.

See also: Deconstruction, Discourse, Feminist Criticism, Poststructuralism.

PHALLUS The symbolic value of the penis that organizes libidinal development and which Freud saw as a stage in the process of human subjectivity. Lacan viewed the Phallus as the representative of a fraudulent power (male over female) whose "Law" is a principle of psychic division (conscious/unconscious) and sexual difference (masculine/feminine). The Symbolic order (*see* Symbolic Order) is ruled by the Phallus, which of itself has no inherent meaning *apart from* the power and meaning given to it by individual cultures and societies, and represented by the name of the father as lawgiver and namer.

POSTSTRUCTURALISM The general attempt to contest and subvert structuralism initiated by deconstructors and certain other critics associated with psychoanalytic, Marxist, and feminist theory. Structuralists, using linguistics as a model and employing semiotic (sign) theory, posit the possibility of knowing a text systematically and revealing the "grammar" behind its form and meaning. Poststructuralists argue against the possibility of such knowledge and description. They counter that texts can be shown to contradict not only structuralist accounts of them but also themselves. In making their adversarial claims, they rely on close readings of texts and on the work of theorists such as Jacques Derrida and Jacques Lacan.

Poststructuralists have suggested that structuralism rests on distinctions between "signifier" and "signified" (signs and the things they point toward), "self" and "language" (or "text"), texts and other texts, and text and world that are overly simplistic, if not patently inaccurate. Poststructuralists have shown how all signifieds are also signifiers, and they have treated texts as "intertexts." They have viewed the world as if it *were* a text (we desire a certain car because it *symbolizes* achievement) and the self as the subject, as well as the user, of language; for example, we may shape and speak through language, but it also shapes and speaks through us.

See also: Deconstruction, Feminist Criticism, Intertextuality, Psychoanalytic Criticism, Semiotics, Structuralism.

PSYCHOANALYTIC CRITICISM Grounded in the psychoanalytic theories of Sigmund Freud, it is one of the oldest critical methodologies still in use. Freud's view that works of literature, like dreams, express secret, unconscious desires led to criticism and interpreted literary works as manifestations of the authors' neuroses. More recently, psychoanalytic critics have come to see literary works as skillfully crafted artifacts that may appeal to *our* neuroses by tapping into our repressed wishes and fantasies. Other forms of psychological criticism that diverge from Freud, although they ultimately derive from his insights, include those based on the theories of Carl Jung and Jacques Lacan.

READER-RESPONSE CRITICISM An approach to literature that, as its name implies, considers the way readers respond to texts, as they read. Stanley Fish describes the method by saying that it substitutes for one question, "What does this sentence mean?" a more operational question, "What does this sentence do?" Reader-response criticism shares with deconstruction a strong textual orientation and a reluctance to define a single meaning for a work. Along with psychoanalytic criticism, it shares an interest in the dynamics of mental response to textual cues. *See* "What Is Reader-Response Criticism?" pp. 521–37.

REAL One of the three orders of subjectivity (*see* Imaginary Order and Symbolic Order), the Real is the intractable and substantial world that resists and exceeds interpretation. The Real cannot be imagined, symbolized, or known directly. It constantly eludes our efforts to name it (death, gravity, the physicality of objects are examples of the Real), and thus challenges both the Imaginary and the Symbolic orders. The Real is fundamentally "Other," the mark of the divide between conscious and unconscious, and is signaled in language by gaps, slips, speechlessness, and the sense of the uncanny. The Real is not what we call "reality." It is the stumbling block of the Imaginary (which thinks it can "imagine" anything, including the Real) and of the Symbolic, which tries to bring the Real under its laws (the Real exposes the "phallacy" of the Law of the Phallus). The Real is frightening; we try to tame it with laws and language and call it "reality."

See also: Imaginary Order, Psychoanalytic Criticism, Symbolic Order.

SEMIOLOGY, SEMIOTIC *See* Semiotics.

SEMIOTICS The study of signs and sign systems and the way meaning is derived from them. Structuralist anthropologists, psychoanalysts, and literary critics developed semiotics during the decades following 1950, but much of the pioneering work had been done at the turn of the century by the founder of modern linguistics, Ferdinand de Saussure, and the American philosopher Charles Sanders Peirce.

Semiotics is based on several important distinctions, including the distinction between "signifier" and "signified" (the sign and what it points toward) and the distinction between "langue" and "parole." *Langue* (French for "tongue," as in "native tongue," meaning language) refers to the entire system within which individual utterances or usages of language have meaning; *parole* (French for "word") refers to the particular utterances or usages. A principal tenet of semiotics is that signs, like words, are not significant in themselves, but instead have meaning only in relation to other signs and the entire system of signs, or *langue*.

The affinity between semiotics and structuralist literary criticism derives from this emphasis placed on langue, or system. Structuralist critics, after all, were reacting against formalists and their procedure of focusing on individual words as if meanings didn't depend on anything external to the text.

Poststructuralists have used semiotics but questioned some of its underlying assumptions, including the opposition between signifier and signified. The feminist poststructuralist Julia Kristeva, for instance, has used the word *semiotic* to describe feminine language, a highly figurative, fluid form of discourse that she sets in opposition to rigid, symbolic, masculine language.

See also: Deconstruction, Feminist Criticism, Formalism, Oppositions, Poststructuralism, Structuralism, Symbol.

SIMILE *See* Metaphor.

SOCIOHISTORICAL CRITICISM *See* New Historicism.

STRUCTURALISM A science of humankind whose proponents attempted to show that all elements of human culture, including literature, may be understood as parts of a system of signs. Structuralism, according to Robert Scholes, was a reaction to "'modernist' alienation and despair."

Using Ferdinand de Saussure's linguistic theory, European structuralists such as Roman Jakobson, Claude Lévi-Strauss, and Roland Barthes (before his shift toward poststructuralism) attempted to develop a "semiology" or "semiotics" (science of signs). Barthes, among others, sought to recover literature and even language from the isolation in which they had been studied and to show that the laws that govern them govern all signs, from road signs to articles of clothing.

Particularly useful to structuralists were two of Saussure's concepts: the idea of "phoneme" in language and the idea that phonemes exist in two kinds of relationships: "synchronic" and "diachronic." A phoneme is the smallest consistently significant unit in language; thus, both "a" and "an" are phonemes, but "n" is not. A diachronic relationship is that which a phoneme has with those that have preceded it in time and those that will follow it. These "horizontal" relationships produce what we might call discourse or narrative and what Saussure called "parole." The synchronic relationship is the "vertical" one that a word has in a given instant with the entire system of language ("langue") in which it may generate meaning. "An" means what it means in English because those of us who speak the language are using it in the same way at a given time.

Following Saussure, Lévi-Strauss studied hundreds of myths, breaking them into their smallest meaningful units, which he called "mythemes." Removing each from its diachronic relations with other mythemes in a single myth (such as the myth of Oedipus and his mother), he vertically aligned those mythemes that he found to be homologous (structurally correspondent). He then studied the relationships within as well as between vertically aligned columns, in an attempt to understand scientifically, through ratios and proportions, those thoughts and processes that humankind has shared, both at one particular time and across time. One could say, then, that structuralists followed Saussure in preferring to think about the overriding langue or language of myth, in which each mytheme and mytheme-constituted myth fits meaningfully, rather than about isolated individual paroles or narratives. Structuralists followed Saussure's lead in believing what the poststructuralist Jacques Derrida later decided he could not subscribe to—that sign systems must be understood in terms of binary oppositions. In analyzing myths and texts to find basic structures, structuralists tended to find that opposite terms modulate until they are finally resolved or reconciled by some intermediary third term. Thus, a structuralist reading of *Paradise Lost* would show that the war between God and the bad angels becomes a rift between God and sinful, fallen man, the rift then being healed by the Son of God, the mediating third term.

See also: Deconstruction, Discourse, Narrative, Poststructuralism, Semiotics.

SUPERSTRUCTURE *See* Marxist Criticism.

SYMBOL A thing, image, or action that, although it is of interest in its own right, stands for or suggests something larger and more complex—often an idea or a range of interrelated ideas, attitudes, and practices.

Within a given culture, some things are understood to be symbols: the flag of the United States is an obvious example. More subtle cultural symbols might be the river as a symbol of time and the journey as a symbol of life and its manifold experiences.

Instead of appropriating symbols generally used and understood within their culture, writers often create symbols by setting up, in their works, a complex but identifiable web of associations. As a result, one object, image, or action suggests others, and often, ultimately, a range of ideas.

A symbol may thus be defined as a metaphor in which the "vehicle," the thing, image, or action used to represent something else, represents many related things (or "tenors") or is broadly suggestive. The urn in Keats's "Ode on a Grecian Urn" suggests many interrelated concepts, including art, truth, beauty, and timelessness.

Symbols have been of particular interest to formalists, who study how meanings emerge from the complex, patterned relationships between images in a work, and psychoanalytic critics, who are interested in how individual authors and the larger culture both disguise and reveal unconscious fears and desires through symbols. Recently, French feminists have also focused on the symbolic. They have suggested that, as wide-ranging as it seems, symbolic language is ultimately rigid and restrictive. They favor semiotic language and writing, which, they contend, is at once more rhythmic, unifying, and feminine.

See also: Feminist Criticism, Metaphor, Psychoanalytic Criticism, Trope.

SYMBOLIC ORDER One of the three orders of subjectivity *(see* Imaginary Order and Real), it is the realm of law, language, and society; it is the repository of generally held cultural beliefs. Its symbolic system is language, whose agent is the father or lawgiver, the one who has the power of naming. The human subject is commanded into this preestablished order by language (a process that begins long before a child can speak) and must submit to its orders of communication (grammar, syntax, and so on). Entrance into the Symbolic Order determines subjectivity according to a primary law of referentiality that takes the male sign (phallus, *see* Phallus) as its ordering principle. Lacan states that both sexes submit to the Law of the Phallus (the law of order, language, and differentiation) but their individual relation to the law determines whether they see themselves as—and are seen by others to be—either "masculine" or "feminine." The Symbolic institutes repression (of the Imaginary), thus creating the unconscious, which itself is structured like the language of the symbolic. The unconscious, a timeless realm, cannot be known directly, but it can be understood by a kind of translation that takes place in language—psychoanalysis is the "talking cure." The Symbolic is not a "stage" of development (as is Freud's "oedipal stage") nor is it set in place once and for all in human life. We constantly negotiate its threshold (in sleep, in drunkenness) and can "fall out" of it altogether in psychosis.

See also: Imaginary Order, Psychoanalytic Criticism, Real.

SYNECDOCHE *See* Metaphor, Metonymy.

TENOR *See* Metaphor, Metonymy, Symbol.

TROPE A figure, as in "figure of speech." Literally a "turning," that is, a turning or twisting of a word or phrase to make it mean something else. Principal tropes include metaphor, metonymy, personification, simile, and synecdoche.

See also: Metaphor, Metonymy.

VEHICLE *See* Metaphor, Metonymy, Symbol.

About the Contributors

THE VOLUME EDITOR

John Paul Riquelme is Professor of English at Boston University. His publications include *Teller and Tale in Joyce's Fiction: Oscillating Perspectives* (1983), *Harmony of Dissonances: T. S. Eliot, Romanticism, and Imagination* (1991), and an edition of essays by the Swiss critic Fritz Senn, *Joyce's Dislocutions: Essays on Reading as Translation* (1984). He is currently at work on a study of the origins of literary modernism in 1890s Britain that deals extensively with Thomas Hardy and Oscar Wilde.

THE CRITICS

Catherine Gallagher is Professor of English at the University of California, Berkeley. Her books include *The Industrial Reformation of English Fiction: Social Discourse and Narrative Form* (1985), *Nobody's Story: The Vanishing Acts of Women Writers in the Marketplace, 1670–1820* (1994), and (edited with Thomas Laqueur) *The Making of the Modern Body: Sexuality and Society in the Nineteenth Century* (1987).

Ellen Rooney, Associate Professor of English and Modern Culture and Media at Brown University, is Director of the Pembroke Center for Teaching and Research on Women. She is the author of *Seductive Reasoning: Pluralism as the Problematic of Contemporary Literary Theory* (1989), and is currently completing *Criticism and the Subject of Sexual Violence*, a study of representations of subjectivity in scenes of sexual violence.

Garrett Stewart is James O. Freedman Professor of Letters at the University of Iowa. He has published books that deal primarily with nineteenth- and twentieth-century fiction: *Dickens and the Trials of Imagination* (1974), *Death Sentences: Styles of Dying in British Fiction* (1984), *Reading Voices: Literature and the Phonotext* (1990), and *Dear Reader: the Conscripted Audience in Nineteenth-Century British Fiction* (1996).

Jennifer Wicke is Professor of Comparative Literature at New York University. Her wide-ranging writings about nineteenth- and twentieth-century literature include *Advertising Fictions: Literature, Advertisement and Social Reading* (1988), which focuses on Dickens, James, and Joyce, and the essay "Vampiric Typewriting: *Dracula* and Its Media" (1992), from her forthcoming book *Born to Shop: Modernity and the Work of Consumption.*

THE SERIES EDITOR

Ross C Murfin, general editor of the Case Studies in Contemporary Criticism and volume editor of Conrad's *Heart of Darkness* and Hawthorne's *The Scarlet Letter* in the series, is provost and vice president for Academic Affairs at Southern Methodist University. He has taught at the University of Miami, Yale University, and the University of Virginia and has published scholarly studies of Joseph Conrad, Thomas Hardy, and D. H. Lawrence.